Play at the Center of the Curriculum

Play at the Center of the Curriculum

Fifth Edition

Judith Van Hoorn
University of the Pacific

Patricia Monighan Nourot
Late of *Sonoma State University*

Barbara Scales
University of California, Berkeley

Keith Rodriguez Alward

Boston   Columbus   Indianapolis   New York   San Francisco
Upper Saddle River   Amsterdam   Cape Town   Dubai   London   Madrid
Milan   Munich   Paris   Montreal   Toronto   Delhi   Mexico City   Sao Paulo
Sydney   Hong Kong   Seoul   Singapore   Taipei   Tokyo

Vice President and Editor-in-Chief: Jeffery W. Johnston
Senior Acquisitions Editor: Julie Peters
Editorial Assistant: Tiffany Bitzel
Senior Marketing Manager: Darcy Betts
Senior Managing Editor: Pamela D. Bennett
Project Manager: Kerry J. Rubadue
Senior Operations Supervisor: Matthew Ottenweller
Senior Art Director: Diane Lorenzo
Text Designer: Aptara®, Inc.

Cover Designer: Diane Lorenzo
Photo Coordinator: Lori Whitley
Cover Image: Corbis
Full-Service Project Management: Jogender Taneja, Aptara®, Inc.
Composition: Aptara®, Inc.
Printer/Binder: STP Courier
Cover Printer: STP Courier
Text Font: New Baskerville

Credits and acknowledgments borrowed from other sources and reproduced, with permission, in this textbook appear on appropriate pages within text.

Every effort has been made to provide accurate and current Internet information in this book. However, the Internet and information posted on it are constantly changing, so it is inevitable that some of the Internet addresses listed in this textbook will change.

Photo Credits: Judith Van Hoorn, pp. 1, 257; Annie Pickert/AB Merrill, pp. 5, 44, 61, 69, 71, 78, 111, 177, 180, 209, 234, 261, 270, 277, 305, 317, 342, 352; Scott Cunningham/Merrill, pp. 15, 206; Robert Harbison, p. 17; Frank Siteman, pp. 26, 30, 151, 158, 163, 231, 327; Laima Druskis/PH College, p. 34; Todd Yarrington/Merrill, pp. 39, 321; Getty Images–Stockbyte, Royalty Free, p. 48; EyeWire Collection/Getty Images–Photodisc–Royalty Free, p. 50; Shutterstock, p. 53; Krista Greco/Merrill, pp. 85, 259; David Mager/Pearson Learning Photo Studio, p. 94; Barbara Schwartz/Merrill, pp. 107, 197; Anne Vega/Merrill, pp. 116, 134, 147, 291; David Napravnik/Merrill, p. 120; Shirley Zeiberg/PH College, p. 125; Barbara Scales, pp. 169, 289, 294; Nancy Sheehan Photography, pp. 191, 239; Bob Daemmrich Photography, Inc., p. 215; Pat Nourot, p. 225; Corbis RF, p. 334; Anthony Magnacca/Merrill, p. 345; Ken Karp/PH College, p. 361.

Library of Congress Cataloging-in-Publication Data

Hoorn, Judith Van.
   Play at the center of the curriculum / Judith Van Hoorn, Patricia Monighan
Nourot, Barbara Scales.—5th ed.
      p. cm.
   Prev. ed. cataloged under title.
   ISBN-13: 978-0-13-706071-9
   ISBN-10: 0-13-706071-8
   1. Play. 2. Education, Preschool—United States. 3. Education,
Preschool—California—Case studies. 4. Cognition in children. I. Scales,
Barbara, 1930- II. Nourot, Patricia Monighan. III. Scales, Barbara. IV. Play
at the center of the curriculum. V. Title.
   LB1137.P53 2011
   155.4'18—dc22

                                                          2010020289

10 9 8 7 6 5 4 3 2 1

www.pearsonhighered.com

ISBN 13: 978-0-13-706071-9
ISBN 10:   0-13-706071-8

This book is dedicated to Millie Almy, beloved mentor to our study of children's play, and to Patricia Monighan Nourot, our beloved co-author, whose life and scholarship were testaments to the power and joy of play.

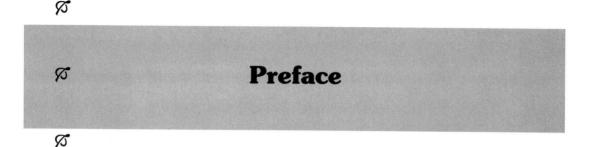

Preface

In this fifth edition of *Play at the Center of the Curriculum*, we reaffirm our commitment to play in the early childhood classroom. The natural link between play and development is becoming increasingly widely recognized. This is an important time and opportunity for changing the way we educate young children. And early childhood is an important time in the lives of our future citizens. The stakes are enormous.

Developmental theory shows that play is critical to the development of intelligence, personality, competencies, a sense of self, and social awareness. Therefore, we believe that a developmentally appropriate, holistic, and integrated early childhood curriculum has play at its center.

The old adage that "play is children's work" is reexamined in this book for teachers. We demonstrate how play can be drawn on to improve developmentally based early childhood education. Early childhood extends into the early primary grades, and we propose that play is a critical dimension to children's learning and development throughout the preschool and primary-grade years.

We believe that an ideal early childhood classroom is characterized by an abundance of play. Our experience tells us that teachers can learn to structure the early childhood classroom environment and to sequence classroom routines so that the learning expectations for children are embedded in spontaneous and guided play activity.

It has always been important that educators assure the community that its youth will receive the necessary abilities and skills to be productive citizens. The articulation of academic standards has evolved as a way of supporting this responsibility. Parents, teachers, and administrators need to be assured that a play-centered curriculum will meet academic standards. In this edition, we have paid particular attention to academic standards, demonstrating how developmentally appropriate standards can be better met in a play-centered curriculum.

> . . . [A]lmost all children can play well . . . [P]lay teaches children how to be sociable and channels cognitive development . . . These capacities serve people lifelong once they go to work (Sennet, 2008, p. 268).

This book carefully blends theory and practice. As seasoned teachers, we demonstrate how to draw both the methods and the content of a successful curriculum from children's play. We interweave anecdotes of children's play, theories of play and development, and instructional strategies that place play at the center of the curriculum.

By combining sound theory with practical illustrations, *Play at the Center of the Curriculum* achieves a solid argument for play in formal education. Teachers and students in the field of early childhood education will find this book to be a valuable resource. This is not merely a "how-to" book, nor is it simply a "thought" book. Rather, it is a blending of each, serving the reader in a number of ways.

Play at the Center of the Curriculum is a resource for those who want to engage children in a developmental zone where children and teachers are learning from and with each other. Current and future teachers are guided in methods of supporting children's progress through play. The teacher becomes the architect of the learning environment, using play and development as the blueprint.

NEW TO THIS EDITION

In this edition, we have enriched and expanded the emphasis in a number of areas, drawing on our own teaching and observations in classrooms, as well as recent research and writing in the field of early childhood curriculum and children's play.

- This fifth edition features a new chapter, "Outdoor Play," by Jane P. Perry, widely recognized for her work on children's play, including the key role of outdoor environments and intentional teacher practices. This chapter highlights insightful anecdotes from the author's research and practice regarding the importance of physically active play, child-initiated play and inquiry, and children's connections with the natural environment.

- This new edition is updated throughout and features discussions of current early childhood education practice, professional literature, and policies that support play-based curriculum.

- A new icon highlights numerous sections and examples that address children and families from diverse cultures and backgrounds, children who are English language learners, and children with special needs.

- The fifth edition includes scores of new anecdotes and current references that illustrate and support important concepts and examples of theory, research, and best practices.

- In response to student and instructor requests, this edition includes elaborated focus and discussion on the importance of spontaneous and guided play.

- All content area–oriented chapters feature new or expanded sections written to ensure that this fifth edition is timely and current.

ORGANIZATION AND STRUCTURE

This text has been written for students with varying experience and knowledge. Chapters 1 through 6 are designed to form foundation concepts and principles. We recommend that these be read first.

Chapters 2 and 3 introduce theory and research that support our understanding of play and development. The reader is introduced to the ideas of major figures in developmental theory—Piaget, Vygotsky, Erikson, and Mead—as well as to the work of contemporary researchers.

Chapters 4 and 5 bring this developmental focus back to the reality of the classroom. We explore the teacher's role in setting the stage, actively guiding, and orchestrating play. The issue of how teachers might respond to violent and aggressive play is addressed through anecdotes and practical strategies.

Chapter 6 looks at how the creation of a successful play-centered curriculum can be used to assess children's developmental progress. Included are many examples of play that embed state and national curriculum standards.

Chapters 7 through 11 explore curriculum areas that are of interest to contemporary early childhood education: mathematics, language and literacy, science, the arts, and socialization. Each chapter begins with an anecdote that focuses on how a potential curriculum is embedded in the children's spontaneous play. The reader will find a rich palette of practical ideas for the articulation of the play-centered curriculum.

Chapter 12, *Outdoor Play*, advocates for the importance of outdoor play that involves children in physical activity, engagement with nature, as well as opportunities for self-initiated play and inquiry. This chapter presents best practices in planning, observing, interpreting, and assessing young children's outdoor play.

Chapter 13 looks at ways in which play, toys, and technology interact to affect the young child's life. We present many ideas and observations useful to teachers and families on the roles of toys and games, media, and technology in the lives of young children.

Depending on the background of students, instructors can vary the order of these chapters and draw on some of the suggested resources to extend students' understanding. Chapters 7 through 13 can be assigned in an order that is compatible with the instructor's course structure.

Chapter 14 extends understandings of developmental theory and play, expanding on the constructivist views presented by Piaget and Vygotsky. The role of play in developing intelligence, personality, competency, and sense of self is explored. We pay particular attention to the role of work and autonomy in the early childhood years as they relate to the broader goals of education. This chapter will, we believe, be more meaningful after reading the more experience-focused chapters that have preceded it.

OTHER FEATURES OF THIS TEXT

Anecdotes

Each chapter anchors its focus in the world of children by beginning with an anecdote related to play and education. Numerous additional classroom anecdotes and examples are provided throughout each chapter. These practical observations ground the reader in day-to-day educational experiences.

Summary and Conclusion

Each chapter ends with a summary and conclusion, giving the reader a brief review of the main points of the chapter and some practical implications. The student might read this first to get an overview of the focus of the chapter.

SUPPLEMENTS TO THE TEXT

All supplements are available online. To download and print supplement files, go to www.pearsonhighered.com and then click on "Educators."

Online Instructor's Manual

This manual contains, for each chapter, learning intentions, a chapter guide and summary, ideas for projects—both in and out of class, and suggested resources for further study.

Online Test Bank

The Test Bank includes a variety of test items, including essay, multiple choice, and short answer.

ACKNOWLEDGMENTS

We gratefully acknowledge those who have shared with us their experiences, ideas, critical reviews, exemplary references, and examples from their own practice: Melinda Bachman, Lyda Beardsley, Libby Byers, Greta Campbell, Shirley Cheal, Suzanne DiLillo, Randi Dingman, Heather Dunlap, Sandra Easley, Johanna Filp-Hanke, Patricia Fluetsch, Buffy Frick, Anita Gensler, Janet Gonzalez-Mena, Suzanne Gray, Cynthia Halewood, Bonnie Hester, Kristin Hope, Jackie Imbimbo, Rochelle Jacobs, Robin Johnson, Richard Karsch, Marjorie Keegan, Susan Kyle, Rose Laugtug, Janet Lederman, Theresa Lozac'h, Kim Lovsey, Christa McCoy, Gail Mon Pere, Virginia Quock, Margaret Potts, Ada Rappeport, Kitty Ritz, Shane Rojo, Kathy Rosebrook, Ann Siefert, Dorothy Stewart, Lisa Tabachnick, Lia Thompson-Clark, Lea Waters, Maureen Wieser, and Professors Millie Almy, Jennie Cook-Gumperz, Ann Dyson, Celia Genishi, Ageliki Nicopoulou, and Diane Levin, as well as Vivian Paley. Their contributions have been practical, often inspiring, and have enriched our text.

We acknowledge the special contributions of Leni von Blanckensee, a specialist in educational technology as well as an experienced teacher, who contributed to our understanding of young children and technology.

We thank the University of the Pacific for the McDaniel Grant and the Merck Foundation Grant, which provided support for developing Chapters 7 and 9. Special thanks to Marcy McGaugh for her excellent work preparing the manuscript.

We are grateful for the continued support and wise counsel we received from our editor, Julie Peters, as well as Carol Sykes, photo department manager. Kerry Rubadue and Jogender Taneja served as production editor and production manager for this fifth edition. We appreciate their technical expertise as well as their encouragement at each stage of the production process. We also wish to thank the following reviewers of the manuscript, who provided valuable comments and suggestions: Susan Catapano, University of Missouri–St. Louis; Sherry Forest, Craven Community College; Mary Jo Graham, Marshall University; and Sandra Stone, Northern Arizona University. Above all, thanks to the children and their teachers who brought life to our presentation of the play-centered curriculum.

Brief Contents

1 Looking at Play Through Teachers' Eyes   1

2 Play and Development: Theory   26

3 Play as the Cornerstone of Development: The Literature   48

4 Orchestrating Children's Play: Setting the Stage   69

5 Orchestrating Play: Interactions with Children   94

6 Play as a Tool for Assessment   120

7 Mathematics in the Play-Centered Curriculum   151

8 Language, Literacy, and Play   177

9 Science in the Play-Centered Curriculum   206

10 The Arts in the Play-Centered Curriculum   231

11 Play and Socialization   259

12 Outdoor Play   289

13 Play, Toys, and Technology   317

14 Conclusion: Integrating Play, Development, and Practice   342

References   368

Name Index   388

Subject Index   395

Contents

1 Looking at Play Through Teachers' Eyes   1

Play at the Center of a Developmentally Based Curriculum   3

    Play as a Fundamental Human Activity   4

    The Power of Play in Development   4

    Grounding Practice in Theory, Research, and the Wisdom of Practitioners   5

    Play at the Center of a Balanced Curriculum   8

    The Play Continuum   11

How Teachers of Young Children View Play   12

    Play Through the Eyes of Brandon's Teacher   12

    Randi: Meeting the Needs of Individual Children in Preschool   15

    Pat: From Worksheeets and Desks to Blocks and Bubbles in Kindergarten   16

    Kristin: Letting Children Develop at Their Own Pace in First Grade   16

Play: The Core of Developmentally Appropriate Practice   17

Addressing Standards in the Play-Centered Curriculum   18

    The Purpose of Standards   18

    Guidelines for Developing Appropriate Standards for Young Children   19

    The Challenges of Standards   20

The Critical Role of the Teacher in the Curriculum   21

Summary and Conclusion   22

2 Play and Development: Theory   26

A Constructivist View of Play and Development   27

Piaget's Developmental Theory and Play   28

    Three Types of Knowledge   30

    Piaget: The Development of Play   32

    Games with Rules   34

Vygotsky: Development and Play   35

    The Zone of Proximal Development   35

    Interpersonal to Intrapersonal Processes in Learning   36

    Acquiring Mental Tools   37

Understanding Rules   38

Vygotsky's Levels of Symbolic Play   38

Mead: Play and the Developing Sense of Self   39

The Play Stage   40

The Game Stage   40

The Generalized Other Stage   41

Erikson: Play and Mastery in the Inner World of Childhood   42

Infancy: Trust and Mistrust   43

Toddlerhood: Autonomy, Shame, and Doubt   43

Early Childhood and the Play Stage: Initiative and Guilt   44

Industry and Inferiority: Play and Work in Middle Childhood   45

Summary and Conclusion   46

3   Play as the Cornerstone of Development: The Literature   48

Play and Intellectual Development   49

Play and the Development of Symbolic Thought   49

Play and the Development of Language and Literacy   53

Play and Logical-Mathematical Thinking   56

Play and Problem Solving   58

Play and Children with Special Needs   59

Play, Imagination, and Creativity   60

Three Aspects of Imagination and Fantasy   62

Play and Social-Moral Development   63

Parten's Research on Play and Social Participation   64

Play and Emotional Development   66

Play and the Harsh Realities of Some Children's Lives   67

Summary and Conclusion   68

4   Orchestrating Children's Play: Setting the Stage   69

Principles Guiding Play Orchestration   71

Taking the Child's View   71

Teacher as Keen Observer   72

Seeing Meaning as It Is Constructed   72

Teacher as Stage Manager   72

A Continuum of Play Orchestration Strategies   73

Setting the Stage for Play   74

Preparing the Physical Space for Play   74

Play Safety   86

Planning the Daily Schedule   87

Extensions for Play   88

Play-Generated Curriculum   89

Curriculum-Generated Play   89

Summary and Conclusion   93

5   Orchestrating Play: Interactions with Children   94

Play and Scaffolding   96

Spontaneous, Guided, and Directed Play   97

The Artist Apprentice   99

The Peacemaker   100

Guardian of the Gate   102

Parallel Player   103

Spectator   104

Participant   104

Matchmaker   105

Story Player   106

Play Tutor   106

Choosing a Strategy   108

Challenges in Play for Children with Special Needs   108

*Challenges in Play for Children Who Are English Language
    Learners*   109

Timing Is Everything: Entering and Exiting Children's Play   109

Play and the Culture of School   110

Responding to Violent Play   112

Ascertaining Children's Purposes in Play   113

Diffusing Violence in Play   115

Addressing Exclusion—Supporting Inclusion   118

Building a Peaceful Classroom   118

Summary and Conclusion   119

6   Play as a Tool for Assessment   120

Assessing Development Through Play at the Bank   121

Examining the Purposes of Assessment   123

Features of Play-Centered Assessment   124

Play and Assessments of Children from Diverse Cultures and Backgrounds   *125*

Play and Assessments of Children with Special Needs   *126*

Communicating with Families about Play and Assessment   127

Assessing Age-Appropriate Development   127

Assessing Development of Concepts and Skills   *128*

Assessing Individual Development   131

Intelligence Is Multifaceted   *132*

How Play Informs Assessment   134

Ascertaining the Child's Viewpoint   136

Principles for Framing Play Questions   *137*

Strategies for Collecting and Organizing Information   138

Anecdotal Records   *138*

Checklists   *139*

Portfolios   *141*

Documentation Assessment   *141*

Videotape   *142*

Assessing Play as Play   143

A Closer Look: Risks and Benefits of Assessments   146

The Risks of High-Stakes Accountability   *146*

Tensions Regarding Play-Centered Curriculum and Early Learning Standards   *146*

Making Schools Ready for Learners   *147*

Serving Students with Special Needs: Benefits of Play-Centered Assessments   *148*

Families, Assessments, and the Play-Centered Curriculum   *148*

Summary and Conclusion   149

7   Mathematics in the Play-Centered Curriculum   **151**

The Playful Nature of Mathematics   152

Mathematical Concepts in the Play-Centered Curriculum   153

Geometry   *153*

Numbers and Operations: Relationships Involving Quantity   *154*

Measurement   *157*

Mathematical Processes: Problem Solving, Communication, Connections, and Representation   *157*

Mathematics in the Early Childhood Integrated Curriculum   158

The Goals of Early Childhood Mathematics Education   *159*

The Nature of Mathematics   *159*

Assessing Children's Development of Mathematical Thinking   *162*

*Mathematics Education Based on the Nature of Mathematics, Children's Development,
    and Children's Interests*   *163*

Play and Daily Life Situations: Two Cornerstones of Early Childhood Education
    Mathematics Programs   164

Play: A Cornerstone of Mathematics Education   *164*

*Daily Life Situations: A Second Cornerstone of Mathematics
    Education*   *165*

*Supporting Children from All Cultures and Children Who Are English
    Language Learners*   *165*

Supporting Children with Special Needs   *167*

Children's Interests   *168*

Orchestrating Play in Mathematics   169

Setting the Stage   *169*

Accessorizing: Transforming the Environment to Extend and Enrich Play   *170*

Play-Generated Curricula   *171*

Curriculum-Generated Play   *172*

The Early Childhood Education Mathematics Curriculum: Principles, Standards,
    and Focal Points   173

Principles   *173*

Standards for Student Learning   *174*

NCTM Curriculum Focal Points   *175*

*Research Findings Support Key Standards and Focal Points: The National Research
    Council's 2009 Report of the Committee on Early Childhood*   *175*

Standards, Expectations, and Professional Expertise   *175*

Summary and Conclusion   176

8   Language, Literacy, and Play   177

Literacy Begins   179

Play, Language, and Literate Behavior: A Natural Partnership   179

Communication as a Prerequisite for Play with Others   *181*

Play as a Form of Communication   *181*

Fostering Literate Behaviors   182

The Value of the Play-Based Curriculum   *182*

Early Story Constructions   *182*

*How the Play-Based Literacy Curriculum Serves Children of All Cultures
    and Languages*   *184*

English Language Learners: Masha's Story   *185*

Honoring the Importance of Literate Behaviors   189

   Emergent Literacy   189

   Writing, Graphics, and Narrative Construction   190

   Awareness of Sounds and Patterns of Language   190

Language and Literacy Learning in the Primary Grades: The Motivating Power of Play   192

   Multimedia Extend Meanings of Literacy   194

Dynamic Approaches to Promoting Literacy Through Play   195

   Using Drama Techniques to Enhance Sociodramatic Play   195

   Story Dictation and Story Playing   197

Balanced Opportunities for Varied Kinds of Play Support Competencies in Language and Literacy   200

   Time for Language and Literacy in Play   200

   Space for Language and Literacy Learning   200

   Materials for Language, Literacy, and Reading and Writing in Play   201

   Guidance for Literacy in Play   201

Standards for Literacy: Calls for Accountability   202

Summary and Conclusion   204

9   Science in the Play-Centered Curriculum   206

Scientists Tour the Kindergarten   208

   Outdoor Area   208

   The Block Area   209

   The Art Area   210

Science in the Early Childhood Integrated Curriculum   210

   The Goal of Early Childhood Science Education   210

   The Nature of Science   213

   The Nature of the Child   216

   Integrating the Child's Interests   219

   Meeting the Needs of Children Who Are English Language Learners   220

   Developing Inclusive Science Curriculum for Children with Special Needs   221

Addressing Standards in the Play-Centered Curriculum   222

Extending the Science Curriculum   224

   Setting the Stage for Learning about the Physical World through Spontaneous Play   224

   Encouraging Further Exploration of the Environment   225

   Interacting with Children in Their Play   226

Orchestrating Extensions for Play   226

Recasting the Curriculum in Play   229

Developing Confidence in Teaching Science   229

Summary and Conclusion   230

10 The Arts in the Play-Centered Curriculum   231

A Guide for Curriculum Design   233

Entering the Child's World of Spontaneous Play   233

Incorporating Artwork   234

Monitoring the Quality and the Challenge of Play: Tactile and Sensory Arts   235

The Arts Enhance Knowledge in All Curriculum Domains   237

Supporting Art and Play: Time, Space, Materials, and Teacher Know-How   238

Presentation of Art Making and Constructive Play Materials   241

Content   244

Cultural Enrichment in the Arts   244

Music and Movement in the Play-Centered Curriculum   245

Diverse Musical Traditions Enrich the Classroom Culture   247

Integration of Children's Experiences and Feelings Through Play in the Arts   249

A Balanced Arts Curriculum   249

Knowledge of the Patterns of Development in Children's Art Making   251

Documenting Change and Growth: Heidi's Horses   251

Important Considerations   255

Children with Special Needs: Guiding for Mastery and Competence   255

Children's Play Interests Reflected in a Play-Centered Curriculum   256

Guided and Directed Play in the Arts   256

Summary and Conclusion   258

11 Play and Socialization   259

Saying Goodbye to Parents   260

From Separation to Integration: John's Fire Hydrants   261

Diversity Creates Social Enrichment for Today's Classrooms   264

Diversity Can Create Challenge for Teachers   265

Inclusion of Children with Special Needs   267

Traditional Research and Practice   269

Current Practice Illuminated by Research   269

Differences in Boys' and Girls' Play and Socialization   270

Children's Negotiations Create a Dynamic Context for Play   272

Newspapers   273

Play Provides a Bridge Between Theory and Practice   274

The Interpretive Approach   274

Teachers Take a Research Stance: Views from the Inside   276

Children's Interactive Strategies   276

Studying the Social Ecology of a Preschool Classroom   278

*Taking an Interpretive Approach to the Social Ecology of the
Classroom*   278

Contrasts in Social Ecologies   278

Play in the Sand Kitchen Reexamined   280

Teacher Support for Play Interactions   281

Children Grant Warrants for Play   281

Supporting Interactive Play at the Environmental Level   285

Social Studies Standards in Early Childhood Programs   285

Social Science for Young Children   286

Summary and Conclusion   287

12   Outdoor Play   289

The Importance of Outdoor Play   291

The Importance of Outdoor Physically Active Play   293

The Importance of Outdoor Nature Play   295

The Importance of Child-Initiated Play and Inquiry   297

*How the Outdoor Classroom Is Different from the Inside
Classroom*   298

Teaching Goals for Children in the Outdoor Classroom   299

Best Practices in Planning for Outdoor Play   301

Serving Children from Diverse Backgrounds   301

Sites with Outdoor Challenges   303

The Adult's Feelings about Being Outdoors   304

Observing and Interpreting Outdoor Play   305

Understanding Children's Outdoor Peer Play   306

The Phases of Peer Play   306

Serving Students with Special Needs   308

Teacher Decision-Making during Outdoor Play   309

Teaching Styles That Support Outdoor Play   311

Indirect Coordination   311

Direct Involvement   312

Fostering Inquiry in the Outdoor Classroom   312

Assessing Children's Play in the Outdoor Classroom   314

Evaluating Outdoor Play Environments   314

Advocating for Outdoor Play for All Children   315

Summary and Conclusion   316

13 Play, Toys, and Technology   317

Types of Toys   319

Toys and Development   321

Games with Rules   322

Robots and Engineering in Early Childhood Settings   323

Children Under Siege: Toys and the Marketplace   324

Toys That Limit Development   324

Toys That Undermine Gender Equity   325

Media-Based Play   328

Racial and Ethnic Stereotypes in Children's Media   329

Teachers Respond to Media Stereotypes   330

Media Literacy in an Age of Consumerism   330

Computer Play and Young Children   332

Computers and Play: Structuring the Physical Space for Computers   332

Computers and Play: Selecting Tool Software   332

Guiding Play with Computers as Tools for Students   334

Play, Computers, and Assisted Technologies   335

Computer Simulations, Games, and Books   336

Technology Guidelines and Standards   336

Addressing Standards for Technology   337

Choosing Computer Software   338

*Using the Potential of Computer Technology to Extend Play and Address
    Standards   339*

Summary and Conclusion   341

14 Conclusion: Integrating Play, Development, and Practice   342

Constructivism and Development   344

What Is Developed?   344

Means-Ends Coordinations and Development   345

Constructivism and Social-Cultural Theories of Play   347

Jean Piaget (1896–1980)   347

Lev Vygotsky (1896–1934)   348

Connecting Piaget's and Vygotsky's Theories   348

A Closer Look at Piaget and Constructivist Theory   349

Schemes: Assimilation, Accommodation, and Play   349

Stages of Development and Play   350

The Construction of Reality   352

Social Experience and the Construction of Reality   354

Play and Development   355

Play and the Development of Intelligence   355

Play and the Development of Personality   356

Play and the Development of Competencies   358

Play and the Development of the Social Self   359

The Meaning of Play in Childhood and Society   360

Play and the Work of Society   360

Autonomy as the Context for Development   362

Development, Developmentally Appropriate Practices (DAP), and Play   363

Expectations for Ourselves and Our Children: Academic Standards   364

Summary and Conclusion   366

Ø   References   368

Ø   Name Index   388

Ø   Subject Index   395

Play at the
Center of the
Curriculum

Looking at Play Through Teachers' Eyes

With dramatic gestures, Brandon loudly sings, "Can you milk my cow?" After he and his kindergarten classmates finish the song with a rousing, "Yes, ma'am!" their teacher, Anna, calls on Becky and Tino to figure out the date and count the number of days the children have been to school. (This is the 26th day.) As other children join in the counting, Brandon takes a toy car out of his pocket. He spins the wheels, turns around, and shows it to Chris. After a moment, he reaches out to touch Kara's shoelaces, whispering, "I have snaps." Then he opens and refastens the Velcro snaps on his shoes.

Anna announces that it's choice time and calls on children to leave the circle and go to the activities of their choice. Brandon sits up straight, wanting to be called on and ready to start. The moment his name is called, he heads to the housekeeping area, where Chris and Andy are opening some cupboards. Brandon announces: "I'll make breakfast." (He picks up the coffeepot.) "Here's coffee." (He pretends to pour a cup and gives it to Chris.)

Mary, a new student in the class, wanders into the housekeeping area holding the pet rat. Brandon interrupts his breakfast preparation and says to Mary, "You can't bring Fluffy in here. You have to keep her near her cage."

Within a few minutes, the theme of the children's play turns from eating to firefighting. Brandon and Andy go to the block area to get some long block "hoses." They spend a few minutes there pretending to hose down several block construction "fires." Brandon knocks one down, to the angry cries of the builders, Valerie and Paul. He then transforms the block hose into a gun, which he uses to shoot at them.

As he and Andy stomp about the block area, Brandon passes Mary, still holding the rat, and says to her, "That's too tight. See, like this." He takes the rat from her, cradles it, looks it in the eyes, and pats it. "Fluffy was at my house during vacation. I got to feed her. See, she remembers me."

Brandon, Andy, and Mary spend the next 10 minutes building a house and a maze for Fluffy. Brandon has chosen to play in the block area each day for more than a month. The children gather five arches for a roof, partially covering a rectangular enclosure they have made by stacking blocks horizontally using long blocks and, when none are left, two shorter blocks placed side by side.

After building the "roof," Brandon rushes to a nearby table, where Rotha and Kai are chatting and drawing. He grabs a piece of paper and hastily scribbles on the middle of it, knocking off a few templates and scissors in the process. "This is my map. This is my map for the maze," he says. Brandon then goes to his teacher for some tape to put on the maze. He points to a figure on the paper where two lines intersect and says, "See my X? That's where Fluffy gets out." ✐

Every observation of children's play illustrates its multidimensional qualities. By observing Brandon's play for just a short time, we can learn about the way he is developing socially. For example, we see that Brandon is able to join Chris and Andy in their play in the housekeeping area by introducing an appropriate topic, offering to make breakfast. This observation also informs us about Brandon's developing cognitive abilities. In his play, he uses a block to symbolically represent first a hose, and then a gun. While building the house for Fluffy, Brandon demonstrates practical knowledge of mathematical equivalencies when he uses two short blocks to equal the length of one longer block. Thus, by observing Brandon's play, we witness how he applies his developing abilities in real situations.

This observation also raises some of the many questions that teachers ask about children's play. How should a teacher respond when a child plays during group instruction? How can a teacher balance children's spontaneous play with more teacher-directed activities? Should teachers redirect children when they select the same play materials or themes day after day? Should gun play be allowed? How can play help us understand and assess children's cognitive, linguistic, social, emotional, and physical development? How can we be sure we are creating an inclusive curriculum that promotes equity and school success for all? How can a play-centered curriculum address mandated frameworks and standards?

Observing Brandon leads us to the central issue this book addresses: Why should play be at the center of the curriculum in early childhood programs?

PLAY AT THE CENTER OF A DEVELOPMENTALLY BASED CURRICULUM

Developmentally based early childhood programs place the developmental characteristics of the young child—the learner—at the center of the curriculum. This book is based on the premise and evidence that play is the central force in young children's development. Consequently, a developmentally based program is a play-centered program. A play-centered curriculum is not a laissez-faire curriculum in which anything goes. It is a curriculum that uses the power of play to foster children's development. It is an emergent curriculum in which teachers take an active role in balancing spontaneous play, guided play, directed play, and teacher-directed activities. Play-centered curricula support children's development and learning in all settings and contexts, both indoors and outside.

In honoring the child's play, we honor the "whole child." When discussing a play-centered curriculum, we think of the child as a developing "whole" human being in whom the processes of development are integrated. Play fosters all aspects of young children's development from birth through age 8: emotional, social, intellectual, linguistic, and physical. It involves the integration of what children have learned. This view contrasts with the ideas that early childhood development involves the linear acquisition of separate skills or that kindergarten and primary-grade children have outgrown developmental benefits of rich play experiences. These views are not supported by research.

In promoting a play-centered curriculum, we make short- and long-term investments in children's development. In the short term, play creates a classroom atmosphere of cooperation, initiative, and intellectual challenge. If we look at long-term consequences, we find that play supports children's growth in broad, inclusive competencies such as self-direction and industry. These are competencies valued by both parents and educators, and ones that children will need to develop to function as adults in our society.

Throughout this book, we emphasize how curricula in particular areas such as mathematics, language and literacy, science, art, socialization, and technology support and enrich young children's play. This idea contrasts with the widespread notion that play serves merely to support subject-matter competencies. Our view also contrasts with the idea of play traditionally found in the intermediate grades—play as a reward for finishing work.

This does not mean that all play is equal in our eyes. Play is fun, but it is more than fun. Play-centered curricula are not opportunities for teachers to stand aside, but require highly competent, involved, and purposeful teachers. The critical dimension is to provide conditions that foster children's development using their own sources of energy. In the following chapters, we articulate the play-based curricula that support children's own developmental forces.

Play as a Fundamental Human Activity

Play is a human phenomenon that occurs across the life span, as well as across cultures. Parents in Mexico teach their babies the clapping game "tortillas," while older children and adults play Loteria. South Asian adolescents play soccer while younger children play hopping games accompanied by singing. Chinese toddlers clap to a verse celebrating their grandmothers, "banging the gong merrily to accompany me home," while the grandmothers, in their old age, play mah-jongg. As humans, we not only enjoy our own engagement in play, but we also are often fascinated by the play of others. The entertainment and sports industries reflect the popularity of observing play.

The Power of Play in Development

What is the specific rationale for making play the central focus of school programs for young children? During early childhood, play is fundamental because it drives young children's development. As we describe in the chapters that follow, play is simultaneously a facet of development and the source of energy for development. Play is an expression of the child's developing personality, sense of self, intellect, social capacity, and physicality. At the same time, through their play, children direct their energy toward activities of their own choice. These activities stimulate further development.

The basic premise of this book is that play is the heart of developmentally appropriate early childhood programs and, therefore, should be at the center of every curriculum. If the young child is at the center of the curriculum, then play should be at the center of the curriculum as well, for play is the basic activity of early childhood.

Play is essential for optimal development and learning in young children. The match between the characteristics of play and the characteristics of the young child provides a synergy that drives development as no teacher-directed activity can.

Play includes interest, motivation, and active engagement.

Grounding Practice in Theory, Research, and the Wisdom of Practitioners

The idea of play at the center of the early childhood curriculum is grounded in work from four early childhood traditions: (a) early childhood practitioners, (b) researchers and theorists who study play, (c) researchers and theorists in the area of development and learning, and (d) educational historians. These four traditions inform our ideas of a practice of play.

Play and the Wisdom of Practitioners. Historically, play has been at the center of early childhood programs. Early childhood educators have observed and emphasized that young children bring an energy and enthusiasm to their play that not only seems to drive development, but also seems to be an inseparable part of development. A kindergarten student playing with blocks might spend an hour focused intently on this task, but might squirm when asked to sit down for 10 minutes to practice writing letters of the alphabet.

Play, Theory, and Research. Theorists and researchers who study play suggest possible reasons for its importance in the development of young children when they describe the characteristics of play. According to theorists, play is characterized by one or more of these features: (a) active engagement, (b) intrinsic motivation, (c) attention to means rather than ends, (d) nonliteral behavior, and (e) freedom from external rules.

When young children are actively engaged, we observe their zest and their focused attention. Adults often marvel at children's unwillingness to be distracted from play that interests them. Brandon, for example, shows his genuine desire to be doing what he does, without encouragement from Anna. This is what we mean by intrinsic motivation, that is, the desire to engage in an activity arises from within the child. When children are actively engaged and intrinsically motivated, they demonstrate their abilities to use language to communicate with others, solve problems, draw, ride trikes, and so on. Children's sense of autonomy, initiative, and industry are rooted in intrinsic motivation and active engagement.

When children pay "attention to means rather than ends," we notice that they are less involved with achieving a goal or outcome than with the activity itself and enjoyment of reaching it. Young children are well aware of the grown-up things they cannot yet do. Even the competencies that are expected of them are often frustrating, such as waiting for a snack, sharing, cutting with scissors, and (in the primary years) learning to read, add and subtract, and carry out simple household chores. In contrast, in their play, children can change the goals and the ways to achieve the goals.

> This shifting among alternative patterns of means and goals appears to contribute flexibility to the child's thinking and problem solving. These new combinations may be accompanied by a sense of discovery and exhilaration. Miller (1974) borrows "galumphing," a term from Lewis Carroll's poem "Jabberwocky," to describe this. "Galumphing" with ideas lacks the smoothness and efficiency that characterize more goal-specific activity, but it is experimentation that may enhance creative thinking. Opportunities for "galumphing" are lacking in curricula that are programmed to have the child arrive at only "correct" responses. (Monighan-Nourot, Scales, & Van Hoorn, with Almy, 1987, p. 17)

Young children's play is often nonliteral, pretend play that is not bound by external rules. How is fantasy play useful to a young child who is learning to function in the real world? Children's symbolic development is fostered through the creation and use of symbols in pretend play as well as in hypothetical, "as if" situations. Through play, children develop boundaries of the real and the imagined, and also visions of the possible, the drive from childhood that turns the wheels of invention.

Play, Development, and Learning.   Additional support for placing play at the center of the curriculum comes from the work of theorists and researchers who have examined the role of play in development and learning. For more than a century, theorists have explored these links.

The work of "classical" theorists reflects the time in which these theorists lived. We discuss these theories from current viewpoints that reflect today's concerns and understandings of development. In the chapters that follow, we turn to the work of Piaget and Vygotsky for understanding the importance of play in cognitive development. We turn to Erikson and Mead to understand the role of play in the child's developing sense of self and ability to establish social relationships, and to Vygotsky and Erikson to understand how play might reflect issues of culture and society. We describe the work of researchers and writers, including Parten, Smilansky, Paley,

Corsaro and others. Throughout this book we discuss recent critical thinking that addresses challenges in early childhood education to promote inclusive, multicultural and peaceful classrooms.

Play and Traditions of Schooling. Writings on the history of schooling also lead us to place play at the center of the early childhood education curriculum. Historians have examined issues such as "What is worth learning?" and, importantly, "Who should learn?" as well as the ways in which formal schools differ from informal apprenticeship structures found in less industrialized, traditional societies (Dewey, 1915/1971).

Early schools in the Middle East and Europe evolved for specific purposes, such as training scribes. Only select groups of boys attended school during middle childhood and adolescence. Later, as formal schools spread geographically, the number of students attending schools began to grow, and the diversity of students began to increase. During the past century, the rationale for schooling changed. In today's formal schools, many activities have become separate from their real-life applications.

During the late 1800s, a greater number of adults needed to have basic competencies in numeracy and literacy, whereas a more elite group of adults needed more technical competencies. It was also during this period and the early 1900s that girls and boys younger than 7 or 8 years old entered "school-like" settings. For the children of factory workers, these settings were child-care institutions designed to keep children out of harm's way. In contrast, for the children of the emerging, more educated middle class, the settings were nursery schools and kindergartens that aimed to support the development of the child. Play comprised a large part of these programs.

By the mid-1950s, the gradual blending of the goals of child care, preschool, kindergarten, and the primary grades led frequently to increased pressure for teacher-directed curricula and programs that stress learning "academic" skills (Nourot, 2005). This trend continues.

Teachers report that young students bring little spontaneous energy and interest to learning addition facts or sight words if only a didactic approach rather than a balanced approach is employed. Many teachers complain that their own work is less creative and challenging when they are required to follow "teacher-proof" lessons. Furthermore, uninformed efforts to increase tests scores have resulted in schools that have even reduced or completely eliminated recess and other outdoor time. Though pressure for performance has increased in preschool and the primary grades, longitudinal studies of student achievement show that children who receive more didactic instruction in the early years fail to demonstrate increased academic performance throughout elementary school and later grades. In fact, there is growing evidence and concern that, today, many young children experience a high degree of emotional stress and show limited abilities to interact with others.

These considerations of the history of formal schooling, as well as current practices, bring us back to our position that play should be at the center of the early childhood curriculum.

Play at the Center of a Balanced Curriculum

Play-centered programs promote equity because they are built around the strengths of young children rather than their weaknesses. At a time when our population is becoming increasingly diverse, we cannot continue these educational practices that fail so many students. To meet the needs of all children, we recommend preschool–kindergarten programs that are firmly play centered, yet complemented by daily life activities and some teacher-directed activities. We see first grade as a transitional year, with emphasis on both play and daily life activities complemented with teacher-directed activities. In second grade, play and work are merged into children's extended projects, thereby integrating areas of academic learning.

In our view, education for children from preschool through the primary grades should promote the development of both the competent young child and the competent future adult. This is best accomplished by means of a balanced, play-centered program in which neither spontaneous play nor teacher-directed activities are the only mode. As Figure 1.1 illustrates, play is at the center of a balanced curriculum.

Play is the central strata. In early childhood settings, play is frequently further characterized as "spontaneous," "guided," or teacher-directed. As Figure 1.1 suggests, rather than considering these rigid categories, we use these terms to highlight the more characteristic feature.

- Spontaneous play.

  Four-year-olds Grace and Sophia stroll over to the maple trees at the border of the yard. It's late October, and leaves cover the ground. Sophia kicks at the leaves. When Grace begins to pick them up, Sophia joins her.

Figure 1.1
Play at the Center of a
Balanced Curriculum

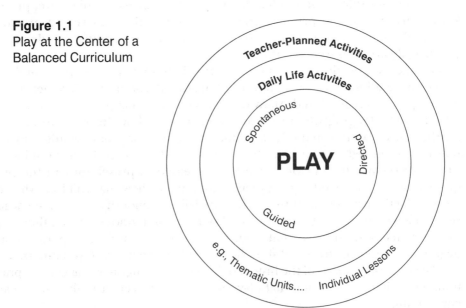

The children spend several minutes gathering the red, orange, and gold leaves. Sophia drops one, and they watch it flutter to the ground. They scatter the leaves, then pick up more. As a large golden leaf twirls to the ground, Grace exclaims gleefully: "They're helicopters!" ⌀

The characteristics of play are most visible in spontaneous play. This vignette reflects all: intrinsic motivation, active engagement, attention to means rather than ends, freedom from external rules, and nonliteral behavior. As an educational term, spontaneous play refers to behaviors that arise from intrinsic motivation, that are self-directed, and that represent expressions of children's own interests and desires.

- Teacher-guided play.

    ❤ Five kindergartners are gathered around the large table, constructing a collage that represents the ocean and hilly shoreline. Roseann, their teacher, made a simple sketch on butcher paper and has set out colored paper and a collection of small objects, including dried flowers, feathers, and shells. She has also put out sheets of brightly colored construction paper, scissors, and glue sticks. She anticipates the children will create collages using these materials as well as others that are always available on a nearby shelf. As she planned the activity and selected materials, Roseann kept in mind that Logan, a child with attention deficit disorder, loves to glue and paste materials that are bright and tactile. Logan carefully selects several opalescent shells and pastes them onto a wave. Roseann notices that Jayden has been observing Logan for several minutes. He hesitates as he examines the materials, moving his hand across a few of the shells. Quietly, Roseann leans toward him and asks: "Which shell do you want to paste first?" ⌀

To guide means to influence someone's thinking or activity. Guided play refers to children's play that is influenced in an intentional manner by adults. In this example, the children are actively engaged. Though they choose to participate, Roseann both initiates and guides their activity.

- Teacher-directed play.
The educational term teacher-directed play refers to children's play that is organized and, literally, directed or controlled by an adult, such as singing a song. Teachers' intentions are clear and specific, even when expressed in a soft tone or even when several choices are provided. Despite the teacher's instructions or directions, the characteristic of the activity may still be defined as play. Inasmuch as the activity is goal directed by adults, it is guided or directed play rather than spontaneous play. The following is a clear example of directed play:

    ❤ It looks like all the children in Molly's second-grade class are giggling. So is Molly and so is Mrs. Kim, Yae Suk's mother. Last week Mrs. Kim made chop-chae with the children and provided chopsticks. Though several children ate the clear rice noodles, vegetables, and beans with ease, most children—and Molly—found it challenging. After class, Mrs. Kim had volunteered to return to teach the children to use chopsticks, the Korean style that is thinner and shorter than most. Today she's returned with dried kidney beans. Molly sets up individual trays so the beans don't fly across the room. Mrs. Kim shows the children how to hold the chopsticks and pick up beans one at a time. She demonstrates, picking up one, then two at a time, then three. What a challenge for hand–eye and small muscle coordination. Though only a few children use the chopsticks with ease, all the children are attentive and involved. Ethan finds that he can pick up one at a time, then two at a time, then three at a time! Others are fascinated with his skill. Mrs. Kim starts chanting: "Hanna, tul, sed" (one, two, three) as Ethan picks up one, then two, then three beans at a time. Pretty soon everyone is chanting, "Hanna, tul, sed," and everyone starts giggling. ✆

Daily Life Activities Are the Critical Second Strata.   Examples of daily life activities include preschoolers setting the table, kindergartners planting a garden, first graders writing and mailing their first letters, and second graders learning to tell time. More teacher-directed activities, including thematic units as well as subject area units, constitute the third strata.

In the play-centered curricula described throughout this book, a constant flow occurs among these three levels. We discuss how children repeat daily life and teacher-directed activity in their play, how teachers plan daily life activities so that they draw on the power of play, how teachers can develop effective assessment strategies, and how teachers can use children's play to promote curricular objectives.

In contrast to the common emphasis on instrumental play, that is, play used to support subject-matter objectives, we emphasize how curricula in content areas can enrich and support good play. By changing our focus from play to daily life activities to teacher-directed activities (and always back to play), our view becomes the opposite of the traditional view. When children play, we believe they are intrinsically motivated and engrossed in what interests them most. They are also practicing and developing competencies at the edge of their potential. In play, self-directed learning engages and focuses attention and provides numerous opportunities for all children to develop self-regulation and to practice self-control.

When children are involved in such daily life activities as writing a letter, sending an e-mail message, cleaning up, or learning to tie their shoes, they are engaged in what is important in the lives of the adults around them. The purpose of daily life activities is readily apparent, if not always enjoyable. There are procedures to learn and social rules to obey. This is not necessarily true of play. For example, when a child like Brandon pretends to make coffee for breakfast, he does not have to adhere to the sequence of how an adult makes coffee. He can choose to turn the cup of coffee into a glass of orange juice or a cup of ice cream if he wants to. Play, too, has rules, but children have more power to determine them.

Children's involvement in play, daily life activities, and teacher-directed activities differs when we compare the rationale for children's activity. Children play because of their own intrinsic interests. In play, no "one task" is imposed on the child by adults. The child does not need to utilize a sense of will or purposeful intention to meet adult expectations. A sense of will is needed to accomplish tasks or daily life activities that are not of one's choosing. This is self-regulation. Unless teacher-directed activities are developmentally attuned to the children's level, it is difficult for the children to adhere to the task. Prior to middle childhood, most children have difficulty maintaining sufficient willpower to learn such adult competencies as reading or writing.

During middle childhood, children become increasingly interested and able to master daily life competencies. Historically, children living in more traditional cultures, as well as those attending formal school, were 7 or 8 years old—the beginning of middle childhood—before such tasks were expected of them. This remains true today in many countries where educators wait until children are 7 or 8 years old before introducing formal reading or mathematics lessons. Until middle childhood, the emphasis is on creating programs rich in opportunities for the informal development of subject matter competencies.

The Play Continuum

Teachers who place play at the center of the curriculum include spontaneous play, guided play, and teacher-directed play. Although these three terms appear to distinguish three separate domains of play, we view them as points along a continuum that goes from child-initiated play to teacher-initiated play, as shown in Figure 1.2.

Throughout this book, we emphasize that the balance among three types of play—spontaneous play, guided play, and teacher-directed play—depends on many factors, such as the developmental level and interests of the children, the cultures of the families, and the culture of the school. Children's school curricula must be viewed in the context of their lives. The child who goes from child care to school to an evening at home watching TV has a different need for play than the child who attends nursery school 2 days per week and plays outside most of the time.

Early childhood educators balance play with appropriate teacher-directed strategies as they address the needs of all children. For example, an older first grader who continues to struggle with letter–sound relationships or basic number concepts may need both more direct adult-guided instruction, as well as more opportunities to integrate developing understandings within the context of spontaneous play.

Figure 1.2
The Play Continuum

Spontaneous Play	Guided Play	Teacher-Directed Play

Child-Initiated ◄– – – – – – – ► Teacher-Initiated

HOW TEACHERS OF YOUNG CHILDREN VIEW PLAY

In the following pages, we return to the vignette of Brandon and his teacher, Anna, from the beginning of this chapter. We also draw from interviews with other preschool and primary teachers who spoke about the implementation of a play-centered curriculum.

Play Through the Eyes of Brandon's Teacher

Brandon's teacher, Anna, uses her observations of his play to gain insight into his growth and development:

> Play gives Brandon opportunities to select activities of his own choosing. I am learning a lot about Brandon by watching him play. He tends to visit several areas during this 30- to 40-minute period, but I've noticed that he often sustains a dramatic theme such as firefighting for a fairly long time or returns to the same theme at several points during the day. He shows much more focused attention during this time than he does when I'm presenting a more structured lesson, like today, for example, in circle time when I introduced counting skills.
>
> He's definitely one of the more verbal children in our group. His social skills are improving, and he often demonstrates a caring attitude toward the other children. I noticed he was also very nurturing toward Fluffy today. He loves to help care for her. I feel this is a wonderful opportunity for him to develop his sense of responsibility, though he has been a bit possessive about her since he took her home. He's really attached to her. He's interested in learning more about rats and brought in a book from the library and copied a picture. Choice time gives him and the other children more of a chance to develop their individual interests.
>
> He generally gets along with the other children, but he can be aggressive at times, for instance, when he knocked down someone's blocks. This year, he rarely gets into direct physical confrontations as he did last year in preschool. I've been keeping anecdotes on this, and it seems that these aggressive acts tend to happen when he's rushed or has too many people around him. Today's episode involving using the blocks as guns certainly raised my classic question about war play: "Should I stop it?" I'm often uncertain about what to do, especially when it is such a momentary theme as it was today.
>
> Along with my written anecdotes, I've been trying to decide what else to include in his portfolio. Today I thought about keeping the map. He was so eager to take it home that I decided to make a copy of it to save. ∅

Anna continues:

> I'm experimenting a lot with play. It's been a gradual process. Observing the children's behavior, I feel that I'm on the right track. It's hard to believe

how different my program is from the way it was only 3 or 4 years ago. I had a desk for each child and all of my "inside" time was teacher directed, either whole-class activities or centers. My program is definitely play-centered. I include materials that foster literacy, math, art, and social development, including some materials that I use in more directed activities. Now we have worktables and a lot more open space. The first thing I did was order blocks. We haven't had blocks in a kindergarten at this school for as long as I've been here and that's 12 years. The kindergarten teacher who has been here the longest said that her old set of blocks was probably still in a district storehouse somewhere.

I also expanded the housekeeping area. In the beginning, I had a very small one, but I never really thought about it as more than a special area where kids could go when they were finished with something else. Now I see how important the playhouse is. I have had a lot of fun making it more attractive to the children who are immigrants. I included more photos of their families, pictures from ethnic calendars showing places and people from different cultures, dolls with ethnically diverse clothing, and objects the children are familiar with from their own backgrounds, like rice bowls and chopsticks. The children seem to feel more at home in my classroom and can play out what they know.

Anyway, I think my kids are a lot more creative and thoughtful than when my program was more teacher dominated. For example, I see this in their stories and journals. Half of the students who were in my class last year are in Kristin's class now. She told me last week that she noticed a difference. The children who were in my class are particularly eager to initiate projects, and they tend to stay engrossed longer. She also sees a difference in the way they cooperate with everyone, not just their good friends, and the way they respect each others' work.

Anna mentioned that Sarah's mother noticed a difference, too. Several years ago, Anna followed only a very structured reading program with prereaders and worksheets. This year the children began their own journals on the first day of school. She put pads of paper and pencils in many places in the classroom to encourage writing. Although Anna still attends to teaching phonic awareness, she now uses a greater repertoire of strategies.

Sarah's mother told Anna that she was very happy that Anna was finally teaching reading. Indeed, Sarah was reading and writing a lot at home as well. Anna remarked that Sarah's sister was in her class 5 years ago when she was only following formal reading lessons and having her students work in workbooks. Anna realized that this story of the two sisters didn't conclusively prove the point, but she thought that in general her students were now much more self-directed in reading and writing.

Anna pointed out that during what she calls *choice time* (which she used to call *play time*), probably a third of the children are reading or writing at any given moment.

I've been joking that I want to "up play" rather than "down play" play! I want to show parents how it benefits their children. We had our first open house last week. I put together a slide show with slides from last year and some slides from the first 2 weeks of school. It made a great difference for parents to see "live" examples of how play is important. As I discussed the development of self-esteem, I showed several slides of Jimmy and Andrea building a tower taller than they are. (I wish I had had a video camera for that.)

The slides also gave me a chance to talk about play and social development. I purposely selected slides that included every student in my class so parents could get a personal message about how important play is to their own child's social development.

Of course, I also emphasized the ways in which children use what they've learned in academic areas and how much more they learn through play. I showed slides of the children building with blocks, pouring and measuring as they played "making chili" at the sand table, and talked about their development of math concepts. I used slides of children writing in their journals, others scribbling on the chalkboard, and one reading to another as I talked about literacy development. The slides helped parents make the connections between play and their children's development in all areas.

I worked out a way to illustrate developmental progress. Four wonderful slides—if I may say so—show how Genette's block constructions became more complex over a 2-month period last year. ✍

In this brief conversation, Brandon's teacher mentions issues vital to the play-centered curriculum—issues that we examine throughout this book. She discusses the development of her program in terms of carefully observing children to understand their interests and development. She uses play anecdotes as part of her assessment program and puts play-created products, such as Brandon's map, in her students' portfolios. Anna reflects carefully on the effects of her interventions in children's play, questioning, for example, "what to do about war play" and "how to help immigrant children feel more comfortable in the classroom." She also experiments with curricular ideas such as using play to support emerging literacy and conceptual mathematics development.

Across the country, preschool and primary teachers continue to examine the role of play in their programs. Teachers are trying to make programs more empowering for all, that is, embracing the full range of diversity of children and their families and meeting the developmental needs of children. As we wrote the fifth edition of this book, we visited and spoke to the teachers and administrators at numerous schools to observe the variety of current practices and understandings about children's play. We highlight teacher conversations from Brandon's school purposely because the preschool, kindergarten, and primary-grade teachers at that school represent a broad spectrum, from those who follow teacher-directed, skill-based programs to teachers who implement play-centered curricula, such as Randi, Pat, and Kristin. Our conversations with these teachers exemplify some of the typical, yet

The child's development is tied to social life.

important, ideas and concerns educators raise as they implement more play-centered curricula.

Randi, a preschool teacher, emphasizes the role of play in meeting the social and emotional needs of individual children. Pat, a kindergarten teacher, raises the question, "What is good play?" and the issue of assessment. Kristin, a first-grade teacher in her second year of teaching, focuses on the importance of choices in children's development. She also discusses how the play curriculum challenges students to use their developing academic skills in a comfortable environment.

Randi: Meeting the Needs of Individual Children in Preschool

I think that play gives children a chance to make their own choices, their own decisions. The chances it provides for socialization also are very important. As they play, children communicate their feelings and ideas. This is especially important in my program, where almost all my children have special needs. For many, English is a second language. Play gives them a chance to express themselves in a less formal and more comfortable situation than circle time, for example. Play also provides opportunities for children to use their own language fluently and to express ideas in nonverbal ways. It's important for developing their sense of self-worth.

Among the questions I have are: "Am I doing the best I can for my students who are learning English as a second language?" It's hard for me when I can't follow the dialogue of their dramatic play. When I think about children like Brandon, I find I have questions about how to handle aggressive play.

Pat: From Worksheets and Desks to Blocks and Bubbles in Kindergarten

I consider play anything children decide to do that's not adult directed, like reading by themselves. If the choice is theirs, logically, they should enjoy it. Play gives young children the time to develop language skills, get along with their peers, make choices, and be responsible. It gives me the chance to learn more about the children, see what they do, and discover what they're really interested in doing. It also gives me time to interact with each child personally.

What I want to happen, what I consider "good play," depends on the child. Yesterday, I observed Marissa in what I consider good play for her. Marissa always seems to follow the other children. Yesterday, however, she was playing by herself with a small playhouse. She had selected what she herself wanted to do. She talked to herself a lot and stayed focused. This is a new behavior for her: selecting her own activity and staying with it.

I've made a commitment to write observations. I need to learn more about what to look for when I'm observing. Also, I want to ask questions to find out what children are really thinking, so they can respond without thinking, "What's the right answer?" I feel as though I'm at a new stage in learning how to intervene. ✆

Kristin: Letting Children Develop at Their Own Pace in First Grade

During free-choice time, my children have access to blocks, Legos and other manipulatives, art materials like paint and markers, and the housekeeping corner. It's also a time when they can dictate a story to me or a parent volunteer, or get some help from their peers in inventing the spelling of words.

I think kids need to have time to work on concepts they are developing at their own pace and by their own choice. Right now, there's a lot of writing going on. Some write letters. Others write whole sentences. In language, as in other areas, there is a wide range of abilities. During free-choice time, children work at a level that's comfortable for them. During the past year, I've extended the amount of play time I provide. Now I plan for at least 30 to 40 minutes a day, usually in the early afternoon. When they've had enough time to make their own choices about learning, the children are much more able to focus on the social studies or science activities scheduled at the end of the day.

Another goal of mine is to discuss my program effectively with parents. Play has never been a traditional part of first grade curriculum in our area. Parents often ask me whether we really have time to play if we are to get the children ready for second grade. ✆

During our visits to schools, we listened to the questions about play, children's development, education practices, and state standards. These visits were fun because teachers shared so many stories, and they were impressive because teachers revealed insights and raised issues. In this book, we address these issues and share stories from some of the teachers we talked to, as well as stories of our own. We create bridges between practice, research, and theory that deal with play in a playful way.

PLAY: THE CORE OF DEVELOPMENTALLY APPROPRIATE PRACTICE

Some teachers with whom we spoke told us that their program consists mainly of play—spontaneous, guided, as well as teacher-directed play. Others, like Kristin, are experimenting with including more play in the curriculum. Some teachers are wondering if play is appropriate, and, if so, what kinds and how much. All are trying to answer questions about the role of play in meeting the needs of the children they teach.

Developmentally appropriate practice (DAP) is the term used by the National Association for the Education of Young Children (NAEYC) to describe programs grounded in child development theory and research and designed to meet the developmental

A play-centered curriculum is emergent.

needs of children (Copple & Bredekamp, 2009). NAEYC's most recent 2009 publication and the organization's Position Statement, *Developmentally Appropriate Practice in Early Childhood Programs Serving Children from Birth through Age 8*, place greater emphasis on the centrality of play in development and learning. Copple and Bredekamp explain that this most recent Position Statement reflects current knowledge from research and recognition of the importance of the broader social context, including the context of children's lives. The 2009 Statement reflects one of the core values of early childhood educators: recognition that childhood is both a time for learning and for "laughter, love, play, and great fun" (p. x).

> Play is an important vehicle for developing self-regulation as well as for promoting language, cognition, and social competence. . . . High-level dramatic play produces documented cognitive, social and emotional benefits. However, with children spending more time in adult-directed activities and media use, forms of child play characterized by imagination and rich social interactions seem to be declining. . . . Rather than detracting from academic learning, play appears to support the abilities that underlie such learning and thus to promote school success. (pp. 14, 15)

Most of the teachers we talked to take these development and learning needs into account with regard to how their teaching practices meet the needs of diverse children and families. For example, in discussing her program, Rosemarie considers both typical development of 3- and 4-year-olds, as well as the particular needs of children who are English language learners. Neil thinks about the needs of 6- and 7-year-olds, including the individual needs of children such Robert, identified as having learning disabilities that affect his working memory.

The premise of this book is that play is at the center of a developmentally appropriate curriculum for all children. This follows from our conviction that play provides the integrative context essential to support the growth of the whole child, particularly through the preschool years and during the primary grades. The position that play is at the center of a developmentally appropriate curriculum leads to our position that a play-centered curriculum can effectively address curriculum standards.

ADDRESSING STANDARDS IN THE PLAY-CENTERED CURRICULUM

Play is the heart of developmentally appropriate practice because it is the driving force in young children's development. Therefore, we consider a play-centered curriculum the most developmentally appropriate way of addressing meaningful, developmentally appropriate curriculum content standards in early childhood education programs.

The Purpose of Standards

What do we hope that children will gain from participating in early childhood programs? A central stated goal of curriculum standards is to ensure equity for children, to ensure that each child receives a quality education. In the best sense, standards reflect the importance of early childhood and are attempts to specify the features of quality educational programs and the most important learning expectations for children.

Although the standards movement had a growing effect on 1–12 grade programs beginning in the 1980s, it was not until 2000 that many national associations and state departments of education considered standards for preschool and kindergarten children. The implementation of standards and the No Child Left Behind legislation led to widespread discussion within the early childhood education community about the appropriateness of various standards and whether particular standards do, indeed, lead to improved outcomes for all children.

Identifying the Most Important Learning Outcomes. The National Association for the Education of Young Children and other national professional organizations have identified the "big ideas" and important processes they consider developmentally appropriate. All underscore the importance of the kind of in-depth curriculum that we advocate throughout this book, curriculum that provides children with numerous opportunities to revisit these big ideas and processes—in their spontaneous play as well as in more teacher-directed activities. Many national educational associations have developed academic subject-oriented frameworks and standards: the International Reading Association (IRA); the National Council of Teachers of Mathematics (NCTM); the Consortium of the National Arts Education Associations; the National Science Teachers Association (NSTA); the National Council for the Social Studies (NCSS); the National Association for Sport and Physical Education (NASPE); and the International Society for Technology in Education (ISTE).

Several of the associations have issued joint position papers with the National Association for the Education of Young Children. These position papers advocate that curriculum content standards for children in preschool through primary grades must be meaningful and recommend that such standards be based on children's active, engaged experiences. These associations also advocate that curriculum reflects the cultures and languages of children and their families, and that curriculum meets all children's special needs. We agree with such major position statements of the national professional organizations. Our analysis of the frameworks and major goals finds that the majority are consistent with the play-centered early childhood curricula we describe.

Guidelines for Developing Appropriate Standards for Young Children

The opportunities and challenges that standards provide for promoting effective early childhood programs are discussed in *Early Learning Standards: Creating the Conditions for Success,* the joint position statement from NAEYC and National Association of Early Childhood Specialists in State Departments of Education (NAECS/SDE; 2002). This key position statement emphasizes that to be effective, early learning standards result in high-quality educational experiences and outcomes for young children when four conditions are met:

1. The content and outcomes of early learning standards are developmentally appropriate to children's current developmental abilities as well as their life situations and experiences. (See pp. 4–5.)

2. Numerous stakeholders are engaged in developing and reviewing early childhood standards. Stakeholders include parents and other community representatives and early childhood educators, including early childhood special education specialists. (See p. 6.)

3. "Early learning standards gain their effectiveness through implementation and assessment practices that support all children's development in ethical, appropriate ways" (p. 6). This means that teaching practices promote social interactions and curricula promote engagement and depth of explorations.

   "Tools for assessing young children's progress must be clearly connected to important learning represented in the standards; must be technically, developmentally, and culturally valid; and must yield comprehensive, useful information." (p. 7).

4. Standards are accompanied by strong support for early childhood programs, including adequate support for professionals and professional development, and respectful support for families as partners in their children's education. (See pp. 7–8.)

We agree with these guiding principles for the development of standards for early learning as well as the guidelines of the national content area associations. Within this context, play-centered curricula optimize children's learning and can effectively address standards.

The Challenges of Standards

In our discussions with early childhood educators, we found that most concerns and challenges arise when the four conditions outlined earlier are not met. Many teachers point to particular state and district content and outcomes that show a lack of understanding of young children's development and learning, including cultural and individual differences. Second, teachers explain that neither those with expertise in early childhood development and education nor community members had opportunities to contribute their expertise to the development or review process.

A primary concern many teachers have about standards is that the assessment practices—rather than the standards—are developmentally inappropriate, particularly the practice of "high-stakes testing." Teachers point to the use of one-time assessment instruments that identify a small range of specific skills. The result of this assessment is then used for a "high-stakes" decision, such as telling parents that their child is not ready for kindergarten or first grade. In fact, the position statement *Early Learning Standards: Creating the Conditions for Success* (2002) emphasizes that "such misuses of standards-related assessments violate professional codes of ethical conduct" (p. 7).

Last, teachers find that, in trying to address the numerous standards in each area, they rely more on teacher-directed instruction. Some teachers remark that as a result their program has not only become less engaging for their students but for them as well. Wien (2004) explored this problem in great detail in her book, *Negotiating Standards in the Primary Classroom: The Teacher's Dilemma*. She presents detailed portraits of eight primary-grade teachers and the ways that they addressed standards. Wein described how each of the teachers responded, all struggling with the issues of developmentally appropriate practice, fostering children's interests, and trying to maintain their own engagement in teaching. Wein described their reflections as well as their classroom practices. Several tried to address the hundreds of standards in an organized, linear manner. Others maintained a greater interest in teaching by integrating standards within an integrated, holistic curriculum that drew on children's interests.

Similarly, Seefeldt (2005) described how standards can actually assist teachers in integrating the curriculum more effectively. She pointed out that if teachers are to implement numerous standards in diverse subject areas, they must identify the "big ideas" and develop a framework identifying the relationships among these major standards. It is through this careful analysis that teachers can create a richer integrated curriculum that uses the power of play to address standards (e.g., Drew, Christie, Johnson, Meckley, & Nell, 2008; Van Thiel & Putnam-Franklin, 2004). This is the approach that we take throughout this book. In the chapters that follow, we describe best practices to address standards in a play-centered curriculum.

THE CRITICAL ROLE OF THE TEACHER IN THE CURRICULUM

If play is at the center of the early childhood curriculum, how is the curriculum developed? How does a teacher foster literacy, mathematical thinking, artistic expression, socialization, self-esteem, scientific thinking, and other concepts, dispositions, and skills valued in early education? How does a teacher address and integrate standards in a meaningful, purposeful way?

We believe that the teacher is the key to the play-centered curriculum. This is a curriculum in constant development—an emergent, evolving curriculum. The knowledgeable teacher uses a wide repertoire of techniques to orchestrate carefully the flow from spontaneous play to guided and directed play, to more subject-oriented instruction, and back to play. This flow is in tune with and arises from the developmental needs of individual children in the class.

> Scott introduced himself as a "third-grade teacher just promoted to kindergarten." This was the first year that he had tried to "incorporate any play . . . much less make play the major part of my program." With little opportunity to visit other programs, Scott started the year feeling that he was sinking as much as he was swimming. "In my sinking mode, I went for teacher-structured activities as life rafts. They felt safe. They were like the curriculum I knew."

It took Scott most of the year to set up an environment where his students could have choices and sustained time to play through activities. Scott needed to read enough to convince himself that play was truly the cornerstone of development for young children. Then he could begin to make changes based on that conviction.

He concluded: "This has become the most intellectually challenging year for me. I am learning how to plan for play and how to use play to assess students' growth. I like the concept of an evolving curriculum, but it takes patience as well as creativity to work it out each day. Things don't always work out as I had imagined."

"Because I'm an experienced teacher, I sometimes feel that I should be able to do this right away. But it doesn't work out that way. It involves a major shift in the way I'm thinking as well as in the way I structure the program: a paradigm shift."

Scott also mentioned how he felt at times when his colleagues from the "upper grades" come into his classroom. "I know they're thinking that I'm 'just' playing. I'm finally feeling that I can defend what I do, explain why play is so important." ✆

As the examples throughout this book illustrate, a play-centered curriculum is orchestrated carefully by the teacher. It is not a step-by-step, teacher-proof didactic curriculum. Consequently, this is not a step-by-step curriculum guide. However, the play-centered curriculum we discuss is also very different from laissez-faire play, such as recess time at many schools, in which no one observes or intervenes. A play-centered curriculum involves teachers in careful planning and preparation, both inside and outside the classroom. A play-centered curriculum needs playful teachers who enjoy being spontaneous, involved, and creative, as well as reflective and analytical.

SUMMARY AND CONCLUSION

In this introductory chapter, we present the rationale for placing play at the center of early childhood curricula. We consider this a pivotal moment in early childhood education. It is a time when young children have fewer rich opportunities for play in schools and in communities, indoors and out. At this same time, researchers and practitioners are learning more about the central role of play in all interrelated facets of development: social–emotional, cognitive, linguistic, and physical. The evidence-based early childhood literature demonstrates the important role of play in development. This is the time to place play at the center of the curriculum and reconcile program practices with the wisdom of practitioners and the evidence from research. Chapter 2 examines the development of play, drawing on major "classical" theories. Chapter 3 provides perspectives on how play supports the development of children's symbolic thought, language and literacy, logical-mathematical thinking, problem solving, imagination, and creativity. Chapters 4 and 5 detail the many levels at which teachers can carefully orchestrate numerous and complex opportunities for children's play in early childhood programs. These chapters examine the many factors regarding intervention strategies, environments, materials, and timing that educators must consider in program implementation. In each chapter, we discuss general guidelines as well as specific considerations and provide numerous anecdotes as illustrations.

In a play-centered, emergent curriculum, ongoing assessment is essential. Chapter 6, "Play as a Tool for Assessment," provides a multitude of examples and strategies for tracing children's learning and development through play.

An inclusive, play-based curriculum addresses issues of diversity and special needs, not as "add-ons" but as integral to the emergent curriculum. Throughout this book, we discuss how play-centered curricula reflect and build on the children's diverse heritages, their cultures, languages, and family backgrounds. Play-centered curricula build on the strengths as well as the challenges of children with special needs, including, for example, children with learning disabilities, communicative disorders, orthopedic disabilities, or attention deficit disorders and children who are gifted or talented.

Chapters 7 through 10 focus on the relationships between play and traditional subject areas: mathematics (Chapter 7), language and literacy (Chapter 8), science (Chapter 9), and the arts (Chapter 10). In each of these chapters, we discuss how play relates to the development of competencies in that area of the curriculum.

We include a primary grade focus to highlight the continuum of children's development and to remove the traditional distinctions among preschool, kindergarten, and primary grades. Throughout this text, we discuss how play-centered curricula can meet the challenge of addressing standards in a developmentally appropriate manner.

In the subject-oriented chapters, we emphasize the important question: "How do activities in academic areas support good play?" This complements the traditional question of how play fosters development in a particular area, for example, "How does play support development in math?" Each chapter emphasizes that play always remains an integrated whole—greater and far more significant than the sum of its parts.

Chapter 11 considers relationships between play and children's socialization by closely observing children's play interests. Chapter 12 highlights the critical role of the outdoor classroom in promoting children's physical development, children's connectedness to the natural world, as well as their self-initiated play and inquiry. Chapter 13 considers toys and technology in the context of young children's play. Chapter 14, "Conclusion: Integrating Play, Development, and Practice," provides a more detailed perspective of the central role of the play-centered curriculum in children's development, drawing on and expanding on issues discussed throughout the book.

Although each chapter in this book has a different focus, play is central to the entire curriculum because it integrates *all* aspects of children's development, as the following example illustrates. Lisa and Peter are working in the "post office," wrapping packages and sending them "to the Philippines." As you read this anecdote, what do you learn about Lisa's and Peter's language, their social abilities and knowledge, and their development of mathematical concepts?

     Lisa: "Do we have enough paper to wrap this package (three books)? They're for my Grandma Venecia from Cebu." Peter picks up two sheets of newspaper.

    Peter: "We're going to have to tape these together. Wait, here's the tape. I'll hold this."

          They tape the two sheets together by cutting and sticking two short pieces of tape horizontally from one newspaper sheet to the other. They then try to cut a long piece, but the tape gets twisted. Lisa cuts four short pieces and tapes the paper together.

    Lisa: "OK, put the books down here." They wrap the books, trying to make the package smooth around the edges, a difficult task because the books are not the same size. "This is going to be expensive! I bet it weighs a ton."

          They put the package on a scale that has numbers to indicate ounces as well as a teacher-made, nonstandard measurement chart with three different colors indicating three different degrees of heaviness.

    Peter: "See. It's green. That's heavy. It's going to be 3 dollars!" He takes the star stamps and pad and stamps three green stars at the top left of the package. "Wait. You need to put her address on it."

          Lisa picks up a thin blue marker and slowly writes GRUM VNSESSA 632 SEEBOO. Then she carefully selects a thick red marker and draws a heart with a butterfly to the left of the address.

In this episode, Lisa and Peter demonstrate that they know some basic information about the applications of mathematics to everyday situations. They know that one weighs a package before sending it, and they have some beginning understandings of the concept of weight. Both Lisa and Peter demonstrate that they understand that the weight of the package relates to the price of mailing it. Lisa also demonstrates that she is aware that numerals are used to write an address. Lisa and Peter are also learning about geometry and spatial relationships as they estimate how much paper they need and wrap their parcel. At the post office, they are able to take information about weight, prices, addresses, and area; coordinate the information; and apply it.

Observations of Lisa's play also inform us about her dramatic gains in speaking English. At the beginning of the year, Lisa spoke comfortably and fluently with her family members in her native Visayan but was hesitant to speak English with the other children. This observation of Lisa's play indicates that she has gained considerable mastery of English, with dramatic gains in sentence length and complexity, as well as vocabulary. She is now comfortable initiating and developing conversations in English with her peers.

As we watch Lisa and Peter, we notice that they are able to sustain their cooperative play for more than 20 minutes. During this time, they encounter several problems. For example, Peter notices that one piece of paper is not large enough to wrap the package. Each time, one or the other or both come up with a solution that the other accepts. For example, Lisa solves the problem with the tape. Their play is goal oriented, good-natured, and without conflict.

Throughout this book, we examine numerous anecdotes. In the preceding episodes, we see how Lisa and Peter's play-centered activities provide opportunities for socialization and their development of language, as well as logical mathematical thinking. Each time we view this vignette from a different perspective, we become more certain that the children's play contributes to their development in that particular domain. We look at the complex, integrated whole of the children's dramatic and creative interactions and creations and feel a certainty about the value of play in the development of these young human beings.

Play and Development: Theory

Five-year-old Sophie brings home a large painted butterfly with her own writing "B T R F Y" carefully drawn in the corner. Her parents approach her teacher concerned that allowing her to spell words incorrectly will hinder her success when she begins kindergarten in the fall. ∅

The children in Roseanna's multiage primary class are deep into the third week of their project on restaurants. They've made paper and play dough pizzas, menus, uniforms for the waiters, and paper money for their transactions. A group of children have finished making placemats and ads for the "Don't Forget the Olives" Pizza Parlor and are contemplating adding sushi to the menu. The school principal questions the value of this play-centered project and how it encompasses the district's academic standards. ∅

What answers can teachers give to questions about play in the classroom? Perhaps the most frequently quoted clichés are, "Play is the child's way of learning" or "Play is the child's work." How does play contribute to development and learning? Is play related to work in some systematic manner, or is play simply evidence of the flights of fancy and freedom we associate with childhood?

To answer these and other questions related to the role of play in curriculum for young children, we as teachers first need to formulate our ideas about the nature of play and how it develops. Although other species engage in physical or sensorimotor play, the range of play from motor play to pretend play to games with rules is a uniquely human capacity. The development of play through these stages forms the foundation for the development of intellect, creativity and imagination, a sense of self, the resolution of feelings, and the capacity to interact with others in positive and morally sound ways. In this chapter and those that follow, we view play through each of these various developmental lenses, discussing how play contributes to each in turn and to the integration of physical, social-emotional, and cognitive competencies for the whole child.

Play is more than a means to an end, however, even though these ends may be highly valued by educators and some parents. Play is the source of laughter and humor, of inventiveness and beauty. It allows us to entertain possibilities and to envision the future. It helps us to persevere in our efforts and to explore the full range of our emotions. It fosters the spontaneity and joy that make us truly human. Keeping this in mind, we invite you to consider how each lens reflects the ways development contributes to play itself as an essential aspect of human existence.

In this chapter, we look at major theories that address the development of play in childhood and explore the levels and stages suggested by these theories. In developing a theory of practice that is based in the daily lives of children and their teachers, we begin by discussing the more "classic" theorists in developmental psychology whose general theories are well articulated.

A CONSTRUCTIVIST VIEW OF PLAY AND DEVELOPMENT

Throughout history, people have tried to understand how humans develop from helpless infants to functional adults. In the West, this has given rise to the debate between "nature" and "nurture." The "nature" argument proposes that the form of adult capacities is contained in the seed of the infant and only needs to be nourished. The "nurture" argument holds that the adult is formed through experience and that the form of the adult is a reflection of this experience. This debate takes different forms, depending on the period in history. Though constructivism has been characterized as involving the interaction between "nature" and "nurture," this explanation is insufficient for early childhood educators in their daily work with children.

Constructivism reflects a different way of understanding human development. It emerged in the late 19th century and early 20th centuries and is being developed further today. At the core of all constructivist theory is a belief that the developing child, in the context of the social and physical environment, explores and adapts to the environment by coping with everyday challenges.

Also core to major constructivist theories is the recognition of the central role of play in young children's development. In this chapter, we highlight the ways that four "classic" constructivist theorists inform the ways early childhood educators understand and support children's development through the play-centered curriculum. These theorists are

- Jean Piaget (1896–1980)
- Lev Vygotsky (1896–1934)
- George Herbert Mead (1863–1931)
- Erik Erikson (1902–1994)

These theorists shared similar constructivist orientations in the way they wrote about children's development in relation to the social and cultural context. In fact, this similar orientation is reflected in the titles of their books: *Mind, Self, and Society* by Mead (1934), *Childhood and Society* by Erikson (1950/1985), *Mind in Society* by Vygotsky (published in translation, 1978), and *Sociological Studies*, essays by Piaget (published in translation, 1995). In many ways, the differences among their theories reflect the historical time and place in which they lived and their interests, background, and professional education. Perhaps most important, the theories reflect the specific questions these theorists asked about how humans develop.

PIAGET'S DEVELOPMENTAL THEORY AND PLAY

Though Piaget was primarily focused on intellectual development, his theoretical work addresses social, moral, linguistic, and emotional development as well. Piaget viewed the development of knowledge as a gradual process of restructuring earlier ways of knowing into more adequate and more generalized ways of knowing. His theory places the child at the center of this construction with a high premium on the child's spontaneous, autonomous activities. In the early childhood years this is always linked to play, both alone and with peers.

Imagine a world in which every experience you have is new, without mental pictures of previous events in your life to help you organize your perceptions and expectations. Life would be very confusing. Fortunately, human beings do have the means for organizing experiences so that we can make sense of the events in our lives.

In Piaget's constructivist view, knowledge is not simply acquired by accumulating information from the environment or copying the behavior of others, but is based on what the individual child brings to each situation. The *schemes* or mental patterns that children have already constructed are modified and built on as children try to make sense of new experiences in light of what they already know.

> Four-year-old Kim explains the word *invisible* to his friend Tony when the word comes up in a story read by a parent to the two boys. "It's like you go inside *visible*, and then no one can see you when you're in *visible*!" Kim asserts, and Tony nods his head in understanding. Kim bases his explanation on what he has experienced about not being seen in the game of hide and seek; if you hide inside something, then you can't be seen.

According to Piaget, the means of organization is intelligent *adaptation*. In adaptation, humans modify their means of interacting with the environment to fit their personal needs (e.g., Piaget, 1962b, 1963a, 1969b).

Piaget proposed an interactive process between two aspects of adaptation, which he called assimilation and accommodation. This interaction is the source of development and learning. In assimilation, new experiences are incorporated into and interpreted by existing structures of thought. Most important, elements of experiences are not simply added to the thoughts already there, like items tacked onto a grocery list. Instead, elements are transformed to fit into the structure or "template" of that individual's thinking.

An example is the assimilative pattern developed in playing with playdough or clay. Claylike substances can be pinched, patted, molded, and rolled using patterns from previous experiences.

> What happens when Kaya encounters "oublek," a substance made of cornstarch and water that has some of the properties of clay, but also some different ones? Perhaps she is surprised that the new material oozes through her fingers rather than molding into a form. Kaya's efforts to accommodate to the differences that the new material offers cause a change in the assimilative structure that Kaya will apply to claylike substances in the future.

In Piaget's theory, accommodation is a complement to assimilation. Accommodation allows the structure of our thinking to change in adapting to new experiences. Accommodation is the process through which new schemes or mental patterns for potential behavior are created. Existing patterns are modified to incorporate new information. Accommodation allows us to meet challenges presented by the environment such as resolving the cognitive surprise generated by playing with oublek when playdough was expected.

The assimilation process allows us to make sense of our experiences in light of what we already know. It allows us to consolidate, generalize, and apply our current structures of thinking to new situations and materials. The accommodation process challenges us to change and adapt our mental structures in the face of new information.

According to Piaget, there is constant interaction between these processes, alternating states of tension and balance concerning what "fits" into our schemes or mental models about experience and what doesn't fit. Awareness that a new idea or perception does not fit into our structure of thinking calls for a change in our mental models and results in the continuing development of thought. Through the interaction of assimilation and accommodation, children balance their internal states and meet their personal needs for intelligent adaptation.

In the early childhood years, assimilative and accommodative processes are constantly fluctuating. First, the mental patterns fit the new situation. Then new elements are introduced that contradict. Mental structures then change to accommodate these new elements. This process of construction and expansion marks the development of children's early thinking from idiosyncratic concepts about the way the world works to more stable and predictable relationships between internal mental models and the external world.

Because the young child's understanding of the world is closely tied to immediate contexts and lacks the stability of adult thought, their behavior is largely governed by play, by a predominance of assimilation in which reality is assimilated to the immediate needs and perspective of the child. Through play and assimilation, young children bend their view of reality to their own immediate needs and wants.

Three Types of Knowledge

Piaget delineated three major types of knowledge: physical, logical-mathematical, and social. In their play, children develop all three. *Physical knowledge* is derived from

Symbolic thought develops through make-believe.

activities with objects that allow children to make generalizations about the physical properties of objects. For example, through physical manipulation in play, children may discover that rocks sink and corks float, blocks stacked too high may fall, and sand and water may be used to mold forms.

Logical-mathematical knowledge, knowledge about the relationships among objects, people, and ideas, is constructed as children reflect on the relationships between actions or objects, for instance by comparing the sizes of two balls, or the relative lengths of blocks. In logical-mathematical knowledge, the concepts used by the child come not from the objects themselves but from the relationship invented by the child. These two types of knowledge, physical and logical-mathematical, are constructed through the child's own experiences. Play is critical to the development of both physical and logical-mathematical knowledge.

In contrast, *social knowledge* is knowledge imparted by other people and includes names for things as well as social conventions such as proper behavior at snack or group time. This type of knowledge falls closer to the accommodative end of the continuum, relying on processes of imitation and memorization for its acquisition. However, social knowledge also depends on the mental structures created through logical-mathematical knowledge for its application. As Kamii (1982) pointed out, categories such as "good words" and "bad words" are derived from social experiences, but it is the logical-mathematical capacity for classification that enables children to decide when a word might meet with the disapproval of adults.

In practice, physical, logical-mathematical, and social knowledge are closely connected in any situation involving the education of young children, as we see in this example:

> Four-year-old Enid helps Madeline, the assistant teacher, bring food to the snack table. "We need one cracker for each place," Madeline coaches. Enid takes the crackers from the box, places one on each plate, and looks expectantly at her teacher. "There," Madeline says. "Let's count these together—1, 2, 3, 4, 5, 6, 7." Enid counts with her teacher. "Now let's count the crackers—1, 2, 3, 4, 5, 6, 7." They count together again. Madeline asks, "How many cups will we need if we have one for every person?"
>
> Enid carefully takes one cup at a time from the stack and places each next to a plate with a cracker on it. Two of the cups tip over as she sets them down, and as she replaces them upright, Enid looks intently at the uneven places in the tabletop that have pushed the empty cups off balance. She runs her hand over the table next to the remaining plates to find a smooth spot before she sets down the next cup.
>
> Enid looks expectantly at Madeline, pointing her finger at the first cup. "1, 2, 3," Enid begins, then hesitates. Madeline joins her by counting "4, 5, 6, 7," and they finish the sequence of numbers. "Seven plates, seven crackers, and seven cups," summarizes her teacher, and Enid beams at her accomplishment. "Would you like to ring the bell for snack?" Madeline asks. Enid nods and goes off to ring the bell. 🐚

In this example, we see Enid constructing physical knowledge about strategies for placing crackers and cups on the snack table. She learns something about balance on even and uneven surfaces. Enid also constructs logical-mathematical knowledge about the relationship of cups to surfaces and about one-to-one correspondence. Madeline helps her count using one-to-one correspondence and presents the idea of equivalent sets for the seven plates, seven crackers, and seven cups. Madeline also helps her to learn social conventional knowledge about the names and sequence of numbers in English, as well as the position of cups in relation to plates. Enid uses her knowledge of the purpose of the snack bell to call her classmates to enjoy her handiwork. Teachers' abilities to understand and support children's learning depend on their skill in identifying the types of knowledge being constructed by the child and finding strategies to enhance that construction. Teachers are challenged to provide opportunities for children to construct their own learning and apply what they have learned from others through playful activity, Both kinds of learning are important—knowledge derived from inner sources and knowledge derived from outer sources—and a balance between the two is necessary for development.

Piaget: The Development of Play

Piaget's theory is intimately tied to the study of play. Many of his important works are filled with observations of his own three children at play during their first 2 years of life and of other children he observed in preschool settings in Geneva, Switzerland.

His important work, *Play, Dreams and Imitation in Childhood* (1962b), made play a central part of his theory. Here he showed how children develop the ability to represent their world through a series of stages in which assimilation and accommodation are increasingly better coordinated with each other. Children's ability to represent their inner concerns and understandings is revealed in their play, which progresses through a series of stages. As each new stage develops, it incorporates the possibilities for play of all the previous states (Figure 2.1). In the following sections, we present a brief description of these stages. (See also Chapter 13.)

Figure 2.1
Piaget's Stages of the
Development of Play

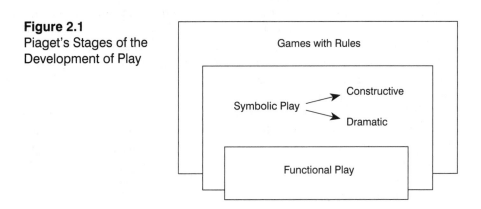

Practice or Functional Play.   The first stage is termed practice or functional play and is a major characteristic of the stage of sensorimotor intelligence. Practice or functional play is what Piaget (1962b) called "a happy display of known actions" in which children repeatedly practice their schemes for actions with objects or their own bodies. It is exemplified by the play of the infant, the grasping and pulling, kicking, and propelling of arms that infants engage in for the pleasure of mastering the movement. It continues as children take part in activities such as splashing water or sifting sand, honking a horn, or riding a bike. Practice or functional play remains a major form of activity throughout childhood and adulthood. How many adults doodle while talking on the phone or enjoy the exhilaration of jogging or moving to music? Opportunities for practice play remain an important source of development and pleasure throughout life and provide an essential feature of school curriculum, as we illustrate in subsequent chapters.

Symbolic Play.   The second stage, symbolic play, begins at about 18 months of age and is a major characteristic of the stage of preoperational intelligence. Symbolic play involves the use of mental representation to pretend that one object stands for another in play or to take on a make-believe role in play. It forms a foundation of future abstract thinking and the ability to organize both work and play experiences as human beings develop. Three major forms of symbolic play are described by Piaget: constructive, dramatic, and games with rules, which demonstrate the beginnings of conceptual thought.

The first, constructive play, provides a natural link between practice or functional play and more sophisticated forms of symbolic play. In constructive play, the child uses concrete objects to create a representation of an object: blocks or playdough manipulated to represent a house are typical examples. The intent in constructive play is to approach one's mental representation of the symbolized object as closely as possible.

> Three-year-old Sandy searches for just the right size and number of sticks to make five candles on her birthday cake. ✲

Following closely on the heels of constructive play, and often overlapping it, comes dramatic play. This play involves the creation of imaginary roles and situations and frequently accompanies the construction of pretend objects. But the representation is more abstract. Instead of simple object symbols, children use gesture and language to create imaginary roles and situations with complex themes, characters, and scripts. Sometimes this play is sociodramatic in nature, involving the negotiation of roles and pretend themes with others. At other times the play may be solitary, with characters, themes, and situations enacted by a single player.

> As Josh finishes his garage of blocks and parks a toy car in it, he pretends that an imaginary family piles into the car for a trip to the beach. ✲

> Sally invites several children to play the part of guests at the birthday party as she enacts the role of the birthday girl. She "blows out" the stick candles, and the group shares her sand birthday cake. ✲

Both stages of symbolic play, constructive and dramatic, are intellectually and socially complicated. Their mastery sets the stage for playing games with rules, which appears about the age of 6 or 7 and continues as the predominant form of overt play throughout middle childhood, adolescence, and adulthood. Overt play is an important concept because older children and adults continue to engage in constructive and dramatic play long after early childhood, but in a more covert manner. Dramatic and constructive play take the form of private fantasy and hypothetical thinking and accompany the daily internal lives of adults in many of the same ways that overt dramatic play enriches the lives of young children.

Games with Rules

The games with rules stage involves adherence to an external set of social rules that governs play. This type of play marks the transition from preoperational to concrete operational thought in Piaget's theory. In this play, rules may be negotiated and agreed on by the players before the game begins or negotiated on the spot as children spontaneously invent a game. The ability to negotiate and adhere to mutually agreed-on rules has its roots in the ad hoc negotiation of rules common to sociodramatic play at earlier stages of development (e.g., Piaget, 1965d).

Piaget (1962b) also theorized about the emotional nature of symbolic play, discussing the cathartic or "liquidating combinations" in play that allow children to discharge emotions associated with disturbing experiences. He also discussed the compensatory function of symbolic play that provides opportunities to "correct" reality that is confusing or unpleasant. So, for example, a child spanking a baby doll might discharge anger about their own punishment. Replaying a situation in which the child was not allowed to stay out after dark might prompt a dramatic play sequence of hunting monsters all night in the forest. Even though Piaget discussed the emotional

Realistic toys support and motivate play.

nature of play and believed that social experience is essential for the development of cognition, his work largely focused on individuals rather than social interactions.

VYGOTSKY: DEVELOPMENT AND PLAY

Vygotsky was primarily concerned with how development and learning takes place through social interactions within historical and cultural contexts. The English title of his major work, *Mind in Society,* is literal. The title conveys that the mind can never be considered or discussed as separate from the social, cultural, and historical context.

The influence of Vygotsky's work continues to grow in early childhood education practice and research. This theoretical perspective is central to current work on pretend play. Vygotsky was a constructivist who was particularly interested in the social dynamics that support development. He believed that conflict and problem solving in social situations are essential features of child development. In this chapter we discuss four important social–cognitive processes that are central to his theory: the zone of proximal development, the movement from interpersonal to intrapersonal knowledge, the acquisition of mental tools, and the transition from implicit rules to explicit rules.

The Zone of Proximal Development

Vygotsky coined the term *zone of proximal development* (ZPD) to refer to the context in which the child's understanding is furthered as a result of social interactions. He wrote that children perform beyond their usual level of functioning when engaged in the social and cognitive collaborations that create this zone. Vygotsky explained that play was essential to development and, in fact, the source of it: "Play is the source of development and creates the zone of proximal development" (1967, p. 16).

By observing children's symbolic play, teachers discover how new concepts, skills, and competencies emerge in the play of each child in relationship to others.

> Steven and Anthony are playing near the tunnel in the outdoor play yard. Steven, lying on his stomach with a face full of mock agony, moans, "Pretend you gave me medicine." Anthony pretends to feed him medicine, and Steven leaps up, announcing, "All better." Then Anthony becomes the patient, and Steven feeds him pretend medicine. They each take two turns. Then Anthony says, "I'm hungry," and they rush inside to get their lunch boxes, returning to the outdoor play area with a snack of pretzels. Steven holds up a pretzel and asks, "What letter?" "No letter," responds Anthony, and Steven takes a bite. "Now it's a B," shouts Anthony, and he bites his pretzel. "What letter?" "An O," shouts Steven. The final bite is eaten. "Now what letter?" asks Steven, holding out his empty hand. "No letter!" shouts Anthony delightedly, and they both fall on the ground laughing. ✑

Anthony and Steven have created a zone of proximal development where their understanding of letters is further developed. In viewing play as the source of the zone of proximal development, we focus on the collaborative construction, the *co-construction,* of a pretend reality that is invented by the players and sustained by the rules they negotiate. Because relationships are of primary importance to young children, their desires to participate in imaginary worlds shared with others lead them to accept and invent new symbolic meanings, regulate their own impulses, and collaboratively construct pretend realities. As this vignette illustrates, teachers observe that children's co-construction of knowledge can be observed across a wide range of early childhood settings.

Interpersonal to Intrapersonal Processes in Learning

Another of Vygotsky's important contributions to understanding play and development is his assertion that every function in development occurs first at the social or interpersonal and, later, at the individual level or intrapersonal level (Vygotsky, 1978). In this view, social activities between children and adults or among peers promote development and are of primary importance.

In most cultures, this includes lullabies and baby games. Infants hear patterns of communication, not only the structure of language but also rhythm and intonation.

> ❤ Mrs. P. plays a tickle game in a Filipino dialect with her son, who is 18 months. As she holds him with her left arm, she moves her right hand high above his head:
>
> "Banog-banong sa Cagon."   (Kite, kite of Cagon.)
>
> He watches intently as she moves it toward him, her voice growing more and more dramatic.
>
> "Asa matagdon?"   (Where will it alight?)
>
> She moves her hand downward, tickles his chest, and they both laugh.
>
> "Dinhi-Dinhi!"   (Here! Here!) ✇

Young children frequently learn a new concept or skill with others, such as Amy learning to use a funnel to try to fill a water balloon with her playmates at the water table. She then tries her new concepts and skill in the bathtub at home.

In schools, children learn from adults and from other children in both formal and informal activities. In this way, they develop understandings of activities and adult roles that are time and culturally specific.

At her retirement dinner, Leni is asked how things have changed in the thirty-plus years since she started teaching.

> Things are the same when I think about painting and drawing activities. But it's different for writing and even pretending to write. I started teaching before there were computers. Back in the 80s when they played office, the kids pretended to type using the old upright typewriter we had. Now kids use computers—and not only for pretend play, but to write and send class e-mails. And, I remember, when I was in second grade I was taught to write with a fountain pen and we had bottles of ink on our desks.

When I started teaching, this area was agricultural. When the kids played outside, they pretended to drive tractors and trucks. They'd "pick" food to "cook." Sometimes they'd set up fruit stands. Now the kids in my class pretend to go to the megastore—and they drive vans and SUVs and "commute to work."

Part of the difference reflects what the children bring to school. But I think a large part of the difference stems from the differences in what I do.

I always purposely set up the environment and plan the curriculum to reflect the lives of the families. If you walked in my classroom this year you'd know there are families from many cultures and different countries. We've always used simple phrases from each child's home language. And the languages have changed in the last decades. I've spoken Spanish for many years and now I'm learning Mandarin as well. ⌀

Acquiring Mental Tools

Vygotsky (1978) explained that humans use tools to make activities possible and easier. Some tools are concrete objects, like levers and wheels, that make physical work easier. Levers and wheels are simple tools; other tools are complicated and often combine a number of simple tools (e.g., a car motor).

Mental tools have been essential to human evolution and cultural development. Mental tools are sometimes referred to as "tools of the mind" (e.g., Bodrova & Leong, 2007). Mental tools often make cognitive as well as physical activities possible and easier. For example, the use of language, whether spoken or signed, is a mental tool central to communication, particularly the communication of more abstract ideas and concepts. Children, from all cultures and all times, learn the use of mental tools from others—peers as well as adults. Teachers know that some mental tools may seem quite simple to adults but are challenging to young children. The chapters that follow provide numerous examples of the acquisition of mental tools and their application in areas related to language, technology, science, mathematics, and the arts.

In the following vignette, use of a metacognitive strategy is a mental tool. Elijah chants, "Over one, under two" to make sure that he follows the pattern he is weaving.

Sam and Elijah go to the same after-school child-care program. This afternoon Sam (age 5) watches Elijah (age 8) weave on a handloom.

Elijah:	Do you want to try?
Sam:	I don't know how. How do you know what to do next?
Elijah:	Here. See. I'm making this design. I put this yarn over one, under two. See, it goes over one, under two. Try.
Sam:	Over one. Ok, under. This isn't right.
Elijah:	Help me do this row. Hold down that one (green). Now I go over (the green). O.K. Now pick up those two—the red and orange—and

I go under (the red and the orange). Remember, over one, under two. Over one, under two. Just say it with me, "Over one. Under two."

Sam: That's too complicated.

Elijah: Maybe next time. ✆

Understanding Rules

Vygotsky clarified how children develop their understanding of rules. He asserted that all play has rules and that with new levels of development, these rules become more explicit. In this way dramatic (pretend) play, where rules are implicit, forms the foundation for games, where rules are explicit. Rules in dramatic play govern the organization of roles and behavior in play and events. For example, "Daddies shake hands like this" and "Firefighters have to hook up their hoses first." Yet following these rules is largely taken for granted during children's dramatic play until conflict among players occurs when their expectations differ. Then children assert their versions of the rules governing characters' behavior and hypothetical events.

As children begin to articulate their ideas about rules that govern social behavior from their experiences and their family and cultural backgrounds, they also confront the ideas of their peers and the adults around them. They develop the capacity to negotiate rules of play that are set forth before play begins such as a game of checkers or four-square. Negotiating rules of play can be particularly challenging for children with developmental delays, children with emotional challenges, or children from families in which the expectations from home and those from school are a mismatch. Yet basic to a play-centered curriculum are mutual understandings of social rules, for example, that throwing blocks or sand might hurt other children. In this way, children begin to understand why agreed-on rules are essential to the functioning of society.

Vygotsky's Levels of Symbolic Play

Vygotsky also contributed to our understanding of how play relates to levels in the development of symbolic thinking. He observed that very young children merged the meaning of objects with the objects themselves and thus could not think abstractly. In symbolic play, children use objects to represent ideas, situations, and other objects. Objects that represent other objects are called "pivots." Children use pivots to anchor their mental representations of the meanings of words. For example, when Sam selects a book to represent a taco in his kitchen play, he anchors his concept of "taco-ness" with an object that opens and closes, and thus resembles a real taco. When children's representational competence grows, pivots become less necessary, and meaning may be carried completely in the mind, for instance, through the use of an imaginary object. For Vygotsky, the use of objects in play as support for the development of meaning-in-the-mind marks a key stage in the development of thought (e.g., Vygotsky, 1967, 1978).

For Vygotsky, the use of objects in play marks a key stage in the development of thought.

MEAD: PLAY AND THE DEVELOPING SENSE OF SELF

In all early childhood settings, teachers attempt to understand and support children's developing sense of self. Though currently not widely known, "Mead's writing is still as relevant to today's educators as it was to previous generations of teachers. In *Mind, Self, and Society,* Mead (1934) described the relationship of play to the development of a stable sense of self.

For Mead, play is the major vehicle for young children to learn to differentiate their own perspectives from those of others in their social worlds. As children take on pretend roles of others and coordinate those roles with the roles taken by their playmates, they come to view their own behavior from the perspectives of other people.

> Robert is playing at being a waiter in a restaurant. He incorporates the perspectives of his "customers" when he asks them if they are ready to order. He then communicates with his "cook" in the kitchen and tells his customers: "It will take a long time to get a burger here. Better go to McDonald's." ∅

This negotiation between the self and others also takes place outside play scripts as we see when Robert, his cook, and his customers have to figure out how they will put away the props and furniture for their restaurant when the teacher announces that it's cleanup time.

The Play Stage

According to Mead (1934), the preschool and primary-grade years provide the impetus and context for children to see themselves as unique human beings within the community of others. In Mead's theory, the young preschool child operates in the play stage of the development of the self, accomplishing simple role transformations from self to others. This is what Smilansky (1968) described as the beginning stages of role play. The child simply becomes a tiger, or an astronaut, or a veterinarian, and then returns to being the self, with limited expansion of the components or complementary roles involved in the transformations.

> Three-year-old Jed announces "I'm a fireman! RRRRRRR!" and races around waving an imaginary hose. Five minutes later he becomes a puppy, barking and crawling on all fours. ⌀

In Mead's terms the child is just beginning to differentiate the "I" or spontaneous aspect of the self from the "me," or the sense of the self as a social object. In transforming himself into a puppy, for example, Jed is beginning to figure out how others might view him from their perspectives. This is the stage in which children often create imaginary companions, representing the companion's viewpoint as well as that of the self. Children at this stage form the rudiments of a sense of self that include their own perspectives as well as representations of how others view them. Emphases may differ according to culture; for example, cultural values and interpretations of children's behavior within an individualistic cultural orientation may be different from those with a collective or mutual interdependence cultural orientation.

The Game Stage

As role playing becomes more complex, children enter into what Mead called the game stage of the development of the self. In this stage the "I" aspect of self is coordinated with complex representations of the viewpoints of others about the "I."

> Five-year-old Cindy simultaneously plays the role of mother to her child, who is eating breakfast, wife to her husband, who is on his way to work, and ballerina to her coach, who has just called her on the phone in a typical "morning in the playhouse" enactment. ⌀

Not only does Cindy need to adjust her voice tone, gesture, and language to what she believes is appropriate for each role, but she must also imagine the complementary roles of others to each of her roles and coordinate them. All the while she uses cardboard chips to represent scrambled eggs and pours milk from a wooden block.

At this point, the child in the game stage of development of the self is learning to coordinate her representation of herself with the multiple perspectives that others might take. She can think about the various aspects of her "pretend selves" in relation to the other players. She shifts fluidly from the "I" to the "me" and considers herself a social object as well as an actor in her play.

The Generalized Other Stage

The third stage of the self that Mead describes is that of the generalized other. In this stage the child not only coordinates the "I" of the self with multiple "me's" but adopts a metacognitive stance regarding the framework within which action takes place. For example, Cindy might begin to comment on the rules of her culture that define authentic roles of mother or ballerina or spouse. Early childhood educators frequently see children in this stage discuss the components of their roles with comments such as, "Doctors talk like this" or "Babies walk this way."

Initially, such negotiations may be particularly challenging for children who are bicultural and bilingual. However, it is precisely these very capabilities that can support children's abilities to take the perspectives of others.

In the dramatic play area, Eun Mi and Hyun Jae are engrossed in cooking, speaking in Korean as they prepare the pretend food.

Eun Mi: This special rice and kimchee is for grandfather.

Hyun Jae: And bring one rice bowl for grandmother! And this is for our "brother" Chung Shik.

By speaking Korean, they can express nuances of perspective taking, relationships, and customs that are hard to translate into English. For example, with this short, two-sentence exchange, they have indicated that they honor their grandparents, not only by their terms for grandparents but also when Eun Mi uses the honorific term for rice. Hyun Jae uses the term for brother that communicates that their pretend brother Chung Shik is older than she. She has also shown that she is aware of the two different counting systems and has used the correct system for counting bowls. In these sentences, both children use verb forms that show they know that are talking to peers.

The generalized other stage is one in which games with rules become of interest as children coordinate the perspectives of players with their understanding of the framework that governs the rule structure of the game. Mead (1934) emphasized the importance of the social context in which children learn a game. This behavior reflects the understandings children have about the social rules of our culture, as expressed in both their role behavior within the play and in their negotiations about roles outside the play. This development takes time. Older preschoolers and kindergartners may follow game rules presented and played out in a rigid manner. Teachers find that children delight in creating their own games or devising their own rules for such games as Candyland or Chutes and Ladders (Monighan-Nourot, 1987).

> Sally, 4½ years old, has been playing Candyland intently, by herself, for thirty minutes. She began by sitting on the floor and placing all the cards in front of her, in straight rows—face up. She then carefully opens the board and puts all the markers on Start. She selects one marker. At that moment, she notices Pat, her teacher, observing her and invites her to sit and play.

> *Sally explains:*   "First, you have to pick a bunny or something to be your marker thing. Then you look at the board and see where you want to go, and pick the card that matches it!" (Monighan-Nourot, 1987). ✆

Pat explains that Sally invented her own version of this game with rules. She delights in this game that reverses the rules so that they match her desires: she first decides where she wants to go, then picks the card.

ERIKSON: PLAY AND MASTERY IN THE INNER WORLD OF CHILDHOOD

Erikson stressed the importance of the early years and wrote extensively about the importance of play for young children's emotional development (e.g., Erikson 1950/1985, 1977). When naming his theoretical orientation, he combined "psycho" and "social" to emphasize that the individual's inner psychological state is inseparable from the social context.

Psychosocial theory continues to influence early childhood education practice for several reasons. Teachers are concerned with supporting children's emotional and social well-being. Teachers turn to psychosocial theory in their efforts to foster children's mental health. Erikson described the development of the healthy personality from infancy through old age. In numerous writings, he theorized about how children's social and emotional development relates to their families, school, and the cultural contexts in which they live. Psychosocial theory, as Erikson explained, extends Freud's psychoanalytic theory by considering both the inner, psychological dimensions and the outer, social and cultural dimensions of children's developing identity (Erikson, 1950/1985).

Erikson described eight major stages of psychosocial development that build on previous stages (Erikson, 1950/1985). The first four stages describe development from infancy through early childhood. Rather than being stages that individuals "pass through," Erikson stressed that although the healthy personality exhibits the strength of a particular stage (e.g., trust), healthy individuals continue to rework the balance of the strength of the stage and its antithesis (e.g., mistrust) throughout their lives. For example, it is adaptable for healthy individuals of all ages to exhibit mistrust in situations where it is dangerous to be too trusting, such as being challenged to jump from a high wall.

Infancy: Trust and Mistrust

During the first year of life, infants are totally dependent on their caregivers. In fact, the word *caregiver* means one who "gives care" as well as "cares about" as well as "cares for." The caregiver's sensitivity and consistency in care lead not only to the infant's attachment to that caregiver, but also to the infant's developing a sense of trust in self and the outer world. The emotionally healthy infant's basic sense of trust is central to the toddler's development of autonomy.

Akinyi rides comfortably on her mother's hip as they walk to the early morning market. She is turned sideways and sees her mother greeting several women that Akinyi sees every day. One of the women smiles, reaches over, and rubs Akinyi's back. Akinyi can feel her mother laughing softly. As her mother bends to choose vegetables for the afternoon meal, Akinyi rocks gently to one side, tied securely to her mother.

Toddlerhood: Autonomy, Shame, and Doubt

During their second and third years of life, children's growing motor and cognitive competencies contribute to their psychosocial development. This is a time when children develop a sense of their own power, a sense of "I can do it." Children's developing sense of autonomy is shaped by their schools, families, and society. Erikson emphasized that we examine what young children are allowed or expected to do and how adults set limits or boundaries on children's behavior, so that a sense of autonomy is the outcome overall rather than children's sense of shame and doubt regarding their efforts.

Ethan, 2 years old, has delayed gross motor development. Nadia, a special education specialist, has visited Ethan's home several times each month since he was born. She watches on as Ethan and his mother play one of his favorite games: "Can you get me?" Ethan's mom gets down on her hands and knees. She makes a quick move toward him as she looks at Ethan in the eye and, in a playful, higher voice says, "Can you get me?" She turns around and starts crawling away, with Ethan crawling after her. She takes quick backward glances to make sure that he's able to stay close enough behind her as she modifies her speed. Faster and slower. Faster and slower. Ethan is never more than a foot or two away. "Oh, Ethan, you're getting me! You got me!" She slows just enough so that he catches her as he crawls along at his full speed.

Later, as his mom talks with Nadia, Ethan continues to crawl around the furniture. At one point, he remains behind the couch for several minutes. Nadia calls, "Ethan, where are you? Are you hiding?" Ethan emerges with a wide grin.

Even for the child who is developing a healthy sense of autonomy, teachers find that the balance between autonomy, shame, and doubt shifts from month to month and even from activity to activity within each day.

Play links imagination with social life.

William has made a high pile of plates, forks, and spoons and begins to set the table. He brushes against a chair, and forks and spoons fall everywhere. His teacher, Ron, notes that this usually self-sufficient, confident child looks doubtful of his ability and turns to Ron as if for reassurance. Ron stays where he is and responds in a quiet voice, "Go ahead. You'll fix it." ✍

Early Childhood and the Play Stage: Initiative and Guilt

Erikson called the next stage, usually from about 4 to 6 years, "the play stage." This is the stage of initiative and guilt. The sense of autonomy seen in younger children's activities slowly develops into more sustained, complex initiatives. Guilt arises when initiative is inappropriate or overreaching. For example, despite her aunt's admonition to watch out for her baby cousin, Breann attempts to leap from one post to the other, misses, and falls on Duane, who wails in protest.

As they develop, children's greater motor, cognitive, and social capabilities mean that they are able to initiate complex play with others and sustain play for a longer time. As a toddler, Ethan's hide-and-seek play is complemented by his mother's efforts to support his growing autonomy. Older preschool children and kindergartners enjoy related, but greatly extended, games of hide-and-seek.

Children's sense of initiative is supported by their increased small and large motor coordination and strength, as well as their developing cognitive abilities.

Matthew, age 5, sits on the rug next to the puzzle rack. He selects a challenging puzzle with more than 30 pieces and a rather abstract picture. He starts with one edge of the puzzle, speaking to himself quietly, "Is this one it? This one? There, I got you!" ✍

For Erikson, this is the stage where imagination holds sway as children create their own "microreality" (Erikson, 1977). He described how, at this stage, children express their initiative in play by developing complex plots with conflicting turns and twists and create a wide range of characters.

Children at this stage initiate play to work through past failures and present contradictions. Conflicts between archetypes of good and evil expressed in power roles such as superheroes and space aliens are common themes. Conflicts between child initiative and adult prohibitions are also expressed through fantasy play, such as the "naughty baby." In dramatic play, children enter into fantasies that allow them to explore their concepts of initiative and independence. Play themes that portray children as orphaned or separated from their parents, having to fend for themselves in the woods or at sea, are common in preschool and kindergarten.

Play-centered curriculum supports children's exploration of the psychosocial issues of taking initiative and feeling guilt over violating adult prohibitions. In contrast, curriculum that emphasizes learning by imitating models may undermine the development of initiative. In every teacher-initiated curriculum, judgments of right or wrong are consistently made by adults with regard to children's processes and products, and children learn to rely on adult judgment and approval rather than their own internal resources. For example:

> In completing a teacher-modeled project, Rebecca places the precut green strip of "grass" above her name on the page and then places the "trunk" of the tree at a right angle above it. She begins to tear pieces of tissue paper for her "fall leaves." As the teacher circulates about the classroom, she pauses and says, "You've done a good job on your tree trunk, Rebecca, but your grass needs to go along the bottom edge of the paper." The teacher removes the green paper strip of grass as well as the brown trunk, placing them to match her own model. Rebecca puts her hands in her lap and stares desultorily around the room, as the teacher moves on to guide another child's activity. ✆

Too much activity forced on the child by others, claim Katz and Chard (2000), leads to "damaged dispositions" of intrinsic motivation, concentration, initiative, confidence, and humor that are essential to the learning process throughout children's lives.

Adults can support children's play by providing a safe environment in which developmentally appropriate limits are set to support children's developing sense of initiative. The child who is supported in taking initiative during this stage of development forms a firm foundation for the sense of competence and purpose that develops during middle childhood in the stage of industry and inferiority.

Industry and Inferiority: Play and Work in Middle Childhood

The flexible goals of the initiative stage, where process takes precedence over product, evolve gradually into goal-oriented projects where children's "I can do it" attitude is expanded to include perseverance and self-evaluation.

Several groups of children in Leslie's second-grade class are writing plays that they will act out in the two kindergarten classes. For the past week, Peter, Lisa, and Leah have discussed dozens of ideas of how to write and perform a play, based on the story of Homer Price and the donut machine. They are writing the scene where the machine is making dozens and dozens of donuts and the three children helping at the store race around stacking the donuts everywhere. They draft, read aloud, and agree on each section, then work with their fourth-grade mentor to correct errors.

Oh! More donuts!
Wow! More and more donuts!
Fast, catch that one!

They stop and evaluate the script. "Let's use real donuts." "How can we show that there are so many?" "Can we make it look like they're coming faster and faster?" Next week the children will revise and rehearse. Next Friday is their opening day in the kindergarten classrooms. ✆

Erikson (1977) wrote that play remains important during middle childhood and throughout adulthood. In middle childhood, children also have the cognitive and motor competencies to participate more fully in the work that their culture values. Children construct their sense of industry or inferiority based on these cultural expectations. At this stage each culture provides some forms of formal education or training for adult roles (Erikson, 1950/1985). For example, children participate in chores at home, begin formal instruction in literacy and mathematics, or, in some more traditional cultures, may apprentice to a local artisan.

SUMMARY AND CONCLUSION

Teachers of young children gain support for their use of play in the classroom by understanding the role of play in development as expressed in the important developmental theories of Piaget, Vygotsky, Mead, and Erikson. These theorists suggested that each child, in every classroom, develops through a constructive process that is shaped by family, community values and histories. In early childhood programs, these processes result in a peer culture of play that reflects the children's collective and individual understandings of the world. By learning as much as one can about the sociocultural factors children bring with them to school, and by observing and listening with care and understanding, teachers can enhance the learning and development of children in their care.

By placing play at the center of the curriculum, we make an investment to protect both the short-term and long-term futures of our children and our society. Play supports the development of specific concepts such as those needed to understand physics or our language system. It also supports more general qualities related to socialization, mastery, imagination, and flexibility of mind that help to ensure a legacy of adaptation to change and freedom to make choices.

Although not all play may be seen as furthering children's development, in our view, play is the necessary core to curriculum for young children. Play provides the teacher with cues and vehicles for assessing children and implementing curriculum goals. Most important, it allows children to develop to their fullest potential intellectually, socially, morally, physically, and emotionally as they learn to negotiate their developing sense of self with the demands of the group. Awareness of the possibilities inherent in play for understanding each child in the classroom opens many new doors for teachers. This awareness enhances both the professional knowledge and artistry that make teaching preschool and primary-grade children a fulfilling and important profession.

Play as the Cornerstone of Development: The Literature

In this chapter we examine the growing empirical research as well as professional literature regarding how play influences various aspects of child development, beginning with intellectual development, followed by a look at its effects on creativity and imagination, its influences on socialization and moral development, and its relationship to emotional development. In doing so, we also illustrate how the play-centered curriculum can meet national standards for early education.

Historically, early childhood education teachers believed that childhood was valuable in and of itself (Bergen & Fromberg, 2006; Elkind, 2007; Nourot, 2005; Singer & Singer, 2006; Wolfe, 2002). As early childhood educators became more focused on specific outcomes of educational practice, the role of play became instrumental to curriculum goals for young children. Many advocates of children's play asked: "What aspects of desirable academic and social knowledge are constructed through play in early childhood?" Much of the recent research has followed this instrumental focus and argues for the central role of play in constructing and consolidating particular knowledge, skills, and competencies in preschool and the primary grades, or "educational play." (See, for example, Fromberg & Bergen, 2007; Hirsh-Pasek, Golinkoff, Berk, & Singer, 2009; Jones & Cooper, 2006.)

PLAY AND INTELLECTUAL DEVELOPMENT

For both Piaget and Vygotsky, play is intimately tied to representation, that is, how in symbolic play and symbolic role playing the child expresses ideas, feelings, and needs. Additional elements of intellectual development include how children come to understand the perspectives of others, how children invent strategies for play with others (as in games with rules), and how children solve problems. We round out our focus on intellectual development with a look at language and literacy, and logical-mathematical thought.

Play and the Development of Symbolic Thought

Symbolic thought is an important component of representational intelligence and underlies the pretense we associate with the play of preschool and primary-aged children. It forms the foundation on which children construct their abilities to engage in abstract thinking in literacy, mathematical reasoning, and problem solving. Symbolic activities entail creating meaning and expressing that meaning through gesture (driving a pretend car), language, intonation ("OK, honey, it's bedtime."), and objects (using sand and rocks to make a birthday cake). The development of symbolic behavior has been frequently studied (Bergen, 2002; Fromberg, 2002; Honig, 2007; Johnson, 2006; McCune, 1985; Rubin et al., 1983).

> Sally picks up a wooden block and holds it to her ear. She makes pushing button motions with her fingers and says, "Hello, is Mickey Mouse there?" ∅

Beginning at about 18 months, symbolic thought becomes possible, evidenced by the use of language and pretend play. From this point on, the ability to transform

Play with concrete materials supports children's imagination and pretense.

objects or situations, through the use of imagination, into meanings that are different from the original object or situation forms the foundation for intellectual development and communication (Piaget, 1962b; Vygotsky, 1976).

Symbolic Play with Objects.   Building on Vygotsky's notion that concrete objects serve as pivots to "anchor" children's imagination and pretense, researchers have studied young children's play with objects. They have discovered that, as children's play develops, they seem able to use objects that are increasingly different from the object represented in play, building the foundation for abstract thinking (Gowen, 1995; Nourot, 2006).

This ability to abstract the essential features of an object and to mentally represent those features rests on the notion of symbolic distancing. Sigel (1993) coined the term *symbolic distancing* to denote the degree to which an object looks like what it is intended to symbolize. For example, to represent a car, a particular block might serve better than another because of its shape and size. A child's ability to use an object that looks different from what it is used to symbolize develops with age and is largely constructed through play. When this competence is well developed, children do not have to interrupt their ongoing scripts of pretend play to search for an object that closely resembles the one they wish to symbolize (Fein, 1981; Scarlett et al., 2005).

Symbolic Role Play.   Children also make symbolic transformations in their role play. Research indicates that as children's capacities for representing ideas develop, they increasingly create pretend roles and situations without the use of costumes or props, using more subtle behaviors such as gesture and intonation to mark their transformation into make-believe roles in play. Teachers may note the subtle markers, such as a tone of voice, a walk, or a gesture that children use to enter make-believe (Fromberg, 2002; Henderson & Jones, 2002; Morgenthaler, 2006; Nicolopolou, 2007; Smilansky, 1968, 1990).

Supporting Symbolic Play for Children with Special Needs. The concept of symbolic distancing is particularly useful when working with young children and children with developmental delays. Some children with special needs have difficulty in separating reality from fantasy (Bergen, 2003; Mindes, 1998, 2007; Odom, 2002; Preissler, 2006). When symbolic distancing is a challenge, most would select an object that is a replica or closely resembles the actual object in appearance and function. Teachers can support the success of children with special needs in integrated classrooms by including a range of play materials. Wolfberg (1999) reports her research on the scaffolding of imagination and pretense in the play of children with autism. She contends that both teachers and peers can support children's use of increasingly abstract symbolic representations through modeling and play orchestration.

> Four-year-old Edna and 5-year-old Jonah, both children with autism in a full-inclusion preschool class, are playing parallel in the dramatic play area. Edna drives the grocery cart around the classroom, returning in a ritual fashion to tap the toy cash register on each round. Jonah is also in the pretend store, packing and unpacking toy plastic food in shopping bags repeatedly. Their teacher takes the role of cashier and orchestrates some cooperative play between Edna and Jonah by modeling and coaching how Jonah might load the groceries into Edna's cart and help her to her "car" in the block area. The teacher gradually reduces her coaching role from direct modeling, to verbal prompts, to observation as the two children master the sequence of pretend.

Taking the Perspectives of Others. Playing with peers requires perspectivism, or the ability to mentally represent the viewpoint of others to negotiate group play situations.

> Both Samantha and Estelle want to play the part of the princess for the castle they have built of blocks. Play cannot continue until a compromise is reached. Their teacher suggests that one princess has a cousin who visits from another kingdom, and the girls promptly begin discussing how the two princesses' clothing and crowns might look different, and the carriage that they could build to make the journey between the two castles.

The continuity and stability of the players' joint creation depends on their abilities to mentally represent and consider the perspectives of others in negotiating their roles and the plot of their play (Ariel, 2002; Curran, 1999; Sheldon, 1992; Sluss & Stremmel, 2004). Although young children with cognitive and emotional developmental delays can be observed playing with their peers in integrated classrooms, they may have particular difficulties taking the perspectives of their peers. For example, many have difficulty evaluating how their behavior affects others. Many children with social and emotional special needs are egocentric. Such children might fail to greet peers, but might become upset if peers failed to greet them. Play-centered curricula provide all children numerous opportunities to engage in behaviors, such as compromising and negotiating, that foster the development of friendships (Bergen, 2003; Buchannan & Johnson, 2009; Coplan, Rubin, & Findley, 2006; McCay & Keyes, 2001; Mindes, 2007; Newcomer, 1993; Odom, 2002; Panksepp, 2008).

Weighing the Demands of Play.   Children who are new to the group or who may be having difficulties in social negotiations with peers may need the comfort and security of a fantasy script that is not too different from what they know. Almost everyone knows the script for playing house or blocks and trucks, or riding trikes. The less demanding the symbolic distancing requirements of the play scenarios, the more attention children can devote to social negotiation with peers. This may be a particularly important issue for children with developmental delays who may have difficulties with the distancing demands of the play as well as challenges entering the play setting. It is also a consideration for teachers of children with difficulty in self-regulation, or children who are fearful and anxious and may respond aggressively to such frustrations (Ariel, 2002; Bretherton, 1984; Farver, 1992; Göncü, 1993; Green, 2006; Haight, Black, Ostler, & Sheridan, 2006; Scarlett et al., 2005).

Cultural and Linguistic Contexts for Symbolic Play.   Weighing the social and cognitive demands of play situations also has implications for assessing and supporting the development of children from all cultural and linguistic backgrounds. Kirmani (2007) emphasizes the key role of early childhood programs in empowering children and families from diverse cultural and linguistic backgrounds. All children need the support of familiar play accessories. Children who are English language learners and those from all cultural backgrounds benefit from scripts and play accessories that are familiar as well as those that offer opportunities for both repetition and expansion (Espinosa, 2006, 2010; Göncü, Jain, & Tuermer, 2007; Reynolds, 2002). Depending on temperament or family expectations, some children will naturally engage in more solitary play or parallel play as a way of meeting their own needs. When children come from family or cultural contexts in which play in school is not valued or encouraged, it is important that their teachers be sensitive to these concerns (Cooney, 2004; Hughes, 2003; Joshi, 2005; Roopnarine, Shin, Donovan, & Suppal, 2000).

Inventing Strategies.   The most complex level of play, games with rules, requires players to reflect on the relationship of all the players within the framework of the rules. For example, a Monopoly player might want to figure out who is playing fairly according to the rules and who is not, or even whom she might make an alliance with to borrow from the bank. These and similar meta-cognitive demands on the skilled game player require advances in mental development to view both social and symbolic behavior from an objective stance—and then use that information to formulate a strategy (DeVries, 2006; DeVries, Zan, Hildebrandt, Edmiaston, & Sales, 2002; Kamii & Kato, 2006).

This kind of strategy-taking does not often appear until children are 6 or 7 years old. As an example, when 3-year-olds play Duck, Duck, Goose, after the goose is tapped and named, all the children get up and run. They understand the basic rule of the game, but cannot coordinate the perspectives of different players with their own. Four-year-olds understand that only the "goose" and "it" run and that the goose must chase and catch "it." But the players chase each other around the circle and the "goose" inevitably fails to tag "it." At 5 or 6 years of age, children begin to employ a strategy with "the goose," often circling in the opposite direction to tag "it" before "it" can manage to run back to the empty spot.

When children begin to spontaneously invent strategies and discuss and negotiate rules before games begin, games with rules become an appropriate addition to the school curriculum. Game materials and boards may be available, but children should be encouraged to invent and negotiate their own rules. In the primary grades, the playing and inventing of games with rules becomes a major component of play. Children use this newly emerging stage of play development to consolidate their understanding of rules and strategies and as an opportunity to display and elaborate their new cognitive accomplishments.

Play and the Development of Language and Literacy

Much of the research on children's use of symbols has linked play to language and literacy development. Some researchers have focused on parallels between early language development and the use of symbols in play (Bergen & Mauer, 2000; Christie,

Everyday objects scaffold children's symbolic play.

2006; Pellegrini & Galda, 1993; Uttal et al., 1998). Others have studied the ways in which children play with the elements of language such as with sounds or meanings. Children's exploration of sounds, arrangements of words, and meanings of words form the context for children to invent unique forms of language and to master new forms as they are acquired. This play with language and sound also forms the basis for phonemic and phonological awareness. Language play is ubiquitous in classrooms with young children and often occurs in the most mundane of circumstances.

> It's juice time in a preschool setting, and James and Eva begin to giggle as they wait for their turns to pour juice. "You're juicy-goosey," contributes James. "You're juicely-goosely-foosley," chortles Eva, and they both dissolve in laughter. ⌀

Yopp (1995) and Wasik (2001) report ways in which play with the sounds of language contributes to the development of phonemic awareness. Phonemic awareness includes the ability to recognize and to manipulate individual sounds of words. It involves insights about the sounds of oral language and the segmentation of sounds used in speech communication.

The spontaneous play in the juicey-goosey example might be supplemented by teachers of young children with songs that play with sounds of language such as "Apples and Bananas," or rhyming in "Down by the Bay"; nursery rhymes such as "One two, buckle my shoe"; and children's books like *The Cat in the Hat, Chicka Chicka Boom Boom,* or *Barnyard Dance.* The key to playing with sounds is to truly focus on listening and speaking the sounds rather than to focus on print.

As illustrated by the following examples, state and national standards for planning curriculum for early literacy include such concepts as narrative and story comprehension as well as the phonemic and phonological awareness needed to decode sounds and symbols. When Tyler makes a road sign while playing with toy cars, he is "making letter–sound correspondences." When Isabella sings "Down by the Bay," she "recognizes and generates rhymes through songs and stories." When Kyle copies names from cubbies to send a letter in the play post office, she "demonstrates growing awareness of beginning, ending, medial sounds of words."

Literacy in Play: Decoding the Symbols.   Research in the field of emergent literacy has looked at how children incorporate literacy play into their make-believe activities. Such play incorporates the social functions of literacy into pretend play scripts and addresses the early literacy academic standards related to concepts of print and early writing (Christie, 2006; Davidson, 2006; Einarsdottir, 2000; Neves & Riefel, 2002; Roskos, 2000; Roskos & Christie, 2000a, 2004; Singer & Lythcott, 2004).

> In one kindergarten classroom, children set up a bank, a store, and a restaurant, all built with blocks. To obtain money from the bank to spend elsewhere, "tellers" in the bank asked their "customers" to pick one of the blank books from the library corner and write their names on it. After counting out

paper to represent money, the teller wrote CRTO ("credit to") in the book, and stamped it with a rubber stamp. ✇

In addition to understanding the social functions of print, children's schooling in the written symbols of language and mathematics requires the ability to perform symbolic transformations. For example, the ability to understand that *H* and *K, bat* and *14,* are combinations of lines that represent sounds, words, and numbers is similar to the capacity to use a block to represent a truck or a telephone.

Children who become skilled at symbolic transformations in their play are also preparing conceptually to understand some of the subtleties of culturally shared symbolic systems used in written language, aspects that adults take for granted, but that children find confusing. For example, children are frequently bewildered by the arbitrary meaning assigned to symbols that look the same. The letter *C* is sometimes pronounced as a *K* such as in the word *cake,* sometimes as an *S* as in *city* and sometimes as a new sound *CH* as in *chicken.* This inconsistency among assigned meanings for symbols that do not change in appearance can be very confusing to a child who has not developed the concept of "multiple transformations" in his or her pretend play. For example, the idea that a rectangular block can be a car, a person, or a sandwich, depending on the child's imagination, prepares children to understand these differences when they begin to operate with our system of written signs and symbols. In both symbolic play and phonetic decoding, the concept that one object (that continues to look the same) may be transformed by the mind into several different meanings is essential.

A related concept is the idea that several objects that look different may be symbolically transformed to carry the same meaning. In play, for example, you might see Jennie use a block, a Lego, or a toy car to represent a walkie-talkie on a spaceship. These choices depend in part on what is available and also on the child's ability to abstract salient features of objects to use them as symbols for alternative meanings. This concept is called on when children learn to identify symbols of written language, for example, in understanding that *A* and *a* both represent the same sound in our alphabet.

These competencies are closely related to the following academic standards for print and early writing. For example, when Kira says, "K starts my name," as she surveys the labeled photos at the sign-in table, she "understands that letters make up words and distinguishes between print and pictures." When Michael pretends to read to the teddy bear in the book area, turning pages and orienting the book with pictures on top and text below, he "handles books appropriately and respectfully." When Alysha uses a note pad and pencil to take Riordan's order in the classroom restaurant, she "uses symbols and forms of early writing to create more complex play." When Emily makes a sign to lean against her completed block tower, "Du not dstrub!" she "uses letters and/or phonetically spelled words and basic punctuation."

The Development of Narrative.   The capacity to enter the "as if" or hypothetical frame of reference in which animals talk, such as that created by E. B. White in *Charlotte's Web,* or the ability to create such a frame oneself in telling or writing a story, rests on understandings constructed in dramatic play. The ability to negotiate multiple roles and hypothetical situations in housekeeping play or to dictate and enact an episode of superheroes' adventures calls on the same capacities in young children's symbolic thought as those needed to write a poem or a narrative of one's own.

Taking on the roles of different characters and sequencing events to tell a story form the foundation for the important aspect of literacy learning called "narrative." Reading comprehension, particularly with characters, motives, and plots, also rests on alternative perspectives and sequencing events to create and interpret meaning (Bruner, 1986; Fein, Ardeila-Ray, & Groth, 2000; Fromberg, 2002; Gallas, 2003; Kim, 1999; Nel, 2000; Nicolopolou, 2007; Roskos & Christie, 2000a). This ability to demonstrate a concept of story also appears in early education standards for literacy development.

These and other aspects of play and literacy are considered in detail in Chapter 8 and relate to academic standards in a variety of ways. For example, when Ethan says, "Let's read the frog book first, it's my favorite," he "chooses to read books for enjoyment." At circle time, Noah dramatizes the Scarecrow's walk from the *Wizard of Oz* seen the week before. In doing so, he "retells, reenacts, or dramatizes stories." When Emma, while listening to *Charlotte's Web* at story time, predicts that Charlotte will go to the fair with Wilbur, she "reads or listens to a story and predicts what will happen next."

Play and Logical-Mathematical Thinking

Another relationship between play and development is the construction of logical-mathematical knowledge. One expression of this is seen in children's construction of cause–effect relationships through physical activities. Block building, bike riding, and sand and water play all foster the construction of spatial relationships, gravity, and other concepts of physics. These real-life experiences are essential to children's future understanding and abilities to solve problems, and form the foundation for learning science concepts as children develop (Bodrova & Leong, 2007; Chalufour & Worth, 2004, 2006; DeVries et al., 2002; Forman, 2005; Kamii & DeVries, 1993; Kamii, Miyakawa, & Kato, 2004; Wolfe, Cummins, & Meyers, 1998).

Numerous examples in Chapter 9 show how play activities relate to early science academic standards. When Jeffrey finds an equivalent block for a racing track construction, he is "engaging in play as a means to develop questioning and problem solving." When Megan weighs her baby doll at the pretend hospital, she is "beginning to use scientific tools and methods to learn about the world." When Matthew and Renee mix playdough to make their farm animals just the right color, they are "learning that properties of substances can change when mixed, cooled, or heated." When Adrian uses straw and clay to make adobe bricks, he is learning "that earth is made of materials that have distinct properties and provide resources for human activities."

In the development of logical-mathematical thinking, children construct their own schemes or mental patterns for organizing and interpreting meaning in the environment. In doing so, they develop the ability to classify and put objects and ideas into relationships with each other (e.g., ordering objects from least to most). Play provides children a wide array of opportunities to construct concepts at their own pace.

> For the past two weeks Marie has been playing almost daily with a set of thick crayons, eight colors. Today there is something new. She chooses a large box of thin crayons, a total of 40 colors. She picks out all the crayons that have a red color and arranges them separately from crayons of orange and pink shades. As she colors a piece of scrap wood with multiple shades of red, she comments, "This is for my mom." Lily sits down next to her. Marie turns, offering a crayon. "There's more reds over here." ⌀

In this example, Marie is coordinating relationships of "more than" and "less than" and "similar" and "different." The coordination of these relationships is the beginning of logical reasoning in early childhood. Intellectual development leads to more mature play in preschoolers.

Dramatic play can also contribute to the development of classification and relational concepts in another way. In the following example, for each symbolic transformation, David identifies similar characteristics of familiar objects to form the basis of his decision of what to use as a prop. Before choosing the cookbook, presumably because of its qualities of opening and enclosing that are compatible with his idea of a hot dog, he scans the area, rejecting the pencil and a tennis ball in favor of the book. He later uses the pencil to represent the mustard bottle. This selective attention to similar characteristics of objects is another concept essential to the development of classification abilities.

> Six-year-old David is fixing dinner for his "son" Peter. Peter says, "But I want a hot dog for dinner!" "OK. I can make good hot dogs," notes David as he scans the playhouse area for a prop that exemplifies "hot dog-ness" for him. He selects a paperback cookbook from the shelf, opens it, and "stuffs" it with a plastic marker. "Do you want mustard?" he asks. Peter nods emphatically and David shakes a pencil over the "hot dog," pretending that it is a bottle of mustard. ⌀

Another relationship between play and logical-mathematical thinking rests on the symbolic transformations inherent in role play. The child who transforms himself or herself into a veterinarian, a puppy, or an astronaut, and each time returns to the mental concept of self, is beginning to show evidence of reversibility, a feature of thinking that accompanies the development of logical thought in middle childhood and participates in such competencies as basic addition and subtraction. Some researchers have hypothesized that mental transformations in pretend play form the foundation for the Piagetian notion of conservation (Golomb, Gowing, & Friedman, 1982). Conservation involves the understanding that quantity does not decrease or increase with a change in its position or form just as role play involves understanding that the identity of a person remains the same when a role is taken (Forman & Kaden, 1987).

Four-year-old Cassie asks as the family leaves a performance of *Seussical,* "Those people don't really look like that, do they? I mean they had to be real people in costumes?" Her parents went over the program with her and noted the names of the actors who had played particular roles. The next week, Cassie dressed her stuffed animals and dolls in feathers and bits of cloth and yarn, creating "weird animal" costumes, and confirming her concepts of how identities change. ⊘

All aspects of logical-mathematical thinking show up in children's play. Everyday examples of ordering, classifying, quantifying/measuring, and comparing can be seen throughout children's play and can be related to early math and science academic standards. For example, when Naomi counts aloud to time the baking of pretend cookies in the oven, she is "counting by rote memorization." When Elliot asks for more red paint at the easel, he is "appropriately using comparative words." When Quinn counts out six coins to pay for ice cream at the pretend restaurant, he "understands numbers and simple operations and uses coins in daily activities." When Tyson lines up the toy dinosaurs from smallest to largest, he is "seriating and ordering."

Play and Problem Solving

The flexibility in thinking that allows one to solve a problem from a fresh perspective, or use a tool in a unique way, is part of critical thinking. Play contributes by allowing children to play through their ideas, in the same way that adults talk through alternatives to problems they face and imagine consequences from varying perspectives. This process also leads to the discovery of new problems or new questions to be asked as children play and think more deeply about their experience (Chalufour & Worth, 2006; Holmes & Geiger, 2002; Wolfe, Cumins, & Myers, 2006).

This playing through of alternatives may be nonverbal, as in the first example below, or it may include verbal communication as in the second example of negotiating with peers.

Second graders Chrissie and Jake are making a sand mountain with a road around it designed for a ball to roll down. The moist sand is beginning to dry in the hot sun, and pieces of the road are crumbling. They first try a "patching" job with more sand, but it is too dry to stick. When that doesn't work, they dig under the dry sand to find more of the damp sand they originally used. ⊘

Research on children who are popular with peers indicates that children who are flexible in their thinking frequently come up with unique alternatives for resolving disputes and suggesting compromise (Howes, 1992).

Four-year-old Erica and 3-year-old Melisa are playing with a hospital bed, medical props, and two dolls. They agree to have their "patients" share the toy bed, but there is only one pillow. Erica takes a blanket and folds it several times, placing it under the head of her doll. "Now we both have pillows," she concludes, and the play continues, uninterrupted by disputes. ⊘

Researchers who have studied children's play speculate that the conflicts and subsequent negotiations that occur as children shift from actors "in play" to directors "out of" play force children to consider the perspectives of their playmates. In play, children enact roles and move the story line forward with action and dialogue. Out of play, children step out of make-believe roles to negotiate new roles, behavior appropriate to roles, and ideas for the plot of their play. If one wants play to continue, then compromises must be made (Fromberg, 2002; Göncü, 1993; Reifel, Hoke, Pape, & Wisneski, 2004; Reifel & Yeatman, 1993; Sheldon, 1992).

All of the state standards for early education that we reviewed include the ability to negotiate and resolve social problems, be empathetic with others, and try hard to be successful. These competencies and dispositions occur in everyday play. For example, Garrett and Lilly play space ship and negotiate the roles of pilot and copilot, thereby "negotiating with peers to resolve social conflicts and cooperation in play." Mischa falls and hurts her knee. While the teacher is coming from across the yard, Jack hugs her and says, "You'll be OK!" thereby "expressing empathy or caring for others."

Shawn and Heather set up paint cups for Josa and tilt her easel so she can reach it from her wheelchair, thereby "demonstrating respect for differences in interaction with others from diverse backgrounds and with different abilities." For 3 days in a row, Emily returns to the road project, adding new signs and persisting at building a bridge with buttresses, thereby "demonstrating persistence in play and projects."

Play and Children with Special Needs

Play-centered curricula can be beneficial for those children who are often unable to resolve problems when they arise. This includes many children with social and emotional disabilities and children with developmental delays (Bergen, 2003; Buchannan & Johnson, 2009; Koplow, 1996; Odom, 2002; Wolfberg, 1999). Flexibility is an important dimension of problem solving (Holmes & Geiger, 2002). Because of the links between flexibility, language, and cognition, certain children with special needs lack this flexibility and react to the environment in a rigid manner. Extended opportunities to interact with peers in play can support the development of problem-solving skills. For example:

In a second-grade integrated classroom, Joe and Harold are playing with small race cars. Joe has a learning disability, which includes challenges with visual processing and visual discrimination. As Joe pushes his car on the carpet, he says, "I want my car to go faster." Harold looks around the classroom, spots a table and says, "We can use a table 'cause it's smooth." Joe then looks around the room and exclaims, "Let's go over there," and points to an area of the classroom that is covered in shiny tile. The children take their cars to the slick surface of the tile floor and begin racing them.

Although some of the research and writing in the field of special education, such as that cited earlier, suggests that children with special needs are unable to solve problems, this example of Joe's success in problem solving in collaboration with Harold demonstrates that it is important to observe each child's abilities in different contexts.

A related issue is the role of the teacher. Genishi and DiPaolo (1982) and Pellegrini (1984) suggest that the teacher's presence during peer play negotiations may inhibit children from solving their interpersonal problems on their own. On the other hand, researchers such as Smilansky (1968, 1990) discuss the ways that the teacher's presence may support children's ability to work out solutions to disagreements during play. Teachers may find the issues of roles and timing especially challenging when working with children who have cognitive, social, or emotional delays or who are overly aggressive when others do not play according to their wishes.

In these and all interventions in play, the teacher's sensitivity and support for children's capabilities and patience for their intended meanings is paramount (Bergen, 2003; Brown & Marchant, 2002; Clark, 2007; Fromberg, 2002; Mindes, 2007; Wolfberg, 1999).

The idea that play promotes children's development is a major feature of Vygotsky's notion of the zone of proximal development (Vygotsky, 1967, 1978). He set forth the idea that children function above their normal level of ability when challenged by peers in their play. Children's desire to maintain social interaction and to encounter and coordinate perspectives other than their own contributes to the developmental stretch evident in play. Researchers studying children's play in mixed-age groups or classrooms with mainstreamed children report that younger or less sophisticated players play at higher levels of complexity when playing with older or more expert peers (Katz, Evangelou, & Hartman, 1990; Stone & Christie, 1996). Children who are imaginative in their symbolic play transformations and flexible in their negotiations with peers are building concepts essential to critical thinking expertise and social problem solving.

PLAY, IMAGINATION, AND CREATIVITY

Imagination and creativity are qualities that are sometimes taken for granted when reviewing the value of play in development. Much has been written concerning the curriculum appropriate for the 21st century. Bruner (1976) perhaps stated this dilemma best by asking, "How can a system that prepares the immature for entry into the society deal with a future that is increasingly difficult to predict within a single lifetime?"

One possibility is to foster adaptive, flexible, and creative thinking. These qualities are essential because "whenever the environment is changing, it selects for playful individuals" (Ellis, 1988, p. 24). Concerns about the effects of didactic teaching and skills-based curricula have led to research and writing urging educators to consider

Solitary play fosters concentration and imagination.

more carefully the need to foster imaginative and flexible minds and to provide rich and varied opportunities in the visual and performing arts (Brown, 2009; Elkind, 2003, 2007; Gallas, 2003; Holmes & Geiger, 2002; Isenberg & Jalongo, 2001; Singer & Singer, 1990, 2006; Singer & Lythcott, 2004; VanderVen, 2006).

Academic standards for the arts are met in numerous ways in everyday play, as these examples show. When Robin appropriates scarves from the dress up box and creates a dance on the stage built in the block area, she is "developing self-expression through visual arts, dance, music, and drama." When Patty becomes the wicked queen, snarling and lowering her voice to threaten the sad princess, she is showing an "appreciation, interest and knowledge of the arts." When Leslie says, "I'll use collage like Steve does," as she cuts parts for a tree and flowers, she is developing "an appreciation, interest, and knowledge of the arts."

Singer and Singer have written extensively about the contribution of play to the imaginative thinking of children (e.g., Singer & Singer, 1990, 2005, 2006; Singer, 2006). In the Singers' view, make-believe play is essential to the development of the capacity for internal imagery. It contributes to the development of creativity by opening children to experiences involving curiosity and the exploration of alternative situations and combinations. In addition, their research emphasizes the psychosocial benefits of imaginative play: Children who engage in much make-believe play are likely to be happier and more flexible when they encounter new situations.

Three Aspects of Imagination and Fantasy

Egan (1988) developed Vygotsky's claim that play leads development in early childhood. He claimed that fantasy and imagination are the appropriate content of early childhood curriculum because they highlight for teachers the passionate concerns of young children. Egan's work emphasized three major aspects of imagination and fantasy in early childhood: (a) the oral nature of the peer culture in the early years, (b) the importance of binary opposites in creating dramatic tension in play themes, and (c) the sense of wonder, magic, and joy inherent in pretend play.

The Oral Culture of Early Childhood.   Egan (1988) found the seeds of the ability to create a story in the orally expressed fantasy of early childhood. As each aspect of a story told in the fantasy play unfolds, its meaning is clarified and extended in relation to other aspects of the play. In solitary dramatic play, fantasy stories are told to the self, and in sociodramatic play the play's meanings are communicated and negotiated within the peer culture of the classroom (Ariel, 2002; Dyson, 1997, 2003; Fromberg, 2002; Katch, 2001; McEwan & Egan, 1995; Nicolopoulou, Scales, & Weintraub, 1994; Paley, 1981, 1994, 1995; Perry, 2001).

The accompanying ability to extend knowledge of characters, situations, and events from the everyday into the realm of the improbable or impossible is a primary form of logic that encompasses ambiguity and paradox and merges thought and feelings. This ability to make meaning through narrative forms is one of the first examples of the ordering and classification of human experience (Bruner, 1986, 1990). This early use of contradictory forms of logic in play is what Egan calls "mythic thinking," and it is seen in both the fantastic series of events that children may imagine in play and in role play. For example, when 4-year-old Erin pretends that she is an undersea monster, she knows that she simultaneously is and is not the role that she plays. This early embrace of paradox lays the foundation for noncontradictory forms of logic that emerge in middle childhood. Egan believes that one must create and entertain a variety of possibilities before narrowing them through logical thought. Young children's grasp of reality begins by stretching the borders of the known world into new dimensions and possibilities in play (Nourot, 2005).

Bipolar Opposites in Play.   Children's play is often structured around binary opposition themes such as love/hate, danger/rescue, the permissible/the forbidden, big/little, good guy/bad guy, death/rebirth, and lost/found (Bettelheim, 1989; Corsaro, 1985; Egan, 1988; Garvey, 1977/1990; Katch, 2001; Paley, 1988). These oppositional tensions help children discriminate features of their physical and social worlds and to define themselves within those worlds. The unity of thought and emotion animates their abilities to make sense of life through the stories told in dramatic play. The following anecdote shows how children move flexibly between sense and nonsense, the physically possible and impossible, the mundane and the exotic, the safe and the threatening, and, for some, the permissible and the forbidden.

Dolly and Ruth are pretending to be witches and pretend they are taking blood from their playmates by touching their arms with a spoon, and then running back to the pot on the stove in the housekeeping area to add the imaginary blood of each victim, cackling as they stir the brew. Quincy is a witch too, wearing a sparkling cape and carrying a cup with a plastic lemon in it. "This drink has poison and fingernails in it," he announces.

Later Quincy holds up his cup. "But if you drink this magic potion, you can come alive again," and he offers some to John, who has just joined the play. "Can I play?" John asks. "Yes," agrees Dolly, "but you have to be a witch, like us." John pretends to take blood from Ruth, imitating the high cackling laugh he has heard Dolly use. Then Quincy offers his cup to Ruth, "This will turn you from a witch into a princess." She pretends to drink the princess-making potion, and then the other witches try to turn her back into a witch. "No, no, drink this one." The tension between the bad witches and the good witch Quincy with his magic potion continues a few more minutes until cleanup time is called. ✇

The framing of ideas for character, plot, and setting through bipolar oppositions, such as the good witch/bad witch/princess, and the death and rebirth in the preceding anecdote also define these emerging aspects of story, even as it clarifies children's sense of themselves. Children want passionately for play to continue despite the potential pitfalls of differing ideas about characters or events in the play. The shared understanding that comes from framing play themes and characters in binary themes such as good guy/bad guy or danger/rescue supports the shared understanding and the subsequent negotiation that allows play to flourish (Nourot, 1997, 2006).

Wonder, Magic, and Joy. Although the development of logical thinking and skill in negotiating meanings with others are important aspects of imaginative play in early childhood, the essence of play is captured in the magical and ecstatic experiences that define creative processes throughout life (Ariel, 2002; Brown, 2009; Csikszentmihayli, 1993; Nachmanovitch, 1990). The joy and wonder encompassed in imaginative play are powerful links to others and an incentive to self-regulation and perspective-taking. The desire for this sense of wonder and joy creates a powerful incentive for children to move beyond their own viewpoints to encompass the perspectives of others. In doing so, children experience the power of both friendship and fantasy in their play (Jones & Cooper, 2006; Jones & Reynolds, 1992; Reynolds & Jones, 1997).

PLAY AND SOCIAL-MORAL DEVELOPMENT

Every day in preschools, child-care centers, kindergartens, and primary-grade classrooms, differences in the nature of social interaction and the complexity of fantasy, constructive play, and games with rules are observed. These differences reflect aspects of children's cultural, familial, and individual styles, as well as moral and social development. Teachers are better equipped to support play when they understand its developmental sequences and range of behaviors, as well as children's families and cultural context as observed in the play (e.g., Bowman & Moore, 2006; Gaskins, Haight, & Lancy, 2007).

> In one kindergarten classroom, Jon and Rio were happily engaged in building a "ranch" out of blocks. Their intimacy was evident as they giggled and whispered to one another their plans for the fantasy. "And then pretend the bad guys can get in here," one boy said to the other. Paul watched from the sidelines and finally began to build his own structure next to Rio and Jon. "But what about me?" Paul said plaintively, as the ranch builders began to expand their construction site. "I know," said Rio, "we'll make a line right here and you can build, too. We won't cross the line." ⌀

In this example, we see Paul learning to assert his rights, and Jon and Rio learning to understand and accommodate the perspective of a third player, without giving up their investment in keeping their ranch to themselves.

DeVries and Zan (1984) and Kamii (1982, 1990) draws on Piaget's theories of moral development (Piaget, 1965d) when she discusses autonomy and heteronomy in classrooms for young children. Moral autonomy is characterized by being governed by oneself. Moral heteronomy means being governed by others. Children who develop moral autonomy come to see moral values as internal guides, independent of whether they may be "caught" doing something inappropriate by a parent or a teacher. In a classroom that promotes moral autonomy, children construct beliefs about what is fair and unfair based on their experiences with their peers. Through social-moral dilemmas that involve reciprocal interactions with their playmates, children learn to make informed choices about their behavior and practice factoring in the perspectives of others (DeVries & Zan, 2005). In the preceding example, Jon and Rio were able to factor in Paul's desire to play with them and still preserve their own interactive play space. They compromised, treating one another with respect and consideration.

Parten's Research on Play and Social Participation

Parten (1932) studied the social behavior of children in a parent-cooperative preschool. Based on her observations, she hypothesized a continuum of social participation in play, ranging from onlooker behavior to solitary, parallel, and two forms of group play.

Onlooker Behavior.   Onlooker behavior is when a child watches as others play, either because of reluctance to join, or as a way of scanning for an opening. Less-sophisticated players may hang around the edge of a play scene to learn by observing and imitating others—at times they may be unsure how to enter a play episode. More sophisticated players use onlooker behavior to help them make choices, to decide which activity to select, or to ascertain the most effective strategy for gaining entrance into an already-established play episode. Sometimes onlookers are simply interested in the play or behavior of others. Sensitive teachers are aware of these possible functions of onlooking and use observation and intervention skillfully to determine what role, if any, he or she might take to help children make choices about their play activities. Onlooker behavior is not simply immature behavior, but, in fact, represents time for children to contemplate their actions.

Solitary Play.   Solitary play is defined as play alone, without overt interaction with peers. For example:

> Four-year-old Amani carefully paints a heart shape at the easel and fills it in with bright pink. She stops to contemplate her painting briefly, then adds arms and legs. "There!" she says softly. "It's a heart person!"

Parten found solitary play to be typical of the youngest children in her group, but more recent research has shown solitary play performs several functions, depending on the age of the child and the context of play. For example, solitary play may provide the context for complex dramatic play, such as enacting a family drama with toy dinosaurs, or it may provide an occasion for needed respite from the demands of negotiating with others, such as solitary play with pegboards. The sensitive teacher is aware that children need opportunities for privacy and solitary play as well as opportunities for sharing and group play in the classroom. For some children who have been traumatized by violence and loss, the need to play alone is paramount (Scarlett et al., 2005).

Parallel Play.   Parallel play is defined as play with shared materials or physical proximity without attempts to coordinate play. Nonverbal negotiation of materials may occur, but joint play themes and/or constructions are not elaborated. For example, Juliann and Helen are playing parallel to one another with small wooden blocks and a large dollhouse. They each carry on quiet dialogues animating their characters. As one child puts down a block or a piece of dollhouse furniture, the other may pick it up, but they do not overtly acknowledge each other's play. This type of play is thought to represent the earliest, undifferentiated form of group play, and teachers may often see it as a prelude to full-blown group play as children test the waters with their peers and gradually begin cooperative efforts.

Group Play.   Parten differentiated two forms of group play. The first, associative play, is seen when children share and coordinate materials and space in proximity to one another, but lack true cooperation. It is similar to parallel play in its form but includes some of the elements of group cooperative play as well. For example, Frank and Sandra are playing with Lego blocks at a small table. They negotiate with one another over the number of wheels they may each use out of the basket of parts, but they each continue to work on their own projects, rather than focus on a joint project.

The second form of group play, cooperative play, involves sophisticated efforts to negotiate joint play themes and constructions with peers and is characterized by children stepping in and out of their play to establish roles or events. For example, three children playing restaurant may alternate their roles in the play as customer, cook, and waiter/waitress with comments about the plot made from outside the play, such as "Pretend the hamburger got burned."

PLAY AND EMOTIONAL DEVELOPMENT

The sense of connection and joy that children experience in play is closely related to emotional development. Children's emotional development refers to their capacity to feel or experience a wide range of emotions such as happiness, sadness, anger, jealousy, excitement, wonder, and fear. Emotional development also involves children's capacity to manage or regulate their emotions and their expression. Piaget, Vygotsky, and Erikson wrote about the importance of play in emotional development.

Dramatic play themes that portray children as orphaned or separated from their parents, having to fend for themselves in the woods or at sea, are common in preschool and kindergarten. Other common themes involve life and death. At times, conflicts between child initiative and adult prohibitions are expressed in the classroom through fantasy play, such as the "naughty baby."

Erikson's (1950/1985, 1977) work shows that, through their sociodramatic and pretend block constructions, children respond emotionally to the major life themes that their new cognitive capabilities present. Themes such as death and life, love and hate, care and jealousy occur frequently in the play of young children. Erikson wrote, "The play age . . . offers the child a micro-reality in which he can use toys (put at his disposal by those who sanction his play) in order to relive, correct, and re-create past experiences . . ." (Erikson, 1977, p. 99).

In their play, children reassure or frighten themselves, often at the same time. Erikson also reminds us that, in play, children further develop their sense of purpose. In dramatic play, children enter into fantasies that allow them to explore their concepts of initiative and independence.

> For example, Bebbie, Betty, and Helen are playing in the sand area. They have constructed a volcano and invented a danger and rescue plot for their characters. Bebbie and Betty laugh with delight as the water cascades over their wet sand volcano. They use their voices to protest when Helen begins to stomp on the sand. Later in the play, the three children express conflicts between archetypes of good and evil in their superhero rescue roles. ∅

Piaget (1962b) also wrote about play as a cornerstone of emotional development. Like Erikson, he described the "liquidating" function of play that allows children to neutralize powerful emotions and release them by reliving them through make-believe. He also described the "compensatory" nature of fantasy play that helps children rewrite events in which their feelings of helplessness or fear are overwhelming.

Similarly, Vygotsky (1976, 1978) discussed play as the primary matrix for children to develop self-regulation of their behavior and emotions in early childhood.

Contemporary theorists and writers emphasize the importance of emotional development. Entry into school presents additional challenges to emotional development centered on the home and family. With school comes the advent of social comparisons and the need to come to terms with challenges such as insecurity, envy, humiliation, pride, and confidence. Learning to interact with others in a responsible manner, to wait for one's turn, and to regulate one's own emotions presents major milestones in the development of emotional competence. Gardner (1993) wrote that "interpersonal and intrapersonal intelligence" is characterized by the ability to accurately read and respond to the feelings, motivations, and desires of others and access one's own feelings and use them to guide behavior. Similarly, Goleman (1995) explained that "emotional intelligence" is characterized by empathy and self-regulation, a construct that he and Lantieri have developed for educators and families in their book, *Building Emotional Intelligence: Techniques to Cultivate Inner Strength in Children* (2008). Indeed, a growing trend in the early childhood research and literature is the emphasis the importance of young children's play in the development of emotional development (e.g., Bowman, 2006; Bedrova & Leong, 2007; Honig, 2007; Jones & Cooper, 2006; Landreth, Homeyer, & Morrison, 2006).

Play and the Harsh Realities of Some Children's Lives

The degree to which contemporary play invites realities that are both incomprehensible and frightening to children remains a thorny issue for both teachers of young children and researchers of play (Ariel, 2002; Katch, 2001; Lancy, 2002; Levin, 2003b; Waniganayake, 2001). Much of play that teachers see as risky or full of violence and aggression may stem from children's need to repeat and revise frightening or confusing experiences through imagination in much the same way that adults talk through emotional distresses (e.g., see Clark, 2007; Haight et al., 2006; Katch, 2001).

Six-year-old Jason organizes his classmates to pick dandelions from the school lawn at recess time. They create bouquets and stash them in their cubbies when they return to their first-grade classroom. At their play and project time later in the day, the children construct a pretend casket from blocks complete with handles for pallbearers and enact a pretend funeral with Jason coaching them on the prayers and songs. Other children join, and the bouquets of dandelions are shared and thrown on the "casket" as it is lowered into the grave site marked by tape on the classroom rug. Jason's 19-year-old aunt was killed in a drive-by shooting the previous Saturday.

Jason's teacher understands that "righting" the imbalance in a world in which community violence is frequent, and the evening news shows vivid and repetitive images of catastrophe and violence is an important aspect of play in schools. The children are all playing through a disturbing event in their community, and their active collaboration with Jason contributes to his healing. She wonders what to do.

Children also try to make sense of frightening images and scripts from the national media. For example, in the aftermath of September 11, 2001, teachers across the nation reported children repeatedly crashing toy planes into buildings in their play and confusion about the continual replay of the images on television.

Children often play out the frightening themes and challenge school-based rules regarding weapon play, violence, or use of language in efforts to create meaning for themselves. These emotional roots of play and the possibilities for healing they present must be carefully interpreted by teachers (Katch, 2001; Koplow, 1996; Levin, 2006).

But sometimes stress levels are too high for children to use play to cope with their emotions. It is important that teachers seek professional resources when children's play takes forms that are disruptive or upsetting to the other children or to the teachers themselves. School counselors and psychologists have long explored the ways in which children struggle to make sense of frightening and/or confusing events (Axline, 1969; Erikson, 1950/1985, 1977; Landreth, Homeyer, & Morrison, 2006; Winnicott, 1971). Erikson (1950/1985) wrote about "play disruption" in children as they reached levels of stress and anxiety that were high enough to curtail play. Children who have been severely traumatized may not be able to use play to represent and work through stress and conflict in more typical ways. These children may require sensitive and careful orchestration from specialists as well as teachers in school and in therapeutic settings (Goleman, 1995; Koplow, 1996; Scarlett et al., 2005).

SUMMARY AND CONCLUSION

In Chapter 2 we explored the role of play in four major developmental theories. In examining the research and literature on play, we explored some of the many ways in which play influences development and learning and how play provides experiences that correspond with academic standards.

We have seen that play has a critical role in all facets of human development. These include, but are not limited to, the large domains of social, emotional, and intellectual growth. We have examined some of the specific ways that play influences symbolic thought, expressive language, literacy, perspective taking, a sense of self, social cooperation, logical-mathematical thinking, imagination, creativity, and moral reasoning and peer cultures. (See Chapter 14 for a more general discussion of the link between play and development.)

Orchestrating Children's Play: Setting the Stage

In Ann's K–1 combination classroom, the environment invites play. The house-keeping area includes kitchen furniture and accessories and a small couch and rocking chair. A girl doll with Asian features and two boy dolls, one with African-American and one with Caucasian features, rest in two small beds near the rocker. The children have made a VCR and a television screen from different-sized cardboard boxes. Hats and costumes are stored on shelves and hooks, doll clothes in drawers. An accessory box with props for hospital play sits open on a shelf adjacent to the house, along with the ever-useful blank clipboards with paper and pencils attached. Ann considers these staples of her play environment. She explains that a local pediatrician had visited the class the day before and introduced children to terms and medical tools that she hoped would be recast in today's play.

Outdoors, the three-level climbing structure invites children to create their own degree of challenge. Soft rubber matting provides a cushion below, and ramps lead to the slide. There is ample space for Angie, who uses a wheelchair, to get out of her chair and maneuver onto the slide. The pathways around the structure are constructed so that the wheelchair can easily be moved for entering and exiting the play structure. There is a small garden area, with benches and a table for potting plants that is wheelchair accessible. Drawing and painting supplies are stored in a small cart, as many children like to draw and paint representations of the plants and rabbits housed in the outdoor yard.

Using the knowledge of theories and research that guide teachers' understanding of the development of play presented in Chapters 2 and 3 is the first step in the complex and rewarding process we call "play orchestration." Awareness that 3-year-olds are more dependent on replica objects to sustain their play because of their emerging ability to symbolize, or that 5- and 6-year-olds frequently play games with rules that shift with each round, gives teachers a frame of expectations for behavior and learning.

The next step in the orchestration process is to bridge expectations based on knowledge and understanding of development and learning with practical strategies for supporting play in settings for young children. These strategies are illuminated by an interpretive approach to teaching. In this approach, teachers always view children's behavior within the sociocultural context in which it occurs, noticing the history and social hierarchy of the group. They are alert to a change in the dynamics of the play of a group at the entrance of a newcomer, a child with special needs, or an English language learner. Teachers draw on their knowledge of multiple theories of development and learning to interpret what they observe (Corsaro & Elder, 1990; Corsaro & Miller 1992; Henderson & Jones, 2002; Hughes, 2003; Paley, 1999; Reynolds, 2002).

This book addresses curriculum in settings for young children as well as the phenomenon of childhood play. We value teachers' keen observation, planning of explicit strategies for orchestrating play, and the assessment of learning and development evident in play. A play-centered curriculum is not made of fixed components but is emergent, finding its direction in the themes and concepts children generate in their play. For a play curriculum to be effective, the teacher must orchestrate the dynamic flow of its elements by matching play to the child's developmental level and by providing opportunities for stretch to occur for each child and for the group as a whole. Skilled teachers employ myriad strategies for "upping the ante" to encourage developmental stretch, as they foster feelings of trust and safety within play contexts (Barnes & Lehr, 2005; Bowman, 2005; Clawson, 2002; Derman-Sparks & Ramsey, 2005; Joshi, 2005; Singer, Golinkoff & Hirsh-Pasek, 2006; Singer & Singer, 2005; Swick, 2002).

PRINCIPLES GUIDING PLAY ORCHESTRATION

Four general principles guide our thinking about the ways that teachers may support play across contexts that involve spontaneous play and those that involve guided and directed play. In examples that follow, we describe how these principles may apply for different ages of young children and in classrooms that include children with special needs and children from a variety of cultural, socioeconomic, and linguistic backgrounds.

Taking the Child's View

The first principle involves the teacher taking the child's view of experiences and materials in the classroom. Developmentally appropriate practice (DAP), a term coined by the National Association for the Education of Young Children (NAEYC), involves understanding age-appropriate development in young children (Bredekamp, 2004; Copple & Bredekamp, 2009; see Chapters 1 and 3).

Developmentally appropriate practice involves understanding the individual development of each child and the cultural context in which development occurs. What does Raul bring to school from his home that is unique and different from the concepts

Teachers can create bridges from teacher-initiated activities to spontaneous play.

and attitudes brought by Miko or Frances? How does the impending divorce of Jo Ann's parents affect her development and behavior? What special accommodations does Brian, who has spina bifida, need to have access to the slide or have an opportunity to swing? In taking the child's viewpoint, teachers work with aspects of developmentally appropriate practice: understanding the normal development of a particular age group and understanding the life experiences in and out of school that shape meaning for each child. For example, what does Emil's preoccupation with gunplay and soldiers mean in light of his family's recent immigration from a war-torn country to the United States? Will the addition of a private small space outdoors, and a few of the miniature ponies, encourage Fran and Celine to interact, rather than just watch others play?

Teacher as Keen Observer

The second principle of orchestrating play in the curriculum involves the teacher as a keen observer of children's behavior. His or her observation skills are supported by planning specific times to circulate through the classroom, to jot anecdotal notes on peel-off labels, or to sit and observe for a longer period in a specific area of the indoor or outdoor classroom. The teacher also uses observational strategies when working with a small group of children on a focused activity and takes time to write down children's observations, questions, experiments, and hypotheses as they work and play.

Seeing Meaning as It Is Constructed

Under the auspices of this third principle, the sensitive teacher recognizes that children construct meaning through many aspects of their experience. Sometimes meaning emerges as playmates suggest a new block to support a building or offer a costume for a role. Sometimes meaning emerges as teacher and child sit together to figure out the spelling of a new word. Knowledge that is derived from children's interactions with adults and other children is contextually relevant. Knowing what is relevant through observing and interpreting children's play enables teachers to skillfully intervene in ways that fall along a continuum of subtle to active participation in play. Such knowledge may enable them to decide to step back and allow children the autonomy to resolve their own challenges or conflicts. Or it may enable them to decide if it is necessary to more actively guide or redirect play.

Teacher as Stage Manager

The fourth principle involves the teacher's skill in organizing the environment. The teacher plans experiences or projects for children, anticipating the needed spatial arrangements, basic materials, accessories, and time frames to enable children to construct knowledge through their play. In this role, the teacher supports play by indirectly orchestrating the physical environment, including the dimension of time for children's play (Cryer, Harms, & Riley, 2006; Curtis & Carter, 2003; Greenman, 2005; Hand & Nourot, 1999; Katz & Chard, 2000).

In this chapter we first present some general definitions of strategies and concepts for setting the stage for play in early childhood programs. In Chapters 5 and 6 we follow with more detailed descriptions and examples of orchestration strategies as well as illustrations of how assessment and a play centered curriculum go hand in hand. Greater numbers of children with special needs are now included for part or all of the day in preschool and primary-grade settings. Adaptations to the environment, careful selection of play materials, and curriculum are described extensively in the early intervention literature, and we include many of these strategies in our examples and suggested resources. We believe that play "leads" development for all children, those who develop in atypical as well as more typical ways.

A CONTINUUM OF PLAY ORCHESTRATION STRATEGIES

The model we present in Figure 4.1 represents play orchestration strategies ranging from very indirect to very direct roles on the part of the adult. The most indirect of these strategies involve arranging and accessorizing the physical environment for play, and then planning curriculum based on observation and recording of children's play. Increasingly directive techniques for guided play orchestration are described in depth in Chapter 5. Although we present these as separate play orchestration strategies, skilled and observant teachers frequently employ several strategies in supporting children's play, often beginning with more indirect strategies, perhaps moving to more directive ones, and then, as they fine-tune adult involvement, returning to a less-directive role on the part of the teacher.

Figure 4.1
Continuum of Play
Orchestration
Strategies

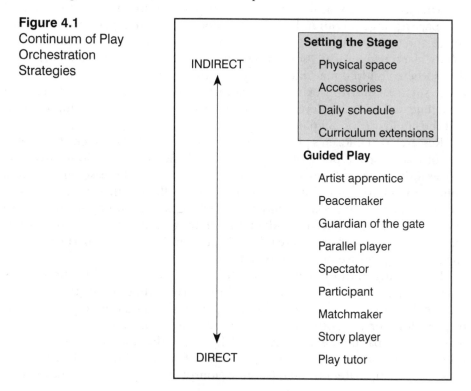

INDIRECT

Setting the Stage

Physical space

Accessories

Daily schedule

Curriculum extensions

Guided Play

Artist apprentice

Peacemaker

Guardian of the gate

Parallel player

Spectator

Participant

Matchmaker

Story player

DIRECT

Play tutor

SETTING THE STAGE FOR PLAY

As adults, we look at an office, a restaurant, or an outdoor barbecue and know what kinds of activities and behaviors are expected. As children play in different areas of both the indoor and outdoor classroom, they learn the implicit and explicit rules about what is expected and, in effect, come to read the social and physical cues of that particular area. The environment, then, is not only "responsive," but children also respond to it by bringing their own knowledge of their cultures, situations, events, and people and recalling what they may have done before in this area to bear on their understanding of what may be expected of them (Cook-Gumperz, & Corsaro, 1977; Qvortrup, Corsaro, & Honig, 2009).

At the indirect end of the continuum, teachers orchestrate play by setting the stage for it to occur. They first provide the physical space conducive to children's play needs, a process that reflects their respect for children's special abilities, needs, families, and communities. Teachers also use their professional skills to elaborate and extend curriculum based on the children's play that they observe. Accessories for play are changed frequently as the teacher responds to children's advancing needs or are readily available for children to appropriate on their own (Chalufour & Worth, 2004; Curtis & Carter, 2003; Reynolds, 2002).

Preparing the Physical Space for Play

In structuring the physical environment for play, questions to consider are: How is the space arranged, both indoors and outdoors? Is there a place to safely engage in rough-and-tumble play, an area to vigorously run and jump and chase? Are there clearly marked areas with "soft" spaces such as soft chairs or a small grassy area outdoors where children may find privacy? Are there other areas that have clear boundaries, such as the housekeeping, reading, and block areas? All these features contribute to children's developing play complexity by fostering autonomous choice and the familiarity of ongoing play episodes.

Research on children's play environments indicates that between 30 and 50 square feet of usable space per child represents an ideal size for indoor environments. Spaces with less than 25 square feet per child may lead to increases in aggression and unfocused behavior for children (Smith & Connolly, 1980). For teachers, crowded physical spaces promote more directive teaching and limit opportunities for social interaction among children. Outdoors, a variety of choices and natural environments that include trees and grassy areas have been found to increase participation in play and reduce aggressive play (Moore & Wong, 1997).

In thinking about environments, teachers need to consider both units (the spaces arranged for children's play) and the surrounding space (the area around a unit needed for people to move about). Space invites children to pause and attend, to play alone or with others, to move randomly or purposefully, and to combine materials or separate them. Space generally shapes the flow of play and communication in the classroom or outdoors (Clayton & Forton, 2001; Curtis & Carter, 2003; Frost, Wortham, & Reifel, 2005; Hand & Nourot, 1999; Kostelnik, Onaga, Rohde, &

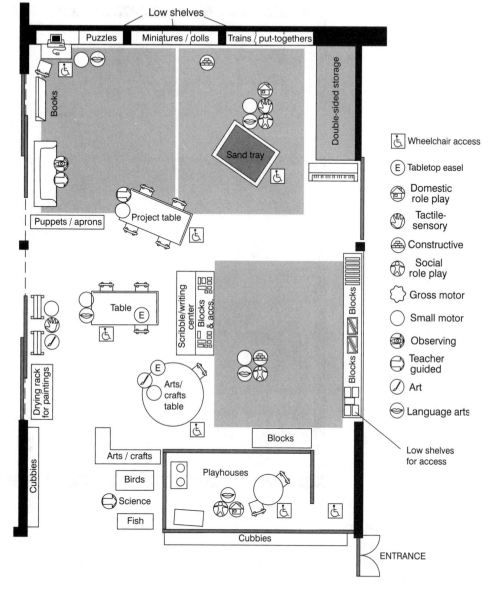

Figure 4.2
Preschool and Kindergarten Setting

Whiren, 2002; Kritchevsky, Prescott, & Walling, 1977; Trawick-Smith, 1992; 2010). (See Chapter 12, "Outdoor Play.") Figures 4.2, 4.3, and 4.4 show indoor and outdoor plans that support play-centered curriculum.

Adapting Spaces for Special Needs. Considerations of the physical space are extremely important when integrating children with special needs into the classroom.

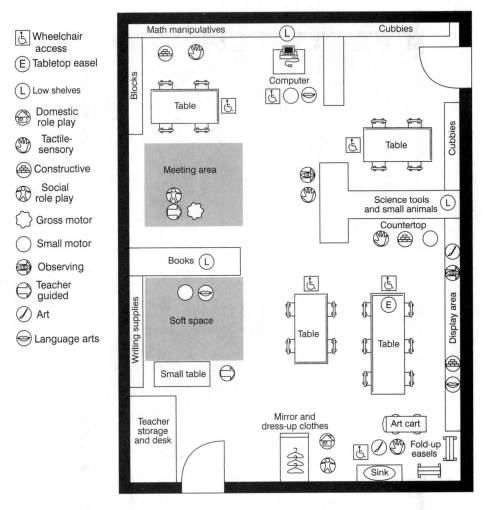

Figure 4.3
Primary Grade Setting

According to McEvoy, Shores, Wehby, Johnson, and Fox (1990), educators cannot assume that children with special needs will be socially integrated merely by placing
them in classrooms with nondisabled children. It is imperative for teachers to be
aware of the particular alternative learning strategies of each child (Barnes & Lehr,
2005; Erwin, 1993). In some cases, adaptive equipment for children who cannot
stand for long periods of time, such as a tabletop easel or exercise ball placed at a
regular easel, may be needed to promote active engagement (Hanline & Fox, 1993;
Sandall, 2003; Thomas, 2005). Based on this awareness, teachers can then plan
environments that support the child's development of self-initiated solitary play as
well as play with peers. For children in wheelchairs, or in the case of Jake, a child whose
wide rigid leg braces made movement around the classroom a challenge, less may be

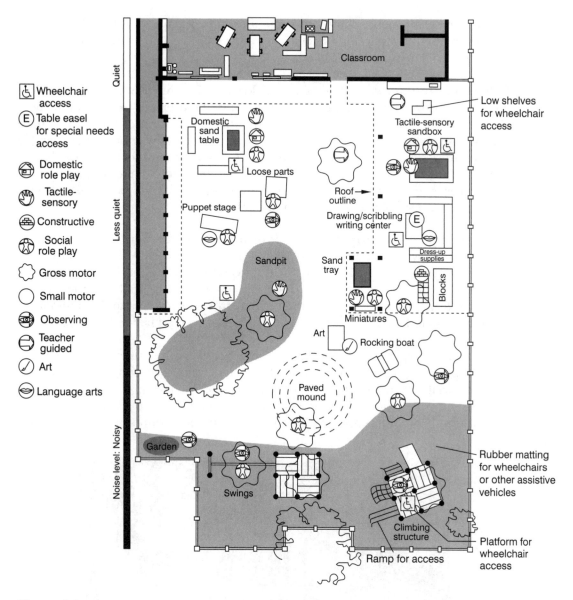

Figure 4.4
Outdoor Setting—Preschool and Primary Grade

more. Teachers and children may need to think about what furniture or materials could be left out of the room or stored to provide more access or movement.

Outdoor environments that provide linkages among play areas such as platforms, slides, or tires and nets are most conducive to sustained play. Multiple levels of challenge and diverse materials help children to make choices. Pathways need to accommodate wheelchairs and other mobility aids. Ramps, decks, and stationary bridges are useful for parking wheelchairs so that children may access climbing areas (Burkhour, 2005; Frost et al., 2005).

Paths and Boundaries.   Research on children's environments indicates that clear boundaries between interest areas, and clear paths of movement between them, help children to focus on their play and support their protection of interactive space (Perry, 2001; Ramsey & Reid, 1988). Boundaries must be low enough, however, for children to view available possibilities in the environment and for adults to observe children. Low adult–child ratios also contribute to the maintenance of play themes. Merely having an adult nearby can act as a buffer against interlopers or distractions, lending indirect support to established play interactions

> John and Sara are playing airport in the block corner. They have just painstakingly completed a control tower and runway when Andrew and Colin chase through the block area on their way outdoors to try out the magic capes they have made from yarn and paper. The block structures fall, and there are angry tears and accusations. If the pathway from the art area to the outdoors were rerouted around the block area, such events would be less likely. ✇

Quiet and Noisy Areas.   Another setup strategy involves separating quiet and noisy, or private and group, activities in different parts of the setting. Activities likely to foster social interaction and busy noise are blocks, dramatic play, reading and writing corners, number activities, and climbing structures. Sandboxes, water tables, art activities, and computers are variable—in some situations with some children, they

Teachers express their own playfulness while orchestrating children's play.

may be conducive to social interaction; in others they may promote more parallel and solitary play than cooperative play (Curtis & Carter, 2003; Ramsey & Reid, 1988). In general, activities that encourage gross motor play, such as tricycles and outdoor climbing structures, foster more social interaction than those that encourage small motor skills, such as puzzles, table toys, miniatures, or Montessori materials and, in fact, may support more sociodramatic play. Teachers may find that small motor toys promote more solitary and parallel play (Hendrickson, Strain, Trembley, & Shores, 1981).

Activity units that offer children privacy for playing alone or with one or two friends are created by furniture that defines the space. These "hidey-holes" for children to find respite from the group seem particularly important for children who may spend 8 to 10 hours a day in group settings.

Including Children with Special Needs. 🖤 Areas that support social activities are critical in classrooms practicing inclusion. Many children with special needs are challenged by the social skills necessary for appropriate development, and it is important that teachers do not make assumptions about these social skills and instead carefully observe and support children's efforts, even if they appear to be characteristic of much younger children (Creasey, Jarvis, & Burke, 1998; Kostelnik et al., 2002; Odom, 2002; Sheridan, Foley, & Radlinski, 1995). Beckman and Kohl found that providing interactive toys leads to increased social interactions among disabled and nondisabled children (Beckman & Kohl, 1984, as cited in McEvoy et al., 1990). Similarly, Horner found that disabled children's adaptive behaviors were increased by adding large numbers of toys to a free-choice setting (Horner, 1980, as cited in McEvoy et al., 1990).

Children with health impairments may benefit from play spaces that foster less physically demanding play while allowing children to be part of the group and to make choices about when to observe and when to join play (Burkhour, 2005; Frost et al., 2005). Quiet places are particularly important for some children who are easily distracted or frustrated (Bronson, 2000; Kostelnik et al., 2002; Kranor & Kuschner, 1996; Odom, 2002).

Hannah is a student with special needs, diagnosed as having ADHD and language delays. With the supportive teamwork of her parents, the school psychologist, and the special education teacher, Hannah has been fully integrated into Pam's first-grade class. Pam finds that Hannah frequently has difficulty sustaining interactions with the other children. As part of Hannah's Individualized Education Plan, Pam and the school psychologist are attempting to assess and support her progress in social activities with peers.

In addition to interacting with peers in Pam's class, Hannah's participation in after-school day care means that she is with large groups of children for 10 hours each day, from 7:30 a.m. to 5:30 p.m. Pam observes that Hannah spends quiet time each day by herself in the classroom's reading loft, looking at picture books or talking quietly to the stuffed animals. When Hannah becomes frustrated, Pam finds that she can help Hannah self-monitor her behavior by suggesting that she go to the loft or another quiet place. 🖉

Soft Spaces.   Children also benefit from soft areas in the classroom that provide privacy and refuge. The cozy nature of a corner with pillows and rocker, carpeting, and materials that invite sensory exploration such as sand or clay evoke comfort, collaboration, and friendship in the environment. When children become angry or frustrated, teachers can give them a chance to retreat to a quiet, soft space by themselves, a place with no hard objects to throw or hurt themselves. Adults may need to accompany children who are, at that moment, very aggressive or have behavioral disabilities.

> The book corner is in a central area of the room. It is carpeted in a warm-toned tweed, which was selected both for its sturdiness and softness. The rug is bounded on one side by a piano that faces a low couch. Several thin rectangular pillows, covered in a washable velour, are available for sitting on or leaning against the piano legs during circle time. At the wall end of the rug, two birch book display stands each put five rows of picture books within easy reach of rug sitters. (Beardsley, 1991, p. 52)

Some of the outdoor spaces may be soft as well. A tree for shade, a grassy carpet to just sit on and watch or read or play alone or with a friend provide havens from the frequently active pace of outdoor play. For example:

> In the outdoor garden area Josh and Taylor sit with their backs against a row of hay bales quietly looking at picture books. They're propped on the edge of the planter box that holds the newly blooming daffodils and crocuses planted by the children the previous fall.

Freidrich Froebel (1782–1852) wrote about the importance of nature and forms of life and forms of beauty as elements in a kindergarten or "garden of childhood." Providing materials that invite real-life experiences with plants and small animals, such as gardens, and terrariums, and opportunities to care for these living things is essential. Activities such as gardening or woodworking, or washing dishes or furniture, give children a sense of competence as they use real tools. Forms of life also include culturally diverse objects and representations of experiences from children's lives such as photographs and music.

Patterns, color, light, and visual and auditory harmony are all aspects of forms of beauty in the environment. The use of texture, paintings, color on walls or floors, music, and plants all convey a feeling of respect and care for the environment and for children themselves in aesthetically pleasing forms. Access to water and to natural environments outdoors are all important aspects of forms of beauty (Hand & Nourot, 1999; Wolfe, 2002).

Outdoor Play Spaces.   Although much of what we have discussed as important in play environments applies across indoor and outdoor spaces, outdoor play environments offer unique opportunities for learning and development. Outdoor play offers choices to children in the use of natural materials such as sand, water, and plant life that are constrained indoors. Outdoor play offers opportunities for children to develop the "naturalistic intelligence" that Gardner (1999) describes, and to reap the benefits of fresh air, live plants, and perhaps the care of small animals to which many children have little access. Opportunities for fine and gross motor play abound. Natural materials such as pebbles, leaves, sticks, flowers, and feathers find their way into children's dramatic play. These materials become treasures to sort, to touch, and to use in creating art pieces (Topal, 2005; Torquati & Barber, 2005). In Berkeley, California, an asphalt playground was replaced with soft spaces, a grassy field, and small garden areas and trees. The outcomes were reduced rates of accidents and aggressive behavior (Moore & Wong, 1997). Barbour (1999) looked at the effects of outdoor playgrounds on peer relationships among physically disabled children and typically developing peers. She found that outdoor playgrounds that offered more options than the typical open "exercise" play space fostered more integration of children with physical limitations in play with typically developing peers. Fisman (2001) studied children's responses to actual and ideal playgrounds and discovered that children expressed a desire for many more choices, flexible use areas, and soft private spaces for their outdoor play.

In another urban school setting, a working farm is at the school site. Teachers in this district often take their classes there in the fall, winter, and spring to observe the changes in the seasons. Gardens, ducks, chickens, rabbits, goats, two horses, and a pig offer opportunities for children to observe and care for plants and animals, and teachers at the school use the farm as part of their planned curriculum.

Unfortunately, in the rush to promote academic achievement in the early years, some educators have begun to limit access to outdoor play for children, especially in elementary school settings; however, there is growing research indicating that this is counterproductive (Jarrett, 2003; National Association of Early Childhood Specialists in State Departments of Education [NAECS], 2002; National Association for the Education of Young Children [NAEYC], 2009).

When Space Is Limited. In classrooms where space is at a premium, often in public school primary-grade settings, teachers may be creative in the use of portable accessories or "Murphy space." For example, in one first-grade classroom, where desks grouped as tables occupy a large part of the classroom, the teacher constructed easels that fold into the wall, much like a Murphy bed, that can be pulled out and set up during free play time. He complements this with a rolling cart that includes art and carpentry materials that may be transported outdoors or to a table area.

Other teachers have decided that table space for all children to sit down at one time is not necessary in a room where the play goes on in specific areas of the classroom. For one teacher, freeing the room of large tables has enabled him to rotate the use of center areas according to the play experiences he has planned and has left open space in the room for block play and a large dramatic play area.

Adjacent Areas. When setting up, teachers might also think about the effects of placing activity areas adjacent to one another to invite opportunities for the cross-fertilization of the ideas of children engaged in play, even when the play areas remain distinct. For example, in one first-grade classroom, ongoing play at the carpentry table adjacent to the block area prompted the construction of airplanes and helicopters to be housed at the block area airport. In a second-grade classroom, a post office created to encourage letter writing soon expanded to a bank and an office on either side, where children integrated literacy and mathematics concepts.

To encourage the cross-fertilization of ideas in activity areas, Griffin (1998) recommends that teachers keep a box of game parts, puzzle pieces, rocks, and miscellaneous small objects that children may use in their dramatic play. In this way, the puzzle pieces and objects associated with more structured activities are more likely to remain in their respective areas, while allowing children to appropriate flexible materials for their own uses. Cultural and family factors may affect children's understanding of the school culture's conventions for returning objects to their original storage places. For example, a child who lives in a trailer or a crowded home may have learned to store toys out of view rather than displayed on a shelf. Conversely, children who come from families where the adults do the cleanup may have no rationale for the expectation that they put classroom materials away.

Accessories for Play.   The provision of accessories in the environment relates to our discussion of symbolic distancing in Chapter 3. For sociodramatic play, younger or less-sophisticated players need more realistic props to support or scaffold their play themes and roles. Their symbolic distancing skills are not well enough developed to appropriate a block or an imaginary gesture when a real-looking prop such as a toy telephone is not available. Generally, younger children (ages 2–3) prefer to have several sets of realistic props to use in their dramatic play. Multiple sets of brooms and phones, toy food and dishes, fire trucks, and toy animals are necessary elements for the scaffold supporting their dramatic play. If not available, play fantasies may give way to object disputes, and the symbolic distancing of roles and situations has little chance to get underway.

On the other hand, sophisticated dramatic players like to have lots of unstructured props—that is, props with limited specific use of their own—available for their dramatic play. Cardboard packing, rocks, sticks, and blocks are examples of unstructured props. Such nonrealistic props offer much leeway to the child to make successive transformations—for instance by using pebbles as money, food, buried treasure, and circus tickets—all in the course of a single play episode.

Primary-grade children enjoy having hats and scarves available for more formal play and dramatic enactments and will generally use both unstructured props and imaginary ones in such activities (Heathcote & Bolton, 1995). (See Chapters 8 and 10.) They also use miniatures, models, and games with rules as accessories to their fantasy play. Many children in this age group also enjoy collections and are supported by trays or boxes with compartments for organizing their collections.

> Randall and Amber have been making a volcano scene in a cardboard box for several days. After constructing the volcano from play dough, they use red and orange tissue paper to represent flames from the volcano and toothpicks and paper to make trees and homes on the sides of the volcano. They spend time coloring branches of their trees to represent ash and burned wood and

discuss the escape and rescue operations of the people and animals who lived in the houses. ✑

Timing in the introduction of props is important. Replicas of real objects and props that relate to familiar scripts are appropriate at the beginning of the year, as children get to know one another. Accessory boxes that augment the familiar scripts of housekeeping or cars and trucks in the preschool and kindergarten may be introduced later in the year. Many teachers have a large selection of accessory boxes built around themes such as restaurant, office, beach trip, and camping that they introduce to correlate with curriculum themes or have available on request by children. Accessory or prop boxes may be made from cardboard boxes, ice cream containers, or plastic bins (Desjean-Perrotta & Barbour, 2001; Myhre, 1993). Figure 4.5 provides suggestions for themes and contents for prop boxes. Some teachers offer a rotating variety of theme boxes in a designated area of the room; others periodically replace or augment equipment in the housekeeping area or outdoor climbing structure. In the primary grades, these accessory boxes are valuable as prompts for enacted plays and story writing.

Play Materials for Children with Special Needs. ♥ Older children with special needs characterized by autism, some speech disabilities, or developmental language delays may benefit from having multiple realistic or replica play accessories to support their fantasy play. Such costumes and props for pretend play enable children who are challenged to communicate their ideas with language to more fully participate in pretend play role and situations (Marvin & Hunt-Berg, 1996; Wolfberg, 1999).

Adaptive toys with technological features such as a battery-operated bubble blower or electric dice roller enable some children with physical disabilities to more easily participate in play (Locke & Levin, 1998; Stone & Stagstetter, 1998).

Familiarity Balanced with Novelty. ♥ Children need a balance of the familiar and the novel. In addition to the traditional housekeeping props, the teacher must consider the cultural backgrounds of the students. Does the family eat with chopsticks and cook in a wok? Does the family use a barbecue? Might cherry-picking baskets, beads and yarn, western hats or coal miners' hats be familiar objects in some children's homes? If we want all children to find a familiar script in the classroom, we must scaffold their symbolic behavior on what is comfortable and homelike to them (Derman-Sparks & Ramsey, 2005; Genishi & Dyson, 2009; Genishi, Huang, & Glupczynski, 2005; Hughes, 2003; Reynolds, 2002).

Areas where materials for art and music are available open opportunities for new accessories or modifications of old ones (Bronson, 1995). In one classroom, small cans filled with rice, beans, or pebbles and then taped closed were placed next to the xylophone and rhythm instruments, with materials for creating individual shakers set out nearby. In another setting, a discussion of a Pisarro painting prompted the

Office
stapler
tape
old adding machine or fax machine
copier made from cardboard box
telephones
computer keyboard
computer monitor made from box

Paint Store
painter's hat
bucket
brushes, scrapers
paper color chips in graded colors
cash register and "money"
order pads and pencils
home improvement catalogs
telephone

Flower and/or Fruit Stand
plastic flowers, fruits, vegetables
boxes or crates, tables for display
cash register and "money"
chalkboard for prices

Bakery
playdough, paper confetti
cookie sheets, tubes for decorating
oven
telephone
labels or chalkboard for prices
cash register and "money"
blocks for display cases
cookbooks

Gas Station
trikes, wagons
large boxes for pumps plastic hoses

cash register and "money" or "credit cards"
window-washing supplies (spray bottles, squeegies)
large box for car wash

Restaurant
aprons
chef's hat
menus
tablecloths
silverware
dishes
play food
chalkboard and chalk for "specials"
order pads and pencils
cash register and "money"
telephone

Bank
tellers' windows
cash boxes
bank books
office supplies
play money

Shoe Store
shoes and boxes
foot measure, tape, ruler
socks
telephone
receipt book
price labels
cash register and "money"

Camping Out
sleeping bags
tent
camp cookware
flashlight
backpacks

Travel and Passport Office
computer keyboard, box for monitor

toy camera
drawing and writing supplies
blank books
travel brochures

Hospital or Doctor's Office
bandages
toy medical tools (e.g., blood pressure cuff, syringe)
cots or mats
waiting room with magazines
white coats
medical hats
rubber gloves
files, clipboards, and paper for patient information
telephone
computer keyboard, box for monitor

Pet Shop
toy animals
boxes for cages, aquariums
cash register, receipts, "money"
materials to make collars, pet toys, and animal food

Laundromat
washers and dryers made from cardboard cartons
plastic or straw baskets
clothing to "wash," sort, and fold
toy iron and ironing board
clothes rack and hangers
cash register or change machine
bulletin board and notices
magazines

Figure 4.5
Some Suggested Accessory Box Themes and Contents

Teachers help children sustain their play by sensitively entering into their activities.

teacher to mix muted pastel colors and thicken the paints so that children might try the "painting in pokes" that they had noticed in the print borrowed from the public library (Beardsley, 1991).

Play Materials Offer Alternatives. Teachers may set up environments that encourage a particular kind of play by combining or rearranging materials. For example, setting out toothpicks with clay may encourage more social interaction than clay alone, as children link structures they build or construct birthday cakes or bridges in play that involves others.

Quiet and private materials offer children opportunities for exploration before they begin to play. In initial exploration, the focus is on "What can this object (or material) do?" After time to explore the material at hand, children begin to truly play, when the implicit question becomes, "What can I do with this object or material?" (Hutt, 1971; Wohlwill, 1984).

Sandy approaches the used adding machine that another child has just left. She pushes keys and watches the numbers print for about 10 minutes. The next day she returns and continues her exploration, systematically trying each key to note the number it produces on the tape. On the third day she invites Mark to play. "Come to my store. You can buy cookies," and she rings up a pretend purchase. ✆

Materials that offer opportunities for exploratory and self-correcting activity includes pegboards, form boards, miniatures, and picture lotto. These activities give children a relaxed time away from the mental effort of negotiating with their peers and help them restore a sense of order and control to their lives. Materials that support solitary play may also provide important relief from the pressures of social interaction for children learning English as a second language or those with language disabilities (Clawson, 2002). This function seems to be age related. McLloyd (1983) found that 3-year-olds used these materials in more solitary ways, whereas 5-year-olds engaged in more cooperative play, regardless of the structure of the materials. This relates to the finding that solitary play represents one of the many options for older children because they are better able to verbalize their needs for privacy.

Play Safety

One of the most compelling issues related to play environments for young children is the question of the safety of toys and play environments. Each year, hundreds of children are injured while playing with commercial toys. Many of these injuries occur in school settings. Therefore, teachers need to be knowledgeable and observant.

Government regulation of toy safety standards increased with the Hazardous Substance Act of 1973 and the Consumer Product Safety Act of 1978. These standards include the important requirement that toy manufacturers clearly label products with age appropriateness. For example, toys containing tiny pieces or sharp edges must be clearly labeled to warn adults that they are not designed for children under the age of 3. Toys that are electrical in nature, and thus present a potential hazard of burning children, must be labeled as hazardous for children age 8 and younger.

Consumer publications inform teachers and parents about toy safety issues. The U.S. Consumer Product Safety Commission offers resources such as *For Kids' Sake: Think Toy Safety* (2005) and *Shop CPSC Toy Safety Tips Before Shopping for Holiday Gifts* (2008), as well as the Consumer Product Safety Improvement Act of 2008, available online at no cost, that are designed to help prevent toy and playground injuries. The American Academy of Pediatrics lists toy safety tips for the holidays. The Toy Industry Association offers a Toy Safety Hotline, and Safechild.net offers tips for toy safety as well as updated information on toy recalls.

The Toy Manufacturers of America, in conjunction with the U.S. Consumer Product Safety Commission (2005), has developed and published guidelines for guarding against potential accidents involving toys. These guidelines include:

1. Select toys that are appropriate for children's interests and stages of development. This includes avoiding toys with long strings or small parts for infants and toddlers. "Choke tubes" are available to measure the size of pieces in toys that are suspected of being dangerous.
2. Read labels on packaging carefully and dispose of packing material (such as plastic wrappers) that might be dangerous to children. Choose toys with non-toxic paints and flame-retardant fabrics.
3. Keep toys clean and in good repair. Store toys designed for older children out of sight and reach from those at earlier developmental stages.
4. Supervise the play of children, particularly very young children, to see that they do not use toys in ways that are dangerous to their health or safety.

Not all products are screened under consumer safety guidelines. Parents, teachers, and other professionals who work with children and families still must be vigilant. Many products available by mail from overseas do not meet these standards. Toys that children acquire from someone's attic could be in poor repair, have parts painted with lead-based paint, or have pieces missing that make them potentially hazardous.

Playground Safety.   Another issue is playground safety. Although space limitations do not allow us to treat this topic in depth, we have read several resources useful for planning safe, outdoor play areas that have high playability. The NAEYC requires 75 square feet of play space outdoors per child as part of their accreditation criteria and recommends the following six elements of playground safety:

1. Careful supervision of children
2. Arrangement of space that protects against access to streets, standing water, and other hazards
3. Provision of sturdy and safe equipment designed for the physical and developmental level of children
4. Provision of resilient surfaces for landings
5. Provision of regularly scheduled maintenance and cleanup
6. A variety of choices for play (NAEYC, 1996)

One of the most user-friendly resources is the manual on playground safety written by Jambor and Palmer (1991). These authors offer general guidelines and specific criteria for playground safety in a checklist. They discuss three general principles for school playground safety. First, enclosures that shelter play environments should have no visual barriers so children are supervised adequately and protected from hazards outside the play area. Second, adequate space is needed to accommodate children safely using equipment on their own. Jambor and Palmer include guidelines for space surrounding slides, swings, and climbing structures. Third, play surfaces must minimize the impact of children's falls. In general, Jambor and Palmer recommend that softer surfaces (such as grass or packed dirt in contrast to cement or asphalt) are less likely to contribute to injury when children fall. (See Frost et al. [2005] for a detailed review of playground safety issues.)

Planning the Daily Schedule

Another element of the infrastructure of curriculum is the daily schedule of activities. Powerful messages are sent to children about the value of their own choices and the activities they construct for themselves by the way that teachers structure the days. This scheduling includes not only the content of the classroom, but also how much time is allotted for playful purposes (Cryer, Harms, & Riley, 2003; Hand & Nourot, 1999; Harms, Clifford & Cryer, 1998; Trawick-Smith, 1998, 2010; Wassermann, 2000). The daily schedule is also an effective way to verify how much actual time is being made available for children's play. If an examination of the schedule indicates that most of the children's time is booked for circle, group, housekeeping, or other directed activities, there is probably too much "teacher choice and teacher voice" in the program. In full-day programs, 50 minutes of time for spontaneous play and self-directed choice time during the morning as well as the afternoon is ideal. (See Cryer, Harms, & Riley, *All About the ECCERS-R* [2003] for detailed examples.)

In the most free-flowing environments, the room is arranged with activities available for children to choose. Furniture and materials are flexible, and the teacher floats, interacting with small groups of children more often than the entire class. Traditional nursery schools and open classrooms based on the British Infant School model are examples of this design. Teachers who use this design in their classrooms have noted that lengthening the total time for free choice activities and play increases the focus and engagement of children in their chosen activities and also encourages children to try new experiences after they have touched base with their old favorites (Paley, 1984).

In other environments, more teacher direction and less child choice is evident. Small- and large-group direct instruction alternates with free-choice time. Teachers spend more time with designated groups and less time attending to the flow in the total classroom. The pitfall of this model is that what teachers perceive as play (e.g., building an airport with blocks) may be seen by the children as labor because their choice of activities really rests with the teacher. Teachers may also miss out on important learning events when they attend to only one group.

The most structured environment leaves little time for free play. Play is regarded as recreational rather than as a vehicle for learning. Small- and large-group direct instruction characterize this design, and the teacher's attention to children's play rests primarily on concerns about safety rather than on aspects of social or intellectual development. Skills-based academic programs exemplify this model.

A play-centered curriculum that serves children's intellectual development and construction of new and meaningful knowledge achieves a delicate and important balance between teacher-initiated and guided play and child-initiated and directed play. Teachers who are sensitive to the distinction between labor required by others and playful work selected by children in their settings will note the importance of choices for children, as well as ample time for children to elaborate and complete activities they have begun. In any activity, teachers need to ask themselves: How much of it is truly chosen by the child? Does the child have choices about where, when, how, and with whom she or he plays? How engaged are children in their play? Assessing children's opportunities for spontaneous self-directed play through examination of the daily schedule is an effective reality check on how much time is actually being allocated for play.

EXTENSIONS FOR PLAY

Setting the stage for play and curriculum planning go hand in hand. It represents the backstage versus the onstage aspect of teaching when we focus on play as the center of the curriculum.

Play-Generated Curriculum

One facet of curriculum planning is play-generated curriculum, or curriculum that emerges directly from the interests of the children. Teachers draw on their observations of children's interests and themes in their play to provide opportunities to extend and elaborate their learning. For example:

> In one first-grade classroom, several of the children had participated over the weekend in a community art fair called "Art in the Park." They had all contributed their efforts to a huge wall mural. On Monday, three of the children asked if they could have some large paper to show the other children "how you make a really big picture." The teacher set up large sheets of butcher paper. The children were provide a complete palette of paints in multiple small milk cartons, which were housed as a set in small tote boxes. Children experimented with recipes for making paint and mixing colors. Later in the week the teacher brought in books from the library depicting murals in other communities around the world. The following week, the teacher introduced new media such as collage and group wood sculptures for the children to try. ✑

Curriculum-Generated Play

This facet of curriculum planning involves a more direct role for the teacher. In planning curriculum-generated play, a teacher's observation of children's play leads her to include materials or techniques that she suspects will create a match with children's spontaneous interests (Bennett, Wood, & Rogers, 1997; Hand & Nourot, 1999; Stegelin, 2005). In this way, the teacher's knowledge of the content area such as science, mathematics, art, or literacy intersects with her sense of children's previous experiences and their current interests.

> The teacher of a second-grade science program noticed children's interests in the concept of water pressure as they experimented with dish soap bottles outdoors. She related these interests to requirements for physical science activities and the introduction of scientific terms in the state department of education's science framework and state curriculum standards. The teacher placed holes in containers at different levels and set up plastic piping material with a water source, challenging the children to find out which arrangements would make the water squirt farther. She introduced terms like *pressure* in the context of their observations and introduced the term *hypothesis* in conjunction with the "guesses" that the children made about their experiments. ✑

> A kindergartner named Jennifer spent her choice time over several days creating a book she called "The Very Hungry Clowns," which consisted of clowns with butterflies in their tummies, a new one drawn for each day. Jennifer's merging of a phrase she had heard at home with the format and structure of Eric Carle's book *The Very Hungry Caterpillar* read earlier in the week were evident in her play creation. ✑

The technique of curriculum-generated play has elements in common with the thematic curriculum design seen in many programs for preschool and primary children. We believe curriculum-generated play enhances the best of thematic curriculum. Some thematic curriculum is based on the teacher's interests, children's families, past experiences, and resources. Truly play-centered curriculum integrates teachers' interests and concerns with those observed in children as they play (Katz & Chard, 2000).

This continuity among families, community, and school curriculum is reflected strongly in the Reggio Emilia approach to early schooling (Edwards, Gandini, & Forman, 1993; Forman, 2005; Hendrick, 1997; New, 2005; Wien, 2008). Within this approach, the contributions of families and community and the relationships and interaction among children as they construct knowledge in small groups are all highly valued aspects of curriculum planning. Time for themes, concepts, hypotheses, and multiple representations to emerge and evolve to completion is valued.

The spiral curriculum approach that revisits and revises representations of experience is shared by both children and teachers. Bruner (1963) coined the term *spiral curriculum* to represent the idea that, at many stages of their development, children may grasp basic concepts, each time returning to the same ideas at a more sophisticated level of understanding. So, rather than focusing on the themes of curriculum, such as whales or dinosaurs, the teacher focuses on the concepts that might be revisited as children encounter those themes several times during their school experience.

Play-Centered Curriculum Addresses Experiences from a Variety of Cultures.

One drawback of thematic curriculum that is not directly based in children's experiences is the unsatisfactory treatment of multicultural issues. Topics such as ethnicity and race, culture, and language may be overlooked or misrepresented. For example, teachers with good intentions may address cultural diversity in a manner that has come to be known as the "tourist curriculum" (Derman-Sparks & ABC Task Force, 1989; Derman-Sparks & Ramsey, 2005). In this approach, foods, festivals, and music from different cultures are introduced once a year, often in conjunction with a holiday. In addition, some teachers have fallen into the routine of presenting out-of-context knowledge of culture, such as depicting stereotypes of American Indians at Thanksgiving or Chinese culture at Chinese New Year, without addressing the real issues of cultural diversity in our daily lives. Instead, the "antibias" approach advocated by Derman-Sparks and ABC Task Force includes diversity as a regular aspect of the curriculum, where teachers foster children's positive attitudes toward the acceptance and celebration of differences among cultures. It is important that the environment reflects children's cultures and languages, and that the physical space and materials for play become vehicles for learning about our country's rich diversity (Gonzalez-Mena, 2008).

Consistent with this view, in a play-centered curriculum, aspects of the physical environment and accessories for play reflect diversity of culture, through such items as the tortilla press, yogurt maker, seaweed toaster, rice bowls, and chopsticks, as well as day-time planners and briefcases that are available in Janice's kindergarten room.

In a play-centered curriculum, art, music, literature, science, and mathematics experiences reflect cultural diversity in a manner that makes it part of everyday life in the classroom, not just an infrequent glimpse of fragmented information or a song or two. For example:

> In Consuelo's first-grade classroom, she observed the Southeast Asian children pretending to make rice and shrimp dishes in their sand and water play. She contacted one of the parents of the children and included frequent cooking projects. The projects introduced some of these foods and the techniques used to cook them to everyone in the class and offered the Southeast Asian children foods that seemed familiar and delicious to them as part of the regular snack menu. ✇

> In a second-grade classroom, the teacher incorporated literature describing the legends of several cultures into his curriculum on astronomy. He invited families of children to tell bedtime stories and family stories to the class and was pleasantly surprised when over half of the families participated. Family members, including parents and grandparents, aunts and uncles even took time off work to come to school and share stories from their childhoods or family traditions and rituals. ✇

The cultural values of some families may provide an additional challenge in advocating for play-centered curriculum. For example, Joshi (2005) describes a common response of Asian Indian families to play at school, reflecting the belief that education should be focused on learning correct behaviors and habits, rather than playfulness and creativity. He recommends that teachers take the time to explain and describe how concepts, skills, and academic standards are embedded in play-centered curriculum at school and to respect the families' beliefs by offering suggestions for activities at home to enhance these academic goals. Documenting children's play and projects through photographs, visual arts, and writing can make the links between play and academic learning more evident to families. Another curriculum strategy represents subtle orchestration on the part of the teacher and calls for finely tuned observation skills. In this strategy, the teacher provides opportunities and asks questions that encourage children to use newly constructed knowledge derived from the curriculum in their play. We return to the notion presented in Chapter 2 that play is a predominance of assimilation and represents opportunities for children to consolidate and generalize their emerging mental concepts. We see this aspect of play as extremely important. The true test of whether experiences orchestrated by the teacher help children learn a specific concept or skill, such as counting money or using a calculator, is to see it "replayed" spontaneously by children in their play.

Integrating Academic Standards. In one first-grade classroom, the teacher complemented a mathematics unit on measurement with the creation of a shoe store in the dramatic play area. She was delighted to hear children use terms like "same size" and "half an inch shorter," as they used rulers, yardsticks, and shoe measurers in their play. As part of the language and literacy curriculum, she facilitated the making of a shoe sale sign and sales receipt books, while children wrote about shoes they love to wear. The unit was expanded to include other stores that children knew about in their local shopping mall, and integrated literacy, mathematics, art, and social studies concepts in the play. Table 4.1 illustrates the curriculum standards addressed by the shoe store project and the environmental supports provided for the children's play.

Table 4.1   Examples of Standards Addressed by the Shoe Store Project

Curriculum Standards	Play Example	Environmental Support
Phonemic and Phonological Awareness		
Makes letter-sound correspondences	Children make signs for shoe sale and labels for shelves	Supply blank signs and pens in block area
Demonstrates growing awareness of beginning, ending, medial sounds of words	Sandra writes receipts for shoe sales	Provide signs with words for sneakers, sandals, running shoes, dress-up shoes
Numeracy		
Uses comparative words, such as many–few, big–little, more–less, fast–slow appropriately	Discusses small, big, long, short in trying on shoes	Different size shoes are available in play props
Understands numbers and simple operations and uses math manipulatives, games, toys, coins in daily activities (adding, subtracting)	Counts out 6 coins to pay for shoes at pretend store	Pretend money and cash register
Measurement		
Uses measuring implements	Measures using foot measure	Yardstick and shoe measure from local shoe store
Estimates	"I need a smaller sandal"	
Ordering and Seriating		
Orders objects from smallest to largest	Lines up shoes on shelf in order	Shoe rack and shelves with space for ordering pairs of shoes
Sorting and Classifying		
Describes how items are the same or different	"Those shoes have Velcro and these have buckles"	Shoes of similar kind (e.g., running shoes) but with different features

SUMMARY AND CONCLUSION

Teachers use knowledge of developmental theories and research when setting the stage for a play-centered curriculum. Rather than following a fixed curriculum, the teacher guides orchestration by providing opportunities for development. Guiding principles include (a) taking the child's view, (b) being a keen observer of children's behavior, (c) seeing meaning as it is constructed, (d) serving as stage manager to organize the environment, and (e) planning new curriculum.

The various strategies discussed in this chapter are subtle and complex. Therefore, it is helpful if teachers work with others and think of themselves as working within their own zones of proximal development. For many of us working in classrooms, new challenges are related to addressing the needs of all children, including those with identified with special needs and children whose cultural and socioeconomic backgrounds are varied. Children who are learning English in addition to their home languages offer further stretches to the imaginations and resourcefulness of teachers. All teachers continue to develop and refine their abilities to set the stage, prepare the physical space, plan the daily schedule, and develop curriculum-related extensions for play. In these extensions, teachers think about children's play to inspire and generate more formalized curriculum, as state and national curriculum standards and benchmarks affect even the youngest children in our schools. The chapters on the arts, science, mathematics, and language and literacy that follow will provide further consideration of these extensions.

Orchestrating Play: Interactions with Children

Pam, a first-grade teacher, watches as three children begin to play a board game, counting out marbles as they move to designated spaces on the game board. Peter counts whatever numbers come to mind, although he uses one-to-one correspondence as he pulls them from the barrel (1, 2, 3, 4, 7, 10). Marcia counts hers quite precisely, using the conventional number sequence, and one-to-one correspondence. Emily grabs a handful without counting, and Peter shouts, "You're cheating!" Pam asks if she may join the game and models counting in sequence and with correspondence when it is her turn. Soon Emily is imitating her strategy, and Peter is attempting to master the sequence for counting from one to 10. ✄

The 3- and 4-year-olds in Grace and Dorothy's classroom had just returned from a field trip to the outdoor farm at their local regional park as part of their project curriculum on the theme of mothers and babies. The mother pig at the farm, "Sophie," has four piglets and the children were excited about their opportunity to observe the piglets nursing and watch them as they learned to move on their own. When the local news reported that the baby pigs at the regional park's farm had been stolen, the children were distressed and worried. They contributed their theories about what happened. "One day the baby pig woke up, and Tilden farm was gone," "Maybe they just rolled down the hill" were two suggestions. After a phone call to the park ranger they had met during their visit, the news was not promising for the pigs' safe return. Grace and Dorothy supported the children's discussion and play speculating about the pigs' fate for a few days. Then they turned the discussion from the fear and violence that first dominated to the ranger's plan that the park would build a pig-napping-proof pen, and to feelings of empathy for Sophie and her babies. "She is missing her babies," went one dictated story. "The baby pigs are scared and sad without their mama," went another. The children set to work eagerly, using clay, blocks, sticks, and drawings to work on their designs for the "safe pigpen." They use the toy farm animals to test their designs and to play through their fears. "Where did all my piggies go? Cow, will you help me find them?"

"Here we are—in the barn!"

"You scared me silly, babies! I couldn't see you. Remember, stay close to me!" (Stewart, 2001b). ✄

In each of these anecdotes, we see how the teacher's ability to set up, observe, enter, and exit play with sensitivity and grace is crucial to the successful sustaining of children's play. Each teacher does this by considering factors of age-appropriate activities and individual development. For example, Pam knows that 5- and 6-year-olds are just beginning to understand games with rules, and that children's emerging abilities to use both conventional numerical sequences and one-to-one correspondence in counting vary at this level of development.

Grace and Dorothy understand the fears raised by the pig-napping at the local park, especially because the children have already begun to think about the mother pig–baby pig relationship they had observed firsthand. After supporting a discussion of their fears, Grace and Dorothy introduced ideas that shifted the children's thinking from fear and violence to empathy for the pigs and more positive alternatives, such as imagining ways to keep baby pigs safe.

A key role for the teacher lies in the ways he or she interacts with children as they play and think. The most important aspect of this role is the attitude that teachers maintain toward children's play. Teachers' respect for both individual and cultural variations in play themes and activities is essential, along with the cultivation of their own disposition of playfulness and humor (Bergen, 2002; Cooney, 2004; Lancy, 2002).

PLAY AND SCAFFOLDING

The notion of "scaffolding" was developed by researchers who studied the ways in which adults support and elaborate children's early language. Just as scaffolds on a building support the new construction, adults' interventions in play assist children's attempts at effective communication (Cazden, 1983; Ninio & Bruner, 1976).

Scaffolding includes the ways that teachers support and facilitate meaning making in children's play. As we noted in Chapter 4, the environment acts as a context for play at school. Various environmental elements scaffold for certain kinds of play. For example, the housekeeping corner supports both constructive and dramatic play as well as the use of cooperative language; seriated cups, funnels, and pitchers in the water table suggest extensions for water play; small tables and chairs scaffold solitary or parallel play; and rugs and cushions scaffold opportunities for cozy sharing or privacy (Beardsley, 1991; Henderson & Jones, 2002).

The impact that a teacher's presence has on children's play is an important aspect of scaffolding. In one classroom, interaction among children at a project table was considerably muted because much of the interaction was dominated by the teacher, who took over such tasks in conversation as initiating topics and controlling turn-taking. In a contrasting setting, teachers lingered close to children's play areas doing productive work of their own such as weeding the garden or untangling a ball of yarn, remaining available but unobtrusive as children sought to negotiate turns on a rope swing (Lederman, 1992).

Acquiring skills to negotiate their own interactions is basic to children's social and communicative competence, and it does not rest solely on adult modeling. Play provides the occasion for children to corroborate, question, experiment, and stretch their understandings of the world and their places in it.

Other examples of scaffolding include the use of music to encourage persistence at cleanup time or while on a hike. Along with scaffolding the group's efforts, songs with open-ended phrases also support children's developing abilities to hear and reproduce rhymes.

> Ted sings, "Exploring we will go, exploring we will go. We'll catch an ant and put him in our. . . ." He pauses as Sarah and Luis complete the phrase with "pants." Nessa calls out "bants" and Anthony offers "shoe." More children join in as the singing continues, "And then we'll let him go!" (*Beardsley, 1991, p. 115*)

❤️ Scaffolding also supports children whose play reveals and expresses frightening or confusing experiences, such as some of the children in Dorothy's class. Scaffolding is also important for children for whom the construction and negotiation of a pretend reality is a challenge, such as children with autism or pervasive developmental delays (Clark, 2007; Griffin, 1998; Koplow, 1996; Kostelnick, Onaga, Rohde, & Whiren, 2002; Phillips, 2002; Wolfberg, 1999). In the following example, two children with autism are supported in their efforts to engage in cooperative play.

Jeremy enters the rug area where Todd is building with blocks. Jeremy watches, and jumps up and down in place. The teacher suggests, "Jeremy, ask if you can help." Jeremy says tentatively, "Can I help?" as he looks at Todd. Todd nods his head, and Jeremy sits down. They begin to build a tower cooperatively. With a sudden kick, Todd knocks the tower down. They begin rebuilding the tower, and this time Jeremy kicks it down with his foot. Todd admonishes Jeremy, "No kicking!" as Jeremy jumps up and down in place. They rebuild the tower twice, taking turns knocking it down with their hands until it is time to clean up (Lovsey, 2002). ✍

Questions that arise for most teachers are: How much scaffolding is helpful, what form should it take, and when should it be modified or removed?

Teachers need to consider both the physical environment and the ways in which they intervene (or refrain from intervening) as integral elements of scaffolding. In the sand or water area, for example, the teacher might move an arrangement of water hoses with multiple outlets into the area, or by using a play voice direct attention to a "flood" or an "avalanche." Keen observational skills and a willingness to wait and watch as children construct their own meanings are key elements of successful scaffolding in play (Henderson & Jones, 2002; Jones & Cooper, 2006; Perry, 2001, 2003).

SPONTANEOUS, GUIDED, AND DIRECTED PLAY

Play orchestration is possible in three contexts of play among young children. In spontaneous play, the teacher's role is nearly invisible, just as setting the stage represents a prelude or backdrop to a drama. In guided play, the teacher's role is more directive, although these strategies, too, range along a continuum of less to more teacher direction. Guided play strategies differ slightly, depending on the nature of the materials and the content area of the curriculum. For example, art play and music play may call for more guidance when new materials and techniques are introduced. The strategies listed in Figure 5.1 are appropriate for orchestrating children's exploration, sociodramatic, and constructive play in the classroom. Subsequent chapters delineate guided play strategies appropriate to specific content areas such as language and literacy, science, and art.

In each case, the teacher orchestrates play in all its facets—intellectual, social, physical, and emotional—by being first and foremost a keen observer. In addition to possessing keen observational skills, the teacher who orchestrates children's play

Figure 5.1
Continuum of Play
Orchestration
Strategies

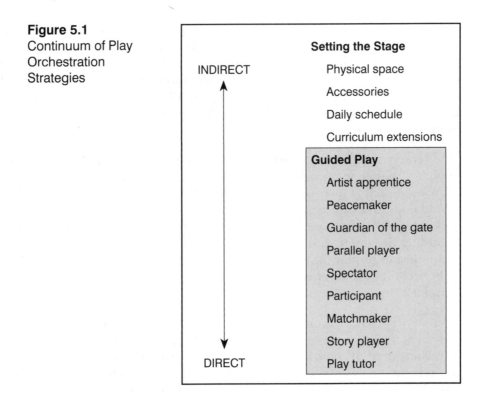

needs to learn to "dance" with the children as she facilitates their play. The first element of this dance is determining if and when she should join the children (Roskos & Christie, 2001). First she needs to ask herself: Will the children benefit by my intervention, or shall I simply watch?

Many teachers are uncomfortable with this notion of simple observation because it seems at odds with cultural stereotypes of teaching as adult-directed activity (Henderson & Jones, 2002; Jablon, Dombro, & Dichtelmiller, 2007; Joshi, 2005; Yang & McMullen, 2003). One useful strategy to help teachers extend their observation skills and at the same time model representation, reflection, and recording is by taking the role of "scribe." In this role, the teacher draws or writes about children's play and then shares her recordings of her observations with the children (Jones & Reynolds, 1992; see also, Jones & Cooper, 2006). For example:

> In Gail's kindergarten classroom as part of a thematic unit on airports, Tom and Alexis have built "a machine for seeing inside your suitcase" out of blocks, playdough, cardboard, and paper. Gail draws their constructions and then invites the children to label parts and discuss their functions with their classmates at group time. Alexis points out that Gail has forgotten to draw an essential piece—a small ball of aluminum foil. "You forgot that important shiny part that makes the light go inside the suitcase," she says, and Gail adds it to the drawing, writing a label next to it. ✆

Vivian Paley (1984, 1986, 1992, 1995, 1997, 1999) is masterful at recording children's play and then using it as a frame for group discussion or as raw material for drama. Paley reports frequently asking children, "I noticed that you were playing." Remarking on an aspect of their play that she found interesting Paley might ask, "Can you tell me more about it?" This form of authentic questioning, in which the teacher asks questions he or she does not already know how to answer, both acknowledges play for the children and adds to the teacher's information about them as individuals and as a group.

♥ Sally, a first-grade teacher who teaches in an ethnically diverse community with many English language learners, frequently uses this technique in her classroom. For example, Sally took handwritten anecdotal records during the candy store sociodramatic play in her classroom. She noted that Javier modeled the invention and use of pretend money for Lee, who seemed at first confused, then enthusiastically began to count his change: "1, 2, 3, 4, 5—that is five dollars!" Sally noted this in Lee's portfolio and then used the event to launch a discussion at group time about objects that could be used as pretend money.

"We could use those plastic buttons, because they're round," suggested Frank, representing in language his thinking about a perceptual feature of both money and buttons.

"Or shells," contributed Fran.

"Or make our own dollar bills with paper," shouted Emilia enthusiastically. A plan was made to extend their play by adding a bank the following day. ✆

What are some ways teachers can be more directly involved in children's play? Table 5.1 shows some orchestration roles that involve direct teacher intervention in children's play and range from the most subtle and indirect to the more active and direct.

The Artist Apprentice

The most subtle of these guided play strategies is what Griffin (1998) calls the Artist Apprentice role. In this role, the teacher helps to remove clutter in the physical space around an ongoing play episode or offers accessories for play, much like a set assistant in a theater.

As Mark, Donelle, and Beth launch their spacecraft, land on a planet, and discover aliens, Ms. Toms, their teacher, helps to tidy the blocks when the spaceship "crashes," and the players move their play to the housekeeping corner. She provides a red scarf for their flag and a cardboard box for their control panel. ✆

♥ In doing this, Ms. Toms helps the children to maintain their thematic focus in play. If the blocks were to become scattered, the space travel might degenerate into block throwing. Alternately, the extended theme might become sidetracked in the search for appropriate accessories to represent the flags and the control panel. In the

Table 5.1   Spontaneous, Guided, and Directed Play

Curriculum Standard	Spontaneous Play	Guided Play	Directed Play
Demonstrates equivalency with blocks	Eric uses four triangular blocks to finish his yellow brick road of squares.	Teacher sets out tangram blocks and patterns; Sara and Ari negotiate use of smaller rectangles to complete a house pattern.	Teacher sits with Matt and Brita and asks them to help her stack the blocks so they are all in squares.
Uses scientific tools and methods to learn about the world	Sandra uses a toy thermometer to take her doll's temperature. "Oh, it's 100. She needs to go to the doctor!"	Teacher sets out ice cubes and containers of warm and cold water and thermometers, asking the children, "What do you think will happen? How can you tell?"	Teacher directs small group to measure temperatures of pans of water placed in the sun with varying numbers of ice cubes and to measure and mark time for melting the ice.
Uses pictures and letters to express thoughts and ideas	Jeff answers the phone in the playhouse. "She's not here. Can I take a message? She will be glad you can come!" and scribbles on a notepad, using M for mom and drawing a smiley face.	Teacher sets up card-making center with templates for Valentine hearts and paper letters to glue or copy.	Teacher directs children to make labels for their block structures, asking them to label parts of their constructions so they can photograph them.

Artist Apprentice role, the teacher does not intervene with accessories or action unless she perceives that her action is helpful to sustaining children's play. Phillips (2002) described another example: Teddy, a 6-year-old, is a child with autism who repeatedly takes books from shelves and stacks them on the floor. The adult intervenes first by clearing space for his purposeful play with books and then uses her words to give voice to his actions.

Another technique used by the Artist Apprentice is to physically protect an ongoing project and help others set up their own projects in adjacent spaces. In one preschool, a plastic hoop was used to designate "in-progress" constructions in the block area, so that new players would know that someone was saving the materials to play with later (Beardsley, 1991).

The Peacemaker

The next intervention role along the direct–indirect continuum is the Peacemaker, who may help children resolve conflicts that appear in their play in several ways. First, the teacher may offer accessories that help to resolve disputes. For example, as

3-year-olds Mary and Jesse argue over a toy typewriter for their office play, the teacher might find another toy typewriter or help the children to imagine how they could use blocks to make another typewriter.

In terms of roles, teachers can help children resolve conflicts by suggesting related alternatives for disputed roles. In Chapter 3 we described a situation in a kindergarten classroom in which several children wanted to play the princess role in an ongoing dramatic play episode. The teacher asked if the princess might have a sister or some cousins who weren't in the movie the children had seen, and the children agreed on new but related roles. These kinds of suggestions model for children the flexible thinking and problem solving that ideally occur in play and help them to generate solutions to role disputes on their own as teachers encourage them to invent their own alternatives.

Teachers also act in the role of the Peacemaker when they help children to invent roles that stretch their thinking beyond the need to possess disputed materials.

> An observer to Mrs. Paley's classroom in Chicago noticed a child standing, arms flung across the front of the unit blocks. No one else was able to use the blocks, as a consequence. When the children complained to Mrs. Paley, who was seated at the story dictation table, she asked, "Ben, how can they get the blocks they need?" Ben replied (after a long pause), "They have to order them!" The other children immediately picked up blocks and "telephoned" their orders to Ben. ⌀

Mrs. Paley remarked later that she could see that Ben "was a character in search of a part." Her one-line query to Ben provided the scaffold for successful negotiation and maintenance of the play episode by inviting the player to stretch himself and invent a part.

The teacher may serve as an interpreter of children's motives to their peers when conflicts occur, or when children disrupt the play of others. Some children slip easily in and out of play and learn to give their fellow players "meta-messages" about their intentions. Bateson (1976) coined the term *meta-communication* to describe the behaviors that people use to signal play. Such behaviors include winks or smiles, laughter, play voices, or exaggerated movements. Verbal markers may be as obvious as "Let's pretend that I'm the babysitter and you're the bad baby" or as subtle as the change in voice pitch to mark the role of the "Papa Bear."

Children whose play is characterized by imitation of content derived from media such as television or whose speech and language are delayed are frequently misunderstood by peers in their attempts to initiate and maintain play (Katch, 2001; Levin, 2003b; Ogakaki et al., 1998; Wolfberg, 1999). These misunderstandings also occur in settings in which children speak different languages or dialects. In group settings children develop their own ways of initiating and sustaining talk with others that are relevant to the local context of their classroom.

Teachers can help children interpret communicative cues and invent explicit strategies for finding out meanings of others when they feel confused. Such techniques may be particularly important in helping children interpret the cues of play fighting or rough-and-tumble play so that the play remains a healthy and safe exercise in physical challenge rather than an escalation into violent confrontation (Ariel, 2002; Blurton-Jones, 1972; Pellegrini 1998, 2002). For example, in an anecdote in Chapter 11, the teacher intervenes directly for a child with speech impairment by asking if he wishes to engage in the rough-and-tumble play fighting that his play partners have initiated, signaling to the children that rough and tumble is permissible only with consent of the parties, and then only if it seems safe.

Guardian of the Gate

How can the sensitive teacher help a newcomer gain entry to ongoing play without disrupting an already-established episode or, alternatively, to judge when it may not be appropriate to interrupt?

Corsaro (1985, 2003) reported that in his observations, 75% of the time preschool children's initial bids to enter ongoing play episodes are rejected. Young children seem to intuitively protect their shared fantasies from interruption by interlopers. After two or three attempts at entry, 50% of children seeking to enter others' play are successful.

How can teachers help children develop effective strategies for entry and the confidence to try again if rejected at first? Intervention strategies on the part of the teacher to monitor the gates of play parallel those for the Peacemaker role.

One way teachers can encourage children is by introducing an accessory. Griffin (1998) tells of a child who rode a trike every day around the periphery of other children's play, watching but never joining. She gave him an old camera, simply saying, "Take this with you on your travels." Other children soon noticed the camera and asked to be "photographed." Gradually, the child became included in playgroups and developed the confidence to play with others through the accessory that was uniquely his.

Sometimes teachers may suggest a new role. One teacher, seeking to help a child she had observed as an onlooker on the edge of play, asked her to help deliver a large package to the ongoing houseboat play. The "delivery people" were then invited to stay for lemonade, and the onlooker child became included in the play, with her teacher there as security. In another classroom, the teacher asked a group of children who were playing camping, "What could Carl be, a Forest Ranger?" In this way, the teacher opens up possibilities for the children to negotiate new roles within their play without interfering with the integrity of the ongoing episode.

Teachers also can interpret the social context of play. Schwartzman (1976) wrote that play offers teachers "sideways glances" at make-believe. First, it reflects the social status of children in the group. Children with high status often play the most powerful roles and also assign roles to their peers. Children with lower status in the group may hold that status due to unskilled attempts to enter the play of others. Play also reflects children's understanding of the peer culture in the classroom. Teachers can explain children's motives to others in terms such as, "I see Sandy really wants to join your group. She is looking for a friend to play with. Would you like to be her friend?"

Orchestrating Play Entry for Children with Special Needs. Teachers may find that some children with special needs have less experience, confidence, or ability when engaging in play activities. Some consistently look to adults to help them enter the play of others. This is often true of children who are unable to communicate their needs clearly. Some children with special needs may have lower status than their nondisabled peers because of the difficulties they have in entering play. In the role of Guardian of the Gate, teachers can provide the additional involvement that might be needed without increasing children's dependence on adults (Neeley, Neeley, Justen, & Tipton-Sumner, 2001). For example, a teacher might make a child's motives known to increase social interaction between disabled and nondisabled students (Allen & Brown, 2002; Bartolini & Lunn, 2002; Hanline & Fox, 1993).

> Emma, a kindergartner with delayed expressive language, loves to play catch and frequently approaches other children holding the ball and saying "Emma, Emma" pointing to her chest. Her teacher has helped other children understand that Emma is asking them to play ball, and prompts Emma to say "to me" as the ball play begins.

Parallel Player

An even more active role for the teacher involves playing parallel to children. In this scenario the teacher plays next to but not with the child, using similar materials, but not interacting. The teacher might first imitate the child's behavior, such as pouring sand into a container, establishing a basis for reciprocity. Next, the teacher might introduce a variation in the play, such as using a funnel and watching to see if the child imitates the variation. In this way, reciprocity builds at a nonverbal level. In dramatic play, the teacher might use a prop in a new way, subtly extending the child's symbolic distancing, for example, by using a pretend gesture or an unstructured prop to make a telephone call within the child's view (Forman & Kuschner, 1977).

Parallel play is a strategy children frequently use for entry into ongoing play, and it works for teachers as well.

> In Jackie's multiage primary-grade class, Ted, Martha, Elisa, and Kim were calling themselves "ocean scientists" as they played on the carpet. They were sorting, ordering, and counting seashells, discussing their criteria for classification, and speculating about which was bigger, a large, flat, thin shell or a smaller, round, dense one. Periodically, one child would say "We're scientists doing our work," and the others would nod in agreement. Jackie sat down on the carpet with the children, first manipulating shells and informally observing and joining their discussion. She then brought out a small plastic balance scale from the shelf and began to place large shells one at a time in one bin of the balance scale and count smaller shells into the other bin, watching until it balanced. The children began observing and commenting on Jackie's actions. Jackie then began to verbally describe her own hypotheses and behavior as she

manipulated the shells and the balance scale. Soon another scale was produced and the children began to play in pairs, returning to their original questions about which shells were bigger, now reframed as which ones weighed more. Jackie gradually withdrew from the play context, continuing to take anecdotal records for later inclusion in their portfolios and to support the class debriefing about choice time that would occur later in the day. ✍

Spectator

The teacher comments from outside the play about the themes and content of play when she orchestrates play from the perspective of spectator. In this way she indirectly coaches play from the sidelines by taking the role of an interested spectator or a peripheral participant. For example, as Maggie and Keisha approach their teacher carrying their suitcases, the teacher might ask about their imagined travel plans, "Have you bought your tickets yet? Do you have enough suitcases?" By referencing a present context and extending it to a future event, the teacher invites the children to elaborate their play to incorporate the teacher's comment. In this way, teachers validate children's dramatic play and may subtly suggest extensions.

As with all intervention strategies, particularly those that involve a more active role for the adult, teachers must be careful to gauge the situation and determine if comments, even from outside the play frame, might disrupt the flow of children's play or introduce elements incongruent with their intentions (Ghafouri & Wien, 2005). Williams (2002) suggests that this form of orchestration may be typical of some parents who, while valuing play, see it as a means of teaching cultural skills by directing play through their comments to children.

Griffin (1998) developed a scheme for analyzing strategies that children use to coordinate shared meaning in their make-believe play from both outside the play frame and as players inside the frame. For example, teachers, as spectators outside the pretend frame, can support children by implicit pretend elaboration, such as in the travel and suitcase example described earlier. In this role, the teacher is an implicit and undefined onlooker to play and may suggest extensions or clarifications that help move play forward.

Participant

In the next role, the participant, the teacher moves from outside the pretend frame into an active role in the play, perhaps as a neighbor knocking on the door to borrow eggs, or as an ambulance driver bringing an injured person to the hospital. Once the teacher is part of the enactment of a shared script, she can indirectly communicate actions, themes, and verbalizations in her role as participant.

After the make-believe theme of an airplane trip had been established in Matt's kindergarten class, he noticed that children were boarding the pretend airplane and just sitting in the seats. He boarded as a passenger, and asked Carlos, the flight attendant, what was on the menu for dinner. Carlos responded with,

"You could have pizza or fried chicken," and then began to enact the rolling of a food cart down the aisle of the pretend plane. ⌀

Another participant strategy that allows adults to enter the play space is the use of a direct or indirect comment to shift or extend the play in a particular way by interjecting high drama into the script. The teacher might report a warning or foretelling of an imaginary event as if it were real. "Quick, we need a nurse! Call 911," prompts Matt, as he enters his kindergartners' superhero play and encourages them to extend the make-believe play beyond the fight, die, and resurrect sequence he has observed in this play all week.

Through both dramatic underscoring and storytelling, teachers can interject verbal comments into the stream of play without disturbing the shared illusion of the pretend frame. In underscoring, the teacher might sing or use a sound effect to model the communication of pretend actions, roles, or objects.

Matt speaks urgently to children playing firefighter, as they have arrived at the burning house with sirens blaring and limited action. "I'll turn on the hose-sh-sh-sh-sh" (making water sounds as he mimes turning on a faucet) to douse a pretend fire. ⌀

Storytelling is a verbal strategy that allows the player (adult or child) to communicate pretend transformations using narrative forms. For example:

First-grade teacher Sally shops at the pretend candy store in her classroom, elaborating the plot to extend children's problem solving as she tells her story. "It's my sister's birthday and she really likes gummy bears, do you have those? We are having a big party for 10 people and we need two bears for everyone. Can you sell me enough? Also, I need a birthday card. Do you have those?" ⌀

As in the spectator intervention, the teacher must be sensitive to cues from children and not enter into play unless it is called for (Bennett et al., 1997). If the teacher does enter the play as a participant, then he or she needs to play a supporting rather than starring role. Many teachers of young children enjoy engaging in play as a participant and may have a tendency to control the flow of play without realizing they have usurped the power of the children. For example, in one preschool classroom, an overenthusiastic volunteer offered to play the injured party in hospital play. She ended up directing the entire play episode, assigning roles to children and suggesting what the doctor and nurse players should say and do.

Matchmaker

In this role the teacher may deliberately set up pairs or groups of children to play with one another. He may, for example, pair a more sophisticated player with a less sophisticated player. Providing there is not too great a difference in their play styles and personalities, both children may benefit from this arrangement. Complementary emotional needs may also serve as a basis for matchmaking.

In one classroom, Sandy, whose parents were divorcing, sought out situations she felt she could control and in which she could feel power. Paul, on the other hand, distressed over the birth of a baby sister, created a baby role for himself whenever possible. These two children were a perfect match in terms of their complementary emotional needs and spent long hours in house play with Sandy as a powerful and nurturing mother to the helpless baby Paul.

Wolfberg (1999) recounts her research in which she paired children with varying severity of autism with typically developing playmates in playgroups. Situations in which the child with more skilled play was able to bring his or her peer into a zone of proximal development in play abound in this interesting and valuable research.

Matchmaking may also be an effective strategy for orchestrating play with English language learners. Children who are more proficient in English may be able to smooth communication among players with less fluency in English.

Story Player

Vivian Paley (1981, 1986, 1990, 1999) introduced the technique of story play for supporting children's play that structures its form, but not its content. In her approach, children dictate stories to a teacher who writes them out to be enacted by the class later in the school day. The text is written down exactly as it is dictated and reread in the child's language. Each author selects who will take the parts to be enacted. The author serves as director as the teacher reads the story aloud. Elaborations of the plot are often enacted as the story unfolds in drama. Comments such as, "I forgot, the little bear does come home to his mom at the end," are sometimes added to the story's text. Props are not usually used to ensure that the children's imagination is exercised, although teachers may want to consider the developmental level of the child in making decisions about props. In Chapter 8, "Language and Literacy," story playing is described in greater detail.

Play Tutor

The teacher as play tutor takes on the most direct role of all by re-creating the emotional security of the caregiver–infant dyad that is the source of human beings learning to play. In this context the child feels safe and is able to take risks involved in using symbols and language to represent the meaning of the concrete. The teacher models and directs children's play in this role, providing reinforcement to their efforts to symbolize and interact.

Researchers who study childhood play have been guided by the work of Smilansky (Smilansky, 1968; Smilansky & Shefatya, 1990) for many years. Smilansky focused on intervention with preschool children whose dramatic play lacked complexity. Direct tutoring may benefit those children whose play consists of repetitive one-liners

Playful interactions with adults are just as essential as those with peers.

imitated from television, or whose attempts to enter the play of others are awkward and intrusive (Bartolini & Lunn, 2002). Smilansky's strategies guide teachers in their attempts to help children elaborate their play through such elements as extended role play, social interaction, verbalization, persistence, and object transformations in a process she calls sociodramatic play training. Smilansky's scheme for assessing play complexity is presented in detail in Chapter 6.

Other researchers have employed a technique they call "thematic fantasy role play" (Saltz & Johnson, 1974), in which the teacher assigns roles and directs the enactment of stories read aloud to the children. This technique assigns more control to the teacher than sociodramatic training, where children form their own story lines with teacher support. It also differs from Paley's story-playing approach in its emphasis on stories authored by adults and roles selected and directed by the teacher.

Another strategy involves both matchmaking and play tutoring. Teachers may ask children to serve as "play coaches" and help other children invent roles, pretend with objects, or join in a play episode. In many classrooms, children are given this role with regard to computer use, writing, or other activities in which the status of "expert" encourages children in particular roles to reflect on their own thinking and communicate it to others. It adds the dimension of expert–novice to the already powerful zone of proximal development created in pretend play. Smilansky (1990) found that the play coaches as well as their players benefit from this process.

Because play tutoring represents a very direct role for the adult, it must be used carefully (Trawick-Smith, 1998, 2010). Children who have difficulty with symbolic play distancing and/or social play negotiations might be better served by less-direct teacher strategies. For example, a multiage setting often encourages more advanced play on the part of younger children and prosocial behavior on the part of older children and may be a more desirable alternative than play tutoring.

CHOOSING A STRATEGY

Considerable skill and thought is required to determine which context, in combination with which child, calls for a given strategy. For example, the child who plays parallel functional play with blocks or sand is a likely candidate for the parallel player strategy. The child who hangs around the edges of playgroups might benefit from an accessory or entry strategy. As a general guideline, wise teachers intervene with the most indirect strategy possible. Many teachers begin by changing the setting for play, perhaps by adding new accessories. If that doesn't work, then the teacher proceeds to increasingly more direct strategies along the continuum.

Challenges in Play for Children with Special Needs

In intervening with all children in their play, there are several factors to consider. We believe it is essential for teachers to keep in touch with the power of the zone of proximal development created through play. All children, regardless of their current developmental capacities, stretch their competencies in play with others. For some children, playful interactions with adults are just as essential as those with peers. Smilansky's play tutoring approach and the overt modeling of pretense may be called for. For most children, however, the teacher in his role as matchmaker and stage manager serves to support play opportunities that are productive and engaging for all. The matchmaking and tutoring roles present promising avenues for orchestrating pretend play with children with special needs (Bartolini & Lunn, 2002; Henderson & Jones, 2002; Kostelnik et al., 2002; Mindes, 2006; Odom, 2002; Phillips, 2002; Preissler, 2006). Wolfberg (1999) described an ongoing playgroup consisting of normally developing peers who are coached by the teacher to interpret, elaborate, and scaffold the play of autistic playmates.

One drawback of play in inclusive environments is that, although young children frequently empathize with their peers who have special needs, most young children are unable to take the perspective of another child and act altruistically on that understanding. For example, in one kindergarten classroom, Pauline, a child with Down syndrome, was consistently manipulated by two of her peers into giving up her play materials in exchange for less-desirable objects.

Another consideration is that children who are typically developing sometimes feel pressured to include peers who have special needs. They may subsequently comply with adult expectations by allowing the child with special needs in the play area and then ignore him or her (Trawick-Smith, 1994, 2010). Conversely, peers may overdo their helpfulness by treating special needs children in a patronizing manner or by doing too much for them. For example, in a preschool classroom, 4-year-olds Alicia and Emily consistently spoke for Theresa, a child with communicative delays. In doing so, they often squelched Theresa's efforts to communicate with others and her developing sense of initiative.

Challenges in Play for Children Who Are English Language Learners

Play with peers provides a safe context for negotiating turns, roles, and problems that arise in play. Linguistic skills are evident in these negotiations and in the enactment of play themes and entry in play. Given the importance of language for social competence and success in play interactions, English language learners present some unique challenges to orchestration (Saracho, 2001).

One challenge is the observation made by many teachers that children prefer to play with peers who speak the same language (Clawson, 2002). Whether the groupings occur as a result of English speakers or from English learners, the results call for sensitivity on the part of the teacher. Matchmaking children who are interested in similar things may be one approach. In this way, children who do not speak the same language begin to form a social history with one another as they share play (Orellana, 1994).

Other challenges call for different orchestration strategies. For example, in observing children, a teacher may notice that the onlooker behavior of a child masks a desire to join the play (Derman-Sparks & Edwards, 2010; Espinosa, 2010; Kirmani, 2007; Ramsey, 2006).

> Selena hovers at the edge of the restaurant area watching as Mark and Cecilie cook a pretend dinner. Ann, their teacher, is a customer in their play restaurant. She comments from the participant role, "I'd like some cake after my dinner. Is it on the menu?" "Oh I don't know if we have any," responds Mark. Ann asks Selena in Spanish if she knows how to make cake. Selena nods, and slowly begins to approach the pretend restaurant. "Selena knows how to make cake," Ann suggests to the two other players, and they hand her a bowl and spoon, as she joins them in the kitchen. Selena begins to mix pretend cake ingredients, and asks Ann in Spanish, "Do you like chocolate?" ✄

Timing Is Everything: Entering and Exiting Children's Play

When teachers enter and exit children's play or shift from one strategy to another, timing is crucial. Manning and Sharp (1977) and Reynolds and Jones (1997) suggest guidelines for entering play. First and foremost, teachers need to observe play long enough to see if any intervention is called for or if the children are best served by the teacher in a less-direct role. As part of this observation phase, the teacher has an opportunity to ascertain the themes, characters, plot, and vocabulary negotiated by the children.

If the teacher chooses to enter the dance of interaction played out by the children, she must do it seamlessly, joining the flow of the play without disrupting its progress or integrity. Respect for children's ongoing shared make-believe is critical. Adult entry is more suitable at transition points during which children are "stepping out" of the play frame to negotiate rules about the play or ongoing themes or roles, rather than at the times when children are deeply engaged in pretend play (Bennett et al., 1997).

Leaving the play and returning control completely to the child players is just as important as a sensitive and flowing entry. Because the teacher's purpose is always to support children in their efforts to sustain and elaborate play on their own, the timing of exits is critical. Phasing out of play is one exit strategy that gradually returns the control of the play to children. As a participant within the play frame, a teacher might use storytelling to explain her departure or take a less active role. For example:

> Karen entered the train play of a group of five preschool children with the intention of facilitating Heidi's entrance into the play. Karen sees that Heidi is now engaged with others eating "lunch" in the dining car. Karen announces, "Oh good. The next stop is mine, so I'll see you next Friday on the train." She says to the engineer, "I'll be getting off at the next station." $\varnothing$

Sometimes teachers may unobtrusively leave the area when children are very involved in play, as Jackie did when the children appropriated the seashell balancing activity. At other times, the teacher may speak from a different stance: "I promised some children in the block area I'd come visit their airport. I'll come back to watch you when I finish." This effectively places the teacher on the outskirts of play as a spectator and reminds the children of her real-life responsibilities as the teacher (Trawick-Smith, 1994, 2001, 2010).

PLAY AND THE CULTURE OF SCHOOL

Play always occurs within a social context and in relation to the various cultures that coexist within the classroom and the school. The "school culture" (Heath, 1983) represents the norms of school behavior commonly accepted in our society and shaped through teacher behavior. The peer culture represents an alternative and, to some degree, a complement to the school culture in the classroom.

Three types of play commonly occur in school settings: instrumental play, recreational play, and illicit play. Each is defined by the way in which the teacher responds to children's play and the context in which it occurs.

Instrumental play is sanctioned and often employed by the teacher to meet goals consistent with school curriculum. Examples include blocks, teacher-initiated games with rules that teach concepts or vocabulary, and dramatic play. In dramatic role play, teachers find that the negotiation of the features or implicit "rules" of adult roles provides fertile ground for children to test their mental concepts about gender and adult occupations with other children whose backgrounds may have created a different set

Children learn through guided play experiences.

of rules and expectations. In one preschool classroom, Nat and Katherine argue over who will fix the dinner, the mom or the dad. In Nat's home, his father is the primary caregiver and usually prepares the evening meal. In Katherine's home, her father commutes to work in a large city and her mother generally prepares the meals.

Recreational play is sanctioned by the teacher as a means to let off steam. It often occurs outside the teacher's view. Playground play at recess and free play outdoors in some preschool and kindergarten settings are examples of this type of play.

Illicit play is not sanctioned by the teacher and, in fact, may be expressly forbidden. Children engage in illicit play either behind the teacher's back or as a direct challenge to the teacher's authority. Such play is thought to provide children with a sense of mastery and autonomy within the school setting that limits the range of acceptable behavior. Examples commonly seen in early childhood settings include transforming Tinker Toys into guns when such play is prohibited, "group glee" activities, such as coughing or snapping Velcro shoes, and passing secret notes or pictures (Corsaro, 2003).

One aspect of illicit play that proves to be increasingly difficult for teachers are the consequences of outlawing weapon and violent play in the classroom (Katch, 2001, 2003; Levin & Carlsson-Paige, 2006). Strategies for coping with the behind-the-scenes strategies that children use to circumvent teacher-made prohibitions about the content of play are addressed later in this chapter.

Other kinds of illicit play are described by Scarlett, Naudeau, Salonius-Pasternak, and Ponte (2005) as "risky play" in which children endanger themselves and others, for example by throwing sand or rocks. In this "mean-spirited play," characterized by teasing and bullying, and "mischievous play," children deliberately flaunt school rules, such as rolling around on the carpet at circle time. Scarlett et al. (2005) also describe "ambiguous play," in which children seem to be using play as a means of mastering strong emotions, such as putting the baby doll in the oven (Ardley & Ericson, 2002) or tearing apart the housekeeping area as "naughty" kittens.

Although instrumental play in educational settings or, as Sutton-Smith (1995, 1997) calls it, "play in the rhetoric of progress," is sanctioned by educators, we wish to remind ourselves and other teachers of the importance of play that is not sanctioned by adults. This mischievous or silly play represents another arena in which we find the social skills and concepts of young children developing.

Just as play serves an "equilibrating" or balancing force in our lives, by its paradoxical nature, play also allows us to invert reality, to throw off balance what we know to be normal or sensible. This represents the power of both nonsense and festive play (Fromberg, 2002; Sutton-Smith, 1995). One of the outcomes of this kind of play that is mischievous, rebellious, and nonsensical is the powerful social bonding that occurs among players as they jointly oppose traditional social norms and a sensible view of the world in a playful manner.

> David and Brad are playing with a squirrel doll in the playhouse. David squeaks the squirrel and taps it on Brad's shoe. Brad shouts "Stop, squirrel!" "I'm not a squirrel. I'm a squirmmy!" responds David in a high-pitched voice, hopping the squirrel doll up and down. He grabs a baby doll out of Brad's hand and makes a pouring motion over his head with it. "Sh-h-h." Brad questions, "Hot coffee?" "No, hot caw-caw," David responds, laughing loudly. "Hot caw-caw!" He and Brad fall together onto the floor, laughing hysterically. ✆

In their evolving peer culture, children confront the differing perspectives of one another and also that of the school culture represented by the teacher. As Corsaro (1985, 2003) advises, teachers must walk a fine line between respecting children's needs to ally themselves against the constraints of adult authority (to look the other way on occasion) and their own need to provide firm and consistent limits about what is acceptable in the school setting. "Adult ideas, materials, rules, and restrictions can be seen as frames or boundaries within which features of peer culture emerge and are played out" (Corsaro, 1985, p. 289). A good example of this dilemma is the ongoing debate in early childhood education centered on the use of toy and imaginary weapons and fantasies involving violence in preschool and primary-grade settings.

RESPONDING TO VIOLENT PLAY

Although pretend weapons and war play issues have plagued the curriculum and classroom culture decisions of teachers for decades, the increased numbers of children in schools whose lives are filled with violence and the increased access for all children to violent media imagery as seen on television, computer games, and video games have sharpened the debate. Educators and families can collaborate in early childhood programs to reduce aggression and violence. To begin this process, we as teachers have to examine our own beliefs and experiences. Many teachers of young children cope with frustration about violent play by outlawing toy weapons and violent themes, hence driving the play "underground" into the peer culture. Is it more effective to illuminate children's fears by openly discussing the violent content of play or by creating more empathetic and rich contexts for play than to ignore children's fears (Ardley & Ericson, 2002; Katch, 2001; Levin, 2003a; Levin & Carlsson-Paige, 2006)?

When pretend play is largely an attempt to order what is confusing, chaotic, or frightening to children, then is it more important to consider the sources before invoking classroom rules about weapon play or violence? For example, in the days and weeks following the September 11, 2001, attack in New York, many teachers believed that the block play, dramatic play, dictated stories, and story play enacting the violence were appropriate avenues for healing and making sense of fear. Similarly, Dorothy and Grace's children needed to play out their fears regarding the lost baby pigs to move to a more empathetic stance. Does replay of violent imagery desensitize children or offer them an avenue of control?

Ascertaining Children's Purposes in Play

When considering the motives for children's aggressive play, teachers need to identify the sources of violent imagery. When does children's play reflect media violence that is pretend, and when does play reflect real-life violence? Many teachers report impatience, anger, and frustration with pretend media-based violent play. "How can their parents allow 5-year-olds to watch those teenage horror videos?" one teacher laments. On the other hand, teachers express more empathy for children whose play includes violent images and themes that arise from violence in their home lives and experiences of their families.

A related question that calls on teachers to ascertain children's purposes is the relationship of development to violent play. Young children are just learning to reliably negotiate the lines between reality and fantasy. Crossing those boundaries frequently in pretend play helps children to clarify the meaning of violence in our contemporary culture. But how much of this play is too much? What are the fine lines between "playing through" confusing or frightening images or experiences and becoming obsessed with them?

Some war play or aggressive "good guy/bad guy" themes such as that in superhero play is often typical for many young children in our culture, though not in other cultures. The loud noises, fast pace, and especially the thrill of the chase that have been elements of diverse forms of sociodramatic play for decades often appeal to children. The themes of good versus evil, life and death, lost and found, and danger and rescue that occur in war play and other aggressive play give children opportunities to deal with these archetypal concerns.

In considering that there are frequently multiple motives for children's aggressive play, teachers need to examine several issues. To what degree does the play reflect the desire to be powerful in the world? To what extent are the children playing out a script from violent media? To what degree does it reflect children trying to make sense of the real violence they have seen on the evening news or even in their own neighborhoods? Schwartzman (1976) pointed out that an important aspect of play is its "inward perspective" or the process by which children repeat experiences that are puzzling, confusing, or disturbing to them.

One source of violent play that reflects real violence is the personal stories of children related to community violence. For example:

> Tracy's home had been fire-bombed and her older brother injured. For several weeks, her kindergarten peers, in their roles as paramedics and firefighters, carried the "injured" Tracy to hospitals they constructed in the block corner, under tables, and in the sandbox.

A second source of such play is the violence of war. The meaning of war play is different for children whose families have experienced war directly. Millions of children are from refugee families who have fled the direct effects of war, recently or in the past generations. There is considerable literature on the effects of war on children and families (Levin & Van Hoorn, 2009).

> Aashna's family are recent refugees who moved to a small American town directly from a refugee camp where his sister died. Deborah, the student teacher in the class, noticed that Aashna startles frequently in response to sudden noises. During the past week, several children in the class have been initiating a war game. Each time, Aashna runs around the periphery of the group, then goes closer to the children, making rapid shooting sounds. Despite his limited English, he knows the script. Today, after a few minutes, Aashna is clearly agitated, repeating, "Garan, Garan" as he asks for his fourth-grade brother.

Millions of children in the United States have direct experience with war due to the deployment of parents and other relatives to Afghanistan and Iraq. As of 2010, more than 800,000 children have had a mother or father deployed in combat. Researchers report that when their parents are deployed, preschoolers act out more and are more aggressive (e.g., Chartrand, Frank, White, & Shope, 2008). Some of their teachers are unaware that the child has a parent deployed in the National Guard or Reserves and, therefore, may not understand changes in behaviors.

Looking at Pretense versus Reality in Violent Play.   Teachers are concerned about violent pretend play suggested by media and toys. The explicit violent details of television, movies, and computer games, as well as the many toy weapons on the market today, seem to spur children on to greater heights of aggression, as we shall discuss further in Chapter 13, "Play, Toys, and Technology." In "firing" a toy gun, for example, children may lose sight of the story line of the pretend play and end up hurting one another through their aggression (Carlsson-Paige & Levin, 1990; Katch,

2001; Levin, 2003a; Levin & Carlsson-Paige, 2006). Children who are unduly repetitive in their imitation of characters' dialogue and scripts gleaned from television, movies, and videos need intervention from teachers to expand on their limited repertoires to more complex representations of characters, settings, and plots. Teachers struggle with alternatives to outright censorship to help children make sense of frightening and confusing images seen in the media, such as themes of bullying and violence that occur in the following example of Leo and Jeremy playing out an episode from the television series *Survivor*.

> Seven-year-old Jeremy and 6-year-old Leo are playing in the outdoor lawn area of their elementary school playground. "I'll make you eat these worms!" snarls Jeremy, attempting to stuff a handful of leaves and wood shavings into Leo's mouth. When Leo protests, Jeremy counters, "But that's how your team can win! You want us to win, don't you?" ⌀

What can teachers do to mitigate the themes of violence in their classrooms? In what situations might children be playing out confusing and disturbing images from their own lives, rather than imitating scripts from television, movies, video, or even video games? These and other questions regarding violence and play have surfaced in our work with teachers, children, and families.

Diffusing Violence in Play

When does the discharge of frightening feelings become obsessive? How can teachers and families work together to diffuse violence in children's play?

Observe Play Carefully.   Many teachers report that they can follow the plot of the latest violent movies or the morning's TV cartoon shows by observing children's play. However, teachers can help children to use the characters, play themes, and props derived from popular media in constructive ways.

By keeping informed about popular cartoons, videos, films, and television series, as well as toys that may be popular in the peer culture of the classroom, teachers are better able to understand the play they observe. Through close scrutiny of children's play, teachers may determine if some children are "stuck" in repetitive imitations of what they have viewed. Teachers may then orchestrate play to enable children to expand character roles, elaborate story lines, and transform themes (Carlsson-Paige & Levin, 1998; Levin & Carlsson-Paige, 2006).

Look Beneath the Surface of Play.   When teachers are sensitive to the underlying themes of play, they may suggest nonviolent alternatives that appeal to children. Good guy/bad guy play encompasses themes such as danger and rescue that are central to children's socioemotional development (Corsaro, 2003; Katch, 2001; Levin, 2006; Paley, 1990; Perry, 2001). Once the theme is identified, teachers may introduce literature with new characters and plots that elaborate these themes in new ways.

Children engage in complex fantasy play that may involve danger and rescue themes.

In a preschool directed by one of the authors, teachers and parents embarked on an experiment to diminish the frequency of television-limited play that imitated cartoon violence. Noting that themes of good and evil, life and death, and lost and found dominated much of this play, the teachers and parents read various versions of *Peter Pan* and helped the children create and act out their interpretations of the characters and events in their play. Later in the year, *The Wizard of Oz* and *Peter and the Wolf* and other literary works were explored in similar ways. Children still used pretend weapons and fought and chased adversaries, but their repertoire of characters and actions for these themes was expanded. For example, after the *Peter Pan* theme was explored, one child noted that "turning bad guys into toads or rocks was better because if you shot them, they just came alive again." ⊘

Set Limits.   Teachers may also keep children "safe" by setting limits. For some children, the appeal of war play or media-derived play is especially irresistible when it is violent in nature. Because the script for war play or media play is usually simple and well known, children with limited social skills or language abilities are often drawn into the vortex. As the cast of the play grows, the level of aggression can become out of the children's control. By setting limits and carefully monitoring this play, teachers can help ensure that at-risk children are protected. It is also important for teachers to understand the circumstances in children's personal lives that might be leading to an overabundance of this type of play.

Several teachers we know set these limits by banning real-looking weapons from their schools, while acknowledging children's need to do battle with imaginary ones. In this way they avoid the phenomenon of children imitating action from television with single-use weapon toys. Other teachers make a point of talking to children about alternatives for their play plots when aggressive play careens out of control, perhaps suggesting strategies for tricking bad guys instead of shooting them. The following is one teacher's pragmatic approach to managing the problem of guns in her play yard.

Out of concern for the lack of peacefulness in the play yard, the teacher asked the children at circle time to help her make a set of rules about gun play, as she was worried because some children often wound up getting hurt. The teacher said she was also getting tired of trying to stop the gun play and settle arguments all the time. She asked the children to vote on how many liked to have pretend shooting in the play yard. Most children, except for a small coterie of boys, voted against gun play. The teacher wondered if it would be fair to those who wanted to engage in pretend gun play to be prohibited from it. She thought perhaps they could work out some rules that would make others feel safe about people who wanted to pretend to use guns. She suggested that there be a place in the yard where people who wanted to pretend with guns could go and play in that way. A second rule would be that only people who consented to play this way could go there. A third rule was gun players could not point their guns at people who didn't want to play. They had to ask permission from the targeted person.

The group then went on to discuss the best place for the gun-toting players. The large climber did not seem to be the fair choice because too many non–gun players wanted to use the climber for other games. The sand pit likewise. And the sand kitchen was obviously not a good place. Finally it was decided to move the blocks from under the semishelter to another location and designate this space with traffic cones as the gun players' area. The area had a small carpet that also helped define its area.

By this strategy the teacher was not prohibiting gun play directly but limiting its range to a space where it could be monitored effectively. When gun players left the pretend gun play area and started shooting at someone who had not elected to play in this way, the teacher could ask the targeted child if they had chosen to be part of the gun play game. If the targeted child said no—and usually they did—the logic of pointing out the lack of agreement was obvious to all. If they said yes, they would be directed to the gun play area. In this way the teacher had the support of the group in limiting gun play. After pursuing this approach for a week or so, the gun players became more and more isolated, and their numbers diminished greatly. Gun play began to be less and less interesting as the majority of the children now had the space to peacefully pursue other more elaborate themes without interruption from gun players. ✍

A strategy such as this requires some courage on the part of the teacher, and watchful monitoring without giving gun players too much attention requires sensitivity. For those children who persisted in gun play, the teacher might work one on one with them in creating drawings of their guns for a display of kinds of weaponry. This could lead to doing research on ancient weaponry, or the invention of gunpowder and so on. While drawing with the gun players, she could learn more about the meaning that this play had for the child.

Addressing Exclusion—Supporting Inclusion

One compelling question that intersects with some of the thinking regarding violence in schools is the relationship of violence to exclusion, both for the child who is excluded and for those who are sought as play partners. Katch (2001) addresses these issues with her powerful insights to the hearts and minds of children whose violent imagery in play both attracts and repels others. Both the rejected children who retaliate with violence and the popular children who strike out in frustration at being continually solicited to play have feelings with similar roots.

Paley (1992) writes eloquently of the problem with the tradition of early childhood educators to accept children's often painful rejection of one another in play as a natural part of growing up. In implementing a "You can't say you can't play" rule in her own classroom, she brings the issues of inclusion and exclusion and their accompanying social and emotional consequences to the forefront of the debate.

Building a Peaceful Classroom

In the preceding sections we focused on the multiple ways that teachers can respond to children's violent play, both directly and indirectly. We conclude this chapter by going beyond strategies for violence prevention to integrated strategies for peace promotion. Peace promotion is central to our ideas of a play-centered curriculum.

> In Dorothy and Grace's preschool classroom, the children began to consider remedies to the sadness of Sophie the mother pig on losing her children. They decided to paint a mural and to learn "Old MacDonald Had a Farm" on the bells. After weeks of mural construction and practice, the children went back to the farm to present Sophie with the mural and play their bell concert for her.

In the classroom, just as at the international level, peace is more than the absence of violence. Violence is not only direct and clearly visible, but also can be insidious at a structural level. At the structural level, violence refers to inequalities in schools, communities, and societies that disadvantage some and privilege others, such as racism, sexism, religion, nationality, and inequalities based on economic class (Christie, Wagner, & Winter, 2001).

Peace educators and psychologists make the useful distinction between a negative peace and a positive peace. Teachers have seen many K–12 curricula that are promoted as violence-prevention programs—focusing on negative peace (i.e., stopping violence). Conflicts exist, but they are resolved or managed nonviolently.

A positive peace is marked not only by the absence of violence, but also as equity and opportunities to enhance growth for all. Peace education is truly an "umbrella concept" (Gustafson, 2000). This has long been the view of early childhood. Reviews of early education for peace and nonviolence theory, research, and practice show that traditional early childhood education has always been multifaceted in attempts to foster peaceful classrooms (Van Hoorn & McHargue, 1999).

In *Teaching Young Children in Violent Times—Building a Peaceable Classroom,* Levin (2003b) provides an example of a multifaceted play-based approach. She discusses and illustrates how teachers can build community, promote cooperation and peaceful conflict resolution, help children learn about and appreciate diversity, and help children deal with media-related violence, as well as real violence in the news. Today, early childhood educators are finding a growing number of books and curriculum materials that describe play-centered approaches to promoting peaceful classrooms (Adams & Wittmer, 2001; Derman-Sparks & Edwards, 2010; Derman-Sparks & Ramsey, 2005; Jones & Cooper, 2006; Kreidler & Whittal, 1999).

SUMMARY AND CONCLUSION

We think of *Play at the Center of the Curriculum* as "play at the center of a curriculum for peace and nonviolence," for these are the values that are embedded in each chapter. Many of the classroom examples of play described in this book show children cooperating, considering the feelings of others, developing friendships, and playing with peers who speak different languages and come from diverse family configurations and ethnic backgrounds. These are all aspects of building a culture of peace.

The considerations for setting the stage discussed in Chapter 4 lead to more peaceful classrooms. There are subtle strategies as well as more visible ones. For example, teachers consciously set the stage so that children have sufficient space as well as materials that foster cooperation. Teachers plan a time schedule that balances activities so that children do not become overly tired and consider children's needs for private play. Environments welcome all children and their families and help all to learn about living in a diverse society.

Strategies discussed in this chapter for intervening in children's play promote children's development of dispositions and behaviors inherent in a peaceful classroom: empathy, prosocial behavior, and cooperation. How can newcomers to the United States find a place in the social group? What about children with physical limitations? When play is at the center of the curriculum, children are more autonomous and have multiple opportunities to develop social problem-solving abilities and to take the perspective of others.

Early childhood programs that promote peace are characterized by a pervasive culture marked by inclusiveness, empowerment of all, nonviolent conflict resolution, cooperation, and empathy. We firmly believe that the play-centered curriculum leads to a peaceful classroom and nurtures peaceful children.

Play as a Tool for Assessment

In Kathy's kindergarten classroom, four children have set up a "bank." They have stacked two rows of large hollow wooden blocks to form a counter and built chairs for themselves out of smaller blocks. Additional small blocks on the countertop form windows and have the "teller's" names taped to them. Pat, an adult visitor to the classroom, walks up to the teller's window. Shawna, one of the tellers, asks Pat if she brought her bank book. When Pat responds "No, I don't have one," Shawna directs Pat to the basket of small blank paper books that Kathy makes available in the classroom. "Write your name on it," Shawna tells Pat, and Pat prints her name on the front. "P-a-t," Shawna says as she touches each letter, and then remarks that her grandmother's name is Pat too. "Does she spell it like this?" Pat asks. "I don't know," replies Shawna, "I'll ask her."

Returning to her place behind the bank counter, Shawna takes the bank book and opens it to the first page. She carefully writes "CRTO," and then asks Pat how much money she wants. Pat says, "Fifty dollars." "I can't count that much, you know," says Shawna, "How about 10?" Pat agrees, and Shawna takes out a piece of 8 × 11 white paper, folds it in half and makes a series of horizontal cuts. She then cuts the paper down the middle and counts out 10 pieces of paper. She writes a "1" on each "bill" and counts them out carefully on the counter in front of Pat. "Here you go," Shawna says as she uses a rubber date stamp and a stamp pad available for children's play to stamp the bank book. "Just come back when you run outta dollars." ✇

ASSESSING DEVELOPMENT THROUGH PLAY AT THE BANK

Later that day Kathy, the teacher, discusses the dramatic and constructive play at the bank with Pat, who teaches kindergarten in a neighboring school. She talks about the ways in which Shawna's play yields information about her developing concepts and skills in literacy, mathematics, and social studies, as well as her social and emotional development.

Kathy has taken digital photographs of the bank in its various stages of construction over 2 days of free play periods. Both Pat and Kathy are impressed with the complexity of the block representation of the bank environment. Kathy's anecdotal records indicate that the children who built the structure discussed and negotiated their experiences of how banks look. They used spatial reasoning, including part–whole relationships, to select blocks for the counter, the chairs, small blocks for the name plaques, and long rectangular blocks for the teller's windows. Her notes indicate that Shawna was one of the children who persisted with the project over several days' time, while two other children lost interest after the first day. Shawna and her "new" best friend Emily continued the project and directed the creation of the tellers' roles, which they were eager to play. The tellers have each written their names and fastened them to the "name plaques," using a social form of literacy they have observed in banks and, at the same time, practicing their own renditions of their names.

Kathy and Pat discuss the conversation about Pat's name, and how Shawna spontaneously identified each letter. "Shawna is still working on the idea that some names are spelled the same way every time—probably because not all the adults who work in this classroom know how to spell her version of 'Shawna,'" Kathy informs Pat.

Another example of how Shawna is working on the consistency of letters to spell words is shown in her careful writing of "CRTO" in the bank book. Apparently there was quite a bit of negotiation when the bank "opened" before the children agreed on "the thing you hafta write in the book." Emily's mother works in a bank and had apparently used the term "credit to" in talking about accounts. Emily was quite emphatic that this was the proper term and used her invented spelling concepts to create the notation "CRTO." The date stamp is another form of social literacy that children have observed in the real world.

> "Shawna's awareness of the limitations of her counting amazed me," said Pat. "I thought of offering to help her count to 50 and then realized she had already come up with her own, better alternative. I also wondered how she learned to cut paper that way." ✍

Kathy explained that weeks earlier they had experimented with paper folding and cutting to make shapes for valentines. Shawna was apparently replaying this skill and applying it in a new situation. Kathy and Pat agreed that Shawna's writing of a "1" on each bill and then counting them out carefully for the customer not only showed Shawna's counting skills, but also informally contributes to the concept of place value she will construct in the future.

Kathy is interested in Shawna's progress as an individual and as part of her kindergarten group. Kathy uses information from her assessments of children to plan curricula for her classroom and to monitor the learning that has taken place. State standards in the curriculum areas of language and literacy, mathematics, science, social studies, physical education, and visual and performing arts provide a framework for Kathy's assessment of learning and development in her kindergarten classroom. Gullo (2006) points out that "kindergarten offers teachers a unique opportunity to develop and engage in a regular, ongoing routine of informal assessment that looks at children's learning and development in multiple developmental ways in multiple contexts" (p. 142). In her program, we see Kathy systematically using "multiple ways in multiple contexts." Her portfolios of the children include written observations, photos, samples of student work, developmental charts, and checklists that she organizes and updates regularly.

Play is a natural "piece" of the assessment "pie" because it offers perspectives on children's progress in all areas of development as they are spontaneously integrated into daily experience. Ongoing observation of spontaneous play such as the "bank" is an ideal complement to assessments made during guided play with specific goals and to more direct measures of children's achievement in subject-centered activities.

In play, many facets of children's development are revealed. These examples from Kathy's classroom, for example, illustrate age-appropriate development for 5- and

6-year-olds in the areas of emergent literacy and mathematical concepts. Educators increasingly call for a refocusing of our goals for young children's programs based on what we know from child development theory and research. Many standardized tests target attention to surface skills such as memorizing the alphabet or numbers, and away from deeper concepts such as classification or the nature of narrative. We need to use assessment practices that recognize the value of easily observable skills, as well as the more subtle concepts children construct during their early years of education. Play assessment allows us to observe both.

EXAMINING THE PURPOSES OF ASSESSMENT

Assessment of children's progress is a complicated and multifaceted issue in early childhood education. The primary goal of assessment in a play-centered curriculum is to inform educators' professional judgment about curriculum to support the development of all children and benefit their lives. Although most early childhood educators, researchers, and professional organizations agree, other purposes of assessment frequently cloud these goals. Adding to and sometimes supplanting the primary purpose of assessment to determine children's strengths and approaches to learning are recent initiatives at local, state, and national levels in the United States and many countries to assess the progress of young children based on expectations for learning from preschool through the primary grades (Meier, 2000; Seefeldt, 2005; Wien, 2004; Wortham, 2005).

About a decade ago, early childhood educators across the country began discussing the implications of the Federal No Child Left Behind Act of 2001. The National Early Childhood Assessment Panel, a policy group comprised of respected early childhood educators, identified four major purposes of assessment for young children (Shepard, Kagan, & Wurtz, 1998a):

- Inform the teaching–learning process for children and their teachers.
- Identify children in need of special education services.
- Inform program evaluation and staff development.
- Focus on accountability for students, teachers, and schools.

The first three purposes are widely recognized as critical to quality programs for all young children (e.g., Copple & Bredekamp, 2009). These purposes provide a rationale and natural context for play-centered assessment. All children benefit when programs address children's needs, abilities, and interests. The first two purposes focus on improving the teaching–learning process in the play-centered curriculum. The third purpose, serving program evaluation and staff development needs, also links to play through evaluation of the learning environment for play and the observed and self-identified needs of teachers to improve their skills at orchestrating play. Ongoing, purposeful teacher–family communications regarding the processes and outcomes of play-centered curriculum also relate to this purpose.

However, the fourth purpose, "high-stakes" accountability, is not a good fit for play-centered curriculum and assessment, nor is it a fit for children aged 3 to 8. The NAEYC/NAECS/SDE position statement on Early Learning Standards (2003) states, "Assessment and accountability systems should be used to improve practices and services, and should not be used to rank, sort, or penalize young children" (p. 7). The National Early Childhood Assessment Panel recommends that the standardized tests that characterize such high-stakes assessment be postponed until the end of third grade and preferably until fourth grade (Shepard et al., 1998a). As we discussed in Chapter 1, ethical concerns arise when the results of group measures for accountability are used to make decisions regarding individual children, teachers, or schools. Early childhood educators, family members, and professional organizations raise serious questions. Merrill, a second-grade teacher, expressed it this way:

> 💔 In my school, most of us are concerned that results from the mandated tests don't accurately reflect most of our students' capabilities. I know people are aware of how this problem impacts some of my students, including students identified with special needs and students who are English language learners. But what about Madison and Amparo who seem to have special needs but don't quite meet the criteria to get services? And probably another quarter of my class have stressful personal situations that I'm sure affect how they do on these tests. What about the student in my class whose mother has been unemployed for months? Or the one whose parents are separating? Or the girl who just transferred into my class because she was just placed with a new foster family? The whole school is gearing up for tests next month. I ask myself, "How can I add more stress to these kids' lives?"

Features of Play-Centered Assessment

In contrast to standardized tests are classroom-based, or "performance-based," assessments, carried out under typical conditions, and centered on children's play. As examples from Kathy's kindergarten class show, this kind of assessment involves complex and ongoing measures that focus on children's individual styles and pace of learning. In addition, play-centered assessment serves as a means of learning and reflection for the students as well as the teachers and families. If children are to develop the ability to reflect on their own developing concepts and take responsibility for their own learning, their participation in their own assessment process is critical.

Play is the window to view both age-appropriate development and individual development. In play, teachers may discern whether children's understandings of concepts such as correspondence or classification fall within a range expected of a given age group. For example, they may determine which children in their group exhibit complex sociodramatic play and which may need support from particular orchestration strategies to enhance their development of symbolic thought.

Play also illuminates the development of individual children. It allows teachers to notice and appreciate the interests and values a child brings from home and the

Play offers perspectives on children's progress in all areas of development.

special kind of intelligence he or she may use to express thoughts and feelings. Play allows us to see the cognitive as well as the emotional aspects of children's development and the ways in which they are interconnected.

Play-centered assessment also naturally includes social–moral development in addition to the more traditional questions of cognition and attitudes toward learning. In a society that is increasingly diverse in its values and perspectives, the development of children's abilities to negotiate, to understand the perspectives of others, and to communicate effectively becomes essential. Play-centered assessment helps teachers shift their thinking to see social–moral development as a priority on a par with cognition and motivation. It offers a window to document progress and plan curriculum in these areas (DeVries & Zan, 1996; Kamii, 1990).

Play and Assessments of Children from Diverse Cultures and Backgrounds

In numerous writings about assessment, Gullo emphasizes, "To obtain valid and reliable results, assessments must be free from linguistic or cultural biases. Assessment instruments and procedures must be chosen with care" (Gullo, 2006, p. 144). We advocate that play-based assessments provide opportunities for teachers to meet these criteria, in keeping with NAEYC's Recommendations on Screening and Assessment of Young English-Language Learners (2005).

NAEYC emphasizes that the central purpose of assessment is to foster children's development and learning (i.e., assessments are implemented to benefit the child). For assessments to truly reflect what children can do, to be valid and reliable, anyone carrying out an assessment needs to know the child and be bilingual and bicultural. These recommendations also underscore that educators and families work closely together whenever assessments are conducted, are interpreted, and results are implemented.

Pamela and Ben are kindergarten teachers in a rural school district that serves many English language learners. The following interviews show how their play is an opportunity for formative assessment that leads to insightful curriculum decisions.

"We do more small-group directed play early in the day," explains Ben. "We focus on specific skills such as phonemic awareness using rhymes and songs, and letter and numeral formation using mazes and patterns, but we have 60 minutes of play time as well. Then the children are free to make choices about their learning, and we have many opportunities for block building, cooking, painting, clay, puppetry, and dramatic play that have always been the 'bread and butter' of good kindergarten programs. We also offer projects such as our Bubble Unit that integrate social studies, science, math, literacy, and the arts."

Pam continues, "The combination of free-flowing play and small-group teaching and assessment gives us both very focused and spontaneous information about each child. It's a critical time of the day for our students who are English language learners to develop both receptive and expressive language. I also think kids will take more risks when they are creating and solving their own problems in play. For example, Gary loved our bubbles project. His enthusiasm inspired him to measure his bubbles every day for a week and to record their widths. A month ago he out and out refused to try to write any numerals—context is everything!" ✆

Play and Assessments of Children with Special Needs ♥

Another purpose of assessment in programs for young children is identification and intervention for young children with disabilities. Transdisciplinary, play-centered assessments are being incorporated in some early childhood special education programs. Play-centered assessments provide valuable information regarding all children's development and practical information on functional abilities that teachers find essential to make appropriate accommodations.

Eva is a kindergartner with an orthopedic disability. She has just returned to school after an operation to increase her stability. She will be using use a wheelchair for the next few months. Several days prior to her return, Eva's teacher, Melinda, met with Eva, her mother and aunt, the school's special education specialist, as well as Eva's physical therapist (PT) and occupational therapist (OT), to make sure that accommodations were in place for a smooth transition back to the classroom.

Eva was excited for her PT and OT to meet her teacher and see her classroom. As she wheeled around the room, her mother emphasized to Melinda that Eva had become quite skilled: "She's pretty independent and very social. It's important that we encourage her and stand back as much as possible. That's really important to us." As Eva navigated easily between the tables, the occupational therapist pointed out accommodations that needed to be made. Several accommodations were one-time fixes such as adjusting the height of several tables. Others involved ongoing checks, like making sure that pathways remained uncluttered. When Melinda discussed the varied activities, it became clear to everyone that although the tables were positioned to accommodate the wheelchair, there were not enough table blocks and not enough space around the easels.

Eva's aunt asked about time outdoors. Eva echoed her question. She missed playing outside with her friends. When they all went outside, Eva pointed with delight at the ramps. How welcoming! They'd already been thinking about her.

The special education specialist assured them that she would be there for Eva's first morning back. Next week, after Eva's first few days and ongoing observations, they would meet to identify goals and formulate a detailed plan.

COMMUNICATING WITH FAMILIES ABOUT PLAY AND ASSESSMENT

As noted in the preceding example, play is a valuable tool teachers can use in communicating with families about their children's progress and illustrates for families the individual flavor of their child's expression. Play anecdotes also offer an opportunity for the teacher to explain what is being learned in the play-based curriculum as examples of the child's progress are cited. Brandon, the child in the opening anecdote in Chapter 1, spends part of his 26th day in kindergarten building a maze for Fluffy, the pet rat, and then represents his play with a map. He gets carried away with firefighting fantasies, and some of the aggressive behavior his preschool teacher saw comes out in his play with others. Brandon's parents will appreciate hearing of his progress in map making and of the complexity of his maze. They will enjoy hearing about his nurturing concern for Fluffy. They may be able to help the teacher understand his aggressive outbursts of behavior at school by comparing his behavior at home and at school.

ASSESSING AGE-APPROPRIATE DEVELOPMENT

These vignettes and those from Kathy's classroom illustrate practices that the 2009 National Association for the Education of Young Children Position Statement recommends as "sound assessment that is developmentally appropriate for children from birth through the primary grades" (Copple & Bredekamp, 2009, p. 22). For example,

- "Assessments of young children's progress and achievements is ongoing, strategic, and purposeful. . . .
- Assessment focuses on children's progress toward goals that are developmentally and educationally significant. . . .

- There is a system in place to collect, make sense of, and use the assessment information to guide what goes on in the classroom. . . .
- The methods of assessment are appropriate to the developmental status and experiences of young children, and they recognize individual variation in learners and allow children to demonstrate their competence in different ways. . . ." (p. 22)

Kathy uses assessments that are "authentic" because both content and methods of collecting data on children's progress align with widely held expectations about the development of kindergarten children. Authentic assessments include the teacher's knowledge of the typical stages of development for children in a given age range on a variety of skills and concepts, and the assessment process itself promotes learning and development (Shepard, Kagan, & Wurtz, 1998b). The criteria of authenticity in both content and assessment strategies is a key element in ascertaining the developmental appropriateness of assessment for children in preschool and primary grades (Copple & Bredekamp, 2009; Hyson, 2008; National Association for the Education of Young Children & National Association of Early Childhood Specialists in State Departments of Education, 1991; National Educational Goals Panel, 1998).

Assessing Development of Concepts and Skills

For example, Kathy and Pat examined Shawna's assessment portfolio, which contained handwritten observations, called "anecdotal records," of Shawna's spontaneous and guided play since the first week of school. They compared Shawna's rendition of her name with well-formed letters and adequate spacing in March to the shakily written backwards "s" followed by a series of curved lines that Kathy had placed in Shawna's portfolio in early October.

Pat and Kathy looked at Shawna's early attempts at spelling words other than her name, beginning with the pictures and letters on a shopping list made in the playhouse in November, and then random letters in December and January. Her most recent writing, like the "CRTO" (Credit to) at the bank showed attempts to use some beginning and ending consonant sounds. "I lk wtrmln" (I like watermelon) is Shawna's recent contribution to a class book about favorite letters of the alphabet.

In the area of geometric and spatial reasoning, Kathy collected snapshots of Shawna's block structures, some built along with peers and others individually. Kathy also showed Pat an observation form on which she records anecdotal records of children's spontaneous and guided play (Table 6.1), and links them to the state academic standards for kindergarten.

Kathy also records notes from guided and directed play, as in this example from earlier months of the school year when she informally questioned Shawna regarding her understanding of number concepts.

In the playhouse, Shawna was setting the table for "breakfast" for four stuffed animals. She had each animal sitting at a chair at the table and was passing out napkins. She took the napkins one at a time from the playhouse

Table 6.1   Record of Mathematics Skills and Concepts for Kathy's Kindergarten

Curriculum Standard	Play	Dates	Contexts
Number Concepts			
Counts to 10 by rote memorization	S. and E. press leaf patterns into sand, counting to 10 and laughing as they check results.	9/27	Outdoors—sand area
Counts with one-to-one correspondence	Sets table for stuffed animals, counts 1 to 4 to place cups and napkins.	11/6	Housekeeping area—play alone
Uses comparative words, such as many–few, big–little, more–less, fast–slow appropriately	"I need more blocks; you have too many."	12/4	Block area—negotiates with boys; "Girls need blocks too!"
Understands numbers and simple operations and uses math manipulatives, games, toys, coins in daily activities (e.g., adding, subtracting)	"I need 2 more to make 10 dollars."	3/27	Pretend bank—customer role
Sorts and Classifies			
Describes how items are the same or different	"Put all the red food in this basket and the yellow food in here."	9/14	Pretend store—packing groceries

cupboard and placed each at an animal's place, walking across the playhouse each time. She went through the same process with spoons and cups until each diner had a place setting. After discussing Shawna's breakfast guests and the menu with her, Kathy asked Shawna how many of each—napkins, spoons, and cups—there were. Shawna counted each set aloud, "1-2-3-4." "Four and four and four," she said, smiling, "for my four friends." Kathy noted Shawna's competence with number concepts, including one-to-one correspondence in counting to four on the record of mathematics skills. ✑

Later, in January, Kathy's anecdotal records showed that Shawna had set the table for her snack group of six children. She had carefully counted the number of places aloud, then gathered sets of six napkins and six cups and placed one of each at each setting.

"Sometime in those three months Shawna learned to count and mentally match equivalent sets. In October, when I discovered that many of the children were just beginning to construct the idea of one-to-one correspondence, I planned a series of guided play activities where I set up materials like straws and cups and brushes and paintboxes. I asked children to help me set the places for children to work and found out how they were thinking about counting. My observations of play helped me plan a curriculum that was a good match for children's needs and also see how successful my ideas were." ✐

Development of Fine Motor Skills: Scissors.   Kindergarten is a critical time for the development of children's motor skills. Kathy's assessments include both fine and gross motor skill competencies. She collected samples of Shawna's cutting projects over the course of the school year. Shawna's early attempts at using scissors were characterized by cutting straight short lines and then tearing the paper with the scissors the rest of the way. Kathy recalled guiding Shawna's hand to show her how to close the blades of the scissors on each cut, and how Shawna and a group of friends spent most of their time for nearly 2 weeks in November making collages for people from magazines and paper scraps. After that, Shawna's cutting showed smooth edges and control over different shapes. By February, she was cutting circles and hearts with ease and her subsequent use of folding to make multiple sets of a cut shape were a great advance from her cutting skills earlier in the year.

Documenting Social Development.   Up to this point Kathy and Pat had discussed the aspects of Shawna's development seen in her portfolio and through anecdotal records that reflected Shawna's progress in "age-appropriate development" in academic subject areas. Shawna's development of such concepts as the use of letters to represent spoken language, one-to-one correspondence, and spatial representation with blocks are aspects of development Kathy focused on in her observations. Skills such as counting in conventional order, using scissors, and writing her name also fell within the range of accomplishments Kathy expects of kindergarten children. More important, Shawna's records indicated growth in all areas from September to April.

Kathy's anecdotal records and samples of Shawna's writing also document the development of Shawna's friendship with Emily. Although Shawna still chooses to spend part of each day in solitary play, Kathy was pleased to see the development of a close friendship with Emily because Kathy finds that, typically, kindergarten children can develop at least one friendship during the year. Her district has taken the lead among others in the state by incorporating standards of social and emotional development in their systematic assessment instruments. An example of standards is shown in Table 6.2.

Kathy felt that Shawna's ability to negotiate with other children seemed to have been bolstered by the bond she formed with Emily. For example, Kathy believed that part of the reason Shawna was able to confront a group of boys over taking more than their share of blocks was because she felt she was speaking for her friend as well as herself. Kathy also showed Pat samples of notes with pictures and Emily's name on them that Shawna had written. She recalled that Shawna had proudly spelled out Emily's house number when she drew a picture of Emily's house after visiting one day after school.

Table 6.2   Curriculum Standards for Approaches to Learning and Social and Emotional Development for Kathy's Kindergarten

Date	Curriculum Standard	Play Observation	Notes
9/14	Children become more comfortable with taking risks and with generating their own ideas.	Sam finally joins the block play. "I can make good garages!"	B
	Children are increasingly able to persist in and complete a variety of tasks, activities, projects, and experiences.		
11/7	Children show growing capacity to maintain concentration despite distractions and interruptions.	Maddy and Joan continue to build their sand restaurant despite the noise and disruption from the nearby chase and rescue game.	C for M O for J
	Children use more and more complex scenarios in play.		
	Children develop greater self-awareness and have positive feelings about their own gender, family, race, culture, and language. Children identify a variety of feelings and moods (in themselves and others).		
2/27	Children increase their capacity to take another's perspective.	"I think she's sad because her dad went on a trip," comments Doug in response to Carrie's tears.	C
	Children show progress in developing and keeping friendships.		
	Children manage transitions and follow routines most of the time.		
	Children use materials purposefully, safely, and respectfully, and take care of their own needs with the support of adults.		

B = Beginning; O = Occasionally; C = Consistently

ASSESSING INDIVIDUAL DEVELOPMENT

The second aspect of assessment, that is equally important as widely held expectations for a given age, is that of individually appropriate development (Copple & Bredekamp, 2009). This aspect takes into account children's talents and special needs, their cultural, linguistic, and family background, and their personal qualities such as temperament and interests. Teachers often intuitively assess children's development with regard to individual personality and temperament, and consider factors related to language, culture, and family background. Unfortunately, because these factors do not appear on report cards or find their way into "developmental norms" charts, these important individual aspects of development may go by the wayside in favor of more skills-oriented goals.

In her assessments, Kathy makes a point of including children's "dispositions" or "approaches to learning," such as taking initiative, curiosity, and cooperation. These approaches to learning are now more frequently included in state and national standards regarding appropriate assessment for children ages 3 to 8. Kathy also looks for ways in which children's play reflects their experiences at home, their styles of interaction, and ways of representing their ideas (Espinosa, 2010; Hughes, 2003; Katz & Chard, 2000; Murphey & Burns, 2002; National Educational Goals Panel, 1992). The trusting, reciprocal relationship that she has established with Shawna's mother is an example of mutuality that allows both of them to support Shawna's development (Copple & Bredekamp, 2009). For example:

> Shawna comes from a family where she has two teenage brothers. Kathy and Shawna's mother have speculated that some of her interest in block building and her ability to assert herself with the boys in the classroom may come from this experience with her brothers. Kathy continues, "As a much younger sibling, her situation is somewhat similar to that of an only child in the family—Shawna seems to need a lot of time to play by herself. Although she has Emily and one other blossoming friendship in the room, she often will go to the library corner or the table toys and play alone. I also think her home situation has fostered her ability to assert herself with adults and talk easily with them. She often includes parents who visit the classroom in her play, just as she did with you today." ✍

Intelligence Is Multifaceted

The issue of addressing multiple facets of children's learning and development is the subject of ongoing local and national debate. Current assessment efforts at local, state, and national levels have been criticized for overreliance on language and mathematics (Chen, Krechevsky, Viens, & Isberg, 1998; Kamii, 1990; Krechevsky, 1998). Early childhood educators are concerned that schools recognize the need to support a variety of modes of expression and understanding to acknowledge the potential of each individual (Epstein, Schweinhart, DeBruin-Parecki, & Robin, 2004; Kohn, 2001; Meisels, 2000; Seefeldt, 2005; Shepard et al., 1998a, 1998b; Wesson, 2001; Wien, 2004).

Given these concerns, another aspect of individual development that is essential for teachers to include in assessment is the interests and aptitudes observed in children's play in the classroom. Gardner (1993, 1999) extended the notion of "intelligence" beyond the paper-and-pencil language and math evaluations traditionally seen in school settings. He discusses how abilities in music, spatial reasoning, and other aspects of personal expression are more often seen as special "gifts," but not integral to adapting to the world in an intelligent manner. Gardner reminds us that all these intelligences are present to some degree in everyone. Most of us have strengths in two or three intelligences that shape the way in which we see the world and express ourselves. Gardner believes that educators need to pay serious attention to alternative avenues of expression as well as the traditional *linguistic* and *logical-mathematical* intelligences emphasized in schools and assessed on standardized tests.

Gardner has proposed five other intelligences that operate in people's daily lives. One of these is *musical intelligence*. Musical intelligence is expressed as children hum and sing to themselves. They often find patterns of sounds in language such as alliteration and are interested in musical instruments, dance, and singing in the classroom. Another intelligence is *bodily kinesthetic intelligence*. Children who readily express this intelligence are very active, expressing their thoughts and feelings through bodily movement. They may dance or leap across the room, exhibit coordination beyond their years in large motor activities, and be particularly interested in and skilled at the mechanics of objects. *Visual-spatial intelligence* may be seen in children who are very interested and skilled in constructive play. Their block structures are very sophisticated in terms of design elements such as symmetry, color, and form, and their dramatic play is often characterized by elaborate use of objects to represent settings for their play. They may be very interested in art, using several different media to convey their ideas. In the example given earlier, Shawna exhibits several qualities associated with spatial intelligence.

Gardner (1993) also described the personal intelligences that teachers see in young children. Children who express themselves through *interpersonal intelligence* are very interested in and savvy about other people's thoughts, feelings, and perspectives. They are often very social and well liked by other children and adults. Others may exhibit more *intrapersonal intelligence*. These children are very introspective, reflecting on their own thoughts and feelings and are often able to discuss just how they solved a particular problem or how they felt in a certain situation. As noted in Chapter 3, interpersonal and intrapersonal intelligences are linked to the concept of "emotional literacy" described by Goleman (1995).

More recently Gardner (1999) posited a *naturalistic intelligence* that is characterized by particular sensitivity to the natural world. We see this in the child who loves to watch spiders spin a web, watch sowbugs move in the garden, and care for plants and animals.

Careful observation of children's play, in terms of both the process and content of their activities, offers teachers important clues on the individual development of each child within this framework of multiple ways of making meaning. Case studies, such as the information Kathy has collected on Shawna, are excellent examples of holistic assessment. (See Gallas, 1997; Genishi & Dyson, 2009; Katch, 2001; and Paley, 1986, 1990 for detailed and informative case studies.)

Children Need to Reflect on Their Own Learning.   A major element of assessment approaches that provide multiple forms of representation is the provision of opportunities for children to reflect on their own learning and development. NAEYC's 2009 Position Statement recognizes "children's own evaluations of their work" as a key element of developmentally appropriate assessment practice (Copple & Bredekamp, 2009, p. 22). For example,

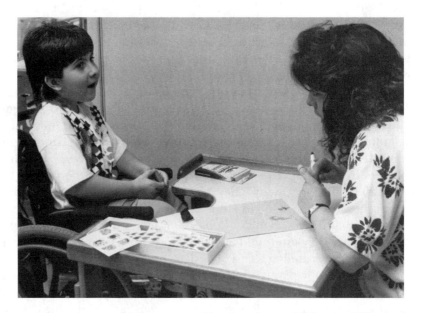

One-on-one interactions provide opportunities to assess children's skills.

As Shawna and Emily sorted through photos of the bank in its various stages of construction, Shawna remarked, "We got the name tags for the tellers, but next time we have to make a sign that shows people where to get in the line." ✆

The many projects described in this book, such as Kathy's "bank project" described at the beginning of this chapter, the post office project described in Chapter 1, and Sophie and the lost pigs project and others described in Chapter 5, are examples of how play and representations of play claim a central role in how children reflect on their own experiences and learning.

HOW PLAY INFORMS ASSESSMENT

Play is the ultimate "integrated curriculum." Play offers teachers windows to view all aspects of children's development, including concepts, skills, dispositions, and feelings. All aspects of development, such as classification concepts or cooperative behavior, inform teachers about how to orchestrate more complex play.

Play occupies a privileged role in constructivist theories of learning and development. Therefore, it is the natural vehicle for assessing children's understanding of their experiences. Play also offers a multidimensional look at skills, concepts, and dispositions that are valued by teachers and appear in state and national curriculum standards. It helps teachers to see myriad different avenues for developing and expressing understanding of these concepts among individual children.

Because play is central to development, it is central to our efforts to assess and develop programs that serve the needs of all children. Although there is much discussion in the early childhood community regarding the developmental appropriateness of many curriculum standards and benchmarks imposed by schools, much of this discussion comes down to the means by which these competencies are assessed, rather than the benchmark itself. Play-centered assessment enhances the developmental appropriateness of many curriculum standards.

For example, one competency often seen in state curriculum standards for understanding of numbers in kindergarten, "counts with one-to-one correspondence," is reflected in Kathy's goals. But each child approaches this concept in a slightly different way. Jonathan develops his understanding by counting the number of blocks he needs to make the fence around his "lion cage" exactly the same on each side. Shawna sets the table in the housekeeping corner, and Emily arranges the paintbrushes and the cups in correspondence to one another as she mixes colors for the day's easel painting.

A play-centered curriculum provides an atmosphere for assessment that is both comfortable and challenging. Children have many opportunities to make choices regarding their modes of expression and their playmates. In a classroom well equipped for play, children will find familiar objects and means of expression that scaffold their performances and allow them to create and problem solve in ways most comfortable to them.

Play enhances reliability of assessments by ensuring that the results of an assessment are based on many opportunities for observing children at play with familiar materials and playmates. In this way, play-centered assessment differs from assessment that occurs only once or twice during a school year in which children are confronted with unfamiliar materials and intimidating contexts and are expected to perform to a standard of achievement.

Play also enhances the validity of assessments. Children are best assessed by their performances in real contexts. For example, it makes sense to evaluate children's spatial reasoning while they are constructing with blocks or collage materials instead of administering a paper-and-pencil task.

💙 In Roseanna's K–2 multiage primary class in an ethnically diverse community, a pretend restaurant begins as the "Don't Forget the Olives Pizza Parlor" and evolves to include Chinese food. The first week, children labor over a large wall menu that depicts the food choices and combinations in both print and pictures. After making pretend pizzas with playdough made from a posted recipe, Matt and Sam introduce potstickers, rice, and noodles made from playdough as well. Celia, Mei Lin, and John write menus that show the pizza choices on one side, the Chinese food on the other, and drinks and desserts on the back. Their teacher helps them make copies to color and mount on colored paper for their customers as they enter the restaurant. "Then everyone can see what we have on the wall, and at their table!" exults Angie, as she dons her chef's hat. 🐚

Embedded in these experiences, Roseanna plans several of the curriculum standards from her state:

- The standard, "Writing with a command of standard English, including sentence structure, grammar, punctuation, capitalization, and spelling" as part of understanding the conventions of written language for grade 2, is illustrated in the signs and menus children make for their restaurant.
- The standard, "Identifying, sorting and classifying objects by attributes," as part of the concept of sorting and classification for kindergarten, is embedded in the arrangement of food on the serving trays and in grouping items for the menu.
- The standard, "Learning that properties of substances can change when mixed, cooled, or heated" as part of the physical science concept that "matter comes in different forms" for grade 1, is evident in the playdough recipes that the children follow.
- The kindergarten-level visual arts standard, "Using a variety of art materials such as paint, clay, wood, and markers to express their ideas," is addressed by the making of playdough food, costumes for restaurant employees, placemats, tablecloths, menus, and advertisements.
- The standards, "Understanding the concept of exchange and use of money to purchase foods and services" and "The specialized work that people do to manufacture, transport, and market goods," are part of learning basic economic concepts for grade 1. They are exemplified in the group's study of ingredients for foods for the restaurant and the pricing and pretend sale of foods and drinks.

ASCERTAINING THE CHILD'S VIEWPOINT

A major challenge for the teacher in implementing play-centered assessment is the development of observation strategies and questioning strategies that illuminate children's progress, while at the same time respecting children's right to control their own play. When Pat discovered Shawna could not yet count to 50, she might have asked Shawna how high she could count. Pat decided, however, that interrupting the flow of Shawna's play to do direct teaching or to ask her to perform a task was not appropriate in that context. Kathy's anecdotal record in which she questioned Shawna about the numbers of spoons, cups, and napkins demonstrated a situation in which questioning was not disruptive to the play. Shawna seemed pleased to show off the setting, "Four and four and four—for my four friends" to her teacher.

This judgment call on the part of teachers is one that requires sensitivity, thoughtfulness, and a repertoire of strategies for determining when to assess by careful observation and when to guide or directly question a child. As teachers use their careful observations of children's play, they grow in their understanding of how children think and feel. Through observations of children and ongoing conversations with families, teachers develop a deeper insight into children's purposes and conceptions concerning the world. Teachers also gain a greater appreciation of how the peer culture in the classroom influences learning.

As teachers gain an understanding of children's worlds, they become better able to plan curriculum that is relevant and appropriate to children's development. In guided play experiences, teachers have specific, intentional goals in mind. They may use these guided play contexts to assess children's progress in ways that pinpoint the questions they have about the development and learning of individual children and the group.

In the following sections, we turn to the work of Selma Wassermann (2000), who developed principles for assessing and guiding children's play through questioning strategies and the introduction of new materials. Her model involves setting up materials for children to investigate concepts through their play and asking questions that encourage children to communicate their thoughts and to elaborate their thinking.

Principles for Framing Play Questions

According to Wassermann (2000), the first principle in formulating questions for children regarding their play is to *carefully attend to the child's behavior and/or verbalization.* This may involve making eye contact with the child and certainly listening to children with full attention and interest. It may mean getting down to the child's level or moving close enough so the soft-spoken child may be heard. Attention also means looking for nuances of feeling in the child's behavior, voice pitch, or tone. For example, many young children sing as they play with objects, sometimes creating a running monologue about what they are doing.

A second principle emphasized by Wassermann *is respect for the child's intentions and autonomy.* This means, in the most basic way, not passing judgment on the child's play behavior or on the product of that play. Respect may take the form of the teacher's decision not to ask a question, but instead to subtly and quietly put forth a new object or material the child might choose to use, and see what he or she does with it. This is part of the Artist Apprentice strategy for orchestrating play that we discussed in Chapter 5.

If the teacher does decide to ask a question after determining that it will not be too intrusive, then a third consideration arises: *Does the adult's question empower the child, or does it foster dependence on adult judgment?* For example, if Pat had offered to teach Shawna to count to 50, rather than accept the alternative of 10 dollars offered by Shawna, she might have conveyed that her adult knowledge was the only alternative in this situation. On the other hand, Pat might have felt that Shawna was eager to perform her counting skills and asked, "How high can you count?" In this way she would have invited Shawna to show off her rote counting skills. Instead, Pat chose to accept Shawna's suggestion of 10 dollars, believing that to do otherwise would have interrupted the flow of the play.

Ask Authentic Questions. Paley (1981) noted that she tries never to ask a question to which she already knows the answer. Along with others, such as Duckworth

(1996), Paley suggests that teachers' questions need to represent an authentic curiosity about how children are thinking about their experiences. This is qualitatively quite different from finding out if the child knows what the teacher knows. The challenge is not to impart the teacher's knowledge to the child, but to objectively and without judgment observe the process the child uses to interpret his or her environment. In addition, many educators have noted that children who do not come from middle-class homes are frequently bewildered by teachers asking questions to which there are obvious answers, such as, "What color is the grass?" Genuine interest in children's own thoughts and perspectives is a more respectful and more meaningful approach to questioning (Delpit, 1995; Tizard & Hughes, 1984).

Successful assessment of children's development in their play depends largely on keeping these principles in mind. Our viewpoints as teachers are transformed as we listen to children and open ourselves to children's purposes and meanings.

Challenge Children's Thinking in Play.   Other questioning strategies challenge children to analyze or to generate hypotheses about their play. Asking children to predict, verbalize, or draw their plans for play or to explain how their ideas might be tested are all examples of questions that challenge children to stretch their thinking. Ask, for example: I wonder if there's another way to do that? What do you suppose the lion would do if you allowed him out of his cage? Do you think you could make that same color again with paints?

Context is another dimension to assessing children's viewpoints as expressed in play. In an extension of the matchmaking strategy for orchestrating play described in Chapter 5, teachers wisely might consider structuring individual, small-group, and whole-group contexts for play. Wolfberg (1999) and Elgas and Peltier (1998) describe how teachers can use small-group projects and stable play groups to assess the development of children with special needs, as well as their typically developing peers.

STRATEGIES FOR COLLECTING AND ORGANIZING INFORMATION

In Kathy's classroom, several strategies for systematically collecting information about children's progress are evident.

Anecdotal Records

The first and most essential strategy is observation and anecdotal recording of spontaneous and guided play. Kathy says that she identifies one or two children each day to observe during play and project time. She records her thoughts on Post-it Notes or on sticky mailing labels and then completes her notes after school. She says she finds that keeping observations to a maximum of three children a day makes the task easier to accomplish and that she can put together her notes on each child rather quickly. The dated observation then goes on the form. (See Table 6.1 on page 129 and Table 6.3 on page 140, for example.)

Other teachers simply place their notes taken on Post-it Notes or mailing labels on a paper in the child's folder, but Kathy says she prefers to "log" the observations as she takes them. "Then I can see where a child is spending most of her time. I can also see if I am really getting a good picture of the child's activities or if all my observations are too narrowly focused. For example, I looked at Mario's chart a few days ago and realized that nearly all my observations of him were taken on the outdoor climbing structure playing with the same group of boys. I have to make an effort to find him on his own and record his play."

Another strategy for collecting information about children's development is through anecdotal observations of guided play experiences that teachers set up. For example, in her first-grade classroom, Anita frequently sets up a store as one of the centers. She is often a participant as well as an observer, focusing on children's counting and understanding of money. A center where leaves and rocks are available for classifying, or one with a variety of objects and a tub of water, are setups that afford teachers opportunities to observe children's play and converse with them about their thinking.

Checklists

Yet another useful strategy in assessing development through play is a checklist. Checklists might include stages of early writing (Table 6.3) or stages of sociodramatic play drawn from Smilansky's work (see Table 6.4). Other checklists might include strategies observed in children's problem solving, block building, or cooperative group play. A comprehensive checklist for assessment of young children on many dimensions of development is the 1993 Work Sampling System developed by Meisels and his colleagues (Marsden, Meisels, Jablon, & Dichtelmiller, 2001; Meisels, 1993; Meisels, Xue, & Shamblott, 2008).

Checklists have the advantage of giving the teacher "quick glance" feedback regarding the stages of development of both individuals and the group. For example, if in looking at a class checklist for stages of block play, a kindergarten teacher notices that many of the children are not yet constructing elaborated structures, she may want to consider some of the intervention strategies suggested in Chapter 4. She may want to introduce some accessory boxes for new play themes that might stretch children's block representations to more complex levels. Checklists may also work to help summarize information from audiotaped or videotaped sequences of children's play, guiding the teacher to organize a large quantity of information into a succinct form.

Checklists have the disadvantage of giving the teacher too little information about the context or detail of children's play when the observations are made. Just marking the stage and date of the observation is useful as a broad measure of development but may lack the richness of detail provided by anecdotal observations, videotapes, audiotapes, and portfolios.

Many teachers combine checklists with portfolios and observations. In his first-grade classroom, Mark takes observations and materials from portfolios every 3 months

Table 6.3   Checklist of Beginning Writing for Kathy's Kindergarten

Dates	Observed Behavior	Evaluation	Comments and Play Context
9/14	Uses scribble writing or approximations of letters	Beginning___ Consistently_X_	Kayla holds a pen and makes a row of circles. "This is my letter!"
	Tells about writing	Beginning___ Consistently___	
	Uses strings of letters	Beginning___ Consistently___	
12/5	Writes left to right	Beginning___ Consistently_X_	K. begins "Happy Birthday" at left side of card.
	Knows difference between writing and drawing	Beginning___ Consistently___	
	"Reads" pictures	Beginning___ Consistently___	
	"Reads" writing	Beginning___ Consistently___	
12/3	Dictates "art notes" to pictures	Beginning_X_ Consistently___	"And write sun here and then the moon, 'cause it's night" as K. points to images she has painted.
	Dictates stories	Beginning___ Consistently___	
	Copies name	Beginning___ Consistently___	
10/7	Writes first name, last name— Copies words other than name	Beginning___ Consistently_X_ Beginning_X_ Consistently___	K. writes first name with reversals.
12/5	Writes independently	Beginning___ Consistently_X_	K. begins "Happy Birthday" pretend writing of card.
2/18	Uses upper- and lowercase letters	Beginning_X_ Consistently___	"Does 'Mom' have a big M or little?" K. asks.
	Spaces writing	Beginning_X_ Consistently___	
	Uses begin/end consonants in writing	Beginning___ Consistently___	
	Invents spellings	Beginning___ Consistently___	
		Beginning___ Consistently___	

and summarizes the stages of development they represent on a checklist of early writing. This way he gives himself a more detailed picture of individual children's progress, as well as the progress of the whole group, and ensures that he has collected a representative sampling of each child's experiences in his classroom.

Portfolios

Portfolio assessment at all levels of education is currently widely discussed. Historically, teachers have gathered samples of children's "work" and collected them in files. But too often this work represents only a child's efforts to copy a set of sentences from the board, a teacher-modeled art project, or a set of math workbook computations. Contemporary children's portfolios reflect much more of children's processes (Smith, 2000; Strickland & Strickland, 2000; Wortham, 2005). For example, Tierney and his colleagues (1991) recommend that children select their own samples for a language and literacy portfolio and include drafts as well as their final writing and drawing projects.

A preschool teacher holds a monthly art show in which children display their work. She asks children each month to pick out a piece of their artwork that they would like to be included in their portfolios.

> Tommy's father is Chinese, and he has recently become interested in the written forms of both the Chinese and Japanese languages. The family hosted a Japanese exchange student in their home for the summer. Tommy was impressed by the Japanese writing on the boxes of Japanese toys he was given as gifts and by the student's translation of the symbols for him. Tommy's pretend writing "in Japanese" is clearly marked from the pretend writing he has also done "in English." His teacher has a short audiotape of him "reading" his writing to her. For the Japanese symbols, he makes sounds that he thinks are like the language he has heard. Then he translates it into English for his teacher.

Documentation Assessment

Teachers can also take photographs of projects in process and write captions and ongoing questions and insights. For example, in Greta's second-grade classroom, open-choice playtime, called "project time," was the context for group projects that extended over several days or weeks.

> As part of a project in social studies focused on tools and inventions in the past, present, and future, one group designed a whole series of robots, starting with the "X-100 model" that could serve soft drinks, extending to the "X-500 model" that could clean the whole house. The children created a collection of promotional brochures for their robot series, and Greta helped them videotape their pretend television commercial showcasing their products. She kept records of their constructions as they developed and the drafts

of their brochures and scripts for the television commercial. She marked the development of their thinking as a group as well as their individual contributions to the project. Over time, it became clear that Sonia was the budding engineer of the group, suggesting additional functions and parts for the robots each day. Mauricio carefully wrote their scripts and illustrated the brochures. Lila, a child who recently moved from Mexico and who had been reluctant to speak English, starred in their commercial, which was presented in both English and Spanish. This project addressed Grade 2 social studies, technology, and literacy standards for Greta's district. ✆

A key feature of documentation assessment is the opportunity for children to revisit their experiences and to elaborate their play in new ways. Documentation assessment also provides a powerful avenue for communicating with families about the play-centered curriculum and its outcomes for children.

Documentation assessment has been described in detail by educators who have studied at Reggio Emilia in Italy and draw from that approach. Classic and more recent resources include work by such educators as Edwards, Gandini, and Forman (1993); Gandini, Hill, Cadwell and Schwall (2005); Helm and Benecke (2003); Wein (2008); and Wurm (2005).

Videotape

Richard teaches a kindergarten–first-grade combination class in a rural area. Many of the children in his classroom speak English as a second language, and their parents work in the nearby electronics industry. The parent group at Richard's school purchased a video camera a year ago. Richard videotapes children's open-choice playtime and, occasionally, their large-group-time discussions. Sometimes Richard sets the camera on a tripod in a given area of the classroom and lets it run. In this way he sees what goes on over time with a play project. He recalls two boys who came into his kindergarten without preschool experiences or much contact with other children. Both boys were limited in their social negotiation strategies, and both chose to play in the block corner nearly every day. Richard videotaped their play periodically over 2 months, documenting on videotape their progress from grabbing blocks and shouting "Mine!" to cooperative constructive play projects.

He often tapes play in the housekeeping area as well. Because Richard does not speak Korean, he is frequently at a loss to discover the content of some of the children's dramatic play sequences. With videotape as a tool, he is able to record sequences of play and then show them to a colleague who speaks Korean. She helps him to determine both the content and developmental level of the play he has taped.

"Letting the tape run" is also a strategy that Richard uses to assess what happens "on the periphery" of his classroom, and to plan curriculum accordingly. He observes and reflects on what the camera picks up. He often invites the children to watch some of the tapes and solve the problems they reveal. For example, Richard noted that some of the block and manipulative accessories were not being used much by the children. Through the videotape, it was revealed that the children seemed to have difficulty taking out the materials and putting them away. The class watched the tape together and some of the children explained their frustrations as they watched. They brainstormed a new way of storing the materials in the future.

Interview Children About Their Play.   Another technique that Richard developed is interviewing children about their play during playtime. He circulates through the room with the camera, and children explain their constructive play projects, science experiments, or dramatic play. For example:

> 💟 During one play period, Juan described the three-story house he built with Cuisenaire rods while he and Richard conversed in Spanish. In the housekeeping area, a group of children had opened a restaurant and took Richard's order for spaghetti, writing his order on a clipboard and using invented spelling.
>
> Richard checked in with children at various stages of their play. Richard's tape showed that Amanda and Jerry persisted for 45 minutes in making "magic potions," proudly reciting their newest ingredients each time they were interviewed.
>
> He recorded Juan and Marty arguing over their block play early in the hour, then returned much later to two smiling boys peeping out of a structure. "You wanted to build a firehouse and you wanted to build an office. What did you finally decide?" asked Richard. "A police," announced Marty, and they proudly showed off their telephone for "when people call 911" on the desk they built.

ASSESSING PLAY AS PLAY

One of the major points of this book is that there is a reciprocal relationship between the development of play and the development of other aspects of cognitive and social-emotional functioning in childhood. Therefore, although play serves as a context for assessing the development of such qualities as representational thinking, emerging literacy, problem-solving strategies, and mathematical concepts, the development of play as play in a variety of contexts also concerns teachers of young children (Bergen, 2006; Gross, 2006; Harris, 2009).

Smilansky (1968) developed a system for viewing children's sociodramatic play that is still widely used for assessing young children. Sociodramatic play might appear in several contexts, such as the housekeeping area, around the climbing structure, in the sandbox, or with the blocks. In all contexts the features of socio-dramatic play that mark social, linguistic, and cognitive complexity are the focus of assessment. The six components of Smilansky's system for evaluating play complexity appear in Table 6.4. Sophisticated sociodramatic play of preschool and primary-grade children includes all these elements in good measure. Children's developing

Table 6.4 Complexity of Children's Play

Benchmarks	Evaluation/Date	Play Examples
Using Make-Believe Roles		
Children declare their roles ("I'm the firefighter.") and engage in behavior consistent with that role (hosing down a pretend fire).	**Not yet___** **Occasionally** <u>10/18</u> **Consistently___**	Sandy announces "I'll be baby—you're the sister." "Help me, sister! I'm stuck!"
Using Make-Believe Props		
Children use objects to represent other objects (a block for a walkie-talkie); gestures or words to represent pretend action ("Whoosh! Whoosh!" while pretending to hose a fire), and/or verbalize a pretend situation ("Pretend the baby was trapped in the house").	**Not yet___** **Occasionally** <u>2/13</u> **Consistently___**	"9-1-1 please," says Zack, as he picks up a block and hold it to his ear. "We have a fire!"
Using Make-Believe Episodes		
Make-believe play is coordinated into an elaborated episode ("Call the ambulance. This baby is really hurt bad.")	**Not yet___** **Occasionally___** **Consistently___**	
Persistence		
Children sustain their dramatic play over time (5 minutes of more sustained play for preschoolers and kindergartners; 20 minutes for first and second graders and even continue story lines over several days' time)	**Not yet___** **Occasionally___** **Consistently** <u>1/25</u>	Selena and Chris play princesses for a week, each day making more rooms for their castle out of blocks and playdough.
Social Interaction		
Two or more children are engaged in enacting a play episode.	**Not yet___** **Occasionally___** **Consistently___**	
Verbal Communication		
Children use words to communicate make-believe transformations in play and to "direct" the play, by assigning roles or planning story sequences ("I'll be the ambulance driver, and you give me the baby").	**Not yet___** **Occasionally___** **Consistently___**	

Sources: Information from *The Effects of Sociodramatic Play on Disadvantaged Preschool Children* by S. Smilansky, 1968, New York: Wiley. *Facilitating Play: A Medium for Promoting Cognitive, Socioemotional, and Academic Development in Young Children* by S. Smilansky and L. Sheftaya, 1990, Gaithersburg, MD: Psychosocial and Educational Publications.

complexity in their play may be traced through anecdotal observations or video-taping of dramatic play episodes.

For example, in Kathy's kindergarten class, two children, Amanda and Curt, spent much of their time in the housekeeping area arguing over who would use objects such as the toy telephone or the teapot. Both children's capacities to perform make-believe transformations were unsophisticated according to Smilansky's scale. In story play activities that Kathy offered three times a week, Amanda and Curt watched as others used gestures to represent imaginary objects and tried it themselves as actors in story play productions. Kathy modeled for them the use of blocks for a variety of pretend objects, as she guided the resolution of their play disputes. After 6 weeks, Kathy repeated her play observations using the Smilansky scale and determined that both children had made progress in their use of make-believe props for play.

Although the Smilansky scale is the most concise assessment of symbolic play that we have found, teachers who care to look in more detail at the kind of play children engage in and its relationship to language might also wish to use the play complexity instrument described by Sylva, Roy, and Painter in their 1980 study, *Child Watching at Play-groups and Nursery School.*

In their work on "master players," Reynolds and Jones (1997) present a useful scheme for assessing the sophistication of play. They report that children who were skilled at pretend play with others coped effectively with social constraints, showed mutuality in their interactions, added new elements to play, and were able to see patterns or to structure play for themselves and others.

The Penn Interactive Peer Play Scale (PIPPS) is an instrument developed for teachers to assess children's interactive skill and social competence in play. In contrast to other measures to assess play as play, the PIPPS was specifically designed to be responsive to the strengths in the play of young children who live in urban environments characterized by poverty. Head Start teachers, parents, and children were involved in the development of this assessment. The PIPPS guides teachers in identifying techniques that children use to sustain play with one another. It includes descriptors for positive play interaction such as sharing ideas, leadership, helping, and inclusive behaviors. Descriptors for negative play or disruption include starting fights or arguments, refusal to share or take turns, and physical and verbal aggression. A third factor labeled "disconnection" in play is characterized by behaviors that indicate nonparticipation in play, such as aimless wandering, refusal of invitations to play, and unhappy demeanor (Fantuzzo et al., 1995).

Rubin and his colleagues developed a system for combining Piaget's and Parten's levels of play (Rubin, 1980; Rubin, Maioni, & Hornung, 1976). They nested Piaget's categories of functional, constructive, dramatic, and games with rules within Parten's social categories of solitary, parallel, and group play (Figure 6.1). In their research, Rubin and his colleagues pointed out that play sophistication ranges from the simplest combination, solitary functional, to the most complex, group games with rules.

Figure 6.1
Stages of Cognitive Com-
plexity of Play Nested within
Categories of Social Play

Solitary Play	Parallel Play	Group Play
functional	functional	functional
constructive	constructive	constructive
dramatic	dramatic	dramatic
games with rules	games with rules	games with rules

Source: Information from "Free Play Behaviors in Middle- and Lower-
Class Preschoolers: Parten & Piaget Revisited" by K. Rubin, T. L. Maioni,
and M. Hornung, 1976, *Child Development, 47,* pp. 414–419.

A CLOSER LOOK: RISKS AND BENEFITS OF ASSESSMENTS

Because teachers, administrators, and policy makers use standardized assessment to evaluate programs and to come to decisions about groups of children, these assessments are by their nature designed to be cost and time efficient. The assessment instruments selected frequently reduce complex capabilities to a single score that may be interpreted readily by those who are not educators (Pellegrini, 1998; Shepard, 2000; Shepard et al., 1998a, 1998b; Wesson, 2001). All too frequently, these pressures have lead to practices that undermine positive outcomes for children.

The Risks of High-Stakes Accountability

Inequitable access to schooling results when narrowly focused, single assessments determine when a child is "ready" for school. Many early childhood educators believe that readiness and redshirting are practices closely linked to the "high-stakes" testing prevalent in public schools, which make scores on standardized tests the primary, if not the sole, measure of individual and school success (Andersen, 1998; Graue, 2001; Kohn, 2001; Meisels, 2000; Wesson, 2001; Wien, 2004). The notion of *readiness* to enter kindergarten, preschool, or the next grade is tied to debates about what expectations for concepts, skills, and behaviors are age and individual appropriate. Varying interpretations of the term *readiness* begin early in the schooling experience to position some children disadvantageously.

Gullo (2006) warns that as the result of didactic kindergarten curriculum and limited notions of readiness, children may be barred from attending kindergarten or required to attend "developmental" kindergartens. In school systems, pressures to exclude children to raise the school's scores in order to demonstrate "school success" are exacerbated by recent trends in early education, particularly the trend to push didactic, narrowly focused curriculum into primary grades, kindergarten, and preschool.

Tensions Regarding Play-Centered Curriculum and Early Learning Standards

In addition to questions regarding school readiness, the adoption of curriculum standards for programs serving young children presents multiple challenges. As we

A teacher may assess dispositions to learn such as taking initiative, curiosity, and cooperation.

discussed in Chapter 1, in our review of state and national standards we find that many are consistent with play-centered curriculum. However, tensions are created between basic principles of developmentally appropriate practice and the simplistic skills and concepts listed in some standards documents. Honoring children's interests and choices about learning and offering time for exploration, play, and reflection to construct meaningful knowledge are frequently threatened by pressures for teachers to isolate skills and concepts and teach in a didactic fashion. Another serious concern is the damage to children's self-esteem and dispositions to learn as side effects of these measures (Meisels, 2000; Wien, 2004). A related issue is the narrowing of curriculum, a trend increasingly reported by teachers in light of high-stakes assessment pressures.

Making Schools Ready for Learners

Developmental approaches to school entry view children as coming to school with their own strengths and styles of learning, as we see in Pamela's class. This turns the question of readiness to one that asks, "Are the schools ready for all learners?" (Graue & Diperna, 2000; Hand & Nourot, 1999). This perspective is essential to implement standards in a play-centered curriculum that supports all children's development (e.g., Bergen, 2006; Jacobs & Crowley, 2010).

In a thoughtful review, Murphey and Burns (2002) identified community notions related to school readiness that include separation from caregivers, play with other children and appropriate interactions with adults, social problem-solving skills, appropriate expression of emotions, flexibility in adapting to transitions, persistence, enthusiasm, and curiosity. In our own conversations with teachers and families, we have found that these social and dispositional competencies are at the top of the list for readiness criteria for children as they enter kindergarten.

Serving Students with Special Needs: Benefits of Play-Centered Assessments

A number of researchers have developed play-centered scales that are appropriate for determining eligibility for special education services and making program decisions. For example, Eisert and Lamorey (1996) report on research using their Play Assessment Scale (PAS). The scale includes 45 items that measure both spontaneous and elicited play development in infants and preschool children. They emphasize that play-centered assessments allow us to observe children with special needs using their skills functionally in natural environments.

Using Videotape for Assessing Special Needs.   Richard has found that video records of children's behavior have been very helpful in documenting his assessments of children who have special educational needs. In one instance, the parents of Maureen, a child whom Richard believed needed special help, refused to believe that their daughter needed to be referred for further assessment. Richard documented Maureen's behavior at group time where her need to be touching Richard at all times was evident. He documented Maureen's play with other children in which she would frequently lash out and hit others. Because Maureen was an only child and their home was at the outskirts of this rural community, she had had few playmates. Consequently, her parents had little opportunity to compare their daughter's behavior with that of other children her age. The videotape helped Richard and Maureen's parents agree on special-needs assessment for Maureen and helped them to plan some strategies together that would smooth Maureen's relationships with others.

Families, Assessments, and the Play-Centered Curriculum

Teachers find that when families are involved in assessments, some children feel more comfortable and less hesitant. Families are an integral part of some assessments and can contribute to physically support a child or help elicit responses. Play-centered assessment may increase family involvement, as Meyers and his colleagues found (1994) in their research. They also reported that parents felt more comfortable in seeking information from professionals during play-centered assessments and perceived the identified goals as important.

In Richard's K–1 combination class, videotape became useful in giving family members an opportunity to observe their children in particular and the whole curriculum in general. Twice a year, he prepares a videotape with edited segments of children's activities and progress. At "Back to School Night" in the fall, he shows parents scenes from a typical day in his classroom and examples of play projects children have done in previous years. At "Open House" in the spring, Richard shows video clips of children's block constructions, dramatic play sequences, story plays, science experiments, and other events and projects that he has captured on tape. He creates a video "yearbook" for children and their families from clips of classroom life throughout the year so that children may keep a permanent record of their kindergarten experience.

SUMMARY AND CONCLUSION

In this chapter we have looked at some of the ways that play episodes inform teachers in their efforts to assess children's progress. Play provides information to guide teachers' future designs for curriculum and serves as a means of evaluating the progress of groups of children as well as the progress of individuals.

Play-centered assessment paints a portrait of the "whole child," as individuals express their unique views of the world through play. Teachers' anecdotal observations of children's play and portfolios of the products of play offer an ongoing record of children's development in cognitive, linguistic, and social-emotional domains.

Play-centered assessment is a means for teachers to evaluate the success of their curriculum planning, to see if children replay the concepts and skills embedded in the curriculum and use them in their own play. Play-centered assessment is appropriate for use with all children. It may have special advantages for assessing the development of children with special needs and children who are English language learners.

We have discussed multiple means of collecting information on children's play, including forms for organizing anecdotal observations, checklists of age-appropriate development, and audiotaping and videotaping techniques. We have looked at ways to assess how play contributes to development in traditional academic areas such as literacy and problem solving. We have also looked at ways to assess play as play, to highlight the reciprocal relationship of play to other aspects of early childhood development.

In this chapter we have addressed some of the major issues relating to the use of standardized tests for children. We contrast these methods with the more spontaneous, contextualized assessment that play provides in classrooms for young children.

Finally, we have discussed some of the ways that teachers use play-centered assessment to communicate with families. Using observational records, photographs, and audiotaped or videotaped samples of children's experiences in the classroom helps families understand what their children are learning through their play as well as appreciate their children's unique styles of development and expression.

Critical to all assessment issues is the notion of time. Time for children to inhabit their classrooms, develop relationships, competencies, and dispositions, as well as time for them to develop their concepts of themselves as learners and meaning makers is the missing element in the ubiquitous press to have children perform more and sooner. As Almy (2000) wisely advised, the adults in children's lives are the ones responsible for ensuring that children do indeed have time to play and to enjoy childhood in the 21st century.

Our view is that play-centered curriculum is the avenue that offers the opportunity for children to develop and learn in ways led by children's own strengths and interests as they enter school. Careful observation, orchestration, and documentation of children's play across a variety of contexts build the foundation for more formal instruction in traditional school subject areas such as mathematics, literacy, science, social studies, and the arts, as children develop and construct new knowledge in more formal school contexts. This will inspire teachers to think beyond traditional means for assessing children in the elementary grades and to document interests and dispositions as well as competencies revealed in the full spectrum of children's behaviors, including play.

Mathematics in the Play-Centered Curriculum

The blocks have arrived! After weeks of anticipation, the students in Virginia's first-grade class get their first opportunity to create with blocks. Some of the 27 children have never played with unit blocks before. Until this year, the school's three first-grade classes had no blocks. Virginia is the first of the first-grade teachers in the school to use them.

Chhoun runs to the blocks purposefully. He builds a two-tiered structure and divides it into symmetrical sections. Several towers add an interesting touch of asymmetry. In front of the structure he builds four small, separate constructions that look like animals. He groups three to his right and a single one to his left. Leah and Becky work together to build a castle. It has a triangular base, so that one looks into the structure as if looking onto a stage. They also emphasize asymmetry by adding a second tier on one side. ⌀

Virginia was surprised at the children's skillfulness in block building and their sense of design. She wondered about their previous experiences with block building. When discussing their constructions, Virginia emphasized their use of balance and symmetry, and how they "decorated" the more regular, symmetrical structures with small shapes to make them a bit asymmetrical. She pointed out that the limited number of blocks available sometimes led to exchanges in which children discussed issues of fairness concerning the number of blocks each child could take. Children traded one longer block for two shorter blocks. They counted the total number of blocks different children had. They searched for particular triangular or cylindrical blocks to complete their structure or provide greater stability.

As Virginia's comments show, block play provides opportunities for children to consolidate and extend their mathematical thinking. When children construct with blocks, they deal with concepts that are basic to mathematics during the early childhood years, such as space (geometry), quantity (number), measurement, and patterns. Blocks have always been a favorite play material of young children. Early childhood educators and researchers have long recognized that blocks support the development of mathematical abilities within a playful context, fostering the development of the whole child. A play-centered curriculum supports the development of children's mathematical interests and understandings.

THE PLAYFUL NATURE OF MATHEMATICS

Mathematicians write about the playful, creative aspects of mathematics. As Holton, a mathematician, and his colleagues (2001) explain,

> Mathematical play involves pushing the limits of the situation and following thoughts and ideas wherever they may lead . . . it is designed to allow complete freedom on the part of the solver to wander over the mathematical landscape (p. 403).

In this playful spirit, mathematicians creatively generate new ideas and experiment to solve problems.

This description of mathematical play in the work of adult mathematicians characterizes the play of young children as they explore the mathematical dimensions of their environments. Spontaneous and guided play help children develop dispositions central to doing mathematics such as curiosity and the desire to explore and experiment. The vignettes in this chapter show children immersed in problem solving and inquiry that involve "wandering over the mathematical landscape" as well as trying a particular path to reach a solution.

MATHEMATICAL CONCEPTS IN THE PLAY-CENTERED CURRICULUM

Through spontaneous and guided play, children begin to understand basic mathematical concepts. Concepts related to such fundamental mathematical understandings as spatial relationships, number and operations, measurement, and patterns begin to develop during early childhood. In the sections that follow, we illustrate how typical spontaneous play helps children develop, consolidate, and extend their understanding of these and other mathematical concepts.

Geometry

Spatial relationships and basic geometric concepts are just as fundamental to children's understanding of the physical world as numerical concepts. As we observe children's interactions with their surroundings, we find that many of young children's experiences involve spatial relationships; yet, most adults—and mathematics texts—emphasize children's understandings of numerical concepts.

Young children's initial understandings of spatial relationships and knowledge about shapes form a foundation from which more sophisticated geometric concepts can develop as children grow. Young children often explore and play with their spatial environment. As infants, they crawl around and over furniture. Later, they construct mazes with pillows or obstacle courses with chairs. They roll down hills, slick slides, and beanbag chairs. They play with their bodies' shapes as they dance, their round, fluid movements becoming linear and staccato. Perhaps this is the first awareness of spatial relationships—awareness of one's body and its environment. As adults, we see that this fundamental exploration and play involves basic concepts of spatial relationships. These include proximity, enclosed versus open space, vertical versus horizontal movements, and numerous shapes. All these concepts take time to develop, literally from infancy to adulthood.

Proximity. Proximity refers to the closeness or separation between objects. When one object is near another, we can say that it is in close proximity.

> Janet paints a tree right next to the house she has just finished painting. She paints grass around it so that the green fills in the space between the tree and the house. In one spot, the tree almost touches the house. Janet selects a narrower brush that her teacher has made available and carefully traces around the area between the house and the tree. ∅

Vertical and Horizontal.   When something is vertical, it is perpendicular (upright) to the ground or another reference point. When something is horizontal, it is parallel to the ground or another reference point.

> Tomás uses red and blue pegs to make four horizontal rows of alternating colors across the pegboard. He then constructs a brilliant strip of yellow pegs that runs vertically to the bottom of the pegboard. ∅

Shapes.   The concept of shape refers to the form of an object. Children frequently have experiences that involve regular, Euclidian shapes such as triangles, circles, and squares. In this vignette, we see the children collaborating to develop a complex design with hexagons and octagons, and their teacher responding to the children's curiosity by introducing vocabulary so they can discuss their joint activity.

> Together, Nick and Emma stretch rubber bands across the nails of a geoboard, making hexagons and octagons. Noticing the students' interest, their teacher first informally introduces the terms *hexagon* and *octagon*. When the children show interest in these unusual words, he explains the derivation of *hex* (meaning six) and *oct* (meaning eight). He then introduces more advanced pattern cards for the geoboard and suggests that they try making their own cards, as well. ∅

Children also have numerous experiences with irregular or non-Euclidean shapes. For example, 2-year-old Peggie delights in squeezing the light green playdough through her fingers. She then opens her hand and looks at the play dough form in her palm. It certainly is an irregular, though very interesting shape!

Numbers and Operations: Relationships Involving Quantity

"Five little monkeys jumping on the bed. . . ." How many monkeys were jumping? When people think about math, they generally think about relationships involving quantity. When we describe aspects of the physical world, we often use concepts that indicate how much there is ("That's too much milk.") or how many there are ("Six glasses of milk!").

Young children's construction of number concepts involving quantity develops over several years. Before children can truly understand number concepts, they begin to understand the concepts of one-to-one correspondence. They learn number names and to count by rote. They also learn the numerals that represent number concepts and begin to understand the difference between ordinal and cardinal numbers.

Continuous Quantities.   Continuous quantities refer to those objects whose amounts we don't count, like "that's too much milk" "and "that's a little rice." Preschool and kindergarten programs traditionally include materials that foster the exploration of continuous quantities, such as sand, clay, water, and even mud. Many primary-grade teachers also recognize the value of providing these special materials that playful people of all ages enjoy.

Steve takes big handfuls of playdough to make giant hamburgers. He rolls out two large, circular forms, and exclaims, "These buns are still too small," and places the hamburger inside. ∅

Discrete Quantities. These are the objects whose amounts we count, like "seven cookies" or "three grains of rice." Discrete quantities are also called noncontinuous quantities.

In sustained, spontaneous play, Laurie, Sandra, and Marie are jointly exploring a large shell collection. They divide the shells into three sets with 26 shells each. They then begin to classify their sets (e.g., large, multicolored spiral and small, multicolored spiral). Linda, their second-grade teacher, notes that Marie, who is learning English, is participating enthusiastically in this group as well as showing her understanding of the relationships between the supraordinate class, all multicolored spiral shells, and the subordinate classes, large and small multicolored spiral shells. ∅

Estimation. We see young children estimate when they form a judgment of the approximate quantity.

Sandra says they need two big blocks. However, Melinda finds only small ones and returns to Sandra with an armful of five small blocks. ∅

People use estimation processes throughout life to make preliminary judgments and to assess how reasonable an answer might be. For example, a fifth grader estimates that 31 times 33 is about 900. When she calculates that the answer is 10,230, she knows there's an error. In play-centered curricula, children have many opportunities to develop estimation abilities.

Quantifiers. When children are learning to deal with quantities, initial concepts include "some," "fewer," "all," "more," and "none."

Bradley selects all the red pegs. When none are left in the tray, he asks Cheryl if she has any red ones. "No," she answers, "none of these are red." ∅

Equalities and Inequalities. At a young age, children develop the ability to make judgments as to whether two objects or groups are equal or unequal. Indeed, some children seem to spend much of their time focused on whether they have the same quantity of whatever it is that their classmates have.

Steve: "You took more red [playdough] than me."
Karen: "Well, I'm the grandma so I get more."

Seriation. Children often delight in ordering objects according to a common property such as color, shape or size. We see this when children spontaneously line up cars, counters, or other objects by length, height, or even the shade of color (light green to dark green).

A second-grade teacher has worked with the children to create flannel board cutouts of dolls of four different sizes, each having backpacks and objects of corresponding sizes that fit in the backpacks. Some children are intrigued by these multiple seriation problems and create others of their own, such as making cars of different sizes for the dolls to ride. ∅

One-to-One Correspondence.   The understanding of number is complex and includes several concepts. Children's growing understanding of one-to-one correspondence is essential to their understanding of numbers.

In the block area there are farm animals, including horses, cows, and sheep. Craig and Atsmon place four horses on top of the four blocks in front of them. They demonstrate one-to-one correspondence by selecting a set of four horses with the same number of objects as their set of four blocks.

Tomás has placed the red and blue pegs in one-to-one correspondence in two horizontal rows. ∅

Livi and William set the table with five places. In front of each chair, they have placed one placemat, one cup, one spoon, one fork, and one napkin. ∅

Number Names.   Number names are the names we use to represent the number concepts.

♥ Maria tells Jason, "I got three, three buttons." Later, in playing in the housekeeping area, she talks to Rosa in Spanish, "Tengo tres, tres botones." ∅

Rote Counting.   Children first develop the skill to say the names of numbers in correct order before they know the meaning of the number concepts, including, the importance of the order. In rote counting, the order of numbers has no special significance, like the order of letter names when chanting "a, b, c, d. . . ."

While filling a jar with cupfuls of water, Jeremy counts "five, six and seven, eight." (But the words do not correspond to the actions of either filling or pouring the cups.) ∅

Numerals.   Numerals refer to the notation or symbols we use to represent the number concept. The same number concept is represented by *15* and *XV.*

Jeffrey sits outside next to the compact pile of weeds pulled from the garden. He bends a stem into different configurations, exclaiming, "It's a 7. . . . Look, now I put a foot on it and it's a 2!" ∅

One of the girls in Kristin's first-grade class is seated at a desk, working by herself. She draws a picture of a woman with a bubble caption above her head. In the bubble she has printed the numerals in order from 1 to 21. When she notices Kristin looking at the picture, she explains that "she's counting in the picture." Then she begins to draw another picture of a counting lady. ∅

Ordinal Numbers.   Ordinal numbers indicate the place order of the object such as "the third child in line." They answer the question, "Which one?"

Alvin looks at the line forming behind him for turns on the new scooter. "I'm first!" he announces. ∅

Cardinal Numbers.   Cardinal numbers indicate the quantity of the set. They answer the question, "How many?"

Mary turns over a Candy Land game card: "I've got two yellows." ∅

Number Concepts.   When children truly develop concepts of number, they understand the relationships among numbers, for example, eight is "bigger" than seven. They also understand that a set of objects can be rearranged without changing the number of objects in the set.

Tomás: "I need three red ones to fill this line."
Karen: "We don't have three. We just have two. Do you see one more?"

Measurement

In early childhood, children begin to develop an understanding of the many ways in which we take measure of our world. Young children begin by comparing the attributes or properties of objects such as size ("I want the bigger one"), height ("she's taller"), and length ("that's longer"). Kindergartners and primary-grade children are fascinated with measurements that use nonstandard units and enjoy making estimations and approximations: "The school is as long as . . ." "From my house to the school is as long as . . ." "That (block) tower is taller than our teacher!"

Mathematical Processes: Problem Solving, Communication, Connections, and Representation

As the preceding examples show, as they construct their understanding of mathematical concepts, children are actively engaged in mathematical processes. Problem solving is central to mathematics (National Council of Teachers of Mathematics [NCTM], 2010) as it is in science (National Science Teachers Association [NSTA], 2009). For example, as Ricky builds a symmetrical design with attribute blocks, he has to figure out what to add to the left side to match the green triangle and a yellow hexagon he's just placed on the right side. Problem solving is frequently a social

Mathematical knowledge is constructed by acting on objects.

activity in which ideas are represented and communicated to others though pictures, photos, and graphs, as well as numbers and letters. In Chapter 1 we described the activities of Lisa and Peter, who were busy wrapping packages at the post office. They talk about how much paper they needed to cover the package. They need to know not only how to measure, but also to integrate their understanding of numerical and geometric concepts. After several attempts, they figure out how to solve the problem that arose when the sheets of paper were too small.

Problem Solving Is Basic to Mathematics.   The problems children face in their spontaneous play and everyday life situations are their own problems. Perhaps it is their ownership of these problems and the social nature of their play that contributes to the extraordinary competencies that Vygotsky saw in children's play that led him to hypothesize that play leads to development (see Chapter 2.)

MATHEMATICS IN THE EARLY CHILDHOOD INTEGRATED CURRICULUM

Play-centered mathematics curricula are based on the understanding of mathematics as well as the understanding of children's development and interests. Although adults may think about students' learning as occurring in separate subject areas, young children who participate in engaging, inclusive activities experience no such boundary. They don't think of themselves as being in "math land." Instead, they experience involvement in thought processes related to a variety of areas, such as the arts, science, and literacy as well as social interactions with lively communication. This is one important rationale for considering the full continuum of play, from spontaneous play to play in which the more didactic curriculum is recast in children's play.

The Goals of Early Childhood Mathematics Education

In their joint position statement, *Early Childhood Mathematics: Promoting Good Beginnings,* the National Association for the Education of Young Children (NAEYC) and the National Council of Teachers of Mathematics (NCTM; 2002) explain,

> Throughout the early years of life, children notice and explore mathematical dimensions of their world. They compare quantities, find patterns, navigate in space, and grapple with real problems such as balancing a tall block building or sharing a bowl of crackers fairly with a playmate. Mathematics helps children make sense of their world outside of school and helps them construct a solid foundation for success in school. (p. 1)

These national organizations emphasize that we must commit our efforts to supporting children's interests and competencies in mathematics learning, just as we have in literacy, if we are to have successful mathematics programs. In setting goals for mathematics education in early childhood programs, *Early Childhood Mathematics: Promoting Good Beginnings* (2002) includes important recommendations that are consistent with a play-based curriculum. For example:

1. Enhance children's natural interest in mathematics and their disposition to use it to make sense of their physical and social worlds. . . .
2. Provide ample time, materials, and teacher support for children to engage in play, a context in which they explore and manipulate mathematical ideas with keen interest. . . .
3. Build on children's experience and knowledge, including their family, linguistic, cultural, and community backgrounds; their individual approaches to learning; and their informal knowledge. . . .
4. Base mathematics curriculum and teaching practices on knowledge of young children's cognitive, linguistic, physical, and social-emotional development. . . .
5. Introduce mathematical concepts, methods, and language through a range of appropriate experiences and strategies. (pp. 4–7)

The Nature of Mathematics

Mathematical thinking involves dispositions such as curiosity, playful risk taking, and experimentation. When young children think mathematically, they use their developing logical abilities to solve problems.

Mathematics involves all three types of knowledge that Piaget described: physical knowledge, social knowledge, and logical-mathematical knowledge. Mathematical thinking involves physical knowledge because we use mathematics to describe relationships in the real world. For example, we decide to buy 3 pounds of tomatoes at a reasonable price. We select ones that cost $1.29 per pound, estimate the total, and put them in the basket.

Mathematical thinking also involves social knowledge, information we learn directly from others. English-speaking children learn the number name *seven,* just as French-speaking children learn the number name *sept.* Not only do children in different places call numbers, shapes, and mathematical procedures by different names, but this socially constructed knowledge also includes a particular way of seeing the world. For example, most people in the world use the metric system for measurement. Young children learn that their weight is measured in kilograms, the distance to school is measured in kilometers, and the amount of milk in a container is measured in liters. Procedures for arithmetic operations also differ from culture to culture, sometimes based on differences in systems for counting (Ma, 1999).

The basis of mathematics is logical-mathematical thinking because solutions to mathematical problems involve the logical relationships that our mind constructs, rather than the information our senses observe (physical knowledge) or that we obtain from others (social knowledge). As children and later as adults, each of us constructs our own mathematical concepts over time with help or interactions with others and based on our culture and time in history. In this way, children reinvent for themselves what adults and older peers in their social environment already know (Kamii, 1984, 2000, 2003; Kato, Honda, & Kamii, 2006).

What do we mean by logical-mathematical thought?

Sally is taller than Marie. Marie is taller than Melody. Although we've never seen Sally and Melody together, we know that Sally is taller than Melody.

The relationship of Sally's height and Melody's height is a logical relationship that "must be." As adult thinkers, we are certain that Sally is taller than Melody without seeing the physical evidence. We do not have to see Sally, Marie, and Melody standing next to each other. Young children have not yet constructed this logical way of thinking about problems involving height, volume, or area, or even ideas that seem as simple to us as the idea of number (see Chapter 13).

Logical-mathematical thought is the foundation of our understanding of many everyday aspects of the physical world. How many floor tiles do we need to cover the kitchen? How many miles per gallon does our car get? Children also grapple with problems requiring applications of logical-mathematical thought. How many large rectangular blocks do we need to build a ramp so the cars can get off the highway without falling over? How many forks do we need to set the table for four children? Logical relationships are at the heart of all mathematical thinking—all everyday problem solving.

Logical-operational thought does not emerge at once, like a butterfly emerging from a cocoon, but occurs from infancy into adulthood. Like studying the metamorphosis of a butterfly within the cocoon, we can assess evidence of the many small changes in a child's development. (See, for example, Clements & Sarama, 2009; Kamii & Kato, 2006; and the review of the research by Baroody, 2000). Three- to

Table 7.1 Five Logical Mathematical Relationships

Type	Example
1. Classification relationships	"Smocks" vs. "ordinary clothes"
2. Seriation relationships	The "big" vs. the "small" paintbrushes
3. Number relationships	"Three paints at the easel"
4. Spatial relationships	The paint drips down the paper
5. Temporal relationships	Wet paint takes time to dry

Source: Information from "The Development of Logico-mathematical Knowledge in a Block-building Activity at Ages 1–4," by C. Kamii, Y. Miyakawa, and Y. Kato, 2004, *Journal of Research in Childhood Education*, 19(1), p. 46.

5-year-olds might delight in showing that they can arrange four "candles" in multiple ways on the "cake" they have made out of sand and know they still have four (see Table 7.1). Older children attain a more mature understanding when they realize, in this example, that no matter how large the number is, merely rearranging the "candles" does not alter the number.

Geist and Geist (2008) suggested that it is useful to consider mathematical understandings as "emergent," just as we consider the development of literacy. When early childhood educators and other adults attempt to rush the processes of development, young children's lack of a firm foundation can lead to frustration and damaged dispositions not only in preschool and the primary grades but later on as well (e.g., Helm & Katz, 2001). The development of basic concepts such as number sense and abilities such as problem solving is a complex process that takes time and experience. The Joint Position Statement of the NAEYC and the NCTM (2002) emphasizes that teachers of young children must take time to provide a variety of strategies, activities, and materials. If we are to address the needs of all students, we need to provide adequate time for rich experiences that draw on what children already know.

Children often show that they have informal knowledge developed from their everyday experiences rather than from direct mathematics instruction.

> Two girls in Shelley's kindergarten class are playing with a flannel board. There are a dozen flannel pieces for the story. The girls divide them evenly before beginning to make up their own story. They put out one piece for each of them until they both have six. ✺

Throughout the day, young children show that they can use informal strategies to solve problems. Informal knowledge forms the basis of more complete conceptual mastery (e.g., Cameron, Hersch, & Fosnot, 2004; Geist & Geist, 2008; Ginsburg, 2006; Ginsburg, Inoue, & Seo, 1999; Kamii, Miyakawa, & Kato, 2004; Smith 2009; Wallace, Abbott, & Blary, 2007).

Assessing Children's Development of Mathematical Thinking ❤

It is often difficult for teachers to assess the children's understanding of mathematical reasoning, both what they can do on their own and what they can do with the support of others. In their series *Young Mathematicians at Work*, Fosnot and Dolk (2001) emphasized the importance of assessments that take place while children engage in mathematical thinking. Teachers use assessments to make children's thinking processes visible to arrive at valid assessments and make informed curriculum decisions.

This is particularly true when assessing the understandings of English language learners, who face challenges in assessments that require understanding English and providing oral or written responses. Teachers find that varied play-centered assessments, described in Chapter 6, provide insights into all children's use of mathematical reasoning in situations that are relaxed and not stressful.

Sometimes, more formal, teacher-directed assessments are appropriate to complement informal assessments. For example, when a child understands that a given number of objects can be rearranged and that a change in the arrangement does not result in a change in number, the child is able to conserve number. The ability to conserve is fundamental to a true understanding of number.

> Amy is a student in Leni's first-grade class. She can draw the numeral *9* under the circle with nine ducks. When Leni asks her to show with her fingers "how many" nine is, Amy counts on her fingers from one to nine and holds up nine fingers. At first glance, it seems that "nineness" is a concept that Amy understands.
>
> Leni models her assessment on one of Piaget's procedures (Piaget, 1965a). She places a pile of pennies on the table. She then selects nine pennies and places them in a row. Leni asks Amy to take pennies from the pile and make a new row that will have the same number of pennies as Leni's row. Amy does this easily. Next Leni moves the pennies so they are closer together than Amy's row. She asks Amy whether they now have the same number of pennies or whether she or Amy has more.
>
> Amy replies without hesitation: "I have more pennies because my row is longer." ✍

Although Amy can count and recognize the numerals used in mathematical recording, she does not completely understand the concept of number. Young children like Amy rely on their perceptions of how things look. Amy might be able to tell us that when four pennies are rearranged, four pennies are still present. However, when the number is too large to grasp perceptually, she becomes confused. When nine pennies are rearranged, she looks at the two groups to determine which group looks bigger. Answers to problems involving logic are not "out there" in the physical world through better observation. Amy must use logic to construct the answer that rearranging the pennies does not change the total number of pennies.

Block play supports mathematical thinking.

In time, Amy will master the concept that "the number nine" refers to a relationship among objects that remains stable, even when the arrangement of the nine objects changes. Children's abilities to understand these logical relationships between objects develop during the primary grades.

Assessments of children's abilities need not be as formal as the example just given. As we discussed in Chapter 6, ongoing, formative, informal assessment, particularly observations of young children's play, provides teachers with the information they need to respond to the needs of each child. Anecdotal records can provide detailed narrative portrayals of how children explain what they understand as well as what they do. Many teachers are augmenting anecdotal records with digital photos or video documentation of children's spontaneous and guided play. Checklists help teachers get a quick overview of a single child's progress or the progress of all children in the class. Teachers can use portfolios to keep samples of children's work. For example, children may select samples of patterns they have made across the year. We recommend that a mix of varied approaches is the most useful strategy for both formative and summative assessment as well as useful communication with parents.

Mathematics Education Based on the Nature of Mathematics, Children's Development, and Children's Interests

A play-centered mathematics education is based on an understanding of mathematics and of children's development and interests. *Early Childhood Mathematics: Promoting Good Beginnings,* the Joint Position Statement of the NAEYC and the NCTM (2002), emphasizes the importance of providing "ample time, materials, and teacher support for children to engage in play, a context in which they explore and manipulate mathematical ideas with keen interest" (p. 4). This joint statement recommends that high-quality education programs for young children build on children's individual and cultural experiences and foster their interest in making sense of their world.

PLAY AND DAILY LIFE SITUATIONS: TWO CORNERSTONES OF EARLY CHILDHOOD EDUCATION MATHEMATICS PROGRAMS

We think that play and daily life situations are the cornerstones of mathematics education in early childhood. A mathematics program centered on play and daily life situations can be a vital dimension of partnerships with parents, particularly because most parents recognize the importance of children's developing competencies in mathematics. Teachers and parents can share examples of how play and daily life situations can foster play and mathematical thinking at school and at home.

Play: A Cornerstone of Mathematics Education

Purposeful opportunities for spontaneous, guided, and teacher-initiated play provide numerous possibilities for children to use their emerging logical-mathematical abilities. Some play situations are children's own reconstructions of events in daily life: setting the table in the housekeeping area so that everyone will have one of each utensil or making playdough hamburgers that are "just as big" so no one will complain. When the children in Pat's kindergarten class begin to play "gas station," they talk about how much gas they need and how much it costs as an extension of their play with trikes and wagons.

Play has two characteristics not always found in everyday life situations that offer further advantages. First, play is flexible. Situations from everyday life sometimes have a single solution, but problems encountered in play more often have many possible solutions and provide the opportunity to "wander over the mathematical landscape."

Second, play involves children in problems of their own choosing. In play, as the joint NAEYC and NCTM statement (2002) points out, children explore mathematical ideas with "keen interest." We believe that children's interests are heightened when they, themselves, select both the content and the level of difficulty. When children are engaged in problems of their own choosing it is more likely that they are working within their own zone of proximal development.

> Four-year-old Miriam discovered yesterday that she could make smaller triangles within the larger triangles she constructed on a geoboard. Today she is using colored rubber bands and four geoboards combined to make a square and is "going to town on triangles," Mrs. Ward, a participating parent, reports. Miriam's play with the geoboards illustrates how she integrates and extends her mathematical understanding through play. ✇

> In Susan's kindergarten class, some children carefully count out stamps, "take money, and make change." They write numerals in the receipt book. Susan notes that other children simply take the letters, stamp them, and put them in the box. ✇

Games with rules are one form of play that DeVries, Kamii, and others strongly recommend as experiences that encourage the use of logical-mathematical thinking. *Young Children Reinvent Arithmetic* (Kamii, 2000) provides an account of how, through collaborative research, Kamii works with teachers to develop math curriculum based on group games and situations from everyday life. It includes a chapter by DeClark that chronicles her change from a teacher who relied on direct instruction and worksheets to one who advocates a game-centered curriculum. In *Developing Constructivist Early Childhood Curriculum*, Hildebrandt and Zan (DeVries, Zan, Hildebrandt, Edmaiston, & Sales, 2002) described vividly how group games help children take the perspective of others because they must understand and play by rules others have proposed.

Daily Life Situations: A Second Cornerstone of Mathematics Education

Daily life situations provide opportunities for children to make sense of their world and to develop mathematical understandings informally within the context of their own lives and the lives of people in their community. This now-classic principle of John Dewey is emphasized by many math educators. As children encounter and try to solve problems in daily life that involve logical-mathematical thinking, they realize that as their understanding grows, they will become better at solving problems that matter to them, not simply problems on a worksheet.

As children enter the kindergarten classroom each day, Theresa places a survey at the front door, allowing children to "vote" on different classroom decisions for the day, like whether to have snack inside or out. A few weeks after this classroom routine had begun, Ila and Erin began taking "surveys" of their classmates' preferences, using classroom clipboards, scratch papers, and tally marks to query friends about their favorite color or their favorite place to play at school. ✄

In *Young Investigators: The Project Approach in the Early Years,* Helm and Katz (2001) include a wonderful example of a fire truck project that drew on the spontaneous interests of many children. As the project developed, the children were involved in such activities as making a map of the fire station and counting the fire truck's doors and ladders. They mirrored their understandings in their own construction, using materials such as blocks and Legos. Through experiences such as these, children come to regard math as something that "happens in your head," rather than as the mindless repetition of drills and worksheets.

Supporting Children from All Cultures and Children Who Are English Language Learners

Today as in the past, we see that laws that ensure an appropriate and free education to all have not yet led to equal education. Consistently, national and state statistics show that school success in mathematics is less typical of children who live in poverty and who are members of linguistic and ethnic minority groups (e.g., see the NAEYC and the NCTM Joint Position Statement, 2002). The vignettes discussed throughout this chapter show that an inclusive play-centered curriculum addresses the needs of children from diverse backgrounds, cultures, and who speak a language other than English.

> Marie, an English language learner, plays with Laurie, and Sandra, and her teacher observes the ease with which she participates with her peers who speak only English. They are examining and sorting a large collection of shells, a gift from Marie's cousins. Marie first makes two groups: larger shells and smaller shells. She sorts the shells in the group of large shells into what she calls "more shiny" and "not shiny." She sorts the small shells in the same way. Her teacher notices that Marie demonstrates her understanding of relationships among the supraordinate classes of shells—pointing out to her friends the two groups that are "not shiny." ✆

The Joint Statement of NAEYC and NCTM (2002) provides guidance regarding the developmental appropriateness of standards as well as guidelines for connecting current and future expectations. This is in keeping with practice that is developmentally, culturally, and individually appropriate. The statement underscores the importance of building on the experiences and knowledge that children bring to school from their family and community cultures. The concept of the play continuum, from spontaneous play to guided play to teacher-directed play, as well as the principles related to orchestrating children's play, is the basis for principles that promote inclusiveness and equity in mathematics as in all areas.

The Environment.   Play is the cornerstone of logical-mathematical thinking. Even though logical-mathematical thinking is central to many disciplines, mathematics is a specific discipline with a specific vocabulary. Although most early childhood educators pay careful attention to opportunities for supporting literacy, mathematics education may not be an important program focus for all students in all programs. It is critical to assess the curriculum carefully, lest we discover that by assuming that "math is everywhere," we find instead that "math is nowhere."

First, we can make sure that we intentionally orchestrate the play-centered curriculum to promote rich mathematical experiences for all children. As indicated in Chapter 4, this includes attention to providing time, space, and materials so that children can become deeply engaged in activities that support mathematical thinking.

Consistent efforts to promote equity lead teachers to reexamine the environment to ensure that multiple possibilities for mathematical thinking as well as the use of mathematical language are everywhere. Are graduated containers provided for measuring and pouring in several areas? Are instruments for measuring, such as calculators, rulers, and scales, accessible? Are materials such as blocks and manipulatives organized so that differences in size and shape are readily apparent? What accommodations may be needed? For example, are numerals and shapes large enough for children with visual impairments to see clearly?

How is space organized? Are there places for children to play alone in quiet spaces, with peers, and in small groups? A table at the math center permits children to work in small groups and provides a consistent, defined space for teacher-directed mathematics activities.

Culturally Relevant Mathematics. Ensign (2003) introduced the concept of culturally relevant mathematics, especially in urban schools. How can the classroom mirror aspects of the community? For example, could we make signs in children's home languages for the dramatic play, block, or outdoor areas that are similar to signs in the community? Are there photos of familiar places in the community? In addition to numerous books that illustrate numbers and shapes, can children who are learning English as a second language also turn to books with pictures or simple but interesting texts that follow a sequence of events? As we have mentioned, it is also essential that we use assessments that reveal the abilities and understandings of children who are learning English. Informal and formal assessments of mathematics usually have a strong language component so that all English language learners are at a disadvantage, even those gifted in mathematics.

Considerations for Teacher-Initiated Activities. Mathematics in a play-centered curriculum includes teacher-initiated activities as part of the continuum. In some programs, we might consider a special area designated for mathematics. Based on her observations in numerous classrooms, Scales (2000) noted that few preschool classrooms had areas designated for mathematics, as they did for literacy and science. In addition to an environment where math happens "everywhere," teachers can consider a designated "math happens here" area. Scales and her colleagues emphasize that many preschool programs lacked a mathematics curriculum that can result in "hidden disparities in informal math learning." In such programs, teachers might not assess children's development of spatial reasoning and numeracy and might not consistently support children's development in these areas.

Supporting Children with Special Needs

A commitment to equity does not mean that we always respond by maximizing direct teacher instruction for children who are not learning number concepts or operations as quickly as their peers. How can we address children's strengths as well as their needs?

Eight-year-old Brendt has a keen eye for symmetry and yet experiences developmental delays in many areas. He has spent several days cutting squares and triangles of various colors and sizes, using large, beginners' scissors. He carefully places them on the large mosaic he is constructing, exploring the relationships between shapes and sizes by superimposing the triangles on the squares.

Inclusive mathematics curricula address the wide range of children's needs (Ginsburg, 2006; Smith, 2009). For example, some children have disabilities related to mathematics, such as disabilities with calculations (*developmental dyscalculia*); those who understand mathematical concepts but have limited language ability; those with developmental delays; and children with auditory and visual impairments. Last, it is important for teachers to be skilled observers so that children's special needs and individual interests in the area of mathematics can be identified during the early years.

Children's Interests

Throughout this book, we have discussed children's interests in the play materials found in traditional early education programs, such as clay, blocks, manipulatives, sand, and water. In this chapter, we see that children are often actively engaged in mathematics when it might have appeared that they were doing something else. In a rich, play-centered curriculum, children develop mathematical understandings in all areas of the environment and all times of the day. Art materials lend themselves to explorations of geometry and arithmetic. If we listen closely, much of the conversation in the dramatic play area involves math in some way. We see children count out plates for the table, count out money at the store, seriate teddy bears by size, and measure cups of sand for a pretend soup. Though teachers have often thought of mathematics as part of the "indoors" curriculum, teachers of young children can promote the playful development of both informal and formal mathematical concepts outdoors (see Chapter 12).

> In a community near the ocean, 3-year-old Nicky and 2-year-old Schyler are playing outside on a wooden boat. While Jo, their teacher, rocks their vessel, the children sing "Row, row, row your boat." They finish the song by counting, "one, two, three, we all fall out!" Laughing and tumbling out, they quickly board the ship to play again. ✄

Also reflected in children's play is their desire to learn about the adult world and to understand the things adults do. We see this when they play house or store or pretend to read or write because they are in a literate environment. Similarly, their interest in numbers is shown when they use calculators when playing store, yardsticks to measure a block structure, or telephones and computers when playing office, thus reflecting their life in a number-literate environment. Young children also want to learn about serious issues in the adult world, many of which have an aspect that is mathematical in nature. Even young children hear adult conversations about the economy, the price of gas, or homelessness. In "Mathematics and Social Justice in Grade 1," Murphy (2009) describes how a discussion of *The Rabbits*, a children's book about Australia and the inequities of power between native peoples and Europeans settling in Australia, lead to activities in his first-grade class in which children spent many days using Cuisenaire rods in their efforts to represent these power relationships.

A long number line allows children to think about quantity in many modalities.

ORCHESTRATING PLAY IN MATHEMATICS

The general guidelines for setting up the physical environment and developing schedules of routines presented in Chapter 4 apply to our specific concerns about setting up an environment that fosters the development of mathematics, particularly logical-mathematical thinking.

Setting the Stage

How is the physical space arranged? Do the children have room to work on block constructions without constant interruptions from others in a crowded space? Should the small wood table be located near the water table so children can have a place for their assortment of measuring cups and containers?

Are sufficient materials available that will allow children to explore with shapes and number concepts as they play? For example, are blocks of many kinds available? Is an adequate quantity of differently shaped unit blocks set out for creating diverse structures? Are there several kinds of table blocks, such as pattern blocks, attribute blocks, Construx, and Lego blocks? Different types of clay provide opportunities for children to explore non-Euclidean shapes. Pattern boards, tangrams, and pattern blocks give children experiences with Euclidean shapes that they can also use to sort. The multitudes of peg-type manipulatives give children chances to think about quantity as well as patterns.

The sandbox and the water table are sometimes neglected areas stocked with cast-off materials and odd containers. Although it is useful to have containers of different shapes, it is also important to provide graduated sets. A measuring set with a quart pitcher, a pint pitcher, a cup pitcher, a half-cup pitcher, and measuring spoons of differing amounts gives children a chance to explore equivalencies. As Murray

(2001) points out, "If we are to make math experiential, we must present children with tactile tools with which they can learn, opportunities to interact with each other and the teacher, and diverse methods of arriving at the correct answer" (p. 29).

Time considerations are important here as in all aspects of play. How long do children have to work uninterrupted? What are the rules about leaving a Lego construction overnight? What should be done about Cindy, a student with special needs who tends to need close supervision after 15 minutes in the block area? And if Jonny has been working intently on his Lego construction for 20 minutes, must he stop because it is his turn to make an apple snack?

Accessorizing: Transforming the Environment to Extend and Enrich Play

Virginia observed that block play in her classroom had settled into a routine after 5 weeks. At the beginning, she enjoyed the great variety of construction. Now she wondered whether things had gotten into a rut. Day after day, block play involved building ramps and racing. The same boys tended to play in the same groups with the same repetitive themes. When car racing first came into vogue, several girls were involved, and the ramps had become more complex each day. This was no longer the case.

Rather than intervene directly through out-of-play suggestions or through entering and redirecting the play, Virginia decided to experiment with accessories placed near the blocks. She placed a box of toy people and animals on the block shelves. This brought several children, including several girls, back to the block area. New themes evolved. The castlelike structures that had been built during the first few days reemerged. The car races even seemed more complex, with drivers and teams. ∅

Pat decided to use an explicit approach to include measurement with her kindergartners. Three of the children riding trikes had appropriated a hose to play gas station. Pat asked them what other things a gas station had and what they could use. Within a few days, the drivers were busy adding measured oil, checking tire pressure, and pumping gallons of gas. ∅

Accessorizing is a playful activity for teachers as well as for children. All parts of the environment can be enriched further to stimulate mathematical thinking. This not only helps children acquire mathematical abilities within a meaningful context but also helps them apply their skills and abilities in numerous situations. What can we add to the housekeeping area? Are measuring spoons, food cans of different sizes, and silverware settings for six or eight available? Dramatic play accessory boxes can be assembled easily. What is needed to play store? Post office? Bank? Office? What can be added to support mathematics learning and foster social interactions in ways that support the inclusion of all children? In programs where all children and their families feel welcome, their ideas for making connections between home and school enrich the curriculum.

Play-Generated Curricula

Children's play in a rich environment leads to curricular innovations that are more challenging and sophisticated than most traditional curricula. Martine is building a *pyramid* of cubes. Stevie needs another *cylindrical* block. Many preschool and primary standards and benchmarks include problem solving that goes well beyond identifying and naming the basic two-dimensional Euclidean shapes: triangle, circle, square, and rectangle. As experienced block builders, sand castle designers, and artists, children have the background to support a much more sophisticated mathematical vocabulary. Furthermore, as these examples illustrate, children have a need to use these terms in their daily activities.

Ideas for numerous activities and extended curriculum units that relate to mathematics and address standards arise through careful observation and reflection on children's play. (See Murphey & Burns, 2003; Copley, 2000; Ginsburg, 2006; Sarama & Clements, 2006; Seefeldt & Galper, 2004; Smith, 2009.)

> After discovering that the "car racers" were fascinated with measuring, Virginia developed a unit on measurement that addressed state curriculum benchmarks such as using nonstandard and standard units of measurement and mathematical processes such as communication and problem solving. She introduced a measured roadway for cars, which she marked with colored paper. She then removed the paper and introduced nonstandard units such as Popsicle sticks, knots on a string, and Unifix cubes, along with standard measuring units such as rulers, yardsticks, and the popular tape measure. Based on her observations of children's play and her knowledge of children's interests, she included activities that reflected children's fascination with the minuscule and the gigantic, from tiny sprouting radish seeds to measuring the length of the playground. Many children spontaneously wrote about measuring in their journals, reflecting their interest in numeracy as well as literacy. ✄

> Pat decided to extend her kindergartners' gas station play by including the gas station in her school's social studies curriculum, "our neighbors." Pat's emergent curriculum built on their interests. Pat was able to explain to parents and administrators how this project addressed standards because of her knowledge of the state's mathematics and social science frameworks and standards.

> The children discussed their own experiences at gas stations. Many shared vivid memories—cars breaking down and being fixed, getting stuck on the highway with flat tires, tales of stolen cars, and accidents. These were important communications, and the storytellers received serious attention and sympathy from their classmates. The children then drew and wrote about these experiences in their journals. A trip to the school's library resulted in a great assortment of books about vehicles and transportation.

> Pat then arranged for a tour of the local gas station. The children saw where the big gas truck pumped the gas into the underground tanks. They first estimated, then asked the truck driver, how many gallons were in the tank.

The garage mechanic showed them different tools. Many, like wrenches, came in graduated sizes. He demonstrated how he measured the oil and how he used a funnel when he added oil. ✇

Play-generated curriculum forges critical links between math, literacy, and science. The article, "Reading in Math Class: Selecting and Using Picture Books for Math Investigations," recommends that teachers select books that include meaningful math connections and stimulate children's sense of wonder (Thatcher, 2001). It is our view that books that relate to the children's interests, as shown in their play, are particularly powerful. Kroll and Halaby (1997) remind us that children not only read to learn mathematics but write to learn mathematics as well.

Curriculum-Generated Play

Children consolidate and extend the experiences they have in their math education program through their spontaneous play. As we have shown, teachers can consciously create bridges from mathematics programs that address standards when they provide and create environments that support playful activities. This presents a serious challenge, however, when the curriculum involves adopted texts or dittos that rush from topic to topic. This results in an emphasis on memorization rather than the approach taken by the NCTM. When the mathematics curriculum involves children interacting with each other to address real problems, both children and adults find numerous bridges to play. (See, for example, Clements & Sarama, 2009; Copley, Jones, & Dighe, 2007; De Vries et al., 2002; Eisenhouer & Feikes, 2009; Ginsburg, 2006; Griffin, 2004; Kamii, 2000; Sarama & Clements, 2009; Seefeldt & Galper, 2004; Smith, 2009.)

The number and scope of early childhood mathematics curriculum projects is growing. Projects include "Making Sense" (Richardson, 2004); the *Berkeley Math Readiness Project* (see Klein & Starkey, 2004); "Number Worlds" (Griffin, 2004); *Building Blocks,* a technology-based curriculum (Clements & Sarama, 2007a); *Big Math for Little Kids* (Greenes, Ginsburg, & Balfanz, 2004); and a language-arts-based supplementary program focused on the development of spatial sense (Casey, 2004).

When providing an environment with the basics for rich play, accessories can be chosen that relate to specific aspects of math curriculum goals, including the focal points, standards, and benchmarks defined by the teacher, district, state department of education, or national organizations like the NCTM. As in all other subject areas, teachers can promote curriculum-generated play by ensuring that a wide selection of materials that promote mathematics activities is available during choice time

Souvanna has been working with her second- and third-grade students to put together several boxes with materials for playing store. They decided on a post office, a grocery store, and a computer store kit. Souvanna makes sure that students have multiple opportunities to practice adding, subtracting, and multiplication by including scales, timers, calculators and computers, and student-made pads of sales slips. ✇

According to her state and district's kindergarten math curriculum, Marilyn is expected to teach rote counting and recognition of numerals from 1 to 20. She also decides to experiment with turning the dramatic play area into a store. In addition to a balance scale, she is lucky to find an old hanging scale. She includes a Bates stamp with numbers that the children can rotate and change. She has several hand calculators and an old adding machine borrowed from a third-grade teacher. She also includes tubs of small objects, like Unifix cubes, that can be sold. She is delighted to find that she now has a use for out-of-date coupons and the weekly ads from local supermarkets. The pictures and the numbers make the messages understandable for kindergartners. The store is now open for business! On opening day, workers and customers discover that Marilyn has forgotten an important component: They need money. This leads to a group project of making bills and coins. ∅

THE EARLY CHILDHOOD EDUCATION MATHEMATICS CURRICULUM: PRINCIPLES, STANDARDS, AND FOCAL POINTS

In 2000, the first national conference was held that addressed the issue of standards for prekindergarten and kindergarten mathematics education. The goal of the conference was to bring leaders in early childhood mathematics together "to help those responsible for framing and implementing early childhood mathematics standards" (Clements & Sarama, 2004, p. xi).

One outcome of the conference was a series of recommendations for early policy makers and leaders. The first recommendation for the area of Learning and Teaching relates to the central role of play: "Mathematical experiences for very young children should build largely upon their play and the natural relationships between learning and life in their daily activities, interests, and questions" (Clements & Sarama, 2004, p. x).

Since that initial conference, national associations of teachers, mathematicians, and researchers have issued guidelines, recommendations, and reports to guide teachers as we develop coherent curricula. During the past decade, the NCTM has attempted to address teachers' concerns by crafting articulated principles, standards, and focal points.

Principles

The NCTM and the NAEYC Joint Position Statement (2002) articulates six guiding principles to guide practice that are key considerations in discussions of focal points, standards, and assessment:

1. Equity: Excellence requires equally high expectations and strong support for all students.
2. Curriculum: A curriculum must be coherent, focused on important mathematics, and well articulated across the grades.
3. Teaching: Effective teaching requires understanding of what students know and need to learn and then challenging and supporting them to learn it well.

4. Learning: Students must learn mathematics with understanding, actively building new knowledge from experience and prior knowledge.

5. Assessment: Assessment should support the learning of important mathematics and furnish useful information to both teachers and students.

6. Technology: Technology is essential to teaching and learning mathematics; it influences the mathematics that is taught and enhances students' learning (pp. 2–3).

Standards for Student Learning

In 2000, NCTM published *Principles and Standards for School Mathematics*, which addresses the questions: What should students learn? When should they learn it? The standards can be understood as a well-articulated, coherent framework that answers these questions with "big ideas" to guide curriculum across grades, rather than lengthy, unrelated lists of what students should know. NCTM describes five content standards and five process standards for student learning for preschool, kindergarten, and through 12th grade. (See the NCTM Web site for numerous resources and publications for educators, including thorough explanations and illustrations of principles and standards for children at all levels. Resources for parents are also available.)

As Table 7.2 shows, all the vignettes in this chapter can be used to illustrate the ways that play-centered curriculum addresses both content and process standards.

Table 7.2   Addressing Mathematics Standards in the Play-Centered Curriculum

Examples of Content Standards	Vignette
Numbers & Operations	
Learners apply kindergarten mathematics to solve problems that connect everyday experiences in and out of school.	Marilyn has turned the dramatic play area into a store. The children select food to buy, decide on the quantity they need, count out "money," and make change.
Geometry	
Learners identify, name, and create common two-dimensional shapes in the environment and play situations.	Using the colored rubber bands near the geoboard, Nick and Emma make multiple hexagonal and octagonal shapes.
Measurement	Pat's kindergarten students pretend to measure oil, check tire pressure, and pump gallons of gas as they play in the gas station she has helped them create.
Examples of Process Standards	
Problem Solving	
Learners make decisions about how to identify and solve problems.	In their play, Lisa and Peter estimate the amount of paper they need to wrap the package to mail to Lisa's grandmother.
Communication	Laurie, Sandra, and Marie talk about what they're doing as they divide a shell collection into three sets of 26.

NCTM Curriculum Focal Points

Whereas standards address the question: "What should students learn?" curriculum focal points address the question: "What should teachers teach?" NCTM's 2006 publication, *Curriculum Focal Points for Prekindergarten through Grade 8 Mathematics*, represents the Council's continued effort to identify the most important considerations, the "big ideas" for teaching mathematics curricula that are intentional, coherent, and comprehensive.

The curriculum focal points closely track the key curriculum standards for students. NCTM (2006) identifies three curriculum focal points for students in prekindergarten, kindergarten, and the primary grades:

- Number and operations
- Geometry
- Measurement

As teachers examine their own teaching and students' problem solving, communication, and mathematical reasoning, they become aware of important connections to other aspects of mathematical thinking. In addition, NCTM identifies three "Connections to the Focal Points" that relate to and interconnect with the three focal points, "giving them additional depth and breadth. For instance, the Number and Operations Connections asks children to apply the knowledge from the three Focal Points in solving problems" (Clements & Sarama, 2008, p. 364).

Research Findings Support Key Standards and Focal Points: The National Research Council's 2009 Report of the Committee on Early Childhood

Mathematics in Early Childhood Education, Paths toward Excellence and Equity presents an analysis of 20 years of research (Cross, Woods, & Schweingruber, 2009). The committee found that "the potential for most (young children) to learn mathematics in the early years of school is not currently realized" (p. 1). The major recommendation is consistent with key standards and focal points: mathematics for young children should focus on (a) number concepts and (b) spatial relationships, geometry, and measurement. This finding is consistent with the emphasis we place on play and daily life experiences as the cornerstones of the early childhood curriculum, complemented with developmentally appropriate early childhood education mathematics curricula.

Standards, Expectations, and Professional Expertise

In speaking with teachers, we continually hear concerns about state and district interpretations of state standards and also about high-stakes, standardized assessment tests for young children. In our examination of state standards, we found that problem solving and computational skills as used in daily life were embedded in the written standards. Many schools and districts, however, encourage teachers to address math standards mainly through drill worksheets that are unrelated to the contexts of daily life. This is one example of how the implementation of standards, rather than the learning standards or curriculum focal points themselves, can be developmentally inappropriate.

What can teachers do? *Early Childhood Mathematics: Promoting Good Beginnings* (NAEYC & NCTM, 2002) emphasizes the importance of educators and families being key participants in decisions:

> The process of developing and reviewing early learning standards involves multiple stakeholders. Stakeholders may include community members, families, early childhood educators and special educators, and other professional groups. In all cases, those with specific expertise in early development and learning must be involved. (p. 7)

Early childhood educators have great expertise to contribute to the dialogue and decisions about developmentally appropriate practices in mathematics education.

SUMMARY AND CONCLUSION

Marilyn's and Virginia's curriculum development flows from the formal math curriculum implemented in their districts to guided and spontaneous play, and back to the development of math curricula activities related to play. This flow is characteristic of integrated and appropriate early childhood education mathematics curricula. When early childhood environments provide opportunities for play with blocks and materials such as clay, sand, and water, children develop and consolidate mathematical concepts as they play. The centrality of play in quality mathematics programs for young children is recommended by the national associations for teachers of young children and teachers of mathematics. We can observe activities in which children deal with spatial concepts such as proximity, symmetry, Euclidean shapes, and non-Euclidean shapes; with concepts of measurement such as area, volume, and weight; and with relationships involving number, classification, and patterns.

Children think mathematically as they use their developing logical abilities to solve the real problems that confront them in play. In solving their own problems, children develop an appreciation for the usefulness of mathematics.

Teachers then can extend play activities into the more formal curriculum. The play-centered curriculum provides the conceptual framework to address mathematics curriculum focal points and standards in an integrated, developmentally appropriate manner. In programs that provide a balanced continuum from child-initiated to teacher-initiated activities, we find children who bring energy, joy, and imagination to their own relationships with mathematics.

Language, Literacy, and Play

At Patrick's school, "story playing" is a regular activity. Daily, children have the option to dictate a "story play" to a teacher. Later, it will be enacted by their friends during circle time. Three-year-old Patrick has attended his school for only 2 weeks. He has not yet made friends with anyone. He spends most of his time near his teachers, where he has observed the story play dictation frequently, but has not yet dictated a story of his own.

An important breakthrough happens when Patrick quietly tells the teacher he has a story to tell. His first story dictated, he is assured it will be enacted at circle time.

At circle time, Patrick is invited to the "stage" (a taped rectangle on the rug). He shyly steps forward. Patrick's story is "I have lots of friends." He picks himself to be one of his friends, along with Margaret and Barbara (two teachers). His teacher begins to read Patrick's story.

> *Teacher:*   Now, listen to what Patrick's story said. "I have THOSE friends."
> Who wants to be THOSE friends? If Patrick points to you, come
> right on the stage. All right, Patrick, pick someone who has a
> hand raised. All right, Sophia, you were picked. Who else?

With the teacher's active assistance, Patrick chooses Mary, Ian, and Catherine.

> *Teacher:*   Good! All right, now, those are THOSE friends. Now the last part
> of Patrick's story is "I have THESE friends." If you want to be
> THESE friends, raise your hand and Patrick will pick. Patrick,
> would you like to pick Kelly? You want Felix to be one of THESE
> friends? All right, Felix, you're one of THESE friends.

Patrick then picks Nathan, who comes on stage, and then follows with Jessica and Sam.

> *Teacher:*   Now, Patrick, you've got THESE friends and THOSE friends. What
> would you like them to do?

Looking at the piano just outside the circle, Patrick says, "Play piano."

> *Teacher:*   Good, all Patrick's friends are piano players. ✄

What an important day for 3-year-old Patrick! Not only has his story launched him as a member of a community of "storytellers," but it has also established him as a person who, having started with only two friends, his teachers, now has new friends, his peers. For sure, Patrick will be chosen to have a part in the plays of others.

Patrick's story playing is guided-play, in which the teacher's presence, comments, and questions serve to scaffold learning. Patrick's teacher has supported his first tentative effort to engage in a responsive dialogue with others. Participation in the story play activity leads children to an early awareness that language contains within it the expectations of a responsive "other." Patrick must tell his listeners what to do. With their response, his own sense of self within a social world will grow (Bahktin, 2000; Richner & Nicolopoulou, 2001).

LITERACY BEGINS

Literacy is commonly defined as reading and writing. Current thinking, however, has expanded this view to include a broader range of kinds of literacies, such as digital and visual literacy, as well as musical literacy, cultural literacy, and so on. The acquisition of literacy reflects family and cultural values and is affected by the context in which it emerges. Despite the ambiguity of its definition, the achievement of literacy is considered to be a necessity not only for academic success, but also for the acquisition in life of what Bourdieu (2006) has referred to as cultural capital, which leads to economic well-being, status, and power. The view taken in this chapter is that literacy, particularly for young children, arises from the child's early and strong motivation to communicate desires, needs, feelings, and what they are beginning to know about the world to others. Children, as well as adults, communicate in a variety of forms—verbal, nonverbal, gestural—that are shaped by cultural, ethnic, and family conventions and patterns (Cook-Gumperz, 1986; Erickson, 2004; Genishi & Dyson, 2009; Heath & Mangiola, 1991).

Play provides the motivating context for the "literate behaviors" that precede the development of more specific literacy skills. Literate behaviors have numerous forms of expression, both verbal and nonverbal, that fulfill the fundamental purpose of communicating the child's needs, interests, and desires. For the young child, these larger purposes of language provide the motivation and framework for later literacy development (Heath & Mangiola, 1991). Taking a broad sociocultural perspective derived from Vygotsky (1962), we see language and literacy being constructed not solely in a dyadic mentoring relationship with the teacher, but also from the collective resources of families and the classroom (Heath & Mangiola, 1991).

PLAY, LANGUAGE, AND LITERATE BEHAVIOR: A NATURAL PARTNERSHIP

In play-centered programs, communication through gesture, action, talk, and written symbols supports both play and literacy everywhere, from the library corner and the language arts center to the sand table and the dress-up corner. This opportunity to communicate allows children to establish a theme in play and a role for themselves in that play. Signs, even when not legible to everyone, can label things, allocate turns, and designate a territory.

For example, children communicate through talking to themselves in solitary play and to their peers in social play. Noah is talking to himself at the easel—"Now

Many children spontaneously read in a print-rich environment.

there is blue, blue, and now white"—thus, schooling himself in the creation of a new color. Or, as Maria answers Juan, "I know what to do to help make a tunnel! You have to dig another hole." Children also create and share imaginary worlds and participate in the beginnings of narratives. Lizzy, whose mother is ill, wants to play hospital. She needs to communicate and use language to get the play going, attract other actors, and carry out the theme. Additionally, language makes such collaboration in play possible and facilitates the development of "friendship." Patrick had just two friends before he dictated his "I have lots of friends" story, but a whole classroom of buddies thereafter.

Collaborative activities with others enhances the complexity of play by deepening, lengthening, and diversifying play forms. For example, Lizzy's hospital starts with one ward, but it expands as the children pursue the theme to include everything from an operating room to an eye clinic, a pharmacy, and an ambulance unit.

The partnership of play and language also supports the development of children who are English language learners. Through her interest in the class's story play activity, Russian-speaking Masha communicates her desire to play with others and rapidly acquires English skills in this motivating context. Lastly, language in play enables children to share and exchange their knowledge about literacy skills. For example, in the social context of one first-grade classroom, children are encouraged to exchange ideas spontaneously and share what they know about writing during their regular "Booklet Writing Time." In this way, not only the teacher, but also classmates are resources for language learning.

Communication as a Prerequisite for Play with Others

In spontaneous play with peers, children recast their knowledge of the world in terms that are compatible with their interests, competencies, and levels of cognitive, social, and affective development. Play in the home corner is not simply a copy of what "mommies and daddies" do, nor is such play merely the children's attempt to repeat stories that have been read to them or seen on television.

Spontaneously created play narratives are occasions for children to share and develop a sense of "topic" and "sequence"—the basic elements of written texts. In such collaborative literate behaviors, a topic and an ordered sequence are coordinated with play partners, thereby successfully maintaining the narrative thread of a cohesive interaction (Corsaro, 1997; Jaworski & Coupland, 2006).

> Jelani, playing at a sand tray, initiates the topic of "saving freezing bunnies" by hiding several miniature bunnies in a "safe sand mountain." Cody stays on topic by sprinkling dry sand over the mount, exclaiming, "It's raining, it's raining." He has followed with an appropriate sequence of activity and expanded the initial topic as the two collaboratively construct a theme in their play discourse. ✆

In this vignette, Jelani and Cody verbally coordinated their constructive and dramatic play. Nonverbal expression, however, also contributes to and often provides the communication needed for shared spontaneous action sequences. Tag, chase, or superhero games immediately come to mind. One child sounds familiar superhero music, and others take up the theme. Soon a highly coordinated activity of swooping or "flying" gets underway.

Other nonverbal initiation of topic and sequencing actions occurs in such settings as the home play corner, where the function of the props is familiar to many of the children. For example, when Josh brought the laundry basket to Amanda, who had just picked up the iron and ironing board, he was on topic. When Ethan entered the play and began wielding a plastic carrot like a sword, he was clearly off topic and not in synchrony with the ongoing interaction.

Play as a Form of Communication

Long before acquiring verbal competency, young children are able to convey their needs and desires, likes and dislikes, competence, and knowledge in the language of their culture. They do this through gesture, expression, and choice of objects and activity, in solitary as well as interactive play. In dialogue, children express their unique personal identity and cultural heritage and learn to adapt to the communicative needs of others in the sociocultural diversity of the classroom (Dyson, 1997, 2003; Genishi, 2002; Genishi & Dyson, 2005, 2009; Hughes, 2003; Jaworski & Coupland, 2006; Reynolds, 2002). The wise teacher closely monitors the language of play, finding in it much of the source of a culturally and developmentally appropriate play-based curriculum and the grounding for an authentic assessment.

FOSTERING LITERATE BEHAVIORS

The natural processes of language learning are turned upside down when we attempt to teach isolated skills, such as letter formation and phonics rules, to children before they have shown interest and motivation in spontaneous efforts to dictate a text or write a letter themselves. Although they often play at letter formation, young children do not use or learn a word's component sounds before they articulate the word—they do not practice the "d," "o," and "g" sounds before saying "dog"—and they do not start with simpler sentences before expressing complex emotions or desires. It is through nonverbal communication—gesture, interaction, expression—that children initially communicate desire or pain. Only after using language in these ways do they come to consider adult norms (Heath & Mangiola, 1991).

The Value of the Play-Based Curriculum

Contrary to traditional views, the rate and direction of the language learning process are not necessarily linear and progressive. Research tells us that for some children, the direction might be curvilinear or cyclical, and even sometimes regressive, only to spiral out again later (Heath & Mangiola, 1991). For example, in guided-play activities, Nathan dictated many stories, all of which revolved around stories about the Beatles that his father had read to him. His stories seemed to be attempts to mimic the adult fiction he had heard. As he became more integrated into the peer-group culture of the school, his stories began to have greater personal meaning. At that point, teachers noted that his previously long-winded and convoluted narrative style seemed to shift to a more age-appropriate level. The urgency of Nathan's need to express something meaningful to his peers took precedence over seemingly advanced literacy skills that were not well established.

Learning for young children is determined largely by what they want to know and when they need to know it. To illustrate this point, we look at the development of an accurate concept of gender in children's storytelling efforts.

Early Story Constructions

Three-year-old children typically begin story constructions with fuzzy, gender-undifferentiated bunnies and cuddly creatures. Often, 4-year-old children, as they achieve greater narrative competence, may begin repetitively to relate gender-stereotypic stories derived from the media and peer culture, which marks their membership in the peer group (Nicolopoulou, 2001; Nicolopoulou, McDowell, & Brockmeyer, 2006; Nicolopoulou & Scales, 1990). It is followed, generally at about ages 5 and 6, by a spurt of more creative and elaborate narrative, encompassing and interweaving this same stereotypical material with material based on personal interests and family experiences and expectations (Nourot, Henry, & Scales, 1990).

As Dyson (1993, 1997, 2003), Paley (1995, 1997, 2004), Genishi and Dyson (2009), and others (including Tobin, 2000) have noted, children's narratives are often centered around issues of power, fairness, gender, ethnicity, and culture. Dialogue about such issues provides not only a motivating context for the growth of language and literacy, but it can also provide the context for the construction of more accurate and more equitable notions of a social self within a social world.

When children have opportunities for spontaneous play and authoring in all its multiple forms, they integrate their experience and knowledge and generate a curriculum that is naturally relevant to their cultural and personal lives. (Fein, Ardlila-Ray, & Groth, 2000; Genishi & Dyson, 2009)

Angela's Story. This is poignantly revealed in the case of Angela, who illustrated her traumatic story of poverty and homelessness (Figure 8.1), then dictated its text to a teacher she trusted.

Angela's story reveals not only the sadness of her life outside school, but also her need to communicate her special story. It demonstrates the efficacy of the play-based curriculum to meet that need. Furthermore, the story's wording—"Once there was" and "The End"—reveals that Angela is beginning to grasp the social conventions surrounding the literate activity of storytelling. For homeless Angela, "school" learning was intertwined with other more basic lessons in basic survival.

In preschool and kindergarten, drawing, along with scriptlike scribbling, is a form of early writing. It reveals much about the child's beginning knowledge of writing conventions and the function of texts. We find many correspondences to the competencies Angela has learned through play in the Continuum of Children's Development in Early Reading and Writing, laid out in a Joint Position Statement of the International Reading Association (IRA) and the National Association for the Education of Young Children (NAEYC) on appropriate standards for reading and writing (1998) and early indicators adopted by a number of states. For example:

- Angela uses illustrations or pictures to represent oral language.
- She describes people, places, and things in her story.
- She identifies the purpose of illustrations in a story.
- She includes a main idea in oral descriptions and drawings.
- She has dictated sentences.
- She has dictated the beginning, middle, and end of the story.
- (And more advanced) She uses her illustrations and dictation to create a consistent writer's voice and tone.
- She uses descriptive words and dictates a complete thought.
- She recounts experiences or presents the story in a logical sequence.
- When her story was bound and its pages stapled together like a book, she demonstrated the ability to use correct book handling skills (e.g., the book is right side up and the pages turn in correct direction). (Scales, 2004)

Once there was a
lady who lived
in a house and
didn't have anything
to eat.

Figure 8.1
Angela's Drawings

How the Play-Based Literacy Curriculum
Serves Children of All Cultures and Languages

Today's classroom is richly peopled with children of diverse backgrounds, who bring to school markedly different cultures, languages, and ways of handling the English language (Genishi & Dyson, 2009). Traditionally, educators have attempted to ignore sociocultural differences in the classroom. In attempting to attain equity by neutralizing our classrooms, we fail to notice that children of different backgrounds bring rich variety to play patterns and language (Derman-Sparks & Ramsey, 2005; Genishi, 2002; Genishi & Dyson, 1984, 2005, 2009).

In one classroom, parents helped to create a print rich environment by labeling the centers and materials in English, Russian, and Chinese, reflecting the various cultures and languages of the students. Some of the English language learners in this classroom had younger siblings, parents, or other relatives who frequently volunteered. Opportunities to use both their first language as well as English were, therefore, available. This created an atmosphere in which all cultures were recognized, accepted, and celebrated, and all children felt valued (Genishi, 2002).

Figure 8.1
(*continued*)

Play-centered environments provide opportunities for second language acquisition. In contrast to classrooms where adults often control the language spoken, the play-based program exposes children to the full range of their peers' language abilities. Play encourages young English language learners to develop their language competence for its strategic value in social relations. But it is also important to involve native speakers who can extend children's opportunities to use their primary language and to learn English as well. Books and recordings used in a classroom where there is a variety of languages, along with the presence of bilingual teachers, aides, parents, volunteers, and cross-age tutors—all of these can support a program that is language-varied for all students (Genishi & Dyson 2009; Genishi & Godwin, 2008).

English Language Learners: Masha's Story

In the following, more lengthy anecdote drawn from records of story plays created by an immigrant child, we document Masha's acquisition of a second language, as well as her integration into the play culture of an American preschool classroom (Scales, 1997).

Having recently arrived from Russia, Masha spoke little or no English. She was very accomplished in arts activities and contented herself with these

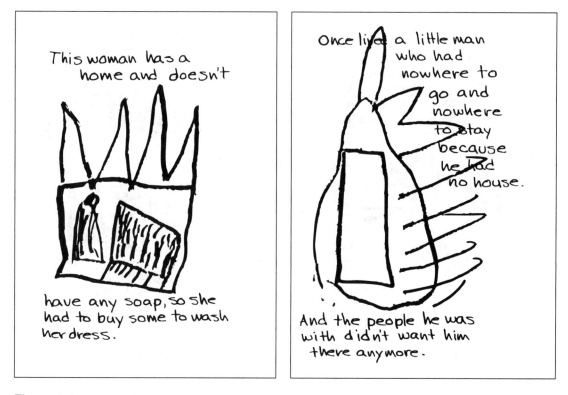

This woman has a home and doesn't have any soap, so she had to buy some to wash her dress.

Once lived a little man who had nowhere to go and nowhere to stay because he had no house.

And the people he was with didn't want him there anymore.

Figure 8.1
Angela's Drawings (*continued*)

pursuits for most of the fall and winter, rarely going outside to the play yard. At circle time she was very attentive when children's story plays were enacted. Despite this interest, Masha had laboriously dictated only one story in October, near the beginning of the school year. This is what Masha dictated:

"My head and my eye.

My veil . . . white.

And play veil.

Someone pull my veil and play."

In her beginning English she has tried to recapture the excitement of whirling with colorful scarves in the language of dance with the other children.

After this first attempt, Masha did not dictate any stories for many months. But she had begun to make friends at the drawing table, where she was also near a teacher most of the school day. Finally, early in April, Masha rushed to Janet, her favorite teacher in the school, announcing urgently that she had a play to write, her first since October. It was a pivotal story that reflected her social development at the time. In her story, we hear a poised 4-year-old obliquely announcing that she is now ready to enter

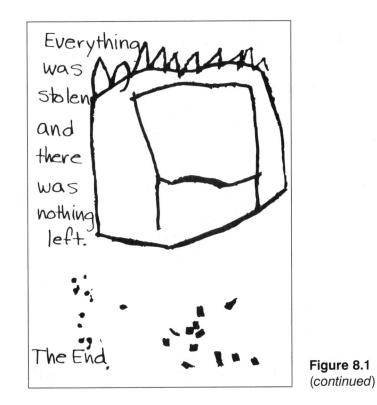

Everything was stolen and there was nothing left.

The End.

Figure 8.1
(continued)

fully the world of her peers. She symbolically bids her teacher and mentor (and the drawing table as well) a gracious farewell. Tactfully, she honors her teacher by giving the only character in this play the teacher's name. Listen to Masha's story:

> "Once upon a time there was a little girl named Janet. And she so much liked to draw pictures, beautiful pictures. And she stopped drawing beautiful pictures and then she started to climb up the tree. And that's the end."

Masha furiously dictated 19 stories between April and the 1st of July. They vividly reflected her advancing development through the expression of her changing social motivations, her acquisition of greater and greater fluency in English, and her grasp of the peer culture. First to appear was the familiar character of Cinderella, which she also knew in Russian. Soon other Disney-inspired figures began to enter. She made sure that there were many roles so that all her new friends could participate; sometimes she multiplied the characters so that no one was left out. Some stories involved two Cinderellas and several others had multiple characters named Pocahontas, distinguished as "a big one" and "a little one." She wrote several stories about "Fly Horses" and, much to the teacher's consternation, many little horses began "flying" about the play yard as Masha's Fly Horse theme daily became more integrated into the peer culture. Masha, despite admonitions to slow down, kept flying. She had made the whole school her own, and she was not about to stop flying at this point. ✇

By June, a few months before kindergarten, Masha's stories began to express her growing awareness of herself as ultimately becoming independent not only from her teachers, but also from her parents. Listen to Masha reflect on growing up.

"Once upon time there was a little baby with her mother. And then the mother said to her little child, 'Look, child, there's your father who's coming.' The father, he come and he showed the little child a toy. And the little child grew up into a grown-up girl and that's the end." ⌀

Masha's stories are a vivid record of one child's growth in language acquisition and social integration and reveal, in a minor way, how her personal play theme (Fly Horses) was integrated into the culture of her American classroom (Scales, 1997).

Seefeldt and Galper (2000) suggest that young English language learners generally follow a pattern of second language acquisition that parallels the development of their first language (Otto, 2010). In this example we find

- A silent period (throughout which Masha conversed in Russian with her mother and her bilingual cousin, Alex).
- A tentative use of new language (Masha's first story) marked by use of simple syntax and grammar, and very short sentences.
- Complexity of language structures increases gradually (e.g., use of verb tenses includes past and future as well as present). (This was transitional for Masha at school's end.)
- Use of very short sentences.
- Moving from present verb/noun construction to past and future (transitional for Masha at school's end).

We see this pattern reflected clearly in language Masha used to dictate her stories.

Variations in this pattern may, of course, occur, as is the case for Masha's younger cousin, Sonia.

In the second month of school, after beginning to tentatively use English, Sonia acquired an English-speaking friend who began to "speak" for her. Sonia stopped using English in the preschool and did not speak in Russian while at school. No more of the "ABC" song was heard at nap time. Sonia and her new friend were inseparable, although their interactions did not involve speech. Teachers were alarmed and saw this as a possible indicator of a speech or emotional disorder. They consulted frequently with her parents, who reported that their child was becoming ever more fluent in English at home. Everyone doubted this until evidence of Sonia's bilingual competence finally arrived many months later in a tape recording Sonia's father shared with teachers. Sonia's English was more fluent than her parents'! However, Sonia continued to remain mute at school until she separated from her new friend on entering kindergarten. ⌀

This anecdote certainly indicates the complex ways that second language learning may impact socioemotional development. It also illustrates that the idea that a "one size fits all" way of learning language or literacy must be resisted. This anecdote also demonstrates how difficult it is to be a young English language learner in a classroom where English is the primary language spoken. It gives us a greater appreciation of the countless, sometimes unruly, but always original, ways children learn (Dyson 1997; Genishi, 2002; Genishi & Dyson, 2009; Genishi & Goodwin, 2008).

HONORING THE IMPORTANCE OF LITERATE BEHAVIORS

A group of fast-paced 4-year-old superheroes elaborated their play when their teacher suggested they draw pictures showing the features of their characters' costumes. The children excitedly drew their characters. The teacher then labeled each character's essential items of apparel—one character, for example, wore a special belt. As superhero experts, the children used their language skills to give the teacher the information she needed to label their characters accurately. Had the children been older, the teacher might have asked for their help in spelling, some of the children could have rendered their own labels, and language certainly would be used to verify and dispute the details of the pictures and the order of the story's sequences. Because they require consideration of a responsive other, all these types of communication— writing, drawing, oral expression, and the use of different media—serve as stepping stones to more developed literacy concepts (see Figure 8.1).

Emergent Literacy

In examining children's early drawing, scribbling, and mark making, researchers note that children seem to know what writing is for before they learn the forms. For example, Graves (1983) asserted,

> Children want to write. They want to write the first day they attend school. This is no accident. Before they went to school they marked up walls, pavements, newspapers with crayons, chalk, pen or pencils, anything that makes a mark. The child's marks say "I am." (Morrow, 2009, pp. 232)

The concept known as emergent literacy was first used by Clay (1966). The following is an adaptation of some of its key features:

- Literacy development begins early in life and is ongoing.
- There is a dynamic relationship between reading, writing, oral language, and literacy as each influences the other in the course of development.
- Development of literacy occurs in everyday contexts of home, community, and school.
- The settings for the acquisition of literacy are often social, often in collaboration with an adult or other children.
- Literacy activities are embedded in contexts such as art, music, play, social studies, and science, where purposeful meaning occurs.

Literacy development approached in this way accepts children at any level of development and provides a program for learning based on individual needs (Morrow, 2009).

The whole language approach is similar to the emergent literacy perspective. As defined by Bergeron (1990). It is

> . . . . a concept that embodies both a philosophy of language development as well as the instructional approaches embedded within, and supportive of, that philosophy. This concept includes the use of real literature and writing in the context of meaningful, functional, and cooperative experiences in order to develop in students' motivation and interest in the process of learning. (p. 319)

Writing, Graphics, and Narrative Construction

Writing is critical in helping young children grasp the concept of "story" or "narrative" and the perspective this implies (see, for example, Dyson, 1989, 2003; Dyson & Genishi, 1994; Genishi & Dyson, 2009). Writing, in turn, occurs as part of a social context. It often emerges from the shared verbalizations surrounding scribbling, drawing, labeling, letter writing, or dictating that lead to an early understanding of the requirements of written communication. Whether the subject that is shared with friends is superhero lore or other fantasy creatures, children come to grasp the relationships of an author to a text and a text to a reader.

Subsequently, children come to understand that stories follow specific narrative conventions characteristic of their cultures. Angela began her story by marking new episodes with "Once there was . . ." and closed with "The End," and marked sequences within her story with "and then." Later she linked events causally (using "because," "and so") as she encountered the need to explain her sequencing.

Opportunities for writing in the classroom should be abundant (Morrow, 2009). Children can be encouraged to send notes to each other by making a mailbox for intraclass mail from sturdy, 12-section beverage boxes. Bookmaking and publishing are encouraged by setting out a few pages of paper stapled together or with holes punched to receive yarn ties. In one class, an autograph book proved a successful activity for all when one child introduced the idea (Koons, 1991). More high-tech activities for children in the primary grades can involve computer journals, PowerPoint presentations, e-mail, and speech-to-text programs (see Chapter 13 for more examples).

Another exciting possibility involves journal writing: the child creates a written and/or drawn record of his or her experiences. The child can do the writing independently, with the assistance of a speech-to-text program, or the journal can be dictated directly to the teacher. Journals can be prepared by adding pages to a construction paper cover or using binders with fairly sturdy paper—unlined for younger children, with lines for older beginning writers.

Awareness of Sounds and Patterns of Language

Letter–sound correspondences are arbitrary and must be taught. The more meaningful the context for introducing such correspondences, the more effective they are.

Computer stations can extend a library.

An example of a meaningful context would be starting with a child's name. What is the sound of the letter that begins it? What is the sound of the letter that ends it? Patterns in the rhythm and structure of language, such as syllables, can be introduced by clapping on the accents in the child's name. Seefeldt and Galper (2000), in *Active Experiences for Active Children: Literacy Emerges,* include many activities for children that provide a meaningful context. They suggest that phonemic awareness includes

- The ability to detect rhythm and alliteration
- Phonological memory
- The ability to break down and manipulate spoken words and isolated sounds in words

Although the terms sound similar, phonemic awareness and phonics are not one and the same (IRA/NAEYC, 1998). While phonemic awareness is a precursor to understanding letter sounds in words, it is not the systematic presentation of letter sounds in words. Whatever the method used to teach reading (whole language, systematic phonics, or a combination of the two), children first need a strong basis in phonemic awareness (Wasik, 2001).

Another key to developing phonemic awareness is in knowledge of *rimes* or *word families.* Whereas recognition of rhymes develops relatively early and easily, awareness of rime may require explicit instruction. With knowledge of rimes, along with onsets, such as *will* and *still,* children are able to decode words that are new to them. With knowledge of common and familiar rimes, such as *ack, ail, est, ice, ink,* and *ight,* children are able to read nearly 500 words typical to primary-level reading books (Seefeldt, 2005).

Teachers can introduce letter–sound correspondence with one of the most meaningful things children have—their names. For example, pronounce the initial consonant of a child's name; then ask, "Whose name am I thinking of?" (Seefeldt & Galper, 2000). Phonological units consist of syllables, rimes and onsets, and phonemes (Yopp & Yopp, 2009).

Changing the beginning letters of children's names to create a new variation is another game that draws attention to letter sounds and creates a hilarious response. Patterns in the sequence of sound in language can be foregrounded in a game that changes a vowel following a consonant in a little chant (e.g., "I Like Apples and Bananas"). Children delight in its silliness and quickly pick up the pattern by changing the vowels to "o" or "i" or "u."

LANGUAGE AND LITERACY LEARNING IN THE PRIMARY GRADES: THE MOTIVATING POWER OF PLAY

Erikson (1985) noted that elementary-school-age children become interested in mastery and the need to prove themselves competent in the activities that their culture values. For example, by first grade, they are more ready to participate in the lives of adults and are coming to terms with social expectations of their teachers and parents in academic areas, like literacy.

Parents of children involved in play-centered, emergent literacy programs sometimes question how children progress from drawing, scribbling, dictation, pretend writing, and invented spelling to the necessary formal conventions of literacy. Harriet, a primary-grade schoolteacher, provides an answer. Having participated in workshops conducted by the Bay Area Writers Project (University of California, Berkeley), she views herself, her classroom environment, and her students as the major resources in a sociocultural context that enhances language and literacy learning (Scales, 1997). She believes in teaching specific skills (she gives spelling tests, for example). But, importantly, she is wise enough to provide ample time for children to integrate their emerging knowledge through playful engagement with the social resources of this classroom. The motivation and practice necessary to acquire skills in letter–sound recognition, rules for capitalization, punctuation, and dictionary spelling augmenting children's invented spelling are provided primarily through the children's spontaneous acts of writing about things that interest them, rather than through unrelated repetition.

A respect for "authoring" in many forms manifests itself in the centrality of a small-group activity called "Booklet Writing Time," during which Harriet and trained parent volunteers support children in guided play surrounding writing and drawing. After Booklet Writing Time, children are provided an opportunity to take the "author's" chair to read or tell the class about what they have written or drawn. Sometimes Harriet points out special features of children's stories, like, "Listen to Michelle's story and when we get to the point where people are talking, put your hand up, and when they stop, put your hand down. That's called 'dialogue.' Doesn't it make this piece of writing more interesting?" These intrinsically engaging activities not only involve children in learning about the function of language, but also offer the occasion for teaching necessary social knowledge, such as vocabulary, the structure of language, spelling,

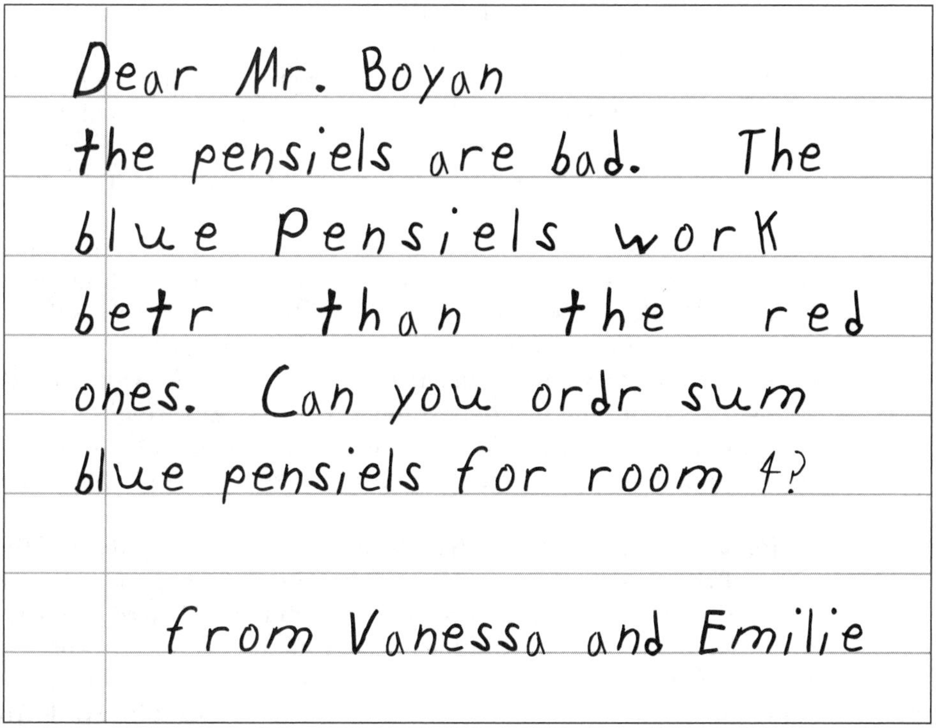

Dear Mr. Boyan
the pensiels are bad.   The
blue Pensiels work
betr   than   the   red
ones. Can you ordr sum
blue pensiels for room 4?

from Vanessa and Emilie

Figure 8.2
Vanessa and Emilie's Pensiels Letter

letter–sound correspondence, and phonemic awareness. Such social knowledge arises from the context of self-directed, developmentally appropriate activities.

After lunch, a period of spontaneous play again presents opportunities to write and draw, and children produce numerous pieces at this time. These can be as simple as a block builder's sign saying, "Don't shake the table," or a "Kwyot plas" sign, or as complex as the letter to the principal (Figure 8.2) Emilie and Vanessa wrote, requesting better "pensiels." Some groups may even create more extended pieces, such as a play or a class newspaper.

During these spontaneous and guided play periods, the generative power of play motivates children's authoring. Like the ephemeral quality of play itself, the creative flow of writing is fleeting, not to be interrupted by premature corrections of "form." In this classroom, neither the teacher nor parent volunteers spell words for children; they encourage the children to try to figure out for themselves how words should look. Later, children are guided to learn correct form as individual development dictates. Here is an observation from this classroom:

It is Booklet Writing Time, and Jomar invites his teacher to look at his booklets. He has filled the pages of several. Each entry is dated, and he and his teacher start with the earliest. A vivid illustration accompanies this first story: "THiS Is MY SPASMANHEEIZFLIEEN."

Pointing to the word *THIS*, Jomar's teacher, Harriet, comments, "I noticed you changed *THIS*. How did you know the dictionary spelling?"

Jomar murmurs, "I learned it and I changed it."

"It was a spelling word and you went back and fixed it," his teacher responds.

Carefully drawing a line with a ruler well below Jomar's writing and illustration, she says to Jomar, "Let's do some dictionary spelling because you already know a lot about dictionary spelling." She carefully copies the first word of Jomar's story and then comments enthusiastically that *Is* is spelled "just right too, except would we put an *I* like that there?" Jomar has used a capital *I*.

"No, we would dot it," Jomar replies. His teacher carefully writes *is* with a lowercase *I* after *This*. Harriet and Jomar read through his story and invite Jomar to point to the three words in his story that he would like to be able to spell the "dictionary" way.

Jomar points to SPASMANHEEISFLIEEN, and they discuss the "soft" sound of *c* in *spaceman*. Then his teacher invites Jomar to spell along with her as she writes the word *spaceman*. Later she comments, "You remember, we have just learned about 'ing' endings," and Jomar is guided in his dictionary spelling of the word *flying*. As they proceed through his story, she demonstrates that a "two finger space" is a good rule for separating words from each other (Morrison & Grossman, 1985). ✆

Jomar's teacher talks not about his most recent piece of writing, where he still may be integrating recently acquired knowledge, but about one of his earliest efforts. In this way, Jomar comfortably appropriates formal skills he has already nearly acquired in the context of his own writing. In the process of "proofing" his earliest efforts at "authoring," Jomar becomes what Harriet likes to call a witness to his own growth and development. As Michelle, one of Harriet's other students, reflects on her own growth as an author, she exclaims: "At first you couldn't even read what I wrote!" In this classroom, Michelle knew she was an author before she knew how to write (Morrison, 1985). The varied pieces of writing children produce in this first-grade classroom as well as the story plays created by preschoolers provide documents through which the children can observe their own personal progress as authors or playwrights.

Multimedia Extend Meanings of Literacy

The wealth of today's various media argues against narrowly defining literacy as the acquisition of specific reading skills. Consider the range of possibilities. Oral storytelling stimulates the listener's imagination and contributes to reading as a habit. Books, of course, contribute to knowledge of literature and, if illustrated, appreciation for art. Recordings and radio contribute strongly to imagination and can influence speech ability and comprehension. Movies, videos, and television, today's principal storytellers, contribute to the child's imagination, speech, and ability to listen and comprehend, as well as to an appreciation of music and art. Interactive computers may make the broadest contribution across all areas, from imagination to potential for control of the medium and creativity in its use (Bellin & Singer, 2006; Brown, 1986; Christie & Roskos, 2006; Sarama & Clements, 2002; Singer & Singer, 2005; Singer et al., 2006; Singer & Lythcott, 2004; von Blanckensee, 1999). (See Chapter 13 for more examples of technology-based literacy; and Morrow, 2009, for an index of computer games.)

DYNAMIC APPROACHES TO PROMOTING LITERACY THROUGH PLAY

Young children spontaneously initiate sociodramatic play. Careful observation of the cadence of children's speech and gestures reveals (a) when sociodramatic play is coordinated and cohesive, (b) whether the children know who is taking part in it and who is not, and (c) what the play is about (Cook-Gumperz & Scales, 1982, 1996; Sawyer, 2001; Scales & Cook-Gumperz, 1993). A well-coordinated play scenario is, in a sense, a story the children are telling with an agreed-on theme and cast of characters.

Sensitive teachers can enhance the development of this literate behavior by responding to or even helping establish sociodramatic play interactions by taking a participant role (see Chapter 4). They will want to avoid dominating the dramatic play with their power as grownups, but on the other hand, abdicating educative responsibility must also be avoided. In other words, a balance must be struck between spontaneous and guided play.

Using Drama Techniques to Enhance Sociodramatic Play

One way to support more complex sociodramatic play is for the teacher to enter into what English drama educator Dorothy Heathcote called "role" within children's sociodramatic play (Heathcote & Bolton, 1995; Wagner, 1999). Heathcote developed an extensive repertoire of drama techniques for the classroom, emphasizing strategies that enable children to create and elaborate roles in spontaneously created dramas that center around historical, ecological, or social themes. One example of a drama that might be developed could center around caretaking in an animal habitat. Other scenarios she developed for elementary-age children involved the impact of changes due to technological advances: How does one fishing village confront the loss of its livelihood when a neighboring village upstream begins fishing with large nets instead of the old traditional ways (Heathcote, 1997)?

Drama themes are generated from the children's suggestions with minimal props and direction. Children playfully elaborate these dramas based on their own knowledge and understanding. These methods have been particularly successful with elementary school-age children. Heathcote suggested that in initial phases of a dramatic interaction (or a play interaction), the teacher's interventions must be subtle.

By taking a role that enables the teacher to speak indirectly about the unfolding play or drama, its context can be supported and shaped.

By this indirect means, for example, one teacher was able to facilitate the expansion of a theme from random shooting play to more cohesive hospital play that involved many more players in meaningful roles. Indirectly invoking this prior play experience on a later occasion, the teacher enhanced the focus of chaotic play by merely giving each player an armband marked with a red cross. This new focus allowed less mature players to be included, and the older children assumed more complex roles in an elaborated play theme that entailed greater interactive challenge.

Later the teacher, in role, may shift responsibility for advancing the play to the children. The teacher, who in the earlier example is only a member of the "hospital governing board," may now appear to be "helpless" to know what to do next or who is in charge. In this way, the teacher can subtly shift her "teacher power" and authority to invent over to the children (Heathcote & Bolton, 1995; Heathcote & Herbert, 1985).

> Entering a hospital play scenario, the teacher addresses Jason as a colleague: "Jason, have you been 'certified' by the governing board of the hospital to serve as its 'director' of emergency units?" After assurances, the teacher retreats from the play to set up a "disaster control center equipped with cell phones." Jason and his friend, Juan, begin to man the dual steering wheels of the emergency truck and direct the flow of "casualties" to the "intensive care unit." ⌀

Avoiding Some Pitfalls.   The teacher in a "role" must not forget that it will be necessary to return to being the teacher—signaling this shift in relationships by a change of voice or posture—for it is inevitable that the children will have to go home, no matter how much fun they are having. Shoes, socks, jackets, and sweaters must be found, projects stored, and the school tidied for the following day. Hence, whatever part in the play teachers create for themselves, the roles must allow movement in and out of the play. Again, the teachers' roles should never be central ones; they should only allow the teachers to be available when needed to support, guide, and sustain the play, but never to direct or dominate.

Moreover, in assuming their "role" in play, teachers must communicate clearly that the drama is part of the world of pretend, in which things are only make-believe. Otherwise, the children may become confused about the reality of their play.

Consider the teacher who failed to do this. After spending several days with a child constructing a robot out of cardboard boxes, tape, and wires, she was shocked when, on completion of the robot, her partner demanded that she "plug it in!" It is impossible to describe the look of disappointment on the child's face when told, "It's only make-believe." One can only speculate that the child's confusion arose because he thought he had entered the powerful world of adults, where things "really" happen, whereas the teacher felt she had entered the child's world of make-believe, where all things are possible because they are only pretend. The teacher had much to learn from this episode.

Story Dictation and Story Playing

Do you remember 3-year-old Patrick, who dictated the story "I have lots of friends"? By encouraging a child to dictate stories to be acted out later by classmates, the teacher provides an outlet for the child's deeply felt needs—in Patrick's case, the need for friends. Furthermore, because of the urgency of the child's desire to communicate those needs, and because of the autonomy allowed by virtue of the child's being the one to choose the subject, story, and players, the teacher establishes fertile ground for the development of literate behaviors.

The story dictation/story play curriculum, articulated largely by Vivian Gussin Paley (1981, 1986, 1992, 1999, 2004), recalls Sylvia Ashton-Warner's (1963) discovery that reading is mastered easily if the words to be used are autonomously chosen (for these are the words that have personal and emotional impact for the child). It is a literacy and play curriculum that lends itself to applications in prekindergarten, kindergarten, and elementary classrooms, allowing opportunities for children to move from dictating story plays to eventually writing their own creative texts to be presented at a Readers Theater or Author's Chair (Dyson, 1997, 2003; Owacki, 2001).

In the following section, we discuss stories dictated to teachers in one school over the course of several years. In this classroom, the story dictation and story play curriculum is quite simple. The opportunity to dictate a story is offered every day. A record of who has dictated and who has not is kept so that all may have a turn.

Reading can be a social as well as a solitary activity.

In some first- and many second-grade classrooms, children write their own stories and read them or enact them for their classmates (Dyson, 1997, 2003; Scales, 1997).

Minimizing the addition of props to enhance children's use of their imagination, the child-authors and others whom they select act out the stories. For children who are not yet reading, the teacher can read the story, and the acting can spontaneously be performed with a bit of minimal direction from the child-author and the teacher. A record of these stories, along with field notes on the dramatization, is kept in each child's portfolio.

Laronda. 💟   Laronda comes from a large, hard-working, strict family, where pretense is frowned on. She differs from her peers in class, who are, for the most part, offspring of university-based, academically oriented families. She dictated a number of story plays during her second year at preschool when she was 4 years old. An enthusiastic storyteller, she quickly grasped the conventions of storytelling and story playing.

Laronda was popular with her classmates, and her stories mentioned many of her friends by name. In content, the stories were tied to themes and activities of a devoutly religious home life, the world of work, and the domestic comings and goings of an extended family. Laronda's stories rarely mentioned play as an activity and incorporated few fantasy elements. From her field notes, the teacher noted that Laronda was called on frequently by other children to play the role of "Queen" but never the "Princess." This, despite the fact that in some of her own stories Laronda created a "princess" role for herself, although one who "left because she had to cook." Apparently the children recognized something "adult" about Laronda's pragmatic world. There were few parties and no birthdays to celebrate there. There were domestic chores to be performed, and there was work to "go to" and "come home from."

Other children in this mostly middle-class group placed themselves at the center of the worlds they created, often being taken to the park to play, whereas the voice of Laronda was part of a choir of family voices. The teacher wondered about the impact of Laronda's group-oriented culture, which discouraged too much focus on the self, play, and imaginative expression. How much of Laronda's intellectual energy in future schooling would be spent in managing and bridging two disparate worlds in this cosmopolitan university community (Giddens, 2000; Gonzalez-Mena, 1998; Zapeda, Gonzalez-Mena, Rothstein-Fisch, & Trumbull, 2006)?

Jason.   Jason, a kindergartner, is the only child of an adult-dominated household. His parents are adamantly opposed to gun play and vigilantly monitor his television viewing to minimize his exposure to violence.

During the year, Jason cautiously attempted to establish himself as a member of the peer group, particularly with a group of the more vigorous boys in the class. The first of the last two stories he dictated shocked his parents:

> Once upon a time, there was a dragon and he went home. And he went to his friend's house. And then he went to another friend's house. And then he saw a horse. And then he saw another horse and killed the horses. And then

he went back home. And then he saw ten hundred million horses and killed them. And then he saw some people and he killed them. And then he saw everything that's alive in the whole wide world and he saw all his friends and he killed them.

Building the dramatic momentum of this chronicle of devastation, Jason's dragon went to "New York," where "he killed everything else." He then went to school and killed his teachers, all his friends, and the people at school, and "knocked down all the trees of the whole school."

Finally ". . . he knocked down the whole world and the whole sky and every plant. The End." ☙

When Jason's alarmed mother queried him about this play, he turned to her with twinkling eyes and said, "I was a dragon, you know." This did not surprise the teacher, who had already seen in Jason's previous stories a little dragon shyly trying to show its face. She sensed that this story was Jason's declaration of independence. It unleashed the full power of his imagination, as well as his ability to express latent aggression in a literate, creative way.

Here is Jason's next (and final) story:

Once upon a time there was a Ghostbuster. And then the Ghostbuster went to his friend's house and instead of his friend there was a dragon. And then the dragon said, "Bye, bye. I don't want to play with you. I'm going to the park!" And the dragon went to the park and he got to the park and then when he was at the park he went on the swing. And then a girl came and she said, "What are you doing here?" And then the girl played on the slide. And then the dragon played on the slide. And the girl played on the swing. And then a spider came and then a spider found a web. And they both said, "How are you doing?" (Stage direction: One says it first and then the other.)

And then the dragon went home and he drank some tea. And when he was done he went to bed. And the robbers came in and they looked around and then they went out. And then the little girl played a little more and went home and ate dinner and went to bed. And when she went to sleep some robbers came in, and they looked around, and they stole everything that she had. And they went out. And they all woke up in the morning and ate their breakfast. And they all went to the park and had a party. (Stage direction: All the characters hold hands and begin their singing.) The End. ☙

Here we see a competent and vigorous 6-year-old very much in command of the story writing conventions he has acquired. He uses a formulaic opening, "Once upon a time," and, although most of the occurrences are physical, one represents a mental event: Jason indicates expectation in the second sequence when he says, "instead of his friend there was a dragon." Jason supplies stage directions to clarify and expand the story and presents a mixture of popular media characters (Ghostbuster, robbers), fairy tale characters (dragon, spider), and others, all using direct speech and reciprocal conversation. Sentences are complex and include subordinate clauses, such as "when she went to sleep."

Using these conventions with style and poise, Jason constructs a story that successfully integrates the strands of his life (e.g., going to bed or to places like a friend's house or the park) and incorporates expectations derived from his family and teachers (you eat dinner, then go to bed; the girl and dragon take turns on the slide). In the style of many traditional tales, all of his characters, good and bad, end up as friends; they all go to the park and have a party. Furthermore, by including such details as Ghostbusters and robbers, Jason incorporates the demands of his peer culture. He now has established himself as not only his own "person," but as a full-fledged "member" of the group.

The story dictation activity of the preschool evolves naturally into journal and booklet writing activities in the later elementary years. The motivating power of this activity is augmented by the social opportunity to share stories from an "author's chair," as in a second-grade class mentioned earlier in the chapter, or in a third-grade classroom's "author's theatre" described so powerfully by Anne Dyson (1995, 2003). Gretchen Owacki (2001), also using drama in the classroom, devotes a chapter to describing a primary-school curriculum called "Readers Theatre."

As children think and talk about their experiences, they learn that what they talk about can be written and what can be written can be read. In doing so, they begin to learn to listen, to speak to others, and thereby to learn the specifics of language and print conventions.

BALANCED OPPORTUNITIES FOR VARIED KINDS OF PLAY SUPPORT COMPETENCIES IN LANGUAGE AND LITERACY

Literate behaviors are best supported by a wide range of diverse classroom resources and activities that include story dictation and story acting and that are balanced on a continuum from spontaneous to guided play. Careful consideration of time, space, materials, and staff provides a planning context for achieving diversity and balance.

Time for Language and Literacy in Play

First, does the program permit sufficient time for literate behavior in play? The pattern of the day should allow for long, uninterrupted periods of spontaneous play in all centers. If children are rushed and the day is chopped up with teacher-directed "inside time," "group time," "sharing time," "snack time"—that is, with too much teacher choice and teacher voice—the children will have little opportunity to integrate and contextualize their play themes through literate behaviors.

Space for Language and Literacy Learning

Is sufficient space provided for literate behavior in play? Work tables, writing centers, and play areas should be spacious enough to accommodate communication and be set up in such a way that the children can establish face-to-face engagement and visually share materials (i.e., draw on materials such as miniature toys that serve as a source for topics) or comfortably share and exchange with one another their knowledge of language and literacy, as in Harriet's Booklet Writing Time.

Materials for Language, Literacy, and Reading and Writing in Play

Materials for language and literacy play include all kinds of writing and printed materials, such as books, catalogs, tablets, clipboards, and sticky notes. Ample amounts of attractively displayed and maintained supplies of paper, crayons, and markers are needed. Books, paper, and writing materials should be not only in the reading or writing center, but also in the dress-up and home play corners, near the outdoor climber, in the block play area, and adjacent to the fishbowl (to record the daily development of the cluster of baby snails!). With the teacher's help, items can be labeled, directional arrows drawn, and symbols and signs made to identify activities and projects. A well-balanced collection of factual and fantasy books, biographies, poetry, and alphabet books is a valuable resource for both teachers and children. To enhance children's awareness of categories of literature, some books may be organized by topic in plastic bins or on shelves in a library area.

Guidance for Literacy in Play

In promoting literate behaviors, the staff should know when and how to join imaginatively, but not take over, the children's play and know when and how to withdraw. The need for guidance is suggested in some of the following issues that arise in classrooms.

Negative Talk. Social emotional learning is enhanced when teachers help children turn negatives into positives through language. Concern is often expressed about negative ways children use language, such as name calling or disrespect for others. The worst is to say, "I'm not your friend." In one classroom, teachers thought children might be helped by being invited at circle or meeting time to create a chart with columns that listed words written in the "happy" or "sad" columns. Teachers discussed how to change negative words to positive ones that make the classroom a happy place. Grownups call this "diplomacy," a competency we need throughout our lives (Mitchell, 1993).

Relating to Children with Special Needs. These same teachers wondered how they could help children communicate in play with a hearing-impaired child. Some suggested inviting someone fluent in signing to teach children to sing and sign. The teacher asked the children to place their hands over their ears and try to communicate with each other. Wisely, the children, themselves, contributed nonverbal modes of communicating, such as suggestions to "look right at him" and "talk with your hands and eyes."

STANDARDS FOR LITERACY: CALLS FOR ACCOUNTABILITY

Many early childhood teachers are experiencing pressure to implement standards with emphasis on early literacy skills. These assessments are based on a range of standards that vary from state to state. In some cases these standards are in conflict with what teachers consider developmentally appropriate practice and may consequently narrow the efficacy of a play-centered program. Some teachers believe that too much testing could be detrimental to the emotional well-being of children and erode their sense of self-esteem (Fein, Ardlila-Ray, & Groth, 2000; Genishi & Dyson, 2009; Genishi & Goodwin, 2008; Wien, 2004). Guidelines in The Continuum of Children's Development in Early Reading and Writing, in the joint position statement of the IRA and the NAEYC (1998), are helpful tools for implementing developmentally appropriate standards. Response to current calls for accountability through standards and assessment has opened a dialogue among early childhood professionals and educators about ways to ensure that equity of opportunity to develop competencies in a broad range of literacy skills is available to all children in the play-centered classroom (Fein, Ardlila-Ray, & Groth, 2000; Roskos & Neuman, 1998; Seefeldt, 2005).

The many anecdotes in this and other chapters illustrate how standards can be addressed in classrooms where the purposes of language are honored and supported by a language and literacy rich, play-centered environment. The motivating power of the story play curriculum for young English language learner Masha comes to mind. Matthew, a child with special needs, struggles to use language to interact in fast-paced fantasy play with peers (Chapter 11). Three-year-old Patrick's introduction to early literacy with his "I Have Friends" story and Angela's compelling narrative reveal the agency and motivation in children's learning and demonstrate the acquisition of specific language and literacy competencies. In these vignettes we witness an advance from the range of literacy learning displayed in the story play dictation of 3- and 4-year-olds like Patrick and Laronda to the more sophisticated story play productions of kindergarten-age children like Jason. In conferencing with Jomar's primary-school teacher, we observe Jomar integrate social knowledge about the conventions of writing as he "edits" his booklet writing. Emergent literacy is seen in Emilie and Vanessa's letter to their primary-grade school principal about the quality of the "pensiels" in their classroom. These anecdotes reflect the role teachers play in supporting these children's advancing development. In large part, evaluation of children's progress in the early years has been based on compilations of documents the children produce and on systematic recording of teacher observations. Educators are now involved in a new dialogue about how to establish accountability to ensure equity of educational opportunity for all children (Chapter 6).

Teachers know that children of any age function at varying levels along a continuum of emerging competencies in reading and writing. In Table 8.1, phases of development derived from the NAEYC and IRA's joint position statement (1998) provide an illustration of the range of expectations and suggested curriculum for young children.

Table 8.1 Expected Competencies in Reading and Writing

Expected Competencies	Examples	Teacher and Environmental Support
Phase 1: Awareness and exploration (goals for preschool). Children explore their environment and build the foundations for learning to read and write.	Children listen to stories and may pretend to read. They acquire book handling skills. They engage in drawing and scribble writing as they develop competency in using writing tools. Many begin to write their names and attempt other favorite words such as favorites *rainbow*, *I love you*, and *Dear Mommy or Daddy*. Children enjoy labeling their paintings, drawings, or many will want to dictate a narrative to go with their drawings.	Time, space, and materials for language and literacy are provided on a daily basis at multiple sites for storytelling and dictation. Many opportunities for spontaneous and guided exploration of book handling skills, scribble writing, and spontaneous letter formation. Photographs of family and pets provided throughout the classroom.
Phonemic awareness developed through familiar songs, rhymes, and games.	Children begin to recognize written forms of favorite words.	Group activities emphasize phonemic awareness and beginning and ending letter sounds.
Phase 2: Experimental reading and writing (goals for kindergarten). Children develop basic concepts of print and begin to engage in and experiment with reading and writing while continuing to develop phonemic awareness as they engage in beginning reading. Children go from scribble writing to formal writing of words for notes, labels, and their own names.	May use invented spelling to enhance play such as a "kwyot plas" sign.	Formation of upper- and lowercase letters is introduced through models and templates; appropriately ruled paper is available for spontaneous use in a print rich environment. Clapping on the syllables of children's names develops awareness of phonemic units as well as of the beginnings and endings of words.
Phase 3: Early reading and writing (goals for first grade). Children begin to read simple stories and can write about a topic.	Children may read their own stories and story plays. Children begin to want to learn dictionary spelling of invented words, such as Jomar's "spasmanheeizflieen."	Opportunities are provided for writing in journals and booklets on a daily basis. Writing materials are made available throughout the classroom to support children's spontaneous writing. Developmentally appropriate conventions of text construction, spelling, and writing are introduced in a small group or at circle time or to individual children in conference.

(*continued*)

Table 8.1   (Continued)

Expected Competencies	Examples	Teacher and Environmental Support
Phase 4: Transitional reading and writing (goals for second grade). Children begin to read more fluently and write various text forms using simple and more complex sentences.	Children may begin to create writing tasks for themselves, such as a class newspaper or letters to parents or to others, such as Vanessa and Emilie's letter to the principal about the "bad pensiels" in their classroom.	Writing continues to occur on a daily basis; abundant books for independent and directed reading are available every day. Guidance in conventions of text construction, spelling, and writing is presented in whole or small groups and in conference. Features of a written text, such as dialogue, are considered in activities such as the "Author's Chair" or in reading and discussions of the writing styles of familiar authors.

Source: National Association for the Education of Young Children & International Reading Association (1998). *Learning to Read and Write: Developmentally Appropriate Practices for Young Children:* A joint position of the International Reading Association (IRA) and the National Association for the Education of Young Children (NAEYC). Washington, DC: National Association for the Education of Young Children.

SUMMARY AND CONCLUSION

A play-centered language arts curriculum arises from a context that honors the purposes of children's communication and the responses they might evoke, before it stresses isolated strategies for literacy learning, such as letter formation and phonics rules. Literate behaviors, particularly in pretend and sociodramatic play and storytelling, are seen as precursors to a grasp of the concept of "story" or "narrative" and the necessary perspective-taking this implies. Such understanding emerges through play as, together, children talk, draw, and share their early attempts to write. In one classroom, the story play activity is a catalyst for second language learning and a mirror of development in the case of one Russian-speaking child. Happily, in her case, advances in second language learning, socialization, and literacy move as an integrated whole. Other patterns may emerge in other situations (Genishi & Goodwin, 2008).

Through ample opportunities in guided and spontaneous play, children become participants in and authors and readers of their own stories. Reading widely and writing in many forms lead to an understanding of the many genres of authoring. Children become motivated to begin to learn dictionary ways to spell words, develop phonemic awareness, acquire letter and sound recognition, appropriately utilize upper- and lowercase letter forms, and master the rules for capitalization and punctuation and other conventions of literacy.

Although a classroom that is rich in language and literacy is a powerful resource for children, sources, agents, and settings for learning language are not limited to teachers and schools. In many contemporary classrooms, children's classmates and their worlds beyond school are also resources that provide a broad sociocultural context. Through a play-centered language arts curriculum, we tap into the richness of the full range of diverse cultures and languages in our classrooms and communities.

9

Science in the Play-Centered Curriculum

> Rosa is playing with a boat at the water table under the shade tree. She slowly pushes the boat down and looks as the drops of water gradually fill it. She watches it sink, whispering, "Come up now!" She lifts it up. She collects small rocks and bark chips from the base of the tree and fills the boat with six large bark chips. "Here you go—Toot! Toot!" She adds three rocks and the boat slowly begins to take on water. Quickly, she piles on two more rocks and the boat sinks. The rocks go down with the ship, but the bark chips come floating to the top. "Pop! Pop!" Rosa pushes one of the chips down again and watches as it pops up as soon as she lets it go. ∅

Young children are involved in inquiry as they seek answers to their own questions, even though this spontaneous play is not the formal, analytical process of the scientist or older student. Let's take a brief look at Rosa's water play, a typical activity in early childhood education programs.

How does Rosa's spontaneous play relate to science? When Rosa carefully pushes the boat down, she is investigating what will happen—a scientific process. She observes the water entering the boat. Observing is another basic scientific process. Scientific processes relate to Rosa's actions and developing understandings of the physical world. She is also extending her knowledge of scientific concepts or "big ideas" in science. She does not yet understand that objects that are heavier than their equal volume of water will sink and those that are lighter will float. However, through activities such as this, Rosa extends her beginning understanding of weight. Rosa is also learning more about the content of science—factual knowledge about the properties of the bark chips such as their specific color, shape, and size. Scientific processes, concepts, and content are central to appropriate science curriculum for young children.

Why should early childhood education programs emphasize science? Young children need to learn about the physical as well as the social world and consider the physical world as being understandable. Science is a natural and necessary part of development. Children's own inquiry, their attempts to learn about the world and how things work, should be at the heart of their science curriculum.

Science is an implicit, often hidden, part of the early childhood education curriculum that centers on play. However, many early childhood educators lack the background in science to make the connection explicit. It can be a challenge to bridge the play-centered curriculum that emerges from the children's own interests with standards-based science curriculum.

The focus of this chapter is different from the focus of most books on science activities for young children. Other books usually suggest ways for teachers to set up teacher-initiated science activities, such as growing seeds and sorting minerals. The teachers we talked with described some excellent investigative projects, themes, and units from resource books as well as science curriculum materials adopted by their districts. Although we agree that excellent science programs can be found that are developmentally appropriate, such programs are not necessarily based on children's own expressed interests. In that sense, they represent only a small range of the science curriculum.

To design a program with play at the center, we highlight activities that children initiate through their own exploration and spontaneous play. One purpose of this chapter is to demonstrate that science is already an integral part of the play-centered curriculum. Teachers can help parents, other staff, and administrators see how rich the traditional play curriculum is in the area of science. The second purpose is to point out how teachers can extend the investigation of ideas and processes that arise within the context of children's spontaneous play.

The integrated play curriculum is the foundation for a developmentally appropriate science program for young children. This chapter begins with a tour of the environment of an early childhood program, analyzing how different indoor and outdoor areas offer numerous opportunities for children to be involved in science.

SCIENTISTS TOUR THE KINDERGARTEN

As all young children play, they are involved in activity that scientists would identify as "learning about science." This is what happened when several science professors toured a local kindergarten. Marilyn is a biologist, Bob is a chemist, and Toni is a physicist.

Outdoor Area

Marilyn: I'm amazed at how much goes on in such a short time. I've seen a lot of activity related to the rain we had yesterday. Jerry was watching a snail move along the side of the sandbox. He observed and commented on the silvery trail the snail made and then discovered the many trails already made all over the wooden side of the sandbox. He and Alicia organized a "snail race" with three snails. The road was the slide. They were watching the different speeds the snails traveled. Observing and comparing are fundamental scientific processes. I was surprised that the children pointed out that the snails crawled up at an angle. Many adults wouldn't have discovered all that information about snail behavior.

Bob: Yes, I was also surprised at what I saw happening without any formal instruction. The sand in the sandbox is pretty wet, and several youngsters were making "cakes." There was a lot of investigating going on to find the best "batter," just the right amount of moisture to hold the shape in their cake pans. The kids had all kinds of ideas on how to improve the consistency including adding more water and more coarse sand. Through the scientific process of experimenting, they were learning about the properties of materials. Their attention span and absorption in their activity impressed me.

As the children continued to play, Marilyn, Bob, and Toni pointed out numerous science concepts, processes, and varied content. For example, Soshi was trying to pump on the swings. As she tried to figure out how the rhythmic rocking of her body

Observing and describing are the foundations of science.

would make the swing go higher, she was learning more about cause and effect. Lisa and Peter were "fishing" in a puddle and found a large worm with many rings that the children called "armor rings." Learning about the particular characteristics of living organisms is important content in biology.

The Block Area

Toni: This looks like "pre-architecture." I'm impressed with the children's understanding and use of shapes. This repetition of triangular blocks here and the interesting example of symmetry are important concepts in both science and mathematics.

Marilyn: Aren't these blocks fantastic! Look how the children are experimenting, trying to figure out if the longer block or the two shorter blocks will work better . . . and how they try again . . . and, of course, look at the fun they're having.

Toni: There are so many opportunities for questions, for inquiry. I wonder if he will be able to figure out a way to make that block tower stand.

Marilyn: Yes, Luis just learned about the idea of buttressing . . . another important concept . . . and now, I bet, he's going to use it again over there.

They all fall silent for a moment, watching April and Tanisha build roads for small cars. The children use a block for an arch and several triangles to make a bridge. Tanisha puts a car at the top of the bridge and lets it roll down. April learns from her friend's solution and experiments by giving the car an extra push: "Sooo fast!"

The Art Area

Toni: There's a lot of play and science going on right here. Take a look at that clay table. What strikes me immediately is the way the children explore the properties of the materials. That "food" made out of playdough is not nearly as clearly defined as the food made out of plasticine. The kids have investigated the properties of these different kinds of clay and the limits of what one can do with the clay. Which clay is harder or softer? Which is smoother? I noticed one boy discover that the bridge he made with the playdough doesn't take much stress. The plasticine had more of the tensile properties he needed in a building material.

Marilyn: I'm enjoying watching that girl, Marcia, mix finger paints. It seems like she's learning about concepts relating to shades of color. She's trying to make a shade of green that matches the color of the paper. And she's quite precise about it. Look how she adds such a small drop of white. She's involved in the processes observing, comparing, and experimenting.

SCIENCE IN THE EARLY CHILDHOOD INTEGRATED CURRICULUM

The visiting scientists observed as Soshi, Jerry, Alicia, and the other children followed their own interests. Through their spontaneous play, these children are engrossed in inquiry. In fact, in some of their activities, we see a curiosity about concepts that are milestones in the evolution of science itself: the laws of floating and of distance and velocity, and the physics of the buttress. These interests and the activities they stimulate are common among children playing in environments that are rich in possibilities. How can our observations of young children's natural interests as expressed through play lead us to the formation of a balanced science curriculum?

The Goal of Early Childhood Science Education

If we analyze the nature of science, we recognize that central to all scientific inquiry and discovery is the further development of children's dispositions such as curiosity, a drive to experiment, and a desire to critically assess the validity of answers. We believe the goal of science education for early childhood education is to encourage and support these dispositions.

This is our rationale for seeing play as the core of the early childhood science education program. Children's spontaneous play shows us the children's interests, what they are curious about, and how they pose questions and solve problems.

We believe that a developmentally appropriate science program is based on the similarities between scientists involved in science and children involved in play—the interest plus the energy, knowledge, and skills to pursue that interest. We also find that, in both science and play, the interest is often social—shared by others at home or at school or arising from a particular social context. Therefore, to infuse the early childhood program with the spirit of scientific inquiry, we need to acknowledge the vitality of the children's scientific interests as shown through their play. We can then incorporate these interests, and the social energy that accompanies them, into the curriculum.

This play-based approach to early childhood science education addresses what we believe is the basic weakness of the traditional K–12 science curriculum. Our nation has contributed so much to scientific development and has prospered so much from its applications. Yet, today, many U.S. students graduate with a low level of science literacy, which can hamper future scientific development. Most science curriculum programs are seriously flawed by their focus on science facts and routines. What these curricula lack is that which is central to scientific endeavor: the joy of finding out.

The child who wonders why certain yellow flowers appear in some places in a spring meadow but not in others is a young naturalist involved in inquiry. In contrast, the child who dutifully colors in the outline of spring flowers is involved in activity unrelated to the process of science. The first has put forward a problem to be solved, which at its core is scientific. That child is acting like a scientist. The second child has formulated an entirely different problem: How to respond to the teacher's lesson?

In a play-centered curriculum, young children are not simply studying facts but are pursuing problems of interest and judging the adequacy of their answers. For all children to develop the ability to engage in scientific inquiry, teachers must respect them as emergent scientists. In this way we encourage all children to see themselves as members of the scientific community. If this sense of community with science is not established in the early years, the prospects of attracting these children to science in adolescence and young adulthood are diminished. It is in these later years and not before that children become capable of participating in the more rigorous forms of scientific inquiry that we recognize as scientific thought.

Scientific Literacy for All Children. For decades, the American Association for the Advancement of Science has sponsored the work of scientists, science educators, and classroom teachers in an effort to foster programs that ensure that all students become literate in science, math, and technology. *Benchmarks for Science Literacy* is the report of the association's Project 2061 (1993). How is scientific literacy for children in kindergarten through the primary grades described?

> From their very first day in school, students should be actively engaged in learning to view the world scientifically. That means encouraging them to ask questions about nature and to seek answers, collect things, count and measure things, make qualitative observations, organize collections and observations, discuss findings, etc. Getting into the spirit of science and liking science are what count most. Awareness of the scientific world view can come later. (p. 10)

This vision of the goals of science education is reflected in the eight national standards developed by The National Research Council, the main agency of the

National Academy of Sciences (1996). These national standards provide the foundation for most of K–12 science standards developed by state boards of education as well those for early childhood science education:

- Unifying concepts and processes in science
- Science as inquiry
- Physical science
- Life science
- Earth and space science
- Science and technology
- Science in personal and social perspectives
- History and nature of science

Throughout this chapter we discuss how young children develop their understandings in all these areas through the play-based curriculum.

National associations of scientists and individual science educators underscore the importance of both equity and excellence in science education. Children are curious and eager to learn about the physical world. Early childhood educators can play a critical role in providing equal, consistent support for girls and boys well as for children from all cultures and backgrounds to define themselves as competent scientific investigators.

To develop an appropriate science curriculum, we need to draw on the nature of science as well as what we know about children's development. When we analyze the scientists' comments as they observed the kindergarten program, we find that they discussed scientific processes, content, and concepts, as well as dispositions for learning, such as curiosity. These are the very points made by the American Association for the Advancement of Science (AAAS) in Project 2061 (1993), *Science for All Children*. AAAS and the National Science Teachers Association (NSTA) underscore the importance of focusing on children's depth of understanding, rather than the "topic-a-day" approach to science.

Numerous teacher resources are published by these associations as well as by the National Science Resources Center. This is also the approach taken by national science curriculum projects that foster scientific literacy for all children, including children from diverse cultures and backgrounds and children with special needs. These include the Full Option Science System (FOSS), Great Explorations in Math and Science (GEMS), and the Education Development Council's *Young Scientist Series* (e.g., Chalufour & Worth, 2003, 2004, 2006). Each month, the NSTA journal *Science and Children* includes articles for early childhood educators and reviews science books for both educators and children, as well as Internet resources.

As early childhood educators, we can analyze the scientific nature of children's activities by asking ourselves: What scientific processes are involved? What scientific concepts are the children developing? What is the scientific content of their activity? How do children's experiences in school relate to their lives in families and communities?

The Nature of Science

The following is an out-of-date but typical definition of the term *science*: "a study that deals with an area of facts or truths that are arranged systematically and demonstrate the operation of general laws." Many early childhood educators and parents of young children recall memorizing a definition such as this one.

Today's children are actively engaged in science. One primary emphasis is on the importance of helping students develop their understanding of science by gaining competence in the processes of science as well as acquiring knowledge through participation in meaningful scientific activities. Another primary emphasis is the long-term development of an understanding of scientific concepts—the "big ideas" in science. Although scientific content, "the facts," is still a basic part of science education, the American Association for the Advancement of Science, Project 2061 (1993) and other policy statements emphasize that merely learning scientific facts is not the primary goal of science education. Today's scientists and science educators view science as a social process in which knowledge is constructed through social collaboration with colleagues. Young children think as scientists when they see science as part of daily life, that is, "science in personal and social perspectives."

Scientific Processes.   Young children naturally use scientific processes to seek answers to their questions. We watch them as they engage in inquiry: observing, describing, comparing, questioning, collecting and organizing data, communicating with others (e.g., discussing and recording information), interpreting results, and seeking answers to questions.

> In a first-grade class, 6-year-old Mark and 7-year-old Gillian observe that earthworms have rings, and some of them have a thickening near the front end. They compare several earthworms and find that both small and large worms have a lot of rings, but that "only the bigger ones have a lump near the front." They want to find out what the lump is and if the older worms, like trees, have more rings. With their teacher's help, they find the answer to their question about the lump in a high school biology text drawing of a worm. No information is given about the number of rings, so they go back and count. They find they need a magnifying lens because one worm is tiny so it's difficult to count the rings. ✆

Mark and Gillian collaborate on finding answers to these questions. This vignette shows their obvious delight in learning with and from each other and thereby illustrates their co-construction of knowledge as they answer their questions through this joint activity as well as. As they draw pictures of the worm, they're involved in the scientific process of recording information. By using common tools of science such as the magnifying lens, they are involved in the development of science competencies.

Young children are capable of using many scientific processes. They are often careful observers and hone that ability when they examine the rings on a worm or the legs of a beetle. In spontaneous, playful interactions, they are eager to communicate their observations, another scientific process. With further teacher guidance, young children can compare properties of objects, organize information, and record their data through drawings and technological tools such as photos or videotapes. The availability of low-cost digital cameras offers opportunities for teachers as well as children themselves to document change over time. (See, for example, DeMarie & Ethridge, 2006.) Photos are easily enlarged to accommodate children with visual disabilities as well as group discussions. Some hand-drawn or photo books about changes can be created in a day, such as one about making and baking rolls. Young children also begin to understand the concept of time through digital camera recordings of long-term projects, such as documenting the growth of beans planted in cups, pumpkins planted and harvested in the school garden, or the growth of Bun-Bun, the class rabbit.

Scientific Concepts.   Scientific concepts are organizing principles of "what we know." For example, "cylindrical," "green," "hard," and "life cycle" are examples of concepts that we can apply in many content areas. Ibrahim knows that green is a property that can refer to different objects: the tomato leaf, the harder tomatoes, some of the crayons, and paint at the easel. Many basic concepts young children develop relate to the properties of objects. They learn to describe objects in terms of such properties as color, shape, size, and weight. Teachers can model science conversations that acknowledge children's love of long, unusual, and descriptive words such as transparent, minuscule, and chrysalis.

As children grow older, they are able to understand more abstract, relational concepts such as ideas about motion, light and shadows, changes, and relative position. Young children learn science concepts best when they encounter the same concept in different content areas. For example, Duckworth (2001) reminds us that "we see how early experience, only partially understood, over time contributes to the construction of large ideas" (p. 185).

During their brief tour, the scientists observed the children dealing with a great many scientific concepts. For example, through their spontaneous play, Tanisha and April were learning about concepts of distance and velocity, and Luis was learning about the concept of buttressing.

Science Content.   Science content refers to the subject matter, the factual information. For example, a book on insects might include sections with facts about leafhoppers, aphids, dragonflies, mayflies, moths, and butterflies. It is just as vital that we provide ample opportunities for young children to explore a wide range of science areas. In addition to books on life science, there are numerous developmentally appropriate and engaging books on physical science and earth and space science.

In a balanced science curriculum, children learn science content within an organized framework of unifying scientific concepts and processes. In a play-centered science curriculum with sufficient time for spontaneous play, children's understanding of particular scientific content, concepts, and processes are expressions of their own curiosity, interest, and creativity. If we analyze the touring scientists' observations of the kindergarten in terms of science content, we find that through spontaneous play, some children were finding out about worms, some about sand, some about blocks, and some about different collage materials.

Ibrahim's teacher has documented his involvement with teacher-guided gardening activities. He is one of several children who always return to the garden each day. At 4 years old, Ibrahim has learned a lot about the tomatoes in the small garden outside his child care center. He knows that tomatoes can be yellow as well as red, and he can identify several varieties of cherry tomatoes and beefsteak tomatoes. He can also distinguish a tomato leaf by its shape, texture, and fragrance. He knows when the tomatoes are ripe and how to pick them carefully. When Ibrahim's teacher shares her observations with his parents, she learns that his grandparents, who come from Oman, have several types of tomatoes growing in their garden. She explains to his parents how his playful gardening activities, at home as well as school, relate to specific state standards such as children's understandings of the attributes of objects (e.g., smell, color, shape, and size), understanding of the life cycles of plants, as well as understanding science as a personal and social endeavor connected to their everyday lives.

This vignette shows how important it is for children to have the chance to return to favorite activities again and again. As children work with the same objects over an extended period, they enjoy their growing mastery of specialized science content.

Observing plants and animals in the classroom can lead to a curiosity about nature.

The Nature of the Child

In developmentally appropriate science education programs, teachers continually learn more about the development of the children they teach. What are the interests shown by 4-year-old Madison and 7-year-old Samuel? How can we describe their developmentally different way of understanding the physical world around them?

The Child's Level of Development.   In Chapter 2, we briefly introduced basic principles of constructivist developmental theories. In developing an early childhood education science curriculum, teachers find constructivist theories helpful in looking at children's experiences in context and in interpreting children's interests and responses.

The work of Piaget and others demonstrates that young children do not carry out scientific processes such as experimenting in the same way that adults do (Piaget, 1965a). For example, children might experiment with yellow and blue paint to create a particular shade of green, but their experimentation will not be systematic. Rather than adding a bit more blue and mixing it well, they might add different amounts of different colors. Young children might try different ways to use a set of weights to balance a balance beam, but their efforts are trial and error rather than planned and comprehensive.

A closer look at children's levels of cognitive development leads us to understand why young children will not be able to comprehend many scientific concepts despite well-intentioned instruction. Mature scientific thinking involves such processes as the ability to analyze, to form hypotheses, and to make inferences and deductions. Young children are not able to do this in the way adults do. The deductions and inferences made by young children do not have the generalized application found in the thought processes of most adolescents and adults. As the previous example illustrates, children's thinking is egocentric and perception bound. They are not yet able to understand all aspects of sequences that occur over time.

In *The Child's Conception of Physical Causality,* Piaget (1965b) described children's growing understanding of shadows. He found that young children believed that the objects themselves produced the shadows. When he asked very young children about shadows, they usually told him that the shadow next to a book was an actual substance coming from the book. The somewhat older children he spoke with had begun to understand the relationship between the shadow and the source of light. Not until most children were in middle childhood did they explain to him that the shadow resulted from an absence of light and that the actual object was blocking the light.

This does not mean that we should underestimate young children's abilities or ignore their interests. Shadows illustrate this point well. Many young children demonstrate their fascination with shadows in their spontaneous play. Skillful teachers find guided play as well as teacher-initiated activities that draw on children's interests.

Science Learning and Social Contexts.   Scientists as well as constructivist developmental theorists consider the importance of social contexts. Two national science standards state this: "science in personal and social perspectives" and "history and nature of science." Scientists consider the endeavor of science an outcome of historical, cultural development and therefore social in context.

The development of children's science learning is also influenced by their social and cultural environments. As Vygotsky (1978) emphasized, families, schools, and communities are integral to each child's development. In some cultures, children have many experiences that support the development of particular scientific processes, concepts, and content. Parents and teachers in urban areas, for example, might focus on providing children with different types of building blocks. In Janet's urban kindergarten class, children tend to build cityscapes—apartment buildings, offices, malls, and freeways. They ask numerous questions about the office building that is under construction a block away from their school. In contrast, the parents and teachers of children who live on farms might stress content such as plants and animals, concepts such as "the life cycle," and observational processes such as observing whether plants are ready for harvest.

We see that children's understandings usually develop faster in subject areas in which they have greater experience with the physical world and where important adults and peers share social knowledge with them. With time for further maturation and more interactions with the physical and social world, young children's manner of thinking changes. We need to build our science programs around children's present ways of thinking and provide the experiences that will foster future development.

Nature and the Environment: Developing a Sense of Place.

Jaelitza, a teacher in a rural child-care center, reflects on the children's daily opportunities for rich outdoor adventures in her article, "Insect Love: A Field Journal," published in *Young Children* (1996):

> Teacher Neil found a Promethia moth, a nocturnal moth, which had attached itself to a bottle in the pony shed. Brought into the light, it did not fly away, and so we were able to observe it very closely. Matt and Levi were very interested. Neil showed us its picture in the field guide and went on to answer the two boys' questions by referring to the moth as well as the text of the guide.
>
> Matt and Levi were interested in our new field-study materials—bug "houses" and a new magnifying glass. They were ready to set out immediately, and I followed. Turning over logs that demarcate the tepee garden patch, we found a ready supply of sow bugs, immature snails, worms, ants and spiders. . . . (p. 31)

Jaelitza (personal communication, 1996) and other teachers and naturalists express the concern that few of today's children have opportunities to develop a deep connection to the land, a sense of geographical place, through sustained opportunities to play outdoors in fields, woods, beaches, and even empty city lots.

The need for place is expressed beautifully in Nabhan and Trimble's (1994) classic work, *The Geography of Childhood*. In *Last Child in the Woods: Saving Our Children from Nature-Deficit Disorder*, Louv (2008) writes that for children to develop emotionally, socially, and intellectually, they need unstructured, direct and playful experiences with nature. Sadly, around the world, more children are living in urban areas and spending more time indoors. Louv explains that most children now have a deficit of fundamental experiences in nature. Children are growing up disconnected from themselves as well as from the natural world, at the very time that we recognize a need for all people to develop greater awareness, knowledge, and feelings about protecting the global environment,

Helping Urban Children Develop a Sense of Place.   Although play-centered curricula draw on and reflect children's social contexts, it is critical that we not limit our expectations and curricula to these contexts.

Melben (2000), a teacher in an urban elementary school, views urban children's lack of outdoor nature activities as an example of inequities. In an article in *Science and Children,* she presents examples of efforts to develop science projects that followed the children's own interests and drew from their experiences. Her descriptions of projects with rainwater and pigeons amply illustrate that children's understandings of ecology and sense of wonder can be promoted in urban as well as more rural settings.

This principle is particularly important in science. In cities and suburbs, and particularly in unsafe areas, we need to ask: How can we help urban children, their families, and ourselves develop a sense of place, an appreciation and ease with the outdoors, and a feeling of wonder about life? Fortunately, in recent years there has been an enormous increase in environmental education resources for parents and educators of young children. Numerous books, journals, and articles suggest ways to engage urban children with the natural world (e.g., Arce, 2006; Benson & Miller, 2008; Campbell, 2009; Chalufour & Worth, 2004, 2006; Rosenow, 2008).

As a preschool teacher in New York City, Butler realized that the children in her program had little knowledge about or appreciation for nature (Hachey & Butler, 2009). Her commitment to helping young urban children develop a love of nature and sense of place lead Butler and Hachey to develop experiences that integrated nature-based play and gardening in the urban classroom.

> I wanted to the children to listen to birds and to look at the trees . . . I wanted them to help care for plants and notice the growth, the smells, and the textures of leaves . . . I wanted the children to first notice, then observe, then appreciate and wonder about these things. . . . (p. 42)

Science education literally saved the day for one school in Texas. Haines and Kilpatrick (2007) highlight how student achievement and teacher morale rose after their school became a Project Learning Tree (PLT)–certified school united faculty.

These teachers in the United States are contributing to widespread global education efforts to enhance young children's connections with the natural world and their cultures. In South Korea, for example, an "eco-early childhood" curriculum promotes care for the local and global environment. This curriculum includes activities to promote habits such as recycling and are integrated with traditional Korean practices such as traditional exercises and meditation (Kim & Lim, 2007).

Environmental education challenges all of us to slow down and do more. What Louv (2008) and other writers and educators such as Rivkin (2006) help us remember is that developing a sense of place involves more than "curriculum." Children and adults need time to play, to wonder, and to relax if they are to truly engage with feelings as well as ideas about the natural world. (See Chapter 12.)

Integrating the Child's Interests

Observation of individual children's spontaneous play is central to discovering their interests. These interests are the children's bridge between play and science and home. As teachers committed to equality of opportunity, it is particularly important for us to consider the ways in which children's interests can lead all children to participate in science.

Bee loves to observe the silkworms. She feeds them mulberry leaves, has arranged her own box, and is keeping a daily journal with descriptions and pictures. Her teacher discovers that Bee's grandmother comes from Laos and knows how to spin the silk from the cocoons into thread. Bee, her grandmother, and her teacher work together to plan a series of activities that are multicultural, playful, and scientific.

The urban children in Shelley's preschool program had been sloshing through the snow for weeks as they walked to school, delighting in falling snow, and sharing stories about snow adventures. Shelley first extended these activities by bringing snow and icicles inside in containers so that the children could have unhurried observations and chances to discuss the melting process. She then put water in an ice tray and took the tray out of the freezer throughout the morning so that the children could observe the changes. This led to a weeklong observation of the melting of a 50-pound block of ice that Shelley purchased from an ice company and placed in a baby bathtub.

Ferguson (2001) writes about Thomas, a 5-year-old in her class, sharing her concern that he appeared uninvolved with the other children as well as uninterested in the classroom curriculum. This changed dramatically when, during a class discussion about snakes, Thomas hesitantly shared that he knew all about snakes, that he "had almost 100 snakes in his basement" (p. 6). Of course, he received quite a response from his peers. Ferguson describes how she extended this teachable moment into a lengthy inquiry project, although she felt uncomfortable around snakes. Thomas and his uncle Bob served as enthusiastic resource specialists to Ferguson and the other students. Uncle Bob brought in a large snakeskin. Thomas and several children took a trip to a pet store, where they saw a huge snake. This was followed with related classroom activities that reflected the children's interests, including a collection of plastic reptiles that Ferguson placed in the manipulative area.

Meeting the Needs of Children
Who Are English Language Learners

In her kindergarten, Alia has built a treasure box. This is an example of a teacher-initiated project that requires little knowledge of English while promoting continuous and playful peer interactions. First, her teacher has children who are interested draw a representation of the carpentry project each has designed. With some adult help, Alia carefully measures and cuts the wood. She learns about sanding, first using coarse sandpaper, then a finer grade. This activity is part of the ongoing science program that builds on children's interests and that promotes equity for all children. ✐

This vignette shows how play-centered science curriculum provides numerous opportunities for children to develop greater fluency in English as they explore the physical world and interact with their peers. Teachers show that children are welcomed by including known, familiar objects in the indoor and outdoor environment, particularly things children see at home. This encourages English language learners, including children who are immigrants and refugees, to draw on familiar experiences and show their competencies. In this way, teachers reduce stressful situations and provide support for listening and speaking in relaxed and engaging situations. The National Science Education Standards emphasize the investigation of authentic questions such as those encountered in daily life situations when considering issues of equity and access for all students: "The diversity of students' needs, experiences and backgrounds requires that teachers and schools support varied, high-quality opportunities for all students to learn science" (National Academy of Sciences, 1996, p. 4). Playful teachers consider the innumerable ways that children can relate science processes, concepts, and content to their everyday lives, families, and cultures.

Through science activities, teachers take advantage of the many ways that the development of a new language parallels that of the first language. Central to first language development is a supportive social and physical environment. Similarly, early childhood educators create environments in which children's learning of English can flourish (DeBey & Bombard, 2007; Genishi, 2002; McDonnough & Cho, 2009). As children play and explore, they not only hear language but also wish to communicate their own observations, questions, and desires. Playful science experiences such as Alia's carpentry project and activities with blocks, plants, sand, and water provide daily opportunities for children's gestures to be understood in context. A single word or two- or three-word phrases convey ample meaning and simple sentences contribute to conversations with peers and adults.

From his first day at school, Carlos looked forward to experimenting at the water table. Initially, he spoke mostly with two other children who spoke Spanish as well as English. His teacher noted the complexity of his explorations. Recognizing his interests and level of ability, his teacher bought plastic tubing, funnels, and a series of graduated beakers so that Carlos and his friends would find many challenging problems to solve. ✐

Developing Inclusive Science
Curriculum for Children with Special Needs

In inclusive programs, teachers plan play-centered science curriculum to meet the needs of all young children. This includes those whose special needs have not yet been formally identified, as well as those who are receiving special services. The U.N. Convention on the Rights of the Child recognizes that all young children have the right to play. How can teachers ensure that children with special needs have numerous opportunities to engage in spontaneous and guided play related to science? Just as the scientists toured the kindergarten with an eye toward opportunities for learning science, all teachers can tour their environment with an eye toward equity, serving students with special needs. Such informal tours are even more useful in the company of early childhood special educators, occupational therapists, or speech therapists.

Melva learned that the following year Aiden, a student with visual disabilities, would be a student in her second-grade class. To prepare, she wanted to learn more about his development and his interests, as well his specific visual abilities and challenges. During the last weeks of school, she met with family members, his current teacher, and the special education teacher. As they walked through the classroom, his grandmother commented that he'd enjoy the math manipulatives and really like the terrarium with the desert lizard. Joy, the special education teacher, described a range of computer-assisted technologies including nature Web sites with special features to accommodate people with low vision. Melba learned more by observing Aiden in his first-grade class. She saw firsthand that during spontaneous play Aiden and several peers built with a set of table blocks and made structures with clay. Melva was surprised to confront her own stereotypes when she saw Aiden and a friend working on a large puzzle of a forest scene.

The following questions serve as an initial guide. Do all children have easy access to materials? Are particular accommodations necessary for a child to be able to see or hear or use tools such as scales, magnifying lenses, or scissors? Are there quiet corners for a single child to focus on an exploration as well as open outdoor spaces for active exploration, climbing, and swinging? Are spaces set up so that children can play alone or with one other child without the stimulation of a larger group? What accommodations are needed so that the experiences of children with particular special needs are similar or most equal to those of peers?

Kara teaches first grade in a school where the most common reason for absence is asthma. A fifth of the children in her class have already been diagnosed by age 6. In this school and across the country, an increasing number of children are spending more time in hospitals and at home due to this environmentally related and serious illness. Last year, when children were home for more than a few days, Kara mailed them worksheets. She and several other primary-grade teachers realized that they needed to be more creative because many in their classes had frequent absences. They've invented "make and take" science boxes with donated materials prepared by the children and family members. Their goal is to add another science box each month so children have choices. A science book made by the class about a current class project is always included. Kara makes sure that the boxes have tops that work like trays so objects don't fall on hospital floors. Materials, like collections for sorting, are included so that children can do activities independently or with others. Other materials are provided that can be used for group games with other children or adults, such as science-themed game cards. The accompanying handout of ideas is not only translated into Spanish and Korean, but also includes photos so that the children themselves can "read ideas." Kara and the other teachers visited the nearby hospital, met the child life specialist, and made future plans to collaborate. ✐

As they work with children with special needs, teachers remember that all children have particular strengths and interests. For example, Pat shared one of her treasured memories of a kindergarten child with autism who loved to play with blocks. She honored his joy and involvement with blocks rather than insisting that he "go to another activity first." After many weeks, it was there in the block area that he first engaged in parallel play and later spoke his first word.

ADDRESSING STANDARDS IN THE PLAY-CENTERED CURRICULUM

The National Science Education Standards statement emphasizes the importance of developmentally appropriate curriculum and constructivist teaching practices. According to the National Science Education Standards (1996),

> From the earliest grades students should experience science in a form that engages them in active construction of ideas and explanations that enhance their abilities to develop the abilities of doing science... . Students should do science in ways that are within their developmental capacities. (National Academy of Science, 1996, p. 1)

Our review of national and state standards demonstrates that an integrated primary science curriculum with play at its center can address most national and state science standards and indicators. Indeed, many science strands and specific standards relate to playful activities (see Drew, Christie, Johnson, Meckley & Nell, 2008; Jacobs & Crowley, 2010; Van Thiel & Putnam-Franklin, 2004). In Table 9.1 we draw from vignettes in this chapter to illustrate how teachers develop play-based curriculum that addresses standards.

Numerous national and state science standards can seem confusing and overwhelming. Teachers can simplify the process of addressing standards. The National Science Education Standards (1996) and standards of many states emphasize the importance of integrated, extensive explorations of familiar environments and

Table 9.1 Addressing Science Standards in the Play-Centered Curriculum

National Science Standards*	Illustration
Science as Inquiry	
Children develop abilities necessary to do scientific inquiry, e.g., children pose questions, explore, and investigate.	At the water table, Rosa observes and interacts with objects. She explores what happens when she pushes wood chips below the surface of the water.
	Mark and Gillian find answers to their question about the "lumps" on the worm.
Physical Science	
Children develop understandings of the properties of objects.	Ibrahim distinguishes the tomato leaf by its properties: shape, texture, and fragrance.
Children develop understanding of the position and motion of objects.	As April and Tanisha roll toy cars down the bridge, they explore how incline and force affect speed.
Life Science	
Children develop understandings of the characteristics of organisms and environments.	Jerry observes and comments on the silvery trail a snail makes as it moves.
Earth and Space Science	
Children develop understandings of properties of earth materials.	Matt and Levi examine soil and rocks.
Science and Technology	
Children develop understandings and abilities to distinguish between natural objects and objects made by humans.	Mark and Gillian use a magnifying lens to observe worms.
Science in Personal and Social Perspectives	
Children develop understandings of types of resources.	Matt and Levi live in a rural area. They explore their environment, turning over logs and finding numerous living things.
Children develop concepts relating to changes in the environment.	Children in Janet's class in an urban area use blocks to build cityscapes.

*National Standards for grades K–4. The early learning standards developed by each state are coordinated with these unifying concepts and processes.

materials. The stated goal is for young children to develop deeper understanding rather than superficial information from short, unrelated activities.

To examine your program's standards from an integrated perspective, first identify the program's "big ideas," that is, the processes, concepts, and content identified as most important. At the national level, the K–4 standards address "science as inquiry." These standards focus on children's abilities to understand and engage in inquiry processes such as asking questions, observing, using simple tools, using data to construct explanations and knowledge and to communicate their work to others. Most states' early learning standards include a similar emphasis on scientific processes: children's asking questions about their world, seeking answers, and communicating with others.

Most state standards focus on unifying concepts and processes. Guidelines provide examples of learning experiences that are developmentally appropriate. For example, we find that in many states, children develop understandings in earth science by using wet and dry sand and talking about their experiences. They might compare and describe the rocks found in their neighborhoods. Across the country, many children learn about insect life cycles by discussing and documenting their observations of the lives of butterflies. Table 9.1 illustrates how teachers can relate children's play-centered activities to science standards.

The stated goal of the national standards and most state science standards is to support young children's curiosity, wonder, and engagement with their physical world and knowledge about it. Some state standards and indicators for early childhood programs are very general, whereas others are carefully crafted to articulate with the state's primary science standards. At first glance these often appear more detailed. We find that teachers can address standards in an integrated, meaningful way when they develop an environment that is rich in possibilities for play and exploration. In doing so, teachers consider children's interests and the knowledge children bring from home.

EXTENDING THE SCIENCE CURRICULUM

How can teachers extend the science processes, concepts, and content that children deal with in their own unstructured play? How can we decide when to intervene and when not to? What best supports children's learning?

In Chapters 4 and 5, we discussed principles that guide orchestration and presented a continuum of intervention strategies ranging from setting the stage to guiding play to teacher-initiated activities. When thinking about enriching the science curriculum, we consider strategies at all points along the continuum and implications for extending children's involvement with science. Recognizing the key role of play in development, we focus first on providing an environment rich in possibilities for spontaneous play. This contrasts with science programs that typically begin with particular activities and then consider opportunities for children to explore and create.

Setting the Stage for Learning about the Physical World through Spontaneous Play

The basis for a play-centered curriculum is a well-planned environment that allows for multiple opportunities for spontaneous play. Developing an environment that is rich in opportunities for children is a great challenge for teachers. It takes careful planning to enable children to have the chance to work with a wide variety of materials in

Materials offer children opportunities for playful exploration of the physical world.

a great many ways. Different types of paints, clays, collage materials, blocks in different shapes and sizes, sand and water, climbing structures, plants, animals, and a varied collection of objects, especially recycled ones, are a few of the many materials found in play-centered programs.

The play-centered environment is flexible. Physical space can be rearranged as interests change. If a group of children is interested in working with large blocks, the teacher might decide to extend the space allotted for block activities, as well as provide additional materials. We observed children in one class making an impressive collection of blocks with milk cartons of different sizes fitted together. One fortunate class in a rural area had new possibilities open up when Russell's father brought in a truckload of coarse sand from the river, and the parent group built a sand and gravel pit. The children became more involved in large vehicle construction play.

Encouraging Further Exploration of the Environment

After initially developing the environment, teachers then observe children in their spontaneous play to modify the environment so that children can extend their play. Like a dance, this involves the teachers themselves in a creative and playful process.

Based on her observations of Rosa at the water table, her teacher decided to place a box with an assortment of objects near the water table. She included some large wooden objects that floated and small metal objects that sank. Rosa's teacher understood that she was providing new curricula opportunities for all the children, as well as individualizing the curriculum for Rosa. Jerry and Alicia were interested in snails. What would they do if their teacher turned over a shovelful of soil to expose worms, sow bugs, and larvae? Other children were using blocks to build towers. Perhaps a set of table blocks or pattern blocks would engage children in extended investigations.

These examples show teachers observing the children, following the children's lead, thinking of the many materials that might be added, and adding materials in thoughtful and nonobtrusive ways. Teachers are engaged in an ongoing process of matching and extending. Another preschool teacher describes how digital photos support children's use of technology and provide them with opportunities to examine and talk about what they did and to generate ideas for extending their explorations (Hoisington, 2003).

Interacting with Children in Their Play

Taking the child's-eye view in science education often takes the form of wordless communication. A teacher's smile, returned to a child's questioning glance, is non-verbal communication. In the context of the child's attempt to balance one more block on a tower of blocks, it is a scientific conversation: "When you do it that way, they fall over." "Yes. I was surprised too."

During spontaneous play, teachers help children maintain their focus by assuming the role of the artist apprentice so that play areas remain less cluttered. In guided play, teachers might decide to take the role of parallel player, sitting side by side with children. If teachers enjoy exploring and playing with blocks or with sand or collage materials, their own sense of interest, wonder, and focused involvement through spontaneous play will be communicated. As long as the teachers' explorations and play involve them in experimenting and discovering new ways to do things or the enjoyment of familiar patterns, they can avoid the trap of producing static models that children might copy. Teachers model use of scientific language in the role of spectator. What questions come to mind: "How can you build a tower with connecting turrets using table blocks?" "Can you build a tunnel under the sand pyramid you just constructed?"

Orchestrating Extensions for Play

In Chapter 4, we show how teachers use the idea of the play continuum as they plan play-centered curriculum. We begin with play-generated curriculum that emerges from the interests of the children.

Play-Generated Curriculum

In their play, Sarah, Dean, and Nellan expressed their interest in worms. John, their second-grade teacher, saw this as an opportunity to introduce different science experiences involving worms. He provided pieces of Plexiglas so the children could observe the movements of the worms in greater detail. When this proved a popular activity, John asked the children to find other wormlike animals. Within a week, there was an exciting collection of caterpillars, several kinds of worms, and insect larvae that Nellan had brought in. This led to a conversation between Nellan and the other children about the differences between worms and insects, as well as the sequence of the insect life cycle. ⌀

One teacher in a school-age child-care program enjoyed the enthusiasm that the children brought to their play with light and shadows. She extended this play by showing them how to outline each other's shadows with chalk on the walkway. This led to the question: "How long and how short does your shadow get?" In follow-up activities, they outlined their shadows on butcher paper several times during the day. The children and teachers had fun generating many researchable questions, for example: "Can you shake your shadow hand with someone else's?" "Can you make your shadow stand on someone else's shadow shoulders?" ✆

Teachers turn to curriculum materials developed by science educators, as well. FOSS and GEMS have units for young children that draw on children's interests as expressed in their play. For example, in the FOSS—Full Option Science System— earth and space science unit *Air and Weather* (2005a), children construct and try out parachutes, make balloon rocket systems, and build kites and pinwheels.

Through our selection of science-related activities, we reflect society's social and cultural values as well as our personal interests. For example, when John asks the children to collect other wormlike animals, he is thinking about his state's science frameworks, which include a focus on living things and the life cycle for the primary level. Shelley relates children's explorations with ice to the physical science strand of her state's frameworks, which includes "states of matter" as an important concept. The vignettes throughout this chapter illustrate how teachers support children's spontaneous play in ways that are recognized by society as relevant to science learning.

Curriculum-Generated Play. In a play-centered curriculum, teachers intentionally explore the ways in which the curriculum can lead to play. The connection is seamless when the science curriculum is well integrated rather than a series of unrelated activities.

Although teacher-planned science programs can be integral parts of a play-centered curriculum, teachers need to evaluate the program's philosophy and activities to ensure that program and activities complement play-centered curriculum. Teachers can select or develop units that draw on children's interests and naturally lead back to children's spontaneous play. For example, the FOSS units *Balance and Motion* (2005b) and *Air and Weather* (2005a) and the GEMS units *Treasure Boxes* (1997) and *Ant Homes Under Ground* (1996) often stimulate play in which children draw on what they are learning. *The Young Scientist Series* includes books on nature, water, and building structures and begin with opportunities for open exploration followed by suggestions for more focused explorations and extension activities (Chalufour & Worth, 2003, 2004). Every month, the NSTA journal, *Children and Science,* and the NAEYC journal, *Young Children,* include articles in which teachers of young children share creative ideas for investigations of life science (e.g., Blackwell, 2008; McHenry & Buerk, 2008), earth and space science (e.g., Danisa et al., 2006; Ogu & Schmidt, 2009; Trundle, Willmore, & Smith, 2006), and physical science (e.g., Ashbrook, 2006; Longfield, 2007; Novakowski, 2009).

In *Serious Players in the Primary Classroom,* Wasserman (2000) describes how teachers can plan thematic science units so that children have opportunities to re-play concepts and content they already have encountered in more structured lessons. The following vignettes describe the ongoing thematic ecology unit on arthropods and the continued exploration and play of Jenny's kindergarten and first-grade children.

In September, Jenny teaches the children how to use bowls to collect in-sects and spiders in a wooded area near the kindergarten/first-grade class-room. She models tapping bushes or shrubs with a stick over a white plastic tub. Leaves, dirt, dust, and animals fall into the tub. Ned, Shawn, and Ashley crouch around the tubs eagerly narrating in careful detail the movements of the animals: "There's a tiny green spider. It's *so* small, wait, there's two. How many spiders do you have? Don't let it get out!"

Children's interest in spiders continues. Several weeks later, Ashley, Yumi, Eric, and Ned are on their hands and knees, carefully using sticks to lift and ad-just the position of a metal, wheeled object. Eric lifts the entire object slowly, re-vealing red debris, dirt, and many small insects. Suddenly Ashley yells, "Oh my gosh, a spider! A red spider! It has eggs." A large, rust-colored spider with a round, whitish abdomen is revealed. Quickly it burrows back into the debris and soil. Ned says quietly, "It's a mother spider. It's an egg sac. The white thing is an egg sac." Ashley declares, "It's red like the dirt." Over the next few weeks, the rust-colored spider appears in journals and drawings (such as in Figure 9.1). The children return often to the area to find the spider.

In January, the fourth and fifth graders join the kindergartners outdoors. Shawn walks to the white plastic tubs, chooses one from the wagon and finds a large stick on the ground. He walks with his fourth-grade partner to a bush and silently taps the bushes. He stops, places the bowl on the ground, crouches and looks inside the bowl. His partner watches him. Shawn stands, takes a step back

Figure 9.1
Journal Entry about a
Spider

We foound a Spidere They
was all Red ecsept fer there
was a big White Ovel Thing.
We thinak it Was a Age Sac.
We Thinak it was a Femall.

to the bush and taps again, silently collecting more debris and animals. Again he places the bowl on the ground, squats and bends his head deeply over the bowl and looks. His fourth-grade partner mirrors his stance. ∅

Recasting the Curriculum in Play

The National Science Education Standards recommend that the central strategy for teaching science is the exploration of "authentic questions" (National Academy of Sciences, 1996, p. 30). We find that these explorations are most likely to be replayed in children's subsequent spontaneous play. When science curricula are appropriate for the development and interests of the students, teachers support ways for children to replay what they are learning.

Kogan (2003) relates how kindergarten students in a bilingual (English) school in Mexico City recast a thematic unit about the human body in their play. When children told their personal stories about accidents and broken bones, their teacher tape-recorded the conversations during role play. Kogan describes the in-depth emergent curriculum in which children first drew "memory drawings" of their bones, then viewed x-rays, and examined chicken bones to compare with their drawings. The class visited a medical clinic where a child's grandfather worked. There they had a chance to talk with medical personnel about the x-ray machine and see how doctors checked x-rays on a computer monitor. The kindergartners even used laboratory microscopes to view slides with blood. Back in the classroom, children represented their growing knowledge in numerous ways, including play. Some represented bones, carefully considering what to use for the inside and outside. Others built a complex, pretend x-ray machine, considering how to control the light. These playful activities resulted in further inquiry: "What has bones?" "What bones do different animals have?" And so this inspiring Bone Project continued, involving children and teacher in the full continuum of play-centered curricular activities. ∅

DEVELOPING CONFIDENCE IN TEACHING SCIENCE

Many early childhood educators are concerned that they know too little about science to develop a rich play-centered science program. Unlike the scientists who toured the classroom, many teachers are aware that they have little expertise in the life sciences, physical sciences, or earth sciences. How can teachers who think that they have a weak preparation in this area develop a challenging, play-centered science curriculum?

View yourself and others as members of a community of playful investigators rather than as experts. Think about the science-related activities that you enjoy so that your students will observe your curiosity and your sense of wonder. Become knowledgeable about the interests and abilities of your children and their families, as well as others at school and in the community. By recognizing the scientific expertise of others, you are serving as a good role model for your students. Vignettes such as the example of Bee's grandmother and the silkworm cocoons illustrate that teachers need not feel that they have to be scientific experts. Teachers can enrich their science programs by turning to local resources provided by children, their families, and the community.

Help children learn how scientists investigate by surrounding children with science resource media. By showing your students that you, yourself, turn to science resources including books, DVDs, and science Web sites, you promote children's scientific literacy. In an environment that is rich in science resources and opportunities for play, children and teachers continually extend their knowledge of the physical world and their opportunities for exploring it.

SUMMARY AND CONCLUSION

Young children are curious about the natural world. They are interested in finding out about their physical environment—finding out about how things work. A program based on children's interests therefore includes an emphasis on science. As early childhood educators integrate the curricula with children's spontaneous play as the focal point, they see the great extent to which all children's activities involve science processes, concepts, and content. Like the scientists who toured the kindergarten, teachers begin to "see science" and see opportunities for science activities everywhere. As shown in this chapter, the play-centered science curriculum provides the means to foster children's active, hands-on engagement in ways that promote the inclusion of all children and support equity.

Teachers support inquiry by observing children closely and developing an environment that invites children to explore their physical world through spontaneous play. Further exploration is encouraged through the addition of materials and through supportive teacher–child interaction. Drawing on the children's expressed interests and backgrounds, teachers introduce science activities related to children's play. Teachers' knowledge of guidelines for appropriate practices in addressing standards as well as their knowledge of the unifying concepts and processes in science guide their curriculum decisions so that program standards are addressed in meaningful ways. Appropriate teacher-directed activities complement play-centered activities and lead back to play.

The early childhood years provide a rich and perhaps critical opportunity to draw the natural power and direction of children's reasoning into the community of science. As we incorporate these interests and energies into the early childhood education classroom, we promote equity for all children and promote a scientifically literate generation.

The Arts in the Play-Centered Curriculum

As if in an opera, 4-year-old Noah stands at the easel, reflects, and then declaims in song what he has playfully discovered about color:

> There is some colors which are red, blue, yellow
>
> There is a lot of colors
>
> And there is aqua, aqua,
>
> And there is blue, blue, there is blue, blue . . .
>
> and white and aqua
>
> There is white and aqua

Now he contemplates his palette and sings, "There is some colors," and names the primaries, "Red, blue, and yellow." He dips his brush into the blue: "And there is blue, blue, there is blue, blue," emphasizing blue perhaps because it is basic to aqua. Noah intends to create aqua and knows that one does not do that by starting with white. Finally, the white is celebrated, "and white and aqua," and Noah closes softly, "There is white and aqua." ∅

This delightful image of a child singing while painting accompanies the closing credits of Thelma Harms's classic film, *My Art Is Me* (1969).

What does the image reveal? It reveals the creative transformations in the flow of play that lie at the heart of children's art making. It also tells a lot about what Noah knows about color, and about what he doesn't know about color—there is a bit of green in aqua. And, more importantly, it demonstrates how art (Noah's painting, poetry, and song) and problem solving (his creation of aqua) are intertwined in the context of play. Close observation of children playing within the arts gives teachers sound content for a developmental curriculum. In this chapter, we stress that all curricula in the arts should encompass a balance of play options. These include opportunities to engage in directed and guided play in the arts, such as often occur at circle, project, and small-group time, but equally important, making sure there are ample time, space, and materials for children's spontaneous play as well.

The arts are indispensable to a successful developmental curriculum. This is because children spontaneously turn art into play, and play is the young child's principal means of learning. Indeed, the most successful curricula put art to use at every turn—and, by art, we mean graphic art, construction, poetry, storytelling, music, dance, and drama—so that play and the arts curriculum are indistinguishable from each other.

Now, the spontaneity with which children turn art into play does not mean that specific planning for art need not take place. Such planning embraces a number of considerations:

- When should arts activities be spontaneous? When should they be guided or directed?
- What can be learned from spontaneous engagement in the arts?

- What materials, tools, and resources do the children need?
- What technical homework should the teacher do?
- How can teachers and the environment encourage spontaneity?
- How should they provide guidance and direction?

Considerations such as those listed are discussed next with particular attention to graphic art and construction, but with references throughout to many of the other arts, such as music and drama.

A GUIDE FOR CURRICULUM DESIGN

An effective arts curriculum uses art to support children's play and uses play to support art. Because play occurs throughout the early childhood classroom, so too will the arts. Although we traditionally think that play serves the arts (Noah should discover that aqua has green in it), it is equally important in early childhood settings to ensure that the arts serve play. To see this happen, the teacher must often enter the children's world of play and bring into that world the basic materials and props of art (Gee, 2000; Isenberg & Jalongo, 2010; Zimmerman & Zimmerman, 2000).

Entering the Child's World of Spontaneous Play

A teacher may enter the child's world of play by introducing a new material or a play prop or by modifying a play setting at points when play falters. Sometimes the teacher does this on his own initiative and sometimes at the children's need or request. Sometimes he discusses or demonstrates the new prop or setting directly, and sometimes he does not. Under what circumstances do these variations occur, and what, in the first place, impels the teacher to enter the spontaneous play world at all?

Spontaneous play is often of a "pretend" nature ("I'm the mommy, you be the baby" or "Look at me, I'm a puppy!"). Teachers may fear that entering the child's play requires drama skills in which they are unprepared to engage. The sensitive teacher, having observed children's play closely, knows that even simple modifications in props and settings will stimulate children to initiate more elaborate pretend play. She may pick up a play phone and in a play voice call for an "emergency crew." She may add to the available props an armband with a red cross on it, a badge with "police" written on it, or a few chiffon scarves or transparent curtains. In these instances, little needs to be said to the children. They are likely to pick up the indirect cues instantaneously and create scripts to integrate those props into the ongoing play. British drama educator Dorothy Heathcote utilized this method of indirectly shaping the context to suggest new or elaborated avenues for drama or dramatic play (Johnson & O'Neill, 1984; Lux, 1985; Wagner, 1999).

To stimulate playful engagement and focus in the graphic arts, the teacher might introduce novel painting tools. Sponges, for example, stimulate the creation of patterns and textures. Rollers invite children to paint over the entire surface of the paper

Drawing can be available at the easel as well as the work tables.

rather than merely working in a cramped area in the middle. By demonstrating how the paintbrush can be used to apply paint to the sponge or roller, rather than dipping these tools directly into paint, the teacher helps children gain greater control and mastery over their productions. By modeling these somewhat sophisticated accessories and techniques, the teacher helps children create a new world of pretend.

In dramatic play, the teacher helps a child create his own superhero cape from paper, rather than pulling one from the costume box that he may have used before, when he was 3. By bringing constructive art to dramatic play, the teacher engages the child anew. He makes sure that materials for drawing, cutting, and scribbling are near at hand so that accessories to complement dramatic and fantasy play can be created quickly.

Sometimes children engaged in dramatic play will seek the teacher's assistance, perhaps for new props: "We need things to make a hideout!" Blankets, old sheets, pieces of carpet, and large and small blocks will serve. Or it may be for technical help—say, to design a network of tunnels in the sand (see Chapter 5 for more). Indeed, a young child's technical requirements can become quite elaborate. "There's buried treasure in the sand pit, we need a pirate's map," may signal a need for the teacher as "artist apprentice," to facilitate in constructing a network of lagoons, walkways, bridges, and highways or to devise relevant graphics, such as a skull and crossbones, and DANGER, DETOUR, and other hazard signs.

Incorporating Artwork

Bringing artwork into the flow of play in the classroom environment is not difficult (Isenberg & Jalongo, 2006, 2010). For example, on some bright, sunny day, we may want to trace around children's shadows with the fat chalks we made by mixing plaster of paris and powdered tempera with water in Dixie cups (remembering, of course, to pour the dry mixture into the water, as well as safety concerns about use of powdered mediums). Later the children will wonder why the chalk outlines of their shadows don't fit them when they return to capture them in the late afternoon.

Are the fat chalks still at hand for use on another day (wet and rainy this time) when there are no shadows at all? Then children can use them to create beautiful red, blue, and violet "expressionist" stains on the wet asphalt. Maybe this is the day that Noah will begin to construct his knowledge of color by discovering all the necessary pigments to make aqua. If the teacher is lucky, he may be able to share this epiphany by guiding Noah to notice the many tones of aqua on the pavement.

Abundant access to two-dimensional graphic arts, such as drawing, scribbling, and collage, lends itself to spontaneous exploration of the arts through play. These mediums are provocative adjuncts to children's fantasy play and make important contributions to the child's development of both literacy and small motor skills.

Monitoring the Quality and Challenge of Play: Tactile and Sensory Arts

Teachers know that tactile sensory play with mediums like water, finger painting, and play dough have universal appeal. Children find the tactile/sensory aspects engrossing, and knowledge of the physical properties of materials is acquired through free manipulation of such media. The ease with which finger paint and play dough can be transformed through manipulation also recommends them as valuable adjuncts to fantasy and functional play. Children frequently create songs and stories as they work with these materials. The following anecdote illustrates how what begins as simple tactile/sensory play can bring greater challenge to an art activity. Guided by the teacher, it becomes more deeply complex, resulting in children's acquisition of a whole repertoire of art-making skills and engagement in reflection on what they have learned.

Six-year-old Jason attends a child art studio on Saturday mornings. One of the first activities involves finger painting to music and movement. Children begin by choosing two colors of finger paint. Jason and the other children are encouraged to spread the paint with hands and fingers as far as they can reach on the large sheet of paper that covers the whole table. Today eight children, their teacher, and one parent volunteer are involved. Jason has been willing to don one of his father's old shirts with sleeves rolled, but is very tentative about touching the paint. However, when the music sets up a marching beat and children are encouraged to go around the table using fingers to draw lines, Jason falls in as all march around the table singing in time to the music.

Within a few minutes, the finger paint has covered most of the table. Tools for mark-making, such as twigs, old combs, and toothbrushes, are made available.

The teachers announce, "We're making rivers and mountains and snakes that ripple and wiggle and squiggle around the table." Now a "snowstorm" comes as small scoops of dry tempera are sprinkled into the wet, and children use their hands to make beautiful, blended smudges.

But soon a rainstorm comes up. As mark-making tools are gathered, small brushes and trays of liquid tempera are introduced. As the rain comes faster and faster and faster, teachers and children create patterns of raindrops all over the table, with spatters and splashes of raindrops. As trays of liquid are removed, seeds are sprouting, and plants are growing more lines.

By now the paper is quite wet. Torn and crushed strips and pieces of crepe paper and shiny pieces of gift wrap are distributed for children to press into the wetness to create textures and new patterns. The crepe paper makes multicolored stains, turning red and blue to violet. Finally, confetti is offered, and Jason delightedly integrates his bits into the group's composition.

The handsome piece is allowed to dry as the children clean up. Later it is hung, and at snack time they view their work. As they talk about their composition, they begin to learn the names of the processes they have used; color, line, texture, and space are just a few. Jason liked the bumpy parts the best (Personal observation—Berkeley Child Art Studio). ✆

Manipulation of many tactile/sensory materials is intrinsically satisfying. In some classrooms these may be used in activities merely to keep children occupied, without asking how they can lead to more challenging experiences. The introduction by Jason's teacher of various new materials enhanced the children's acquisition of complex art making skills. Her guidance of the children's reflective discussion of their finger painting experience illustrates also how development can be enhanced around a relatively simple art activity. In the future, these children may utilize particular aspects of their experience, such as line and texture, in more deliberate creations.

With respect to tactile sensory art activities a number of questions can be raised:

- Does the activity have an educational rationale? How much learning does it really promote?
- Does it link with goals for the group curriculum and/or with a learning plan for individual children?
- Does it support extension into pretend play with peers?
- Does the activity have a balanced emphasis not only on aesthetics and the narrative aspects of sociodramatic play, but also on its potential to support children's growth in other areas, such as early math and science?
- Can we be sure that the components of the arts curriculum, particularly for the kindergartner and older child, are sufficiently challenging? Or are we "dumbing down" the curriculum for the older children?
- On the other hand, in mixed-age groupings, are too many aspects of the curriculum overly demanding for the youngest?

The Arts Enhance Knowledge in All Curriculum Domains

The arts, science, mathematics, and play merge when children work on the skeletons they will hang in the haunted house in October. This artful play with bones will get its scientific accuracy from a chart in the school's encyclopedia or, better yet, from our visit to the physiology department of a nearby college. Children may begin to get acquainted with their bodies: how they look and work and what's in them.

Are black paper and a clear plastic jar on hand to make a home for the worms dug up in the moist earth the day after it rained? In this seamless world, the teacher may wonder where art leaves off and science begins.

Constructive play with blocks involves art and math, often replicating architecture, whose interdisciplinary richness has earned it the title of queen of the arts. Blocks are a major accessory for pretend play, creating the context for elaborate fantasies for individuals, pairs, and groups of children. Blocks serve as an important adjunct to extend play. Cardboard box houses (see picture, p. 257) furnished with fabric, wallpaper, and rug scraps, and peopled by miniature clothespin dolls become a small city when blocks laid end to end become "Main Street." Curved units define a small park and provide other needed structures. Here we see several guided play projects evolving and being integrated into the children's spontaneous block play, a sure validator of a play-generating curriculum.

Valuable insights into the child's developing intelligence, competence, and social awareness can be gained by teacher observations, notes, photos, or videotape recording of such play in block areas. (For a review of literature and new insights, see Frost, Wortham & Reifel, 2005, and Reifel & Yeatman, 1991). Teachers will want to use other samples of children's artwork to make authentic assessments of development. What should they look for? Much information is available on universal features of the development of drawing schemas in such classic works as Lowenfeld (1947), Goodnow (1977), and Kellogg (1969).

Special Needs.   Much less information is available on the features of development of drawing by children with emotional, perceptual, or developmental disabilities. Sara, an art therapist working on a kindergarten assessment team, noted that certain features of children's drawings offer early "warning signs." Some of these are a sudden regression to scribbling stage in drawing schemes, drawings that show lesser competence in the execution of some features, the repetition of an obsessively recurring theme, or drawings with all lines leaning in one direction (Wasserman, personal communication, 2005). In the course of this discussion with the art therapist, a cautionary anecdote was submitted to one of the teachers about a smaller-than-average child who consistently painted at the bottom edge of the paper at the easel. Teachers thought this child possibly had a perceptual problem. When they encouraged the child to elevate himself by standing on a large block while painting at the easel, his paintings began to fill the pictorial space.

Supporting Art and Play: Time, Space, Materials, and Teacher Know-How

An arts curriculum becomes established in the play-centered program through the modes of intervention described in Chapters 4 and 5. In the sections that follow, we illustrate how the establishment of a viable arts curriculum depends critically on specific forms of support. When adequate time, space, and well-managed materials are provided—and when teachers have done their technical and conceptual homework and strike an appropriate balance of spontaneous and guided play—engagement in the arts can be explored deeply.

Time.   In ideal programs, ample time for spontaneous and guided play with arts materials is provided throughout the school day. A balance between the two is essential, however. Making spontaneous play the only mode leads to fragmentation and chaos; on the other hand, an overabundance of teacher-directed or teacher-guided activities prevents children from integrating their knowledge by trying things out for themselves. A simple measure of the balance of play options can be achieved by examining the program's daily schedule and staffing pattern. This will enable the teacher to determine whether play options are sufficiently balanced and supported by adequate time and staff. If much of the day is devoted to teacher-directed group activity, it is likely that occasions for spontaneous play are reduced. Research indicates that in early childhood classrooms the most effective learning occurs in small groups (four to six children) engaged in either spontaneous or guided play activities.

Space.   In well-planned programs, space is organized to encourage various configurations of children to engage in arts activities at multiple sites throughout the classroom and play yard:

- Clean, smooth work surfaces free of glue or paint residue from previous projects may be set up in several areas, with seating inviting the solitary play of an individual child or the collaborative or parallel play of pairs and groups. Small trays or Formica-backed blocks for individual work with clay and other wet mediums can be obtained (usually as scrap) from a local kitchen installer or lumber yard.
- Ideally, these areas will be relatively quiet and protected from the flow of fast-paced play, but at the same time be accessible to and visible from active play areas.
- Expectations for the kinds of play to take place are clearly cued by furnishings and accessories, which will distinguish areas where free exploration of materials and resources is expected from those where teacher-guided activities or more structured projects will occur.

If monitored sensitively, both outdoor and indoor centers for drawing, scribbling, writing, dance, and music making can support engagement in the arts as an end in itself or as an adjunct to pretend play.

Musical activities with multiple players need adult guidance.

Pacific Oaks College has developed valuable guides for assessing the complexity of playground spaces. These guides can be used to calculate the play potential of music- and art-making centers and help teachers achieve greater predictability in play patterns (Kritchevsky, Prescott, & Walling, 1977; Walsh, 2008).

Although management and predictability are important elements in any program, inflexible attempts to organize all aspects of arts activities lead to an inhibition and dwindling of children's creative expression. Conversely, too little organization in presentation and sequencing in arts activities can result in the tyranny of chaotic movement and environmental clutter. Both extremes undermine children's chances for mastery, competence, aesthetic development, and understanding.

Materials.   Open-ended arts activities and construction materials ideally complement spontaneous play, providing the raw materials, resources, and accessories for the world of pretend. All the arts, including drama, song, and dance, often merge with and become indistinguishable from play. Not all materials, however, need to be open-ended. For example, older children can use templates for frequently called-on images—stars, various animals, dinosaurs, vehicles, geometric shapes, and even numerals and letters. The use of these materials should be couched, however, in an atmosphere of free exploration, creativity, and problem solving, and they should be well balanced with an abundance of open-ended materials. Music and rhythm instruments fall into a similar category and may need some preliminary introduction in their appropriate use to enhance the quality of spontaneous play.

At a drawing and scribbling table set up for guided play (e.g., with scissors, markers, and plastic templates set out), 4-year-old Toby uses the bus template turned on its side to represent a wind-filled flag fluttering from the main mast of his ship. By tracing the curved edges of the multiple wheels of the bus, he represents the rippling fabric perfectly. Several children immediately seize on the novel potential in the templates, creating flags for their own drawings. ✍

Teacher Know-How.   In doing their homework, early childhood teachers will want to equip themselves with both technical and conceptual information. For example, on a technical level: What colors make pleasing blends? How do primary and secondary colors blend? Knowing this, the teacher can set up the palette at the easel, so that colors that are adjacent to each other blend pleasingly, as in Figure 10.1. Teachers also should be sufficiently familiar with art materials to be able to answer the following questions from their own experience:

- What are the characteristics of paint, paper, and clay?
- How much starch or extender should be added to the paint? The color should not look transparent, watery, and washed out. A creamy texture that flows off the brush pleasingly rather than clumping in globs is desired.
- What kind of clay would be best—a low-fire white clay that takes a glaze or acrylic paint nicely when it is fired, or a rich-toned red clay that is handsome

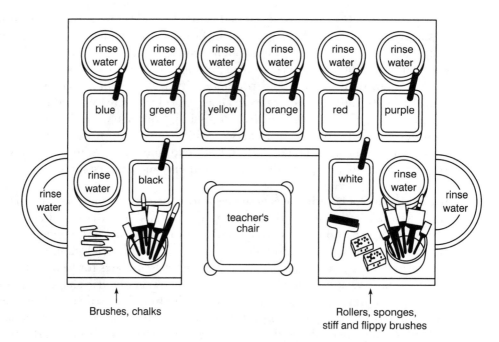

Figure 10.1
Berkeley Child Art Studio Group Palette for Painting Class

in itself when fired but that might stain children's clothing if aprons are not worn?

- Have safety concerns for use of mediums such as glue, powdered pigments, wheat paste, etc., been addressed and children's allergies known to all staff (Isenberg & Jalongo, 2006, 2010)?

Teachers will want to have a good understanding of the peer cultures that emerge in their classrooms. On another level, they will also want to know something about the cultural, historical, and aesthetic traditions of their own heritage and other cultures. What kinds of folk art, music, dance, costumes, or use of color relate to the backgrounds of children in the classroom? What kinds of music or recorded materials are suitable for use with young children during active class time, in or out of doors? What about during nap time and during the late afternoon in after-school care?

Presentation of Art Making and Constructive Play Materials

In addition to the nature and use of art resources and materials, we are concerned with their presentation, accessibility, maintenance, replenishment, and imaginative selection. Children do not use an item spontaneously if they cannot see it, if they do not have some basis for imagining its potential, or if it doesn't work. Therefore:

- Items are displayed at eye level. If possible, use movable shelves as well as some storage units that are equipped with sturdy wheels; this provides flexibility to display materials where they will be used or needed. Musical instruments, movement accessories like scarves and headbands, and recorded music could be stored and displayed for use indoors or out in such movable units.

- Crayons are kept clean and sorted by color with the paper peeled, so a real choice of color can be made.

- Tempera paint is of a good consistency, and tempera paint blocks are kept clean. Each medium is presented in a skill-appropriate choice of colors.

- Water color pans are clean, set up in a skill-appropriate choice of colors and in a self-help setup.

- Paint setups will evolve, starting with (a) primaries, (b) secondaries and tertiaries, (c) black and white, and (d) tints.

- Brushes, rollers, and sponges are introduced as appropriate.

- Appropriate paper for each medium is available.

- Felt markers make a clean and clear mark, scissors cut with ease, and masking tape is readied for use in small strips on a block or two. All items are displayed in a self-help setup.

- Make sure that provocative new items are available from time to time, along with a continuous flow of novel "found" treasures and recyclables, such as the dots from the paper punch, various stickers, or old greeting card pictures and colorful paper scraps. Even the inevitable "anonymous" easel paintings can be recycled into beautiful collage material. Cut into strips or random shapes, they provide incentive for creating new inventions and accessories for fantasy play—headbands, bracelets, and belts—at spontaneous drawing and crafts tables.

- Both large and small unit blocks are made available indoors and outdoors, both with and without props. Block-shaped templates on shelves aid access and storage.
- Stacking blocks too neatly and storing them out of the way or in the same place at all times will diminish children's expressive use.
- Heaping blocks in a box or basket is not recommended, because dumping them out can breed chaos rather than construction, as well as an indifference to the care of the environment.

Attention needs to be given to how different play materials are arranged relative to each other. At a staff meeting to discuss combative play that seemed to occur frequently around the large dinosaurs located in the block area, one teacher reported that on a visit to another school, he had seen an alternative dinosaur display; both large and small dinosaurs were located in a carpeted area within the science center. The area also included attractive books and materials that provided pictorial information on dinosaur habitats from the prehistoric age. In this way the science area was expanded and enriched, and the block area was liberated for constructive play. ✆

On another more general note, constant vigilance is needed to ensure that the children's display areas do not become usurped for teacher or project storage or become catchalls, thereby losing their effectiveness as a support for "choice." This is a particularly pernicious problem when there are multiple users, such as occurs in the necessary rotation of morning and afternoon staffs or when different age groups must be served.

The teacher's respect for the child's expression is reflected in developmentally appropriate expectations as well as in the quality and appropriateness of materials available and the care taken in their presentation. Sometimes the most expensive materials are not always the best. In cases of more costly materials, consider how they might possibly be obtained. For example, although newsprint or recycled computer paper may be adequate for the drawing and scribbling table, it is poor support for tempera applied with a young child's vigorous strokes. With resources parsimoniously husbanded through such activities as the recycling of crayons and diligent scrounging of paper ends from local printers, perhaps a very good quality easel paper (ideally 80#) could be affordable.

Standards for Competencies in the Arts. Teacher "know-how" includes a knowledge of standards of developmentally appropriate competencies in constructive arts, drama, music, and movement and dance, so all children's advances may be extended and supported through guided as well as spontaneous play. Teachers should acquaint themselves with the National Art Education Association's (1999) standards for the arts so that children in the classroom have opportunities to integrate their knowledge and express deep feelings and meaningful ideas through the arts (Isenberg & Jalongo, 2006). See Table 10.1 for samples of standards and suggested curriculum in the arts.

Table 10.1 Addressing Some Standards for Visual and Constructive Arts

Standards	Examples
Children will become responsible users of art media and tools.	Noah spontaneously experiments with mixing colors to make "aqua" at a well-organized painting center, where he has learned routines for independent use of materials. Special tools, such as a paint roller, help him relate to the whole pictorial space rather than one small area only.
Children should have opportunities to gain mastery of a variety of techniques and processes.	In guided play activities Noah and his classmates begin to learn about volume by constructing tunnels out of clay for miniature animals.
Children will become aware of and be able to talk about line, texture, color, and space.	In a special multimedia finger painting activity, Jason begins to learn about line, texture, space, and color. In a feedback session about the activity, the teacher guides the children in reflecting on what they have learned in the activity about line, texture, color, and space.
Children will be able to recognize their own work and that of peers.	At snack time children discuss their paintings that have been displayed for the monthly art show. Later they design invitations for parents and act as docents for an "opening" at "pickup" time later in the day.
Children will develop control and be able to dance and execute rhythmic movement in concert with music.	Masha's mother makes elastic head and waistbands for use in the movement and dance center. Tucking colorful scarves into the waistbands and headbands, Masha teaches other children her "Fly Horse" dance.
	At daily music time, some children learn and use a simple notational system to indicate a pattern of long and short accents and rests in a three-line composition for rhythmic hand clapping.
Children will become acquainted with and share in the classic genres of their own and other cultures.	Isabella interprets a Matisse painting in her own way in her K–1 art class. Matisse is her favorite painter. Her brother, Adrian, prefers the special African masks they have learned about in his second-grade class.

Sources: Information from National Art Education Association. (1999). *Purposes, Principles, and Standards for School Art Programs.* Reston, VA: Author; Seefeldt, C. (2005). *How to Work with Standards in the Early Childhood Classroom.* New York: Teachers College Press; Isenberg, J. P., & Jalongo, M. R. (2010). *Creative Thinking and Arts Based Learning.* Upper Saddle River, NJ: Pearson Education.

Content

In the previous sections we discussed how the classroom environment can be set up to enhance play, particularly spontaneous play, in the arts. In this section we discuss various specific contents that teachers will want to introduce to enhance children's knowledge. These curricula may involve a greater degree of preparation and guidance on the part of the teacher to ensure that much of the learning can occur in spontaneous engagement with the materials provided.

Cultural Enrichment in the Arts

In some school districts, primary grade teachers and art specialists have adapted an arts curriculum that enhances cultural and aesthetic literacy. Children are introduced to the styles of artists from different periods and cultures and then invited to replicate a style in their own drawings or paintings. Isabella vividly emulates the style of Matisse, who became her favorite artist, in a painting she made in her K–1 art class (Figure 10.2).

Figure 10.2
Isabella's Matisse

Through this same program, other older children noted parallels in the African masks they were making and the drawings they had rendered in the styles of Modigliani or Picasso. Some teachers use reproductions as a pivot to conversation with children about great works of modern and classical art forms.

Preschoolers at another school annually create and mount a spectacular display of African figures in what their teacher, Berta, describes as a Gallery of Cultures in their classroom. Berta assists them in preparing an armature for each figure out of a wooden dowel or paper towel spool mounted on a base of heavy cardboard. The heads and hands of the figure are made of baker's clay. Pipe cleaners inserted into the spool provide flexible arms. An array of swatches of brightly colored African textiles, such as kente cloth, along with ample amounts of tape and glue, is the inspiration for creating stunning costumes for the figures. Many books from the library with illustrations of traditional costumes influence the children's choices.

The cultural richness of children's communities is illustrated by the following:

> Karen, an artist and parent who creates dolls depicting characters drawn from traditional African stories, began sharing her dolls and stories in her son's preschool class. She now shares them throughout the primary school classrooms in her school district. Other families enjoy the presentation of her characters and storytelling through the education program at a major museum located in a nearby community. ✇

Music and Movement in the Play-Centered Curriculum

As part of an arts program and each day's routine, teachers present a music and movement curriculum as a directed or guided experience for the whole group. New and traditional movement and music material, as well as ethnic songs and rhythms, can be introduced in this way. One teacher discovered that the movement group became more cohesive and inclusive when she established a "boy/girl–boy/girl" seating arrangement in movement class. This made possible the option for cross-gender dancing when children paired for folk-dancing routines.

Sharing songs generated from children's own cultures can be an effective way to support spontaneous play involving music, and in one case enabled cross-gender play. When two 4-year-old girls, Yolanda and Shani, spontaneously demonstrated their knowledge of a superhero theme song, they were granted roles by a group of 4-year-old boys on the climbing structure in a previously gender-segregated game. Within the framework of teacher-guided musical play, the following are some other familiar possibilities.

Call and Response and Improvisational Routines.   More formally, call-and-response routines, improvisation, and ensemble playing with instruments and voice enhance children's listening skills and perception of pattern and rhythm.

Alternating a single child's improvisation on an instrument such as a xylophone, drum, or triangle, with ensemble playing and singing, are illustrated in the next example, where the teacher rotates turns of improvisation by placing a baker's hat made of paper on the head of a child she selects to improvise after others sing and play:

Baker's hat, just your size,

When it's on your head you improvise.

Similar improvisation with instruments and singing can be utilized around traditional favorites with a strong, simple rhythm, such as "Noah's Ark." Perhaps one would alternate voice and instruments with the children singing unaccompanied at first:

Who built the ark, Noah, Noah.

Who built the ark, Noah did.

And then continue with both voice and rhythm instruments:

Here come the animals, two by two.

If I were there I'd come along too.

This is particularly effective when accompanied by various percussion instruments, such as those utilized in the Orff-Kodaly curriculum (Alper, 1987; Isenberg & Jalongo, 2006, 2010). If the teacher has a piano and can play, this helps children maintain the rhythm and pitch.

Simple echo routines involving rhythmic patterns of hand clapping, finger snapping, knee slapping, and other sound making, with or without rhythm instruments to accompany patterned movement or dance, can be thoroughly satisfactory activities.

At the level of guided play, a well-organized listening center for two or more children, stocked with a diversity of recorded music, could be provided. These recordings can include cards with salient information about the music written out so that the guiding teacher can point out aspects of it to the children. For older children who are beginning to read, the cards can be filed in the listening center for direct use. As many teachers know, children constantly create spontaneous songs and dances as they play, and these songs can be recorded and enjoyed at the listening center (Veldhuis, 1982).

Although much of this chapter deals with graphic and constructive play in the arts, music is an important avenue for the development of children's thinking and aesthetic sensibilities and, therefore, deserves to be carefully integrated into the curriculum.

Rhythmic Patterns and Tonal Discrimination.   Familiar songs and games can be integrated into a more systematic, guided play framework, such as that developed in the Orff-Kodaly method (Alper, 1987; DeVries, Zan, Hildebrandt, Edmiaston, & Sales, 2002; Isenberg & Jalongo, 2006, 2010; Wheeler & Raebeck, 1985). The general objective of this approach is to refine the senses so that the child gains knowledge of and appreciation for various aspects of music, such as rhythmic patterns and tonal discrimination. Furthermore, because the emphasis is on making and enjoying music as a group activity rather than as individual performance, the method has a positive social value and does not emphasize competitiveness.

Furth (1970) writes,

> The opportunity can be given to children to express facets of their personalities that go along with their developing intelligence in the medium of music. To play in rhythm, to control intonation and intensity of tone, to construct musical phrases over time, to symbolize all these things in musical notation, as well as to interact with others and submit one's activity to the group task—all this is part and parcel of human intelligence. It is for this reason the music teacher can justifiably rely on intrinsic motivation. His goal is musical thinking, with the accent on thinking. He is not concerned with turning every child into a professional . . . musician. (pp. 140–141)

To play and enjoy music together as a group without emphasizing competitiveness has a positive social value.

Counting and pattern-making skills can be developed in music activities when a notational system is used to mark accented beats and rests. One first-grade teacher encourages children to compose their own three-line songs in this way. Children then "read" and clap the simple pattern of fast and short beats and rests in unison as each child composer indicates them on a blackboard.

Music promotes auditory discrimination and phonemic awareness through rhyming words and segmentation (Genishi & Dyson, 2009; Seefeldt, 2005). Participating in music involves abstract thinking important to mathematics. Music contributes to social skills, and of course, it can lighten a tense moment and ease transitions.

Diverse Musical Traditions Enrich the Classroom Culture

Teachers can use culturally and linguistically diverse selections of recorded music to accompany children's dance and movement. Parents are a rich resource for this diversity. In one class, a Chinese family provided a recording of popular contemporary Chinese children's songs. These became instant favorites because of their particularly catchy and appealing rhythm. In this same classroom, a Russian parent interested in dance provided accessories in the form of child-sized, elasticized headbands and waistbands decorated with bright ribbons and sequins. Children needed no teacher assistance to create their own dance costumes; they merely tucked brightly colored scarves into the headbands and waistbands. This mother's contribution helped her Russian-speaking daughter establish early communication with other children in dance and movement (See Chapter 8). Once such activities are launched with a small group of children, teachers may be able to withdraw but closely monitor from a distance. In this way, they can help ensure that the music and movement experience will remain focused and evolve as musical play without being diverted into random tag, rough-and-tumble, or chasing games.

Music can enhance the affective tone of an environment. However, musical activities that merely distract or entertain, although possibly useful as "management strategies," cannot be justified as developmental curricula. In guided play in the arts, care should be taken to avoid undue focus on the virtuosity of a teacher rather than the particular needs of children. Such performances may well be enjoyed by and be interesting to children, but they fall into the category of directed play. As such, they should be carefully balanced with opportunities for free improvisation with music.

In addition—and this point is crucial—in high-quality programs, no teacher-guided play or directed circle time activity should be mere preparation for something else. Introduction of materials is important; however, nothing in the early childhood arts curriculum should be simply a "dry run," such as repetitive rehearsal for a play. Every single arts activity should make sense in the context of the children's lives at school, and each step in an art sequence should be intrinsically interesting.

Integrating All Dimensions of the Curriculum Through the Arts. Art activities serve not only as aesthetic development, but also as an integral part of learning throughout the early childhood curriculum, for example, in mathematics and in development of logical and spatial knowledge. This is illustrated in the following example of curriculum-generating play.

In a Head Start classroom, children were introduced to pattern duplication and pattern extension during small-group time. The teacher discussed and demonstrated the difference between patterns and designs. Later at the painting easel on the same day, one of the children spontaneously generated her own pattern sequence using geometric-shaped sponges to create a page full of small, multicolored triangles and circles arranged in an original pattern with accurate extensions. Other children followed suit, and the teacher created a display for the school corridor of the products children created that involved the concept of patterning. These paintings also allowed the teacher to assess who was understanding the pattern concept. ✆

In another case, a kindergarten teacher helped children learn the features of geometric figures—triangles, rectangles, and squares—through a guided play activity using toothpicks and clay balls to construct models of the figures. ✆

Intuitive math is going on "everywhere," including in arts activities. It is the teacher's responsibility to note and support these competencies when and where they occur (Scales, 2000).

Spontaneous play allowed Noah to integrate his new knowledge about colors—he used this growing grasp of color to start creating aqua. Such integration and recasting of experience and the application of knowledge in new contexts also can occur in guided play.

Integration of Children's Experiences and Feelings Through Play in the Arts

A special dictated letter with a picture "for mom" or an e-mail may be called for when distressing experiences, such as the birth of a baby brother or Mom's too abrupt departure, occur.

> Lonnie, a formerly abused child currently healing in his adoptive home, needed to include multiple masking tape "band-aids" in the many self-portraits he produced. ✆

> Jason's only painting for the monthly art show revealed much. His intense interest in depicting trains and the intersecting lines of railroad tracks revealed the cognitive and representational competence of a five-year-old. Teachers were pleased to see that his mark making in art related to his new, spontaneous interest in writing his name and making signs to designate areas of play for himself and his younger friend, Wesley. Although Jason acted as a mentor to Wesley in many collaborative activities, his friend now felt left out because he did not share Jason's interest or capabilities in writing. The teacher was faced with a dilemma when Wesley's mother asked her "not to stress writing," especially because literacy through play was a centerpiece of the curriculum. ✆

As we can see, life in the zone of proximal development can be daunting. It does not always flow smoothly and presents challenges to both the children and their teachers.

A BALANCED ARTS CURRICULUM

Throughout this book and in this chapter, we stress the need to balance curriculum offerings across the continuum of directed, guided, and spontaneous play. When play is at the center, the arts, as well as other options, will be examined carefully to ensure that the balance between spontaneous and guided or directed play is optimal for the group served. In determining the appropriate balance of arts activities, we must always consider:

- The cultural, social, and developmental needs of both the group and individual children
- The dynamic of the group
- The quality and size of the physical environment
- The number of staff and length of program day

As teachers plan curriculum, they will want to examine the types of activities they offer, along with the kinds of demands they make on resources available in their particular settings. Here is where a consideration for a balance of activities is needed. Too much spontaneous play at all sites can lead to chaos, whereas too much directed or guided activity can lead to the erosion of learning that occurs in spontaneous play. Some activities, such as painting, drawing, scribbling, and collage, can be monitored with minimal teacher intervention and so may be a staple offering most of the classroom day. The critical issue here is how well the children can read the cues the environment gives them about what they are expected to do with the available materials.

Establishment of routines for use of the available materials is essential. Caution must be exercised in the introduction of too many teacher-directed projects, as this not only stifles creativity on the part of children, but ties up staff resources as well. In some primary classrooms, children select the centers they will go to at "choice time" during a morning meeting. Minimum and maximum numbers of children at a center can be adjusted as needed. This can work smoothly if centers are well set up and expectations are established.

The following is a discussion of some familiar activities with indications of their demand for teacher setup, monitoring, and guidance or direction. Some groups will need more structure and fewer options, or more complexity with an increase in guided or even directed play; others will need less complexity with more opportunity for spontaneous play. In each case, the teacher will select from various curriculum offerings to create a menu of activities that enhances potential for playful engagement in the arts.

- Various kinds of drawing, scribbling, and collage activities have a high degree of potential for spontaneous and playful engagement. Attention to the setup of materials and space is important, and some degree of monitoring, if only to replenish and refresh supplies, is necessary.

- Many forms of sculpture and three-dimensional work also lend themselves to spontaneous play with materials offered. Clay, play dough, and wood gluing come to mind. Again, some degree of care in setup, introduction to routines, and monitoring are required.

- Printmaking, silk screen, and projects involving pre-cut elements, such as collage portraits, require a high degree of teacher guidance and direction, but some facets involve spontaneous and self-directed action. The process of selecting the textured elements for a relief print (intaglio) and placement of various facial features for a collage portrait involves creativity, challenge, and judgment for many young children. Coloring and rendering eyes, hair, complexion, and clothing in a painted self-portrait also involve creativity and critical thinking.

- Activities like story dictation, journal writing, music, and movement often fall into the category of more directed and guided play. However, these activities can become more spontaneous for children if the teacher creates a context in advance that clearly indicates expectations. For example, a music center can do much to enhance the development of musical sensitivity when routines for use of instruments are established and the available number and kinds instruments lend themselves to a harmonious but not proscribed sound.

- In the same sense, story dictation and journal writing should be collected by the teacher with minimal intervention as to content or demand for use of formal narrative conventions. The subsequent acting out of such stories may involve the teacher directly in reading the story and helping to guide an orderly selection of actors. Although these activities are generally guided and directed, the activity may lead to an enrichment of the content of children's subsequent spontaneous fantasy play.

Many of these activities can be made available in the classroom simultaneously. However, caution must be taken in setting up more than one highly teacher-directed activity because the consequence can be an erosion of overall opportunity for self-directed and spontaneous play.

KNOWLEDGE OF THE PATTERNS OF DEVELOPMENT IN CHILDREN'S ART MAKING

Being aware of evolving patterns in children's art can provide the teacher a mirror to development and a guide for curriculum design. Like archaeological remains, children's paintings, constructions, block building, assemblage and collage, and recordings of songs, stories, and dances are a reflection of development and can be examined and diagnosed as documents of growth and development (DeVries et al., 2002; Griffin, 1998; Veldhuis, 1982). As such, they can be used to assess the effectiveness of the curriculum in supporting playful exploration of the arts.

Documenting Change and Growth: Heidi's Horses

Consider some of the drawings of horses made by one child over a period of about 5 years (Fein, 1984). Heidi's drawings, in Figure 10.3, reveal her interests and follow the general developmental sequence of drawing schemes (Gardner, 1993; Isenberg & Jalongo, 2006, 2010; Kellogg, 1969; Lowenfeld, 1947). Heidi was able to playfully explore her interest (indeed, passion) in a supportive environment that encouraged art making and allowed a free choice of subject matter. The drawings graphically illustrate that it is interest, intersecting with personality and intelligence, that fuels play and the development that results from play.

A compilation of paintings, drawings, or stories can provide a pivot in parent conferences or for assessment purposes, enabling a better understanding of the trajectory of a child's interests, development, and competencies.

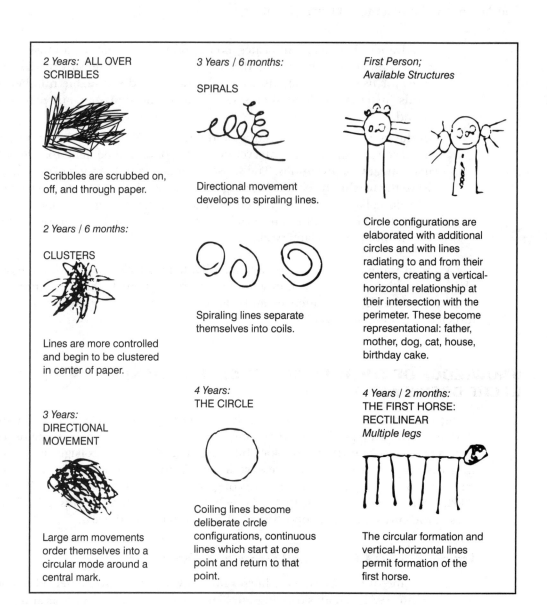

2 Years: ALL OVER SCRIBBLES

Scribbles are scrubbed on, off, and through paper.

2 Years / 6 months:

CLUSTERS

Lines are more controlled and begin to be clustered in center of paper.

3 Years: DIRECTIONAL MOVEMENT

Large arm movements order themselves into a circular mode around a central mark.

3 Years / 6 months:

SPIRALS

Directional movement develops to spiraling lines.

Spiraling lines separate themselves into coils.

4 Years: THE CIRCLE

Coiling lines become deliberate circle configurations, continuous lines which start at one point and return to that point.

First Person; Available Structures

Circle configurations are elaborated with additional circles and with lines radiating to and from their centers, creating a vertical-horizontal relationship at their intersection with the perimeter. These become representational: father, mother, dog, cat, house, birthday cake.

4 Years / 2 months: THE FIRST HORSE: RECTILINEAR *Multiple legs*

The circular formation and vertical-horizontal lines permit formation of the first horse.

Figure 10.3
Heidi's horses
Source: From *Heidi's Horse* by Sylvia Fein, 1984, Exelrod Press. Reprinted with permission.

Breadth and width;
Four legs spaced

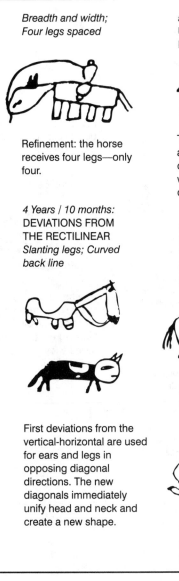

Refinement: the horse receives four legs—only four.

4 Years / 10 months:
DEVIATIONS FROM
THE RECTILINEAR
Slanting legs; Curved back line

First deviations from the vertical-horizontal are used for ears and legs in opposing diagonal directions. The new diagonals immediately unify head and neck and create a new shape.

5 Years:
UNIFICATION OF
HORSE PARTS

The unification of the head and neck is applied to contain the whole horse within one unbroken outline.

5 Years / 3 months:
DEVELOPMENT OF
THE UNIFIED
HORSE
Sturdy shape

Problems of leg-spacing and length are solved.

The new diagonal directions of line allow the horse to run.

Body markings: blazes and dapples

A learning plateau provides time to consolidate, and to enrich the horse's gear and markings.

Heidi's last major construction before her sixth birthday is to extend the horse's head towards the ground, "so he can eat."

6 Years: THE
HORSE MORE
POWERFULLY
CONSTRUCTED
The boxy shape is rounded

The rigid, box-shaped horse is transformed by fluid, calligraphic outline into a powerful horse with flexible stride.

Figure 10.3
(*continued*)

7 Years: THE HORSE IN ACTION
Cowboys and rodeo

Heidi shifts her interest to action-packed performances; the elegant single horse recedes.

As storytelling becomes more restrained, precision returns to the drawings, and the rider receives artistic attention.

8 1/2 Years: HEIDI: SELF-PORTRAITS
Queen Heidi, the very 1st

Heidi assumes importance second to the horse, and appears in favorable roles. She thinks of herself as a horse.

8 1/2 Years: TECHNICAL TASKS: OVERLAPPING

The rider's body turns partially to side view.

Overlapping begins. The horse has two legs on one side of his body, two on the other.

8 Years / 11 months: ADVANCES USING OVERLAPPING
The rider in profile

Overlapping possibilities are extended to arm and stifle joints.

Problems appear when the position of the horse's hind legs are reversed.

Two horses side by side

One horse overlaps another to show that they are standing side by side. Figure/ground relationships have become more complex.

Figure 10.3
Heidi's horses (*continued*)

IMPORTANT CONSIDERATIONS

❤ Guided play often provides opportunities for the teacher to observe closely and learn how the competencies, interests, and personality of a child complement or conflict with the social challenges of the group setting, For example, in a prekindergarten conference with a kindergarten assessment team, Sara, an art therapist, suggested that active and unfocused children often may be helped to gain control by working not with fluid materials such as finger paints or water-based media, but with more resistant materials. Stitchery, when presented on a frame or an embroidery hoop, is an example of a material that can give structure and boundaries. Clearly defined patterns may be included as guidance. In addition, Sara noted that children with perceptual problems may need not only more form, but also activities that provide a calming effect derived from doing what they are good at. The issue here is to allow the child to experience control rather than lack of control (Wasserman, personal communication, 2005).

Children with Special Needs: Guiding for Mastery and Competence ❤

Consider Jerry, an active and often unfocused child:

> Four-year-old Jerry jumps from the jungle gym and dashes across the yard yelling, "Rocket launch! Rocket launch!" Within seconds, he reaches the sand pit, jumps in, and plows through Andre's and Peter's sand towers. Taking Jerry gently by the hand, his teacher productively redirects this explosive energy. "You seem to know a lot about rockets," she says. "How about drawing one with me?" ✍

Through drawing she engages the child in a vivid and expressive rendering of his fantasy. The recognition Jerry may have been seeking in spontaneous play with peers might be accomplished more easily through guided, creative expression. Such expression will serve him better until linguistic ability and his competence in interacting with others advance to meet the need he feels to share his powerful fantasies.

Creating some segments of a cartoon strip about rockets might help Jerry. When the teacher labels aspects of his vigorous, but seemingly meaningless scribbles, by using words in bubbles and arrows that highlight and clarify important information—"here is the launching pad, here is the rocket's nose"—Jerry is led to experience himself as a more effective communicator.

More ambitiously, Jerry's drawings and words become a "movie" when taped together, attached, and wound onto take-up spindles of a paper movie machine a parent made for the classroom. As Jerry's movie is unreeled and narrated for the class, the teacher demonstrates sequence as a feature of a narrative while sharing Jerry's word images. Using today's digital camera and computer technology (e.g., a program like iStopMotion2, www.boinx.com/istopmotion.com) allow Jerry's drawings to become an animated feature.

Lisa frequently has difficulty sharing the available supply of play dough. With this knowledge, the teacher can ask her to assist in the preparation of a new batch of dough to be shared with others, thereby helping Lisa manage her needs, emotions, and impulses in the group setting. ⌀

Enhancing Children's Membership in the Group.   Guided play with art-making materials affords many opportunities for language use and social and cultural sharing and, again, gives the teacher an opportunity to observe quietly. Often the group project is stimulated directly by the children: "I want one like Martha has!" "So do I!" With the help of the teacher, the paper earrings that Martha just made are studied. The required materials are set up at a table so that Martha can teach the others to make earrings of their own.

In the primary grades in particular, projects that enhance group membership may sometimes be ongoing and involve long-range goals. Even so, every step toward the project goal is ideally play centered and intrinsically satisfying. Making a group book, a class poem, a quilt, a mural, or decorations for a school party—all can support the child's growing ability to plan, to look forward, and to share socially. Following an invasion of ants in the classroom, the children mounted a research project about ants. Two girls in a first-grade classroom sent a letter to the principal of their school requesting better pencils. Other children in this same first-grade classroom we discussed in Chapter 8 created a newspaper for all the members of the class. It involved several weeks of research and planning before the first and only edition was published. Group projects such as this one can provide valuable opportunities for children to learn about and participate in the cultural richness of many of today's classrooms.

Children's Play Interests Reflected in a Play-Centered Curriculum

Children's playful engagement in the arts is frequently the source for new and emergent curricula. This is reflected vividly in myriad ways. The monsters of one year's pretend play give way to Robin Hood in the next. The prince and princesses in this year's group book become the daddy and mommy dinosaur in next year's. So, too, with the paintings and constructions. Musical interludes can become a part of children's spontaneous story play dictation, or they can become part of an "author's theatre" in later elementary school. Once introduced as a genre, children will incorporate songs they know, such as nursery rhymes or contemporary media songs, into their plays. British drama educator Dorothy Heathcote (Heathcote & Bolton, 1995) often used child-generated songs and chants in her drama work with children (see Chapter 8 for some discussion of drama as one of the literary arts).

Guided and Directed Play in the Arts

Although we know that young children learn most effectively through play, educational strategies often rely solely on guided or directed play. Such play can become more spontaneous, in some of the following ways. In the role of play tutor—for example, at the clay table—teachers can show children how to model basic clay shapes (as precursors to developing concepts of volume). After such modeling, the teacher can step back and allow the children to integrate their learning on their own. Often other children will pick up the role of tutor in these instances.

To build the children's repertoire of three-dimensional forms, teachers can demonstrate to them how to hollow out a ball of clay to make a dinosaur's cave; or, more playfully, how to extend the hollow to make a tunnel where the hands of two friends meet; or how to make clay coils, slabs, and seriated balls. In one preschool program, Wade integrated knowledge about clay modeling when he added teeth to the jaws of his hollowed-out clay form. Sylvie, a second grader, using slabs of clay that she had rolled out smoothly, cut and shaped a beautiful rectangular jewelry box (complete with a fitted lid) for her grandmother's birthday.

A play-generating curriculum was introduced to children making their first transition from home to school. It involved creating a special room.

To start, a shoe box is provided to each child, along with bits of wallpaper, tile, fabric, wood, and carpet pieces, with an invitation to create a replica of a room for themselves. Child-made models from previous years may be provided at the initiation of this project. Aurora is learning English in her bilingual classroom. Emulating labels on classroom furnishings, she asks that labels in both English and Spanish be placed on the items in her "room."

When guided/directed play in arts activities is linked in some relevant manner to children's fantasy play, or if the teacher can play parallel to children (as suggested in Chapter 5), then such play is protected from becoming merely work disguised as

In play, children recast their knowledge of the world in new ways.

play. The teacher can then stay in touch with the child's developmental needs. In this manner, the teacher participates in what Vygotsky (1967) referred to as the zone of proximal development, that area where children experience their own future, more advanced, self through stimulation and challenge in the context of interactive play with peers or with an adult.

The Reggio Emilia and Project based curriculums (Katz & Chard 2000), referred to as emergent curriculum, are examples of the use of guided play (see Chapters 1 and 5, this volume). Many teachers who have adopted these approaches find that the knowledge and competencies set out in a standards-based curriculum can be readily achieved through child investigations and documentation inherent in the Reggio and Project approaches (Wien 2008).

SUMMARY AND CONCLUSION

In this chapter, we have based our rationale for an arts curriculum in early childhood on the following premises.

A curriculum in the arts for early childhood at the preschool level and in the early elementary grades finds its center in the necessity for children to play. It encompasses not only graphic arts, but also drama, music, dance, movement, and all forms of constructive play. It can be an emergent, play-generating curriculum in which children's autonomy and interests are supported. It can take several forms, orchestrated along a continuum that supports both guided and spontaneous play.

The effectiveness of an early childhood arts program will be measured by the degree to which we observe that children are able to enter into sustained, effective, self-directed play. Is guided or directed art the only form we see? Do we see knowledge gained in guided arts activities being integrated as it is reapplied in spontaneous play? In short, the major question to ask is: What *are* the quality and quantity of children's spontaneous play within the arts curriculum?

An important task for the teacher is to balance the options for kinds of play in the arts program. By ensuring the child's independent choices in play, the teacher supports development and engages the child's interest and authentic expression. Although implementation of developmentally appropriate standards is an important priority that provides equitable access to educational and cultural resources for all children, it is best to remember that children learn most effectively through play and are unable until middle childhood to perform work in the adult sense (Alward, 1995). (This issue is discussed more fully in Chapter 14.)

In conclusion, when teachers find the source for their curricula in play, they link it to child development and thereby discover its validation. In the early years, the arts are core subjects, as important as English, mathematics, or any other subject, and are integral to the entire curriculum. Much of the child's development is revealed most vividly through the documents children produce in the arts and constructive play. When these are shared with children, they, along with their parents, become witnesses to their advancing competence and grow in self-esteem.

Play and Socialization

Andrew lopsidedly heads out the door of his preschool classroom with his mother's large, leather briefcase slung over one shoulder. He insists on carrying it wherever he goes. Andrew's destination today is the swing at the rear of the play yard. Recently he has become willing to set the briefcase on a bench nearby when he uses the swing, but stormy protests can be expected if anyone goes near it.

Andrew is 3 years and 1 month old and a newcomer to this 4-hour program. Separation from his mother has been difficult. To ease his adjustment, his teacher invited Andrew's mother to remain at school until a reasonably amicable separation could be achieved. Andrew's mother was able to accommodate his need when she was on leave from her part-time job, and Andrew played happily when his mother was present. Although the teacher had anticipated that this period of accommodation would be brief, it stretched into weeks, and Andrew, even if engaged, continued to insist on leaving with his mother. With his mother's furlough from her job nearly over, she and Andrew's teacher devised a strategy to allay his anxiety: his mother would leave her large leather briefcase on the bench near the door as a reminder that she would be returning at some predetermined time. First, she stayed away until snack time; then she was to return at story time, and so on for longer periods of time each day.

Andrew's mother was meticulous about returning at the promised times in the preschool day, and eventually Andrew was able to stay for the full 4 hours of the program—not without a catch, however; the briefcase must stay behind to ensure his mother's return. It was many weeks before Andrew allowed his teacher to tuck the briefcase away safely into his cubby, and it was not until the second half of the school year that it did not come to school with Andrew at all. ∅

SAYING GOODBYE TO PARENTS

Some theorists consider separation from parents a major milestone for children, and research on this subject suggests that the character of this achievement is an important indicator of secure or insecure attachment to the parental figure. Attachment theorists assert that when unusual conflict or anxiety surrounds separation from the parent or caregiver, the child may also develop other significant problems in relating to others (Ainsworth, Bell, & Stayton, 1974; Balaban, 1985, 2006). Other studies indicate that such children may have difficulties in persevering and/or varying their attempts to initiate play with peers (Riley, San Juan, Kliner, & Reminger, 2008; Tribble, 1996).

In this chapter we show how children's talk and interactive behavior are significant indicators of their social and communicative competence. Many of the illustrations presented are drawn from teacher observations, anecdotes, and research. They raise many questions, demonstrate some of the dilemmas teachers face, and suggest some solutions.

A comfortable transition from home is important to a child's school success.

We recommend a sociocultural approach as an authentic way to examine the effects of social emotional issues arising from attachment and separation from parents. Such an approach illuminates cultural, ethnic, and linguistic diversities, as well as inequities due to gender differences and, of course, poverty. The following anecdote begins to illustrate this approach, demonstrating how simply beginning school can itself be a complex social emotional event that may affect a child's relations with peers and teachers.

From Separation to Integration: John's Fire Hydrants

John, 4½, appears to teachers to be socially isolated from his peers (Scales, 2005). They believe this may have resulted from the intersection of several factors, which included a reluctance to separate from his father, a new baby brother in the home, and his first experience in a preschool class consisting of children with established relationships from the previous year.

In September, John arrived at school with his father, dressed in a long yellow raincoat, black boots, and a black fire helmet. Rain or shine, John wore this attire for the next 6 months. To help with John's transition, his father spent the better part of each morning at the school's drawing and writing center with his son and several girls. This pattern continued for many months.

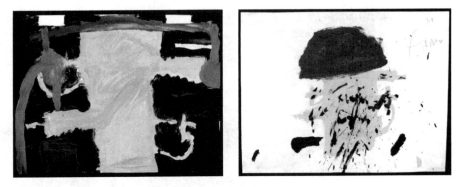

Figure 11.1
John's Earliest Fire Hydrant and One with a Loose Cap That Is Leaking

John and his father studied the fire hydrants they saw on their walk to school. They took photographs and compiled many small books about fire hydrants. John's father drew many models of fire hydrants as he became a fixture with John at the drawing and writing table. John also drew and painted fire hydrants (Figure 11.1) and dictated stories about fire hydrants. John used an adultlike style in his speech and storytelling and preferred the company of either his father or other adults, with whom he talked at length about fire hydrants. Shy offers of fire hydrant pictures by one of the girls at the drawing table were ignored. ✐

Once established, this intense interest in fire hydrants continued relatively unchanged for many months. In enacting his stories at circle time, John always took the role of the fire hydrant and allotted few parts to others, except for the girls who were "regulars" at the drawing and writing table.

His teacher's analysis of his stories and paintings over time revealed that one major change occurred in December, when John depicted his fire hydrants with faces and introduced the character of a "walking, talking" fire hydrant. (Figure 11.2).

Figure 11.2
A "Walking, Talking"
Fire Hydrant

Here is a "walking, talking" fire hydrant story:

December 13 Story

Once there was a fire hydrant and it was a walking, talking fire hydrant. Then another hydrant came and it was the newest one that John the walking, talking fire hydrant had ever seen. The very new hydrant fell down and broke one of its caps!! The cap was made of cast iron; it was old but the model number was new. Then another hydrant came and another hydrant came and then another. Then the hydrants got broken. They did not put out water anymore. Then there was a very, very, very old fire hydrant came and rewinded the camera that they were using. Then a ball popped out of a hose hookup. Then a block came out of the other hookup. ∅

The fire hydrant pattern in painting, drawing, and storytelling persisted until spring. But finally, in a story dictated in May, a major advance was made. This story indicated a shift in John's gradual socialization. He dictated a story about, and took the role of, a very silly firefighter. (There is no fire hydrant present in this story.) Here John abandoned his adultlike narrative style for what seemed to be "baby talk." The teachers wondered if John was emulating what he thought was the language of his peer group. Not accidentally, his awareness of the context of the classroom is indicated in his reference to the fence that surrounds the playground and is near where many of the more active boys congregate in the play yard.

May 1 Story

An Entire Fireman Once there was a fireman and he fell in a puddle and got his suit all wet. And then he got in front of the big hookup and the garbage truck went over his legs! And he went to the hospital and he got da-da yocky-not medicine. He felt much, much, much better. And then they went to the ba-ba fence and jumped in puddles (the ba-ba fence is the fence near the child-care center). ∅

Additional evidence of John's growing interest in the classroom environment is seen in the paintings he produces around this same time (Figure 11.3).

Figure 11.3
Fire Hydrants with Asian-appearing Pagodas and Calligraphy

Although John did not abandon the fire hydrant theme, he began to depict fire hydrants that have an Asian look, with pagodalike appendages and Asian-looking calligraphy in the pictorial space. Is this a reflection of the Japanese calligraphy displayed on the walls of his classroom or a response to the artwork created by his only friend, a Japanese girl who is also a "regular" at the drawing table?

But it was his final story, dictated in June, that revealed a great leap forward in socialization for John.

June 5 Story

Firefighters from all over the city came to a really big fire. There were not enough fireplugs close by. So the firefighters had to take their small hoses and hook them up to each truck. There were 7 trucks. And then they got their monitors but there was not enough pressure! (Monitors are the big nozzles on top of the trucks.) They saved a very, very, very tall building from danger of the fire. The end.

According to the teacher's field notes on the story playing activity, in this story John created many roles—seven firefighters and seven fire trucks. Well over half the class was included. He allocated the superordinate roles of firefighters to boys and the subordinate roles of trucks to girls. He did not place himself in a central role as a hydrant, and when asked about this, he replied, "I wanted to be among the firefighters."

John's integration into the classroom culture was facilitated by the storytelling, story-acting curriculum offered at his school. However, his integration came at a cost. In his selection of choice roles for boys and lesser roles for the girls, we see that John also incorporated the gender stereotypic indicators of power that are often seen in group settings (Cook-Gumperz & Scales, 1996; Nicolopoulou, Scales, & Weintraub, 1994; Nicolopoulou, McDowell, & Brockmeyer, 2006).

The sequence of stories and paintings in John's portfolio provides a vivid picture of his social adjustment and reveal the very unique way in which John, over the school year, constructed his own form of social integration to the school culture. His stories illustrate how effective the story play curriculum can be in facilitating socialization (Paley, 2004). The teachers' analysis of the stories over time gave them a grounded way to assess John's advances in social competence that were embedded in the culture of his classroom.

DIVERSITY CREATES SOCIAL ENRICHMENT FOR TODAY'S CLASSROOMS

Paley, as well as Dyson and Genishi and Heath and Mangiola and many others, have written extensively about how the culturally, linguistically, and ethnically diverse classrooms of today can provide great social enrichment for its members. They describe how such diversity expands the world views of both teachers and children (Genishi & Dyson, 2009; Heath & Mangiola, 1991).

Diversity Can Create Challenges for Teachers

However, along with the values of cultural and ethnic diversity, such open-play settings with mixed-age groups can also represent a challenge to social integration as the anecdote that follows demonstrates.

"Little Dragon"

After a celebration of the Chinese New Year as part of a multicultural program involving the children's astounding creation of a dragon, 3-year-old Christopher began emulating the actions of a dragon. He rigidly strode through the play yard, roaring and imaginatively breathing fire while stalking some of the older boys in the class. At about the same time, Christopher's mother began receiving an unusual number of "Ouch Reports" (see Figure 11.4) for Christopher (Alkon et al., 1994).

She wondered what was going on. Christopher's descriptions of events in the "Ouch Reports" indicated that it was often Alex, the oldest, largest, and most popular child in the program, who had chased him. Was it possible that he, a Chinese American, was becoming a target of abuse for the "rough," older boys in the class? His mother began to wonder if she had made a mistake in enrolling Christopher in this integrated, university-based preschool. Perhaps she would have been wiser to place him in the new Chinese language school that was opening in a nearby community.

The teacher surveyed the file maintained by the school on "Ouch Reports" and found that Christopher did have a few more reports of bumps, falls, and scrapes than other children his age. The implications of these findings were discussed in a staff meeting. Teachers were also able to reference other observations that had been compiled for this child.

In the early days of the program, Christopher had spent most of his time near his early morning teacher, but now he had begun to spend more time in the active outdoor play areas of the school. Teachers noted that when Christopher pretended to be a dragon, the older boys chased him with cries, such as "Here comes the bad guy!" Teachers' attempts to reason with Christopher and the older boys about this pattern temporarily ended the chasing by the 4-year-old boys. Three-year-old Christopher, however, always tearfully insisted that he wished to continue to be a dragon. He seemed to have little interest in integrating himself by taking on a character from the play scenarios of the older boys. The moment the teacher's attention was averted, he approached the group again as a dragon, with the same consequences.

Christopher seemed enchanted with his ability to obtain the attention of the older boys. When conflict arose or when he fell while fleeing from the "superheroes," he seemed developmentally unable to comprehend the teacher's admonitions about the consequences of this entry strategy and the need to thematically coordinate his play with others. Developmentally, he did not yet have the perspective-taking skills to comprehend either the consequences of his own actions or to coordinate them with the interests of others.

University of Califormia   Child Care Services

OUCH REPORT

Child's Name: _John Doe_   Teacher's Name: Jane Doe/Teacher

Today's Date: 7 /25 /97 Time of Accident 4: 40   a.m./p.m.

Location of Event: Far yard

Contributing Factors: "I hurt myself right on the leg.
                          I was being chased and I bumped."

Type of Injury: Location of Injury:

__ Cut
✓ Scrape
__ Bump or Bruise
__ Mouth injury
__ Crush injury
__ Human Bite
__ Insect bite/sting
__ Injury by foreign object
   (splinter, sand in eye etc.)
__ Hair pulled
__ Other

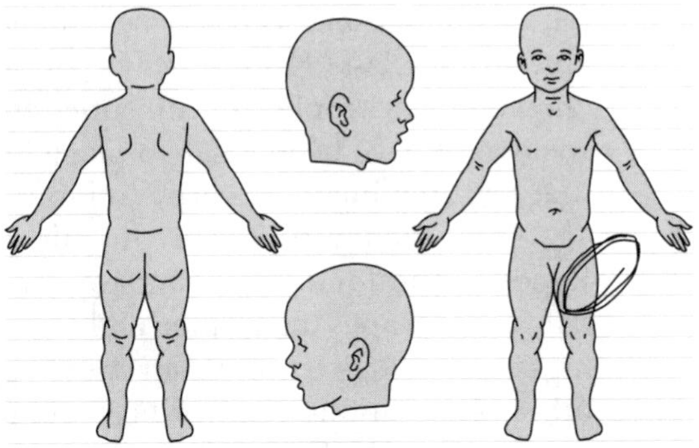

Type of Treatment Given: Recommended Follow-up:

— Cleaned injured site   He seems great - he was
✓ Ice pack applied   a little shaken by
__ Band–Aid or dressing applied   hurting himself.
✓ Child rested or laid down
✓ Given comfort
__ Antiseptic applied
__ Other

                          Head Teacher (initial/date) BJ

Figure 11.4
Ouch Report
Source: Information from University of California head teacher Rebecca Tracy for classroom use.

Luckily, around the time of spring break, another child about Christopher's age adopted the persona of *Tyrannosaurus rex*. Not surprisingly, the two formed a union and soon became the magnet for a small, but cohesive, group of younger children. When the teachers granted this group a special dragon territory on one of the smaller play structures, they were able to rant and rage with each other powerfully but be protected from forays by older "super-heroes" in search of "bad guys." This teacher strategy allowed them to have a protected area within which they could engage in their dragon fantasy at their own developmental level. ✆

Inclusion of Children with Special Needs

Teachers in play-centered classrooms must be realistic about the goals they set for all children, including those with special needs, and the availability of resources to implement them. Support for both inclusion as well as accommodation to special needs is a necessity; experience tells us that failure to establish agreement on goals and a time frame for their achievement with all concerned can hamper a successful inclusion program.

Some of these diverse factors might have confounded support for successful inclusion in play of a child with a speech impairment in the vignette that follows. Teachers were not all in agreement about how to handle this child's efforts to socialize with younger children.

Matthew

Matthew, a large, slow-moving child (age 6 years and 5 months) with a severe speech impairment has been retained for an additional year in the 4-year-old class. His parents and teachers believe that an extra year will help him make advances in social and interactive skills with peers who are a bit younger. ✆

Previously, in the 4-year-old class, Matthew relied solely on the teachers to interpret his needs and support his efforts to socialize with peers. Recently he has been attempting to play and interact more frequently with other children. His teachers, however, still need to closely monitor his play with peers because of his limited speech and physical skills (Scales, 1989, 1996). In this, Matthew resembles many children with special needs, who rely greatly on adults to provide them with support in the interpretation of their needs (Erwin, 1993; Isenberg & Jalongo, 2006, 2010; Newcomer, 1993). According to van der Kooij (1989a), some children with special needs respond to their environment in a single way, often nonverbally, making it difficult for them to effectively enter play situations. The following vignette is an example. Note the manner in which Matthew attempts to enter the play between Greg and François by kicking a tire as an initiating act.

"Quicksand." The following excerpt from a longer text indicates what happens when Matthew attempts to enter into sand play with two boys. Greg, an unusually active child (5 years and 1 month), and François, a child of African American heritage (4 years and 9 months), have just negotiated a tenuous play interaction with one another. They are making "quicksand" by pouring water and sprinkling dry sand into a trench, which has been dug by the teacher.

Matthew has jumped to a mound nearby the two boys and stands opposite Greg above the "quicksand." As they face each other, Matthew attempts to enter the play not by speaking, but by kicking a tire embedded in the sand above the trench. Greg responds by jumping across the trench to a sand mound near Matthew and shoves him over saying, "Take this, Matthew." Matthew responds by picking up a handful of sand and throwing it at Greg.

Greg shoves him over again and says, "Take this." He enlists François's help with a "Help me get him." Both boys are pulling and tugging on Matthew, and François asks, "Are we pushin' him in the quicksand?" Greg gives further directions to François as he points to the center of the quicksand: "No, push him right down there." François stands over Matthew and says, "Now you come here, Matthew, I've got something to show you."

Matthew points to François and says clearly, "I know what you're going to do. I saw it."

Greg and François continue to tug at Matthew, and François says, "Help me lift big boy up. Fat mouth."

Shortly after Greg begins to push Matthew, two teachers intervene. One attempts to encourage Matthew to use his language to tell Greg his objections to being pushed into the sand. A second teacher moves to assist and redirect Greg. She first acknowledges the good aspects of what Greg and François have made together, but also warns that it might need "special attention" because it could be "dangerous." Thus, she signals the boys that they can expect closer monitoring from teachers. Despite this warning, the two boys continue to attempt to push Matthew down into the sand.

The teacher returns to alter the direction this rough-and-tumble play has taken. "Are you playing the game with them, Matthew?" he asks. Without waiting for Matthew to respond, Greg and François chime in. They define the game as one that involves ". . . tryin' to push him [Matthew] down there." They say that Matthew has said, "Yes," he wishes to play the game. At this point Matthew speaks up quite clearly to say, "NO," indicating he does not wish to play. In some cases, teachers may tolerate what is known as "rough-and-tumble" play as an expression of affiliation if all the participants are willing to engage in it and it is not too rough (Bateson, 1976).

Somewhat later, Matthew makes another attempt to enter the play with Greg and François. This time, he has modest success when he uses his language to assure the two boys relatively clearly, "I know what we can do, put sand on top." At this point François acknowledges Matthew's participation by saying, "You're right, Matthew. Then when people walk here, they'll sink in [and go in quicksand]. Kaboom!" Having affirmed the theme of the play, Matthew is not bothered further and appears to have succeeded in becoming a rather passive participant. ⌀

While things turned out well in this episode, the teacher was wary about encouraging Matthew to enter this fast-paced, rough-and-tumble play with two unpredictable partners. This example illustrates the social difficulties that children with special needs may experience with peers during play and the dilemma it can create for teachers.

In the previous vignettes we have illustrated the various factors that may impede children's ability to establish and maintain interactive play with peers in the classroom; the first two involve issues of separation, the third concerns the inability of a younger child to take the perspective of others, and the final episode involves three children attempting to play together. One, Matthew, is a child with special needs; a second is François, a child who is culturally different from his classmates; and the third is a child who often acts out aggressively. From these examples we see that it is not always easy to know precisely how to support play (Kaiser & Rasminsky, 2008).

TRADITIONAL RESEARCH AND PRACTICE

In the past, teachers who turned to research with questions related to play and socialization found relatively few answers. Researchers were sometimes even uncertain that play was really taking place and were not always able to even identify its boundaries. This made it difficult to determine who was playing "what and with whom," or how to intervene in a relevant way. Smilansky's (1968) recommendation (derived from her research) that intervention support elaborated dramatic play is one notable exception (see Chapter 3).

Various checklists and rating scales to assess environmental features, such as boundaries and links between areas, as well as level of play complexity have been devised (Harms, Clifford & Cryer, 1998; Kritchevsky, Prescott, & Walling, 1977; Walsh, 2008; see Chapters 4 and 5). These methods verify the presence or absence of desired features in classrooms and play yards, but do not reveal how these elements in themselves act to generate social and cooperative behavior.

CURRENT PRACTICE ILLUMINATED BY RESEARCH

Starting in the 1970s, play was studied in detail by a number of researchers influenced by Vygotsky and working in a sociocultural tradition (Cook-Gumperz & Corsaro, 1977; Dyson, 1997; Garvey, 1977; Reed, 2005; Vygotsky, 1962). Many researchers collaborated closely with teachers or were teachers themselves (e.g., Cochran-Smith & Lytle, 1993; Cook-Gumperz & Scales, 1996; Corsaro, 1997; Erickson, 1993; Gallas, 1998; Perry, 2001; Qvortrup, Corsaro, & Sebastian-Honig, 2009; Reifel & Yeatman, 1991; Scales, 1996; Tribble, 1996). Drawing on this research, our knowledge of the specific ways that play interactions contribute to socialization has increased (Reifel, 2007; Sawyer, 2001).

Many of these were naturalistic, observational studies that looked at peer play and communication as it unfolded and demonstrated how children develop the skills to monitor varying social and cultural contexts. Some studies showed how school practice constrains or complements the development of essential features of social competence (Cook-Gumperz & Corsaro, 1977; Cook-Gumperz, Corsaro, & Streeck, 1996; Corsaro, 1985, 1997; Corsaro & Schwartz, 1991; Genishi & Dyson, 2009; Genishi, Huang, & Glupczynski, 2005; Qvortrup, Corsaro, & Sebastian-Honig, 2009). Other research brought to light the complex issues involved in the gender socialization of boys and girls (Dyson, 1994; Goodwin, 1990; Nicolopoulou, McDowell, & Brockmeyer 2006; Nicolopoulou, Scales, & Weintraub, 1994; Scales & Cook-Gumperz, 1993).

Differences in Boys' and Girls' Play and Socialization

A year-long study of children's narratives by Nicolopoulou and Scales (1990) found that preschool boys' and girls' stories differed in both content and form (Nicolopoulou, McDowell, & Brockmeyer, 2006).

For girls, the family romance was paramount, with marriage, family relationships, or the frequent themes of arrival, losing, or finding babies. Boys, on the other hand, rarely spoke of any relationship other than that of a "friend"—a friend with whom they more than likely battled as a culminating feature of their stories. These gender differences emerged early and persisted despite teachers' efforts to broaden the repertoires of both boys and girls.

Through interactions with playmates, children learn to negotiate roles with others.

"Tough Guys."   As we noticed in John's fire hydrant stories, the following anecdote also reveals a previously hidden, gender-related social hierarchy in the allocation of roles in children's storytelling (Scales, 1996).

> Near the end of the day at a preschool, 28 children are seated around a square taped on the carpet. This is "the stage" where they enact stories that were dictated earlier to a teacher. At this particular moment the proceedings have stalled: the child-author's originally chosen actor for the part of a particular superhero has refused the role. The children are becoming restless and inattentive. The teacher, hoping to get things moving again, whispers a suggestion: "Why don't you pick Max? He really wants a part in your play!"
>
> "Oh no," responds the author. "He can't be it! It has to be one of the tough guys."
>
> The stalemate is resolved when it is suggested that Max can "pretend" to be a "tough" guy. ✆

Suddenly, a previously unseen aspect of the social life of this classroom has become transparent. We knew that for the girls, "princess" roles were highly prized tokens of social favor, argued for and parceled out in play and story acting. Now, a hidden social hierarchy in the boys' world has been revealed as well.

When stories such as this and the power relationships they reveal are merely suppressed in "gender-neutral" classrooms, they go unnoted as a hidden curriculum. However, through story playing in preschool and an "author's theatre" in the primary school classroom, such issues can become accessible for negotiation and dialogue about who "gets in" and who "gets left out," who owns which social roles, and who has power in the play life of the classroom (Dyson, 1995; Scales, 1996, 2005).

As teachers and researchers are aware, not only do the themes and characteristics of boys' and girls' stories differ, but so, too, does their willingness to engage in play usually associated with members of the opposite sex. As far back as 1977, Garvey and Berndt noted that boys were reluctant to play roles, such as a "prince," that are commonly associated with girls' stories or play. Teachers report that this is still the case in today's classroom.

Paley (1984, 2000), a teacher and writer, examined the differences in the play of preschool boys and girls. She found that when time for spontaneous play was lengthened, boys became more willing to engage in quiet table activities, more typically favored by girls. She also recommended that teachers respect children's role choices, as they are an important part of their developing self-concept.

"Neighbors."   An observational study of one classroom conducted by Cook-Gumperz and Scales (1996) revealed that the social dynamics of group settings alone may sometimes aggravate the occurrence of gender-stereotypic behaviors. Cook-Gumperz and

Scales collected a set of observations of two groups playing adjacent to one another in the block area of the classroom. One group consisted of boys, the other of girls. When the group of boys moved to play more closely to the girls, the girls' interactive communication changed markedly. They began to enact roles of helpless mommies and babies who were in danger. Roles in their previous play had involved grooming and feeding miniature animals. In addition, during this time the boys' play became more assertively aggressive and "macho" as they circled around the girls, ostensibly to obtain blocks from a shelf to the rear of the girls (Cook-Gumperz & Scales, 1996).

At a brief interval midway through this long play event, the constellation of boys marched noisily out of the classroom. One boy remained behind and began inching near the girls' play space, making "strange clucking sounds." A brief conversation between the lone boy and one of the girls occurred when she commented on his strange noises. After this exchange, she turned to the girls and reassuringly said, "It's all right, he's just a neighbor." It was notable that no stereotypic forms were used as attempts were made to negotiate the lone boy's entrance into the girls' play space. However, the noisy return of the larger group of boys to the block area disrupted this negotiation, and the would-be "neighbor" was drawn back into the larger configuration. At this point, the assertive behavior accelerated and included loud singing and chanting. The noise finally aroused the attention of a teacher, who attempted to settle the matter by redirecting the children back into segregated groups to "share" the blocks. The attempt by the two groups to play together as "neighbors" (an inspired solution) went unnoticed (Cook-Gumperz & Scales, 1996). Had the teacher paused to discuss what was going on within the play frame of the girls' game (see Chapters 4 and 5), she might have discovered a way to make the play a bit more gender inclusive.

Instead, rather than make any attempt to scaffold possible cross-gender play, the teacher opted to merely "manage" the conflict. On the discourse boundaries between genders, teachers need to be alert to children's own efforts to define themselves and their relationships in new ways (Dyson, 1993, 2003; Tobin, 2000). In more structured ways teachers might scaffold repertoires for cross-gender play by openly exploring with children at circle or small-group time some of the ways they think boys and girls can play together (see Chapters 4 and 5; Perry, 2001).

Children's Negotiations Create a Dynamic Context for Play

In studies of children's play communication, researchers have found that play interactions are shaped by and, in themselves, shape children's understanding of the social and environmental expectations of situations (Cook-Gumperz & Corsaro, 1977; Cook-Gumperz, Corsaro, & Streeck, 1996; Corsaro & Molinari, 2005). From such studies we find that children's lives in preschool are embedded in particular social contexts, whose impact cannot be ignored without neglecting children's interest, self-direction, and motivation (Scales, 1997). The social work in which children engage as they play has been largely unexamined by practitioners whose valuing of play has its roots in early childhood's psychodynamic heritage.

Constructivists such as Piaget and Vygotsky have had an important impact on our view of children's development. Both researchers and teachers have been stimulated by Vygotsky's (1962) concept of the "zone of proximal development." Many recent articles have failed to note that Vygotsky also asserted that play in itself is the source of development and creates the zone of proximal development (Nicolopoulou, 1996; Nicolopoulou, McDowell, & Brockmeyer, 2006). The vignette about John and his fire hydrant persona is a vivid example of the way in which teachers create a zone of proximal development through the story play curriculum, a guided play activity.

A primary-school vignette also illustrates this possibility. Consider how an open activity period effectively creates a zone of proximal development for children. The play roles that four primary school children set for themselves reflect their developing social competency (Vygotsky, 1962).

Newspapers

At midyear, 6-year-olds Clay, Zoe, Randall, and Michelle decide they will use their daily activity period to make a class newspaper. In this language- and literacy-rich classroom, they have many opportunities to generate their own literacy curriculum with different kinds of writing, such as letters, articles, books, lists, and signs. Their teacher, Harriet, wisely helps them develop traditional competencies in handwriting, spelling, and letter sounds on a daily basis. So Zoe, Clay, Randall, and Michelle have not come to their play project uninformed.

Their interest in the newspaper project extended over several weeks and involved much research and many revisions, additions, and reviews by their teacher and classmates. News articles as well as jokes and cartoons were collected and included in the final comprehensive version. Although only one "edition" was published, every child in the classroom received a copy (Morrison, 1985). In this primary-grade classroom, daily activity time, during which children have ample choices of things to do, provides a "zone of proximal development," or what Newman, Griffin, and Cole (1989) call the "construction zone." The creation of such an activity period is similar to the Project and Reggio Emilia approaches (Bodrova & Leong, 2003; Katz & Chard, 2000; Wien, 2008).

In the play that occurs in the free interaction among peers, children are provided with an opportunity to experience the "give and take," or reciprocity, that is a salient feature of effective social play, where shared needs, interests, and competencies and social and moral development can be mediated (see Chapters 4 and 5; Turner, 2009). "This reciprocity is rarely achieved between children and adults, but in play (among peers) it is the rule rather than the exception" (Alward, 2005, pp. 1–2).

Research on Play and Socialization Within Special Education. Play in inclusive settings has the potential to enhance social competence for children with special needs. Researchers have focused on play and socialization within special education and inclusive classrooms (Erwin, 1993; Hanline & Fox, 1993; Hartmann & Rollett, 1994; McEvoy, Shores, Wehby, Johnson, & Fox, 1990; Ostrosky, Kaiser, & Odom, 1993). They have found that children with severe disabilities in integrated sites spent more time engaging in activities with their classmates than in unoccupied behavior, which broadened their base of social support (Erwin, 1993). The vignette in this chapter about Matthew demonstrates in a realistic way that it is not an easy matter to support children with special needs as they attempt to participate in play with their classmates in inclusive classrooms. It often requires careful observation and sensitive intervention at the environmental level. New play designs for equipment and toys also enhance the potential of inclusive classroom. For example, the acquisition of a wheelchair that is scaled to a height that enables eye contact with peers can contribute to enhancing communication for the child with special needs (Belkin, 2004). However, as Belkin found in his study of one child, such an acquisition may require considerable effort and expense on the part of parents (Isenberg & Jalongo, 2006, 2010; Milligan, 2003). Research on patterns of socialization in inclusive classrooms can render more specific information on how the environment affects children with special needs and the dynamics of the classroom.

PLAY PROVIDES A BRIDGE BETWEEN THEORY AND PRACTICE

Our broad constructivist view of child development does not confine us to relying on any single, rigid theoretical approach. Classical Piagetian theory can serve us well in the study of individuals, but we also look to Vygotsky for a bridge to discover how the social dynamics of the classroom intersect with individual cognitive development (see Chapter 14 in this text; Genishi & Dyson, 2009).

Rather than taking a top-down approach—that is, bringing only a selected theory to bear—teachers might find greater explanatory power in analyzing their own records and observations from an interpretive approach (Corsaro & Molinari, 2005; Gaskins, Miller, & Corsaro, 1992).

Such an approach looks closely at specific play interaction and takes an insider's view rather than that of the detached outsider. It grounds these explanations in contexts well known to participants. By this means, findings can be corroborated and discrepant cases identified and explained (Cochran-Smith & Lytle, 1993; Erickson, 1993, 2004; Gaskins, Miller, & Corsaro, 1992; Perry, 2001; Sawyer, 2001).

The Interpretive Approach

The value of an interpretive approach, which draws on multiple theoretical perspectives, is demonstrated by the "tough guy" anecdote cited earlier in this chapter. Remember that the child-author first resisted letting Max play the role of a superhero in his play because he was not a "tough guy." Subsequently, he changed his mind when it was suggested that Max could *pretend* to be a tough guy. The child-author's acquiescence to the teacher's suggestion could be analyzed from a number of perspectives. A classical Piagetian point of view might suggest that the issue simply involved a matter of relations between classes. In this case, for the child-author someone pretending to be a "tough guy" could be included in the class of "tough guys" and, therefore, be allowed to take such a part in his play.

Developmental and cognitive issues, such as a child's understanding of classification and the ability to conserve, certainly were involved. However, such an analysis does not account for all the child's reasoning and did not account for his agency and motivation. Here an interpretive perspective, with its sociocultural orientation, broadens constructivist thinking to provide further explanatory power (Alward, 2005; Scales, 1996). From a sociocultural perspective, the context of the story-acting activity presented the child with a conflict and an ambiguity that needed to be resolved, and the teacher, as mentor, offered an alternative that helped him find a solution within the collaborative construction of the "play."

From a Piagetian perspective, this might be considered to be a disequilibrating event that possibly helped the child-author advance to a higher level of thinking. However, taking a broader sociocultural view that encompasses the social dynamics of the classroom, this conflict could be seen as the kind of negotiation of power roles that Dyson (1995) referred to in her work on urban classrooms. When teachers take an interpretive approach, they discover that children actively contribute to their own socialization and a sense of themselves as social entities within the group, and to the production and reproduction of the children's culture (Corsaro, 1997; Gaskins, Miller, & Corsaro, 1992; Qvortrup, Corsaro, & Sebastian-Honig, 2009). In play-centered classrooms, teachers have a potent opportunity to observe how children insert elements from the larger culture into their play world. In so doing, they are forced, as was John in his fire hydrant persona, to make sense of both their real and fantasy worlds (Nicolopoulou, 1996; Reifel, 2007; Scales, 2005).

In discussing ethnographic and linguistic research on children's narratives, Dyson noted that individual children assume the voices of others, both past and present, as they use the linguistic forms they have appropriated from teachers, parents, and peers to construct a text (Dyson, 1995, 2003; Dyson & Genishi, 1994; Genishi & Dyson, 2009; Scales, 2005). Dyson also found, however, that when addressing present-day events, such as the ambiguity surrounding gender, the text is, in and of itself, transformative (Turner, 2009). That is, it transforms the child's perception of the past and the future.

For example, when today's child uses a past expression of gender (e.g., "princess"), she is not merely miming in some frozen way an outmoded social attitude. Rather, because the old-fashioned expression is now embedded in the different social context of today's world, it brings about change or transforms by giving rise to ambiguities the child must resolve through dialogue with others. If we merely drive gender expressions underground as a hidden curriculum, we fail to provide any occasion for this transformative mediation to occur as the child struggles to reconcile the tension between gender conventions of the past and emerging ones of the present (Dyson, 1995).

Figure 11.5

Teachers Take a Research Stance: Views from the Inside

Teachers can take a research stance by systematically observing play communication to see how the classroom social environment is being "read" by children. For example, the teachers' videotaped observation of the interactive strategies of the three children in the "quicksand" episode gave teachers important information about how to guide children's interactions and later modify the play environment of the sand pit to support more inclusive play (see Figure 11.5).

Children's Interactive Strategies

The interactive strategies that children utilize provide clues to their ability to understand the views of others. Situational strategies children employ also reveal how actions and speech are coordinated and synchronized to conform to a mutual understanding of the unfolding interaction. Such behaviors are essential to prosocial behavior. Children can be provided with opportunities to learn essential skills such as "turn taking" in play interactions with peers. Turn-taking skills may be learned in play at the swings on the playground, or when children put their names or marks on a waiting list for a turn at the water table or computer station.

In many early childhood classrooms, turns at games start early in cooperative dyads. If groups are not too large or too formally structured, the understanding of a conversational turn can be demonstrated in talk at circle time. Games involving turns, such as lotto, and familiar songs with turns of a chorus or refrain can contribute as well. Children also need to be given ample opportunity to generate and practice their own turn-taking rules within the give-and-take of spontaneous play.

Because play is inseparable from all facets of development, play itself must develop.

Central to this approach to understanding children's socialization is the notion that the play context is dynamic (Vygotsky, 1962). As they play, children develop their understanding of the unfolding activity (Cook-Gumperz & Gumperz, 1982). For example, when negotiating a theme, such as "home play," children come to understand that to successfully enter into play, one must be "on topic," for example, carrots are to be "cooked" and not used as guns.

Research tells us that to maintain social cooperation, children, like adults, constantly signal their mutual understanding of unfolding interactive themes. Mutual understanding is signaled when children initiate a play episode or topic or when a topic is changed; play partners will often be observed to affirm the change with a "right." "We're making soup, right?" "Right!" "And it'll have alphabets, OK?" "OK!" (Corsaro, 1979, 1997, 2003; Gumperz & Cook-Gumperz, 1982; Qvortrup, Corsaro, & Sebastian-Honig, 2009; Sawyer, 2001). In the "Quicksand" episode Matthew acknowledged his understanding of the play theme with his "I know what we can do. . . . put sand on top."

Although this is usually expressed in a coplayer's "right" or an "OK," affirmation also can take a nonverbal form (see Chapter 12). For example, a coplayer may express uptake of a theme of cooking by an appropriate gesture, such as beginning to stir a bowl of "sand soup." Matthew's tire kicking was inappropriate as an entry strategy and, as we saw, was rejected.

Turn Taking and Children with Special Needs. The notion of turn taking is especially important for those with special needs who may have difficulty cooperating with peers. In general, we observe the mutual influence of individuals on each other. However, with regard to some children with special needs, "egocentrism" might block such "mutuality" (van der Kooij, 1989a). Opportunities to practice turn-taking skills in the give-and-take of social play, as was provided Matthew, are important for these children so that they can learn to interact effectively (Koplow, 1996; Odom, 2002; van der Kooij, 1989a; Wolfberg, 1999).

STUDYING THE SOCIAL ECOLOGY OF A PRESCHOOL CLASSROOM

Most of the observational material cited in this chapter is drawn from naturalistic studies of preschool or early primary settings for 3- to 6-year-olds. The basic method of analysis was pioneered in conversational studies of adults conducted by such anthropologists as John Gumperz (Jaworski & Coupland, 1999, 2006). It was adapted for work with young children in preschools and primary grades by sociologists Corsaro and Cook-Gumperz (Cook-Gumperz & Corsaro, 1977; Corsaro, 2003; Corsaro & Molinari, 2005; Qvortrup, Corsaro, & Sebastian-Honig, 2009).

Taking an Interpretive Approach to the Social Ecology of the Classroom

Teachers and researchers, utilizing an interpretive approach to the analysis of their observations of children's interactions and communicative behavior, can answer many questions. Dyson's interpretation of children's authoring in urban classrooms reveals the power relationships operating within the social ecology of the classroom. Studies of the play interactions of boys and girls have exposed vivid contrasts and demonstrate how children, such as John, may adopt stereotypic forms from the wider culture to their own play relationships as they simultaneously advance in linguistic and social competence. Interpretation of the communicative styles of ethnically mixed play partners, Greg and François, reveals how the two boys creatively modify their speech style to establish a mutually agreed-on play scenario.

The research discussed in the following sections indicates how interpretative analysis of observations derived from site-specific interactive behaviors of children demonstrated that implied social expectations for play patterns are contained in the social ecological elements of various centers.

Contrasts in Social Ecologies

Researchers Cook-Gumperz and Corsaro (1977) analyzed four episodes that were drawn from videotapes of a preschool classroom. In this section, we discuss and contrast these episodes to demonstrate how the social and ecological cues of settings influence children's play and socialization.

In the Home Play Center: Rita and Bill.   The first episode involves two children, Rita and Bill, playing husband and wife. It demonstrates how little negotiation is required to establish play themes in the home play center because children bring what the researchers call "conventionalized expectations" to this site (Cook-Gumperz & Corsaro, 1977).

For Rita and Bill, the most difficult portion of their interaction involves their attempt to ward off the incursion of two unruly "kitties" that attempt to enter the playhouse. Corsaro and Cook-Gumperz noted that once a play episode is underway, children are protective of their interactive space. We saw the same issue when Matthew attempted to engage in play with Greg and François, who vigorously resisted his attempt until he acknowledged that he understood their play theme.

Aware that children's interactions are fragile, teachers respect ongoing interactions by helping potential intruders like the "kitties" become established at a site nearby or involved with others who are not already engaged. In this case, Rita and Bill handle the problem themselves by dismissing the "kitties" to the "backyard." In the case of Matthew, discussed earlier in this chapter, the teachers were watchfully supportive of his efforts to enter an ongoing rough-and-tumble play event.

The Sand Table: Constructing a Play Fantasy.   In the second episode, a four-sided sand tray is the site for more inventive and well-coordinated play themes. It challenges children's use of their linguistic and communicative skills to construct a unique collective play fantasy because at this site scenarios are not conventionalized as they are in home play centers. The collective fantasy opens with a "rainstorm." Then a small sand mound is elaborated into a "home for freezing bunnies." The players coordinate the changes of theme and do so again as the sand mound becomes a final safe haven from "lightning" in a "B . . . I . . . G steel home."

In contrast to the first episode, the children at the indoor sand tray are required to structure their activity creatively as it emerges. They cannot rely on conventional expectations, such as those in home play centers. Rather, they must depend on their own communication to collectively create and sustain the order of their talk about their spontaneous and novel fantasy (Turner, 2009).

Although the home play center is ideal for the neophyte communicator, more open settings (such as the sand tray with miniatures) also are needed to provide challenge for older children. At such sites, children stretch their communicative strategies as they cue each other to the meaning of unfolding play events they collaboratively create. Such strategies include some of the following:

1. Using special linguistic cues to signify the fantasy (e.g., taking the role of the bunnies).
2. Using repetition to acknowledge some feature of a previous utterance (such as echoing and repeating key words and phrases like *freezing, rain,* and *lightning*).
3. Tying new material to previous thematic content. For example, using the word *and* plus a phrase containing new material allows an opening for another child to interact. In one episode, a child named Sabrina says, "I'll take the baby to the store." Her friend Sarah links her utterance by adding, ". . . and the big sister will drive the car; and I'll be the big sister."
4. Using an ongoing verbal description of behavior as it occurs; for example, saying, "Help, we're in the forest, and it's beginning to rain," while visually manipulating miniature toys.

Settings That Constrain Peer Talk and Interaction.   Cook-Gumperz and Corsaro (1977) analyzed a third episode, which occurred at a project table where the teacher inhibits the children's language use and development of interactive skills because she does most of the talking, controls the flow of talk, and initiates most topics.

With a greater awareness of the importance of the need for children to spontaneously exercise their interactive skills with peers, teachers might consider how they might support and maintain interactive talk during situations involving, for example, teacher-guided projects.

An Undefined Context.   In a fourth episode, the setting involves an undefined context, where talk is also constrained (Cook-Gumperz & Corsaro, 1977). Here, conflict and confusion in play result from the ambiguous cues that are inadvertently created when the teacher moves a worktable from its usual place. Children do not know whether they are at a table for guided literacy play or spontaneous home-related play. Two of the three children try to establish a play scenario about being "teachers," and the other thinks he is playing "police." The play communication that results is marked by a singular lack of coordination in a short-lived attempt to interact.

Information about the subtle features of this breakdown in communication is derived from very close observation of the uncoordinated features of communication and social ecological factors. An understanding of this event will not be revealed by observational schemes that merely code behavior into categories (e.g., solitary, parallel, or collaborative). Such categories give little information about how teachers can intervene in a way that will be relevant and make sense to children or support their play interaction. Teachers learned from this analysis that although mixing environmental cues can sometimes produce interesting and positive transformations in children's play, it also can contribute to failed communication among participants, as it did in this case. Changing social ecological elements is more than merely "moving furniture" and can have unforeseen consequences, as we noted in the wedding play in Miriam's classroom.

PLAY IN THE SAND KITCHEN REEXAMINED

We can also be misled about children's social skills when we classify play as fixed categories on the basis of one element of an interaction. For example, children do not place speech in the foreground of their communication. Instead, they use all modalities of communication, such as gesture, rhythm, and intonation, to achieve their interactive goals. This is demonstrated in the following example.

Three children, Andrea (age 3 years and 2 months), Celine (age 3 years and 4 months), and Peter (age 3 years and 4 months) are playing with pots and pans at an outdoor sand table. Andrea and Celine are busy chatting about what the "baby" will eat for breakfast, while Peter silently stirs a bowl of sand nearby. ⌀

Pam, their teacher, observes their play and assesses Peter's silent engagement as an example of solitary or parallel play. However, based on her later analysis of a videotape recording, this episode provides evidence of Peter's active participation in the group interaction.

Though close at hand, Pam fails to take note of the role that Peter has been assigned. Only at the end of the episode is she made aware that she and Peter have been filling the roles of "baby" and "babysitter," respectively. This is revealed to her when Andrea, the "mommy," emphatically points her finger at Pam and says: "Baby, you—I'm goin' out to the woods." Then with a gesture toward Peter, she says: "You stay here with the babysitter."

Whether Peter's play is solitary, parallel, or collaborative is not easily determined. However, close analysis of the videotape and Peter's affirmation of his role reveal that even without speech Peter is a significant participant in this interactive play, whereas Pam the teacher, being the most passive, is, of course, the "baby" (Scales & Webster, 1976).

For older children, language plays a more important role, and they do not rely as heavily on environmental cues to guide understanding. With their increasing linguistic ability, they are able to detach play from its situational context and, should play be disrupted, are more capable of reestablishing it. As linguistic skills advance, children are also able to maintain interactive play across multiple sites (Scales, 1997).

Teacher Support for Play Interactions

In this chapter we show that initiating or entering play is a complex matter and involves more than mimicking adult formulas, such as "Hello, may I play with you?" Such an opening probably would be greeted with a resounding "No," particularly among 4-, 5-, and 6-year-olds. Within the children's culture, distinctive forms of communication are constructed.

Children develop their own particular strategies for making an entrance into an established play episode. One successful tactic involves circling about the site of the play event until the players make an overture to the newcomer (Corsaro, 1997, 2003). The teacher (in the role of gatekeeper), noting a child's desire to enter a play episode, can assist by helping the newcomer find an activity or role that complements the play event. The teacher also might set the newcomer up nearby with similar props.

An example of a unique solution to a gatekeeping problem occurred when two girls barred the entrance of a third to the playhouse. The teacher's repeated suggestions of possible roles for the entering child had been rejected again and again. Squabbling and howling ensued for some time until one of the rejecting pair had a marvelous idea: the newcomer could be the "door." This role eminently suited Mia, the newcomer, who on other occasions often took the role of gatekeeper, excluding others. She immediately barred the entrance with widespread arms and legs.

Children Grant Warrants for Play

Sometimes play is established around action alone, as in the game of tag. However, close observation of the natural history of an activity reveals that even such seemingly simple play involves what Cook-Gumperz and Corsaro (1977) called granting a "warrant," or permission to establish or alter a play theme.

A typical example of granting a warrant occurred in connection with the quick-sand segment presented earlier. Greg and François had agreed and established a warrant that an area in the sandpit was "quicksand." However, one of the pair at one point, seeing that the water poured into the sand created a froth, referred to it as "chocolate milk." This constituted an attempt to get a warrant for a new thematic direction and prompted his partner to respond, "You remember, we're makin' quicksand." This correction was quickly affirmed by a cheery, "Oh, right, right," and the previous warrant was reestablished.

Negotiations around granting warrants go on continuously in children's interactions. These warrants provide a thread to link sequences of activities. When a warrant is granted, close observation of the play interaction reveals this as a focal point where communicative modes, both verbal and nonverbal, converge. Teachers can observe that children's posture, rhythm, gesture and action are well coordinated. These focal points are evidence that a mutually satisfactory interaction is taking place.

On further observation, teachers also note sequences of maximal divergence or transition points. At these times, children do not share a mutual understanding of the context. They, therefore, have different views about the ongoing interaction. This lack of mutual understanding is even evident in lack of coordination in the children's body language and posture.

In the following segments of the "quicksand" interaction, because the event consists largely of rough-and-tumble play, most of the transition points involve a teacher intervention. Two of the boys, François and Greg, seem to want to engage in rough-and-tumble play and play fighting (as indicated by their laughter). The third child, Matthew, does not, signaled by the fact that he is not laughing (Bateson, 1976; Perry, 2001; Reed, 2005).

At such transition points, teachers may wish to intervene as peacemakers to clarify and reorient the players to a mutually acceptable focus (Chapter 5). However, if teachers are not observing closely, they may intervene at the wrong point or make an irrelevant suggestion, thereby disrupting rather than supporting the interaction. Even a teacher's well meaning reinforcing behavior, such as registering approval of children's cooperative play, sometimes serves only to distract the players.

"Quicksand" Revisited. We return now to an earlier segment of the "quicksand" episode. Our purpose here is to consider in detail the initiating and sustaining of play. In this segment, we also learn about some of the problems that can arise in multidialectical play interactions. François, a child of African-American heritage, speaks Black English as well as Standard English and a form of English one might hear a TV speaker use. Unfortunately, most of François's teachers generally speak only Standard English. His play partner, Greg, uses Standard English and also a form of English used by TV speakers. At the beginning of the episode, Greg is in the center of the sandpit at the intersection of the three pathways that have been configured by teachers. Greg stations himself there as soon as he arrives, at the beginning of the school day. Only three interactions occur in the sand on this day, and all involve the negotiation of a warrant with Greg to gain access to the sandpit (see Figure 11.5). In environmental terms, an obvious feature of this particular sand "curriculum" is that the physical setup of the sandpit constrains play because the arrangement of intersecting passageways gives dominion over a large area to Greg because he stands at the center of the intersection. It also limits the possibilities for the types of play interactions that might go on. The high mounds of sand, steep slopes, and narrow passages of the pathways invite very close physical contact. They tend to generate virtually a single possibility: rough-and-tumble play.

First Attempt to Establish a Warrant for Play

François enters the sandpit and addresses Greg with, "Hi ya, Greg."

Greg responds, "Hi ya, François." Then François jumps to a mound of sand near Greg as the episode begins:

François:	Let's see what time it is. Oh, yeah, it's time for one by two by two.	Speaks rapidly, using style, rhythm, and tone of Black English.
Greg:	No. No.	
François:	OK—well one by two by two, one by two, by two—ooda do da doo, one by two by two—me and my two by two—one by two by two—one by two by two is over.	François wrestles with Greg. Both boys are laughing.
Greg:	OK, François.	
François:	OK, Fatso.	François moves away.
Greg:	Here you go. Take this!	Throws a handful of sand at François. Boys now begin to throw sand at each other. ✆

In this sequence, François attempts to establish a warrant with Greg for a play fighting game called "one by two by two." François addresses Greg in what is recognized by linguists as Black English because of its rhythm, intonation, and other features (Labov, 1972).

As the two children tussle about in the sand, François continues to address Greg in a distinct rhythm, saying: "Oh, I'm gonna catch you." The teacher begins to monitor more closely. As the children begin to throw sand at each other, the teacher moves in to intervene. The sand throwing, though a prohibited activity, is well coordinated and is not a transition point for the children, as they are enjoying the activity. However, as a prohibited activity, the teacher cannot permit it. A transition that disrupts this interaction occurs when the teacher is required to enter.

Second Attempt to Establish a Warrant

François falls into the trench. Greg moves over and they tussle and toss sand about.

François:	Oh, oh, my goo goo.	
François	Why—I'll get rid of your shirt if you do that again. I'll take your shirt off and I'll tear your shirt right off. That's the first thing I'd do.	Greg moves on mound above trench; turns to look at François.
François:	Tear you [inaudible] come back.	Greg and François tussle about in the sand.
Greg:	(laughs) Ø	

In this second attempt to establish a warrant, François again uses intimate Black English, addressing his friend as if Greg were a member of François's linguistic culture. The attempt ends with the boys tussling in the sand and the predictable entrance of the teacher.

At this point, Greg's complaint to the teacher, "I don't wanta play this," constitutes a rejection of François's second bid for a warrant for play. At this transition point, the teacher attempts to help the children find a more suitable focus.

Third Attempt to Establish a Warrant

Speaking in deeper tones and switching to a TV hero voice, François stands on the mound above Greg and initiates another warrant.

François:	I'm at the cliff of the mountain.	François takes a new posture on the mound.
Greg:	You won't get me, François.	Greg moves from François and the intersection.
François:	You won't get me either. Try to tear me apart.	François moves out upper-left exit. Greg follows. Ø

This warrant is more to Greg's liking, and a well-coordinated game of tag is launched. The warrant attempt has succeeded. The play interaction, though primarily gross motor in nature at this point, is well coordinated and cohesive.

The episode just described is noteworthy because one of the children speaks Black and Standard English, as well as TV English, and shifts from one to the other midway through the episode. We see here that the demand is greater in this setting for the African-American child to adapt his linguistic style to his play partner's speech style. François's initial overtures to establish a play warrant by utilizing Black English are not successful (Labov, 1972; Reifel, 2007). However, because he is multidialectical, François is successful in communicating with Greg when he switches first to a form of TV English and then to Standard English.

The challenge in this play episode for the three children is to find a common/mutually understood communicative style. Teachers, although remaining watchful, do not separate the two boys' play fighting, but give them time to find a common focus for a play interaction on their own. Situations such as this provide an interesting challenge to the skills of teachers in creating a supportive play environment that responds to the diverse social needs of all children (Reifel, 2007).

Negotiation of multiple modes of communication in our increasingly diverse preschool and primary-grade classrooms can be viewed as a richness that expands children's world views (as seen by Genishi & Dyson, 2009.) As in the case with the three boys in the previous anecdote, it also represents a challenge to children and teachers to interact effectively and to amicably share meaning with one another.

Supporting Interactive Play at the Environmental Level

Teachers facilitate cohesive interactive play by defining various areas in the classroom and play yard. Dividers and other spatial markings or arrangements protect interactive space so that players are not easily distracted and play is not disrupted. An example of this is seen when teachers arrange the environment so that block building or other floor play does not occur in the middle of pathways.

Teachers can establish spaces that bring children into proximity with one another, like around a rectangular sand tray or table. The visual array of toys shared by all informs an entering child about the play theme in progress and suggests a possible role to be taken. Such spaces also help establish "face engagement." In this case, the basics of communication are ensured, as is a shared understanding of the theme of the unfolding play (Goffman, 1974, 2000).

Such configurations provide what has been called "defensible space" (Cook-Gumperz, Gates, Scales, & Sanders, 1976). Each child has a territory (his/her side of the table), so that entry into interaction with another in this situation places everybody on equal footing. Such a space also provides for two pairs of children playing side by side in parallel play. This opens up the possibility that the play of two pairs may become socially more coordinated as a foursome (see Chapter 4 for more).

SOCIAL STUDIES STANDARDS IN EARLY CHILDHOOD PROGRAMS

Although the activities we have been describing represent socialization to the classroom culture, teachers are feeling more and more pressure to place more emphasis on and assessment of formal academic curriculum standards. The broad area of socialization covers children's ability to interact with peers and dispositions to learn and what, in later schooling, is called social studies. As a discipline, social studies encompasses a wide array of subject areas representing content from a variety of academic fields of knowledge. A sampling of 4 of the 10 areas of knowledge for social studies identified by the National Council for the Social Studies (1998) are

- Time, continuity, and change
- People, places, and environments

- Production, distribution, and consumption
- Civic ideals and practices

Social Science for Young Children

Many of the social studies content areas can be addressed in concrete ways in a play-centered curriculum grounded in children's day-to-day interactions with one another in the community life of the classroom. This community has its own culture and involves sharing of the social resources of the classroom by participants. In this sense, the classroom is a microcosm of the wider community of adults. Sharing, reciprocity, fairness, and democratic processes are necessities in the child's world as well as ours. Most standards for socialization involve dispositions, such as empathy for others, the ability to interact effectively with peers, and respect for the diversity of others. As this chapter amply illustrates, these attributes are best acquired by children as they engage in interactive play in the community of a caring classroom. Their assessment is best derived from systematic records of observations of the interactive behaviors of the children in guided and spontaneous play.

Table 11.1   Sample of Social Studies Standards

Social Studies Strand	Curriculum/Teacher Examples	Children Learn and Experience
Time, Continuity, and Change	The marking of cyclical events, such as day and night, the rhythms of daily routines and the seasons, by special activities and projects, e.g., a mural of a winter scene; examining children's shadows at different times of the day.	Children become aware of time, continuity, and change through the sequences and patterns of daily rituals, such as meeting time, choice time, small-group time, lunch, clean-up, etc.
People, Places, and Environments	Photographic displays of families illustrate diversity of peers and families. Map making of the local environment, maps illustrating differing origins of our ancestors.	Experiences in interacting with diverse others in the classroom. Noticing features of natural and man-made environments locally and in the wider community.
Production, Distribution, and Consumption	Classroom setup, where children play, learn and participate, are defined areas in the inside and outside that are designated for production and use (the writing table, the art table, the ball area, the lunch tables). Long- and short-term activities investigating where food comes from. Making reports about a visit to a farm, a factory, or a supermarket, the port, an airport, the UPS store, a construction site.	Children begin to become aware that location is an essential feature of community. They share the resources of the classroom—toys, treats, and time—with teachers. Field trips and activities about them widen knowledge.

Social Studies Strand	Curriculum/Teacher Examples	Children Learn and Experience
Civic Ideals and Practices	Provide guidance to children as they negotiate disputes, discuss differences, and generate and establish their own rules for how to make the classroom a more harmonious place. Such rules become a part of the curriculum and relate to governance, civic ideals, and practices. Provide games that build turn-taking skills. Teachers model and scaffold ways to make requests in a diplomatic way. Teachers intervene in play in a relevant way to help children find language that will enable them to amicably negotiate their needs and desires, for example, by finding a role for a newcomer, "Could Andrew be the grandfather coming to visit your house?"	Children begin to become aware of these concepts through day-to-day interactions with their peers and teachers in group situations, such as the classroom. Children adapt strategies modeled by teachers and their peers in interactions with each other in self-directed play. In play they come to learn which strategies are effective and which are not. In play and guided activities they become aware of themselves as a community and gain confidence and poise as members of the classroom culture.

Information from National Council for the Social Studies, Curriculum Standards II. Thematic Strands,
http://www.socialstudies.org/standard/strands *(1998).*

SUMMARY AND CONCLUSION

This chapter assumes that a major way children develop socially is through the exercise of their communicative skills in play and interaction with peers. Adult modeling of verbal skills and interactive strategies is not enough. The child's application of given strategies is not only developmentally determined, but also requires the child to interpret the situated character of meaning in unfolding play events. When teachers take over this interactive work, they rob children of opportunities to develop their own strategies. This makes close observation by teachers a critical factor in providing relevant support, particularly for mixed-age and/or inclusive groups, or in ethnically and linguistically diverse play settings. Such observation allows teachers to

1. Examine play through its communicative features, noting how contexts interact with social expectations to influence children's play.
2. Make and test judgments about the effectiveness of play settings.
3. Utilize this knowledge of the classroom context to create new curricula for play and socialization.

4. Assess children's achievement of developmentally appropriate social emotional learning and social studies standards through systematic observations of guided and spontaneous play and examination of children's products such as drawings, paintings, journal writing, and storytelling.

Categories of play, such as parallel, solitary, or collaborative, have served us well over the years, as has our heritage from the psychodynamic and constructivist traditions in early childhood education. This heritage has been augmented by new technologies, analytic methods, and the fresh theoretical orientation of the sociocultural school of Vygotsky and others, which has begun to influence our thinking on issues of identity, social equity, acquisition of cultural resources, and the impact of globalization in our classrooms (Anderson, 1995; Corsaro, 2003; Corsaro & Molinari, 2005; Jaworski & Coupland, 1999; Swartz, 1997).

Using new theoretical approaches, we can now design and implement curricula that support socialization in much more relevant and specific ways. Through observation and analysis of play in its sociocultural context, strategies for the assessment of the development of children can relate to the local context of the school and children's previous experiences, such as problems with separation, individual and special needs, and the cultural and linguistic diversity of their lives.

12

Outdoor Play

Jane P. Perry
University of California, Berkeley

It is the first day of school in Rebecca's mixed-aged preschool classroom. Children are indoors and outside during activity time. Gabrielle and Tomás, both 4-year-olds returning for a second year, take turns descending halfway down the extra-wide slide, stopping, and draping one leg off the lip of the slide. Other children slide past them, more or less deftly. Rebecca watches cautiously at some distance, looking to see how Tomás' and Gabrielle's coordination holds up to her anticipated fear: a flip off the slide at some distance. New children, a year younger, approach, see this game, and attempt to imitate it.

"Gabrielle and Tomás. Can you keep your legs inside the slide, please? I know you feel safe, but I'm not so sure kids who haven't had as much practice will be safe. They will see you dangling your leg and think it is OK, and they might flip off the slide and get hurt."

"But we are newts, and this is what they do," Tomás says.

"Newts! Of course." Rebecca pauses to gather her thoughts. "Say, newts? I want to help kids play and stay safe also. Would you mind enjoying your moist log with your legs inside the slide?"

Leah, a 4-year-old child with autism, slides down on her belly past Tomás, marking her descent by pressing her face to the slide.

Tomás returns his leg to the inside of the slide.

"Here comes Leah," Rebecca says, marking Leah's entrance into the play area. "Hi Leah. It's Gabrielle and Tomás. They are newts."

"We eat bugs and sleep," adds Gabrielle, lying on her belly midway down the slide.

Rebecca moves to closely shadow Leah as she attempts to climb up a challenging arched ladder.

"You might want to ask Leah if she wants to be a newt too," Rebecca suggests.

The next morning before school, Rebecca is preoccupied with the beauty of Tomás' and Gabrielle's physical re-creation of a newt. *Where could they be newts?* she ponders. Once at school and setting up the playground, Rebecca pulls out two benches from under an overhanging roof. She places the benches next to a vine of wisteria. When Gabrielle and Tomás come running outside, Rebecca hears:

"We're newts, right?"

"Right."

Rebecca casually mentions, "There is a log for newts," pointing at the benches. Gabrielle and Tomás locate their game on the benches, lying facedown, and slinging one leg off, only leaving the benches to explore the tan bark area, where trees offer shade as they dig for rolly-pollies.

The newt game carries on for several months, including younger and older children. Rebecca checks out books about newts and salamanders and forested areas from the library to enrich the children's interest. Some dictate stories about newts, which they act out in Rebecca's circle. Some draw pictures of different kinds of newts and salamanders. In her parent newsletter, she includes directions and hours for a local nature center,

Social coordinations occur in outdoor play.

which features a display of newts found in the region. The class paints a mural of a forest with rocks, logs, and a stream, adding newts and other animals that share this habitat.

THE IMPORTANCE OF OUTDOOR PLAY

Play is central to children's healthy development. Outdoor play is not merely a time to "get the wigglies out," let off some steam, and give teachers a break from classroom learning. Gabrielle's and Tomás' play shows us the multidimensional qualities of children's outdoor play. Gabrielle and Tomás are understanding a sense of themselves as they physically act out being a newt. Their play is cognitive in that Gabrielle and Tomás are examining an interest from their local region of nature by using their whole body to explore what it means to be a newt. They use language to communicate ideas with each other and to others. Gabrielle's and Tomás' play is physically driven, and their play is rigorous. They are using balance, timing, and upper-body strength to control their descent.

Leah also likes to climb. Her aide will help Leah to abandon a self-stimulating behavior of going down the slide face first on her cheek and belly to sit up so she can see peers like Gabrielle and Tomás.

This vignette illustrates joyous, spontaneous, child-centered outdoor play that is physically active, engaged with nature, and focused on a self-initiated interest from daily life. Rebecca acknowledges Gabrielle's and Tomás' interest, recognizes the social entry of Leah as another possible player, and keeps them safe with an enriched set-up to promote their investigation. She supports and extends their play with teacher planned aesthetic and cognitive enrichment that draws on their daily life.

Circumstances in the lives of families, education, communities, and society have led to a critical concern over children's loss of time outdoors. Louv (2008) makes the point that children are experiencing such a reduction in time out of doors that children run the risk of what he calls "nature deficit disorder." Piggy-backing on the Federal No Child Left Behind Act, Louv initiated a Leave No Child Inside campaign, which stresses the imperative of outdoor time during children's development.

Educational funding structures that tie continued funding to test achievement have led to some schools eliminating or severely curtailing recess and the essential experiences gained for children out of doors. Concerns for liability have led to playground designs that lack essential physical challenges. Family lifestyles involving parents working long hours or holding down several jobs leave less time for outdoor play. Commercial marketing to parents' vulnerability in their role as parent has made children's free time into a commodity to sell packaged learning-enhanced activities or suggest that children need organized activities to succeed. Neighborhood safety can be a very real obstacle to outdoor time, whereas inflated fear fueled by media attention misrepresents safe opportunities for children to explore and play outside.

In contrast to this dire picture are the benefits of outdoor play. Children who participate in daily outdoor play:

1. Gain essential physical experiences that contribute to their strength and coordination

2. Feel connected with and learn about the world of nature

3. Use their own curiosities and interests during spontaneous peer play (American Academy of Pediatrics, 2007; Burdette & Whitaker, 2005; Frost et al., 2004; Oliver & Klugman, 2002; Pelligrini & Smith, 1998)

First graders Cella, Indi, and Jamila are on the tire swing, rain gear on, spinning and laughing as the moist, light air fills their mouths and mist blows about their faces and hands. These children are experiencing essential kinesthetic experiences that contribute to physical development. Cella, Indi, and Jamila are also practicing gross motor strength, balance, and coordination to successfully push the combined weight of themselves and the tire and mount the tire during a fast spin. They are rewarded by the sensory stimulation of being outside, especially in the light rain. Cella, Indi, and Jamila are also experiencing the pleasures of social affiliation. Having fun while experiencing the intimacy of face-to-face contact contributes to Cella's, Indi's, and Jamila's social development. ✐

Cella, Indi, and Jamila will remember their tire swing game and what they experienced from it when next they play there. Their teachers advocate to retain recess because it is an essential way to support children's physical activity, engage children with nature, and support self-initiated, spontaneous play.

The Importance of Outdoor Physically Active Play

Physically active outdoor play enhances growth by including a child's whole body in practice and skill development. Young children need to move: run, jump, hop, skip, gallop, walk, climb, swing, skip, throw and catch, and push and pull heavy play props. The National Association for Sport and Physical Education (2004) provides six physical activity standards and guidelines that we use for young children:

- Demonstrates competency in motor skills and movement patterns needed to perform a variety of physical activities
- Demonstrates understanding of movement concepts, principles, strategies, and tactics as they apply to the learning and performance of physical activities
- Participates regularly in physical activity
- Achieves and maintains a health-enhancing level of physical fitness
- Exhibits responsible personal and social behavior that respects self and others in physical activity settings
- Values physical activity for health, enjoyment, challenge, self-expression, and/or social interaction

When we look at the standards from NASPE, we see that Gabrielle's and Tomás' activity illustrates all six standards.

NASPE recommends that preschoolers have at least 60 minutes and up to several hours per day of unstructured physical activity. They recommend no more than 60 consecutive minutes of sedentary activity except for sleeping.

Children need to be physically active to establish endurance. In a study of children's physically active play outdoors, Perry and Branum (2009) introduce 4-year-old Mollie. Mollie is experiencing new coordination and balance after a period of tentativeness and several stumbles. She vocally expresses her displeasure and notes, coincident with her pace, "I'm very slow right now because I'm a turtle" (p. 204). When she picks up speed, notice how her new surety is linked to her imaginative thinking: "But right now I'm a lion" (p. 204). Mollie's physical movement is a companion in her spontaneous play. Running around the climber, she voices feelings of empowerment: "Sometimes I pounce on twigs because I'm a meat eater" (p. 205).

Developmental milestones in physical and motor competence include a continuum of abilities like traveling and changing direction quickly, throwing and catching a ball, and later, active play sequences that combine running, jumping, throwing, and catching. For example, Mollie's physical activity demonstrates competency in fast-paced movement across a rugged tanbark surface, her own understanding of her progressively more coordinated skill, her interest in physical activity, and her enjoyment, self-expression, and social interaction.

Young children learn best when their whole body is engaged in active physical play. Active outdoor play helps children integrate development and new learning (for example, see Frost, Wortham, & Reifel, 2008). Gabrielle's and Tomás' newt play offered them the chance to move and refresh muscles that are more sedentary inside. Their climbing and scampering increased blood flow (Ayres, 1979). The newt game was a physically active exercise while being spontaneous outdoor play. In a study of kindergarten children, Myers (1985) compared motor behaviors during a physical education class and during spontaneous play in a playground equipped with opportunities for a range of gross motor challenges. She found that children engaged in more physically active behaviors during child-initiated play than during their regular physical education class.

When children experience active physical exercise in spontaneous play, they also experience the cognitive and social demands to think, speak, and negotiate with playmates and teachers (Frost et al., 2004; Perry, 2001; Perry & Branum, 2009). The physicality of Gabrielle's and Tomás' newt game required that they talk with and negotiate proper safety standards with Rebecca. They safely adjusted their balance and used upper-body endurance to share space with others on the climber. Cella, Indi, and Jamila used refined turn-taking in trading off turns to physically push each other on the tire. Mollie expresses what her physical exertion means to her in vivid metaphors inspired by her natural surroundings.

Outdoor play provides opportunities for gross motor development.

The Importance of Outdoor Nature Play

Direct exposure to nature is essential for healthy development. Being outside in nature opens children's senses, enriching their play with sights, sounds, smells, touch, movement, and taste. Cella, Indi, and Jamila experience lively play precisely because their active play is outside, where the air is fresh and the precipitation enlivens their skin. Nature play, like Gabrielle's and Tomás' tanbark digging, is intrinsically rewarding and offers children the chance to wonder, explore, observe, and investigate. Gabrielle's and Tomás' play is characteristic of the complexity, flexibility, and open-ended interpretation of materials found in nature play (Frost et al., 2004; Perry, 2001).

> *Gabrielle:*   "We're digging for bugs, 'kay?" She uses a stick to turn over a layer of tanbark and dirt.
>
> *Tomás:*   "Yeah. And I found three bugs." He shows Gabrielle his pail with three pill bugs inside.
>
> *Gabrielle:*   "Three. That means we need enough dirt to cover the bottom. And some leaves for them to eat. No beetles, though."

The newt game is an example of how a pretend game based on children's daily life experiences with nature focuses children's attention to the process of inquiry. Gabrielle and Tomás use observation, exploration, and comparison to enrich their own play by collecting and caring for real bugs.

Play outdoors gives children the opportunity to experience and develop a relationship with nature. Louv (2008) argues that children's early experiences in nature establish a foundation for the attachment and compassion that builds feelings of stewardship and sustainability.

> When Calvert arrives as a transfer teacher to his new elementary school, he finds the playground empty of growing plants. After getting support at the next Parent Teacher Association meeting, Calvert secures the donation of four 3' by 5' planter boxes from the local nursery in exchange for a mention of their generosity in his first/second grade combination classroom parent newsletter. He uses the newsletter to solicit help from parents in donating seeds, and Maurice's mom offers to build another planter box. Children from all grades water the seeds and tend to the weeds during recess because Calvert has sent a willing student into each classroom to talk about the garden. At first, either Calvert or another teacher supervises children's garden care, with children from his classroom teaching others on the playground how to tend the growing sprouts. Children make signs that guide care of the garden, and Calvert laminates the signs. After a rainstorm brings worms out onto the playground, Calvert helps children to nestle worms in the planter boxes. In 2 months' time, children are sampling two varieties of lettuce during recess, with descriptive language like "spicy" and "clean." The planter boxes become a gathering place, where kids go to hunt for bugs, make play plans, and reaffirm friendships.

Like Rebecca and Calvert, when teachers include a nature-based educational component in the outdoor classroom, children experience a sense of wonder and connection with the natural world (Moore & Wong, 1997; Schultz, Shriver, Tabanico, & Khazian, 2004; Sobel, 2004; Wilson, 1997).

Caring and nurturing the health of the planet requires just such a relationship with nature. Play among living things engenders nurturance, as Gabrielle and Tomás show while tending to their pill bug collection. In a study of outdoor play by Perry (2008), the power of this nurturance is so strong as to be infused in these children's play even though the snail in question had escaped. In this episode, three preschool children make sense of the leave-taking of their snail and their desire to ensure its safe future. They play in a puddle of water with a boat and a make-believe snail they call Butty, after the real snail that left its pail one afternoon during nap:

Chase:	We need to find Butty.
Emma:	Where's Butty?
Chase:	In the water. Butty! Butty!
Emma:	Did Butty drop in the water?
Chase:	Yeah.
Andreas:	Let's drain all the water. [*Andreas pulls the hose out of the gutter.*] Now the water is draining out.
Chase:	Hey, we need water. If there is no water, the boats won't be able to rescue Butty! (Perry, 2008, p. 100)

Play in nature allows children to share the habitats of outdoor living things like newts, pill bugs, and snails. Young children are readily empathic. Chase, Emma, and Andreas experience affiliation not just with each other but with the snail.

Play in nature not only stimulates investigation and engenders feelings of nurturance, but offers children a place for feelings of settled calm and wonder as well.

> First-grader Maurice lays under the playground maple tree, watching puffy white clouds blowing across the sky and past the tree branches. He closes one eye, opens it, and closes it again, watching the tree branches shift position with his field of vision. One cloud is thick and dense. Maurice watches it as it spreads out and thins as it travels across the sky. He shifts his attention to the sound of the leaves rustling as a breeze moves across the yard. A crow catches the breeze and Maurice watches it sail in the wind with outstretched wings. ∅

Play in nature is compatible with Maurice's interests and abilities. Like Mollie, Cella, Indi, and Jamila, play outdoors with nature complements children's healthy development with tactile, interactive, sensory-rich experiences (Moore & Wong, 1997). The science chapter continues this discussion of nature and an ecology component in a play-centered curriculum.

The Importance of Child-Initiated Play and Inquiry

Outdoor play offers children healthy developmental experiences in initiating activities and following their curiosity. Outdoor play that is directed by the children, rather than organized by adults, is just plain fun. It is also demanding. Children work hard to talk and listen to each other and find language to express their curiosity.

When children play together with concentration, focus, and planning, they use inquiry to make sense of something they are curious about. Inquiry describes children's use of observation, comparison, exploration, and investigation in all aspects of their physical and social world. Gabrielle and Tomás explore and experiment with the physical feeling and skill of balance in being a newt on a branch, and their curiosity extends to observe and investigate bugs. The connections Gabrielle and Tomás experience with each other and with nature when they play outdoors also contributes to social-emotional development because outdoor play helps children develop and establish relationships as they play, problem solve, and negotiate with fellow playmates (Moore & Wong, 1997; Perry, 2003, 2004; Thompson & Thompson, 2007).

Tomás:	"Now let's say we were done, because a snake is coming to get us!"
Gabrielle:	"But we don't get eaten, right?"
Tomás:	"We *think* we are going to be eaten."
Gabrielle:	"But not for real, right?"
Tomás:	"Right, because we jump to a different branch, and the snake can only slither."

Here we see Tomás and Gabrielle establishing feelings of security as they imagine their independent survival in the wild. They are also gaining practice in using language to express their ideas and clarifying and negotiating the additions of new ideas. Their inquiry is a focus for their play on what it means to be a newt and what might be a predator. Tomás and Gabrielle experience the complexity of moving back and forth between the real and the imagined.

Spontaneous play outdoors enhances self-esteem and confidence in exploring different environments (Swarbrick Eastwood, & Tutton, 2004; Thompson & Thompson, 2007). In Perry's and Branum's 2009 study, Mollie gained access to the fast-paced, vigorous peer play culture once she experienced confident mobility. She expresses her newly accomplished mobility by imagining herself as a lion, known for its dominance in the wild. Children seek out the playground because they see it as a time to make things happen and feel in control of their own curiosity, imagination, and expression. Where the indoor classroom tends to frame children's experiences with specific and fixed expectations, children experience more open-ended themes in their play and inquiry outside (Corsaro, 2003; Perry, 2001). The outdoor environment is flexible in noise, space, movement, and theme. Although children seek out this experience, they may also be hesitant.

🖤 Five-year-old Portia is running with several children on the playground during recess. Everyone but Portia runs up a ladder to the upper deck of the climbing structure. Portia approaches her kindergarten teacher Aziza.

"I can't go up the ladder and my friends are there."

"Oh, let's try! I've seen you balance. Your legs are stable and strong," Aziza says matter-of-factly.

"I want to be with my friends," Portia says.

"Let's go then. I'll be there," Aziza offers.

Portia and her teacher walk up to the climbing structure ladder. "Let's see if you can do this," Aziza says.

Portia does climb up, proceeds down the slide, and climbs back up several times. Aziza moves away as Portia reunites with her playmates. At the end of the day, Aziza crouches down to speak with Portia. "Portia, you are learning a lot these few days. Today you found out you *do* know how to use the ladder." 🖤

We find that when outdoor play incorporates fast-paced routines, those fast-paced routines function to cement peer allegiance. Picture Portia's friends running together, looking back and forth at each other, laughing, and feeling, with their fast movement, their zest and spirit together. When a group of children can run together in a fun chase game, they feel connected.

The power of the peer group during outdoor play is that children can perform with greater competence playing in the company of others than just alone. As Vygotsky emphasized, their abilities, buttressed by the collaborative efforts of the group, support what will be a next step on an individual level (Vygotsky, 1978). In the world of children's play with peers, active outdoor play helps children bond and feel affiliated (Pelligrini, 2005).

How the Outdoor Classroom Is Different from the Inside Classroom

In contrast to the inside classroom, the outdoor classroom can offer space and materials that can be used flexibly and with open-ended imaginative interpretation. Children invent their own themes and roles outside, with natural materials that can be anything: a stick can be a screwdriver, an acorn cap can be a fairy cup, wood chips can be money, sand and water can be mixed into whatever imagination calls forth. Outdoor environments like the ones Calvert, Aziza, and Rebecca designed invite exploration and experimentation. The outdoor environment is also one place where children are more involved in spontaneous play. Table 12.1 compares the differences in learning demands between inside and outdoor classroom.

Rebecca uses the outside classroom throughout the day because she has a classroom where children flow in and out at their inclination. Aziza uses the playground at recess for important healthy experiences. Calvert uses the outside for ecology activities during science and language arts as well and incorporates gardening and habitat activities into choices during recess.

Table 12.1 Contrast Between Inside and Outdoor Classroom

Category	Inside Classroom	Outdoor Classroom
Suggestive features of the activity areas	Specific and fixed expectations	Flexible expectations
Physical space in the activity areas	Confined	Spacious
Typical quality of play	Quieter, task-oriented, teacher-generated as well as child-initiated	Noisier, physically vigorous, child-initiated
Children's ability to interpret	Children rely on explicit cues to guide themes and roles	Children invent themes and roles in open-ended, flexible activity areas
Demand on communication and socialization skills	Less demand	More demand

Source: Information from *Outdoor Play: Teaching Strategies with Young Children* (p. 8) by J. P. Perry, 2001, New York: Teachers College Press. Copyright 2001 by Teachers College Press. Adapted with permission.

TEACHING GOALS FOR CHILDREN IN THE OUTDOOR CLASSROOM

The outdoor classroom promotes the same development through play as we discussed in previous chapters relating to the inside. The teacher's first goal in the outdoor classroom is to promote child-initiated, spontaneous play, which, like the inside, is easy for most children. Teachers establish an expectation for child-initiated play and, like Aziza with Portia, support all children in making this step into physically active play. Then children see the playground as a place where they, rather than the teachers, define play and themes. Promoting spontaneous play ensures that children will receive social and cognitive benefits by initiating interactions ("We're newts, right?" "Right.") and verbally expressing their interests and plans ("Now let's say we were done, because a snake is coming to get us!").

The second goal in the outdoor classroom is to maintain the duration of this peer-guided interactive play. Like Mollie, when children pretend together in self-directed outdoor play of long duration, they cultivate and exercise demanding cognitive and social abilities in creative problem solving, organizing and remembering information, attempting to regulate their impulses to keep the game going, and experiencing these abilities in the context of active play.

The teacher's third goal is to encourage imagination and creativity in the outdoor classroom by establishing nature play as a priority. Most children have the ability to pretend and create imaginary worlds and roles. Nature play is often infused with imagination. When teachers establish nature play as a priority, they are supporting children's use of pretense. Pretend play encourages children to think flexibly, entertain multiple perspectives, collaborate, and increase their use of language literacy abilities and numeracy. In Perry's 2008 study, Chase, Emma, and Andreas manage perspective taking and collaborate to perform complex language abilities. With Rebecca's additional outdoor curriculum, Gabrielle and Tomás transfer their play into aesthetic and literary mediums.

The fourth goal of teachers in the outdoor classroom is to guide and enrich children's wonder, inquiry, connection to, and knowledge about nature.

Celi and Indi are on their hands and knees, nibbling at mature lettuce leaves from one of the planter boxes with their mouths. A child-made sign in the planter box reads: "Ready to harvest."

Calvert:	"Say, Celi, what is that you're eating?"
Celi:	"Arugula! Me and Indi are horses."
Indi:	"Horses eat only arugula."
Calvert:	"And how did you figure out which was arugula and which was kale? The greens are so bushy and close together now."
Celi:	"The arugula has light green leaves."
Indi:	"And they are smaller."
Celi:	"And wavy. See?" Celi gently brushes the lettuce leaves with her left hand. She is quiet as she looks at the sunlight shine through the leaves of lettuce.
Indi:	"Kale leaves are much longer and tougher and harder for horses to bite."
Calvert:	"The horses on your farm have pretty strong jaws. I remember we fed them carrots on our field trip."

Calvert accepts the girls' imaginary game as the mode through which Celi and Indi closely observe, wonder about, ask questions, and communicate their ideas to others (Seefelt, 2005).

The fifth important goal for teachers in the outdoor classroom is to support the development of the whole child with challenges defined as "reasonable risk" so that developmental trajectories proceed (Tovey, 2007). Aziza encourages Portia to make small steps in balance and upper body strength to accompany her social needs. During kindergarten recess, Aziza follows Portia's practice with close observation and firm encouragement. With newly acquired large motor skill, Portia, like Mollie, could keep up physically with the other children's fast-paced play and experience the social and cognitive benefits of active peer play. Rebecca supports reasonable risk by recognizing Gabrielle's and Tomás' physically active needs. She negotiates safety standards while acknowledging the children's point of view and arranges an outdoor set-up to support their interests. Figure 12.1 summarizes a teacher's intentions for the outdoor classroom.

> The teacher's intentions for the outdoor classroom are to promote and cultivate children's connection to and interest in nature, encourage physically active play, and support child-directed, child-initiated play of long duration.

Figure 12.1
Teacher Goals for the Outdoor Classroom

BEST PRACTICES IN PLANNING FOR OUTDOOR PLAY

Active outdoor classrooms give teachers the chance to observe, reflect, and facilitate children's intentions as children direct their own self-initiated play.

Serving Children from Diverse Backgrounds

Not everyone has had the background of growing up around and in nature and the outdoors. This does not mean that children under adult care should be kept inside. Far from it. What some may call "inclement weather," with the proper attire, can, like Cella, Indi, and Jamila, offer unique experiences—for the senses and in the exploration and examination of the physical environment. Not all families may appreciate the developmental value of outdoor play. Cooper (1999) reflects on her strategies in gaining the trust of parents, whose perspectives on play are based on their own educational experiences, social class, and cultural norms and values. She says she shares her observational skills with parents as they mutually watch children in play. Cooper emphasizes the motor skills exhibited, the problem solving taking place, and the language development. Parent confidence in the value of outdoor play will be appreciated more readily when, as Cooper says, "the trappings of school are present." The curriculum chapters highlight the literacy, numeracy, art, and science possibilities for outdoor experiences, which Cooper says can be interpreted to parents. Cooper suggests finding out parents' goals for their children and emphasizing those goals in conversations.

Next, Fong provides opportunities for children to interact in diverse and complex ways to make the outdoor classroom an essential component of early childhood development (Frost et al., 2004; Frost & Woods, 2006; Frost et al., 2008). She also helps interpret those experiences for Tashonda's mother.

> Fortunately Fong teaches at an elementary school known for its outdoor environment. It features an edible garden, outdoor art and music areas, a constructive sand and water area for digging and channeling, and wooded space. The playground and outdoor spaces reflect the early childhood education traditions of Froebel and Dewey in cultivating and observing children's outdoor play. Her school also reflects current research and practice emphasizing the

importance of children interacting with each other, and teachers following the children's own interests and inquiry using child observations guided by Reggio Emilia and the Project Approach.

Fong uses the reflective self-study of NAEYC's Early Childhood Program Standards to assess her program. She rates her classroom yearly using the *School-Age Care Environmental Rating Scale* (Harms, Jacobs, & White, 1996). The playground encourages physically active play, helps children become connected to nature, and is designed to encourage child-initiated play and inquiry. The playground is on the same level as the ground-floor classroom, and doors remain open for children to flow indoors and outdoors much of the year based on their needs and interests. Fong has arranged a full range of developmentally appropriate activities outdoors, including tone bars for music and space for movement next to a garden. Children have nature and art materials accessible throughout the day under an overhanging shelter space in the transition area between the outside and inside classroom. Moving from the building out into the yard, children have separate areas for digging, climbing and running, and organized games.

With guidance from research on the importance of outdoor play, Fong organized several parent workdays to talk with parents about their developmental goals for their children. Fong shared her own beliefs about the value of outdoor play. Lashonda's mother heard about her daughter's accomplishments in language and literacy on the playground. That day, Lashonda's mother and other parents created landscaping that varied in terrain and elevation with a water zone, plantings, bark, and rises.

Fong and the other teachers encourage children's use of tools in activity areas with accessible shelves for working in the garden, sand, and water in a sand kitchen modeled after the indoor playhouse with loose parts that include dishes and cookware; in the digging area with shovels, gutters, and tubes for water channeling; and art and writing tools and constructive materials like glue, tape, and clay under the overhang. The nature area includes a garden with edible plants (a child-written sign in one pot reads: "Our Pizza Garden—thyme, basil, oregano, and sometimes tomatoes") and flowers that attract insects and butterflies for children to observe. Her school is lucky to have shade provided by three trees. Two are in a wooded tanbark area. One is in the middle of the playground with a table underneath for focused nature observation, drawing and writing, and constructive manipulatives.

Fong keeps track of the range of materials she offers children outside, making sure children have materials found in nature such as sand, water, soil, rocks, and materials for stacking and constructing. Fong acquired a lockable storage bench and placed it under the overhang not just for children's daily use, but also for teachers to store extra tools, loose parts, and materials for aesthetic expression. Fong used several resources to help her manage placement of activity areas to ensure accessibility for all children while emphasizing places for all children to construct, tend and care, and be quiet (Dimensions Educational Research Foundation & Arbor Day Foundation, 2007; Frost et al., 2004; Kritchevsky & Prescott, 1977; Olds, 2001; Walsh, 2008). Fong's outdoor classroom offers feelings of emotional attachment to special child-defined places. There are gardening and natural areas shared with plants and animals. The playground includes space for large and fine motor skill and strength development, semi-enclosed spaces for respite while maintaining safety and security, and open space for organized games (see Frost et al., 2008; Goodenough, 2003). ℘

Teachers support all children's outdoor play by:

1. Maximizing face-to-face engagement (having tire swings, extra-wide slides built into a hill, and tables with chairs that face each other)
2. Arranging activity areas to suggest places for imagination and concentration (including soft spots with cushions, use of veils to mark a protected area, photographs of children using the areas in play, and signs written by children)
3. Protecting and defining play areas to draw children's attention (with low shelves or carts on wheels for child-accessible materials and props and spaces for one child to be alone, observe, and/or be quiet)

Sites with Outdoor Challenges

Teachers with outdoor sites that are less than ideal can still cultivate children's physically active outdoor play, engagement with nature, and child-initiated play. The playground at Calvert's school is blacktop with one climber built on sand. Sometimes during recess and free play periods, Calvert turns the space under the active climber into a sand kitchen area using a portable, wheeled art cart supplied with loose parts for kitchen play that he stores in a outdoor shed. Calvert also stores a foldout table and a shade tent, which he uses for child-selected activities. Children can bring out Legos for assembly, a paper and drawing caddy with tape for 3-D constructions, play props to match imaginative play, nature specimens, and clipboards, magnifying glasses, and books from the shed as well.

Aziza takes children outside in her science and math periods because outdoor areas are integrated in her curriculum. She divides a large sand area with two hills, with shovels on both. She arranges a cart of kitchen play props in the sand under a shade tent made from draped cloth on clothesline and a bench underneath. She positions a place for drawing for one so that a shy child can observe play in small groups as part of a next step in growth, or just relax out of the fray of fast-paced play. Aziza stores the props and cart behind her classroom door for quick access when exiting.

Roxanne works in a preschool closed to neighborhood use, so some of her set-up props can be left outside overnight, whereas others she gathers from inside. She uses plastic storage crates instead of tables to balance old and outdated keyboards and office telephones, with a food container for paper and stubs of pencils to spark an array of fantasy play about work, connecting to a missing loved one, space travel, and so on. Roxanne tapes a large swatch of paper from a paper roll to the side of the building on the playground border, adds several containers of chalk, and thereby encourages children to express large motor coordination, strengthening, and balance in a cooperative mural. Roxanne presents music accessibly with a few drums on a rug for impromptu rhythm sessions, and Aziza uses professional paint buckets, large food tins, or cylindrical cardboard oatmeal containers for her outdoor music area.

Whether children are in cities or suburbs, teachers can cultivate nature appreciation with little expense. Stephens (2002) suggests observing for where birds make their homes or go in the rain; listening to sounds in nature; tracking animal paw prints after snow and rain; collecting nature treasures; planting on a windowsill, balcony, or community plot; making nature paints from berries; and cultivating compassion with feeders of water or nuts.

Inexpensive or free ideas to enrich the outdoor classroom are offered by the North Carolina Outdoor Learning Environment Alliance: creating an herb garden in planters, identifying a special place for digging, hanging a bird feeder, partnering with U.S. Forest Service or community extension agencies for native trees, and using a log as a bench (Bradford, Easterling, Mengel, & Sullivan, 2010).

The Adult's Feelings about Being Outdoors

Best practices remind us of the importance of outdoor play in children's health. Recall when you were a young child. Did your childhood include playing outside? If so, where? What did you do? Were you alone or did you also play with others? Were you outside in all weather, or just some? What are your feelings about those times? If you did not play outside, why not? Was it a matter of safety?

Every child and adult needs to have safe, natural environments to explore, take care of, feel nurturance from, and be stimulated by. Some people, including many teachers, have not enjoyed such childhood opportunities. A teacher's readiness to develop children's opportunities for outdoor play directly relates to how comfortably and pleasurably that teacher feels about being outside.

Several organizations in this country, including the American Academy of Pediatrics, the Alliance for Childhood, the Arbor Day Foundation, the National Institute for Play, the No Child Left Inside Coalition, and the National Recreation and Park Association propose that being outdoors to play is a right of childhood. The U.N. Convention on the Rights of the Child recognizes the child's right to recreation.

Safety is also a basic right and necessity for everyone. Roxanne grew up in a neighborhood without access to safe options for play. With child development coursework and a mentor teacher, she was able to take the extra step in imagining the invitation that the outdoors offers. Marisol wanted to do cartwheels and climb trees, but was not allowed to do so because her parents dressed her in skirts and dresses. In her student practicum training, she learned alongside the children about the benefits of active outdoor play in nature. As a child, Beth experienced admonishments about being dirty. We find that other teachers also recall causing adults extra work in managing cleanup after outdoor play when they were children. These teachers are challenged to consider experiences for children in their care that override past experiences.

If the school grounds are situated in a neighborhood that cannot reliably guarantee children's safely, teachers will not feel comfortable encouraging outdoor play. This means that children's right to be safe is compromised and needs immediate attention.

Outdoor play is a right because outdoor play engenders good health. If teachers are in a position where they feel uncomfortable about outdoor play options, consider what contributes to this trepidation. If the outdoors is a real safety concern, than community action is necessary to ensure the health of children. If it is past experiences on the part of the adults that do not offer instances of enrichment, pleasure, and nurturance from being out of doors, then the children and teachers like Roxanne will be exploring together the wealths of the outdoors.

OBSERVING AND INTERPRETING OUTDOOR PLAY

Spontaneous outdoor play allows the teacher to focus on children's development because the behavior is directed by the children: How well can Leah manage balance while using the ladder on the climber? Can she stop herself in mid-descent if Gabrielle scampers up onto the slide? It seems like she will need to learn to go down on her bottom so she can see her peers and be able to respond to their presence.

Wintertime can offer unique outdoor play opportunities.

Children establish familiar and particular play routines and habits in the company of each other. Teachers who understand children's peer play interactions can better appreciate what children are trying to do in the behavior they express.

Understanding Children's Outdoor Peer Play

Outdoor spaces vividly invite the expression of peer play interactions. Children themselves see the playground as a place where they direct their own fun, energy, and interests. Corsaro (2003) identified the unique features of what it means to be children together. He described two major themes in young children's peer play: (a) a strong desire to play with others and (b) persistent attempts to challenge, make things happen, and direct their own actions. Children want to feel their own expertise. Using inquiry, they persevere with diligent focus in response to their own curiosities.

Children challenge and enhance gross motor experience by inventing new ways to swing, climb, hang, spin, pivot, throw, run, jump, and feel strong. When Gabrielle and Tomás scamper up the slide, their teacher watches as well. Rebecca senses the children's attention and focus to this managed risk and is ready to step in with a question to refocus concentration if necessary. Rebecca notices the children's broad smiles as they successfully manage this climbing challenge, as well as Leah's initiative to be on the slide at the same time. All three children are feeling the pleasure of being in control, managing a physically demanding task in which they use their whole body and, for Gabrielle and Tomás at least, sharing fun with peers. Gabrielle's and Tomás' conversation and their use of give-and-take comments indicate not only the physical, but also the social and cognitive, challenges of the activity.

Children interact during peer play by:

- Including others in their play based upon agreed imagined roles ("You have to be Rope Girl to be in our game.")
- Remembering past episodes of play, oftentimes in specific areas ("I know!" "Member we played horses and we cozied next to the garden?")
- Claiming territory ("This is our pirate ship!")
- Challenging adult authority ("Let's not get in line, 'kay?")
- Playing games of flee and chase
- Exhibiting rough-and-tumble play
- Feigning fear and "playing dead"
- Using singsong voice to accompany the game and its progression ("Nanny, nanny, boo, boo!")

The Phases of Peer Play

When left to their own devices, we find that children develop their play interactions in three phases. In the first phase, the *initiation phase*, children need to figure out who they are playing with. Sometimes this is easy when children have regular playmates. Even then, children exchange mutual recognition with woops, smiles, or a verbal invitation and acceptance like, "Let's play, OK?" "OK." Or "We're friends, right?" "Right." Some children, eager for interaction, will provoke peers and receive shrieks of irritation and anger, but still attention: "Quit it!" or "She wrecked our tunnel!" or "He stole our stuff!" Teachers facilitate inexperienced children in making this first step in child-directed interactions, with a comment like, "Gee, I think Portia wants to play with you," or coaching the inexperienced Portia with, "Say, 'What are you playing?'" as an initial entry strategy, or by commenting: "I think Tomás wants to play. What could he do instead of knocking your stuff down if he wants to play?"

The second phase of young children's peer play is the *negotiation* phase. Children decide the theme of their game and perhaps their roles. Here again, children must agree to proceed: "Let's say we were dragons, 'kay?" "OK." Or "We're collecting these [acorns] for treasure, right?" "Right." Each new idea involves a negotiation. Often children will need to be persistent: "This is our space ship, 'kay? We're going to flying, right? Right?" "Yeah, but I know the way, 'cause I have the map." "Right." Notice how each new idea or proposal must be acknowledged for the interaction to proceed. Children often use higher-order cognitive and language functions during self-generated outdoor play. Here, too, teachers help children by supporting pretend elements. Teachers can use sound effects to enrich the theme ("Dragons coming!"—teacher makes the sound of wind whooshing) and comments to support children's agreements ("OK, here is the rocket station."). Teachers can offer a complementary idea, question, or prop to deepen the play ("Dragons! Where is your cloud for resting after flying?" or "Here is a keyboard for a control panel.").

The third phase of peer play is the *enactment* phase, where children expand, develop, and transform the theme as play develops. Here, too, children mutually agree over the progression of ideas for the interaction to continue. Perry and Branum (2009) describe how Michael experiments with the mechanics of balance, requiring him to negotiate his investigation with playmates Morgan and Emma. Notice how Michael needs Emma's agreement to proceed.

> Michael tried to balance his fulcrum so that the lower, inclined end of the board will be off the ground. He turned back and looked at Morgan, establishing facial engagement. "I think you're too heavy," he said, offering a hypothesis for the board's persistent downward angle.
>
> "Why don't you try me," suggested Emma. "I'm a little lighter than her," she added picking up on the element of weight as these children interpret Michael's arrangement.
>
> "Kay," said Michael, accepting Emma's involvement in the interaction.
>
> Emma got into the crate. (p. 202) ✂

When adults understand that children's interactions in physically active play are purposeful and follow a sequence, then adults can better support the children's intentions as the children drive the progression of their play.

Serving Students with Special Needs ♥

Teachers accommodate the outdoor classroom to children's emerging physical and social capacities and special needs. Grounds and equipment may need to be adapted for wheelchair accessibility or visual impairment. Signs and photographs can be posted to support children with a hearing loss or developmental disability. These strategies encourage all children to be active and be with their peers.

> Leah's Individual Educational Plan includes an aide to facilitate her language and social interaction. Rebecca observes that Leah's engagement with peers is infrequent. When in the company of others, Leah frequently cries in distress or anxiety but is calmed with adult reassurance and adult physical closeness. Leah's IEP includes practice playing alongside peers to encourage facial engagement with others her age. Adults will help Leah experience the success of having a plan by providing play experiences where Leah can look across a play spot at another child. Today Leah is standing on the opposite side of a sand table.

Leah:	"Help!"
Aide:	"Help me?"
Leah:	"Help me?"
Aide:	"Sure, I can help you." The aide holds down the block structure Leah is assembling vertically. Leah reaches for another block. She looks briefly at Gabrielle who is across the table.
Aide:	"You see Gabrielle building too? Gabrielle is building. Leah is building."
Leah:	"Help me."
Aide:	"Help me build?"
Leah:	"Help me build."
Aide:	"Yes, I can help you build. Oh, look, Leah. Gabrielle is building too. What are you building, Gabrielle?"
Gabrielle:	"I'm building a mall so we can go shopping." ✍

Outdoor play can also offer benefit for children to concentrate with the sensory rich and calming experiences of sharing nature (Kuo & Taylor, 2004).

> Seven-year-old Kendrick is trying hard to settle in Calvert's math activity involving the addition and subtraction of sets. After repeated encouragements to return to the dinosaur counters, Sonia, the librarian decides to help Kendrick calm and focus by inviting him outside to look at the new corn growing. They weed together. Kendrick finds a ladybug and lets it crawl on his hand. Together they gather mint leaves and munch on them. They locate the daisies, some white, some yellow and some orange. Using petals from each, they laugh, add, subtract, multiply, and unexpectedly notice recess has started without them. ✍

TEACHER DECISION MAKING DURING OUTDOOR PLAY

Chapters 4 and 5 emphasized orchestration strategies that support play. Three questions guide a teacher's choice of strategies when supporting spontaneous outdoor play of long duration:

1. Can the child engage alone and with others independent of adults?
2. During peer play, is the interaction losing focus or becoming unsafe?
3. What is the purpose of the teacher's intervention?

Figure 12.2 reviews these teacher decisions during outdoor play, with accompanying strategies to use.

Teachers encourage children to engage with each other because peer exchange and feedback is a powerful means for promoting development. Aziza arranges outdoor classroom areas so her kindergarten children have reliable spots to play repeatedly over days and weeks and months. She arranges wall ball games against the cafeteria wall after lunch is over, horses in a basket next to the garden, jump ropes at the blacktop near the garden, and a picnic table with paper, markers, tape, clipboards, and a few binoculars. Just like the inside classroom, Aziza arranges outdoor areas so small groups of not more than two to five children can concentrate, talk, and listen, protected from interference of traffic and undue noise from other small groups. She uses identified play spots to support complex interactions that encourage imagination, planning, and problem solving.

When preschool children are not yet able to play independent of a teacher, Rebecca uses regularly set-up play spots to encourage adjacent play. Like the example of Leah building with blocks, the opportunity to play across from more experienced players gives most children the chance to recognize their next step. If outdoor play is not losing focus or becoming unsafe, the teacher continues to support children's experience by using play areas to encourage imagination, planning, and problem solving. When outdoor play has lost focus, or when physical or psychological safety is compromised, teachers must decide how best to intervene.

> Six- and 7-year-olds Celi, Kendrick, Eli, and Jamila are playing superheroes during recess. Calvert watches as the game escalates into pushing and wrestling. ∅

Calvert wonders: Have they all agreed to play together? Eli looks uncertain at times. Do they know or have they agreed on what they are playing? Are they aware of new ideas that have been proposed for the game?

> Calvert watches Celi, Kendrick, Eli, and Jamila run gleefully throughout the playground but sees little verbal interchange. When he sees them running though spots where other playmate groups are concentrating on a different interest, he approaches them.

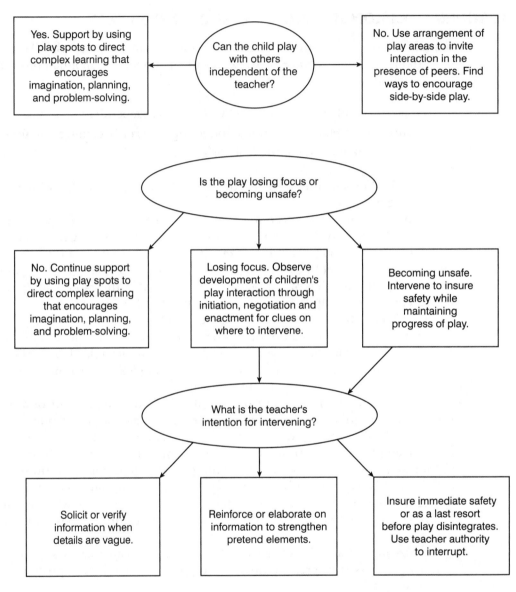

Figure 12.2
Teacher Decisions during Outdoor Play
Source: Information from *Outdoor Play: Teaching Strategies with Young Children* (p. 85) by J. P. Perry, 2001, New York: Teachers College Press. Copyright 2001 by Teachers College Press. Adapted with permission.

Calvert wants to slow the group down to gather information and help them regain focus: "Say, kids, hold on a second, please. What game are you playing?" After listening, he adds a further clarifying question: "And are all of you playing?" Calvert decides to enrich the children's mission of wrestling bad guys by adding to their play options: "You all are in charge of safety and security, right?" He pauses for their nods of tentative approval. "Can you do a security check of the playground for the school? Help us out with some security maps? Maps that show the different places on the playground and what happens there?" ⌀

Calvert's probing questions and prompts help Celi, Kendrick, Eli, and Jamila elaborate, verbalize, and listen to each other. Calvert's questions strengthen pretend elements and encourage creativity while keeping the focus on safety. He encourages the play interaction to continue with renewed focus. With Tomás and Gabrielle, Rebecca requested compliance with a safety rule. She, like Calvert, speaks to the children in their pretend roles as newts. This has the effect of gaining the children's compliance and keeping their game going.

Recall that one of the teacher's goals for supporting child-initiated play outside is to promote interactions of long duration. Rebecca identifies and elaborates on the newt game by setting up an area for continued play as well as adding additional activities like literature, drama, and art expression.

TEACHING STYLES THAT SUPPORT OUTDOOR PLAY

Teachers have a choice of styles when supporting play and development in outdoor areas, making the outdoors an exhilarating place for teachers as well as children. In a year-long reflective study of how teachers support children's self-initiated play outside, Perry (2001) describes two equally valuable, effective teaching styles that support outdoor play. Chapter 5 also elaborates on teacher strategies when interacting with children.

Indirect Coordination

One type of style involves the *indirect coordination* of play areas through preparation, observation of developmental progress, and refinement based on children's use of the play area.

> Roxanne intentionally provides sand and water in an outdoor sand kitchen to stimulate preschool children's experiences not only in social-emotional and language areas, but also in the science of changing physical states of sand and water and the numeracy of categorization and counting when they "set the table."
>
> *Roxanne:* "So, you are making cake AND soup! Sounds like a café. Do you need menus? You can make them at the writing table." ⌀

Roxanne uses the sand kitchen to direct complex learning. She indirectly participates as an artist apprentice, observing the children's progress, noting their interests, and determining if enrichment is necessary in terms of additional materials like clipboards, pencils, and extra paper for taking orders.

Indirect coordination is especially effective when the teacher uses observation to "step into" the life of the children's play, as we saw when Rebecca refers to Gabrielle and Tomás as newts. Roxanne uses open-ended questions to reveal how children are thinking and the intentions behind their actions: "Waiter? Can you tell me what types of soup you have today?" Roxanne uses her observations and reflections to follow children's progress of play: Who makes pretend suggestions to move the game along? What vocabulary does she hear? What instances of counting and one-to-one correspondence does she see?

Direct Involvement

Perry (2001) identifies a second style of *direct involvement* by the teacher as a player. Fong participates as a play organizer and promoter. She uses imaginative imagery to set up a play area as "a place where things can happen." Fong prepares a rocket ship, or a fire station, or a forest. She uses visual cues and play area adjustments like keyboards, milk crates, draped fabric, changes in elevation in sand areas with hills or trenches, and imaginative use of nature props like branches for trees, to suggest themes for interactive play. She uses play voice, sound effects, models negotiating phrases, and ensures mutual agreements with prompting words at the end of suggestions like, "Right?" and "OK?" Fong also provides verbal commentary as a means to cue inexperienced players.

"Do you hear me command central? We are ready for takeoff. 10, nine, eight . . ."

Fong is elaborating on the children's game to strengthen the meaning of their planning. Sometimes children need even more direct organization.

During lunch recess Calvert hears several children sitting off to the playground periphery talking about their Game Boys. He organizes games of Connect 4 at a picnic table, staying to play. ✗

Perry (2001) found that supporting outdoor play is almost always more effective when teachers take into account the children's play theme and intervene from inside the theme of children's play and include the children's play point of view when interrupting to secure compliance. Table 12.2 provides suggestions for when to use either style.

With either style, teachers use direct involvement when play becomes unsafe.

FOSTERING INQUIRY IN THE OUTDOOR CLASSROOM

Inquiry describes children's use of observation, comparison, exploration, and investigation in all aspects of their physical and social world. Roxanne, Rebecca, Aziza, Calvert, and Fong foster inquiry by encouraging children's observation, exploration, and investigation. These teachers focus on children's own curiosities and interests to extend their inquiry with "next steps." Teachers base intervention on their own observation and reflection: Were Gabrielle and Tomás ready to take information from picture books and use it when painting a mural with other playmates? Cella is doing most of the pushing on the tire swing. Calvert asks her, "Cella, Jamila LOVES the tire swing. I wonder if you could show her the tricky part about jumping on after pushing?"

Table 12.2 Teacher Styles to Support Outdoor Play

	Indirect Coordination of Play Areas	Direct Involvement
Goals	To establish areas of play where children can initiate interactions, verbally communicate needs and desires, and negotiate actions with others	To promote focus and ensure safety
What to observe	How children use and interpret cues of the play areas	How children's play progresses through the three phases of initiation, negotiation, and enactment
When to support	Prior to and during peer play	When play loses focus and/or becomes unsafe
How to support	• Daily set-up • Provision of materials • Observation • Definition and separation of play groups	• Soliciting, verifying information • Reinforcing or elaborating on information • Interrupting
Types of support	Preparation of the play area • Creation of space • Creation of an imaginary place	Use of play voice, sound effects, and modeling negotiating phrases inside the context of the play theme
	Refinement of the play area • Settling play groups in areas • Separation of play groups • Stepping into the life of the play theme by referring to imaginative elements as if they were real • Elaboration of play theme with enriched materials based on theme	Interrupt outside the context of the play theme to ensure safety when immediate danger is present

Source: Information from *Outdoor Play: Teaching Strategies with Young Children* (p. 86) by J. P. Perry, 2001, New York: Teachers College Press. Copyright 2001 by Teachers College Press. Adapted with permission.

Katz (2007) includes several guidelines for fostering inquiry during outdoor play, including that children

• be involved in sustained investigations of aspects of their own environment and experiences worthy of their interest, knowledge, and understanding.
• experience the satisfaction that results from overcoming obstacles and setbacks and solving problems.
• have confidence in their intellectual powers and questions.
• help others to discover things and to understand them better.
• make suggestions to others and express appreciation of others' efforts for what is accomplished.
• apply their developing literacy and numeracy abilities in purposeful ways.
• feel that they belong to a group of their peers.   (p. 94–95)

These guidelines show us that children's outdoor play can be purposeful and planned. The chapter on science elaborates on children's process of inquiry.

ASSESSING CHILDREN'S PLAY IN THE OUTDOOR CLASSROOM

Assessments of children's play in the outdoor environment involve follow-up observation and reflection on how children are using activity areas to make sense of a focused interest. Teachers use the same process of inquiry that children follow to collect information and investigate children's progress. Rebecca wonders, is Leah observing what peers in the play area are doing? Can Leah stay to follow through on a plan in the sand and fill a bucket, for example? She records Gabrielle and Tomás for instances of how they each describe their observations as they dig for bugs, whether they ask questions, and what they dictate and/or write in their journal. After engaging children in playground design plans, Calvert watches how Eli uses new sand and plantings independently. Calvert looks for behavioral evidence that children previously refraining from physical activity show interest in recess participation. Does Kendrick evidence pleasure and pride in accomplishments after respites in the garden? In staff meetings, Roxanne and her staff ask themselves if all children willingly spend time outside or do some need invitations and teacher facilitation? Aziza watches Portia. Can she play cooperatively and exhibit teamwork during investigative play? After children make "How We Care for Our Pizza Garden" signs in circle time, Fong looks for how children demonstrate knowledge of how to care for outdoor classroom life. For example, can Anna look at the flowers in the garden and refrain from picking blossoms that will be turning to tomatoes? Does Maurice show respect for classroom areas that have been intentionally set up to care for living things? He may be able to hold the class snake gently, but might step on a beetle encountered in the yard as a demonstration of power.

Evaluating Outdoor Play Environments

Tools for assessing space for outdoor play are available to preschool, kindergarten, and primary-grade teachers. Most assessment tools begin with a plan or suggestions for outdoor design. Some have an explicit evaluative component. Others suggest that teachers follow a protocol of preparation, observation, refinement, and enriched direct interaction.

Frost (2007) in Frost et al. (2008) offers The Playground Checklist to help in the design, use, and evaluation of school and community playgrounds for preschool, kindergarten, and primary settings. The Playground Checklist is a 60-item rating scale under three headings:

1. What does the playground contain?
2. Is the playground in good repair and relatively safe?
3. How should the playground and the play leader function?

The *Learning with Nature Idea Book: Creating Nurturing Outdoor Spaces for Children* (Dimensions Educational Research Foundation & Arbor Day, 2007) provides a research review for why young children need to connect with nature to be healthy and grow. The book provides 10 principles for outdoor classroom design, recommends activity areas, articulates appropriate natural materials, and emphasizes durability, low maintenance, beauty, visual clarity, and safety. It also offers problem-solving considerations for age of children, individual needs, and climate, as well as information on integrating with community resources.

The *Early Childhood Environmental Rating Scale*–Revised Edition (Harms, Clifford, & Cryer, 2004) is an internationally used assessment of outdoor as well as indoor preschool environmental design features, materials, and routines. The *School-Age Care Environment Rating Scale* (Harms et al., 1996) is a counterpart for kindergarten and primary grades. The 43-item ECERS assessment falls under seven subscales: space and furnishings, personal care routines, language-reasoning, activities, teacher–child and child–child interactions, program schedule and structure, and provisions for parents and staff. Each item is rated on a seven-point continuum that offers next steps for quality improvement.

Preschool Outdoor Environment Measurement Scale (POEMS; DeBord, Hestenes, Moore, Cosco, & McGinnis, 2005) is a 56-item checklist for learning about, planning, evaluating, and conducting research on outdoor environments in preschool settings. POEMS groups items into five domains:

1. Physical environment
2. Child–environment interactions, teacher–child interactions, child–child interactions, and parent–child interactions
3. Materials and loose parts in the play settings
4. Program support features
5. The role of the teacher

ADVOCATING FOR OUTDOOR PLAY FOR ALL CHILDREN

Increasingly, professional organizations and researchers are highlighting the importance of outdoor play, while at the same time outdoor play opportunities for children are being curtailed. Calvert is concerned that some children are rarely active. He notices that several children in his elementary school are obese. During recess and afterschool care, they sit against the playground wall and trade cards. His district has mentioned a recess reduction to 10 minutes. Calvert contacts the Alliance for Childhood, who sends him a free DVD copy of a documentary prepared by Michigan Television called "Where Do the Children Play?" He organizes a free screening of the movie for parents, teachers, and neighbors. An advocacy group forms after the movie to petition the school board to *increase* recess time and include a nature component in the elementary school curriculum.

Calvert not only has planter boxes that attract butterflies and grow vegetables now, but the children also run a small "farmer's market" on Fridays after school, where they sell greens, squash, cucumbers, beans, and tomatoes. With their money, the children start a collection to purchase "things to keep us strong and healthy," which included their ideas for active play: an A-frame climber and ladder, jump ropes, balls for organized games, and walking boards.

Teachers of young children are advocates ensuring children's health by making sure children get physical activity, feel connected with the world of nature, and receive the social and cognitive benefits by following their own curiosities and interests during spontaneous outdoor peer play.

We recommend several policy implications for advocating for outdoor play. Children need several periods each day of active play to be healthy. Teachers ensure that outdoor spaces allow for children to use the props and tools of play and to run, jump, hop, skip, gallop, walk, climb, swing, skip, throw, and catch. Teachers provide for nature and natural materials with water, sand, wood, sun, shade, height, slope, and growing plants. Teachers create and maintain outdoor spaces to promote children's relationships with each other in child-initiated spontaneous play. Teachers support outdoor play by providing child-accessible areas for the care of living things and the investigation of living creatures, including tactile experience as part of use of materials, and engaging children in open-ended questions ("I wonder how. . .?").

We recommend that teachers receive professional training in using the outdoor classroom as part of their curriculum and reflectively address their own thoughts and feelings about being outdoors. Outdoor play happens in all weather because the classroom includes provisions for appropriate clothing and healthy options to explore and investigate the unique learning opportunities in nature.

SUMMARY AND CONCLUSION

In this chapter, teachers have prepared outdoor learning areas, observed developmental progress through the social and material interactions, refined outdoor play spots based on children's use of materials and what they enjoy doing with materials in the area, and enriched children's play and inquiry with direct teacher interaction.

Children's health depends on how teachers weave outdoor time into children's daily educational experience. While outside, teachers guide and enrich children's wonder, inquiry, connection to, and knowledge about nature, encourage imagination and creativity, and evaluate the outdoor environment so that children experience challenges of "reasonable risk."

Children want to feel their own expertise. They will persevere with diligent focus in response to their own curiosities. When adults understand that children's interactions in physically active play are purposeful and follow a sequence, then adults can better support the children's intentions as the children drive the progression of their play.

13

Play, Toys, and Technology

To begin their Night Sky project, kindergarten teachers Suzanne, Christa, and Margaret orchestrate their annual Friday sleepover at school, which is accompanied by sky watching through a telescope. They follow this with a mural that over time acquires children's renditions of objects that move in the sky. This includes objects they read about—such as planets, moons, stars, galaxies, black holes, and aircraft—as well as imaginary creatures and objects such as unicorns, aliens, and fairies. The children research their drawings and paintings on the Internet, in books from the library, and from resources contributed by families of children in the three classrooms.

In the next phase, children build a spaceship from a large cardboard box, complete with a mission control. They use walkie-talkies and pretend computers to orchestrate play landings on planets and moons and begin to construct a space ABC word wall that will later become a book for their kindergarten library.

Third graders who visit the kindergarten present a provocation; they say that the kindergartners don't have the right number of moons for Saturn on their mural! So the kindergartners plan a pretend space mission to Saturn to count the moons. They create characters for their spaceship crew on the Saturn mission. Each day, a new episode is imagined at group time. Their crew includes paper-doll representations and histories for each character. One character is Princess Squirty Cupcake Pumpkin, the crew photographer, who on Earth is a full-time princess, 30 years old, and when in space, takes pictures of planets, aliens, and stars. Another character is Sonic Timor, who lives in Japan in a tent, is 65 years old, has five children, and builds electrical things for fun. His mission-control job is radio monitor. ✆

Toys are objects that represent tools for stimulating children's imaginations and skills with communication. Children use them to fashion their experiences with sensori-motor play, constructive play, dramatic play, and games with rules. They use toys such as blocks to construct settings and tools for their pretend play. They use replicas of objects from our adult world, such as microwave ovens and radios to carry out their pretend scripts. Children may even use computers, either as they were designed to be used or as accessories to their own dramatic purposes in which they represent the social uses of technology in their play.

However, toys themselves are not the only ingredient of children's play. We also need to examine the cultures and social interactions that are the broader context for children's use of toys and technology in school settings.

In the curriculum project on the Night Sky, a positive aspect of children's relationship to technology is depicted. The project evolved from earlier in the school year. This school is located in a small city surrounded by a rural area. Children live close to fields and streams, and they see the night sky clearly. The Night Sky project developed from earlier that year when children in the three classes investigated the nearby stream. The questions generated about land, water, and the sky stimulated the Night Sky project, which served to integrate technology in numerous ways.

Technology related to space travel is represented by the children in their projects and in their dramatic play. The teachers use the soundtrack from the movie *Apollo 13* as part of the mission-control environment for dramatic play and walkie-talkies to simulate the landing of the kindergarten spacecraft during their space journey. Details of their mural are researched using the Internet. Overhead projectors are used to project images for the space simulations. To celebrate the return from their mission, families are invited to come to school after dark to view Saturn through the telescope of a local amateur astronomer.

Toys and technological media influence children's play. We invite you to consider how the objects themselves and the social contexts in which children and adults use these objects shape children's play in early childhood settings. We explore the social issues relating to the impact of media-based play and toy marketing on children and schools as well as the role of the Internet in play-centered projects.

TYPES OF TOYS

The category of toys is large and composed of many subcategories. Purely sensorimotor toys give rise to repetitive activity and the joy of making things happen with an object. Bouncing balls, shaking rattles, spinning tops, rocking horses, and monkey bars are a few familiar examples. Representational toys look like other objects in the culture or in nature. Miniatures of animals, vehicles, houses, utensils, furniture, and dolls are familiar examples. Construction toys can be manipulated and used to create new objects. Bristle blocks, wooden blocks, Legos, Kapla or Keva blocks, and Zoob building sets are examples we see in early childhood programs. Locomotion toys include tricycles, bicycles, scooters, and wagons.

Toys affect development in profound and sometimes subtle ways. For one thing, they orchestrate both individual and social activity. Toys have a "logic of action" that suggests how the toy is to be used. For example, a toy telephone suggests or cues particular forms of motor, representational, and social behavior.

Some toys are specific in their cues. Legos and pattern blocks cue children for constructive play. Action figures, dolls, stuffed animals, and toy vehicles cue for dramatic play. Game boards suggest games with rules. Toys also cue teachers for specific play expectations. The toys that teachers designate as math manipulatives might include collections of miniature animals, vehicles, or furniture for children to arrange in sets and thus construct logical-mathematical relationships. Manipulatives might also include pattern blocks or Cuisenaire rods for similar purposes. In the case of miniature objects, experience with logical-mathematical thinking is linked to children's dramatic play accessories. In the case of patterning materials, these relationships are linked to constructive play.

Other common "teacher categories" for classroom toys are fine and gross motor toys. Pegboards, pattern boards, and puzzles aid in developing fine motor coordination, whereas trikes, scooters, swings, and climbers help children develop large muscle strength and coordination. Materials for sensorimotor play outside as well as in the classroom include raw materials for art and construction such as sand, water, paint, mud, and playdough.

No matter how adults classify toys and raw materials for play, the key point is that children will use toys in their play in ways that suit their own agendas, not necessarily those of adults. The essential question is, "How does the child see the play potential of a given toy or material?"

Along these lines, Griffin (1988) suggests that teachers categorize toys by the effects they have on children's inner feelings and social interactions, rather than by the intellectual concepts and skills the toys are thought to develop. Some toys suggest active group play, such as blocks, housekeeping toys, and art materials. Others—such as pegboards, puzzles, miniature animals, and books—cue for quiet, solitary play. Griffin notes that toys that are self-correcting in nature, such as bead strings and pegboards, are soothing to children because they give children an opportunity to create order and control in their physical environments. They are calming in the same way that gardening might be for adults. Many of Montessori's self-correcting toys have this appeal for young children (Montessori, 1936).

In a solitary context, toys such as miniatures and books encourage children's flights of imagination without the challenge of negotiating pretend play with others. Children can use miniatures to represent emotionally laden experiences, thus allowing them to process confusing or troubling experiences at a more comfortable distance. For example:

> Sean had trouble separating from his mother at the start of the preschool day. Each day for the first few weeks of school, after a tearful good-bye, Sean took out the tiny family dolls and a small, plastic playhouse. "Bye Mommy," he said as he walked the little boy doll into the house. "I love you," he whispered, as he put the Mommy doll into a toy car and "drove" it away. He then brought the Mommy doll back to the house and said, "It's time to go home now. Did you have a good day?" as he put the Mommy and little boy into the car. ∅

This kind of play allows children to project their feelings onto toys without having to play just one role. It also allows them to control the situation from the outside. Accordingly, Griffin (1988) suggests that classrooms have an ample supply of toys that are potentially "charged" for children: baby bottles and high chairs, spiders, dragons, capes, magic wands, and hats. Teachers have long found that sensorimotor "raw" materials such as water, sand, mud, paint, glue, and collage materials are pleasing to the senses and afford all children opportunities for mastery and control and foster emotional equilibrium.

💜 Three first graders have spent 30 minutes engrossed in making a collage, an extension of a science unit on the properties of material objects. Angelo searches through the collected objects for brightly colored feathers and beads. He and his peers negotiate the design details and assist each other as they place and paste. Children's individual needs are accommodated in this setting. Angelo, a child with cerebral palsy, participates fully in this social activity that promotes his fine motor coordination. ∅

Special education teachers point out that natural materials meet the needs of many children with special needs, including children with autism spectrum disorder and attention-deficit/hyperactivity disorder.

TOYS AND DEVELOPMENT

As development proceeds, we see a change in children's primary uses of toys. The best toys for young children have the quality of flexible "play-ability," which allows children to adapt the toy to their individual needs and stages of development over an extended period of time. Blocks are a good example of a toy with high play-ability. A 2-year-old might experiment with stacking and falling blocks, repeating the process over and over in sensorimotor play. Three- to 7-year-old children might use the blocks to construct objects they have seen ("This is the dolphin pool at Marine World") or as a prop in dramatic play (a telephone or walkie-talkie). Finally, blocks might serve as the pieces for a game with rules, as children stand blocks on end and "bowl" them down with a pitched tennis ball, giving points for each "hit."

In pretend play, children explore technology from daily life.

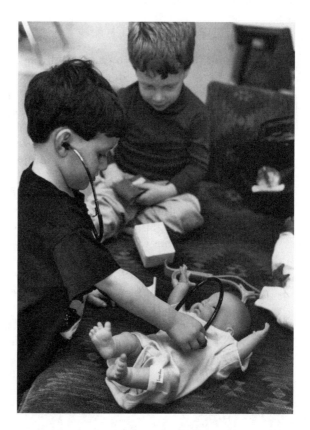

In addition to providing highly flexible toys, teachers provide toys that meet specific needs at particular developmental stages. For example, the process of symbolic distancing described in Chapter 2 calls for sensitivity on the part of the teacher to provide toys that are a good match of structure to the child's developing symbolic concepts. Structure is the degree to which a toy or other object resembles the object that the child is symbolizing. To scaffold their play scripts, 2- and 3-year-olds might require high structure in their toys, such as replicas of tools, vehicles, or housekeeping accessories. Play may easily break down in disputes over who gets to talk on the toy telephone or use the toy fire engine, so many teachers have multiple sets of realistic toys available. Having multiple sets of replica toys also allows several younger children to explore similar interests or roles.

Older children, 4- to 8-year-olds, are more likely to use "unstructured" toys such as blocks, marbles, or sticks in their play. The representational abilities of older children have developed to the point that meaning exists in their own imaginations rather than depending primarily on the characteristics of the objects themselves. For example, an older child might appropriate a block to stand for a sandwich, a helicopter, a wallet, and a cup of coffee, all within the course of a single play episode.

Teachers who carefully observe children's sociodramatic play can ascertain the levels of symbolic distancing in role play and in play with objects. Then they can provide an array of toys ranging from structured replicas to unstructured objects for children to use.

Games with Rules

As children move from early childhood into middle childhood, games with rules become increasingly evident in their play. Board games and games of motor skill—such as hand games, jump rope, soccer, hopscotch, and tetherball—have long been favorite games with rules for children in primary grades. Most of us have vivid childhood memories of ball and rope games, as well as clapping and chanting games played spontaneously on our school playgrounds or neighborhood streets.

Some games with rules such as hopscotch or tic-tac-toe require no special equipment and can be played in a variety of settings. Others, such as jump rope or soccer, require some purchased materials. In contemporary society, we have an increasing variety of commercial toys in the category of games with rules. These range from traditional board games such as Candy Land to developmentally appropriate video and computer games with rules.

Planning for Development in Game Play.   Whatever the form—playground game, board game, or computer game—teachers need to be sensitive to the cognitive leap represented by children's entry into the play stage of games with rules beginning at about the age of 6, as we see a shift in the relationship of rules to fantasy. Now the fantasy becomes implicit or taken for granted by the players, such as the "as-if" frame of reference for Candy Land or Monopoly. The rules are explicit, formulated by the manufacturer, and often are negotiated further by the players before the play begins. Verbal discussion shifts from "Let's pretend . . ." to "The rule says. . . ."

Games need to honor this developmental progression. Games with rules marketed for preschool and kindergarten children need to be used with caution and sensitivity by teachers. Board games and sports equipment have their place in the early childhood classroom but should not be used in place of the more appropriate constructive and dramatic play materials for this age group. Instead, sensitive teachers will encourage children who use balls and bats, jump ropes, board games, and computer programs to create their own rules and construct their own understandings of winning and losing (e.g., see DeVries, Zan, Hildebrandt, Edmiaston, & Sales, 2002).

Selecting Appropriate Games for All Young Children. Understanding the development of play is only one aspect of selecting appropriate games for young children. Other features of game design are important when choosing games for children to play in early childhood classrooms. As children develop the competencies to understand games with rules, electronic games are increasingly appropriate. Good games include simple graphics and a sense of engagement in the "as-if" world created through technology. Simulations and roles that children can identify with are characteristics of this engagement. Good games have defined goals but uncertain outcomes. Levels of challenge escalate as children play repeated rounds and solve problems with more variables and create alternative strategies. These games engage children's minds and creative capacities. Another quality of good games, whether they are traditional board or dice games or electronic ones, is the option of interaction among players, frequently providing more options for multiple players than computer games. However, in computer play, young children enjoy discussing their problem solving and their pretend landscapes. Teachers and researchers believe that such collaboration enhances the cognitive and social value of these electronic games (Scarlett, Naudeau, Salonius-Pasternak, & Ponte, 2005; Singer & Singer, 2005).

Robots and Engineering in Early Childhood Settings

Researchers and teachers have been studying young children's capacities to problem-solve and invent with robotics using Lego blocks. In *Blocks to Robots: Learning with Technology in the Early Childhood Classroom*, Bers (2008) shows children's creative engagement with toys and technology. She describes how a group of teachers and student teachers gained confidence and expertise.

Bers makes robotic technology accessible for teachers and demystifies children's use of robotic technology. In the following example, children explored the stages of insect metamorphosis:

> After reading *The Hungry Caterpillar* (preschool), children sequenced the story and did dramatic play, movement, and art activities to explore change. They used the Mindstorms kit to make a robotic vehicle, representing the heart of the caterpillar, that would travel the journey of the "hungry caterpillar.". . . (Bers, 2008, p. 82)

In his enthusiastic introduction to the book, Elkind explains why this approach is groundbreaking:

> Bers, however, has (extended) the notion of allowing children to create their own object-created environments—to the creation of social environments. The Zora program she has created allows children to construct their own spatial reality . . . (and) make this approach extend to all facets of early childhood education, from curriculum to assessment to classroom management. (p. xii)

Technology can support developmentally appropriate ways for young children to use toys that are engaging, open ended, and developmentally appropriate. As raw material for creative thought, they have untapped potential to contribute to a rich store of imagery for playing with ideas. They also have the potential to help adults and children create common play scripts, characters, and themes that may guide play. Bers provides numerous illustrations of how classroom teachers in varied settings supported creativity and imagination as they introduce young children to engineering.

CHILDREN UNDER SIEGE: TOYS AND THE MARKETPLACE

Children and parents as well as teachers are continually under siege from the toy industry to purchase toys and games that undermine imaginative play. By considering developmental stages of play and the structure of children's games, teachers inform themselves about what play materials are most appropriate for their classrooms. Much of what is marketed to children is not only developmentally inappropriate but also exploits the very vulnerabilities of childhood, such as the desire to be more grown up, have more power, and have friends. This is not accidental as Carlsson-Paige (2008), Levin and Kilbourne (2008), and Linn (2008) point out in recent books on consumerism and children. Marketers of toys rely heavily on the media portrayal of childhood in which socially constructed phenomena such as coveting of toys to love, or accessories to become glamorous or "cool," become part of the assumptions about typical children's development in the United States.

Toys That Limit Development

As potential tools of the imagination, good toys range from pebbles, sticks, and feathers found in nature to "classic" commercial toys such as balls, blocks, and clay. Ideally, these unstructured toys invite children to incorporate their own fantasies, images, roles, and scripts into their play. However the commercial exploitation of play is rapidly eclipsing the freedom inherent in many of these "classic" toys. A walk down the toy aisle in most stores shows the profusion of electronic, single-use toys on the market. Even when teachers don't purchase them, these toys appear in classrooms when children bring them to show in school or when they play out scripts suggested by these toys. To develop abstract concepts and the capacity for imagination, we have to give young children opportunities to apply their own meanings and actions to toys. Toys that have only one use do not provide children with the flexibility they need to use their imaginations in alternative ways.

The action figure whose role or behavior is narrowly defined by the toy's features or the doll whose body movements and talk are produced by the machine inside restricts children's emerging imaginations. Such toys can interfere with the development of distancing strategies that underlie abstract thinking. These one-use-only toys make millions of dollars for toy manufacturers, but they are not conducive to children's play development. In fact, the limiting characteristics of some toys not only negatively affect the development of cognition and imagination for young children, but also limit development in other areas. For example, some of the media character dolls are packaged to persuade children that each character performs only one role or function in play, often a gender-stereotyped role. Some action figures, even ones found in block areas, now suggest violent play.

Even unstructured constructive play toys such as Lincoln Logs, Legos, or animal action figures now come with templates for using the toys in specific arrangements. Many are marketed in "kits" with only the pieces for a particular model pictured on the package included. Such marketing practices may affect the ways children use toys in schools as children imitate what they have seen in ads and toy packaging. This limited and often stereotyped marketing stifles development as children grow accustomed to models to imitate rather than use toys to fulfill possibilities in their own imaginations.

Toys That Undermine Gender Equity

Numerous toys are marketed in gender-stereotyped ways and restrict gender equity in school as well as home settings. Many toys are marketed in dainty pastels for girls and bold primary colors for boys, with the accompanying packages that show gender-typed models for construction so that children get the message that there is an expected "right way for them to play."

As they construct ideas about gender, children eagerly classify information learned from the people and popular media in their out-of-school environments into categories of "boy behavior" and "girl behavior." Once a characteristic behavior or object has been classified as gender specific, then the reasoning continues: "If I am a boy, I must do boylike things and play with boys' toys" or "If I am a girl, I must behave as girls do and own girls' toys."

Like all stereotyping, gender stereotyping limits the range of experiences that children have in their play in all settings—including school—as well as the concepts and skills development associated with those experiences. Teachers report marked differences in the play of boys and girls in their classrooms and discuss the possible influences of "boy toys" and "girl toys," particularly those that represent media-themed characters. Even when they don't have any of these toys at home or school, children learn these stereotypes from peers and the wider culture. Boys are more likely to dramatize these themes using toy weapons, vehicles, and superhero and GI Joe dolls. Girls are more apt to select Barbie or Moxie dolls, house accessories, and toy or pretend cosmetics.

Has it always been like this? Yes and no. Before the 1960s and 1970s, toys were stereotyped according to the prevailing adult, gender-specific occupations of men and women. Boys might play at being firemen or doctors; girls pretended to be mothers or nurses. In the 1970s, parents and educators made concerted efforts to diminish the gender stereotypes promoted in children's literature, television, film, and toys. These efforts were somewhat successful. It became more acceptable for girls to be assertive and independent and for boys to be sensitive and nurturing.

In the 1980s much of this ground was lost with the deregulation of TV. Newly permitted commercials shown during children's programming allowed toy manufacturers to specifically target children's interest in conforming to social perceptions of gender identity to sell more toys.

More stereotyped play reemerged. We still see this today. Messages regarding gender stereotyping are insidious. When we examine more structured toys such as dolls and "action figures," we find that they promote a restricted and dangerous gender identity. As Levin and Kilbourne (2008) emphasize in their book *So Sexy So Soon*, both boys and girls are learning that being a boy is linked to violent play and being a girl is linked to play characterized by precocious sexuality: ". . . they all learn damaging lessons about what to value in themselves and their own gender as well as about one another" (p. 33).

Toys That Promote Early Sexualization.   One of the marketing strategies to emerge in recent years is the concept of "age compression" in which gender-related, sexualized products designed for older children or teens are heavily promoted for younger children (American Psychological Association, 2007; Levin & Kilbourne, 2008; Schor, 2004). For example, Barbie dolls are now more popular with preschool age groups than with the older girls for whom they were originally designed. Popular dolls are marketed with names like "Barbie Fashion Fever Fashionista." Another marketing concept is the image of "edge," which Schor (2004) describes as a younger version of "coolness" with peers usually associated with teen music and sexuality. For many years, the Bratz dolls, ostensibly marketed for preteen girls, were on the wish lists of many 5- and 6-year-olds. Current Barbie, Moxie, and Liv dolls are advertised with "cool fashions" and give the message that fashionable clothing is the key to any girl's success "at the top of her game." Teachers witness the effects of this marketing as girls check to see if they're wearing the "right clothes."

"Boy" Toys That Portray Power Through Violence.   Teachers also report that many toys marketed to young boys have ratcheted up an ever-increasing focus on violence and bullying. For example:

> Four-year-old players Jeremy, Seth, and Mark are playing Teenage Mutant Ninja Turtles in and around the outdoor play structure. Though their topic involves the 25-year edition of the ever-popular ninjas, their play draws from a number of different cartoon action figures and video games marketed to younger children. They make swift martial arts moves, such as strikes and

karate kicks, interspersed with sounds like "Ooph!" and "Whaaa!" as they pretend to fight. Plant stalks used as swords supplement the fighting gear. Mark later points out the pinecone he wielded was "one of those spiky things" that kill the robots.

The robots in this scenario are the bad guys. When their teacher, Shane, intervenes in their increasingly frenetic and violent moves, the children argue that "we aren't really hurting anyone. They are just machines!" Shane remarked that the most troublesome thing about the play is that because none of these children wanted to "be the bad guy," the boys coerced younger, less-powerful players to be the robot victims of their violence. ✇

War-themed toys are examples of toys that promote violence and stereotypes. All young children, born since 2001, have grown up during the wars in Afghanistan and Iraq. Many of today's war toys look like realistic news photos. For example, ads for the Forward Command Post depict a dollhouse that appears to have been bombed. The soldier in battle fatigues carries an assault rifle. The 2010 version of GI Joe advertised is Rise of Cobra Ice Dagger with Frostbite. Accompanying warnings that these toys are not intended for children under three suggest that they are intended for and being marketed to preschool children.

Teachers Respond to Gender Stereotyping. Early childhood educators can use the same repertoire of techniques to address the presence of all forms of stereotyping in classrooms with young children.

Computers in classrooms may engage children in a number of ways.

Leslie, a K–1 teacher, has purposely selected a wide range of play materials for her classroom. "I want both boys and girls to develop the fine motor skills, such as the cutting, pasting, and using a paintbrush, that accompany art play," she comments. "I want both genders to develop large motor skills in climbing, running, sliding, and riding. A wide range of toys helps both the boys and the girls in my group to develop spatial reasoning and the bodily kinesthetic intelligence associated with constructive play. Building a spaceship of Legos or a fort of blocks enhances these experiences for all children. To encourage this, we as teachers need to consciously arrange for children to move beyond stereotyped conventions of what boys and girls do and try new activities." ✏

There are numerous resources for teachers and parents confronted with children's frenzied, violent, and stereotyped play in school and at home. For several decades, Teachers Resisting Unhealthy Children's Entertainment (TRUCE) has distributed a toy guide for parents and teachers that highlights specific toys and commercial trends to avoid, strategies for how to respond, and recommendations for both new and classic toys (www.truceteachers.org).

MEDIA-BASED PLAY

Early childhood educators face dilemmas arising from the link between play and media. The most obvious culprits here are television, CDs, tapes, DVDs, video games, and computer software, which have become increasingly problematic.

Critics of television and other media have long argued that television viewing deadens children's imaginations and social interaction skills in two ways. First, the process of television viewing puts young children in a passive role, absorbing the products of others' imaginations in full color and sound, rather than stimulating the children's own imaginations. Second, if children weren't watching television, DVDs, or game media, they could be playing. In that play they would develop their own symbolic concepts, extend their capacities for problem solving and creativity, and increase their abilities to negotiate and cooperate with others (Levin, 1998; Singer & Singer, 2005).

Critics also argue that the stereotyped and often violent content of media aimed at children is detrimental to their play and future development. Media influence on children's play takes several forms, one of which involves the characters and plots that children create for their play narratives. Young children are just learning to develop their sense of story. Bruner (1986) described character and action as the first "landscapes" of the human capacity for narrative. When these formative landscapes are filled with violent and destructive characters and action, they can have pervasive and long-lasting effects on development. The imaginative process involves playing and replaying images from life experiences, including images from media. Children organize these images into scripts for ascertaining and expressing meaning. When much of the content of this imagery is violent, it may lead not only to "desensitization" for violence but also to a preference for violent imagery that "normalizes" and justifies one's own violent behavior (Ackerman, 1999; Katch, 2001, Linn, 2008).

Action is the second "landscape" in Bruner's model for the structure of narrative. In this aspect of narrative, children construct plots and themes for their play. At worst, teachers find the action in television/video-derived play is limited and repetitive, as well as violent. Children often resist creative alternatives to these limited scripts and imitate what they have seen with great attention to detail of the characters, events, and actions. Singer and Singer (2005) described this as "imitative" imagination rather than creative imagination. This limited play often is accompanied and exacerbated by commercial accessories with explicit details that cue children to use them in only prescribed ways.

Although classic characters such as Peter Pan or Luke Skywalker and Princess Leia from the *Star Wars* trilogy represent positive forces, they repeatedly resolve conflicts through violent actions. Other characters such as Darth Vader represent villains that might help children define their understanding and resolution of good and evil, but again, the resolution of evil influences is achieved by violence. Children watch these characters enthusiastically kill and injure others. Because young children are very literal in their thinking, they understand that "using violence is how we do things." In each generation, the battles that ensue between the positive and negative forces, whether in *Star Wars,* Harry Potter films, or the film *UP* influence children's emerging beliefs about the manner in which good vanquishes evil. Unfortunately, most media examples convey the message that violence is an acceptable way of solving conflict as long as the motive is good.

Fortunately, positive role models are also available and illustrate alternative possibilities. TV and video characters have an attraction for young children that rests on their warmth, humor, and caring behavior. Teachers can talk to children about the personalities and powers of their heroes and heroines. They can then help children imagine nonviolent alternatives to resolving conflicts between good and evil.

Racial and Ethnic Stereotypes in Children's Media

Teachers and parents are concerned about the impact that children's media and toys have on children's stereotypes of cultural, racial, and ethnic groups. How do young children make sense of the portrayal of race, ethnicity, and gender as portrayed in the images they encounter? Stereotypes of race, gender, or ethnicity conveyed through toys and the media are not benign. A major developmental milestone for preschool, kindergarten, and primary-grade children is the establishment of a positive identity. We believe that another important milestone is the establishment of positive feelings toward people in other groups. During the preschool and primary years, children further differentiate the multiple aspects of "who I am" as well as "who they are," often turning to popular characters in toys, films, and television.

Cortés (2000) argues that toys and media products function as "public textbooks" in our society. How do children "read" Barbie? Aladdin? Mulan? Pocahontas? GI Joe dolls? What about the characters largely missing from these "textbooks"—people of color in commercials, Latinos and Asians in movies and on prime-time television? And what about persons of color who are female?

Invisibility supports stereotypes. Media ads for children's toys show fewer children of color. Most of the time these children are minor characters, rarely at the center of action. "Children of color and girls of all races are dispersed to the sidelines as mascots, companions, victims" (Seiter, 1995, p. 7). How does this absence or invisibility influence children's sense of themselves and others? We also need to examine the social context in which characters interact. Is the media and toy world a segregated one? Who plays with whom? Who is rich or poor? Who is violent? Who shows emotion?

In *"Good Guys Don't Wear Hats": Children Talk About the Media,* Tobin (2000) points out that to understand the complex influence of the media, it is necessary to do more than simply analyze the content. We must look at the interaction of the media text with particular children and the particular environments where children live. In his research in Hawaiian classrooms, Tobin found that the same movie or television program was understood differently depending on the viewer and the context. Children from different families living in different communities interpreted media images and behaviors differently.

Teachers Respond to Media Stereotypes

Many teachers express concern about children's words and behavior regarding race, culture, and gender that they find unsettling, sometimes offensive. Teachers also wonder how to respond when parents look to them for advice. Fortunately, as our population is becoming more diverse, an increasing array of resources is available to teachers to use in developing anti-bias, multicultural curriculum (e.g., see: Bowman & Moore, 2006; Derman-Sparks & Edwards, 2010; Espinoza, 2010; Gonzalez-Mena, 2008; Levin, 2003b). The strategies we discussed in the section "Responding to Violent Play" in Chapter 5 are useful here: Observe play carefully, look beneath the surface of play, and ascertain children's purposes in play. Communicate with families about stereotypes observed in children's play. Advocate for appropriate content in children's media.

Media Literacy in an Age of Consumerism

Most young children spend many hours watching television and other media each day (Kaiser Family Foundation, 2005). Regulations that used to limit the length, type, and number of commercials during children's TV programming that were present in the 1960s and 1970s were suspended by government actions in the 1980s. Deregulation has resulted in a rash of television commercials disguised as children's cartoons, whose major purpose is to convince children that they can't "play" the themes they see on television without purchasing all the toys. Each character in the line of toys, such as GI Joe, Power Rangers, or Barbie, has specific features designed to lead children to believe they need to own the complete set.

One first-grade teacher found her daily sharing time to be a good avenue for consumer education. She helped children discuss the features of toys they liked. As a group they brainstormed different play alternatives for a particular vehicle, action figure, or doll, rather than on their plans to collect them just for the sake of collecting.

Ironically, even the weak regulations that now prohibit unrealistic and unsafe depictions of toy usage placed on toy advertisements do not apply to the television shows that depict the character toys and have given rise to "copycat" dangerous play in which children mimic the violent actions of toy and media characters (Schor, 2004). Children do not have a well-developed sense of what is fantasy and what is reality, particularly when confronted with the special effects of audiovisual media. Nor do children have the life experience or self-reflective concepts needed to make wise consumer choices by asking themselves such questions as, "Will this toy last?" or "How will I use it?"

Hesse and Lane (2003) developed an integrated approach to media literacy that promotes children's understanding of editing and point of view. It addresses such concerns as how the media stereotypes people (e.g., all good/all bad) and blurs distinctions between reality and fantasy. They used books to promote discussions about the effects of media as well as active alternatives. They recount a discussion after Lane read *The Bionic Bunny Show* with her class.

> The children had a lively time struggling with the notion that people can be both good and bad, with some arguing, "No, a bad guy would not do a good thing.". . .
> . . . Fiona (Lane) observed, "I think that sometimes television only shows characters that are all good or all bad—I want you to think about how everyone can be a little bit of both." The group continued to talk, now about how all of us have done good and naughty things at one time or another. One child confessed, "I have done both!" (p. 25).

Children who have experienced media literacy lessons that help them understand how special media effects are created have been found to engage in less violent behavior than children who have not had such instruction (Singer & Singer, 2005). Hobbs and Frost (2003) report that older children who received media literacy training improved in reading comprehension, writing, and critical thinking compared to children not receiving such instruction. Robinson and colleagues (2001) studied the effects of reduced television viewing among 8- to 10-year-olds in a community in California. Children whose viewing declined made 70% fewer toy requests of their parents than those in the control group, whose viewing patterns remained the same.

Advocating for Quality Children's Programming.

In addition to talking to children, teachers can alert parents to the ways children are using toy commercials and shows as limited, repetitive scripts for stereotyped play. Teachers also advocate for good programming for children by working with educators and parents at the local level and by supporting the efforts of such national organizations as Children's Defense Fund, TRUCE, Alliance for Childhood, and Campaign for a Commercial Free Childhood. Teachers find that there are numerous resources to share such as Levin's *Remote Control Childhood? Combating the Hazards of Media Culture* (1998) and Carlsson-Paige's *Taking Back Childhood* (2008).

COMPUTER PLAY AND YOUNG CHILDREN

We take the view that computers should be treated much like any other tools or materials for children's play in classrooms for young children. In fact, this was the view of computers set forth by Seymour Papert (1980), creator of Logo, in his now-classic work, *Mindstorms*. In discussing the potential for the graphics program Logo to influence education, Papert referred to computers as "powerful objects to think with" and predicted that they would revolutionize classroom practices.

Now that computers are being used in most early childhood classrooms, many educators, including advocates such as Papert (1993), acknowledge that the educational revolution once predicted has not occurred. Nor have computers harmed development direly, as the early critics predicted. Rather, teachers tend to design computer activities and choose software that reflects their own continuum of instructional strategies. Teachers who emphasize drills that require convergent thinking tend to use computers primarily as "tutors" for skill-oriented tasks—such as matching shapes, letters, or numbers. However, many of these skills, such as learning vocabulary for directionality (above, below, right, left), are learned more appropriately in the context of active play with concrete objects. In contrast to the "computer-as-tutor" approach of animated workbooks, teachers who promote divergent thinking and value play tend to choose "computer-as-tool" and the "computer-as-tutee" types of software, which offer children more opportunities to control computer play (Kafai, 2006; Silvern, 2006).

Computers and Play: Structuring the Physical Space for Computers

If computers are to be used as a tool for children's play, they must be part of the classroom rather than isolated in a computer lab. A prime consideration is creating an optimal environment for children's play. We suggest a table large enough for two to three children to work together, with space on both sides of the computer for children to place materials related to their computer play. A printer should also be connected to the computer so children can keep the products of their play.

Physical placement in the room becomes an important consideration. First, there are health and safety issues for the children and the computers. The computer needs to be placed near a grounded electrical outlet, away from water, other potential spills, and food. A surge protector is necessary to protect the hardware as well as to provide additional outlet space if necessary. The computer center also needs to be far enough away from rigorous physical activity to avoid potential accidents. When positioning the computer, protect children's vision by placing it at an appropriate distance and avoiding places where direct sunlight creates glare on the screen.

Computers and Play: Selecting Tool Software

A variety of software is available for young children that provides the same tools that we adults use but with more child-friendly user interfaces. Art and other graphics programs, word processing, and multimedia programs that combine the child's written words with images, sound, and sometimes animation are readily available. As young children first begin to read and write in kindergarten and the primary grades, they can use some adult software such as e-mail programs successfully as well.

In the context of their play, children use these programs to create and illustrate stories; make books, greeting cards, and gifts of their creative work; or, in the same way as "real" drawings or paintings, to express their artistic inclinations. Whether children use multimedia programs to integrate images with words or use graphics programs alone, it is important to apply the same standards as with traditional art materials. Children always should be encouraged to create original artwork rather than rely on clip art or electronic coloring books. As educators, we focus our attention on the processes of children's play, not their products, but it is also important to think about both process and product from the child's view.

E-mail is a wonderful communication tool for children's play. The speed of sending and receiving e-mail makes it especially exciting for children who have a hard time waiting for a response by "snail mail." Teachers often find that children write more, write in greater detail, and correct their writing more when they use computers to write for a real audience as in using e-mail.

In Nancy's first-grade class, students have same-age e-mail buddies at another school, adult e-mail buddies through a corporate partnership, and fifth-grade buddies at their own school. The children have partners in their class and, together, they write to their e-mail buddies. Nancy finds that the children not only benefit by helping each other, but also enjoy the social aspect of composing written language together.

When the computer sounds to signify that a new e-mail message has arrived, a child rushes to the computer and announces that Lily and Brian have e-mail. They head for the computer and find a message from their adult e-mail buddy. The children love getting mail and want to write back right away. In response to their question, their buddy has written about her pets and asks, "Do you have any pets?"

Twenty minutes later, Brian and Lily send off the following message:

1. I have a gol fis. My gol fis is bubbles.
2. I have a dog. My dog is very ol.
3. Do you like gol fis?
4. Do you like hres?
5. Do you like cows?
6. Do you have a cow?

Nancy finds that the students write differently to their different buddies. They write quickly and informally to their same-age buddies. They try hard to correct mistakes when they write to their adult buddies. Because their fifth-grade buddies come to class to read to them, they usually write with a

Technology can aid discovery.

purpose, asking for a particular book or commenting on a book that has been read. Although participating in e-mail is always a matter of choice, most children rush to answer their messages and wait with expectation for a response. ⌀

Teachers exchange exciting stories about how their classes are using e-mail to communicate with students and families around the country and around the globe. Salmon and Akaran (2006) write of their "cross-cultural e-mail connections" (p. 36) between Salmon's kindergarten students in urban New Jersey and Akaran's primary-grade students in Kotlik, Alaska, where her students live far from a large city, and Native American families maintain a more traditional way of life.

💟 Elijah and Zoë's grandparents live far away in the Netherlands. Since the children were babies, they have communicated weekly with each other using Skype, a free Internet service requiring a Web camera. They share family stories, sing together, and the children show their *oma* and *opa* what they can do, from clapping games to first tricycle rides to skateboarding, with lively communication in Dutch. ⌀

Guiding Play with Computers as Tools for Students

Teachers can guide all children's play with computers by scaffolding its use as children explore its features and begin to use it for their own imaginative ends. For many years, teachers have reported that when children use computers, their work is more complex and imaginative. By using computers to write, children are freer to compose story lines and construct concepts about letter–sound relationships in invented spelling. The formation of letters no longer claims the lion's share of their attention. The teacher helps children review what they have written and plan more complex texts by asking questions such as, "How did the boy feel about that?"

Another computer-based tool for literacy found in classrooms for young children is text-to-speech. This common tool supports children as they develop the concept of letter-sound correspondences as they play. In *Technology Tools for Young Learners* (1999), von Blanckensee describes children using text-to-speech tools:

> Nina is sitting at my Macintosh lap computer in the library of her school. She is 4½ years old, one of the youngest students in her kindergarten class. She types a string of letters and tells me that she is writing a story. I ask her if she would like the computer to read it to her. She watches me highlight the letters and select "speak selection" from the tools menu. She laughs with glee as the computer voice pronounces, "slifmefmaemf."
>
> We do this several times, changing the voice on the computer. This produces more laughter, until Nina has an idea. "Let's hear it say my name," she says as she starts to search for the *N*. After some effort, she has typed her name—the only word Nina currently knows how to write.
>
> Now the computer says "Nina." Nina's laughter turns to sheer joy . . . after several replays of her name, she wants to try my name. She is already thinking about the words she will write. (p. 52) ✆

As these examples illustrate, teachers' guidance as children shift focus among the various tasks of writing composition, such as taking the perspective of one's audience, and transcription, serve as an example of what Vygotsky called the *zone of proximal development*. Such support or scaffolding helps children construct patterns of their own and eventually will lead them to coordinate independently all aspects of the writing process.

Play, Computers, and Assisted Technologies ♥

Technology recommendations and standards for technology promote equity for all children in developing computer literacy. Assisted by families, teachers find there are numerous resources to support children with special needs as they develop independence and competency. NAEYC's recommendations that teachers work with parents, collaborate with others, and access numerous educational resources is paramount (see, e.g., Council for Exceptional Children, Division for Early Childhood and the National Early Childhood Technical Assistance Center). Many materials for educators are appropriate for parents and cross-age tutors as well (e.g., *Digital Storytelling* by Frazel, 2010).

> Maria is a fifth-grade mentor who helps in Andrea's kindergarten computer center twice a week. On this day, Joshua, a student with developmental delays, has been playing with a graphics program. He has made a line drawing of a bunny, and Maria guides him as he fills in the area with different colors. After several minutes, Josh frowns. "I don't want this bunny for my story. I want that bunny," he says, pointing to the painting he had made earlier. Maria, who recently learned to use a scanner for her own work, asks the teacher if she

can take Joshua to the school library to scan his painting. Later, he dictates his story using the scanned image of his bunny. When Joshua's writing is printed with his scanned drawings, the result looks much like a printed book. ✍

Teachers promote inclusion when they review computer programs with photos or human characters to make certain that children with a range of special needs are included and their behaviors are not stereotyped. Similarly, Ella's parents pointed out to her teacher that they wanted to make sure there would be no assumptions that because of her physical disabilities she would be encouraged to use the computer inside rather play actively outdoors.

Computer Simulations, Games, and Books

"Tutee" software for young children offers opportunities to extend their play with computers. Some are simulations in which children enter as characters into the play and control characters' actions on the screen. Others allow children to manipulate objects in interesting ways. One program, for example, allows children to create buildings and towns and then change their perspective gradually, as if they were able to fly overhead like a bird. Other forms of computer programming software, such as Logo, were developed especially for young children. In these types of software, children encounter challenging problems to solve that are built into the software design.

Interactive books are another popular form of tutee software. A quality interactive book begins with a good story that is worth reading again and again. Children are able to control the story by clicking on objects to begin animations, hearing the story in different languages, turning off the "reader" altogether, and in some cases, choosing alternative events and endings. Though interactive books are available on the Internet, some teachers report that the pictures load too slowly for younger children.

Computer simulations, games, and books are attractive to children and offer many opportunities to develop problem-solving strategies and creative thinking. Teachers need to be diligent in applying the same criteria in their selection as with other books or games (i.e., gender equity, nonviolent content, sensitive awareness to culture and ethnicity, child-centered and developmentally appropriate).

TECHNOLOGY GUIDELINES AND STANDARDS

Teachers increasingly view computers as simply another valuable part of the young child's environment, rather than as a panacea for all learning or a threat to social play. The ways that the computer fits into the culture of the classroom and children's play within that culture become the important issues to consider. The social context and manner in which children come to use computers as objects for play determine their comfort level with this aspect of technology in their lives. When computers are used to serve children's imaginative purposes, this process is enhanced. This point of view humanizes the machine through a playful stance, rather than allowing the machine to dehumanize the child in situations where only the machine has the right answers. Play with computers that allows the child to be in control fosters attitudes of competence and flexibility.

Recognizing that appropriate use of technology can foster learning and self-esteem in young children, in 1996 the National Association for the Education of Young Children (NAEYC) developed a position on technology. NAEYC recommends that educators:

- Apply the principles of developmentally appropriate practices in choosing and using technology.

- Integrate technology as one of many options available to children in the learning environment.

- Be conscious of promoting equal access to technology to all children, including children with special needs.

- Take responsibility for avoiding software that includes stereotypes or violence, especially if the violence is controlled by the child. Software selection, like selection of other materials, should reflect the diversity of today's world.

- Take responsibility for working with parents in choosing appropriate software.

- Use technology in their own professional development, such as using e-mail as a tool to collaborate with other educators and to access educational resources on the Internet.

We agree with these recommendations and also emphasize the following: Teachers should encourage children to play with technology in ways that are open-ended, allowing children to determine the outcome of their play.

Addressing Standards for Technology

National Education Standards for K–2 have been adopted by the International Society for Technology Education (ISTE; 2007). The ISTE notes that these standards were written to be consistent with the NAEYC Position Statement and that early childhood educators can implement them in practices consistent with NAEYC guidelines. The six standards are shown in Table 13.1. For each, an example of a performance indicator relevant for play is illustrated with a reference to a chapter vignette.

The ISTE Web site includes information on ISTE publications and online several resources for kindergarten and primary teachers, some of which preschool teachers may adapt for their programs. In IT's *Elementary!: Integrating Technology in the Primary Grades,* published by ISTE, Hamilton (2007) recounts how her school implemented an award-winning program with limited funds. She describes how teachers can develop expertise and includes the comprehensive details needed to implement developmentally appropriate programs. Several chapters describe computer use that is play centered, including drawing and word-processing projects. ✂

Table 13.1   National Education Technology Standards for Students

Standard with Example of Performance Indicator*	Examples from Chapter Vignettes
1. Creativity and Innovation	
Create original works as a means of personal or group expression.	Joshua dictates a story using a scanned image of the drawing he made using the computer.
2. Communicate and Collaborate	
Communicate information and ideas effectively to multiple audiences using a variety of media and formats.	Elijah and Zoë use Skype to communicate with their Dutch grandparents.
3. Research and Information Fluency	
Locate, organize, analyze, evaluate, synthesize, and ethically use information from a variety of sources and media.	Children in Halewood's class experiment with pulleys and levers. They use digital photos in their journals to document their findings.
4. Critical Thinking, Problem Solving, and Decision Making	As part of their Night Sky Project, kindergartners use the Internet to find accurate information to inform their drawings and paintings.
Identify and define authentic problems and significant questions for investigation.	
5. Digital Citizenship	
Exhibit a positive attitude toward using technology that supports collaboration, learning, and production.	First graders in Nancy's class work together and use e-mail to communicate with children and adults.
6. Technology Operations and Concepts	
Understand and use technology systems.	With adult assistance, Nina uses text-to-speech tools. She types her name and is delighted to hear, "Nina."

Source: National Education Standards for K-2 adopted by the International Society for Technology in Education, 2007.

Choosing Computer Software

Because new software becomes available constantly and existing software is upgraded frequently, we have avoided recommending specific software. Rather, teachers need a framework for judging software themselves or access to software reviews that share their point of view.

To help teachers choose instructional activities that are technology based, von Blanckensee (1999, personal communication, January 7, 2010) designed the following scale: *Choosing Technology-Based Activities for Young Children, Ages 3–7.* These include activities that use audio recorders, cameras, video recorders, computer simulations, games and books, and e-mail. This rating scale includes three issues for teachers to consider when evaluating the appropriateness of an activity: (a) content/method,

(b) technology design issues, and (c) computer software design issues. The items used for ratings help teachers ensure that they use technology in ways that reflect individual needs, promote gender equity, and respect cultural diversity. (See Table 13.2.) The scale takes technical and interface design into consideration. It provides an excellent framework for considering the many issues involved in selecting software that we have mentioned throughout this section (diversity, equity, and nonviolent content) and whether the software supports constructivist learning in ways that are age appropriate.

Teachers also can turn to ratings of software based on criteria that are in keeping with NAEYC guidelines such as degree of child control, nonviolence, clear instructions, expanding complexity, and quality of technical features. Evaluations of children's software are available through teacher resource Web sites, including those of various state departments of education. When choosing software rated by others, teachers will want to make sure that the criteria used for rating are philosophically consistent with a play-centered curriculum.

Using the Potential of Computer Technology to Extend Play and Address Standards

In the Night Sky Project vignette that begins this chapter, the three kindergarten teachers embarked on a month-long project on space travel, using sources on the Internet to view images of planets, stars, and space journeys. Internet sites especially designed for children abound.

Children also use computers to create representations of their play and projects. Wang, Kedem, and Hertzog (2004) describe the benefits of K–1 children creating their own PowerPoint presentations. Impetus to reflect on children's own interpretations of content and collaboration with others develops perspectivism and creates the context for the zone of proximal development. Wang and colleagues illustrate that the use of PowerPoint technology can be very effective in bringing children more fully into the self-reflective aspects of documentation assessment, a prominent feature of play-centered curriculum and projects. In this study, teachers used Kidspiration to help children write or dictate concept webs and Kid Pix to create drawings for their presentations about their class project on measurement in their community. The PowerPoint presentations began with prompts from teachers about what children found most important about the concept of measurement and expanded to children's reflections on field trips, visits by "experts," and their own exploration and play with measurement tools.

At the University of Toronto laboratory school, teacher–researchers Pelletier, Halewood, and Reeve (2005) enhanced their traditional journaling process with the use of digital photos. They combined the use of a database called Knowledge Forum with photo journals in a class of kindergarten students. In one class, children kept electronic journals complete with digital photos as they were investigating the topic of simple machines:

> The students had been doing experiments in class with pulleys and levers. They were using Knowledge Forum to comment on photos of our experiments.

Table 13.2 Choosing Technology-Based Activities for Young Children

Ratings: 0 = poor 1 = adequate 2 = good 3 = excellent
Teachers may want to redesign or avoid activities that are poor on any criteria.

Content/Method

The activity supports learning objectives which are developmentally appropriate and consistent with the curriculum. The activity:

- relates to the child's direct experiences at home, school, and community.
- is integrated into the curriculum through connections to other hands-on activities which support the same learning objectives.
- is interesting and challenging to students at a wide range of ability and skill levels, including students with special needs.
- is open-ended, allowing children to learn through their own playful investigation.
- supports language development either directly, through interactive use by children in groups, or through extensions of the activity.
- is appropriate to children with varied learning styles.
- can involve two or more children working cooperatively.
- positively addresses or is sensitive to issues of multiculturalism.
- positively addresses or is sensitive to issues of linguistic diversity.
- positively addresses or is sensitive to issues of gender equity.
- positively addresses or is sensitive to issues of individual differences.
- has nonviolent content, in the case of computer games and simulations.

Technology Design Issues:

- The child can learn to physically operate the technology independently.
- The technology is safe for the age level intended.
- The technology is chosen and set up to minimize the risk of breakage.
- The technology can be adapted, if necessary, for students with special needs.

Computer Software Design Issues:

- The menu is uncluttered and uses picture clues with words for menu choices.
- The child can navigate through the software easily, go back to the main menu, or exit the software at any time.
- The program provides help. The child can escape and/or get help at any time.
- The design is attractive to children: It may include colorful graphics, sound, animation.
- The program can be used in more than one language.
- The program can be used by students with special needs.
- Children can print and save their work.

Source: Copyright 1997, revised 2010 by Leni von Blanckensee (personal communication, January 7, 2010).

At recess one day, the children became very excited when they discovered a shovel that had become wedged between the shed and the fence. They suggested that I could take a picture of it and to put it in our Machines view in Knowledge Forum. The children then decided that the question to go along with the photo would be, "How do we get it out?" The ensuing ideas and debate were quite lively—someone suggested putting tape on the end of a stick to retrieve the shovel. Someone else said that a lever might work. Yet another student wrote "uusrhns" (use your hands). Ultimately, the shovel came out in a river of water once the snow melted and the children had gone on to other investigations. It is still a lovely example of how children's ideas inform and direct the learning in a meaningful way. (C. Halewood, personal communication, October 8, 2005). ⌀

SUMMARY AND CONCLUSION

We began and concluded this chapter with vignettes that illustrate how teachers select classic and recent toys and technologies that serve as powerful tools to support children's cognitive and social development. We considered several difficult issues that confront educators. For example, commercial marketing affects children's classroom behaviors when toys limit development and support stereotyping by gender, race, and ethnicity.

We have also examined the effects of media-based play on children's development and outlined strategies that teachers might use to control the influences of popular media culture on the play in their classrooms. Finally, we considered the influences of technology on children's play, focusing on computers in early childhood programs. NAEYC's Position Statement and the National Education Standards can be implemented in ways that foster the development of computer literacy as children's imagination and self-initiated activities drive their activities.

Computer literacy, like book literacy, occurs in a social context, nested in the culture of the classroom, the school, the community, and society at large. The same might be said of "television literacy" and "video literacy." These literacies are in turn affected by what children bring to school from home as well as what they experience in their classrooms. By expressing literacy in any medium, children and adults exercise the knowledge and skills that are approved by others in the social contexts we value.

In this broad view, we see toy and computer literacies as "an encounter between thought and reality, between desire and possibility, that takes place in the symbolic realm and thereby vastly multiplies human capacity to process, analyze, criticize and reinvent experience" (Easton, 1980, cited in Emihovich, 1990, p. 230). From this perspective, all toys in the classroom—from the blocks to the computer, from lotto games to superheroes—contribute to children's emerging literacy in our culture as they find ways to express themselves and communicate with others through play.

Conclusion: Integrating Play, Development, and Practice

Two boys and a girl are walking up a hill. Four-year-old Charlie shudders and throws his arms up, making explosive sounds interrupted with calls for help. "I need your help; the bad guys are surrounding me."

Jerry, wearing a baseball cap, shouts acknowledgment and comes to the rescue. "It's OK, they're gone. Let's go." They link arms and descend.

Sheila follows. "I have to go to the bathroom."

The two boys look around. "The bathroom's over there," one says and points to a concrete building buried in the shadow of trees.

"Come with me." Her request is ignored, and the boys commence another episode. "I'll be Zelda," she says as she joins the play, but her body reminds her of other needs, and she descends toward the picnic tables. She later returns, holding her father's hand. They head toward the bathroom. Having addressed her own and her parent's concern for safety in unfamiliar places, she returns and reenters the play with an assertion of her competence. "I was right. That is the bathroom."

A few hours later, the children chase Jerry's father across the field. He turns and gently tosses his son to the ground. The chase continues, out past the concrete bathrooms, down to the beach, back up the hill. The two boys temporarily drop behind and plan their attack. "Listen, all we have to do is. . . ."

As the chase ends, they huddle and plot the afternoon's play. Sheila is excluded. Some distance away she sits down on the hillside, pulling at weeds. Shortly afterward, she and Jerry begin walking together. She has a long face. "You weren't nice to me," she says.

Charlie comes toward them, yelling, "Jerry, wait up! Wait up! There isn't a bee in it. I got it out (of the Coke can)." Sheila and Jerry wait for Charlie to catch up. The three old friends are again one. ✆

Look at all that is occurring in this simple vignette. These 4-year-olds are collaborating on common themes that are agreed to and adhered to. They are imitating and reproducing elements of their culture. They are using language to guide their play and to provide its content. They display practical knowledge, as in recognizing the bathroom, as well as understanding when parental protection is needed. Sheila is able to express her feelings of exclusion and to reinstate herself in the triad after her temporary absence. Last, Charlie figured out how to get a bee out of a Coke can.

We see in play the expression of intelligence, the management of needs and emotions, the elaboration of common themes and efforts, and the reproduction of culture. We see the give-and-take of cooperation. The evolution of social consciousness and of sexual identity also is evident. The world of childhood and the world of play are inseparable. Play is evident from infancy through adulthood and unquestionably occupies a central role in human development. Our purpose is to put play at the center of classroom curriculum. In this concluding chapter, we revisit in somewhat broader terms the theoretical basis for our faith in the value of play as a focal point in curriculum planning and classroom management.

CONSTRUCTIVISM AND DEVELOPMENT

The term *constructivism* is used to express the belief that development is not simply maturation or biological unfolding, nor is it the result of the environment or experience imprinting itself on the developing mind, through, for example, reinforcement. The term is derived from the word *construct* and is meant to suggest that the child plays an active role in constructing that which is developed. Constructivism is a theme in education that resulted largely from an interpretation of Jean Piaget's work on child development.

What Is Developed?

Each of the main theorists who have written about child development could tell us something different about what is going on in the opening vignette. Piaget could help us understand the representational methods and coordination of concepts used in the play. Mead could help us understand the way in which this play affects the developing sense of self in these three children. Vygotsky could show us how the collective activity of the children is creating a context for their own understanding. This context is a microculture developing among the children with its own history that intersects with the broader culture. Freud could help us understand how the play addresses deeper emotional themes associated with the control of instinctive forces. Erikson would show us the development of trust and autonomy represented in the play. For example, notice how Sheila asks the boys to escort her to the bathroom and how she comfortably tells Jerry he wasn't nice to her. Dewey might point out the competence and industry represented here.

Even in the simplest scenes of spontaneous and unguided play, development is occurring in all areas of human growth. For the sake of summary, we identify these areas as intelligence, personality, competence, and social consciousness/sense of self. We believe that each of these is developed by the child through spontaneous and self-directed activity within social, cultural, and historical contexts. This is the meaning of the constructivist view of development. Development does not result from the unfolding of genetically predetermined potentials, nor as the direct result of social experience in the form of education or selective reinforcement. Intelligence, personality, competence, and sense of self are constructed by the child through self-regulated activity embedded in social, historical, and cultural contexts. We maintain that this view is consistent with the theorists just mentioned and believe that without play, no development would occur.

Our position can be summarized with five points:

1. Play is the primary context in which the four domains of intelligence, personality, competencies, and social consciousness are developed and integrated.
2. These four domains are inseparable from social experience within cultural/historical contexts.

Props support symbolic play.

3. Self-directed activity is necessary for development in these domains and is aligned closely with play.
4. These four domains are functionally interdependent and are each involved in all forms of play.
5. Each domain is constructed through means-ends coordinations.

Means-Ends Coordinations and Development

Another way to view constructivism is to think about the ways by which the child constructs the means of achieving desired goals. This is called means-ends coordinations, and it concerns, for example, how a reorganization of old means can be used to achieve new ends or, conversely, how new means can be constructed to reach old ends. This is similar to evolutionary biology where old structures evolve to serve new functions and new structures evolve to serve old functions; that is, old means change to serve new ends, and old ends are met through new means. For example, early fish gills evolved to oxygenate fish blood. Eventually lungs evolved to oxygenate the blood of land animals. The gill bone of early fish evolved into a middle ear bone in mammals, making modern hearing possible. Old means serve new ends, and new means serve old ends.

Intelligence is the area of development most closely associated with Piaget's means-ends analysis. The fact that intelligence develops through the dynamics of means-ends coordinations establishes the common tie between intelligence and constructivism. In Piaget's view, intelligence is not a measurable trait such as IQ, but, rather, a process of adaptive understanding. Piaget perceived the development of reason to be an evolution in the child's adaptation to the environment that subsequently leads to understanding. This evolution occurs because early understandings ultimately are challenged by the environment. When new experiences are inconsistent or incompatible with earlier ways of understanding, change ultimately results. For example, basing an understanding of quantity on how things look will yield less consistent interpretations of the world than understanding that quantity is a composition of units. Knowing that rearranging objects does not change their cardinal number is universally understood by all children in all cultures, but takes most of early childhood to evolve. This evolution is a result of construction rather than learning, genetic unfolding, or social imitation and instruction.

Personality also entails means-ends relations and is constructed. Personality is each person's unique means of maintaining acceptable emotional states while at the same time satisfying goals. It's how we remain emotionally stable while carrying out daily goal-directed activity. In a sense, personality is the constructed means by which individuals develop emotional self-regulation. Everyday acts—such as playing with friends, doing what others expect of you, going to school, solving disputes, or negotiating turns on a swing—entail emotions. The way these emotions are managed is directed by personality.

Even at birth, some children are calm, some are more active, some accept changes in routines, and some do not. Although such temperaments occur early and sometimes remain into adulthood, the issue of personality is more complex and tied in direct and subtle ways to a child's experiences and to the deep emotional substrata that underlie all human activity. Personality, like intelligence, is constructed and not given at birth.

Competencies are the things that we can accomplish reliably—the abilities that allow us to function in the world. Competencies are largely fashioned through intelligence, but cannot be separated from other areas of development. Like intelligence and personality, competencies also are tied to means-ends relationships because they are either the means of reaching goals or the goals themselves. A competency can be instrumental in achieving a goal, such as knowing how to play effectively with others, or a competency can be a goal itself as when one tries to fashion the means of entering into play with others. Competencies always involve emotions because we always have feelings about what we do. Emotions also entail competencies in the sense of being able to relate our feelings to the feelings of others as well as in the competencies implied in the self-regulation and control of emotions.

Social consciousness refers to the child's evolving sense of self and how the self is related to the other "selves" it comes in contact with. Social consciousness is inseparable from intelligence, personality, and competency and, like these other areas, is constructed through the coordination of means-end relations. Here, however, the means-end coordinations are related to social causality, or how people affect one another. The sense of self is fashioned through an understanding of two types of causality. One is linked to an objective understanding of ourselves, and the other is linked to understanding how we affect others and how social conditions, in turn, affect us. For example, a stable understanding of ourselves must take into account how we affect others and how others affect us. We are affected by the actions and perceptions of others, and we, in turn, create the same conditions for others. Understanding this requires a reflection on the means-end relationships that occur in social causality; that is, how am I affecting others, and how do others affect me?

CONSTRUCTIVISM AND SOCIAL-CULTURAL THEORIES OF PLAY

Two major developmental psychologists, Jean Piaget and Lev Vygotsky, were contemporaries and constructivists. However they had differing views on childhood development. It's important that we understand some of the issues that divide and unite these important thinkers.

Jean Piaget (1896–1980)

People have posed the question of what it means to be human since the beginning of reflective thought. Historically, this question has been left to theology and philosophy, but in the 20th century, it increasingly has become the province of developmental psychology. Jean Piaget, the Swiss biologist, is probably the single most recognized person in developmental psychology. His work spans a large piece of the 20th century and transformed our understanding of human rationality and mental development.

Piaget, born in 1896, was a biologist interested in evolution. He made the startling discovery that some of the most basic of our understandings are not obtained or learned through cultural transmission or even by direct physical experience. The construction of knowledge, according to Piaget, occurs as a series of predictable and universal stages unfolding as a function of a slowly elaborated form of internal consistency in the means-ends coordination of actions that relate, first, to sensory motor patterns of action and later to internal mental representations of actions. His theory assumes that this sequence of stages is universal, occurring in a similar way for all humans who are healthy and active. Piaget's famous conservation experiments provide examples of predictable stages of understanding. The child first conserves number, understanding that rearranging a set of objects does not change the quantity of the set. This typically occurs toward the end of early childhood. It is years later before the child understands that changing the shape of something does not change its weight (i.e., the conservation of weight). It is later still that the child can conserve volume, understanding that changing the shape of a substance does not change its volume.

Development was viewed by Piaget as changes in patterns of action within the individual, which result in increased internal mental consistency. This concept of development gives a completely new twist to the nature/nurture controversy. Piaget believed that developing children are not simply maturing according to a genetic program (nature), or the product of environmental influences (nurture), but, rather, are the active constructors whose constructions evolve in a predictable pattern of stages. For Piaget, the child's development follows from the laws of activity and means-ends coordinations, in the same way that thermodynamics or the movements of objects follow laws. The specific course of development is viewed as common to all people because the laws of activity and means-ends coordinations are common to all people, not because people share the same experiences or the same genetic makeup.

Teachers might find it difficult to derive practical curriculum from Piaget's theory because of his focus on autonomy and self-directed activity and because his theory says little about how social interactions affect development. In fact, Piaget did not address in depth the problems of education and curriculum. Despite this, educational theory throughout the world has been influenced by Piaget.

Lev Vygotsky (1896–1934)

The theories of Vygotsky, however, prompt us to think about what Piaget has left out of his formulations, and many educators today look to him for direction on how to structure the social elements of the classroom to achieve curriculum goals (Bodrova & Leong, 2006).

Lev Vygotsky was born in Russia in 1896, the same year Piaget was born in Switzerland. Both were part of the new modernism that was influencing continental thought. Darwin's theory of evolution, Freud's theory of the unconscious, Einstein's theory of relativity, and Marx's theory of economics and social institutions, were all part of the modernism of the late 19th and early 20th centuries. It was a time of great intellectual and social change and, in some instances, a time of revolutionary change.

Vygotsky was largely influenced by the social theory of his time and by the changes accompanying the Russian revolution. He was interested in how social interactions affect individuals, and how individuals and society are influenced by history and culture. Vygotsky greatly influenced Russian psychology and argued that conceptual activity cannot be separated from social experience. Further, this experience unfolds within a cultural-historical context. This was an extension of his belief that the regulation of conscious activity can take place only within a social context (Davydov, 1995).

Vygotsky believed that all activity happens in a social context and begins as social experience that is later internalized. Because Vygotsky died in 1934, before Piaget published his most significant works, we do not know how the two would have agreed or disagreed on the issue of individual development and social experience.

Connecting Piaget's and Vygotsky's Theories

Those who attempt to understand the relationship between development and education will benefit from understanding how Piaget's and Vygotsky's theories complement one another. Many assume that Piaget is an individualist, believing that development occurs independently of social experience, and that Vygotsky is an environmentalist, believing that learning occurs as a function of the social-cultural-historic environment. In fact, both Vygotsky and Piaget are constructivists, believing that learning is neither a direct function of social activity or individual activity, but rather, an interaction between both forces. For example, Piaget believed that true conceptual activity, by which he meant rational thought, cannot proceed without the use of a referential system that is tied to and dependent on social agreement. Rationality is impossible without language, words, and mathematical symbols embedded in social contexts, where people must coordinate their points of view with those of others and come to agreements and disagreements. Rationality is impossible when the world is viewed only from one's own perspective because a single perspective cannot take into account all points of view (Piaget, 1954, 1962b, 1995; Vygotsky, 1978).

Understanding this position is critical to understanding Piaget's work. He was concerned primarily with how humans establish logically necessary and objectively verifiable knowledge. Objective knowledge concerns our ability to think logically about spatial relationships: time; relationships among time, motion, and distance; geometric relationships; quantitative relationships such as number, volume, length, and weight; laws of causality; and chance. His theory holds that the attainment of objective knowledge is the result of a gradual "decentering" process. This process involves a progressive development from a state in which the child's ability to represent is limited to what is immediately available or "presented" to the senses, to a later period in which "presentation" is still tied to the child's own experiences but less so than before. Eventually, after early childhood, the young adult can give a representation that is freed entirely from specific sensation and experience and is socially coordinated with others through the use of arbitrary signs such as words (Piaget, 1962b).

A CLOSER LOOK AT PIAGET AND CONSTRUCTIVIST THEORY

Schemes: Assimilation, Accommodation, and Play

The concept of "action scheme" is important to Piaget's theory. A scheme is a pattern for action that can be repeated, like a program in a computer. The reflexes of the newborn are the first schemes. Blinking, grasping, sucking, turning the head, moving the tongue, and opening and closing the mouth are examples. By 3 years of age, more elaborate schemes, such as chasing a ball or putting on a shirt, have evolved from a coordination of simpler schemes. This elaboration and coordination of schemes continues on a lawful course throughout development and yields at each stage the possibility of more complex and adaptive activity (Piaget, 1963a).

The universal ways that children interpret experience are evidence that the construction of reality reflects developmental laws. For example, all children at some point overgeneralize language rules for marking time and number ("I played and I goed to the store" or "I put the shoes on my foots"). As another example, all children at some point in their development, reason that a part is larger than the whole—that, for example, the vase contains more roses than flowers, even though only some of the flowers are roses. All children at some point believe that a quantity changes even if only its appearance has changed. They believe that pouring a liquid into a different-shaped container will change its amount, or that rearranging a pile of blocks will change the number of blocks. These ways of interpreting events are constructed and not copied from experience.

Human development is driven by adaptation to the environment and consists of the twin processes of assimilation and accommodation. Assimilation is an incorporation of the environment into the child's own patterns of action or schemes. In a sense, the child uses already-developed competencies to understand new events. Accommodation takes place when schemes or competencies are inadequate and create contradictory results. Accommodation is a change in schemes as they are modified to fit new circumstances and occurs as a result of interactions with the environment. For example, an amount can be changed by adding or subtracting substance. At some point in children's development, they sense the contradiction between this understanding and the belief that an amount can change even when no additions or subtractions have been made. This feeling of contradiction will contribute to the development of an understanding of conservation of quantities.

Assimilation distorts and changes things because it modifies the world according to the child's schemes. Accommodation, on the other hand, is a process of bending to the pressure of reality. Piaget identified play with assimilation. This reflects the link between assimilation and the distorting quality of play, where pretense and fantasy make the world what the child wishes it to be. When the child turns the living room furniture into a spaceship, the nature of the furniture has been distorted in the child's mind and turned, for the moment, into components of the rocket ship (Piaget, 1962b).

Piaget identified accommodation with imitation because in reproducing reality (imitating), the child's action schemas are accommodated to reality. When a child imitates the sounds of a horse while pretending to be a horse, the child is accommodating to the sounds made by horses.

Although Piaget associated pure assimilation with play, assimilation and accommodation cannot be separated. Children's play develops from a coordination between assimilative and accommodative activity. As children develop, so does their play. Play themes become more elaborate, symbols become more evolved, and social coordinations become more complex and cooperative.

Stages of Development and Play

Because play is inseparable from all facets of development, play itself must develop. The first 2 years of life are called the sensorimotor period because during this phase, the child's understanding of the world is tied to physical behaviors and sensory experiences. Play consists of physical actions that are combined and repeated for the simple pleasure of mastering new combinations. During this period, the child gradually develops the ability to mentally represent the world. This development entails six distinct stages, beginning with birth and the exercise of sensorimotor reflexes and ending with the beginning of representational functions, such as imitation, pretense, and language, which emerge at around 2 years of age.

Sensorimotor play lacks the symbolic or pretend quality of later play because pretense requires representation, which is achieved only at the end of this period. During the early stages of this development, infants cannot construct the symbolism and imagery that are needed to support pretend activity, like picking up a piece of grass and pretending to eat it.

The second major developmental period, the preoperational period, begins with the onset of representation or the ability to form images of objects or events that are not immediately available to the senses. The emergence of representational thought is the result of an advance in the coordination of assimilation and accommodation. Assimilation and play are now capable of giving meaning to symbols produced by accommodation and imitation. The ability to create symbols has a profound effect on children's play in terms of its themes, the symbols used to support the play, and the means of communicating the purpose and manner of the play. The play of this period does not replace sensorimotor play, but rather joins sensorimotor play to create a more diverse palette of possible action (Piaget, 1962b).

During the preoperational period, children form early concepts that are limited in stability. Comprehension of everything, from the concrete and familiar (e.g., mommies and daddies, brother and sister) to the abstract (e.g., number, time, movement, measurement), is unstable and in constant risk of contradiction because young children reason from particular to particular rather than understanding how particular cases relate to the whole set of possible cases. For example, at one moment, mommies might be people who help you, even though not all who help you are mommies and not all mommies help. At another moment, a mommy might be anyone with a baby, even if the relationship is not maternal (Piaget, 1966).

Piaget elaborated on the fact that during the preconceptual stage, play is the primary and most suitable way for children to express themselves as well as modulate or understand their emotions. The medium of play allows a direct expression of emotions and allows the child to defuse and explore unpleasant emotional experiences, even to the point of changing reality to his or her liking (Piaget, 1962b).

A third period, the concrete-operational period, begins at about the age of 6 or 7 years and is characterized by the emergence of consistent concepts. The emergence of true conceptual reasoning is brought about by an increasingly reversible coordination between assimilation and accommodation. This, in turn, is facilitation by social coordinations made possible through language and other representational systems that allow for agreement and disagreement with others. These integrations allow the child to decenter from direct sensory data, such as imagery, perception, emotion, and practical behaviors. This decentering allows the formation of concepts that go beyond individual experience and idiosyncratic symbols (Piaget, 1962b, 1995).

Play is still necessary to development, but because of the achievements during this period, the play of 6- and 7-year-olds is directed increasingly toward social coordinations and successful reproductions of reality. This might be seen in formal games with rules or an interest in constructing models.

Because of the new mental power provided by conceptual reasoning, the 7- to 8-year-old child is more easily able to express, regulate and understand emotions through the use of words and concepts rather than pure play. However, play, pretense, and fantasy remain critical components of emotional self-regulation.

A fourth major period, the formal-operational period, begins with the elaboration of hypothetical or theoretically possible interpretations and the elaboration of scientific or logical means of deciding between competing hypothetical propositions. All the earlier forms of play remain a part of the young adolescent's life, but during the formal operational period, play also incorporates the complex refinements that characterize work. Youth group activities, with real tasks of working with others, and making things "that really work" are examples of play-related activity at this stage. Here emotions can become the focus of reflective activity with a gradual expanding of insight into the nature of human experience.

The Construction of Reality

The construction of reality entails gradual progress in the reliable and logical interpretation of experiences and their emotional content. This allows accurate predictions. For example, we know that pouring a liquid from one container into another does not change its amount. We know, without carrying out the activity, that if we were to pour the liquid back into the original container, it would occupy the same amount of space.

As noted earlier, Piaget was interested in how we construct an objective or rational understanding of time (the temporal succession of events), objects (the differentiation of sensation into discrete entities), space (the relative movements and positions of objects), and causality (the attribution of necessary links between events). In each of these areas, human intelligence eventually fashions an objective understanding. Moreover, these understandings successively deepen from those of the infant to those of the most advanced scientific theorists. Modern science is, after all, a continuing quest to understand the nature of objects, time, space, and causality. This quest never will be finished because each new understanding sets the conditions for further questions.

Emotions, intellect, and social life are drawn together in play.

By 2 years of age, most children have constructed a limited, yet reliable, understanding that objects are permanent entities, organized in space and time, and linked in causal relationships. Even this seemingly simple understanding is constructed gradually. Imagine a child of 14 months sitting on the floor. His mother, whom he's been watching, approaches on his right and passes behind him. The infant turns to his left, anticipating seeing his mother reappear. This behavior suggests that objects, time, and space are becoming organized into a whole where objects continue to exist even though they appear and disappear over time; the child realizes that they exist in a space where, for example, the same target can be reached by different routes. He anticipated his mother's trajectory in space and intersected that point not by visually following her, but by taking an alternative route.

This simple understanding takes many months to develop and is a precursor to a more complex mental organization, characterized by logical-mathematical coordinations. Finding objects hidden within or under other objects, finding one's way around the house, knowing that throwing the ball over the fence will be an obstacle to the dog with whom he's playing fetch, and being able to reach the same place by different routes all speak to a spatial understanding in which placements (position in space) are coordinated with displacements (changes in position). The ability to coordinate positions with changes in position is an early form of logical-mathematical thought. It makes possible the problem solving in near space, which we observe in children toward the end of the sensorimotor period. Understanding that objects continue to exist as they appear and disappear marks the first conservations where, in the context of changing sensations, something remains unchanged. It is the reversible coordinations of sensorimotor action that make the first constructions of space, time, causality, and object permanence possible (Piaget, 1954). This cognitive achievement has effects on the whole child and can be seen, for example, in the onset of separation anxiety, which coincides with the emergence of object permanence.

During the early school years, we see advances in the child's understanding of reality. Children begin to understand that reality can be ordered in a variety of ways; for example, things can be ordered in a series from least to most. This may be reflected in the understanding of time and numbers (e.g., history, age, the calendar). Coordination of part–whole relations is beginning, where the child understands that wholes are composed of parts, that a whole can be broken into parts, and that parts can be reassembled into wholes. This can be seen in the child's understanding of words ("There are more children in the classroom than there are boys, because some of the classmates are girls") and beginning arithmetic ("Seven is bigger than 4 because if you take 4 from 7, you have 3 left over").

As understanding becomes logically organized, we refer to the child's thinking as operational, meaning that the internal mental coordinations carried out by the child are organized in a system of reversible operations that allow concepts to remain stable and, further, to obtain the status of objective reasoning. An example of operations is seen in the reversible coordination of part–whole relations and in order relations. For example, two parts can be combined to yield a third (A + B = C), and a whole (C) can be divided into its parts (A and B). The fact that development tends toward these operational organizations shows that it is lawful and universal.

SOCIAL EXPERIENCE AND THE CONSTRUCTION OF REALITY

As discussed earlier, Piaget endeavored to show that the construction of reality, expressed in what may be called objective knowledge, is constructed through the internal regulations of the child. Because the laws of these internal regulations are assumed to be universal, a communality of knowledge exists among all people. However, Vygotsky believed that all conceptual knowledge is encountered first in social interactions. If development is dependent on social experience, one might expect people from different cultures and different social experiences to develop differently. Piaget and Vygotsky complement one another by showing how inter- and intraindividual forces shape development.

Piaget believed that two developmental themes exist, each consisting of coordinations that eventually lead to stable concepts. One is the internal regulations of the child, and the other is cooperation with others. Social coordinations are essentially the conditions that allow us to agree or disagree with another or to cooperate or compete with others. Piaget asserted that these two processes are inseparable and are simply different sides of assimilation and accommodation. Further, he believed that both aspects of development follow a lawful course. Social actions, like mental actions, tend to become organized in logical-operational systems. Social experience provides the possibility of differing points of view—agreeing and disagreeing, understanding and not understanding. Each of these affects the accommodations of our thinking. The corresponding and, at times, conflicting intelligence of others participates in the development of our own intelligence (Piaget, 1995).

The child's evolving ability to think rationally is tied to social life. The child's capacity for reason eventually must detach from the child's own perspective and incorporate the perspective of others. This process of agreeing and disagreeing with others depends on a means of representing reality that is free of the individual means of representation (practical knowledge, images, sensations, perceptions, emotions, dreams, unconscious symbols). It depends on a socially agreed-on system of representation such as that provided by language (Piaget, 1962b).

A child might have developed certain mental operations, but it does not follow that this same child is necessarily competent in the particular cultural forms of knowledge that require these operations. For example, most 8-year-olds throughout the world have developed the operations necessary for understanding simple addition. However, only some of these children know how to respond to the image 4 + 9 = ____. For individuals' intelligence to be applied or expressed in particular cultural forms, individuals must have experience in those forms and express their understanding as a competency in those forms. This is the job of schooling and other informal mechanisms of social transmission. The untutored mind can develop the intelligence to understand something, but without an encounter with the cultural expression of that understanding, the child will not be able to demonstrate or express the understanding in the language of the culture.

What we learn cannot be separated from social experience. Experience occurs only within the embrace of a particular historical-cultural moment; within the envelope of particular values and patterns for work and play; and with the use of particular, largely cultural, representational means. So, although intelligence might proceed by a lawful unfolding coordination of schemes, what are coordinated are actions and representations, and these are inseparable from social experience. Thus, people in differing cultural and historical settings might develop through the same basic developmental stages and yet have different ways of expressing their intelligence in daily life. This is because the demands of daily life differ across cultures, societies, and periods in history. Furthermore, much of human knowledge is not subjected easily to the rigors of logically mathematically governed discourse and is, therefore, subject to complex disagreements. Science, for example, is an attempt to bring common interests into a discourse setting governed by laws of logic and mathematical reasoning, and even as such, science proceeds through a complex process of argument, disagreement, critique, review, and revision.

PLAY AND DEVELOPMENT

In the following sections, we summarize the relationship among play and four domains of development.

Play and the Development of Intelligence

The natural activity of the child feeds the self-regulated development of intelligence. Natural activities in the early years are almost exclusively play-bound because the character of nonplay activity requires a way of understanding and a way of directing one's activity that has not yet developed in the young child. During the early childhood years, the child's intelligence is marked by a lack of coordination between assimilation and accommodation. The child is constantly understanding the world in ways that engender contradictions and fluctuations. The resulting modifications in understanding and behaviors are never complete enough to ward off continued vacillations and contradictions. The ongoing and constant modification of the child's intellectual structures is marked by a progressive coordination or equilibrium among assimilation, accommodation, and social coordinations, but it is not until the end of early childhood that this equilibrium is stable enough to yield a conceptually consistent and logically ordered world. Prior to this, the child constantly is processing contradictory information. A big block cannot fit into a small hole, but a big Santa Claus can fit down a small chimney. The examples are as numerous as the beliefs of children.

Until this equilibrium is achieved, the child's intellectual activity is always bound within the larger domain of play because, not being able to form an objective, reliable, and stable view of the world, there is always a subordination of the world to the child's immediate view. In a sense, because children make of the world what they wish, we say that children are bound by play, where work and practice are tied to pretense, fantasy, and imitation.

In short, intelligence develops through the child's self-directed and natural activities, which are always play-bound because all of a young child's activity tends toward the subordination of reality to the ego. Lacking the means of true work—where assimilation and accommodation are reliably coordinated, and where intelligence is coordinated with others—the child is forced into a playful mode. In this mode, goal-directed activity slips into fantasy, efforts to grasp reality give way to pretense, and attempts to reconcile diverse perspectives slip into a subordination of reality to the child's immediate interests or perspectives. Hence, it is a truth about intelligence that the child, of necessity, must play to one day be able to work. It is practice at play and not work that will one day produce the intelligent worker.

Play and the Development of Personality

The entire range of children's needs and emotions is arranged and expressed in play. Their play themes deal with abandonment, death, power, acceptance, and rejection. Emotions are practiced and linked to needs, but with pretense as a buffer between the real fear of abandonment, for example, and the fantasy expressed in the play, "Let's say our mothers died and we're all alone."

Play, personality, and intelligence all support each other, are inseparable, and are all related to emotions. Play is not simply one of the possible activities in which a child might engage; it is more accurate to say that play is an expression of the child's personality, intelligence, and feelings.

Personality and intelligence are similar in some ways too, and it is here that we find the powerful relationship between the development of a healthy personality and the healthy expression of play. One of the tenets of constructivism is that as the child attempts to understand the world, intelligence becomes more structured, more consistent, better organized, and more powerful. However, sometimes personality and its regulation of emotions remains undeveloped, poorly formed, and maladaptive. For some, the process of living results in the development of adaptive, well-structured, healthy personalities. For others, the early and incomplete personality of childhood remains throughout life.

A process called "reflective abstraction" is inevitable and necessary in the case of intelligence but not inevitable in the case of personality and the regulation of emotions. Piaget created the concept of reflective abstraction to describe the way in which intelligence bootstraps itself up the developmental ladder. In reflective abstraction, the child brings into recognized forms, through representational activity, the unrealized or unrecognized relationships that make practical behaviors possible. That is, a natural, regulative process advances intelligence simply through the activity of bringing unrealized ideas into representational focus (Piaget, 1977).

As adults, we experience the power of reflective abstraction when, for example, we teach others. Teaching requires us to find a way of representing to others what we already know. The regulations underlying our practical knowledge are abstracted when we transform them into a representational form. In development, we might find a child, for example, who understands the conservation of discrete quantities (such as pennies) but who does not yet understand that pouring a liquid from a vessel into a different-shaped vessel does not change the amount of the liquid. Although still confused with the problem of conserving liquids, the child may be able to see that if a jar of pennies is poured into another jar, the number of pennies does not change. In this example, the child's ability to reflect on an earlier understanding assists the shift from the disequilibrium of an earlier stage to the relative equilibrium of a later stage resulting in understanding the conservation of liquids.

A process similar to reflective abstraction is necessary to the development of personality and its regulations of emotions. A child's personality develops toward an equilibrium between psychoemotional needs and possible interactions within the world. This process is furthered when the child can represent latent needs and emotions consciously. In the case of intelligence, reflective abstraction is inevitable because the child attempts to formulate goals and orchestrate means to reach those goals. It forces the child to represent goals and the links between possible actions and the realization of goals.

For example, in trying to put a necklace of beads into a paper cup, an 18-month-old child might imagine (represent) what is happening when the necklace, draped over the edge of the cup, knocks the cup over. The child might succeed by bunching the necklace into a ball and dropping it into the cup. In doing so, the child represents to himself the goal (getting the necklace into the cup), the obstacle (the necklace knocks the cup over), and the solution (bunching the necklace into a ball). In the case of personality, on the other hand, the inner self can remain unconscious, repressed, and fixated in patterns of action that can remain unconscious and not reflected on throughout life. For example, a child might develop a certain personality as a way of fitting into or resolving conflicts within the family. Although this development might be a coping mechanism, its origins can be repressed and unavailable to the child for reflection.

The parallel between intelligence and personality is established by the common process of means-ends coordination and reflective abstraction. For personality to continue to develop, it needs to be embedded constantly in reflective activity. Symbolic play is the way the child represents emotional needs and concerns, as well as how these needs and concerns are resolved. Adults might depend on therapy, analysis, ritual, art, or work, but the child depends on play for the development of personality. This process points to the critical and necessary role that play occupies in the lives of children. Through the free and unconstrained process of play—unrestrained because it is freed from inhibition and bends the world to immediate needs and interests—the child brings into represented forms the unconscious and inner psychoemotional self.

Play and the Development of Competencies

During the early childhood years, children develop an astonishing array of intellectual, physical, social, and emotional competencies. The infant at birth is helpless, lacking in all but the most rudimentary reflexive sensorimotor competencies, such as sucking, grasping, or looking at objects. The simplest of human competencies, such as removing a blanket from the face or purposefully grasping an object, are not present at birth.

By the time they reach preschool, children have acquired control over their bodily functions; can feed themselves; can dress themselves; can jump, crawl, and run; and have acquired a language and a wide range of representational skills. They can initiate social interactions, have begun to learn how to regulate emotions and express needs and feelings, have learned something about what is acceptable and unacceptable behavior, and have developed a problem-solving intelligence. In short, the preschool child has developed the unmistakable qualities of being human. Older children are more competent in how they feed and dress themselves. They can skip as well as jump. They can use language not only to initiate, but also to sustain interactions and solve complex emotional issues with others. The origins and the continued development of these competencies are tied closely to play.

Many competencies are sensorimotor schemes, integrating the senses with the use of muscles. Obvious examples might be eating, dressing, running and skipping, or even talking, which is a complex sensorimotor activity. Other competencies are not sensorimotor, but instead involve internal representations of possible actions and are representational and abstract. The ability of children to think, problem solve, and coordinate their play with others are examples. Whether the competencies are sensorimotor or representational, their development is dependent on play in a number of ways, the most obvious of which is functional practice. All acquired schemes, whether sensorimotor or not, are repeated. The repetition of newly acquired skills gives pleasure. Children play at making the sounds of their native language, play at large- and small-motor activities such as skipping or dressing, and in general, enjoy exploring and practicing new intellectual powers.

Play, in addition to providing the functional practice for competencies, provides their contextualization and meanings. Children embed their emerging competencies in play activity, often with others, thereby refining not only their articulation, but also their meaning. For example, doll play might contain maternal and family themes, or block play might contain themes of construction and destruction. Outdoor play might involve games that define conditions for running, jumping, and skipping. Much of this contextualized meaning making involves the fantasy and pretend elements of play and, therefore, might be thought of as symbolic play. In play, the child is either creating a symbol (for example, by using a plate of sand to stand for a plate of food) or creating a tapestry of meaning in which a variety of symbols are woven into a meaningful whole.

Another role of play concerns the socialization of competencies. In some cases, they are themselves social, as in the ability to initiate and maintain interactions or a dramatic play theme. In other cases, the competencies are not in themselves social but can be brought together to meet social needs. For example, competencies for large-motor activity, language, problem solving, and considering the needs of others might be brought together in a playground chase game with hero figures taken from the culture.

The ability to form social relationships in which common goals can be established and activities between members of the group are coordinated to achieve these goals is an exceedingly complex competency and slow to unfold. It begins with children playing together in proximity only, to eventually playing with each other but without common themes or purposes. Then it proceeds to attempt to establish and sustain common purposes, but with constant changes in direction, manner, and roles. Finally, social relationships develop into sustained and coordinated play with agreed-on purpose, direction, manner, roles, and sustained emotional compatibility. This broad competency is almost synonymous with socialization and is at its core an evolution of the child's play.

In summary, competencies are the manifestations of intelligence and personality in the presence of emotions. They represent children's ability to control means-ends relationships within the context of needs and emotions, and to develop the means of participation within their culture. Their development is from the beginning tied to play, which provides (a) functional practice, (b) contextualization and meaning, and (c) socialization.

Play and the Development of the Social Self

We are individuals from birth, and yet our identity, our sense of self, must be constructed, developing gradually and passing through many stages. During the first few months, infants cannot distinguish themselves from their surroundings because they lack the intentional ability to interact with the world. For example, infants are limited in their ability to purposely cause effects on objects or others because they cannot distinguish between what they are causing and what others are causing (Piaget, 1954). Without an awareness of what one causes, no real sense of self is possible. So it is that the child will pass through the stages of intelligence, slowly moving from an undifferentiated beginning to a gradual recognition of the self as both the cause of effects and the effect of causes.

Because the awareness of self is, by necessity, tied to this reciprocal causality, the self being both a cause and an effect, its development takes two paths, each with its own ends, and yet, due to their common origin, ends that are inseparable. On the one hand is the developing sense of what one can do or who one is (that is, an awareness of one's intelligence, personality, and competence). On the other hand is the gradual understanding of how the actions of others affect us and how we affect others. In the first, the end point of development is the objective self, a sense of self that progresses through a gradual shedding of its egocentric cloak, approaching an undistorted and objective stance where one's sense of self increasingly corresponds to how others see us. It is in the context of play that children learn to incorporate the viewpoints of others into their own sense of self. In the second, the end point of development is the generalized self, a sense of self as one social object among others, where the reciprocities between "self" and other are understood such that what is true for one must be true for others, and vice versa (Mead, 1934).

The sense of self is perhaps the most interesting and profound aspect of human development because its end is not just the self, but rather a social consciousness capable of generating the ethical, moral, and even spiritual conditions that make the human experience possible. It is because of the sense of self and its inexorable tie to the development of a social conscience that we come to understand the necessary links between social experience and the conditions that foster healthy development and a healthy moral social order. The development of a sense of self is, from its inception, bound to play, where one's own efficacy is explored, where one's own view is coordinated with that of others, and where problems of social coordination are encountered and resolved every day. Play is at the foundation of humankind's most profound and necessary ability—the weaving of the individual spirit into a social fabric.

THE MEANING OF PLAY IN CHILDHOOD AND SOCIETY

How does play contribute to children eventually becoming full members of society? We believe that the world of childhood and the world of play are inseparable and that play is critical to social, emotional, and intellectual development. At the same time, we are aware that, if left to play, children would not develop the essential capacity to operate within the adult world. How is it that play rather than work, that play rather than conformity to adult models, and that play rather than compliance with authority, is the major force in child development?

Play and the Work of Society

We distinguish between the work of childhood and the work of society. The first includes the many instances in which the child formulates ends and means, such as when an infant uses a stick to retrieve an object, when a toddler works at solving a puzzle, or when a school-age child works at understanding the rules of a game. The second consists of the many instances in which the purpose and desired ends, as well as the means and even the success of the work, are determined from outside.

Although both forms of work are important and often merge, they have different status in the child's development. Because we view children's work as self-directed activity, it is by definition autotelic, or containing within it its own direction and purpose. The work of society, which also must be faced by the child, is heterotelic, having a direction and purpose imposed from outside. Although the child might engage in both forms of work, autotelic activity is essential to development because the dynamics of development involve accommodations or modifications brought about

In playing with representational objects, children explore their culture.

by resistances that the world presents to the child's understanding. In a sense, the child treats the world according to what he or she knows; with that often being inadequate, what the child knows must be modified. This is assimilation and accommodation. When, for example, children find their goal thwarted, it is within their inner experience that the goal, the obstacle, and the possible means of overcoming the obstacle are synthesized.

The dynamic interplay between the child's assimilations of the world and the corresponding accommodations is, by its very nature, autotelic because the understandings, the perceived sense of their inadequacy, and the willingness to make the necessary modifications are intrapersonal (within the child) rather than interpersonal (outside the child). We assert the primacy of play over work as a source of development because the development follows from the autotelic work of childhood, which, in the early childhood years, is bound to and subordinate to play.

In the schooling of children, we must seek a blend between the work of childhood and the work of society. We must find the balance that allows children to experience fully the inner tensions between what they presently know and the challenges of new experiences. We use the term *play* to characterize the context in which this balance is best achieved. This does not mean that we should not define the expected learning outcomes for the children in our care. It does, however, mean that in doing so, we must never lose sight of the developmentally driven energies and interests of the child. Accordingly, we endeavor to place the issue of academic standards, for example, within the sphere of developmentally appropriate practice within integrated and holistic school environments.

Autonomy as the Context for Development

The child lives in two inseparable, yet irreconcilable, social worlds: the world of adults and the world of peers. The adult society imposes itself on youth, creating a heteronomous rather than autonomous condition, where codes of behavior are sanctioned by adults and derived by forces totally outside the child's control or comprehension. For example, an adult might tell a child to play fairly, but this does not mean that the child necessarily understands why being fair is important or how to be fair.

The social world of peers, on the other hand, constitutes a condition of autonomy rather than heteronomy. Here children elaborate their own rules and codes for behavior, deciding among themselves what is fair, just, and appropriate to the immediate setting. In this world, they test the extension of their own wills, and they orchestrate their campaigns against adult constraint.

Piaget made a strong argument that it is autonomy rather than heteronomy that creates the context for social, moral, and ethical development. Autonomy is essential to true social coordination, that is, the coordinations of one's own activities and needs with those of others (Piaget, 1965d). Such coordinations require a reciprocity in which members of the social group are on an equal footing, addressing shared needs and shared frames of reference. The relationships between children and adults achieve this reciprocity only partially because children never can be on a truly equal footing with adults. We must wonder how it is that children, through their autonomous pursuits, eventually will obtain the adult traits that now separate them from this world. We can offer three answers that support the belief that autonomy among children has an important place in curriculum.

First, children work and play at accomplishing what they believe they will (or must) become. The classroom constitutes a microculture that exemplifies a blend between the child's present level of development and the expectations of the adult world. Nothing is more important to children than participating in the adult world, of having its interest, attention, protection, and acceptance. Therefore, even when left to explore their own interests, children in large measure pursue the interests that correspond with our expectations.

Second, autonomy is necessary to development because social coordinations (and all shared knowledge is a social coordination) are, in fact, dependent on autonomy. Each party of the coordination must take the other party into account. They must operate under rules that are particular to their own purpose, understood by the participants and not imposed from without.

Last, social autonomy creates the zone of proximal development. We presented Vygotsky's concept of the zone of proximal development (ZPD) in Chapter 2. Vygotsky used the concept of the ZPD to characterize the social space where the disequilibrating social perpetrations of the world are close enough to the child's level of development that the child can profit developmentally from these disturbances. It is in the zone of proximal development that formal and informal teaching take place because it is only within this zone that what takes place "out there" can affect what takes place "in here" (Vygotsky, 1967). Autonomy in social relations creates a zone of proximal development. Peers share a common level of development, focus, and interest and, therefore, feed one another's development. The perpetrations that originate in peer relationships fit into the zone of proximal development, where problems and tasks that arise in activity between peers present appropriate stimuli to development.

Development, Developmentally Appropriate Practices (DAP), and Play

Historically, early childhood education in the United States has not been a universal experience. In the mid-1960s the U.S. Congress determined that any national effort to break the cycle of poverty would be effective only if it included preschool education. This was the beginning of Head Start, which nearly half a century later continues to provide quality early childhood education to a diverse national population. Additional social forces such as an increase in the number of working mothers contributed to a push to introduce growing numbers of children to early educational experience.

As part of the national move to provide early childhood education to increasing numbers of children, the National Association for the Education of Young Children (NAEYC) was founded. One of its early presidents, Millie Almy, was also one of the first U.S. educators to study with Piaget. Almy conducted studies with U.S. children replicating Piaget's work on Swiss children (Almy, 1967).

As the NAEYC took on an increasingly larger role in representing the educational needs of young children, it began to fashion the specifications for developmentally appropriate educational practices. It also defined "early childhood" as the period from birth to age 8. This was not an arbitrary choice. Piaget's work shows that, even though schooling begins in many countries with children who are 6 or 7 years of age, children of this age are just beginning to reliably use conceptual reasoning to interpret experience. For example, the coordination of concepts such as "some and all," "more and less," "same and different" are still only partially formed in the early childhood years. Consequently, children of this age do not have a very clear understanding of numbers, time, space, causality, history, geometry, geography, classification, seriation, and so on. Although there are critics of Piaget's theories, there is no question about the universal difficulty that children have with these concepts in the early childhood years. The NAEYC believes, as do we, that the character of early childhood development requires specific concerns for the character of early childhood educational practices. These concerns are codified by NAEYC as Developmentally Appropriate Practices.

We embrace developmentally appropriate practice but go further in expressing our belief that play is the central force in early childhood development and that play provides an ideal foundation for the articulation of an integrated and holistic early childhood curriculum. By "integrated" we mean a curriculum where learning outcomes, such as literacy, are embedded throughout the curriculum. By "holistic" we mean a curriculum that addresses the whole child in terms of social, emotional, and intellectual development and the development of competencies and sense of self.

The fact that the early childhood years overlap with the early schooling years does not dissuade us from our belief in the placing of play at the center of the curriculum. We believe that spontaneous play and autonomous activity are critical in the preschool and kindergarten years. We believe that a blend of guided, spontaneous and autonomous play is a valuable curriculum in the early primary grades.

Expectations for Ourselves and Our Children: Academic Standards

Over the last two decades there has been a nationwide effort to develop academic standards for elementary education. More recently this effort has pushed down into the early childhood years. The stated goal has been to provide quality educational experiences for all children. As such, it is a continuation of many of the same forces that ushered in Head Start and other early intervention programs.

Standards are seen as a way of establishing clarity of curriculum content, raising expectations for the achievement of all children, and ensuring accountability for public education (Kendall & Marzano, 2004). We see the push for standards as another potentially great moment in the quest for quality education for all the children in our care. However, as with many opportunities, there are risks as well.

The biggest risk is that many in the educational community will find it challenging to hold onto traditional early childhood educational values and at the same time be accountable to the expectations for academic standards. In particular, how do educators who recognized the value of a play-centered curriculum assure the various stakeholders that they can also satisfy the attainment of academic expectations? Honoring children's choices and interests in an integrated and holistic curriculum can be threatened by demands that teachers didactically teach isolated facts and concepts. This threat can take on draconian proportions in settings where the allocation of resources and the possibilities of a job are tied to accountability in rigid and overdetermined terms. As one teacher recently said regarding "high-stakes" tests, "Under No Child Left Behind, test scores can result in a 'restructured' school. This means the staff is fired. We give a 7-year-old a No. 2 pencil and a test booklet. The bubble sheet determines our fate. This is an astounding burden to place on a 7-year-old" (Brown, 2005, p. B9).

We share this concern and have witnessed many situations where individuals, schools, and even communities have not fared well under the academic standards movement. As noted in Chapter 1, Wien (2004) has provided an account of how eight Canadian teachers faced the imposition of academic standards on their early childhood curriculum. Only two of the eight were able to create an integrated curriculum where they were able to demonstrate having achieved expected outcomes (Wien, 2004).

These successful classrooms were very similar in character to what we have proposed as a play-based curriculum. According to Wien (2004), they were characterized by:

1. Ample time for children and teachers to explore and discover
2. Curriculum content embedded in social activity with maximum opportunities for peer–peer and teacher–child interactions

3. A climate of psychological safety
4. A sense of community
5. A quality of intellectual curiosity and quest for discovery
6. A teaching process that supported complex multiple contexts for learning
7. An openness to emergent processes

Wien also noted that the ability to create these integrated classrooms required the support of the school culture as well as opportunities for teachers to maintain and pursue professional literature and relationships. Wien concludes somewhat pessimistically that without such professional opportunities and support, it may prove too difficult to overcome a linear segmented curriculum, with classroom time managed as a production schedule, with requirements for grading and report cards, and with a prescriptive, mechanistic school culture (Wien, 2004).

Seefeldt (2005) offers a more optimistic view that, although standards could become a barrier to implementing an integrated curriculum, they in fact require a total, integrated curriculum as well as authentic methods of assessment. "If standards are to have a lasting impact on the field of early education, it may be because of this focus on integration" (p. 43). She claims that standards contribute to an implementation of integrated curriculum in at least four ways:

1. Standards grew out of a support for curriculum integration.
2. The large number of standards requires an organization and unification of the curriculum.
3. The "big ideas" identified by standards provide a framework for creating an integrated curriculum.
4. Teaching for thinking and problem solving is common to nearly every set of standards.

We believe that the standards movement offers an increased opportunity to ensure universal quality education and to increase the articulation of an integrated curriculum. In addition, in many instances state educational standards have specified the nature of ideal educational practices and thus give educators guidance in how to provide quality education. However, there will be efforts in some communities and schools to place the burden of accountability on the shoulders of children with the use of standardized measures of isolated facts and demonstrations of knowledge. We believe that such an approach is misguided and potentially harmful in the early childhood years. As Wien (2004) noted, "grades are unfitting metaphors for young children's learning . . . a linear, segmented curriculum in particular shows no knowledge of the rhythms of living of young children" (p. 150).

Among early childhood educators and researchers, there is a growing movement to examine the ways that teaching practices can meet the needs of children as well as meet standards. In *Reaching Standards and Beyond in Kindergarten: Nurturing Children's Sense of Wonder and Joy in Learning,* published by NAEYC, Jacobs and Crowley (2010) respond to the challenge teachers face. Once again, there is a growing wellspring of recognition that childhood should be playful and joyful and that learning must be engaged. (See for example, Bergen, 2006; Copple & Bredekamp, 2009; Elkind, 2007; Honig, 2007; Hyson, 2008; Singer, 2006; Zigler & Bishop-Josef, 2006).

We believe it is our responsibility as early childhood educators to show that a play-centered curriculum can achieve the developmentally appropriate goals we set for our young children. We believe that this is the best articulation of the meaning of play in childhood and society.

SUMMARY AND CONCLUSION

Play is a dominant activity from birth through early adolescence. It is part of all areas of social, emotional, and intellectual growth. Play is a way of understanding the world and of comforting the self. It takes its material from the social world of the child, as well as from the child's inner emotional needs. When we acknowledge the primacy of play, we recognize the primary vehicle in the child's early development.

A privileged relationship exists between autonomous activity and development. Self-directed activity, as opposed to other-directed activity, is essential to development because the dynamics of development involve modifying existing ways of behaving or interpreting to adapt to new challenges. This process of assimilating experience to already established patterns and modifying these to accommodate surprises cannot take place outside the felt needs, tensions, and intuitively directed groping of the child. Hence, activity that is directed by the child is primary in development.

The issue of social autonomy is similar. The social conditions and regulations that children establish outside adult authority are the necessary and primary conditions for social development. This, too, follows from the constructivists' position that social development is an evolution of social coordinations where children are increasingly able to align their respective goals to become partners in joint activity. This coordination and the ensuing reciprocities (how you treat me, I treat you) require autonomy rather than heteronomy (authority imposed from without) because reciprocity requires that the players be on an equal footing.

The work of developmentalists such as Vygotsky, Piaget, Erikson, and Mead make it clear that if children were not self-directed and engaged in autonomous social alliances, they would not develop. This does not mean, however, that adult guidance is not critical to the intellectual, emotional, and social development of the child. As we come to understand the constructivist point of view, we recognize that the guidance we provide must be a condition for growth, and growth in the early childhood years is indistinguishable from play itself.

We end with an optimistic belief that a play-centered curriculum is ultimately the best integrated curriculum for young children and that it can be articulated to meet whatever reasonable and developmentally based standards might be put forward for young children. We must ask ourselves as we put forth our academic expectations and classroom practices whether we are truly engaging with and enhancing our students' intelligence, personality, emotions, competencies, and sense of self. If we are creating an environment that can accomplish these ends, then we can be assured that whatever standards are applied to evaluating our effort, we will be judged to be successful.

Play at the Center of the Curriculum articulates the practical connections between play and our academic, social, and emotional goals for young children. We have treated in detail the possible links between play and traditional curriculum domains such as the visual and performing arts, language and literacy, mathematics, science, and socialization. In each of these chapters we've addressed the features of a play-based curriculum and the kinds of learning one can expect from such a curriculum. We have also devoted a chapter to the use of play in assessing whether children have achieved the goals we have set for them.

In our view, it is meaningless to talk about a developmentally based curriculum without implying a curriculum based on play. Teaching in a play-based and developmentally based curriculum requires knowing what the child knows, where the child's interests and energy lie, and where the child is going. It requires knowing how to engage the child so that the teacher's understanding of the child and the curriculum is developed along with the child's progress in understanding and acquiring skills. Entering into the child's play, by direct or indirect means, allows the teacher to see what the child knows and where the child is headed. Orchestrating play allows the teacher to support the child's progress through further manipulations of the play and nonplay environments. The teacher, rather than being the guardian and administrator of the curriculum, becomes the gardener and architect of the environment, using play as its nutrients and structure.

References

Ackerman, D. (1999). *Deep play*. New York: Random House.

Adams, S., & Wittmer, D. (2001). "I had it first": Teaching young children to solve problems peacefully. *Childhood Education, 78*(1), 10–16.

Ainsworth, M. D., Bell, S. M., & Stayton, D. J. (1974). Infant-mother attachment and social development: "Socialization" as a product of reciprocal responsiveness to signals. In M. M. Richards (Ed.), *The integration of a child into a social world*. London: Cambridge University Press.

Alkon, A., Genevo, J. L., Kaiser, J., Tschann, J. M., Chesney, M. A., & Boyce, W. T. (1994). Injuries in child care centers: Rates, severity, and etiology. *Pediatrics, 94*(6), 1043–1046.

Allen, B. N., & Brown, C. R. (2002). Eddie goes to school: Facilitating play with a child with special needs. In C. R. Brown & C. Marchant (Eds.), *Play in practice: Case studies in young children's play* (pp. 123–132). St. Paul, MN: Redleaf Press.

Almy, M. (1967). *Young children's thinking: Studies of some aspects of Piaget's theory*. New York: Teachers College Press.

Almy, M. (2000). What wisdom should we take with us as we enter the new century? *Young Children, 55*(1), 6–11.

Alper, C. D. (1987). Early childhood music education. In C. Seefeldt (Ed.), *The early childhood curriculum: A review of current research* (pp. 211–236). New York: Teachers College Press.

Alward, K. R. (1995, June). *Play as a primary context for development: The integration of intelligence, personality, competencies, and social consciousness*. Poster presentation at the Annual Meeting of the Jean Piaget Society, Berkeley, CA.

Alward, K. R. (2005, June). *Construction of gender in the doll corner: Thoughts on Piaget's implicit social theory*. Paper for the Annual Meeting of the Jean Piaget Society, Montreal, Quebec, Canada.

American Academy of Pediatrics/Kenneth R. Ginsburg, MD, MS Ed. and the Committee on Communications and Committee on Psychological Aspects of Child and Family Health. (2007). *The importance of play in promoting health child development and maintaining strong parent-child bonds*. Retrieved from: http://www.aap.org/pressroom/playfinal.pdf

American Association for the Advancement of Science, Project 2061. (1993). *Benchmarks for science literacy*. New York: Oxford University Press.

American Psychological Association. (2007). *APA task force report on the sexualization of girls*. Retrieved November 13, 2009, from http://www.apa.org/pi/women/programs/girls/reportfull.pdf

Andersen, S. R. (1998). The trouble with testing. *Young Children, 53*(4), 25–29.

Anderson, W. T. (Ed.). (1995). *The truth about truth*. New York: Jeremy P. Tarcher/Putnam.

Arce, C. (2006). Molting mania: A kindergarten class learns about animals that shed their skin. *Science and Children, 43*, 28–31.

Ardley, J., & Ericson, L. (2002). "We don't play like that here!" Understanding aggressive expressions of play. In C. R. Brown & C. Marchant (Eds.), *Play in practice: Case studies in young children's play* (pp. 35–48). St. Paul, MN: Redleaf Press.

Ariel, S. (2002). *Children's imaginative play: A visit to Wonderland*. Westport, CT: Praeger.

Ashbrook, P. (2006). Roll with it. *Science and Children, 43*, 16.

Ashton-Warner, S. (1963). *Teacher*. New York: Simon & Schuster.

Axline, V. (1969). *Play therapy*. New York: Ballantine.

Ayres, J. (1979). *Sensory integration and the child*. Los Angeles, CA: Western Psychological Services.

Bahktin, M. M. (2006). The problem of speech genres. In A. Jaworski & N. Coupland (Eds.), *The discourse reader* (pp. 123–140). London: Routledge Press.

Balaban, N. (1985). *Starting school: From separation to independence*. New York: Teachers College Press.

Balaban, N. (2006). *Everyday goodbyes: Starting school—a guide for the separation process*. New York: Teachers College Press.

Barbour, A. C. (1999). The impact of playground design on the play behaviors of children with differing levels of physical competence. *Early Childhood Research Quarterly, 14*(1), 75–98.

Barnes, E., & Lehr, R. (2005). Including everyone: A model preschool program for typical and special needs children. In J. P. Roopnarine & J. Johnson (Eds.), *Approaches to early childhood education* (4th ed., pp. 107–124). Upper Saddle River, NJ: Merrill/Prentice Hall.

Baroody, A. J. (2000). Research in review: Mathematics instruction for three- to five-year olds. *Young Children, 55*(4), 61–69.

Bartolini, V. (with Lunn, K.). (2002). "Teacher, they won't let me play!": Strategies for improving inappropriate play behavior. In C. R. Brown & C. Marchant (Eds.), *Play in practice: Case studies in young children's play* (pp. 13–20). St. Paul, MN: Redleaf Press.

Bateson, G. A. (1976). A theory of play and fantasy. In J. S. Bruner, A. Jolly, & K. Sylva (Eds.), *Play: Its role in development and evolution* (pp. 119–129). New York: Basic Books.

Beardsley, L. (1991). *Good day, bad day: The child's experience of child care.* New York: Teachers College Press.

Belkin, L. (2004, September). Is there a place in class for Thomas? What a year of "immersion" can do for a boy—and everyone around him. *New York Times Magazine,* 40.

Bellin, H. F., & Singer, D. G.(2006). My magic story car: Video-based intervention to strengthen emergent literacy of at-risk preschoolers. In D. Singer, K. M. Golenkoff, & R. Hirch-Pasech (Eds.), *Play = learning: How play motivates and enhances children's cognitive and social emotional growth* (pp. 101–123). New York: Oxford University Press.

Bennett, N., Wood, L., & Rogers, S. (1997). *Teaching through play: Teachers' thinking and classroom practice.* Philadelphia, PA: Open University Press.

Benson, J., & Miller, J. L. (2008). Experiences in nature: A pathway to standards. *Young Children, 63,* 22–28.

Bergen, D. (2002). The role of pretend play in children's cognitive development. *Early childhood research and practice, 4*(1), 2–15. Retrieved February 16, 2005, from http://ecrp.uiuc.edu/v4n1/bergen.html

Bergen, D. (2003). Perspectives on inclusion in early childhood education. In J. P. Isenberg & M. R. Jalango (Eds.), *Major trends and issues in early childhood education* (2nd ed., pp. 47–68). New York: Teachers College Press.

Bergen, D. (2006a). Play as a context for humor development. In D. P. Fromberg & D. Bergen (Eds.), *Play from birth to twelve* (2nd ed., pp. 141–155). New York: Taylor & Francis Group.

Bergen, D. (2006b). Reconciling play and assessment standards: How to leave no child behind. In D. P. Fromberg & D. Bergen (Eds.), *Play from birth to twelve* (2nd ed., pp. 233–240). New York: Taylor & Francis Group.

Bergen, D., & Fromberg, D. P. (2006). Epilogue: Emerging and future contexts, perspectives, and meanings for play. In D. P. Fromberg & D. Bergen (Eds.), *Play from birth to twelve* (2nd ed., pp. 417–425). New York: Taylor & Francis Group.

Bergen, D., & Mauer, D. (2000). Symbolic play, phonological awareness, and literacy skills at three age levels. In K. Roskos & J. Christie (Eds.), *Play and literacy in early childhood: Research from multiple perspectives* (pp. 45–62). Mahwah, NJ: Erlbaum.

Bergeron, B. (1990). What does the term whole language mean: A definition from the literature. *Journal of Reading Behavior, 23,* 301–329.

Bers, M. U. (2008). *Blocks to robots: Learning with technology in the early childhood classroom.* New York: Teachers College Press.

Bettelheim, B. (1989). *The uses of enchantment.* New York: Random House.

Blackwell, A. (2008). Worms out of this world! Earthworms excite young students to develop their observation skills. *Science and Children, 46,* 33–35.

Blurton-Jones, N. G. (1972). Categories of child-child interaction. In N. G. Blurton-Jones (Ed.), *Ethnological studies of child behavior* (pp. 97–129). New York: Cambridge University Press.

Bodrova, E., & Leong, D. J. (2003). Chopsticks and counting chips: Do play and foundational skills need to compete for the teacher's attention in an early childhood classroom? *Young Children, 58*(3), 10–17.

Bodrova, E., & Leong, D. J. (2006). Adult influences on play: The Vygotskian approach. In D. P. Fromberg & D. Bergen (Eds.), *Play from birth to twelve* (2nd ed., pp. 167–172). New York: Taylor & Francis Group.

Bodrova, E., & Leong, D. J. (2007). *Tools of the mind: The Vygotskian approach to early childhood education* (2nd ed.). Upper Saddle River, NJ: Pearson Education.

Bourdieu, P. (2006). Language and symbolic power. In A. Jaworski & N. Coupland (Eds.), *The discourse reader* (2nd ed., pp. 480–490). New York: Routledge.

Bowman, B. (2005). Play in the multicultural world of children: Implications for adults. In E. Zigler, D. Singer, & S. Bishop-Josef (Eds.), *Children's play: The roots of reading* (pp. 125–142). Washington, DC: Zero to Three Press.

Bowman, B., & Moore, E. K. (Eds.). (2006). *School readiness and social-emotional development: Perspectives on cultural diversity.* Washington, DC: National Black Child Development Institute, Inc.

Bradford, M., Easterling, N., Mengel, T., & Sullivan, V. (2010). *Play outside! Getting Started: Ten free or inexpensive ideas to enrich your outdoor learning environment today.* North Carolina Outdoor Learning Environment Alliance. Retrieved from http://www.osr.nc.gov/_pdf/Getting%20Started.pdf

Bredekamp, S. (2004). Play and school readiness. In E. Zigler, D. Singer, & S. Bishop-Josef (Eds.), *Children's play: The roots of reading* (pp. 159–174). Washington, DC: Zero to Three Press.

Bredekamp, S., & Copple, C. (Eds.). (1997). *Developmentally appropriate practice in early childhood programs* (rev. ed.). Washington, DC: National Association for the Education of Young Children.

Bretherton, I. (1984). *Symbolic play: The development of social understanding.* New York: Academic Press.

Bronson, M. (2000). Research in review: Recognizing and supporting the development of self-regulation in young children. *Young Children, 55*(2), 32–37.

Bronson, W. (1995). *The right stuff for children from birth to 8: Selecting play materials to support development.* Washington, DC: National Association for the Education of Young Children.

Brown, C. R., & Marchant, C. (Eds.). (2002). *Play in practice: Case studies in young children's play.* St. Paul, MN: Redleaf Press.

Brown, L. K. (1986). *Taking advantage of media: A manual for parents and teachers.* Boston: Routledge & Kegan Paul.

Brown, P. W. (2005, October 6). Assessing kids' progress at school: Testing isn't teaching. *San Francisco Chronicle,* p. B9.

Brown, S. (2009). *Play: How it shapes the brain, opens the imagination, and invigorates the soul.* New York: Penguin Group.

Bruner, J. S. (1963). *The process of education.* Cambridge, MA: Harvard University Press.

Bruner, J. S. (1976). The nature and uses of immaturity. In J. S. Bruner, A. Jolly, & K. Sylva (Eds.), *Play: Its role in development and evolution* (pp. 28–64). New York: Basic Books.

Bruner, J. S. (1986). *Actual minds, possible worlds.* Cambridge, MA: Harvard University Press.

Bruner, J. S. (1990). *Acts of meaning.* Cambridge, MA: Harvard University Press.

Buchannan, M., & Johnson, T. C. (2009). A second look at the play of young children with disabilities. *American Journal of Play, 2*(1), 41–59.

Burdette, H., & Whitaker, R. (2005). Resurrecting free play in young children: Looking beyond fitness and fatness to attention, affiliation, and affect. *Archives of Pediatrics & Adolescent Medicine, 159*(1), 46–50.

Burkhour, C. (2005). Introduction to playground. Chicago, IL: National Center on Physical Activity and Disability. Retrieved October 12, 2005, from http://www.ncpad.org/fun/fact_sheet.php?sheet=9&view=all

Cameron, A., Hersch, S. B., & Fosnot, C. T. (2004). *Young mathematicians at work: Constructing number sense, addition, and subtraction.* Portsmouth, NH: Heinemann.

Campbell, A. (2009). Honeybees, butterflies, and ladybugs: Partners to plants. *Science and Children, 46,* 29–33.

Carlsson-Paige, N., & Levin, D. E. (1998). *Before push comes to shove: Building conflict resolution skills with young children.* St. Paul, MN: Redleaf Press.

Carlsson-Paige, N. (2008). *Taking back childhood: Helping your kids thrive in a fast-paced, media-saturated, violence-filled world.* New York: Hudson Street Press.

Carlsson-Paige, N., & Levin, D. E. (1990). *Who's calling the shots?* Santa Cruz, CA: New Society Publishers.

Casey, B. (2004). Mathematics problem-solving adventures: A language-arts-based supplementary series for early childhood that focuses on special sense. In D. H. Clements & J. Sarama (Eds.), *Engaging young children in mathematics: Standards for early childhood mathematics education* (pp. 377–392). Mahwah, NJ: Erlbaum.

Cazden, C. B. (1983). Adult assistance to language development: Scaffolds, models and direct instruction. In R. P. Parker & F. A. Davis (Eds.), *Developing literacy: Young children's use of language* (pp. 3–18). Newark, DE: International Reading Association.

Chalufour, I., & Worth, K. (2003). *Discovering nature with young children.* St. Paul, MN: Readleaf Press.

Chalufour, I., & Worth, K. (2004). *Building structures with young children.* St. Paul, MN: Readleaf Press.

Chalufour, I., & Worth, K. (2006). Science in kindergarten. In D. Gullo (Ed.), *K today: Teaching and learning in the kindergarten year* (pp. 95–106). Washington, DC: National Association for the Education of Young Children.

Chartrand, M. M., Frank, D.A., White, L. F., & Shope, T. R. (2008). Effect of parents' wartime deployment on the behavior of young children in military families. *Archives of Pediatric and Adolescent Medicine, 162,* 1009–1014.

Chen, J., Krechevsky, M., Viens, J., & Isberg, E. (1998). *Building on children's strengths: The experience of Project Spectrum* (Vol. 1). New York: Teachers College Press.

Christie, D. J., Wagner, R. V., & Winter, D. D. (2001). *Peace, conflict, and violence: Peace psychology for the 21st century.* Upper Saddle River, NJ: Prentice Hall.

Christie, J. F. (2006). Play as a medium for literacy development. In D. P. Fromberg & D. Bergen (Eds.), *Play from birth to twelve* (2nd ed., pp. 181–186). New York: Taylor & Francis Group.

Christie, J. F., & Roskos, K. A. (2006). Standards, science, and the role of play in early literacy education. In D. Singer, K. M. Golenkoff, & R. Hirch-Pasech (Eds.), *Play = learning: How play motivates and enhances children's cognitive and social emotional growth* (pp. 57–73). New York: Oxford University Press.

Clark, C. D. (2007). Therapeutic advantages of play. In A. Göncü & S. Gaskins (Eds.), *Play and development* (pp. 275–293). New York: Erlbaum, Taylor & Francis Group.

Clawson, M. (2002). Play of language minority children in an early childhood setting. In J. L. Roopnarine

(Ed.), *Conceptual, social-cognitive, and contextual issues in the fields of play: Play and culture studies* (Vol. 4, pp. 93–110). Westport, CT: Ablex Publishing.

Clay, M. (1966). *Emergent reading behaviors.* Unpublished doctoral dissertation. Auckland, New Zealand.

Clayton, M., & Forton, M. B. (2001). *Classroom spaces that work.* Greenfield, MA: Northeast Foundation for Children.

Clements, D. H., & Sarama, J. (Eds.). (2004). *Engaging young children in mathematics: Standards for early childhood mathematics education.* Mahwah, NJ: Erlbaum.

Clements, D. H., & Sarama, J. (2008). Focal points—pre-K to kindergarten. *Teaching Children Mathematics, 14,* 361–365.

Clements, D. H., & Sarama, J. (2009). *Learning and teaching early math: The learning trajectories approach.* New York: Routledge.

Cochran-Smith, M., & Lytle, S. L. (1993). *Inside/outside: Teacher research and knowledge.* New York: Teachers College Press.

Consumers Product Safety Improvement Act. (2008). Retrieved from http://en.wikipedeia.org/wiki/consumer/product_safety_improvement_act

Cook-Gumperz, J. (1986). *The social construction of literacy.* New York: Cambridge University Press.

Cook-Gumperz, J., & Corsaro, W. (1977). Social-ecological constraints on children's communication strategies. *Sociology, 11,* 412–434.

Cook-Gumperz, J., Corsaro, W., & Streeck, J. (Eds.). (1996). *Children's worlds and children's language.* Berlin: Mouton de Gruyter.

Cook-Gumperz, J., Gates, D., Scales, B., & Sanders, H. (1976). *Toward an understanding of angel's hair: Summary of a pilot study of a nursery play yard.* Unpublished manuscript, University of California, Berkeley.

Cook-Gumperz, J., & Gumperz, J. (1982). Introduction: Language and social identity. In J. Gumperz (Ed.), *Language and social identity* (Vol. 2, pp. 1–2). Cambridge, UK: Cambridge University Press.

Cook-Gumperz, J., & Scales, B. (1982). *Toward an understanding of angel's hair: Report on a study of children's communication in socio-dramatic play.* Unpublished manuscript.

Cook-Gumperz, J., & Scales, B. (1996). Girls, boys and just people: The interactional accomplishment of gender in the discourse of the nursery school. In D. Slobin, J. Gerhardt, A. Kyratzis, & J. Guo (Eds.), *Social interaction, social context, and language* (pp. 513–527). Mahwah, NJ: Erlbaum.

Cooney, M. (2004). Is play important? Guatemalan kindergartners' classroom experiences and their parents' and teachers' perceptions of learning through play. *Journal of Research in Childhood Education, 18*(4), 261–277.

Cooper, R. M. (1999, January/February). "But they are only playing": Interpreting play to parents. *Child Care Information Exchange.*

Coplan, R. J., Rubin, K. H., & Findlay, L. C. (2006). Social and nonsocial play. In D. P. Fromberg & D. Bergen (Eds.), *Play from birth to twelve* (2nd ed., pp. 75–86). New York: Taylor & Francis Group.

Copley, J. V. (2000). *The young child and mathematics.* Washington, DC: National Council for the Education of Young Children; Reston, VA: National Council of Teachers of Mathematics.

Copley, J. V., Jones, C., & Dighe, J. (2007). *Mathematics: The creative curriculum approach.* Washington, DC: Teaching Strategies.

Copple, C., & Bredekamp, S. (Eds.). (2009). *Developmentally appropriate practice in early childhood programs: Serving children from birth through age 8* (3rd ed.). Washington, DC: National Association for the Education of Young Children.

Corsaro, W. A. (1979). We're friends, right? Children's use of access rituals in a nursery school. *Language in Society, 8,* 315–336.

Corsaro, W. A. (1985). *Friendship and peer culture in the early years.* Norwood, NJ: Ablex.

Corsaro, W. A. (1997). *The sociology of childhood.* Thousand Oaks, CA: Pine Forge Press.

Corsaro, W. A. (2003). *We're friends, right?: Inside kids' culture.* Washington, DC: The Joseph Henry Press.

Corsaro, W. A., & Elder, D. (1990). Children's peer cultures. *Annual Review of Sociology, 16,* 197–220.

Corsaro, W. A., & Miller, P. (Eds.). (1992). Interpretive approaches to children's socialization. In W. Damon (Chief Editor), New directions for child development (Issue 58). San Francisco, CA: Jossey-Bass Publishers.

Corsaro, W. A., & Molinari, L. (2005). *I compagni: Understanding children's transition from preschoool to elementary school.* New York: Teachers College Press.

Corsaro, W. A., & Schwartz, K. (1991). Peer play and socialization in two cultures: Implications for research and practice. In B. Scales, M. Almy, A. Nicolopoulou, & S. Ervin-Tripp (Eds.), *Play and the social context of development in early care and education* (pp. 234–254). New York: Teachers College Press.

Cortés, C. (2000). *The children are watching: How the media teach about diversity.* New York: Teachers College Press.

Creasey, G. L., Jurvis, P. A., & Berk, L. E. (1998). Play and social competence. In O. N. Saracho & B. Spodek (Eds.). *Multiple perspectives on play in early childhood education* (pp. 116–143). Albany, NY: SUNY Press.

Cross, C. T., Woods, T. A., & Schweingruber, H.(Eds.). (2009). *Mathematics learning in early childhood: Paths toward excellence and equity.* Washington, DC: National Academies Press.

Cryer, D., Harms, T., & Riley, C. (2003, 2006). *All about the ECERS-R.* Lewisville, NC: Kaplan PACT House Publishing.

Csikszentmihalyi, M. (1993). *The evolving self: A psychology for the third millennium.* New York: HarperCollins.

Curran, J. M. (1999). Constraints of pretend play; implicit and explicit rules. *Journal of Research in Childhood Education, 14*(1), 47–55.

Curtis, D., & Carter, M. (2003). *Designs for living and learning: Transforming early childhood environments.* St. Paul, MN: Redleaf Press.

Danisa, D., Gentile, J., McNamara, K., Pinney, M., Ross, S., & Rule, A. (2006). Geoscience for preschoolers: These integrated math and science activities for young children really rock! *Science and Children, 44,* 30–33.

Davidson, J. (1998). Language and play: Natural partners. In D. Fromberg & D. Bergen (Eds.), *Play from birth to twelve and beyond: Contexts, perspectives, and meanings* (pp. 175–184). New York: Garland.

Davidson, J. I. F. (2006). Language and play: Natural partners. In D. P. Fromberg & D. Bergen (Eds.), *Play from birth to twelve* (2nd ed., pp. 31–40). New York: Taylor & Francis Group.

Davydov, V. V. (1995). The influence of L. S. Vygotsky on education theory, research, and practice. *Educational Researcher, 24*(3), 12–21.

DeBey, M., & Bombard, D. (2007). Expanding children's boundaries: An approach to second-language learning and cultural understanding. *Young Children, 62,* 88–93.

DeBord, K., Hestenes, L., Moore, R., Cosco, N., & McGinnis, J. (2005). *Preschool outdoor environment measurement scale (POEMS).* Kaplan Early Learning Company. Retrieved from http://www.poemsnc.org/poems.html

Delpit, L. (1995). *Other people's children.* Boston: Harvard University Press.

DeMarie, D., & Ethridge, E. A. (2006). Children's images of preschool: The power of photography. *Journal of the National Association for the Education of Young Children, 61*(1), 101–104.

Derman-Sparks, L., & ABC Task Force. (1989). *The antibias curriculum: Tools for empowering young children.* Washington, DC: National Association for the Education of Young Children.

Derman-Sparks, L., & Edwards, J. O. (2010). *Anti-bias education for young children and ourselves.* Washington, DC: National Association for the Education of Young Children.

Derman-Sparks, L., & Ramsey, P. (2005). A framework for culturally relevant, multicultural, and antibias education in the twenty-first century. In J. P. Roopnarine & J. Johnson (Eds.), *Approaches to early childhood education* (4th ed., pp. 107–124). Upper Saddle River, NJ: Merrill/Prentice Hall.

Desjean-Perotta, B., & Barbour, A. C. (2001). The prop box: Helping preservice teachers understand the value of dramatic play. *Journal of the National Forum of Teacher Education, 12*(1), 3–15.

DeVries, R. (2006). Games with rules. In D. P. Fromberg & D. Bergen (Eds.), *Play from birth to twelve* (2nd ed., pp. 119–125). New York: Taylor & Francis Group.

DeVries, R., & Zan, B. (1994). *Moral classrooms, moral children: Creating a constructivist atmosphere in early education.* New York: Teachers College Press.

DeVries, R., & Zan, B. (1996). Assessing interpersonal understanding in the classroom context. *Childhood Education, 72*(50), 265–268.

DeVries, R., & Zan, B. (2005). A constructivist perspective on the role of the sociomoral atmosphere in promoting children's development. In C. T. Fosnot (Ed.), *Constructivism: Theory, perspectives, and practice* (2nd ed., pp. 132–149). New York: Teachers College Press.

DeVries, R., Zan, B., Hildebrandt, C., Edmiaston, R., & Sales, C. (2002). *Developing constructivist early childhood curriculum: Practical principles and activities.* New York: Teachers College Press.

Dimensions Educational Research Foundation & Arbor Day Foundation. (2007). Learning with nature idea book: Creating nurturing outdoor spaces for children, field-tested principles for effective outdoor learning environments. Environment Today. North Carolina Outdoor Learning Environment Alliance. *Exchange, 10,* 1–3.

Dominick, A., & Clark, F. B. (1996). Using games to understand children's understanding. *Childhood Education, 72*(5), 286–288.

Drew, W. E., Christie, J., Johnson, J. E., Meckley, A. M., & Nell, M. L. (2008). Constructive play: A value-added strategy for meeting early learning standards. *Young Children, 63,* 38–44.

Duckworth, E. (1996). *"The having of wonderful ideas" and other essays on teaching and learning* (2nd ed.). New York: Teachers College Press.

Duckworth, E. (2001). *"Tell me more": Listening to learners.* New York: Teachers College Press.

Dyson, A. H. (1993). *Social worlds of children learning to write in an urban primary school.* New York: Teachers College Press.

Dyson, A. H. (1994). *The ninjas, the X-men, and the ladies: Playing with power and identity in an urban primary school* (Technical Report No. 70). Berkeley, CA: University of California, National Center for the Study of Writing.

Dyson, A. H. (1995, April). *The courage to write: The ideological dimensions of child writing.* Paper presented at the Annual Meeting of the American Educational Research Association, San Francisco, CA.

Dyson, A. H. (1997). *Writing superheroes: Contemporary childhood, popular culture, and classroom literacy.* New York: Teachers College Press.

Dyson, A. H. (2003). *The brothers and sisters learn to write: Popular literacies in childhood and school cultures.* New York: Teachers College Press.

Dyson, A. H., & Genishi, C. (Eds.). (1994). *The need for story: Cultural diversity in classroom and community.* Urbana, IL: National Council of Teachers of English.

Edwards, C., Gandini, L., & Forman, G. (Eds.). (1993). *The hundred languages of children: The Reggio Emilia approach to early childhood education.* Norwood, NJ: Ablex.

Egan, K. (1988). *Primary understanding: Education in early childhood.* New York: Routledge.

Einarsdottir, J. (2000). Incorporating literacy resources into the play curriculum of two Icelandic preschools. In K. Roskos & J. Christie (Eds.), *Play and literacy in early childhood: Research from multiple perspectives* (pp. 77–90). Mahwah, NJ: Erlbaum.

Eisenhauer, M. J., & Feikes, D. (2009). Dolls, blocks, and puzzles: Playing with mathematical understandings. *Young Children, 64,* 18–24.

Eisert, D., & Lamorey, S. (1996). Play as a window on child development: The relationship between play and other developmental domains. *Early Education and Development, 7*(3), 221–235.

Elgas, P. M., & Peltier, M. B. (1998). Jimmy's journey: Building a sense of community and self-worth through small-group work. *Young Children, 53*(2), 17–21.

Elkind, D. (1990). Academic pressure—too much, too soon: The demise of play. In E. Klugman & S. Smilansky (Eds.), *Children's play and learning: Perspectives and policy implications* (pp. 3–17). New York: Teachers College Press.

Elkind, D. (2003). Thanks for the memory: The lasting value of play. *Young Children, 58*(3), 46–51.

Elkind, D. (2007). *The power of play: Learning what comes naturally.* Philadelphia, De Capo Press.

Ellis, M. (1988). Play and the origin of species. In D. Bergen (Ed.), *Play as a medium for learning and development* (pp. 23–26). Portsmouth, NH: Heinemann.

Emihovich, C. (1990). Technocentrism revisited: Computer literacy as cultural capital. *Theory into Practice, 29*(4), 227–234.

Ensign, J. (2003). Including culturally relevant math in an urban school. *Educational Studies, 34*(4), 414–423.

Epstein, A., Schweinhart, L., DeBruin-Parecki, A., & Robin, K. (2004, July). *Preschool assessment: A guide to developing a balanced approach.* New Brunswick, NJ: National Institute for Early Education Research.

Erickson, F. (1985). *Toward a theory of student status as socially constructed.* Occasional Paper No. 88. Institute for Research on Teaching, College of Education, Michigan State University, East Lansing, MI.

Erickson, F. (1993). Foreword. In M. Cochran-Smith & S. L. Lytle (Eds.), *Inside/outside: Teacher research and knowledge.* New York: Teachers College Press.

Erickson, F. (2004). *Talk and social theory: Ecologies of speaking and listening in everyday life.* Malden, MA: Blackwell.

Erikson, E. (1950/1985). *Childhood and society.* New York: Norton.

Erikson, E. (1977). *Toys and reasons.* New York: Norton.

Erwin, E. J. (1993). Social participation of young children with visual impairments in specialized and integrated environments. *Journal of Visual Impairment & Blindness, 87*(5), 138–142.

Espinosa, L. M. (2006). Social, cultural, and linguistic features of school readiness in young Latino children. In B. Bowman & E. K. Moore (Eds.), *School readiness and social-emotional development: Perspectives on cultural diversity* (pp. 33–47). Washington, DC: National Black Child Development Institute, Inc.

Espinosa, L. M. (2010). *Getting it right for young children from diverse backgrounds: Applying research to improve practice.* Upper Saddle River, NJ: Pearson Education.

Fantuzzo, J., Sutton-Smith, B., Coolahan, K. C., Manz, P. H., Canning, S., & Debnam, D. (1995). Assessment of preschool play interaction behaviors in low income children: Penn Interactive Peer Play Scale. *Early Childhood Research Quarterly, 10,* 105–120.

Farver, J. (1992). Communicating shared meaning in social pretend play. *Early Childhood Research Quarterly, 7*(40), 501–516.

Fein, G. G. (1981). Pretend play in childhood: An integrative review. *Child Development, 52,* 1095–1118.

Fein, G. G., Ardeila-Ray, A., & Groth, L. (2000). The narrative connection: Stories and literacy. In K. Roskos & J. Christie (Eds.), *Play and literacy in early childhood: Research from multiple perspectives* (pp. 27–43). Mahwah, NJ: Erlbaum.

Fein, S. (1984). *Heidi's horse* (2nd ed.). Pleasant Hill, CA: Exelrod Press.

Ferguson, C. (2001). Discovering, supporting, and promoting young children's passions and interests: One teacher's reflections. *Young Children, 56*(4), 6–11.

Fisman, L. (2001). *Child's play: An empirical study of the relationship between the physical form of school yards and children's behavior.* Retrieved September 18, 2005, from http://www.yale.edu/nixon/research/pdf/LFisman_Playgrounds.pdf

Forman, G. (1998). Constructive play. In D. P. Fromberg & D. Bergen (Eds.), *Play from birth to twelve and beyond: Contexts, perspectives, and meanings* (pp. 393–400). New York: Garland.

Forman, G. (2005). The project approach in Reggio Emilia. In C. T. Fosnot (Ed.). *Constructivism: Theory, perspectives, and practice* (2nd ed., pp. 212–221). New York: Teachers College Press.

Forman, G. E., & Kaden, M. (1987). Research on science education for young children. In C. Seefeldt (Ed.), *The early childhood curriculum: A review of current research* (pp. 141–164). New York: Teachers College Press.

Forman, G. E., & Kuschner, D. S. (1977). *The child's construction of knowledge: Piaget for teaching children.* Belmont, CA: Wadsworth.

Fosnot, C. T., & Dolk, M. (2001). *Young mathematicians at work: Constructing number sense, addition, and subtraction.* Portsmouth, NH: Heinemann.

Frazel, M. (2010). Excerpted from Digital Storytelling. Retrieved May 24, 2010 from http://www.iste.org/source/orders/excerpts/digsto.pdf

Fromberg, D. P. (1999). A review of research on play. In C. Seefeldt (Ed.), *The early child curriculum: Current findings in theory and practice* (3rd ed., pp. 27–53). New York: Teachers College Press.

Fromberg, D. P. (2002). *Play and meaning in early childhood education.* Boston: Allyn & Bacon.

Fromberg, D. P., & Bergen, D. (Eds.). (2007). *Play from birth to twelve: Contexts, perspectives, and meanings* (2nd ed.). New York: Routledge, Taylor & Francis.

Frost, J. L. (2007). Playground checklist. In J. L. Frost, S. Wortham, & S. Reifel (Eds.), *Play and child development* (3rd ed., pp. 394–398). Upper Saddle River, NJ: Pearson.

Frost, J. L., Brown, P., Sutterby, J. A., & Thornton, C. D. (2004). *The developmental benefits of playgrounds.* Olney, MD: Association for Childhood Education International.

Frost, J. L., Shin, D., & Jacobs, P. (1998). Physical environments and children's play. In O. Saracho & B. Spodek (Eds.), *Multiple perspectives on play in early childhood education* (pp. 255–294). Albany: SUNY Press.

Frost, J. L., & Woods, I. C. (2006). Perspectives on playgrounds. In D. P. Fromberg & D. Bergen (Eds.), *Play from birth to twelve* (2nd ed., pp. 331–342). New York: Taylor & Francis Group.

Frost, J. L., Wortham, S. C., & Reifel, S. (2005). *Play and child development* (2nd ed.). Upper Saddle River, NJ: Merrill/Prentice Hall.

Frost, J. L., Wortham, S. C., & Reifel, S. (2008). *Play and child development* (3rd ed.). Upper Saddle River, NJ: Pearson/Merrill Prentice Hall.

Full Option Science System (FOSS). (2005a). *Air and weather.* Hudson, NH: Delta Education, Inc.

Full Option Science System (FOSS). (2005b). *Balance and motion.* Hudson, NH: Delta Education, Inc.

Full Option Science System (FOSS). (2005c). *Pebbles, sand, and silt.* Hudson, NH: Delta Education, Inc.

Furth, H. G. (1970). *Piaget for teachers.* Upper Saddle River, NJ: Prentice Hall.

Gallas, K. (1997). *Sometimes I can be anything: Power, gender, and identity in a primary classroom.* New York: Teachers College Press.

Gallas, K. (2003). *Imagination and literacy: A teacher's search for the heart of meaning.* New York: Teachers College Press.

Gandini, L., Hill, L., Cadwell, L., & Schwall, C. (2005). *In the spirit of the studio: Learning from the atelier of Reggio Emilia.* New York: Teachers College Press.

Gardner, H. (1993). *Frames of mind: The theory of multiple intelligence.* New York: Basic Books.

Gardner, H. (1999). *Intelligence reformed: Multiple intelligences for the 21st century.* New York: Basic Books.

Garvey, C. (1990/1977). *Play.* Cambridge, MA: Harvard University Press.

Garvey, C., & Berndt, R. (1977). Organization of pretend play (JSAS Catalogue of Selected Documents in Psychology, Manuscript 1589). Washington, DC: American Psychological Association.

Gaskins, S., Haight, W., & Lancy, D. F. (2007). The cultural construction of play. In A. Göncü & S. Gaskins (Eds.), *Play and development* (pp. 179–202). New York: Erlbaum, Taylor & Francis Group.

Gaskins, S., Miller, P., & Corsaro, W. (1992). Theoretical and methodological perspectives in the interpretive study of children. *New Directions in Child Development, 58,* 5–23.

Gee, K. (2000). *Visual arts as a way of knowing.* York, ME: Stenhouse Publishers.

Geist, K., & Geist, E. A. (2008). Do re me, 1-2-3: That's how easy math can be—using music to support emergent mathematics. *Young Children, 63,* 20–25.

Genishi, C. (2002, July). Young English language learners: Resourceful in the classroom. *Young Children, 57*(4), 66–72.

Genishi, C., & DiPaolo, M. (1982). Learning through argument in preschool. In L. C. Wilkonson (Ed.), *Communicating in the classroom* (pp. 49–68). New York: Academic Press.

Genishi, C., & Dyson, A. H. (1984). *Language assessment in the early years.* Norwood, NJ: Ablex.

Genishi, C., & Dyson, A. H. (2005). *On the case: Approaches to language and literacy research.* New York: Teachers College Press and National Conference on Research in Language and Literacy.

Genishi, C., & Dyson, A. H. (Eds.). (2009). *Children, language and literacy: Diverse learners in diverse times.* New York: Teachers College Press.

Genishi, C., & Goodwin, A. L. (2008). *Diversity in early childhood education: Rethinking and doing.* New York: Routledge.

Genishi, C., Huang, S., & Glupczynski, T. (2005). Becoming early childhood teachers: Linking action research and postmodern theory in a language and literacy course. *Advances in Early Education and Day Care, 14,* 161–192.

Ghafouri, F., & Wien, C. A. (2005). Give us privacy: Play and social literacy in young children. *Journal of Research in Childhood Education, 19*(4), 279–291.

Giddens, A. (2000). *Runaway world: How globalization is reshaping our lives.* New York: Routledge.

Giffin, H. (1984). The coordination of meaning in the creation of a shared make-believe reality. In I. Bretherton (Ed.), *Symbolic play: The development of social understanding* (pp. 73–100). New York: Academic Press.

Ginsburg, H. P. (2006). Mathematical play and playful mathematics. In D. G. Singer, R. M. Golinkoff, & K. Hirsh-Pasek (Eds.). *Play = learning: How play motivates and enhances children's cognitive and social-emotional growth* (pp. 145–167). New York: Oxford University Press.

Ginsburg, H. P., Inoue, N., & Seo, K. H. (1999). Young children doing mathematics: Observations of everyday activities. In J. V. Copley (Ed.), *Mathematics in the early years* (pp. 88–100). Reston, VA: National Council of Teachers of Mathematics; Washington, DC: National Association for the Education of Young Children.

Goffman, E. (1974). *Frame analysis.* New York: Harper & Row.

Goffman, E. (2000). On face-work: An analysis of ritual elements in social interaction. In A. Jaworski & N. Coupland (Eds.), *The discourse reader* (pp. 306–320). London: Routledge.

Goleman, D. (1995). *Emotional intelligence.* New York: Bantam Books.

Golomb, C., Gowing, E. D., & Friedman, L. (1982). Play and cognition: Studies of pretense play and conservation of quantity. *Journal of Experimental Child Psychology, 33,* 257–279.

Göncü, A. (1993). Development of intersubjectivity in the dyadic play of preschoolers. *Early Childhood Research Quarterly, 8,* 99–116.

Göncü, A., Jain, J., & Tuermer, U. (2007). Children's play as cultural interpretation. In A. Göncü & S. Gaskins (Eds.), *Play and development* (pp. 155–178). New York: Erlbaum, Taylor & Francis Group.

Gonzalez-Mena, J. (1998). *The child in the family and the community.* Upper Saddle River, NJ: Merrill/Prentice Hall.

Gonzalez-Mena, G. (2008). *Diversity in early care and education: Honoring differences* (5th ed.). Washington, DC: National Association for the Education of Young Children.

Goodenough, E. (Ed.). (2003). *Secret spaces of childhood.* Ann Arbor: University of Michigan Press.

Goodnow, J. (1977). *Children drawing.* Cambridge, MA: Harvard University Press.

Goodwin, M. (1990). *He-said-she-said: Talk as social organization among black children.* Bloomington, IN: Indiana University Press.

Gowen, J. W. (1995). Research and review: Early development of symbolic play. *Young Children, 50*(3), 75–83.

Graue, E. (2001). Research in review: What's going on in the children's garden? Kindergarten today. *Young Children, 56*(3), 67–73.

Graue, E., & Diperna, J. (2000). Redshirting and early retention: Who gets the "gift of time" and what are its outcomes? *American Educational Research Journal, 37*(2), 509–534.

Graves, D. (1983). *Writing: Teachers and children at work.* Exeter, NH: Heineman.

Great Explorations in Mathematics and Science (GEMS). (1996). *Ant homes under ground.* Berkeley, CA: Regents, University of California, Berkeley.

Great Explorations in Mathematics and Science (GEMS). (1997). *Treasure boxes.* Berkeley, CA: Regents, University of California, Berkeley.

Green, M. (2006). Social and emotional development in the zero-to-three child: A systems change approach. In B. Bowman & E. K. Moore (Eds.), *School readiness and social-emotional development: Perspectives on cultural diversity* (pp. 89–98). Washington, DC: National Black Child Development Institute, Inc.

Greenes, C., Ginsburg, H. P., & Balfanz, R. (2004). Big math for little kids. *Early Childhood Research Quarterly, 19,* 173–180.

Greenman, J. (2005, May). Places for childhood in the 21st century: A conceptual framework. *Young Children, Beyond the Journal.* Retrieved September 16, 2005, from http://www.journal.naeyc.org/btj/200505/01Greenman.asp

Griffin, E. (1998). *Island of childhood: Education in the special world of the nursery school.* Troy, NY: Educators International Press.

Griffin, S. (2004). Number worlds: A research-based mathematics program for young children. In D. H. Clements & J. Sarama (Eds.), *Engaging young children in mathematics: Standards for early childhood mathematics education* (pp. 325–342). Mahwah, NJ: Erlbaum.

Gross, M. G. (2006). The role of play in assessment. In D. P. Fromberg & D. Bergen (Eds.), *Play from birth to twelve* (2nd ed., pp. 223–231). New York: Taylor & Francis Group.

Gullo, D. (2006). Assessment in kindergarten. In D. Gullo (Ed.), *K today: Teaching and learning in the kindergarten year* (pp. 138–150). Washington, DC: National Association for the Education of Young Children.

Gumperz, J. J., & Cook-Gumperz, J. (1982). Introduction: Language and the communication of social identity. In J. J. Gumperz & J. Cook-Gumperz (Eds.), *Language and social identity* (pp. 1–21). Cambridge, UK: Cambridge University Press.

Gustafson, S. C. (2000). *Educating for peace and nonviolence in early childhood.* Unpublished manuscript.

Hachey, A. C., & Butler, D. L. (2009). Seeds in the window, soil in the sensory table: Science education through gardening and nature-based play. *Young Children, 64,* 4248.

Haight, W., Black, J., Ostler, T., & Sheridan, K. (2006). Pretend play and emotion learning in traumatized mothers and children. In D. G. Singer, R. M. Golinkoff, & K. Hirsh-Pasek (Eds.), *Play = learning: How play motivates and enhances children's cognitive and social-emotional growth* (pp. 209–230). New York: Oxford University Press.

Haines, S., & Kilpatrick, C. (2007). Environmental education saves the day: Becoming a Project Learning Tree (PLT)-certified school unified facility, boosted student achievement, and saved one school from closure. *Science and Children, 44,* 42–47.

Hamilton, B. (2007). *It's elementary! Integrating technology in the primary grades.* Washington, DC: International Society for Technology Education.

Hand, H., & Nourot, P. M. (1999). *First class: Guide to early primary education.* Sacramento, CA: California Department of Education.

Hanline, M. F., & Fox, L. (1993). Learning within the context of play: Providing typical early childhood experiences for children with severe disabilities. *The Journal of the Association for Persons with Severe Handicaps, 18*(2), 121–129.

Harms, T. (1969). *My art is me* [Motion picture]. Berkeley, CA: University of California Extension Media Center.

Harms, T., Clifford, R. M., & Cryer, D. (1998). *Early childhood environmental rating scale* (rev. ed.). New York: Teachers College Press.

Harms, T., Clifford, R. M., & Cryer, D. (2004). *Early childhood environment rating scale* (rev. ed.). New York: Teachers College Press. Retrieved from http://www.osr.nc.gov/_pdf/Getting%20Started.pdf

Harms, T., Jacobs, E. V., & White, D. R. (1996). *School-age care environment rating scale.* New York: Teachers College Press.

Harris, M. E. (2009). Implementing portfolio assessment. *Journal of the National Association for the Education of Young Children, 64*(3), 82–85.

Hartmann, W., & Rollett, B. (1994). Play: Positive intervention in the elementary school curriculum. In J. Hellendoorn, R. van der Kooij, & B. Sutton-Smith (Eds.), *Play and intervention* (pp. 195–202). Albany: SUNY Press.

Heath, S. B. (1983). *Ways with words: Language, life and work in communities and classrooms.* New York: Cambridge University Press.

Heath, S. B., & Mangiola, L. (1991). *Children of promise: Literate activity in linguistically and culturally diverse classrooms.* Washington, DC: National Education Association.

Heathcote, D. (1997). *Three looms waiting.* Berkeley, CA: University of California Media Center.

Heathcote, D., & Bolton, G. (1995). *Drama for learning: Dorothy Heathcote's mantle of the expert approach to education.* Portsmouth, NH: Heinemann.

Heathcote, D., & Herbert, P. (1985, Summer). A drama of meaning: Mantle of the expert. *Theory into Practice, 24*(3), 173–179.

Helm, J. H., Beneke, S., & Steinheimer, K. (1998). *Windows on learning: Documenting young children's work.* New York: Teachers College Press.

Helm, J. H., & Katz, L. (2001). *Young investigators: The project approach in the early years.* New York: Teachers College Press.

Henderson, F., & Jones, E. (2002). "Everytime they get started, we interrupt them": Children with special needs at play. In C. R. Brown & C. Marchant (Eds.), *Play in practice: Case studies in young children's play* (pp. 133–146). St. Paul, MN: Redleaf Press.

Hendrick, J. (1997). *First steps toward teaching the Reggio way.* Upper Saddle River, NJ: Merrill/ Prentice Hall.

Hendrickson, J. M., Strain, P. S., Trembley, A., & Shores, R. E. (1981). Relationship between a material use and the occurrence of social interactive behaviors by normally developing preschool children. *Psychology in the Schools, 18,* 500–504.

Hesse, P., & Lane, F. (2003). Media literacy starts young: An integrated curriculum approach. *Young Children, 58*(4), 20–26.

Hirsh-Pasek, K. Golinkoff, R. M., Berk, L. E., & Singer, D. G. (2009). *A mandate for playful learning in preschool: Presenting the evidence.* New York: Oxford University Press.

Hobbs, R., & Frost, R. (2003). Measuring the acquisition of media literacy skills. *Reading Research Quarterly, 38*(3), 330–355.

Hoisington, C. (2003). Using photographs to support children's science inquiry. In D. Koralek & L. J. Kolker (Eds.), *Spotlight on young children and science* (pp. 21–26). Washington, DC: National Association for the Education of Young Children.

Holmes, R., & Geiger, C. (2002). The relationship between creativity and cognitive abilities in preschoolers. In J. L. Roopnarine (Ed.), *Conceptual, social-cognitive, and contextual issues in the fields of play* (pp. 127–148). *Play and Culture Studies* (Vol. 4). Westport, CT: Ablex.

Holton, D., Ahmed, A., Williams, H., & Hill, C. (2001). On the importance of mathematical play. *International Journal of Math Education in Science and Technology, 32*(3), 401–415.

Honig, A. S. (2007). Ten power boosts for children's early learning. *Journal of the National Association for the Education of Young Children, 62*(5), 72–78.

Houck, P. (1997). Lessons from an exhibition: Reflections of an art educator. In J. Hendrick (Ed.), *First steps toward teaching the Reggio way* (pp. 26–41). Upper Saddle River, NJ: Merrill/Prentice Hall.

Howes, C. (with Unger, O., & Matheson, C.). (1992). *The collaborative construction of pretend: Social pretend play functions.* Albany: SUNY Press.

Hughes, F. (2003). Sensitivity to the social and cultural contexts of the play of young children. In J. Isenberg & M. Jalongo (Eds.), *Major trends and issues in early childhood education: Challenges, controversies, and insights* (2nd ed., pp. 126–135). New York: Teachers College Press.

Hutt, C. (1971). Exploration and play in children. In R. E. Herron & B. Sutton-Smith (Eds.), *Child's play* (pp. 231–251). New York: Wiley.

Hyson, M. (2008). Enthusiastic and engaged learners: Approaches to learning in the early childhood classroom. New York: Teachers College Press.

International Reading Association (IRA) and the National Association for the Education of Young Children (NAEYC). (1998). *Learning to read and write: Developmentally appropriate practices for young children: A joint position statement of the IRA and NAEYC.* Washington, DC: NAEYC. Retrieved January 8, 2010, from http://www.naeyc.org/files/naeyc/file/positions/PSREAD98.PDF.

International Society for Technology Education. (2007). *The ISTE national education technology standards (NETS-S) and performance indicators for students.* Retrieved November 28, 2009, from http://www.iste.org/Content/NavigationMenu/NETS/ForStudents/2007Standards/NETS_for_Students_2007_Standards.pdf

Isenberg, J. P., & Jalongo, M. R. (2001). *Creative expression and play in early childhood.* Upper Saddle River, NJ: Merrill/Prentice Hall.

Isenberg, J. P., & Jalongo, M. R. R. (2006). *Creative thinking and arts-based learning: Preschool through fourth grade.* Upper Saddle River, NJ: Merrill/Prentice Hall.

Isenberg, J. P., & Jalongo, M. R. (2010). *Creative thinking and arts based learning.* Upper Saddle River, NJ: Pearson Education, Inc.

Jablon, J. R., Dombro, A. L., & Ditchtelmiller, M. L. (2007). The power of observation for birth through eight (2nd ed.). Washington, DC: National Association for the Education of Young Children.

Jacobs, G., & Crowley, K. (2010). *Reaching standards and beyond in kindergarten.* Thousand Oaks, CA: Corwin & National Association for the Education of Young Children.

Jaelitza. (1996). Insect love: A field journal. *Young Children, 51*(4), 31–32.

Jambor, T., & Palmer, S. D. (1991). *Playground safety manual.* Birmingham, AL: Injury Prevention Center, University of Alabama.

Jarrell, R. H. (1998). Play and its influence on the development of young children's mathematical thinking. In D. P. Fromberg & D. Bergen (Eds.), *Play from birth to twelve and beyond: Contexts, perspectives, and meanings* (pp. 56–67). New York: Garland Press.

Jarrett, O. S. (2003). Recess in elementary school: What does the research say? Retrieved February 19, 2006, from http://www.ericdigests.org/2003-2/recess.html (ERIC Document Reproduction Service No. ED466331)

Jaworski, A., & Coupland, N. (Eds.). (1999). *The discourse reader.* London: Routledge.

Johnson, J. E. (2006). Play development from ages four to eight. In D. P. Fromberg & D. Bergen (Eds.), Play from birth to twelve (2nd ed., pp. 13–20). New York: Taylor & Francis Group.

Johnson, J. E., Ershler, J., & Lawton, J. (1982). Intellective correlates of preschoolers' spontaneous play. *Journal of General Psychology, 106,* 115–122.

Johnson, L., & O'Neill, C. (Eds.). (1984). *Dorothy Heathcote's collected writings on drama and education.* London, Hutchinson, Ltd.

Jones, E., & Cooper, R. (2006). *Playing to get smart.* New York: Teachers College Press.

Jones, E., & Reynolds, G. (1992). *The play's the thing: Teachers' roles in children's play.* New York: Teachers College Press.

Joshi, A. (2005). Understanding Asian Indian families: Facilitating meaningful home-school relations. *Young Children, 60,* 75–79.

Kafai, Y. B. (2006). Play and technology: Revised realities and potential perspectives. In D. P. Fromberg & D. Bergen (Eds.), *Play from birth to twelve* (2nd ed., pp. 207–213). New York: Taylor & Francis Group.

Kaiser, B., & Rasminsky, J. S. (2008). *Challenging behavior in elementary and middle school.* Upper Saddle River, NJ: Allyn & Bacon/Pearson.

Kaiser Family Foundation. (2005). *The effects of electronic media on children ages zero to six: A history of research—Issue brief.* Retrieved November 13, 2009, from http://www.kff.org/entmedia/7239.cfm

Kamii, C. (1982). *Number in preschool and kindergarten: Educational implications of Piaget's theory.* Washington, DC: National Association for the Education of Young Children.

Kamii, C. (Ed.). (1990). *No achievement testing in the early grades: The games grown-ups play.* Washington, DC: National Association for the Education of Young Children.

Kamii, C. (with DeClark, G.). (2000). *Young children reinvent arithmetic: Implications of Piaget's theory* (2nd ed.). New York: Teachers College Press.

Kamii, C. (with Housman, L. B.). (2000). *Young children reinvent arithmetic: Implications of Piaget's theory* (2nd ed.). New York: Teachers College Press.

Kamii, C. (with Joseph, L.). (2003). *Young children continue to reinvent arithmetic—2nd grade*. New York: Teachers College Press.

Kamii, C., & DeVries, R. (1993). *Physical knowledge in preschool education*. New York: Teachers College Press. (Original work published in 1978)

Kamii, C., & Kato, Y. (2006). Play and mathematics at ages one to ten. In D. P. Fromberg & D. Bergen (Eds.), *Play from birth to twelve* (2nd ed., pp. 187–198). New York: Taylor & Francis Group.

Kamii, C., Miyakawa, Y., & Kato, Y. (2004, September). The development of logico-mathematical thinking in a block building activity at ages 1–4. *Journal of Research in Childhood Education, 19*(1).

Katch, J. (2001). *Under deadman's skin: Discovering the meaning of children's violent play*. Boston: Beacon Press.

Katch, J. (2003). *They don't like me: Lessons on bullying and teasing from a preschool classroom*. Boston: Beacon Press.

Kato, Y., Honda, M., & Kamii, C. (2006). Kindergartners play lining up the 5s: A card game to encourage logical-mathematical thinking. *Young Children, 61*, 82–88.

Katz, L. (2007). Standards of experience. *Young Children, 62*(3), 94–95.

Katz, L., & Chard, S. (2000). *Engaging children's minds: The project approach* (2nd ed.). Stamford, CT: Ablex.

Katz, L., Evangelou, D., & Hartman, J. (1990). *The case for mixed age grouping in early education*. Washington, DC: National Association for the Education of Young Children.

Kellogg, R. (1969). *Analyzing children's art*. Palo Alto, CA: National Press.

Kendall, J. S., & Marzano, R. J. (2004). *Content knowledge: A compendium of standards and benchmarks for K–12 education*. Aurora, CO: Mid-Continent Research for Education and Learning (McRel). Retrieved February 11, 2006, from http://http://www.mcrel.org/standards-benchmarks

Kim, E. & Lim, J. (2007). Eco-early childhood education: A new paradigm of early childhood education in South Korea. *Young Children, 62*, 42–45.

Kim, S. (1999). The effects of storytelling and pretend play on cognitive processes, short-term and long-term narrative recall. *Child Study Journal, 29*(3), 175–191.

Kirmani, M. H. (2007). Empowering culturally and linguistically diverse children and families. *Journal of the National Association for the Education of Young Children, 62*(6), 94–98.

Klein, A., & Starkey, P. (2004). Fostering preschool children's mathematical knowledge: Findings from the Berkeley Math Readiness Project. In D. H. Clements & J. Sarama (Eds.), *Engaging young children in mathematics: Standards for early childhood mathematics education* (pp. 343–360). Mahwah, NJ: Erlbaum.

Kogan, Y. (2003). A study of bones. *Early childhood research & practice, 5*(1). Retrieved July 28, 2005, from http://www.lecrp.uiuc.edu/vol5/no1/kogan-thumb.html

Kohn, A. (2001, March). Fighting the tests: Turning frustration into action. *Young Children*, 19–24.

Koons, K. (1991). A center for writers. *First Teacher, 12*(7), 23.

Koplow, L. (Ed.). (1996). *Unsmiling faces: How preschools can heal*. New York: Teachers College Press.

Kostelnik, M., Onaga, E., Rohde, B., & Whiren, A. (2002). *Children with special needs: Lessons for early childhood professionals*. New York: Teachers College Press.

Kranor, L., & Kuschner, A. (Eds.). (1996). *Project exceptional: Exceptional children: Education in preschool techniques for inclusion, opportunity-building, nurturing, and learning*. Sacramento, CA: California Department of Education.

Kreidler, W., & Wittall, S. T. (1999). *Adventures in peacemaking* (2nd ed.). Cambridge, MA: Educators for Social Responsibility.

Kritchevsky, L., Prescott, E., & Walling, L. (1977). *Planning environments for young children: Physical space* (2nd ed.). Washington, DC: National Association for the Education of Young Children.

Kritchevsky, M. (Ed.). (1998). *Project spectrum: Early learning activities* (Vol. 3). *Preschool assessment handbook*. New York: Teachers College Press.

Kritchevsky, S., & Prescott, E. (1977). *Planning environments for young children: Physical space*. Washington, DC: National Association for the Education of Young Children.

Kroll, L., & Halaby, M. (1997). Writing to learn mathematics in the primary school. *Young Children, 52*(4), 54–60.

Kuo, F., & Taylor, A. (2004, September). A potential natural treatment for attention-deficit/hyperactivity disorder: Evidence from a national study. *American Journal of Public Health, 94*, 9.

Labov, W. (1972). *Language in the inner city: Studies in Black English vernacular*. Philadelphia: Pennsylvania University Press.

Lancy, D. (2002). Cultural constraints on children's play. In J. L. Roopnarine (Ed.), *Conceptual, social-cognitive, and contextual issues in the fields of play* (pp. 53–62). *Play and Culture Studies* (Vol. 4). Westport, CT: Ablex.

Landreth, G., Homeyer, L., & Morrison, M. (2006). Play as the language of children's feelings. In D. P. Fromberg & D. Bergen (Eds.), *Play from birth to twelve* (2nd ed., pp. 47–52). New York: Taylor & Francis Group.

Lantieri, L. (with Goleman, D.). (2008). *Building emotional intelligence: Techniques to cultivate inner strength in children*. Boulder, CO: Sounds True.

Lederman, J. (1992). *In full glory early childhood: To play's the thing*. Unpublished manuscript.

Levin, D. E. (1998). *Remote control childhood? Combating the hazards of media culture*. Washington, DC: National Association for the Education of Young Children.

Levin, D. E. (2003a). Beyond banning war and superhero play: Meeting children's needs in violent times. *Young Children, 58*(3), 60–64.

Levin, D. E. (2003b). *Teaching children in violent times—building a peaceable classroom* (2nd ed.). Cambridge, MA: Educators for Social Responsibility; Washington, DC: National Association for the Education of Young Children.

Levin, D. E. (2006). Play and violence: Understanding and responding effectively. In D. P. Fromberg & D. Bergen (Eds.), *Play from birth to twelve* (2nd ed., pp. 395–404). New York: Taylor & Francis Group.

Levin, D. E., & Carlsson-Paige, N. (2006). *The war play dilemma: What every parent and teacher needs to know* (2nd ed.). New York: Teachers College Press.

Levin, D. E., & Kilbourne, J. (2008). So sexy so soon: The new sexualized childhood and what parents can do to protect their kids. New York: Ballantine Books.

Levin, D. E., & Van Hoorn, J. (2009). Out of sight, out of mind, or is it? The impact of the war on children in the U.S. *Childhood Education, 86*(6), 342–346.

Lewis, C. C. (1995). *Educating hearts and minds: Reflections on Japanese preschool and elementary education*. New York: Cambridge University Press.

Linn, S. (2008). *The case for make believe: Saving play in a commercialized world*. New York: The New Press.

Locke, P. A., & Levin, J. (1998). Creative play begins with fun objects, your imagination, and simple-to-use technology. *The Exceptional Parent, 28*, 36–40.

Longfield, J. (2007). A DASH of inspiration (Developmental Approaches in Science, Health and Technology). *Science and Young Children, 44*(5), 26–29.

Louv, R. (2008). *Last child in the woods: Saving our children from nature-deficit disorder*. New York: Workman Publishing.

Lovsey, K. (2002). *Play entry strategies of autistic children*. Unpublished Master of Arts thesis, Rohnert Park, CA: Sonoma State University.

Lowenfeld, V. (1947). *Creative and mental growth*. New York: Macmillan.

Lux, D. G. (Ed.). (1985, Summer). *Theory into Practice, 24*(3).

Ma, L. (1999). *Knowing and teaching elementary mathematics*. Hillsdale, NJ: Erlbaum.

Manning, K., & Sharp, A. (1977). *Structuring play in the early years at school*. London: Ward Lock Educational.

Marsden, D. B., Meisels, S. J., Jablon, J. R., & Dichtelmiller, M. L. (2001). *The work sampling system* (4th ed.). Ann Arbor, MI: Rebus.

Marvin, C., & Hunt-Berg, M. (1996). Let's pretend: A semantic analysis of preschool children's play. *Journal of Children's Communication Development, 17*(2), 1–10.

McCay, L., & Keyes, D. (2001). Developing social competence in the inclusive early childhood classroom. *Childhood Education, 78*, 70–78.

McCune-Nicolich, L. (1981). Toward symbolic functioning: Structure of early pretend games and potential parallels. *Child Development, 52*, 785–797.

McDonnough, J. T., & Cho, S. (2009). Making the connection: Practical techniques for accommodating English language learners in the science classroom. *The Science Teacher, 76*, 34–37.

McEvoy, M., Shores, R., Wehby, J., Johnson, S., & Fox, J. (1990). Special education teachers' implementation of procedures to promote social interaction among children in integrated settings. *Education and Training in Mental Retardation, 25*(3), 267–276.

McEwan, H., & Egan, K. (Eds.). (1995). *Narrative in teaching, learning, and research*. New York: Teachers College Press.

McHenry, J. D., & Buerk, K. J. (2008). Infants and toddlers meet the natural world. *Beyond the journal: Young children on the Web*. Retrieved April 20, 2010, from http://www.naeyc.org/files/yc/file/200801/BTJNatureMcHenry.pdf

McLloyd, V. (1983). The effects of the structure of play objects on the pretend play of low-income preschool children. *Child Development, 54*, 626–635.

Mead, G. H. (1934). *Mind, self, and society*. Chicago: University of Chicago Press.

Meier, D. (2000). *Will standards save public education?* Boston: Beacon Press.

Meisels, S. J. (1993). Remaking classroom assessment with the work sampling system. *Young Children, 48*(5), 34–40.

Meisels, S. J. (2000). On the side of the child: Personal reflections on testing, teaching, and early childhood education. *Young Children, 55*(6), 16–19.

Meisels, S. J., Xue, Y., & Shamblott, M. (2008). Assessing language, literacy, and mathematics skills with Work Sampling for Head Start. *Early Education & Development, 19*, 963–981.

Melben, L. W. (2000). Nature in the city: Outdoor science projects for urban schools. *Science & Children, 37*(7), 18–21.

Meyers, C., Klein, E., & Genishi, C. (1994). Peer relationships among four preschool second language learners in "small group time." *Early Childhood Research Quarterly, 9*, 61–85.

Milligan, S. A. (2003, November). Assistive technologies: Supporting the participation of children with disabilities. *Young Children Beyond the Journal*. Retrieved September 16, 2005, from http://www.journal.naeyc.org/btj/200311/assistivetechnology.pdf

Milne, R. (1995, December). Let the children play: Settling in after immigration. *Resource, 85,* 1–2.

Mindes, G. (1998). Can I play too? Reflections on the issues for children with disabilities. In D. Fromberg & D. Bergen (Eds.), *Play from birth to twelve and beyond: Contexts, perspectives, and meanings* (pp. 208–214). New York: Garland.

Mindes, G. (2006). Can I play too? Reflections on the issues for children with disabilities. In D. P. Fromberg & D. Bergen (Eds.), *Play from birth to twelve* (2nd ed., pp. 289–296). New York: Taylor & Francis Group.

Mitchell, G. (with Dewsnap, L.). (1993). *Help! What do I do about...?: Biting, tantrums, and 47 other everyday problems.* New York: Scholastic.

Montessori, M. (1936). *The secret of childhood.* Bombay, India: Orient Longman.

Moore, R., & Wong, H. (1997). *Natural learning: Creating environments for rediscovering nature's way of teaching.* Berkeley, CA: MIG Communications.

Morgenthaler, S. K. (2006). The meanings in play with objects. In D. P. Fromberg & D. Bergen (Eds.), *Play from birth to twelve* (2nd ed., pp. 65–74). New York: Taylor & Francis Group.

Morrison, H. (1985). *Learning to see what I saw.* Unpublished report of a research project for the Bay Area Writing Project, Berkeley, CA: University of California.

Morrison, H., & Grossman, H. (1985). *Beginnings* [Videotape]. Produced for the Bay Area Writing Project, Berkeley, CA: University of California.

Morrow, L. M. (2009). *Literacy development in the early years: Helping children read and write.* Pearson Education, Inc.: Upper Saddle River, NJ.

Murphey, D. A., & Burns, C. E. (2002). Development of a comprehensive community assessment of school readiness. *Early Childhood Research and Practice, 4*(2), 1–15.

Murphy, M. S. (2009). Mathematics and social justice in grade 1: How children understand inequity and represent it. *Young Children, 64,* 12–16.

Murray, A. (2001). Ideas on manipulative math for young children. *Young Children, 56*(4), 28–29.

Myers, G. D. (1985). Motor behavior of kindergartners during physical education and free play. In J. L. Frost & S. Sunderlin (Eds.), *When children play* (pp. 151–156). Wheaton, MD: Association for Childhood Education International.

Myhre, S. M. (1993). Enhancing your dramatic play area through the use of prop boxes. *Young Children, 48*(5), 6–11.

Nabhan, G. P., & Trimble, S. (1994). *The geography of childhood: Why children need wild places.* Boston: Beacon Press.

Nachmanovitch, S. (1990). *Free play: The power of improvisation in life and the arts.* New York: Putnam.

National Academy of Sciences. (1996). *National science education standards.* Washington, DC: National Academy Press.

National Art Education Association (NAEA). (1999). *Purposes, principles, and standards for school art programs.* Reston, VA: Author.

National Association for Sport and Physical Education (NASPE). (2004). *Moving into the future: National standards for physical education* (2nd ed.). Reston, VA: NASPE.

National Association for the Education of Young Children (NAEYC). (1996). Position statement: Technology and young children—ages three through eight. *Young Children, 5*(6), 11–16.

National Association for the Education of Young Children (NAEYC). (2005). *Screening and assessment of young English-language learners.* Supplement to the NAEYC and NAECS/DSE joint position statement on early childhood curriculum, assessment, and program evaluation. Washington, DC: Author.

National Association for the Education of Young Children and National Association of Early Childhood Specialists in State Department of Education (NAECS/SDS). (1991). Guidelines for appropriate curriculum content and assessment in programs serving children ages 3 through 8. *Young Children, 46*(3), 21–38.

National Association for the Education of Young Children and National Association of Early Childhood Specialists in State Departments of Education (NAECS/SDS). (2002). *Joint position statement: Early learning standards: Creating the conditions for success.* Retrieved July 15, 2005, from http://www.naeyc.org/about/positions/early_learning_standards.asp

National Association for the Education of Young Children and National Association of Early Childhood Specialists in State Departments of Education (NAECS/SDS). (2003). *Joint position statement: Early childhood curriculum, assessment, and program evaluation: Building an effective, accountable system in programs for children birth through age 8.* Retrieved September 22, 2005, from http://www.naeyc.org/resources/position-statements/pscape.asp

National Association for the Education of Young Children and the National Council of Teachers of Mathematics (NAEYC/NCTM). (2002). *Early childhood mathematics: Promoting good beginnings. A joint position statement of the National Association for the Education of Young children and the National Council of Teachers of Mathematics.* Retrieved October 14, 2005, from http://www.naeyc.org

National Association of Early Childhood Specialists in State Departments of Education (NAECS). (2002). *Recess and the importance of play: A position statement on young children and recess.* Washington, DC: Author.

Retrieved September 25, 2005, from http://naecs. crc.uiuc.edu/position/recessplay.html

National Council for the Social Studies. (1998). *Ten thematic strands in social studies.* Washington, DC: Author.

National Council of Teachers of Mathematics (NCTM). (2000). *Principles and standards for school mathematics.* Reston, VA: Author.

National Council of Teachers of Mathematics (NCTM). (2006). *Curriculum focal points for prekindergarten through grade 8 mathematics: A quest for coherence.* Reston, VA: Author.

National Council of Teachers of Mathematics (NCTM). (2010). *Mathematics curriculum: Issues, trends, and future directions: 72nd NCTM yearbook.* Reston, VA: Author.

National Educational Goals Panel. (1998). *Principles and recommendations for early childhood assessments.* Washington, DC: Author.

National Research Council. (1996). *National science education standards: Observe, interact, change, learn.* Washington, DC: National Academy Press.

National Science Teachers Association (NSTA). (2009). *NSTA position statement: Science for English language learners.* Retrieved April 20, 2010, from http://www. nsta.org/about/positions/ell.aspx

Neeley, P. M., Neeley, R. A., Justen, J. E., III, & Tipton-Sumner, C. (2001). Scripted play as a language intervention strategy for preschoolers with developmental disabilities. *Early Childhood Education Journal, 28*(4), 243–246.

Nel, E. (2000). Academics, literacy, and young children: A plea for a middle ground. *Childhood Education, 76*(3), 136–141.

Neves, P., & Reifel, S. (2002). The play of early writing. In J. L. Roopnarine (Ed.), *Conceptual, social-cognitive, and contextual issues in the fields of play* (pp. 149–164). *Play and culture studies* (Vol. 4). Westport, CT: Ablex.

New, R. (2005). The Reggio Emilia approach: Provocation and partnerships with U.S. early childhood educator. In J. P. Roopnarine & J. Johnson (Eds.), *Approaches to early childhood education* (4th ed., pp. 313–335). Upper Saddle River, NJ: Merrill/Prentice Hall.

Newcomer, P. (1993). *Understanding and teaching emotionally disturbed children and adolescents.* Austin, TX: PRO-ED.

Newman, D., Griffin, P., & Cole, M. (1989). *The construction zone: Working for cognitive change in school.* Cambridge, MA: Cambridge University Press.

Nicolopoulou, A. (1996). Narrative development in a social context. In D. Slobin, J. Gearhart, A. Kyratzis, & J. Guo (Eds.), *Social interaction, social context, and language* (pp. 369–390). Mahwah, NJ: Erlbaum.

Nicolopoulou, A. (2001). Peer-group culture and narrative development. In S. Blum-Kulka & C. Snow (Eds.), *Talking with adults.* Mahwah, NJ: Erlbaum.

Nicolopoulou, A. (2007). The interplay of play and narrative in children's development: Theoretical reflections and concrete examples. In A. Göncü, J. Jain, & U. Tuermer (Eds.), *Play and development* (pp. 247–273). New York: Erlbaum, Taylor & Francis Group.

Nicolopoulou, A., McDowell, J., & Brockmeyer, C. (2006). Story reading and story acting meet journal writing. In D. Singer, K. M. Golenkoff, & R. Hirch-Pasech (Eds.), *Play = learning: How play motivates and enhances children's cognitive and social emotional growth* (pp. 124–144). New York: Oxford University Press.

Nicolopoulou, A., & Scales, B. (1990, March). *Teenage Mutant Ninja Turtles vs. the prince and the princess.* Paper presented at 11th Annual Meeting of the Pennsylvania Ethnography and Research Forum, Philadelphia.

Nicolopoulou, A., Scales, B., & Weintraub, J. (1994). Gender differences and symbolic imagination in the stories of 4-year-olds. In A. H. Dyson & C. Genishi (Eds.), *The need for story: Cultural diversity in classroom and community* (pp. 102–123). Urbana, IL: National Council of Teachers of English.

Ninio, A., & Bruner, J. S. (1976). The achievement and antecedents of labeling. *Journal of Child Language, 5,* 1–15.

Nourot, P. M. (1997). Playing with play in four dimensions. In J. Isenberg & M. Jalongo (Eds.), *Major trends and issues in early childhood education: Challenges, controversies and insights.* New York: Teachers College Press.

Nourot, P. M. (2005). Historical perspectives on early childhood education. In J. P. Roopnarine & J. Johnson (Eds.), *Approaches to early childhood education* (4th ed., pp. 3–43). Upper Saddle River, NJ: Merrill/Prentice Hall.

Nourot, P. M. (2006). Sociodramatic play pretending together. In D. P. Fromberg & D. Bergen (Eds.), *Play from birth to twelve* (2nd ed., pp. 87–101). New York: Taylor & Francis Group.

Nourot, P. M., Henry, J., & Scales, B. (1990, April). *A naturalistic study of story play in preschool and kindergarten.* Paper presented at the Annual Meeting of the American Educational Research Association, Boston.

Novakowski, J. (2009). Classifying classification: Teachers examine their practices to help first-grade students build a deeper understanding of how to categorize things. *Science and Children, 46,* 25–27.

Odom, S. (Ed.). (2002). *Widening the circle: Including children with disabilities in preschool programs.* New York: Teachers College Press.

Ogu, U., & Schmidt, S. R. (2009). Investigating rocks: Addressing multiple learning styles through and inquiry-based approach. *Young Children, 64,* 12–18.

Olds, A. (2001). *Child care design guide.* New York: McGraw-Hill.

Oliver, S., & Klugman, E. (2002, September). What we know about play. *Child Care Information Exchange.*

Orellana, M. (1994). Appropriating the voice of the superheroes: Three preschoolers' bilingual language uses in play. *Early Childhood Research Quarterly, 9*(2), 171–193.

Osofsky, J. D. (1999). The impact of violence on children. *The Future of Children, 9*(3), 33–49.

Ostrosky, M., Kaiser, A., & Odom, S. (1993). Facilitating children's social-communicative interactions through the use of peer-mediated interventions. In A. Kaiser & D. Gray (Eds.), *Enhancing children's communication* (pp. 159–185). Baltimore: Brookes.

Otto, B. (2010). *Language development in early childhood.* Upper Saddle River, NJ: Merrill.

Owacki, G. (2001). *Make way for literacy! Teaching the way young children learn.* Washington, DC: National Association for the Education of Young Children.

Paley, V. G. (1981). *Wally's stories.* Cambridge, MA: Harvard University Press.

Paley, V. G. (1984). *Boys & girls: Superheroes in the doll corner.* Chicago: University of Chicago Press.

Paley, V. G. (1986). *Mollie is three.* Chicago: University of Chicago Press.

Paley, V. G. (1988). *Bad guys don't have birthdays: Fantasy play at four.* Chicago: University of Chicago Press.

Paley, V. G. (1990). *The boy who would be a helicopter.* Cambridge, MA: Harvard University Press.

Paley, V. G. (1992). *You can't say you can't play.* Cambridge, MA: Harvard University Press.

Paley, V. G. (1994). Princess Annabella and the black girls. In A. H. Dyson & C. Genishi (Eds.), *The need for story: Cultural diversity in classrooms and community* (pp. 145–154). Urbana, IL: National Council of Teachers of English.

Paley, V. G. (1995). *Kwanzaa and me: A teacher's story.* Cambridge, MA: Harvard University Press.

Paley, V. G. (1997). *The girl with the brown crayon.* Cambridge, MA: Harvard University Press.

Paley, V. G. (1999). *The kindness of children.* Cambridge, MA: Harvard University Press.

Paley, V. G. (2000). *White teacher* (3rd ed.). Cambridge, MA: Harvard University Press.

Paley, V. G. (2004). *A child's work: The importance of fantasy play.* Chicago: University of Chicago Press.

Panksepp, J. (2008). Play, ADHD, and the construction of the social brain: Should the first class each day be recess? *American Journal of Play, 1*(1), 55–79.

Papert, S. A. (1980). *Mindstorms: Children, computers and powerful ideas.* New York: Basic Books.

Papert, S. A. (1993). *The children's machine: Rethinking school in the age of the computer.* New York: Basic Books.

Parten, M. B. (1932). Social participation among preschool children. *Journal of Abnormal Psychology, 27,* 243–269.

Pellegrini, A. D. (1984). The effects of exploration and play on young children's associative fluency: A review and extension in training studies. In T. D. Yawkey & A. D. Pellegrini (Eds.), *Child's play: Developmental and applied* (pp. 237–253). Hillsdale, NJ: Erlbaum.

Pellegrini, A. D. (1998). Play and the assessment of children. In O. Saracho & B. Spodek (Eds.), *Multiple perspectives on play in early childhood education* (pp. 220–239). Albany: SUNY Press.

Pellegrini, A. D. (2002). Perceptions of play fighting and real fighting: Effects of sex and participant status. In J. L. Roopnarine (Ed.), *Conceptual, social-cognitive, and contextual issues in the fields of play* (pp. 223–234). *Play and culture studies* (Vol. 4). Westport, CT: Ablex.

Pellegrini, A. D. (2005). *Recess: Its role in education and development.* Mahwah, NJ: Erlbaum.

Pellegrini, A. D., & Galda, L. (1993). Ten years after: A reexamination of play and literacy research. *Reading Research Quarterly, 28*(2), 163–175.

Pellegrini, A. D., & Smith, P. K. (1998). Physical activity play: The nature and function of a neglected aspect of play. *Child Development, 69*(3).

Pelletier, J., Halewood, C., & Reeve, R. (2005). How knowledge forum contributes to new literacies in kindergarten. *Orbit, 10*(1), 30–33.

Perry, J. P. (2001). *Outdoor play: Teaching strategies with young children.* New York: Teachers College Press.

Perry, J. P. (2003). Making sense of outdoor pretend play. *Young Children, 58*(3), 26–30.

Perry, J. P. (2004). Making sense of outdoor pretend play. In D. Koralek (Ed.), *Spotlight on young children and play* (pp. 17–21). Washington, DC: National Association for the Education of Young Children.

Perry, J. P. (2008). Children's experience of security and mastery on the playground. In E. Goodenough (Ed.), *A place to play* (pp. 99–105). Detroit, MI: Wayne State University Press.

Perry, J. P., & Branum, L. (2009). "Sometimes I pounce on twigs because I'm a meat eater": Supporting physically active play and outdoor learning. *American Journal of Play, 2*(2).

Phillips, A. (2002). Roundabout we go: A playable moment with a child with autism. In C. R. Brown & C. Marchant (Eds.), *Play in practice: Case studies in young children's play* (pp. 115–122). St. Paul, MN: Redleaf Press.

Piaget, J. (1954). *The construction of reality in the child.* New York: Ballantine Books.

Piaget, J. (1962a). Comments. In L. S. Vygotsky, *Thought and language.* Cambridge, MA: MIT Press.

Piaget, J. (1962b). *Play, dreams and imitation in childhood.* New York: Norton.

Piaget, J. (1963a). *The origins of intelligence in children.* New York: Norton.

Piaget, J. (1963b). *The psychology of intelligence.* Totowa, NJ: Littlefield, Adams.

Piaget, J. (1965a). *The child's conception of number.* New York: Norton.

Piaget, J. (1965b). *The child's conception of physical causality.* Totowa, NJ: Littlefield, Adams.

Piaget, J. (1965c). *The child's conception of the world.* Totowa, NJ: Littlefield, Adams.

Piaget, J. (1965d). *The moral judgment of the child.* New York: Free Press.

Piaget, J. (1966). *Judgment and reasoning in the child.* Totowa, NJ: Littlefield, Adams.

Piaget, J. (1977). *The development of thought: Equilibration of cognitive structures.* New York: Viking.

Piaget, J. (1995). *Sociological studies.* New York: Routledge.

Preissler, M. A. (2006). Play and autism: Facilitating symbolic understanding. In D. G. Singer, R. M. Golinkoff, & K. Hirsh-Pasek (Eds.), *Play = learning: How play motivates and enhances children's cognitive and social-emotional growth* (pp. 231–250). New York: Oxford University Press.

Pulaski, M. (1970). Play as a function of toy structure and fantasy predisposition. *Child Development, 41,* 531–537.

Qvortrup, J., Corsaro, W. A., & Sebastian-Honig, M. S. (Eds.). (2010). *The Palgrave handbook of childhood studies.* Roundmills, Basingstoke, Hampshire, England: Macmillan Publishers Limited.

Ramsey, P. G. (2004). *Teaching and learning in a diverse world: Multicultural education for young children* (3rd ed.). New York: Teachers College Press.

Ramsey, P. G. (2006). Influences of race, culture, social class, and gender: Diversity and play. In D. P. Fromberg & D. Bergen (Eds.), *Play from birth to twelve* (2nd ed., pp. 261–273). New York: Taylor & Francis Group.

Ramsey, P. G., & Reid, R. (1988). Designing play environments for preschool and kindergarten children. In D. Bergen (Ed.), *Play as a medium for learning and development: A handbook of theory and practice* (pp. 213–240). Portsmouth, NH: Heinemann.

Reed, T. L. (2005). A qualitative approach to boys' rough and tumble play: There is more than meets the eye. In F. F. McMahon, E. E., Lytle, & B. Sutton-Smith (Eds.), *Play, an interdisciplinary synthesis. Play and Culture Studies* (Vol. 6). Lanham, MD: University Press of America.

Reifel, S. (2007). Hermeneutic text: Exploring meaningful classroom events. In J. A. Hatch (Ed.), *Early childhood qualitative research.* New York: Routledge Press, Taylor & Francis Group.

Reifel, S., Hoke, P., Pape, D., & Wisneski, D. (2004). From context to texts: DAP, hermeneutics, and reading classroom play. In S. Reifel & M. Brown (Eds.). *Social contexts of early education, and reconceptualizing play (II): Advances in early education and day care* (Vol. 13, pp. 209–220). Oxford, UK: JAI/Elsevier Science.

Reifel, S., & Yeatman, J. (1991). Action, talk and thought in block play. In B. Scales, M. Almy, A. Nicolopoulou, & S. Ervin-Tripp (Eds.), *The social context of play and development in early care and education* (pp. 156–172). New York: Teachers College Press.

Reifel, S., & Yeatman, J. (1993). From category to context: Reconsidering classroom play. *Early Childhood Research Quarterly, 8,* 347–367.

Reynolds, G. (2002). The welcoming place: Tungasuvvingat Inuit Head Start program. In C. R. Brown & C. Marchant (Eds.), *Play in practice: Case studies in young children's play* (pp. 87–104). St. Paul, MN: Redleaf Press.

Reynolds, G., & Jones, E. (1997). *Master players: Learning from children at play.* New York: Teachers College Press.

Richardson, K. (2004). Making sense. In D. H. Clements & A. Sarama (Eds.), *Engaging young children in mathematics: Standards for early childhood mathematics education* (pp. 321–324). Mahwah, NJ: Erlbaum.

Richner, E. S., & Nicolopoulou, A. (2001, April). The narrative construction of differing conceptions of the person in the development of young children's social understanding. *Early Education and Development, 12,* 393–432.

Rideout, V., Vanderwater, E., & Wartella, A. (2003). *Zero to six: Electronic media in the lives of infants, toddlers and preschooler.* Menlo Park, CA: The Kaiser Family Foundation.

Riley, D., San Juan, R. R., Klinkner, J., & Ramminger, A. (2008). *Social & emotional development: Connecting science and practice in early childhood settings.* St. Paul, MN: Redleaf Press.

Rivkin, M. S. (1995). *The great outdoors: Restoring children's right to play outside.* Washington, DC: National Association for the Education of Young Children.

Rivkin, M. S. (2006). Children's outdoor play: An endangered activity. In D. P. Fromberg & D. Bergen (Eds.), *Play from birth to twelve* (2nd ed., pp. 323–329). New York: Taylor & Francis Group.

Robinson, T., Wilde, M., Navracruz, L., Haydel, K., & Varady, A. (2001). Effects of reducing children's television and video game use on aggressive behavior: A randomized controlled trial. *Developmental and Behavioral Pediatrics, 22*(3), 179–183.

Roopnarine, J. L., Shin, M., Donovan, B., & Suppal, P. (2000). Sociocultural contexts of dramatic play: Implications for early education. In *Play and literacy in early childhood: Research from multiple perspectives* (pp. 205–220). Mahwah, NJ: Erlbaum.

Rosenow, N. (2008). Introduction: Learning to love the earth . . . and each other. *Young Children, 63,* 10–13.

Roskos, K. (2000). Through the bioecological lens: Some observations of literacy in play as a proximal process. In K. Roskos & J. Christie (Eds.), *Play and literacy in early childhood: Research from multiple perspectives* (pp. 125–138). Mahwah, NJ: Erlbaum.

Roskos, K., & Christie, J. (Eds.). (2000a). Afterword. In *Play and literacy in early childhood: Research from multiple perspectives* (pp. 231–240). Mahwah, NJ: Erlbaum.

Roskos, K., & Christie, J. (Eds.). (2000b). *Play and literacy in early childhood: Research from multiple perspectives.* Mahwah, NJ: Erlbaum.

Roskos, K., & Christie, J. (2001). On not pushing children too hard: A few cautionary remarks about literacy and play. *Young Children, 56*(3), 64–66.

Roskos, K., & Christie J. (2004). Examining the play-literacy interface: A critical review and future directions. In E. Zigler, D. Singer, & S. Bishop-Josef (Eds.), *Children's play: The roots of reading* (pp. 95–124). Washington, DC: Zero to Three Press.

Roskos, K., & Neuman, S. (1998). Play as an opportunity for literacy. In O. Saracho & B. Spodek (Eds.), *Multiple perspectives on play in early childhood education* (pp. 100–115). Albany: SUNY Press.

Rubin, K. H. (1980). Fantasy play: Its role in the development of social skills and social cognition. In K. H. Rubin (Ed.), *Children's play* (pp. 69–84). San Francisco, CA: Jossey-Bass.

Rubin, K. H., Maioni, T. L., & Hornung, M. (1976). Free play behaviors in middle- and lower-class preschoolers: Parten & Piaget revisited. *Child Development, 47,* 414–419.

Salmon, M., & Akaran, S. E. (2001). Enrich your kindergarten program with a cross-cultural connection. *Young Children, 56*(4), 30–33.

Saltz, E., & Johnson, J. (1974). Training for thematic fantasy play in culturally disadvantaged children: Preliminary results. *Journal of Educational Psychology, 66,* 623–630.

Sandall, S. (2003). Play modifications for children with disabilities. *Young Children, 58*(3), 54–57.

Saracho, O. (2001). Teachers' perceptions of their roles in promoting literacy in the context of play in a Spanish-speaking kindergarten. *International Journal of Early Childhood, 33*(2), 18–32.

Sarama, J., & Clements, D. H. (2002). Learning and teaching with computers in early childhood education. In O. Saracho & B. Spodek (Eds.), *Contemporary perspectives on early childhood curriculum* (pp. 177–219). Greenwich, CT: Information Age Publishing.

Sarama, J,. & Clements, D. H. (2006). Mathematics in kindergarten. In D. Gullo (Ed.), *K today: Teaching and learning in the kindergarten year* (pp. 85–94). Washington, DC: National Association for the Education of Young Children.

Sarama, J., & Clements, D. H. (2009). Teaching math in the primary grades: The learning trajectories approach. *Young Children, 64,* 63–65.

Sawyer, K. (1997). *Pretend play as improvisation: Conversation in the preschool classroom.* Mahwah, NJ: Erlbaum.

Sawyer, K. (2001). *Creating conversations: Performance in everyday life.* Creskill, NJ: Hampton Press.

Scales, B. (1989). Whoever gets to the bottom gets the soap, right? In *The Proceedings of the Annual Ethnography in Education Forum.* Philadelphia: University of Pennsylvania.

Scales, B. (1996, April). *Researching play and the hidden curriculum.* Paper presented at the annual meeting of The Association for the Study of Play, Austin, TX.

Scales, B. (1997, April). *Play in the curriculum: A mirror of development and a catalyst for learning.* Paper presented at the annual meeting of The Association for the Study of Play, Washington, DC.

Scales, B. (2000, March). *Math: The missing learning center.* Sacramento, CA: California Association for the Education of Young Children.

Scales, B. (2004, November). *Standards? Not a problem.* Paper presented at the National Association for the Education of Young Children Annual Conference.

Scales, B. (2005, February). *Using technology to track the development of socially isolated child.* Paper presented at the annual meeting of the Association for the Study of Play, Santa Fe, NM.

Scales, B., & Cook-Gumperz, J. (1993). Gender in narrative and play: A view from the frontier. In S. Reifel (Ed.), *Advances in early education and day care: Perspectives on developmentally appropriate practice,* (Vol. 5, pp. 167–195). Greenwich, CT: JAI Press.

Scales, B., & Webster, P. (1976). *Interactive cues in children's spontaneous play.* Unpublished manuscript.

Scarlett, W. G., Naudeau, S., Salonius-Pasternak, D., & Ponte, I. (2005). *Children's play.* Thousand Oaks, CA: Sage.

Schor, J. (2004). *Born to buy: The commercialized child and the new consumer culture.* New York: Scribner.

Schultz, P. W., Shriver, C., Tabanico, J., & Khazian, A. (2004). Implicit connections with nature. *Journal of Environmental Psychology, 24*(1), 31–42.

Schwartzman, H. B. (1976). Children's play: A sideways glance at make-believe. In D. F. Laney & B. A. Tindall (Eds.), *The anthropological study of play: Problems and prospects* (pp. 208–215). Cornwall, NY: Leisure Press.

Seefeldt, C. (2005).). *How to work with standards in the early childhood classroom.* New York: Teachers College Press.

Seefeldt, C., & Galper, A. (2000). *Active experiences for active children: Social studies.* Upper Saddle River, NJ: Merrill/Prentice Hall.

Seefeldt, C., & Galper, A. (2001). *Active experiences for active children: Literacy begins.* Upper Saddle River, NJ: Merrill/Prentice Hall.

Seefeldt, C., & Galper, A. (2004). *Active experiences for active children: Science.* Upper Saddle River, NJ: Merrill/Prentice Hall.

Seefeldt, C., & Galper, A. (2007). *Active experiences for active children: Science* (2nd ed.). Upper Saddle River, NJ: Merrill/Prentice Hall.

Seiter, E. (1995). *Sold separately: Parents and children in consumer culture.* New Brunswick, NJ: Rutgers University Press.

Sheldon, A. (1992). Conflict talk: Sociolinguistic challenges to self-assertion and how young girls meet them. *Merrill-Palmer Quarterly, 38*(1), 95–117.

Shepard, L. (2000). The role of assessment in a learning culture. *Educational Researcher, 29*(7), 4–14.

Shepard, L., Kagan, S. L., & Wurtz, E. (Eds.). (1998a). *Principles and recommendations for early childhood assessments.* Washington, DC: National Education Goals Panel. (Adaptation). Retrieved July 27, 2005, from http://www.state.ia.us/educate/ecese/is/ecn/primaryse/tppse08.htm

Shepard, L., Kagan, S. L., & Wurtz, E. (1998b). Public policy report: Goal 1, early childhood assessments resources group recommendations. *Young Children, 53*(3), 52–54.

Sheridan, M., Foley, G., & Radlinski, S. (1995). *Using the supportive play model: Individualized intervention in early childhood practice.* New York: Teachers College Press.

Sigel, I. E. (1993). Educating the young thinker: A distancing model of preschool education. In J. L. Roopnarine & J. E. Johnson (Eds.), *Approaches to early childhood education* (pp. 179–193, 237–252). Upper Saddle River, NJ: Merrill/Prentice Hall.

Silvern, S. B. (2006). Educational implications of play with computers. In D. P. Fromberg & D. Bergen (Eds.), *Play from birth to twelve* (2nd ed., pp. 215–221). New York: Taylor & Francis Group.

Singer, D. G., Golinkoff, R. M., & Hirsch-Pasek, K. (Eds.). (2006). *Play = learning: How play motivates and enhances children's cognitive and social emotional growth.* New York: Oxford University Press.

Singer, D. G., & Singer, J. L. (1990). *The house of make-believe.* Cambridge, MA: Harvard University Press.

Singer, D. G., & Singer, J. L. (2005). *Imagination and play in the electronic age.* Cambridge, MA: Harvard University Press.

Singer, D. G., & Singer, J. L. (2006). Fantasy and imagination. In D. P. Fromberg & D. Bergen (Eds.), *Play from birth to twelve* (2nd ed., pp. 371–378). New York: Taylor & Francis Group.

Singer, J. L. (2006). Epilogue: Learning to play and learning through play. In D. G. Singer, R. M. Golinkoff, & K. Hirsh-Pasek (Eds.), *Play = learning: How play motivates and enhances children's cognitive and social-emotional growth* (pp. 251–262). New York: Oxford University Press.

Singer, J. L., & Lythcott, M. (2004). Fostering school achievement and creativity through sociodramatic play in the classroom. In E. Zigler, D. Singer, & S.

Bishop-Josef (Eds.), *Children's play: The roots of reading* (pp. 77–94). Washington, DC: Zero to Three Press.

Sluss, D., & Stremmel, A. (2004). A sociocultural investigation of the effects of peer interaction on play. *Journal of Research in Childhood Education, 18*(4), 293–305.

Smilansky, S. (1968). *The effects of sociodramatic play on disadvantaged preschool children.* New York: Wiley.

Smilansky, S. (1990). Sociodramatic play: Its relevance to behavior and achievement in school. In E. Klugman & S. Smilansky (Eds.), *Children's play and learning: Perspectives and policy implications* (pp. 18–42). New York: Teachers College Press.

Smilansky, S., & Shefatya, L. (1990). *Facilitating play: A medium for promoting cognitive, socio-emotional and academic development in young children.* Gaithersburg, MD: Psychosocial and Educational Publications.

Smith, A. F. (2000). Reflective portfolios: Preschool possibilities. *Childhood Education, 76,* 204–208.

Smith, P. K., & Connolly, K. J. (1980). *The ecology of preschool behavior.* Cambridge, UK: Cambridge University Press.

Smith, S. S. (2009). *Early childhood mathematics* (4th ed.). Upper Saddle River, NJ: Pearson Education.

Snow, C. E., Burns, M. S., & Griffin, P. (1998). *Preventing reading difficulties in young children.* Washington, DC: National Academy Press.

Sobel, D. (2004). *Place-based education, connecting classrooms & communities.* Great Barrington, MA: The Orion Society.

Stegelin, D. (2005). Making the case for play policy: Research-based reasons to support play-based environments. *Young Children, 60*(2), 76–85.

Stephens, K. (2002). Nature connections for kids in cities and suburbs. *Parenting Exchange, 10,* 1–3.

Stewart, D. (2001). *Sophie the pig project.* Lafayette, CA: Old Firehouse School.

Stone, M., & Sagstetter, M. (1998). Simple technology: It's never too early to start. *The Exceptional Parent, 28,* 50–51.

Stone, S. J., & Christie, J. F. (1996). Collaborative literacy during sociodramatic play in a multiage (K–2) primary classroom. *Journal of Research in Childhood Education, 10*(2), 123–133.

Strickland, K., & Strickland, J. (2000). *Making assessment elementary.* Portsmouth, NJ: Heinemann.

Sutton-Smith, B. (1997). *The ambiguity of play.* Cambridge, MA: Harvard University Press.

Swarbrick, N., Eastwood, G., & Tutton, K. (2004). Self-esteem and successful interaction as part of the forest school project. *Support for Learning, 19*(3), 142–146.

Swartz, D. (1997). *Culture and power: The sociology of Pierre Bourdieu.* Chicago: University of Chicago Press.

Swick, K. (2002). The dynamics of families who are homeless: Implications for early childhood educators. *Childhood Education, 80*(3), 116–120.

Sylva, K., Roy, C., & Painter, M. (1980). *Child watching at play-groups and nursery school, Vol. 2: Oxford preschool research project*. Ypsilanti, MI: The High Scope Press.

Tegano, D., Sawyers, J., & Moran, J. (1989). Problem-finding and solving in play: The teacher's role. *Childhood Education, 66*(2), 92–97.

Thatcher, D. H. (2001). Reading in math class: Selecting and using picture books for math investigations. *Young Children, 56*(4), 20–26.

Thomas, K. (2005). Indian Island School, early childhood program, Old Town, Maine: Universal design. In S. Friedman (Ed.), Environments that inspire. *Young Children, 60*(3), 53–54.

Thompson, J. E., & Thompson, R. A. (2007). How connecting with nature supports children's social emotional growth. *Exchange, 178*, 46–49.

Tierney, R., Carter, J., & Desai, L. E. (1991). *Portfolio assessment in the reading-writing classroom*. Norwood, MA: Christopher-Gordon.

Tizard, B., & Hughes, M. (1984). *Young children learning*. Cambridge, MA: Harvard University Press.

Tobin, J. (2000). *"Good guys don't wear hats": Children's talk about the media*. New York: Teachers College Press.

Topal, C. W. (2005). Bring the spirit of the studio into the classroom. In L. Gandini, L. Hill, L. Cadwell, & C. Schwall (Eds.), *In the spirit of the studio: Learning from the Atelier of Reggio Emilia* (pp. 119–124). New York: Teachers College Press.

Torquati, J., & Barber, J. (2005). Dancing with trees: Infants and toddlers in the garden. *Young Children, 60*(3), 40–46.

Tovey, H. (2007). *Playing outdoors: Spaces and places, risk and challenge*. Maidenhead, UK: Open University.

The toy manufacturers of America guide to toys and play. (2005). Retrieved September 25, 2005, from http://www.openseason.com/annex/library/cic/X0085-toysply.txt.html

Trawick-Smith, J. (1992). A descriptive study of persuasive preschool children: How they get others to do what they want. *Early Childhood Research Quarterly, 7*(1), 95–114.

Trawick-Smith, J. (1994). *Interactions in the classroom: Facilitating play in the early years*. Upper Saddle River, NJ: Merrill/Prentice Hall.

Trawick-Smith, J. (1998). Why play training works: An integrated model for play intervention. *Journal of Research in Childhood Education, 12*, 117–129.

Trawick-Smith, J. (2001). Play and the curriculum. In J. Frost, S. Wortham, & S. Reifel (Eds.), *Play and child development* (pp. 294–339). Upper Saddle River, NJ: Merrill/Prentice Hall.

Trawick-Smith, J. (2010). Early childhood development: A multicultural perspective. Upper Saddle River, NJ: Pearson Education.

Trepanier-Street, M., Bock Hong, S., & Donegan, M. (2001). Constructing the image of the teacher in a Reggio-inspired teacher education program. *Journal of Early Childhood Teacher Education, 22*, 47–52.

Tribble, C. (1996). *Individual differences in children's entrance strategies into preschool peer groups as a function of the quality of the mother-child attachment relationship*. Unpublished dissertation, University of California, Berkeley.

Trundle, K. C., Willmore, S., & Smith, W. S. (2006). The moon project. *Science and Young Children, 43*(6), 52–55.

Turner, V. D. (2009). *Bridging Piaget and Vygotsky: Discourse between paradigms*. Paper presented at 2009 Annual Meeting of the Jean Piaget Society, Park City, UT.

U.N. Convention on the Rights of the Child. (2008). Retrieved from http://www.unicef.org/crc

United States Consumer Product Safety Commission. (2005). *For kids' sake: Think toy safety* (Document #4281). Retrieved January 25, 2006, from cpsc.gov/cpscpub/pubs/281.html http://www.liveandlearn.com/toysafe.htmlcpsc.gov/cpscpub/pubs/281.html

Uttal, D., Marzolf, D., Pierroutsakos, S., Smith, C., Troseth, G., Scudder, K., & DeLoache, J. (1998). Seeing through symbols: The development of children's understanding of symbolic relations. In O. Saracho & B. Spodek (Eds.), *Multiple perspectives on play in early childhood education* (pp. 59–79). Albany: SUNY Press.

van der Kooij, R. (1989b). Research on children's play. *Play and Culture, 2*(1), 20–34.

van der Kooij, R. (1989a). Play and behavioral disorders in schoolchildren. *Play and Culture, 2*(1), 328–339.

VanderVen, K. (2006). Attaining the protean self in a rapidly changing world: Understanding chaos through play. In D. P. Fromberg & D. Bergen (Eds.), *Play from birth to twelve* (2nd ed., pp. 405–415). New York: Taylor & Francis Group.

Van Hoorn, J. L., & McHargue, T. (1999, July). *Early childhood education for peace and nonviolence*. Paper presented at the International Union of Psychological Science Sixth International Symposium on the Contribution of Psychology to Peace, San Juan, Costa Rica.

Van Thiel, L., & Putnam-Franklin, S. (2004). Standards and guidelines: Keeping play in professional practice and planning. *Play, Policy, and Practice Connections 8*(2), 16–19.

Veldhuis, H. A. (1982, May). *Spontaneous songs of preschool children*. Master's thesis, San Francisco State University, San Francisco, CA.

von Blanckensee, L. (1997). *Scale for choosing technology-based activities for young children, ages 3–7*. Unpublished manuscript.

von Blanckensee, L. (1999). *Teaching tools for young learners*. Larchmont, NY: Eye on Education.

Vygotsky, L. S. (1962). *Thought and language*. Cambridge, MA: MIT Press.

Vygotsky, L. S. (1967). Play and its role in the mental development of the child. *Soviet Psychology, 12*, 62–76.

Vygotsky, L. S. (1976). Play and its role in the mental development of the child. In J. S. Bruner, A. Jolly, & K. Sylva (Eds.), *Play: Its role in development and evolution* (pp. 537–544). New York: Basic Books.

Vygotsky, L. S. (1978). *Mind in society: The development of higher psychological processes.* Cambridge, MA: Harvard University Press.

Wagner, B. J. (1999). *Dorothy Heathcote: Drama as a learning medium.* Portsmouth, NH: Heinemann.

Wallace, A. H., Abbott, D., & Blary, R. M. (2007). The classroom that math built: Encouraging young mathematicians to pose problems. *Young Children, 62,* 42–48.

Wallach, L. B. (1993). Helping children cope with violence. *Young Children, 48*(4), 4–11.

Walsh, P. (2008, September/October). Planning for play in a playground. *Playground Planning Exchange,* 88–94.

Wang, X. C., Kedem, Y., & Hertzog, N. (2004) Scaffolding young children's reflections with student-created power point presentations. *Journal of Research in Childhood Education, 19*(2), 159–174.

Wanigarayake, M. (2001). From playing with guns to playing with rice: The challenges of working with refugee children: An Australian perspective. *Childhood Education, 77*(5), 289–294.

Wasik, B. (2001). Phonemic awareness and young children. *Childhood Education, 77*(3), 128–133.

Wasserman, S. (2000). *Serious players in the primary classroom: Empowering children through active learning experiences* (2nd ed.). New York: Teachers College Press.

Wasserman, S., & Ivany, J. W. G. (1996). *The new teaching elementary science: Who's afraid of spiders?* (2nd ed.). New York: Teachers College Press.

Wesson, K. (2001). The Volvo effect—questioning standardized tests. *Young Children, 56*(2), 16–18.

Wheeler, L., & Raebeck, L. (1985). *Orff and Kodaly adapted for the elementary school* (3rd ed.). Dubuque, IA: Wm. C. Brown Publishers.

Wien, C. A. (2004). *Negotiating standards in the primary classroom: The teacher's dilemma.* New York: Teachers College Press.

Wien, C. A. (2008). *Emergent curriculum in the primary classroom: Interpreting the Reggio Emilia approach in schools.* New York: Teachers College Press.

Williams, K. P. (2002). "But are they learning anything?" African American mothers, their children, and their play. In C. R. Brown & C. Marchant (Eds.), *Play in practice: Case studies in young children's play* (pp. 73–86). St. Paul, MN: Redleaf Press.

Williamson, P., & Silvern, S. (1990). The effect of play training on the story comprehension of upper primary children. *Journal of Research in Child Education, 4*(2), 130–135.

Wilson, R. (1997). The wonders of nature: Honoring children's ways of knowing. *Early Childhood News, 6*(19).

Winnicott, D. W. (1971). *Playing and reality.* New York: Basic Books.

Wohlwill, J. F. (1984). Relationships between exploration and play. In T. Yawkey & A. Pellegrini (Eds.), *Child's play: Developmental and applied* (pp. 143–201). Hillsdale, NJ: Erlbaum.

Wolfberg, P. (1999). *Play and imagination in children with autism.* New York: Teachers College Press.

Wolfe, C. R., Cummins, R. H., & Myers, C. A. (1998). Dabbling, discovery, and dragonflies: Scientific inquiry and exploratory representational play. In D. Fromberg & D. Bergen (Eds.), *Play from birth to twelve and beyond: Contexts, perspectives, and meanings* (pp. 68–76). New York: Garland Publishing.

Wolfe, C. R., Cummins, R. H., & Myers, C. A. (2006). Scientific inquiry and exploratory representational play. In D. P. Fromberg & D. Bergen (Eds.), *Play from birth to twelve* (2nd ed., pp. 199–206). New York: Taylor & Francis Group.

Wolfe, J. (2002). *Learning from the past: Historical voices in early childhood education* (2nd ed.). Mayerthorpe, Alberta, Canada: Piney Branch Press.

Wortham, S. (2005). *Assessment in early childhood education* (4th ed.). Upper Saddle River, NJ: Merrill/Prentice Hall.

Wurm, J. P. (2005). *Working in the Reggio way: A beginner's guide for American teachers.* Washington, DC: National Association for the Education of Young Children.

Yang, H., & McMullen, M. B. (2003). Understanding the relationships among American primary-grade teachers and Korean mothers: The role of communication and cultural sensitivity in the linguistically diverse classroom. *Early Childhood Research and Practice, 5*(1), 1–20.

Yopp, H. K. (1995). Read-aloud books for developing phonemic awareness: An annotated bibliography. *The Reading Teacher, 49,* 20–29.

Yopp, H. K., & Yopp, R. H. (2009, January). Phonological awareness in child's play. *Young Children, 64*(1).

Zan, B. (1996). Interpersonal understanding among friends: A case study of two young boys playing checkers. *Journal of Research in Childhood Education, 10,* 114–122.

Zapeda, M., Gonzalez-Mena, J., Rothstein-Fisch, C., & Trumbull, E. (2006). *Bridging cultures in early care and education. A training module.* Mahwah, NJ: Erlbaum.

Zigler, E. F., & Bishop-Josef, S. J. (2006). The cognitive child versus the whole child: Lessons from 40 years of Head Start. In D. G. Singer, M. Golinkoff, & K. Hirsh-Pasek (Eds.), *Play = learning: How play motivates and enhances children's cognitive and social-emotional growth* (pp. 15–35). New York: Oxford University Press.

Zimmerman, E., & Zimmerman, L. (2000). Art education and early childhood education: The young child as creator and meaning maker within a community context. *Young Children, 56*(6), 87–92.

Name Index

Abbott, D., 161
Ackerman, D., 328
Adams, S., 119
Ainsworth, M. D., 260
Akaran, S. E., 334
Alkon, A., 265
Allen, B. N., 103
Almy, M., 6, 149, 363
Alper, C. D., 246
Alward, K. R., 258, 273, 275
Andersen, S. R., 146
Anderson, W. T., 288
Arce, C., 218
Ardeila-Ray, A., 56, 183, 202
Ardley, J., 112, 113
Ariel, S., 51, 52, 62, 63, 67, 102
Ashbrook, P., 227
Ashton-Warner, S., 197
Axline, V., 68
Ayres, J., 294

Bahktin, M. M., 179
Balaban, N., 260
Balfanz, R., 172
Barber, J., 81
Barbour, A. C., 81, 83
Barnes, E., 71, 76
Baroody, A. J., 160
Bartolini, V., 103, 107, 108
Bateson, G. A., 101, 268, 282
Beardsley, L., 80, 85, 96, 100
Belkin, L., 274
Bell, S. M., 260
Bellin, J. F., 195
Beneke, S., 142
Bennett, N., 89, 105, 110
Benson, J., 218
Bergen, D., 49, 51–54, 59, 60, 96, 143, 147, 366
Bergeron, B., 190
Berk, L. E., 49, 79
Berndt, R., 271

Bers, M. U., 323, 324
Bettelheim, B., 62
Bishop-Josef, S. J., 366
Black, J., 52
Blackwell, A., 227
Blary, R. M., 161
Blurton-Jones, N. G., 102
Bodrova, E., 56, 67, 273
Bolton, G., 82, 195, 196, 256
Bombard, D., 220
Bourdieu, P., 179
Bowman, B., 64, 67, 71, 330
Bradford, M., 304
Branum, L., 293, 294, 297, 307
Bredekamp, S., 17–18, 71, 123, 127–128, 131–133, 366
Bretherton, I., 52
Brockmeyer, C., 182, 264, 270, 273
Bronson, M., 79
Bronson, W., 83
Brown, C. R., 60, 103
Brown, L. K., 195
Brown, S., 61, 63
Bruner, J. S., 56, 60, 62, 90, 96, 328
Buchannan, M., 52, 59
Buerk, K. J., 227
Burdette, H., 292
Burkhour, C., 78, 79
Burns, C. E., 132, 147, 171
Butler, D. L., 218

Caldwell, L., 142
Cameron, A., 161
Campbell, A., 218
Carlsson-Paige, N., 111, 113–115, 324, 331
Carroll, L., 6
Carter, M., 72, 74–75, 78–79
Casey, B., 172
Cazden, C. B., 96
Chalufour, I., 56, 58, 74, 212, 218, 227
Chard, S., 45, 72, 90, 132, 258, 273

Chartrand, M. M., 114
Chen, J., 132
Cho, S., 220
Christie, D. J., 118, 195
Christie, J. F., 21, 53–54, 56, 60, 98, 222
Clark, C. D., 60, 67, 97
Clawson, M., 71, 86, 109
Clay, M., 189
Clayton, M., 74–75
Clements, D. H., 160, 171–173, 175, 195
Clifford, R. M., 87, 269, 315
Cochran-Smith, M., 269, 274
Cole, M., 273
Connolly, K. J., 74
Cook-Gumperz, J., 74, 179, 195, 264, 269, 270,
    272, 277–280, 282, 285
Cooney, M., 52, 96
Cooper, R., 49, 63, 67, 97, 98, 119, 301
Coplan, R. J., 52
Copley, J. V., 171, 172
Copple, C., 17–18, 71, 123, 127–128, 131–133, 366
Corsaro, W. A., 62, 70, 74, 102, 111, 112, 115,
    181, 269, 270, 272, 274, 275, 277–282, 288,
    297, 306
Cortés, C., 329
Cosco, N., 315
Coupland, N., 181, 278, 288
Creasey, G. L., 79
Cross, C. T., 175
Crowley, K., 147, 222
Cryer, D., 72, 87, 88, 269, 315
Csikszentmihayli, M., 63
Cummins, R. H., 56, 58
Curran, J. M., 51
Curtis, D., 72, 74–75, 78–79

Danisa, D., 227
Davidson, J. I. F., 54
DeBey, M., 220
DeBord, K., 315
DeBruin-Parecki, A., 132
Delpit, L., 138
DeMarie, D., 214
Derman-Sparks, L., 71, 83, 90, 109, 119,
    184, 330
Desjean-Perrotta, B., 83
DeVries, R., 52–53, 56, 64, 125, 165, 172, 246, 251, 323
Dewey, J., 7
Dichtelmiller, M. L., 98, 139
Dighe, J., 172

DiPaolo, M., 60
Diperna, J., 147
Dolk, M., 162
Dombro, A. L., 98
Donovan, B., 52
Drew, W. E., 21, 222
Duckworth, E., 137, 214
Dyson, A. H., 62, 83, 133, 179, 181–185, 189,
    190, 197, 198, 200, 247, 264, 269–272, 274, 275,
    278, 285

Easterling, N., 304
Eastwood, G., 297
Edmiaston, R., 52–53, 165, 246, 323
Edwards, D., 90
Edwards, J. O., 109, 119, 330
Egan, K., 62
Einarsdottir, J., 54
Eisenhouer, M. J., 172
Eisert, D., 148
Elder, D., 70
Elgas, P. M., 138
Elkind, D., 49, 61, 366
Ellis, M., 60
Emihovich, C., 341
Ensign, J., 167
Epstein, A., 132
Erickson, F., 179, 269, 274
Ericson, L., 112, 113
Erikson, E., 6, 28, 42–46, 66, 68, 192, 366
Erwin, E. J., 76, 267, 274
Espinosa, L. M., 52, 109, 132, 330
Ethridge, E. A., 214
Evangelou, D., 60

Fantuzzo, J., 145
Farver, J., 52
Feikes, D., 172
Fein, G. G., 50, 56, 183, 202
Fein, S., 251–254
Ferguson, C., 219
Findley, L. C., 52
Fisman, L., 81
Forman, G., 56, 57, 90, 103
Forton, M. B., 74–75
Fosnot, C. T., 161, 162
Fox, J., 76, 274
Fox, L., 76, 103, 274
Frank, D. A., 114
Frazel, M., 335

Freud, S., 42, 344
Friedman, L., 57
Froebel, F., 80
Fromberg, D. P., 49, 50–51, 56, 59, 60, 62, 112
Frost, J. L., 74–75, 78, 79, 87, 237, 292–295, 301, 303, 314
Frost, R., 331
Furth, H. G., 247

Galda, L., 53–54
Gallas, K., 56, 61, 133, 269
Galper, A., 171, 172, 188, 191, 192
Gandini, L., 90, 142
Gardner, H., 67, 80, 132–133, 251
Garvey, C., 62, 269, 271
Gaskins, S., 64, 274, 275
Gates, D., 285
Gee, K., 233
Geiger, C., 58, 59, 61
Geist, E. A., 161
Geist, K., 161
Genishi, C., 60, 83, 133, 179, 181–185, 189, 190, 202, 204, 220, 247, 264, 270, 274, 275, 285
Ghafouri, F., 104
Giddens, A., 198
Ginsburg, H. P., 161, 168, 171, 172
Glupczynski, T., 83, 270
Goffman, E., 285
Goleman, D., 67, 68, 133
Golinkoff, R. M., 49, 71
Golomb, C., 57
Göncü, A., 52, 59
Gonzalez-Mena, G., 90, 330
Gonzalez-Mena, J., 198
Goodenough, E., 303
Goodnow, J., 237
Goodwin, A. L., 185, 189, 202, 204, 270
Gowin, J. W., 50
Gowing, E. D., 57
Graue, E., 146, 147
Graves, D., 189
Green, M., 52
Greenes, C., 172
Greenman, J., 72
Griffin, E., 82, 97, 99, 102, 104, 172, 251, 320
Griffin, P., 273
Gross, M. G., 143
Grossman, H., 194
Groth, L., 56, 183, 202
Gullo, D., 122, 125, 146

Gumperz, J. J., 277, 278
Gustafson, S. C., 119

Hachey, A. C., 218
Haight, W., 52, 64, 67
Haines, S., 218
Halaby, M., 172
Halewood, C., 339, 341
Hamilton, B., 337
Hand, H., 72, 74–75, 80, 87, 89, 147
Hanline, M. F., 76, 103, 274
Harms, T., 72, 87, 88, 232, 269, 302, 315
Harris, M. E., 143
Hartman, J., 60
Hartmann, W., 274
Heath, S. B., 110, 179, 182, 264
Heathcote, D., 82, 195, 196, 233, 256
Helm, J. H., 142, 161, 165
Henderson, F., 50–51, 70, 96–98, 108
Hendrick, J., 90
Hendrickson, J. M., 79
Henry, J., 182
Herbert, P., 196
Hersch, S. B., 161
Hertzog, N., 339
Hesse, P., 331
Hestenes, L., 315
Hildebrandt, C., 52–53, 165, 246, 323
Hill, L., 142
Hirsch-Pasek, K., 49, 71
Hobbs, R., 331
Hoisington, C., 226
Hoke, P., 59
Holmes, R., 58, 59, 61
Holton, D., 152
Homeyer, L., 67, 68
Honda, M., 160
Honig, A. S., 49, 67, 74, 366
Horner, J., 79
Hornung, M., 145, 146
Howes, C., 58
Huang, S., 83, 270
Hughes, F., 52, 70, 83, 132, 181
Hughes, M., 138
Hunt-Berg, M., 83
Hutt, C., 85
Hyson, M., 128, 366

Inoue, N., 161
Isberg, E., 132

Isenberg, J. P., 61, 233, 234, 241, 243, 246,
   251, 267, 274

Jablon, J. R., 98, 139
Jacobs, E. V., 302
Jacobs, G., 147, 222
Jaelitza, 217
Jain, J., 52
Jalongo, M. R., 61, 233, 234, 241, 243, 246, 251,
   267, 274
Jambor, T., 87
Jarrett, O. S., 81
Jaworski, A., 181, 278, 288
Johnson, J., 107, 222
Johnson, J. E., 21, 49
Johnson, L., 233
Johnson, S., 76, 274
Johnson, T. C., 52, 59
Jones, C., 172
Jones, E., 49, 50–51, 63, 67, 70, 96–98, 108, 109,
   119, 145
Joshi, A., 52, 71, 91, 98
Jurvis, P. A., 79
Justen, J. E., III, 103

Kaden, M., 57
Kafai, Y. B., 332
Kagan, S. L., 123, 124, 128
Kaiser, A., 274
Kaiser, B., 269
Kamii, C., 31, 52–53, 56, 64, 125, 132, 160, 161,
   165, 172
Katch, J., 62, 67, 68, 101, 111, 113–115, 118,
   133, 328
Kato, Y., 52–53, 56, 160, 161
Katz, L., 45, 60, 72, 90, 132, 161, 165, 258,
   273, 313
Kedem, Y., 339
Kellogg, R., 237, 251
Kendall, J. S., 364
Keyes, D., 52
Khazian, A., 296
Kilbourne, J., 324, 326
Kilpatrick, C., 218
Kim, E., 219
Kim, S., 56
Kirmani, M. H., 52, 109
Klein, A., 172
Klinkner, J., 260
Klugman, E., 292

Kohn, A., 132, 146
Koons, K., 190
Koplow, L., 59, 68, 97, 278
Kostelnik, M, 74–75, 79, 97, 108
Kranor, L., 79
Krechevsky, M., 132
Kreidler, W., 119
Kritchevsky, L., 74–75, 239, 269, 303
Kroll, L., 172
Kuo, F., 308
Kuschner, A., 79
Kuschner, D. S., 103

Labov, W., 283, 284
Lamorey, S., 148
Lancy, D.F., 64, 67, 96
Landreth, G., 67, 68
Lane, F., 331
Lantieri, L., 67
Lederman, J., 96
Lehr, R., 71, 76
Leong, D., 56, 67, 273
Levin, D. E., 67, 68, 101, 110, 113–115, 119, 324,
   326, 328, 330, 331
Levin, J., 83
Lim, J., 219
Linn, S., 324, 328
Locke, P. A., 83
Longfield, J., 227
Louv, R., 217–219, 292, 295
Lovsey, K., 97
Lowenfeld, V., 237, 251
Lunn, K., 103, 107, 108
Lux, D. G., 233
Lythcott, M., 54, 61, 195
Lytle, S. L., 269, 274

Ma, L., 160
Maioni, T. L., 145, 146
Mangiola, L., 179, 182, 264
Manning, K., 109
Marchant, C., 60
Marsden, D. B., 139
Marvin, C., 83
Marzano, R. J., 364
Mauer, D., 53–54
McCay, L., 52
McCune, L., 49
McDonnough, J. T., 220
McDowell, J., 182, 264, 270, 273

McEvoy, M., 76, 79, 274
McEwan, H., 62
McGinnis, J., 315
McHargue T., 119
McHenry, J. D., 227
McLloyd, V., 86
McMullen, M. B., 98
Mead, G. H., 6, 28, 39–42, 46, 344, 366
Meckley, A. M., 21, 222
Meier, D., 123
Meisels, S. J., 132, 139, 146, 147
Melben, L. W., 218
Mengel, T., 304
Meyers, C. A., 56, 148
Miller, J. L., 218
Miller, P., 70, 274, 275
Milligan, S. A., 274
Mindes, G., 51, 52, 60, 108
Mitchell, G., 201
Miyakawa, Y., 56, 161
Molinari, L., 272, 274, 278, 288
Monighan-Nourot, 6, 41–42
Montessori, M., 320
Moore, E. K., 64, 81, 296, 330
Moore, R., 74, 297, 315
Morgenthaler, S. K., 50–51
Morrison, H., 194, 273
Morrison, M., 67, 68
Morrow, L. M., 189, 190, 195
Murphey, D. A., 132, 147, 171
Murphy, M. S., 168
Murray, A., 169, 170
Myers, G. D., 58, 294
Myhre, S. M., 83

Nabhan, G. P., 217
Nachmanovitch, S., 63
Naudeau, S., 111, 112, 323
Neeley, P. M., 103
Neeley, R. A., 103
Nel, E., 56
Nell, M. L., 21, 222
Neuman, S., 202
Neves, P., 54
New, R., 90
Newcomer, P., 52, 267
Newman, D., 273
Nicolopolou, A., 50–51, 56, 62, 179, 182,
    264, 270, 273, 275
Ninio, A., 96

Nourot, P. M., 7, 49, 50, 62, 63, 72, 74–75, 80, 87,
    89, 147, 182
Novakowski, J., 227

Odom, S., 51, 52, 59, 79, 108, 274, 278
Ogu, U., 227
Olds, A., 303
Oliver, S., 292
Onaga, E., 74–75, 97
O'Neill, C., 233
Orellana, M., 109
Ostler, T., 52
Ostrosky, M., 274
Otto, B., 188
Owacki, G., 197, 200

Paley, V. G., 62, 70, 88, 99, 101, 106, 107, 115, 118,
    133, 137, 138, 182, 197, 264, 271
Palmer, S. D., 87
Panksepp, J., 52
Pape, D., 59
Papert, S., 332
Parten, M. B., 64, 145
Pellegrini, A. D., 53–54, 60, 102, 146, 292, 298
Pelletier, J., 339
Peltier, M. B., 138
Perry, J. P., 62, 78, 97, 115, 269, 272, 274, 282,
    293–295, 299, 300, 307, 310–313
Phillips, A., 97, 100, 108
Piaget, J., 6, 28–35, 46, 49, 50, 64, 66, 145, 159, 216,
    273, 344, 345, 347–356, 359, 362, 363, 366
Ponte, I., 111, 112, 323
Preissler, M. A., 51, 108
Prescott, E., 74–75, 239, 269, 303
Putnam-Franklin, S., 21, 222

Qvortrup, J., 74, 269, 270, 275, 277, 278

Raebeck, L., 246
Ramminger, A., 260
Ramsey, P., 71, 78, 79, 83, 90, 109, 119, 184
Rasminsky, J. S., 269
Reed, T. L., 269, 282
Reeve, R., 339
Reid, R., 78, 79
Reifel, S., 59, 74–75, 237, 269, 270, 275, 284,
    285, 293
Reynolds, G., 52, 63, 70, 74, 83, 98, 109, 145, 181
Richardson, K., 172
Richner, E. S., 179

Riefel, S., 54
Riley, C., 72, 87, 88
Riley, D., 260
Rivkin, M. S., 219
Robin, K., 132
Robinson, T., 331
Rogers, S., 89
Rohde, B., 74–75, 97
Rollett, B., 274
Roopnarine, J. L., 52
Rosenow, N., 2008
Roskos, K., 54, 56, 98, 195, 202
Rothstein-Fisch, C., 198
Rubin, K. H., 49, 52, 145, 146

Sales, C., 52–53, 165, 246, 323
Salmon, M., 334
Salonius-Pasternak, D., 111, 112, 323
Saltz, E., 107
Sandall, S., 76
Sanders, H., 285
San Juan, R. R., 260
Saracho, O., 109
Sarama, J., 160, 171–173, 175, 195
Sawyer, K., 195, 270, 274, 277
Scales, B., 6, 62, 167, 182, 183, 185, 188, 192, 195, 198, 248, 261, 264, 267, 269–273, 275, 281, 285
Scarlett, W. G., 50, 52, 65, 68, 111, 112, 323
Schmidt, S. R., 227
Schor, J., 326, 331
Schultz, P. W., 296
Schwall, C., 142
Schwartz, K., 270
Schwartzman, H. B., 102, 114
Schweingruber, H., 175
Schweinhart, L., 132
Sebastian-Honig, M. S., 269, 270, 275, 277, 278
Seefeldt, C., 21, 123, 132, 171, 172, 188, 191, 192, 202, 243, 247, 300, 365
Seiter, E., 330
Seo, K. H., 161
Shamblott, M., 139
Sharp, A., 109
Shefatya, L., 106, 144
Sheldon, A., 51, 59
Shepard, L., 123, 124, 128, 132, 146
Sheridan, K., 52
Shin, M., 52
Shope, T. R., 114
Shores, R., 76, 79, 274

Shriver, C., 296
Sigel, I. E., 50
Silvern, S. B., 332
Singer, D. G., 49, 61, 71, 195, 323, 328, 329, 331
Singer, J. L., 49, 54, 61, 71, 195, 323, 328, 329, 331, 366
Sluss, D., 51
Smilansky, S., 40, 50–51, 60, 106, 107, 139, 143–145, 269
Smith, A. F., 141
Smith, P. K., 74, 292
Smith, S. S., 161, 168, 171, 172
Smith, W. S., 227
Sobel, D., 296
Stagstetter, M., 83
Starkey, P., 172
Stayton, D. J., 260
Stegelin, D., 89
Stephens, K., 304
Stewart, D., 95
Stone, M., 83
Stone, S. J., 60
Strain, P. S., 79
Streeck, J., 270, 272
Stremmel, A., 51
Strickland, J., 141
Strickland, K., 141
Sullivan, V., 304
Suppal, P., 52
Sutton-Smith, B., 112
Swarbrick, N., 297
Swartz, D., 288
Swick, K., 71

Tabanico, J., 296
Taylor, A., 308
Thatcher, D. H., 172
Thomas, K, 76
Thompson, J. E., 297
Thompson, R. A., 297
Tierney, R., 141
Tipton-Sumner, C., 103
Tizard, B., 138
Tobin, J., 182, 272, 330
Topal, C. W., 81
Torquati, J., 81
Tovey, H., 300
Tracy, R., 266
Trawick-Smith, J., 74–75, 87, 108, 110
Trembley, A., 79

Tribble, C., 260, 269
Trimble, S., 217
Trumbull, E., 198
Trundle, K. C., 227
Tuermer, U., 52
Turner, V. D., 273, 275, 279
Tutton, K., 297

Uttal, D., 53–54

Van der Kooij, R., 267, 278
Vanderven, K., 61
Van Hoorn, J. L., 6, 114, 119
Van Thiel, L., 21, 222
Veldhuis, H. A., 246, 251
Viens, J., 132
Von Blanckensee, L., 195, 335, 338, 340
Vygotsky, L., 6, 28, 35–38, 46, 49, 50, 60, 62, 66, 67,
	179, 217, 258, 269, 273, 274, 277, 298, 335, 344,
	345–349, 362, 363, 366

Wagner, B. J., 195, 233
Wagner, R. V., 118
Wallace, A. H., 161
Walling, L., 74–75, 239, 269
Walsh, P., 239, 269, 303
Wang, X. C., 339
Wanigarayake, M., 67
Wasik, B., 54, 191
Wassermann, S., 87, 137, 228, 237, 255
Webster, P., 281
Wehby, J., 76, 274
Weintraub, J., 62, 264, 270
Wesson, K., 132, 146
Wheeler, L., 246
Whiren, A., 74–75, 97
Whitaker, R., 292

White, D. R., 302
White, L. F., 114
Wien, C. A., 21, 90, 104, 123, 132, 142, 146, 147,
	202, 258, 273, 364, 365
Williams, K. P., 104
Willmore, S., 227
Wilson, R., 296
Winter, D. D., 118
Wisneski, D., 59
Wittall, S. T., 119
Wittmer, D., 119
Wohlwill, J. F., 85
Wolfberg, P., 51, 59, 60, 83, 97, 101, 106, 108,
	138, 278
Wolfe, C. R., 56, 58
Wolfe, J., 49, 80
Wong, H., 74, 81, 296, 297
Wood, L., 89
Woods, I. C., 301
Woods, T. A., 175
Worth, K., 56, 58, 74, 212, 218, 227
Wortham, S. C., 74–75, 123, 141, 237, 293
Wurm, J. P., 142
Wurtz, E., 123, 124, 128

Xue, Y., 139

Yang, H., 98
Yeatman, J., 59, 237, 269
Yopp, H. K., 54, 192
Yopp, R. H., 192

Zan, B., 52–53, 64, 125, 165, 246, 323
Zapeda, M., 198
Zigler, E. F., 366
Zimmerman, E., 233
Zimmerman, L., 233

Subject Index

Accessorizing, 170

Accessory boxes, 83, 84

Accommodation. *See also* Children with special needs
  explanation of, 29, 30, 349, 350
  imitation and, 350
  play and, 351, 355

Accountability
  high-stakes, 124, 146
  in literacy standards, 202

Adaptation, 29

Aggression. *See also* Violence; Violent play
  assessing purpose of, 113–115
  realities in children's lives and, 67–68,
      112–114

Alliance for Childhood, 315

American Association for the Advancement
    of Science (AAAS), 211–213

Anecdotal records, 138–139

Artist Apprentice role, 99–100

Arts
  cultural enrichment in, 244–245
  guided and directed play in, 238, 256–258
  incorporated into play, 234–235
  science and mathematics merging with, 237
  tactile and sensory aspects of, 235–236
  teacher knowledge about, 240–241

Arts education
  balanced curriculum in, 249–251
  for children with special needs, 237,
      255–256
  effectiveness of, 258
  materials for, 233–236, 239–242
  music and movement in, 245–249
  space issues for, 238–239
  spontaneous play in, 233–234, 238, 248
  standards for, 242–243
  time issues for, 238

Assessment
  of age-appropriate development, 127–131
  ascertaining child's viewpoint in, 136–138

benefits and risks of, 146–149
  of children from diverse cultures, 125–126
  of children with special needs, 126–127
  how play informs, 134–136
  of individual development, 131–134
  of mathematical reasoning, 162–163
  of outdoor play, 314–315
  overview of, 122–123, 149
  of play as play, 143–146
  play-centered, 124–125
  purposes of, 123–124

Assessment tools
  anecdotal records as, 138–139
  checklists as, 139–141
  documents as, 141–142
  portfolios as, 141
  videotapes as, 142–143

Assimilation
  explanation of, 29–30, 349–350
  play and, 351, 355

Assisted technologies, 335–336

Associative play, 65

Auditory discrimination, 247

Authentic questions, 137–138, 229

Autonomy
  as context for development, 362–363, 366
  development of, 43, 44
  moral, 64

Benchmarks for Science Literacy (American Association
    for the Advancement of Science), 211

Bipolar opposites, in play, 62–63

*Blocks to Robots: Learning with Technology in the Early
    Childhood Classroom* (Bers), 323

Bodily kinesthetic intelligence, 133

Booklet Writing Time, 192

Boundaries, for play areas, 78

British Infant School model, 88

*Building Emotional Intelligence: Techniques to Cultivate
    Innr Strength in Children* (Goleman & Lantieri), 67

Call-and-response routines, 245–246
Cardinal numbers, 157
Checklists, assessment, 139–141
Child development
    arts education and, 251–254
    assessing age-appropriate, 127–131
    play materials and, 319, 321–324
    role of play in, 5–7, 27, 122–123, 344–345
    scientific concepts and, 216–217
    stages of, 350–352
    toys that limit, 324–325
Child development theories
    constructivism and, 27–29, 273, 275, 344–355
    Erikson and, 28, 42–46, 66
    Mead and, 28, 39–42
    Piaget and, 28–35, 66–67, 159–160, 275, 347–354
    Vygotsky and, 28, 35–38, 60, 269, 273, 335
Childhood and Society (Erikson), 28
Children
    effects of media on, 328–329
    integrating interests of, 219
    need to reflect on own learning, 133–134
    play communication among, 272–273
    readiness for school, 147–148
    that experience violence and aggression, 67–68,
        112–114
Children and Science, 227
Children with special needs
    accommodations for, 267
    arts education for, 237, 255–256
    assessment of, 126–127
    computers and assisted technologies for, 335–336
    computer use by, 335–336
    inclusion of, 267–269
    language and literacy play for, 201
    mathematics education for, 166–168
    outdoor play for, 308
    perspectivism and, 51–52
    physical spaces for, 75–79
    play-centered assessment for, 148
    play-centered curricula for, 59–60
    play entry for, 103
    play materials for, 83
    play orchestration strategies for, 103, 108–109
    science education for, 221–222
    socialization and, 267–269, 273–274, 277–278
    symbolic play for, 51
    turn taking by, 277–278
The Child's Conception of Physical Causality
    (Piaget), 216

Child Watching at Play-groups and Nursery School
    (Sylvia, Roy & Painter), 145
Choosing Technology-Based Activities for Young children,
    ages 3–7, (von Blankensee), 338–339
Commercials, television, 330–331
Communication, 181
Competencies
    development of, 358–359
    explanation of, 346
Computers. See also Technology
    background of, 332
    to extend play and address standards,
        339–341
    guiding play with, 334–335
    physical space for, 332
    software selection for, 332–334, 336, 338–339
    for students with special needs, 335–336
Computer simulations, 336
Conceptual reasoning, 351
Concrete-operational stage, 351
Conservation, 57
Consortium of the National Arts Education
    Associations, 19
Constructive play (Piaget), 33, 34
Constructivism
    explanation of, 28, 29, 273, 275, 344
    means-ends coordinations and development
        and, 345–347
    Piaget and, 28, 29, 33, 34, 347–354
    social-cultural theories of play and, 347–349
    social experience and, 354–355
    views on, 344–345
    Vygotsky and, 348–349
Consumer Product Safety Act of 1978, 86
Consumer Product Safety Commission, 86
Consumer Product Safety Improvement Act of
    2008, 86
Continuous quantities, 154–155
Continuum of Children's Development in Early
    Reading and Writing (IRA/NAEYC), 183
Cooperative play, 65, 66
Creativity, 60–61
Cultural diversity
    arts curriculum and, 244–245
    assessment and, 125–126
    challenges of, 265, 267
    mathematics education and, 165–167
    music and, 247–248
    outdoor play and, 301–303
    play-based literacy curriculum and, 184–185

play-centered curriculum and, 4, 90–91,
    184–185
as social enrichment, 264–269
Curriculum. *See also specific subjects*
    arts, 237, 249–251
    developmentally based, 3–11
    language and literature-based, 184–189
    mathematics, 158–164, 171–176
    play-centered, 3–4, 90–91
    science, 222–229
*Curriculum Focal Points for Prekindergarten through
    Grade 8 Mathematics* (National Council of
    Teachers of Mathematics), 175
Curriculum-generated play
    mathematics in, 172–173
    planning for, 89–90
    science in, 227–229

Daily life activities
    mathematics education and, 165
    in play, 10, 11
Daily schedules, 87–88
Developmentally appropriate practice (DAP),
    17–18, 363–364
*Developmentally Appropriate Practice in Early Childhood
    Programs Serving Children from Birth through Age 8*
    (National Association for Education of Young
    Children), 18
Developmentally based curriculum, 3–11
Directed play
    in arts, 256–258
    examples of, 100
    explanation of, 9–10
    in play continuum, 11
Direct involvement, 312
Discrete quantities, 155
Documentation assessment, 141–142
Dramatic play
    assessment of, 143, 144
    development of literate behavior through,
        195–196
    indirectly shaping, 233
    logical-mathematical thinking and, 57
    materials for, 82, 234
    Piaget on, 33, 34
    rules in, 38

Early childhood
    oral culture of, 62
    play stage in, 44–45

The Early Childhood Environmental Rating Scale,
    Revised Edition, 315
*Early Childhood Mathematics: Promoting Good
    Beginnings* (NAEYC/NCTM), 159,
    163–164, 176
*Early Learning Standards: Creating the Conditions
    for Success* (NAECS/SDE), 19–21
Early Learning Standards (2003) (NAEYC/
    NAECS/SDE), 124
Education associations, 19
E-mail, 333, 334
Emergent literacy, 189–190
Emotional development
    coping with harsh realities and, 67–68
    curriculum standards for, 131
    explanation of, 66–67
    importance of, 67
Emotional intelligence, 67
Enactment phase in peer play, 307
English language learners
    matchmaking strategies for, 106
    mathematics education and, 165–167
    play-based literacy curriculum and,
        184–189
    play orchestration strategies for, 106, 109
    science education for, 220
Equalities, 155
Erikson, Erik
    background on, 42
    constructivist orientation of, 28
    early childhood and, 44–45
    emotional development and, 66
    infancy and, 43
    middle childhood and, 45–46
    toddlerhood and, 43–44
Estimation, 155
Ethnic stereotypes, 329–330

Families. *See* Parents/families
Fantasy play
    function of, 66–67
    major aspects of, 62–63
Federal No Child Left Behind Act of 2001,
    123, 292
Fine motor skills, assessment of, 130
For Kids' Sake: Think Toy Safety (Consumer
    Product Safety Commission), 86
Formal-operational stage, 351–352
FOSS (Full Option Science System) units, 227
Functional play (Piaget), 33

Game stage (Mead), 40–41
Games with rules
    cautions in use of, 322
    function of, 34–35, 52–53, 322
    for logical-mathematical thinking, 165
    selection of, 323
GEMS units, 227
Gender, expressions of, 275
Gender stereotypes
    play differences and, 270–272
    teachers responses to, 327–328
    toys and, 325–326
Generalized other stage, 41–42
The Geography of Childhood (Nabhan &
    Trimble), 217
Geometry, 153–154
Government regulation of toy safety standards, 86
Group play, 65, 66
Guardian of the Gate role, 102–103
Guided play
    in arts, 238, 256–258
    with computers, 334–335
    examples of, 100, 178
    explanation of, 9
    musical, 246–247
    in play continuum, 11
    strategies for, 97, 98

Hazardous Substance Act of 1973, 86
High-stakes accountability, 124, 146
Horizontal, 154

Illicit play, 110–112
Imagination
    major aspects of, 62–63
    opportunities to foster, 60–61
Imitation, 350
Improvisational routines, 245–246
Inclusion, of children with special needs, 267–269
Indirect coordination, 311–312
Inequalities, 155
Infants, 43, 359
Initiation phase in peer play, 306–307
Initiative, 44–45
Inquiry, 312–314
"Insect Love" (Jaelitza), 217
Instrumental play, 110–112
Intelligence
    assessment of, 132–133
    emotional, 67

expression of, 354, 355
    means-ends coordination and, 345–346
    multiple, 132–133
    naturalistic, 80–81, 133
    personality and, 357
    play and development of, 355–356
    social consciousness and, 346
Interactive strategies, 276–278
International Reading Association (IRA), 19
International Society for Technology in Education
    (ISTE), 19, 337, 338
Interpersonal intelligence, 133
Interpretive approach
    to classroom social ecology, 278
    function of, 274–275, 278
Interviews, 143
Intrapersonal intelligence, 133
It's Elementary!: Integrating Technology in the Primary
    Grades (International Society for Technology
    in Education), 337

Journal writing, 190

Kindergarteners, 8, 75
Knowledge
    logical-mathematical, 31, 32, 56–58, 159–160,
        165, 166, 319
    objective, 354
    physical, 30–32, 159–160
    Piaget and types of, 30–32, 159–160
    social, 31–33, 159, 160

Language development
    awareness of sounds and patterns and, 190–192
    literate behaviors, play and, 179–180
    role of play in, 24–25, 53–56
Language learning
    materials for, 201
    in primary grades, 192–195
    space for, 201–202
    time issues for, 200
Last Child in the Woods: Saving Our Children from
    Nature-Deficit Disorder (Louv), 217
Learning
    interpersonal to intrapersonal processes in, 36–37
    reflecting on one's own, 133–134
    technology and, 323–324
Learning outcomes, 19
Learning with Nature Idea Book: Creating Nurturing
    Outdoor Spaces for Children, 315

Letter-sound correspondence
  explanation of, 190–191
  introduction of, 191–193
Limit setting, for violent play, 116–118
Literacy
  emergent, 189–190
  explanation of, 179
  multimedia and, 194–195
  in primary grades, 192–194
  scientific, 211–212
  standards for, 202–204
Literate behaviors
  classroom resources and activities to promote,
    200–201
  drama techniques to promote, 195–196
  early story constructions and, 182–183
  explanation of, 179
  importance of, 189–192
  play and, 53–56, 179–182, 184–185, 201
  story dictation/story play to promote, 197–200
Logical-mathematical intelligence, 133
Logical-mathematical knowledge
  explanation of, 31, 32
  mathematics and, 159, 160, 165, 166
  play and, 56–58
  play materials and, 319

Matchmaker role, 105–106
Materials. *See* Play materials
Mathematics
  culturally relevant, 167
  in early childhood integrated curriculum,
    158–164
  music and, 247, 248
  nature of, 159–161, 163–164
  in play-centered curriculum, 153–159
  playful nature of, 152–153
  play orchestration for, 169–173
Mathematics concepts
  geometry as, 153–154
  measurement as, 157
  numbers and operations as, 154–157
  processes for, 157–158
Mathematics education
  assessment and, 162–163
  for children with special needs, 166–168
  daily life situations as cornerstone of, 165
  for diverse populations and English language
    learners, 165–167
  goals of, 159

play-centered, 153–159, 163–165, 171–172
  principles for, 173–174
  recommendations for, 173
  standards for, 174–176
*Mathematics in Early Childhood Education, Paths
    toward Excellence and Equity* (Cross, Woods, &
    Schwingruer), 175
Mead, George Herbert
  background of, 39
  constructivist orientation of, 28
  game stage and, 40–41
  generalized other stage and, 41–42
  play stage and, 40
Means-ends coordinations
  explanation of, 345–347
  intelligence and personality and, 357
  Piaget and, 347
Measurement, 157
Media
  critics of, 328–329
  literacy and, 194–195
  racial and ethnic stereotypes and, 329–330
  teacher responses to, 330
Media literacy, 330–331
Mind, Self, and Society (Mead), 28, 39
Mind in Society (Vygotsky), 28, 35
Mindstorms (Papert), 332
Miniatures, 320
Moral autonomy, 64
Moral development, 64
Movement, 245–247
Multiple intelligence theory, 132–133
Music. *See also* Arts; Arts education
  cultural diversity and, 247–248
  mathematics and, 247, 248
  in play-centered curriculum, 245–247
Musical intelligence, 133
My Art Is Me, 232
Mythic thinking, 62

Narratives
  development of, 55–56, 62
  research on, 275
National Art Education Association, 243
National Association for Sport and Physical
    Education (NASPE), 19, 293
National Association for the Education of Young
    Children (NAEYC)
  background of, 363
  on curriculum standards, 19, 302

National Association for the Education of Young
    Children (NAEYC) (*Continued*)
  on developmentally appropriate practice, 17, 363
  *Early Learning Standards: Creating the Conditions
    for Success,* 19–21
  on educational resources, 335
  on mathematics, 159, 161, 163–164, 166, 173
  position statement of 2009, 18, 127, 133, 341
  on screening and assessment, 125–126
  on technology, 337, 339
National Association of Early Childhood Specialists
    in State Departments of Education, 19–21
National Council for the Social Studies (NCSS),
    19, 285–286
National Council of Teachers of Mathematics
    (NCTM), 19, 159, 161, 163–164, 166, 173–176
National Early Childhood Assessment Panel, 123
National Education Standards, 341
National Research Council, 211–212
National Science Education Standards, 220, 222, 229
National Science Teachers Association (NSTA),
    19, 227
Naturalistic intelligence, 80–81, 133
Nature
  enhancing connections with, 218–219
  establishing relationship with, 296
  exposure to, 80, 217–218, 295–296
Nature vs. nurture argument, 27–28
Negative talk, 201
*Negotiating Standards in the Primary Classroom: The
    Teacher's Dilemma* (Wien), 21
Negotiation phase, in peer play, 307
Newspaper project, 273
Night Sky project, 318
No Child Left Behind Act of 2001, 123, 292
Noisy areas, 78–79
Number concepts, 154–157
Number names, 156
Numerals, 156–157
Nurture, nature vs., 27–28

Objective knowledge, 354
Observations
  of outdoor play, 305–307
  of teachers, 287–288
One-to-one correspondence, 156
Onlooker behavior
  in English language learners, 109
  explanation of, 64–65
Ordinal numbers, 157

Orff-Kodaly method, 246–247
Outdoor play
  advocating for, 315–316
  assessment of, 314–315
  child-initiated, 297–298
  for culturally diverse children, 301–303
  example of, 290–291
  fostering inquiry in, 312–314
  function of, 80–81, 291–293
  nature, 295–296
  observations and interpretations of, 305–307
  physically active, 293–294
  safety issues related to, 86, 87, 292, 304–305
  science in, 208
  for students with special needs, 308
  teacher decision making during, 309–311
  teaching goals for, 299–300
  teaching styles to support, 311–312
Outdoor spaces
  challenges of, 303–304
  comfort and safety issues related to, 304–305
  indoor vs., 298, 299
  opportunities in, 80–81
  for preschool and primary grades, 77
  as soft spaces, 80

Parallel play, 65, 103
Parallel Player role, 103–104
Parents/families
  communicating about assessment with, 127
  role in assessments, 148–149
  separation from, 260–264
  view of outdoor play, 301
Participant role, 104–105
Pathways, 78
Peaceful classrooms, 118–119
The Peacemaker role, 100–102
Peer relationships
  phases in, 306–307
  problem solving and, 58–60
  role of teachers in, 60
Penn Interactive Peer Play Scale (PIPPS), 145
Personality
  explanation of, 346
  intelligence and, 357
  play and development of, 356–357
Perspectivism, 51–52
Phonemic awareness
  explanation of, 54, 191, 193
  music activities and, 247

Phonological awareness, 54, 191
Physical knowledge
  explanation of, 30–32
  mathematics and, 159–160
Physical spaces. *See also* Outdoor spaces
  adjacent activity areas in, 81–82
  for arts activities, 238–239
  accommodations for children with special
    needs, 75–76
  for computers, 332
  considerations for, 74–75
  interactive play and, 285
  outdoor, 77, 80–81
  paths and boundaries in, 78
  quiet and noisy areas in, 78–79
  soft spaces in, 80
  when space is limited, 81
Piaget, Jean
  accommodation and, 29–30
  background of, 28–29, 347
  child development theories of, 347–348,
    350–352, 362
  constructivist orientation of, 28, 29, 347–354
  emotional development and, 66–67
  logical-mathematical knowledge and, 31, 32,
    159–160
  moral development and, 64
  physical knowledge and, 30–32, 159–160
  social knowledge and, 32, 33, 159–160
  theories of play, 32–35, 275
Pivots, 38
Play. *See also* Outdoor play
  achieving goals through, 6
  binary opposition themes in, 62
  for children with special needs, 51–52, 59–60
  computer, 332–336
  as core of developmentally appropriate
    practice, 17–18
  developmental role of, 4, 23–24
  development of competencies and, 358–359
  development of intelligence and, 355–356
  development of personality and, 356–357
  directed, 9–11, 100
  emotional development and, 66–68
  as form of communication, 181
  formulating questions for children regarding,
    137–138
  function of, 3, 4, 27, 68, 91, 134–136, 366
  group, 65–66
  guided, 9, 11, 97–100, 178, 334–335

illicit, 110–112
imagination and creativity and, 60–63
incorporating art into, 234–235
instrumental, 110–112
language and literacy and, 53–56
logical-mathematical thinking and, 56–58
in mathematics education, 164–165 (*See also*
  Mathematics education)
media-based, 328–331
multidimensional qualities of, 2–3
parallel, 65
Piaget's theories of, 32–35
problem solving and, 58–59
recreational, 110, 111
school culture and, 110–112
social and emotional role of, 15, 16
social development and, 359–360
social-moral development and, 63–66
solitary, 65
spontaneous, 8–9, 11, 97, 100, 181, 207, 224–226,
  232–234, 248, 297–298, 306
symbolic, 33–35, 38, 49–53, 59–60
tactile sensory, 235–236
taking child's view of, 71–72
teachers' view of, 12–15
violent, 67–68, 112–119
work of society and, 360–361
Play, Dreams and Imitation in Childhood (Piaget), 32
Play-centered assessment. *See also* Assessment
  for children with special needs, 148
  function of, 124–125, 149
  implementation of, 136–137
Play-centered curriculum. *See also specific subject areas*
  addressing standards in, 18–21
  arts in, 232–258
  cultural diversity in, 4, 90–91, 184–185
  early learning standards and, 146–147
  explanation of, 3–4, 6, 22
  exploration of psychosocial issues in, 45
  families and, 148–149
  function of, 8–11, 46–47, 135, 150, 366–367
  integrating academic standards in, 91–92
  issues central to, 14
  language and literacy in, 179–205
  mathematics in, 152–176
  peace promotion in, 118–119
  planning for, 89
  role of teacher in, 21–22
  science in, 208–230
Play entry, 102, 103, 281

Play episodes, 281–285
The Playground Checklist, 314
Playgrounds, 87. *See also* Outdoor spaces
Play materials
    for accessory boxes, 83, 84
    for arts activities, 233–236, 239–242
    child development and, 319, 321–324
    for children with special needs, 83
    familiar and novelty, 83, 85
    for language and literacy play, 201
    for mathematics, 169, 170
    overview of, 82–83, 318
    safety issues related to, 86–87
    tactile sensory, 235–236
    that limit development, 324–325
    that offer opportunities for exploration, 85–86
    that promote early sexualization, 326
    that promote violence, 326–327
    that undermine gender equality, 325–326
    types of, 319–321
Play orchestration
    daily schedules for, 87–88
    materials for, 82–86
    for mathematics, 169–173
    overview of, 70–71, 94–96
    physical space for, 74–82
    principles guiding, 71–73
    safety issues related to, 86–87
    for science, 226–227
    spontaneous, guided, and directed, 97–108
    timing issues in, 109–110
Play orchestration strategies
    Artist Apprentice, 99–100
    for children with special needs, 108–109
    continuum of, 73
    for English language learners, 109
    Guardian of the Gate, 102–103
    guidelines to choose, 108–110
    Matchmaker, 105–106
    Parallel Player, 103–104
    Participant, 104–105
    The Peacemaker, 100–102
    Play Tutor, 106–108
    scaffolding as, 96–97
    Spectator, 104
    Story Player, 106
    timing issues related to, 109–110
Play stages
    Erikson on, 44–45
    Mead on, 40

Play Tutor role, 106–108
Portfolios, 141
Position Statement (National Association for the Education of Young Children) (2009), 18, 127, 133
Poverty, 165, 183
Practice play (Piaget), 33
Preconceptual stage, 351
Preoperational period, 351
Preschoolers
    gender differences in play, 270–272
    physical spaces for, 75, 77
    play-centered programs for, 8
    play materials for, 82
    play stage in, 44–45
    social ecology and, 278–280
Preschool Outdoor Environment Measurement Scale (POEMS), 315
Primary grades
    language and literacy learning in, 192–195
    physical spaces for, 76, 77
    play-centered programs in, 8
    play materials for, 82–83
Private areas
    function of, 78, 79
    as soft spaces, 80
Problem solving
    mathematical, 157–158
    play and, 58–59, 323
    scientific, 157
Project 2061 (American Association for the Advancement of Science), 212, 213
Project Approach, 258, 302
Props, 82–83. *See also* Play materials
Proximity, 153
Psychosocial theory, 42

Quantifiers, 155
Questions
    authentic, 137–138, 229
    framing play, 137
Quiet areas, 78–79

Racial stereotypes, 329–330
Rationality, 348–349
Reaching Standards and Beyond in Kindergarten: Nurturing Children's Sense of Wonder and Joy in Learning (National Association for the Education of Young Children), 365–366
Reading competencies, 203–204

Reality, construction of, 352–355
Recommendations on Screening and Assessment of Young English-Language Learners (National Association for the Education of Young Children), 125–126
Records, anecdotal, 138–139
Recreational play, 110, 111
Reflective abstraction, 356–357
Reggio Emilia approach, 90, 258, 302
Remote Control Childhood? Combating the Hazards of Media Culture (Levin), 331
Rhymes, 191
Rhythmic patterns, 246–247
Rimes, 191
Robotic technology, 323–324
Role play
  symbolic, 50–51, 57
  thematic fantasy, 107
Rote counting, 156
Rules, understanding of, 38

Safety
  in outdoor play, 87, 292, 304–305
  of toys, 86–87
Scaffolding, 96–97
School-Age Care Environmental Rating Scale, 302, 315
Schools
  historical background of, 7
  play and culture of, 110–112
  as ready for learners, 147–148
Science
  in kindergarten, 208–210
  nature of, 213–216
  problem solving in, 157
Science content, 214–215
Science education
  child development and, 216
  for children with special needs, 221–222
  for English language learners, 220
  goals of, 210–212
  integrating child's interest in, 219
  nature and environment and, 217–218, 225–226
  play-generated, 226–229
  science content in, 214–215
  social contexts and, 216–217
  spontaneous play in, 207, 224–226
  standards for, 222–224
  teacher confidence and, 229–230
Science for all Children (American Association for the Advancement of Science), 212

Scientific concepts, 214, 216
Scientific processes, 213–214
Self, sense of, 359–360
Sensorimotor period, 350, 358
Separation, from parents, 260–264
Seriation, 155–156
Serious Players in the Primary Classroom (Wasserman), 228
Shapes, 154
Shop CPSC Toy Safety Tips Bfore Shopping for Holiday Gifts (Consumer Product Safety Commission), 86
Social consciousness, 346–347
Social contexts
  play-centered curricula and, 218
  science learning and, 216–217
Social development
  assessment of, 130
  curriculum standards for, 131
  play and, 359–360
Social ecology
  contrasts in, 278–280
  interpretive approach to, 278
Socialization
  children with special needs and, 267–269, 273–274, 277–278
  of competencies, 358–359
  cultural diversity and, 265, 267
  gender and, 270–272
  granting a warrant and, 281–285
  interactive strategies and, 276–278, 285
  interpretive approach and, 274–275, 278
  role of play in, 15, 16, 23–25, 269–270, 273–274
  separation from parents and, 260–264
  social and ecological cues and, 278–280
  social and environmental expectations and, 272–273
  teacher support for play interactions and, 281
Social knowledge
  explanation of, 31–33
  mathematics and, 159, 160
Social-moral development
  assessment of, 125
  overview of, 63–64
Social participation
  group play and, 65–66
  onlooker behavior and, 64–65
  parallel play and, 65
  solitary play and, 65

Social skills
    in children with special needs, 79
    method to determine, 280–281
Social studies education, 286
Social studies standards, 285–287
Sociodramatic play. *See* Dramatic play
Sociological Studies (Piaget), 28
Soft spaces, 80
Software
    selection of, 332–334, 338–339
    tutee, 336
Solitary play, 65
Spaces. *See* Outdoor spaces; Physical spaces
Spatial relationships, 153
Special needs. *See* Children with special needs
Spectator role, 104
Spiral curriculum approach, 90
Spontaneous play
    in arts, 232–234, 238, 248
    examples of, 100
    explanation of, 8–9, 97, 181
    outdoor, 297–298, 305
    in play continuum, 11
    for science education, 207, 224–226
Standardized tests, high-stakes, 124, 146
Standards
    arts, 242–243
    challenges of, 20–21
    development of, 19–20
    emotional development, 131
    historical background of, 19
    literacy, 202–204
    mathematics, 174–176
    physical activity, 293
    play-centered curriculum and, 18–21, 91–92,
        146–147
    purpose of, 18–19, 364–366
    science, 222–224
    social development, 131
    social studies, 285–287
    technology, 337, 338
Stereotypes
    gender, 270–272, 325–328
    racial and ethnic, 329–330
Story constructions, 182–183
Story dictation/story play
    examples of, 198–200
    explanation of, 197–198
Story Player role, 106
Symbolic distancing, 50, 52

Symbolic play
    assessment of, 143–145
    for children with special needs, 59–60
    creating roles in, 50–51
    cultural and linguistic contexts for, 52
    with objects, 50
    stages of, 33–34
    Vygotsky on, 35, 38
Symbolic thinking, 38, 49–53
Symbols
    ability to decode, 54–55
    language development and, 53–54

Tactile sensory play, 235–236
Taking Back Childhood (Carlsson-Paige), 331
Teacher-directed instruction, 21
Teachers
    decision making by, 309–311
    development of confidence in science, 229–230
    entering spontaneous play, 233–234
    goals for outdoor play, 299–300
    importance of observations by, 287–288
    interpretive approach by, 275, 276
    as key to play-centered curriculum, 21–22
    knowledge about arts, 240–241
    as observers, 72, 95, 97–98
    play orchestration roles for, 99–108
    role in diffusing violence, 115–118
    role in peer play negotiations, 60
    scaffolding and, 96, 97
    as stage managers, 72–73
    support for outdoor play, 311–312
    taking child's view of play, 71–72
    view of being outdoors, 304–305
    view of childhood, 49
    view of play, 12–15
Technology. *See also* Computers
    assisted, 335–336
    to extend play and address standards, 339–341
    guidelines for, 336–337
    learning with, 323–324
    software and, 332–334, 336, 338–339
    standards for, 337, 338
    uses for, 318–319
Television
    advocating for quality, 331
    critics of, 328–329
    racial and ethnic stereotypes and, 329–330
Television commercials, 330–331
Tests, high-stakes, 124, 146

Thematic fantasy role play, 107
Tonal discrimination, 246–247
Toy Manufacturers of America, 86
Toys. *See also* Play materials
    child development and, 321–324
    overview of, 318
    that limit development, 324–325
    that promote early sexualization, 326
    that promote violence, 326–327
    that undermine gender equality, 325–328
    types of, 319–321
Turn-taking skills, 277–278
Tutee software, 336

U. N. Convention on the Rights of the Child,
    221, 304

Vertical, 154
Videotapes
    for assessing special needs, 148
    for assessment purposes, 142–143
Violence
    media, 328–329
    realities in children's lives and, 67–68, 112–114
    relationship to exclusion, 118
    toys that promote, 326–327
Violent play
    assessing motives for, 113–114
    methods to diffuse, 115–118
    overview of, 112–113
    peace promotion and, 118–119

pretense vs. reality in, 114–115
Visual-spatial intelligence, 133
Vygotsky, Lev
    background of, 35
    constructivist orientation of, 28, 348, 349
    emotional development and, 67
    influence of, 269
    interpersonal to intrapersonal processes in
        learning and, 36–37
    levels of symbolic play, 38
    mental tools acquisition and, 37–38
    understanding of rules and, 38
    zone of proximal development, 35–36, 60, 273,
        335, 362–363

Warrants, granting, 281–285
"Where Do the Children Play?", 315
Word families, 191
Writing
    expected competencies for, 203–204
    opportunities for, 190

Young Children, 227
*Young Investigators: The Project Approach in the Early
    Years* (Helm & Katz), 165
Young Mathematicians at Work (Fosnot &
    Dolk), 162

Zone of proximal development (ZPD)
    autonomy and, 362–363
    explanation of, 35–36, 60, 273, 335